SOCIOEMOTIONAL DEVELOPMENT IN THE TODDLER YEARS

Socioemotional Development in the Toddler Years

Transitions and Transformations

Edited by
CELIA A. BROWNELL
CLAIRE B. KOPP

THE GUILFORD PRESS
New York London

A Division of Guilford Publications, Inc.
72 Spring Street, New York, NY 10012
www.guilford.com

Printed in the United States of America

This book is printed on acid-free paper.

Last digit is print number: 9 8 7 6 5 4 3 2 1

Library of Congress Cataloging-in-Publication Data

Socioemotional development in the toddler years : transitions and transformations / edited by Celia A. Brownell, Claire B. Kopp.
p. cm.
Includes bibliographical references and index.
ISBN-10: 1-59385-496-X ISBN-13: 978-1-59385-496-6 (hardcover)
1. Toddlers—Development. 2. Child psychology. I. Brownell, Celia A. II. Kopp, Claire B.
HQ774.5.S583 2007
155.42′2—dc22

2007010715

About the Editors

Celia A. Brownell, PhD, is Associate Professor of Psychology at the University of Pittsburgh, where she directs the Early Social Development Laboratory and has served as Chair of the Developmental Psychology Graduate Training Program and as Director of Graduate Studies. She has been a coinvestigator on the National Institute of Child Health and Human Development Study of Early Child Care and Youth Development since its inception in 1990. Dr. Brownell is an associate editor of *Infancy,* the official journal of the International Society on Infant Studies. She has conducted research on social development of infants and toddlers for over 25 years.

Claire B. Kopp, PhD, is a developmental psychologist whose research interests focus primarily on the social and emotional development of young children, with particular emphasis on the development of regulatory processes. Her writings have also addressed biosocial risk factors that adversely influence children's development. Dr. Kopp has published widely in these areas, with research funded by both federal and private agencies. She taught at the University of California, Los Angeles, and Claremont Graduate University. Dr. Kopp is a frequent reviewer for developmental, psychological, and pediatric journals. She is a source of developmental information for parenting magazines, and her book for parents, *Baby Steps: A Guide to Your Child's Social, Physical, Mental, and Emotional Development in the First Two Years* (2003, Holt), is in its second edition. Dr. Kopp also consults with public and private agencies on early development.

About the Editor

Contributors

Nameera Akhtar, PhD, Department of Psychology, University of California, Santa Cruz, California

Jason Almerigi, PhD, Department of Psychology, Michigan State University, East Lansing, Michigan

Jessica Barnes, PhD, Department of Psychology, Michigan State University, East Lansing, Michigan

Martha Ann Bell, PhD, Department of Psychology, Virginia Polytechnic Institute and State University, Blacksburg, Virginia

Celia A. Brownell, PhD, Department of Psychology, University of Pittsburgh, Pittsburgh, Pennsylvania

Kristin A. Buss, PhD, Department of Psychology, Pennsylvania State University, University Park, Pennsylvania

Susan D. Calkins, PhD, Department of Human Development and Family Studies and Department of Psychology, University of North Carolina, Greensboro, North Carolina

Kaye V. Cook, PhD, Department of Psychology, Gordon College, Wenham, Massachusetts

Judy Dunn, PhD, Social, Genetic, and Developmental Psychiatry Centre, Institute of Psychiatry, King's College London, London, United Kingdom

Kurt W. Fischer, PhD, Department of Psychology and Graduate School of Education, Harvard University, Cambridge, Massachusetts

Hiram E. Fitzgerald, PhD, Department of Psychology, Michigan State University, East Lansing, Michigan

David R. Forman, PhD, Centre for Research in Human Development and Department of Psychology, Concordia University, Montreal, Quebec, Canada

Mary Gauvain, PhD, Department of Psychology, University of California, Riverside, California

H. Hill Goldsmith, PhD, Department of Psychology, University of Wisconsin, Madison, Wisconsin

Rebecca Goodvin, PhD, Department of Psychology, University of Nebraska, Lincoln, Nebraska

Dale F. Hay, PhD, School of Psychology, Cardiff University, Cardiff, United Kingdom

R. Peter Hobson, MD, PhD, Tavistock Clinic and Institute of Child Health, University College London, London, United Kingdom

Martin L. Hoffman, PhD, Department of Psychology, New York University, New York, New York

Claire Hughes, PhD, Centre for Family Research, Faculty of Social and Political Sciences, University of Cambridge, Cambridge, United Kingdom

Claire B. Kopp, PhD, private practice, Los Angeles, California

Angeline Lillard, PhD, Department of Psychology, University of Virginia, Charlottesville, Virginia

Carmen Martínez-Sussmann, MS, Department of Psychology, University of California, Santa Cruz, California

Michael F. Mascolo, PhD, Department of Psychology, Merrimack College, North Andover, Massachusetts

Chris Moore, PhD, Department of Psychology, Dalhousie University, Halifax, Nova Scotia, Canada

Katherine Nelson, PhD, Psychology Program, City University of New York Graduate Center, New York, New York

Susan M. Perez, PhD, Department of Psychology, University of North Florida, Jacksonville, Florida

Marilyn Shatz, PhD, Departments of Psychology and Linguistics, University of Michigan, Ann Arbor, Michigan

Ross A. Thompson, PhD, Department of Psychology, University of California, Davis, California

Christy D. Wolfe, PhD, Department of Psychological and Brain Sciences, University of Louisville, Louisville, Kentucky

Contents

Part V. INDIVIDUAL DIFFERENCES AND APPLICATIONS

SOCIOEMOTIONAL DEVELOPMENT IN THE TODDLER YEARS

1

Transitions in Toddler Socioemotional Development

Behavior, Understanding, Relationships

CELIA A. BROWNELL
CLAIRE B. KOPP

EPISODE 1

Setting: Noon, in an almost empty clinic waiting room

Participants: A 16-month-old in stylish cargo pants

Her mom: standing near the clinic doors

Episode length: About 10 minutes

Action: The toddler walks around the room, once, twice, three times. She locates a chair to her liking, and climbs onto the chair. She gets down. She walks along the row of chairs. She climbs another, and gets down. She walks around the room again, selects another chair and climbs up. She gets down. Minutes go by with walking and climbing repeated again and again. Finally, Mom approaches, telling her child it's time to go. Swooping the child into her arms, she nudges her face with her own, and they leave.

EPISODE 2

Report: Grandfather replying to query about 2-year-old grandson

"Thanks for asking about my grandson. He's an absolute treat! Just turned 2—is always running, yapping away, bossing his grandparents around. Last week, I suddenly became "Noddy Poppa" [naughty grandpa], just because I ate some of his fries! Now I know why toddlers are labeled "terrible." My egocentric version of the story is that it must have something to do with how "terribly" a grandparent feels when the little person is not around!" (K. Rubin, with permission)

EPISODE 3

Setting: Approaching end of dinner time at home, in a small dining area

Participants: Mom, Dad, 2½-year-old boy, guest

Episode length: about 8 minutes

Action: Conversation; has included all participants throughout dinner. Toward end, Dad places a piece of food on child's plate while mentioning it's good. Boy says he doesn't want it and places food on table, beyond his placemat. Dad says leave it on the placemat. Boy protests verbally, and moves food to tabletop. Scenario continues with emotions rising until Dad places boy's hand on placemat with food in it. Boy's body stiffens, and with a taut expression, stares at opposite wall. Parents are silent. After a very tense minute, boy's body relaxes, he leaves food on placemat, and opens new verbal exchange with parents. Guest is silent, and thinks: activation of frontal lobes, and behavioral inhibition won out.

These episodes epitomize the extraordinary developmental changes of the toddler period: the emergence of independent walking and with it, increasingly independent mastery of the wider physical and social world; the growth of conscious selfhood ("Look at me!") and concomitantly, expanding understanding of and reflection on self-other relations, including moral evaluations of one's own and others' behavior; increasing participation in cultural practices and acceptance of adults' rules for behavior, along with the growth of regulatory strategies for aligning one's behavior with said rules. Of course, toddlerhood embodies much more. Indeed, the toddler years are a period of momentous significance, when children make the psychological transition from infancy to childhood, and of momentous change, when developments in social and emotional competence are rapid, pervasive, and profound. Virtually every change in this short period from approximately 1 to 3 years of age represents a watershed in development.

Still, it is important to keep in mind that however much the toddler has raced forward in development, much lies ahead. True, she has put infancy behind her with first words, first steps, first use of cultural tools like spoons and crayons, first evidence of self-recognition, and first instances of pretense and peer play. But she remains immature along many dimensions that characterize the more advanced preschool repertoire, including autobiographical memory, planful problem solving, flexible use of emotional and behavioral regulatory strategies, conversational fluency and narrative, and a more abstract and balanced perspective on self and other. It is unlikely that a toddler could converse with the sophistication, yet charming naiveté, of a 4-year-old who asked her mother, "Do you think tooth fairies are smart? If I put this pebble under my pillow, will the tooth fairy leave money?"

We ourselves have long been interested in the toddler period for its remarkable transitions, its contradictions, and its challenges for both child and parent. Most of all, we have been fascinated by toddlers' social and emotional competencies, particularly those related to the emergence of unique dimensions of human functioning such as self-awareness, strategic emotional control and self-regulation, pretend play, empathy and altruism, and complex interpersonal understanding, interaction, and communication. We believe that the changes of this period provide distinct perspectives on fundamental developmental issues concerning the nature of change, processes and mechanisms of change, interdependence among developing systems, and the distinctiveness of human development. It is these dual interests in toddlerhood and development that have framed our thinking and our research and the structure and content of this volume.

For this volume we asked a number of eminent researchers to contribute their ideas about socioemotional development during this watershed period. In particular, we invited contributors who, as a group, conduct research at multiple levels of socioemotional development, including biology, behavior, understanding, and social relationships; across multiple developing systems, including social, emotional, cognitive, and linguistic; appealing to multiple explanatory processes, including regulatory, interactive, reflective, and symbolic–representational; and in both typically and atypically developing children. Readers will find thought-provoking summaries and evaluations of empirical research combined with rich conceptualizations that help to unravel some of the knotty ambiguities of the toddler years.

In this chapter we synthesize and foreshadow the chapters that follow. Our immediate goal is to provide an anchor for the basic issues and questions and the interesting points and provocative challenges raised by the individual authors. In the first part of the chapter we provide a general view of the developments of toddlerhood, emphasizing the complexities of multiple simultaneously developing systems and their interrelatedness. In the second part we highlight several overarching themes in the efforts by individual authors to generate explanatory frameworks, using examples from the chapters to illustrate. We focus in particular on intra- and interpersonal contributors to development, and within these on cross-systemic influences. Throughout, we aim partly to recognize the complexity of the descriptive and explanatory enterprise itself and partly to highlight promising arenas for future research. Our treatment is not exhaustive, only illustrative. The individual chapters provide rich details and nuance that we cannot hope to duplicate in a general integration such as this one. Our hope is that these chapters will inspire new work concerning the transitions of this period and associated models of developmental change.

THE DEVELOPING TODDLER

What Is a Toddler?

The word *toddler* is so often used in American conversation that it may be surprising to find that others are not similarly inclined. In Italian, for example, the noun *bambino* is an inclusive term for babies and young children. However, dictionary definitions for the verb *to toddle* can be found in many languages, with sources that date back some 200 years. Clues to this selective language curiosity may be found in economic history. Cook (2004), a sociologist who studies marketing, economics, and child-oriented goods, has noted that in the 1930s a new American marketing strategy evolved. Its goal was to create a line of clothing specially geared to the bodies and capabilities of children who were between infancy and the preschool years—a group previously not served by clothing manufacturers. Enter the "toddler" as a marketing niche. The rationale went something like this: The newly walking child is often in diapers, has a somewhat protruding stomach, and wants to be "on the go"; parents might be interested in purchasing a specialty clothing size (e.g., a size labeled T18mo) that would provide a better fit, more comfort, and heightened attractiveness. In addition, this specialty clothing line would be ensconced in distinctive departments within large department stores. The strategy was a success. Seamlessly, size "T" toddler clothes gradually created a huge new market. By-products were the increasing use of the word *toddler* and collateral marketing opportunities for goods such as playpens and toddler-specific toys, among others.

Interestingly, developmental scientists rarely define the term *toddler* or provide guidelines for operationalizing relevant age periods. Some authors use the word *toddler* to refer to 18-month-olds, for example, whereas others label the same age as *infants*. Our own preference is to define the period flexibly from the first part of the second year to the end of the third year, a span of roughly 2 years, give or take a few months. For example, dramatic changes occur in the behavioral repertoire between 10 and 14 months, but for the majority of children one of the most dramatic early developmental changes, independent walking, occurs at about 12 months. In like manner, there is major growth in the 2-year-old's explicit awareness of another's feelings or needs, but it may take several additional months for this awareness to be understood and acted on more consistently. A young 2-year-old may attentively monitor her father's face while listening to and nodding at his words about being gentle with a tiny dog, all the while closing her fist around the dog's ears. She may not correctly infer the meaning of his communication about the dog, especially in relation to her own actions, whereas a slightly older child will loosen her grip on the dog's ears as she understands what her father intends with his words. The flexibility of endpoints in demarcating toddlerhood recognizes that development does not occur in stepwise fashion from one month to the next and that there are no clear starting and ending points for any given competence.

Defining Toddler Development (a Bit Like Deciphering the Rosetta Stone)

The toddler years, although recently characterized as "the dark ages" of early development because of the relative dearth of research in this period (Meltzoff, Gopnik, & Repacholi, 1999), nevertheless engender a similar range and intensity of controversy as the relatively plentiful research on infant development and the developments of the preschool years. Of course, we can neither review these nor do justice to the many controversies in this space, nor are they resolved by the chapters in the current volume.

Many disagreements about the toddler period revolve around two related issues, the nature of competence and skill at a given age and how to characterize developmental change more broadly. One core problem is that we must try to infer what lies in the mind of a small, inscrutable being who looks, and even sometimes behaves, very much like one of us. But at the same time this little being may also act very much like one of our pets, and not very much like an older human child at all. The intellectual temptation to "adultomorphize" the toddler is tantalizing and often hard to resist. But, then, why should it be resisted? Why not assert that the 12-month-old understands that others possess minds and feelings and can simulate and reason about others' mental and emotional states if some children at that age respond appropriately to adult communicative requests, use words to refer to a world shared with adults, expect adults to behave in a manner consistent with their emotional expressions, and the like? Why not assert that the 15-month-old understands that others can entertain beliefs that run counter to reality and that they use that understanding to make sense of others' behavior if some children at that age look longer at events in which an adult's behavior appears to violate the adult's beliefs? Or that the 18-month-old's kiss on mom's finger after she pinches it and yelps in pain reflects young toddlers' spontaneous ability to be empathic and altruistic? Or that the imitating toddler has an explicit body image, understanding that she is identical to others even while differing in size and other irrelevant physical features? In fact, there is no good reason to reject such "rich" interpretations out of hand. They are just as consistent with the data as are more conservative, "lean" interpretations. Unfortunately, few methodologies and procedures can adjudicate such interpretive disagreements in preverbal children, and much good scholarship is wasted on argument without the necessary clarifying evidence.

Instead, we believe that taking a developmental stance on the skills and competencies that emerge and morph over the first 3 years of life will yield more productive answers to questions about the nature and course of change and the mechanisms underlying it. Fundamental interpretive differences often hinge on imputing developmental maturity or immaturity based on a single behavior observed at a particular age under circumscribed conditions. It is difficult, perhaps even impossible, to infer the nature of a developing competence when it is viewed at one age and/or under one set of conditions only. Competence, and its development, is most clearly characterized as it changes: Under what social, physical, and psychological conditions is a competence in evidence, or not, at any given age? What supports and resources are necessary for a toddler to appear competent, and under what kinds of demands does the apparent skill or understanding weaken or disappear? How robust is the presumed competence at different ages under similar conditions, and at a given age under varying conditions, or using different measures? For example, we might find that 18-month-old toddlers exhibit apparently empathic, prosocial responses to mother only, and not to others; to mother only when her emotional expressions are intense and exaggerated and there are no other interfering cognitive, social, or attentional demands, and not under more naturalistic circumstances; only when requested and/or only under certain, routinely experienced distress scenarios. But if we also find that 30-month-olds respond prosocially both to adults and to other children, both to intense and to more subtle emotional expressions, to a variety of distressing events, and so on, then our inferences about developments in empathic, prosocial responsiveness will be quite different than if we had studied a single group of 18-month-olds in a single simulated distress episode with mother expressing exaggerated cries of pain as she hurt her finger on the toddler's toy. In a word, we find questions about "when" a child "has" a particular competence far less compelling and productive than developmental questions about how children's competencies change with age, how they vary as a function of setting, task characteristics, and measure, and why. The chapters in this volume reflect this perspective, taking a developmental stance on a fascinating array of perennially challenging phenomena concerning early social and emotional development.

Related to disagreements about empirical interpretations of competence are theoretical disagreements about the nature of change in socioemotional development and the explanatory mechanisms involved. Some theorists call on innate "modules" or discrete arenas of psychological function with which children are born (e.g., Onishi & Baillargeon, 2005), or that mature on a chronological timetable (Baron-Cohen, 1995; Izard, 1991; Leslie, 1994). Others argue that the key explanatory constructs in the development of socioemotional competence in the first 3 years can be found in self-related processes, from innate links between one's own body and actions and others' bodies and actions (Meltzoff & Moore, 1995; Trevarthen, 1979), to an early-appearing ability to mentally simulate others' internal psychological and physical states (Tomasello, 1999). These families of theories tend to equate many of the fundamentals in infant and adult competence, even using infants and toddlers as "informants about adult cognition . . . [and] . . . good sources of information about fundamental principles of human thought" (Meltzoff, 2002, p. 19). Other theories assume fundamental, perhaps even qualitative, differences between infants or toddlers and adults, with unique mechanisms contributing to particular developments such as objective self-awareness (e.g., Lewis, 1994). Still others take a middle ground, arguing for the gradual emergence of socioemotional competencies through continuous interactions between social and cognitive processes, with the complexity and functionality of structures or competencies increasing over time and with experience, and the appearance of qualitatively new competencies from the interaction of structures at earlier, simpler levels (e.g., Nelson & Fivush, 2004). The chapters in the current volume, and we ourselves, tend toward this latter family of theories.

Substrata: Evolution, Brain, and Behavior

Regardless of theoretical orientation, it is apparent that the toddler period is grounded in multiple, interacting systems and processes, is developmentally rich, and can be viewed through vastly different lenses. In this section we focus a developmental lens on three features of the toddler period that serve as important substrates for socioemotional development. The first focus is on several evolutionarily conserved behaviors that emerge in the toddler period. In addition to grounding socioemotional development in toddlers, they also illustrate the critical role of experience in normative development. The second focus highlights key aspects of brain development in the toddler period, particularly in the prefrontal cortex, with important links to executive function and related implications for the essential role of parent input. The third focus is on the emergence of personal agency, another hallmark of the toddler period and, we argue, a critical foundation for concurrent and subsequent socioemotional development. Although some of what follows is speculative and awaits empirical confirmation, it may suggest new avenues for basic research in normative development in this period as well as education- or intervention-oriented research focused on the parents and caregivers of toddlers.

Evolution and Behavior in Toddlers

The emergent behaviors of the toddler period are unique in their evolutionary diversity. Some are shared with nonhuman primates; one (upright locomotion) dates back to a precursor of the *Homo* lineage; some reflect the demands from parents' lengthy psychological investment in children as childhood itself grew longer, and the associated need for more extensive and explicit socialization (dated around the time of *Homo habilis*; for later trends, see Koops & Zuckerman, 2003); and some reflect continuous modifications of parenting and childrearing that are associated with intergenerational cultural transmission of ideas and practices (e.g., Banyas, 1999; Donald, 1991; Flinn & Ward, 2005; Marcus, 2004; Parker, 2000a, 2000b; Roth & Dicke, 2005; Tomasello, 1999). The evolution of human childhood covers some 5 to 6 million years, during which there were intermittent periods of brain and behavioral changes that included elaboration of frontal brain areas, particularly the prefrontal cortex (PFC), progressive extensions of early childhood, growth of a variety of complex cognitive mechanisms, increasing demands related to survival and maintenance of social groups, the expansion and use of sophisticated tools, the creation of art, the emergence of spoken language, and the elaboration of culture. This temporal diversity in human evolution also reflects intermittent periods of acceleration and realignment of developing behavioral systems (Langer, 2000). One implication is that the modern human repertoire includes *simultaneously developing systems* that have multiple possibilities for intersystem coordination (Parker, 2000b, p. 12). However, before systems can become coordinated, such as the use of cognitive resources to facilitate emotion modulation or the use of vision, gesture, and vocalization to signal a parent that help is needed, each individual system must itself develop some degree of functionality.

Of particular interest are systems that are old from an evolutionary standpoint but remain entrenched in modern-day toddlers' behavioral repertoires (perhaps in a modified form). The emphasis here is on three conserved behavioral systems that have been essential for adaptation and survival across human history, possibly reflecting domain-specific brain mechanisms: one cognitive, one social, and one motor. Object permanence and physical aggression are shared with nonhuman primates, and upright locomotion (bipedal walking) extends back some 3 million years. The construct of *conserved systems* draws from the thinking of biologists Kirshner and Gerhart (2005) who have written extensively about evolutionary adaptations, conservation of core processes, and phenotypic variability. Recent research from numerous scientific disciplines confirms and extends theoretical formulations of these constructs, including the fact that phenotypic variability occurs in conserved processes even though in some instances variability can be harmful (e.g., Carroll, 2005; Kirschner & Gerhart, 2005).

Object permanence is a developmental achievement of the second year that marks a relatively sophisticated conceptual understanding that objects (and people) continue to exist when they are out of sight, based on enduring mental representations of objects through variations in time and space. Object permanence is one of the basic foundations of social relationships: to wit, immature organisms must come to understand that others who provide nurturance and care continue to exist and are available whether visible or not, that important others are sometimes located in different (invisible) places at different times, and that surface appearances may change but the fundamental existence and identity of caregivers remain constant. Although initial developmental studies of object permanence and other sensorimotor skills relied on measures derived from Piagetian theory (Piaget, 1952, 1954), nowadays the Piagetian strategy has given way to other procedures. However, older procedures and studies remain relevant because comparative psychologists and other scientists have adopted these techniques to evaluate aspects of sensorimotor intelligence among nonhuman species, sometimes including human toddlers in their studies (e.g., Call, 2001; Collier-Baker & Suddendorf, 2006). Recent studies of object permanence in great apes include procedures similar to those used in a longitudinal study of children from 8 to 18 months (Kopp, Sigman, & Parmelee, 1974). Kopp and colleagues (1974) showed that toddlers could solve one invisible displacement at 12 months and both two and three invisible displacements at 18 months. Call's (2001) and Collier-Baker and Suddendorf's (2006) studies of nonhuman primates and human 1- and 2-year-olds included invisible displacement configurations more complex than those used by Kopp and colleagues, but revealed similar performance by chimpanzees and human toddlers on straightforward object permanence tasks. This suggests that the young of these species are prepared to acquire elemental understanding of their object and social worlds within environments that provide numerous possibilities for visual, auditory, tactile, and kinesthetic inputs; conspecifics who appear, disappear, and reappear; and displacement and recovery of salient, everyday objects. Importantly, it is this fundamental ability to represent the permanence of the physical and social world, shared with nonhuman primates, that grounds the formation of multiple, complex interpersonal relationships and the ability to communicate about this world with others, which begins in the toddler period.

Physical aggression is also a conserved behavior; however, in most human societies it is not a behavior encouraged by parents and other adults, particularly when young children are in nonfamily settings. Physical aggression is observed in the behavioral repertoires of many nonhuman species and at some point among almost all toddlers (e.g., Hartup, 2005; Hay, 2005; Tremblay & Nagin, 2005). In contrast to sensorimotor intelligence, which represents a foundation for more advanced levels of cognitive and social learning, it is toddlers' *inhibition* of physical aggression that supports the development of competent social and emotional functioning. Physical aggression is apparent as early as 12 months, peaks normatively in the second year of life, and declines by the early preschool years (Tremblay & Nagin, 2005). Developmentally, a necessary foundation for toddlers' physical aggression is their motor competence: body stability, the ability to move about rapidly and at will, and sufficient power in the upper and lower extremities to enable hitting, kicking, and biting. Normative declines in aggression are likely a product of growth in inhibitory control, self-regulatory strategies, understanding of others' feelings and intentions, and increasing investment in cooperative peer relationships and friendships. Differential patterns of aggression are partly explained by parents and others' responses to aggression and often mediated by child gender, temperament and neurodevelopmental functioning, as well as family values and resources (e.g., Calkins & Johnson, 1998; Caspi et al., 2002; Fagot, 1984; Hay, 2005; Keenan & Shaw, 1994; Martin & Ross, 2005; Tremblay & Nagin, 2005). Contributors to unusually high and stable levels of physical aggression in the toddler period and beyond are known to include numerous adverse environmental, family, parent, and child factors that operate both additively and interactively on the developing system (see NICHD Early Child Care Research Network, 2004; Tremblay & Nagin, 2005). However, a variety of codeveloping social and emotional competencies may also contribute to this atypical pattern, including the ability to experience empathy, prosocial motivations, ability to read others' intentions, interest in social play, acquisition of coping and self-regulatory mechanisms, and understanding and evaluation of self in relation to others. Phenotypic variability in this conserved behavioral system has important implications for developments in other aspects of social and emotional function, illustrating the potential costs of simultaneously developing systems in addition to their benefits.

The ability to walk upright on two feet—at any time and not just on occasion—is distinctly human. Walking clearly depends on and reveals the action of multiple systems operating at the level of genes, brain, spinal cord, neuromuscular maturity, perceptual inputs, and powerful individual motivations. It is a conserved behavior related to a deeply conserved physical structure (e.g., Carroll, 2005; Kirshner & Gerhart, 2005), which varies in size and sturdiness with contributions from family inheritance, intergenerational changes in diet, health care, and family rearing practices. Bipedal walking is robust despite marked variations in living conditions and parental involvement. In contemporary times, the onset of walking typically occurs between 8 and 17 months of age, with a mid-20th century U.S. average of 12+ months (Bayley, 1965). Historical records indicate this may be the earliest recorded onset period, possibly due to changes in parental attitudes and rearing styles between the turn of the 20th century, when constraints on walking were common (e.g., use of playpens), and the end-of-century style that provides few restrictions and promotes psychological autonomy (see Kopp, 2006). Karen Adolph's imaginative studies of toddler walking reveal that independent walking typically matures into functional competence within a relatively brief time frame of 4 to 6 months (Adolph, Vereijken, & Shrout, 2003). Moreover, her data show an extraordinary willingness on the part of toddlers to engage in endless hours of practice each day to achieve balance, to prevent falling, and to cope with different surfaces as they walk. When unrestricted by parental constraints or environmental impediments, toddlers may walk as much as 6 hours a day in distributed practice and take between 500 and 1,500 steps per hour, such that at the end of the day they may have "traveled the length of 29 football fields" (Adolph et al., 2003, p. 494). Perhaps no other activity during the early toddler period provides as much pleasure, as much of a sense of independent agency, and as many learning opportunities (e.g., Adolph, 2005; Adolph & Berger, 2006; Campos et al., 2000). Adolph's data suggest that toddlers are motivated to control their own walking experiences whether parents support walking or just assume that it will occur without assistance. Parenting is required primarily to channel walking to protect the child and to help him learn. This conserved system, like the others, serves as an important substrate for early socioemotional development. It contributes to toddlers' growing awareness of an independent self and provides novel perspectives on self-other relations, in part by forcing parents and other caregivers to begin socializing cultural and family norms for physical activity and social and moral behavior. It also contributes to parent–child conflict, which serves as a catalyst for socioemotional development, because toddlers rarely willingly accede to restrictions on walking and related activities.

This focus on conserved behaviors that emerge in the early toddler years has emphasized that development is both experience expectant and experience dependent, with typical outcomes across a wide range of social and physical environments, yet with variability in outcome also arising in response to variety in rearing contexts. Important from the current volume's perspective, every conserved behavioral system codevelops with multiple aspects of social and emotional growth. The parent who says "use your words" to help a toddler negotiate situations in which aggression might be the first course of action assists with the integration of language, emotion regulation, and social behavior. The parent who plays hide-and-seek with the active toddler assists with the integration of motor, cognitive, social-cognitive, and affective processes. Thus, specific inputs from parents and others contribute to further development and to functionally important integrations across domains for these highly conserved behaviors.

Brain and Behavior in Toddlers

Evolutionary adaptations have led to unique attributes linked to developments in the frontal lobes of humans, particularly the PFC. Along with crucial learning experiences, these provide the potential to realize individual and cooperative goals, to benefit from a capacious aptitude for intellectual generativity, to consciously enjoy meaningful and lasting social relationships, and to live in and contribute to enduring and evolving sociocultural groups. The frontal lobes, states Oliver Sacks (2001), release humans from rigid programmed behaviors and thus provide the freedom to engage in higher-order purposeful behaviors associated with contemplation and imagination. More specifically, PFC functions are associated with conscious goal setting, planning and organizing the actions and means necessary to reach a goal, predicting outcomes, self-monitoring of progress, comparing options and instigating changes as necessary, and appraising self in meeting the goal (Miller & Cohen, 2001). Adaptive emotion management is a central element for each step in the process as is a sentient self that when necessary evokes cognitive mechanisms to evaluate the self in terms of needs and goals while also taking into account one's relationships and the events one encounters in daily activities. Although there is some disagreement about relative contributions of the PFC's major subregions to socioemotional functioning, with some claiming the ventromedial and the dorsolateral are primary whereas others note distinctive functions associated with the orbitofrontal region (e.g., Amodio & Frith, 2006; Davidson & Irwin, 1999; LeBar & Cabeza, 2006; Wood & Grafman, 2003), reciprocal connections from PFC regions to other brain areas (e.g., amygdala complex, hippocampal area, motor structures, and other cortical regions including cingulate, parietal, and temporal cortex) are associated with a variety of executive functions such as emotional processing and the integration of emotions, memory and environmental stimuli, controlled attention, motor control, performance monitoring and outcome evaluation, and the regulation of behavior (see Ochsner & Gross, 2005; Raz & Buhle, 2006; Rueda, Posner, & Rothbart, 2004). Cognitive control functions related to the PFC are also altered by neurotransmitter systems such as serotonin and noradrenaline (e.g., Chamberlain et al., 2006). In all, the human PFC, with its abilities for temporal analysis combined with motor behavior, action planning, thinking and language, has the potential to lead to uniquely human forms of intelligence (Roth & Dicke, 2005) and socioemotional functioning, including the ability to experience and understand complex emotions such as guilt and empathy, consciously reflect on and evaluate the self, delay gratification, and understand and process others' internal states such as intentions, beliefs, and attitudes (e.g., Frith & Frith, 2001; Sabbagh, 2006; Saxe, Carey, & Kanwisher, 2004; Seitz, Nickel, & Azari, 2006). However, little of this could happen in the absence of basic regulatory processes such as attention control and behavioral inhibition, which are intrinsic to activities that involve planning and evaluation and have their origins during infancy and toddlerhood.

At the beginning of the second year activation increases within and across the frontal lobes, particularly the PFC, with a transition from initial organization of primary structures to increasing connectivity with other brain regions and within the major regions of the PFC itself (Casey, Tottenham, Liston, & Durston, 2005; Wood & Grafman, 2003). Development in the PFC is protracted, however, extending into late adolescence, particularly in dorsolateral PFC with associated competencies in impulse control and decision making (Casey et al., 2005; Lenroot & Giedd, 2006). In considering the growth of social and emotional behavior related to frontal lobe developments among young children three complex interrelated systems come into play. One is cognitively and linguistically driven and relates to gaining information about one's social world, including the knowledge that others have minds and needs that may differ from one's own, memory systems that permit more efficient retrieval of information about people and events, more complex social reasoning skills, growing ability to define and appraise emotions and other internal states, elemental planning, goal monitoring, decision making, and more (Bauer, 2006; Saxe et al., 2004; Zelazo, 2004). Cognitive systems are bound to language abilities that both facilitate communication with others and serve as a tool for verbal self-rehearsal and self-regulation. A second component relates to children's conscious knowledge of self, including the growth of personal identity and awareness of roles in peer and family relationships, reflection on one's own goals, feelings about the self and valued others, and awareness of self-conscious emotions such as pride, shame, and guilt. All are part of self-consciousness, which is essential for investing in and evaluating one's actions, goals, emotional states, beliefs, and social relationships (e.g., Decety & Grezes, 2006; Seth, Baars, & Edelman, 2005). Responses that are modulated by self-consciousness and the sense of social or moral obligation that surface in an emotionally charged social interaction, for example, contrast with responses that are devoid of self-aware modulation and are primarily visceral and emotionally reactive (see Eisenberg, Hofer, & Vaughan, 2007). The third element concerns regulatory systems such as those related to physiological management, behavioral inhibition, controlled attention, modulation of emotions, and behavioral management with respect to sociocultural norms (see chapters in this volume by Bell & Wolfe; Calkins; Fitzgerald, Barnes, & Almengi; Thompson & Goodvin).

A key theme in this chapter and throughout the volume is the similarly timed, mutually constraining growth in multiple aspects of toddler development. These three systems have particular relevance for early developments in executive function. First, the differentiation and integration of developing domains or systems (Johnson & Munakata, 2005) serve regulatory functions (e.g., toddlers begin to use language to describe emotional upsets). Second, conscious awareness of an objective self, especially in relation to self's and others' actions (e.g., Hauf & Prinz, 2005; Zelazo, 2004), permits self-monitoring and self-correction. Third, regulatory processes can be deployed in the service of meeting self-generated goals, as exemplified by a 2-year-old who becomes frustrated while working on a puzzle but avoids a meltdown by first paying careful attention to the puzzle configuration that resists solution and then finding a parent to help with the problem. As a result of such behavioral integrations, toddlers begin exhibiting executive processes such as controlled (or effortful) attention (e.g., Ruff & Rothbart, 1996), behavioral inhibition (e.g., Kochanska, Murray, & Coy, 1997), error correction strategies (e.g., DeLoache, Sugarman, & Brown, 1985), and emotion modulation (e.g., Calkins & Johnson, 1998). To date, regulatory processes like these are mostly studied in relation to individual differences (e.g., Calkins & Fox, 2002); however, as part of normative development they merit detailed longitudinal research to identify how each process changes and how and when integration occurs across processes and domains of functioning (see Bell & Wolfe, this volume).

Executive functions are relatively immature in the toddler period and their development depends importantly on caregiver inputs and child-organized learning experiences, especially experiences related to growth in PFC insofar as "the brain is exquisitely sensitive to experience" (Marcus, 2004, p. 45). In his book, *A Mind So Rare: The Evolution of Human Consciousness*, Donald (2001) indirectly lays out what we, and by inference young children, require to take conscious control of behavior: surveying and monitoring the environment, attentional selection, maintaining vigilance, allocating priorities, updating working memory, planning, and self-monitoring, and self-evaluation. Donald also indirectly provides suggestions for caregivers to help toddlers master these challenges, including communicating unambiguously about expected behaviors, finding ways to remember the value of individual social relationships within a social group such as the family, using everyday routines to narrow the range of attention and reduce other resource demands to help with setting goals, using language to facilitate attention and to describe mental states, and helping children learn to use the signs and signals of others to evaluate their own behavior. These interesting ideas can provide testable hypotheses about specific parenting contributors to the development of regulatory processes and to problematic self-regulation (e.g., Davidov & Grusec, 2006), as well as offer information about the role of experience in development of "the social brain."

Personal Agency in Toddlers

Bruner (1990) defined the construct of agency as creating meaning from social and object oriented interactions. Although this activity characterizes all of human development, there are important and far-reaching developments in agency during toddlerhood. In particular, toddlers develop a sense of their own personal agency with the mix of walking, self-awareness, autonomy seeking, and emotional upheavals that occur in this period (see Mascolo & Fischer, this volume). This newly emerging agency awareness partly derives from cognitive advances, including those related to executive functions (e.g., Zelazo & Müller, 2002), and it permits self-initiated, goal-defined activities that lead to a sense of mastery (e.g., Bullock & Lütkenhaus, 1988), social interactions with others that involve intentional gestures to refer to objects and events with the goal of sharing experiences or knowledge (e.g., Tomasello, Carpenter, Call, Behne, & Moll, 2005), cooperating with others (e.g., Brownell, Ramani, & Zerwas, 2006; Warneken, Chen, & Tomasello, 2006), self-protective responses in reaction to a mildly fearful stimulus (Gunnar-von Gnechten, 1978), intentional use of various objects as self-soothers, and various forms of teasing, noncompliance, and negotiation that test the limits of agency and autonomy in interactions with adults and siblings (e.g., Kuczynski, 2003; Kuczynski & Navara, 2005).

Early in the toddler period children's awareness of agency emerges in the context of walking, goal-directed activity, and primitive communicative activities that dominate the first half of the second year of life (e.g., Adolph et al., 2003; Bullock & Lütkenhaus, 1988; Wenar, 1976). The latter part of the second year and early months of the third year feature the powerful ascendancy of self-awareness, including a sense of ownership and personal space (e.g., Hay, 2006; Lewis, 1994; Lewis & Brooks-Gunn, 1979) language for describing oneself and one's wants and feelings (Shatz, this volume), symbolic representations of self's and others' actions in play (Lillard, this volume), and the self-aware use of strategic behaviors to modulate negative emotions (Kopp, 1989). The third year reflects culturally mediated socialization and the emergence of social partnerships that require learning to balance one's own wants against those of caregivers, siblings, and peers, all of which implicates behavioral inhibition, verbal regulation of behavior, attention and emotions, reduction in refusals, aggression, and confrontations, along with the deployment of verbal negotiation and active management of social interchanges with a variety of partners. Thus, with toddlerhood comes the recognition of one's own agency and with it, pleasure in one's goal-directed achievements, recognition that it is "me" who is in control—doing and feeling and being good or bad. This necessitates the complementary awareness and understanding of others' agency as well and permits increasingly complex and sophisticated sharing of one's own experiences with others, testing the limits of one's agency, and accommodating to the behavior and feelings of others.

The development of a conscious awareness of one's own agency is thus critical for subsequent socioemotional achievements, and it may be useful to consider ways to integrate more fully the construct of agency into theoretical approaches and conceptual models of transitions in socioemotional development during this period. Figure 1.1 depicts agency and intentionality as core

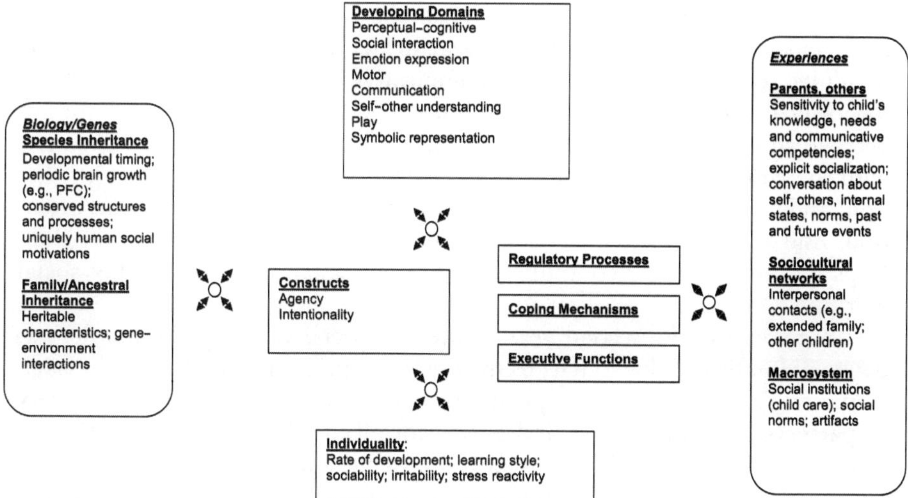

FIGURE 1.1. The toddler years: Agency and intentionality—contributors and integrations.

constructs in the toddler years, at the nexus of multiple developing behavioral systems interacting with various processes and mechanisms. Of course, this is only one possible representation. We have touched here on several interrelated developments that are foundational for socioemotional development in the toddler period. Other behavioral integrations are represented in the chapters in this volume and have been studied by other scholars (e.g., Bloom & Tinker, 2001; Carlson, 2003; Gopnik & Meltzoff, 1984; and others). We turn now to a discussion of the common themes that emerge from and integrate this collection.

PROCESSES OF SOCIOEMOTIONAL DEVELOPMENT IN THE TODDLER YEARS

Humans are continuously, deeply, and pervasively embedded in, schooled in, and supported by social interaction, whether engaged with the object world or with other people. Emotionally imbued social interaction is the fundamental context of development. How do children come to participate in and make sense of their social and emotional worlds? How do *intra*personal developments interface with the changing demands and supports of the *inter*personal world to generate fundamental developments in social and emotional competence? The toddler years are unique in the landscape of socioemotional development. It is during this period that the child's active participation in human culture as "symbol-infused engagement" begins to take precedence (Adamson, Bakeman, & Deckner, 2004).

The first 12 months of life have set the stage for this most human of achievements. The infant has made great strides in perceiving and responding to adults' social, emotional, and communicative behavior, whether others' behavior is directed to the infant herself or to the outside world. The infant has become an enthusiastic participant in social interaction with skilled partners, with some measure of control over her own emotional arousal during interaction, and a new ability to share the outside world with adults via joint attention. And she has established enduring, emotionally grounded social relationships that motivate her continuing urge to understand and engage her social world.

Beginning in the second year of life, the social world of the toddler expands dramatically, due in part to the onset of upright locomotion and associated increases in autonomy, opportunity, and choice, as well as a wider variety of partners, notably siblings and peers, not all of whom are socially skilled. The social world expands, too, as a result of the emergence of conscious self-awareness. Objective self-awareness enables the beginnings of self-regulation, conscience, and moral emotions as the child's own self becomes an object of attention to be shared with, and evaluated by others via social exchange. The toddler's expanding social world also includes the onset of symbolic communication and play, arising out of and supporting reciprocal, cooperative social engagement that takes as its focus objects and events beyond the dyad and beyond immediate, observable behavior, to include things remembered or anticipated, and things unseen such as mental states or imagined phenomena. These developments are both intrapersonal and interpersonal. They are also physiological, attentional, cognitive, social, and emotional, with competencies and developments in each domain both driving and constraining the others.

As noted previously, no developmental achievement occurs in isolation from others, leading us to favor descriptive and explanatory frameworks that are integrative across systems of development. The most successful models of development will recognize and call on this massive codevelopment, which is often dynamically organized and features complex patterns of intersecting causes. In our view, the most productive models of socioemotional development must include both intra- and interpersonal processes as engines of growth rather than assuming the primacy of one source of change over the other. As illustrated in Figure 1.1, explanatory frameworks for the development of socioemotional functioning should also draw from and be consistent across multiple levels of analysis: structurally from gene to physiology to brain to behavior; socially from relationship to group to culture; comparatively from mammal to primate to human; evolutionarily from phylogeny to ontogeny.

Each of the chapters exemplifies some aspect of this multifaceted approach to description and explanation of developmental change in socioemotional functioning over the toddler years. Several chapters refer specifically to the multidimensionality of developmental processes. For example, Thompson and Goodvin note that growth of emotion regulation relies on "a network of loosely allied developmental processes arising from within and outside the child." Bell and Wolfe refer to "interlocking developmental trajectories" in their discussion of relations between cognition and emotion in the development of self-regulation. Hobson argues that the emergence of objective self-awareness and other uniquely human forms of cognition depend on the fundamental inseparability of cognitive, conative, and affective dimensions of mental life.

In this section, we attempt to integrate and synthesize several core themes that emerge from the chapters as a group, using illustrative examples from the chapters themselves. We begin by discussing three *intra*personal processes that repeatedly appear as likely domain-general contributors to socioemotional development in this period: emotion; reflective self-awareness; inhibitory and attentional control. We then turn to the role of social experience and *inter*personal processes in toddler socioemotional development, emphasizing that intrapersonal developments must also enter into any characterization of interpersonal contributors to development. Again reflecting repeated emphases in the individual chapters, we discuss the emergence of explicit socialization in the toddler period and the role of conversation in the development of social skills and knowledge, and we end with the contributions of other children to socioemotional development in the toddler period.

Intrapersonal Processes

What intraindividual mechanisms and processes underlie the normative transitions in toddler socioemotional development? How do they influence the development of competence? What are the general and specific rate-limiting parameters, and how do they operate on various developing subsystems? The answers to these questions vary by domain of development and by level of analysis. However, three fundamental organizers of normative development in the toddler period emerged consistently across the chapters: (1) emotion; (2) objective self-awareness; and (3) inhibitory and attentional control.

Emotion as a Central, Organizing Factor

Emotion motivates behavior and cognition, as nearly every chapter in this volume attests, thereby contributing both directly and indirectly to developing social competence in the toddler years, including self-reflection, self-evaluation, and self-regulation, empathy and prosocial behavior, sociomoral standards, pretense, communication, and interactive skills. At the same time, multiple aspects of emotion are also influenced by developmental processes in other domains, including self-awareness and empathic other-awareness (Hobson; Hoffman; Mascolo & Fischer); autonomy (Forman); attention, effortful control, and executive function (Bell & Wolfe; Buss & Goldsmith; Calkins; Thompson & Goodvin); and relationships, socialization, and cultural processes (Forman; Hay & Cook; Hughes & Dunn; Mascolo & Fischer; Perez & Gauvain; Thompson & Goodvin). Thus, as Mascolo and Fischer discuss in detail, emotion organizes all aspects of behavior and development, and as Calkins and Thompson and Goodvin also point out, emotion is organized, in turn, by these other aspects of development.

Hobson argues that beginning at birth, emotional experiences during social interaction ground a fundamental, human-specific, emotion-based identification with others. In this view, primitive emotional connections with others constitute the foundation for later critical developments in sharing others' mental and affective relations with the world. These include the emergence in late infancy of shared attention and emotional responses to the world outside the dyad, as well as joint object play, social referencing, and the like (Akhtar & Martínez-Sussman; Moore), which then explode in a cascade of new skills over the second and third years of life. In the toddler years children build on these emotional connections with others to achieve a primitive awareness of subjective emotional and mental states that can be shared with others much like behavior and attention were shared in late infancy (Akhtar & Martínez-Sussman; Hoffman; Moore); to initiate the first instances of joint play subordinated to joint goals and themes, including pretend play (Hughes & Dunn; Lillard); to produce empathically motivated prosocial behavior (Hay & Cook; Hoffman); and to begin to see self through others' eyes (Moore), exhibiting the emotionally based motivation to be positively evaluated by others (Forman; Hobson; Mascolo & Fischer), which roots autonomous self-regulation (Calkins; Forman; Mascolo & Fischer; Thompson & Goodvin) and the earliest forms of morality (Forman; Hoffman; Mascolo & Fischer). These early developments eventuate in sharing and identifying with others' abstract mental and emotional stances toward the world and actively contributing to cultural practices during the preschool years and beyond (Moore; Perez & Gauvain). Thus, the socially shared emotions of infancy ground the psychological identification with others that makes its appearance in the toddler years and that lies at the core of socioemotional development throughout childhood.

Emotional experiences are also transformed themselves by developments in social and emotional competence. As toddlers become more engaged in a wider variety of emotionally charged interactions with caregivers, siblings, and peers (Forman; Hay & Cook; Hughes & Dunn; Thompson & Goodvin), they become aware of and begin to reflect on the subjectivity of desires and emotions, about their causes and consequences, about how emotions are evaluated by others and others' expectations for regulating them, and about strategies for doing so (Forman; Mascolo & Fischer; Moore; Thompson & Goodvin). Emergence of an objective self in the second year (Moore) introduces emotional experiences associated with reflecting on self in relation to others (Hobson; Shatz), including self-evaluative emotions such as pride and moral emotions such as guilt (Forman; Mascolo & Fischer) as well as empathically experienced emotions (Hay & Cook; Hobson; Hoffman). The growth of autonomous self-regulatory processes also induces changes in emotional experiences as the child becomes able to modify arousal and expression of emotions (Bell & Wolfe; Buss & Goldsmith; Calkins; Thompson &

Goodvin). This ability, in turn, produces changes in the child's social relationships (Calkins; Hay & Cook; Hughes & Dunn; Thompson & Goodvin) and organizes learning and cognition (Bell & Wolfe). Finally, being able to reflect on and to regulate emotions permits the child to participate in conversations about emotion (Hughes & Dunn; Mascolo & Fischer; Nelson; Shatz), to respond empathically to others' emotions (Hay & Cook; Hoffman), and to recruit and understand emotions used in play (Lillard). Thus, emotions both transform toddler social functioning and are transformed by it.

Self-Awareness and Self-Reflection: The Social-Cognitive Revolution of the Toddler Period

As scholars have long acknowledged, the world of the infant consists of distinct islands of information and experience: first person, agentic, subjective information that arises from acting in and on the world, and third person, objective information that arises from observing actions, objects, and events in the world (Hobson; Hoffman; Moore). These two sources of information, while distinct, are also interconnected, as confirmed in recent neuroscience research (e.g., Decety & Jackson, 2006; Decety & Somerville, 2003). For example, visual or auditory information about others' actions activates brain regions associated with self-produced movement. Thus, others' behavior may be perceived in terms of self's own embodied experiences and subjective sense of agency.

The objective, reflective, or conceptual self emerges during the second year of life, making the "I" of personal agency and embodied subjective experience available to conscious reflection (Lewis & Brooks-Gunn, 1979). With this profound development, apparently unique to humans and the great apes, the child's own experiences, feelings, expectations, actions, and physical characteristics become objects of the child's own thought, much like objects and events external to self had been heretofore. Previously invisible background aspects of the child's interactions with and experiences in the world can now be brought into the foreground; the child's subjective experiences can be explicitly represented and are available for mental comparison and manipulation. Categorical aspects of self can thereby enter into representational and propositional relationships with objective aspects of the world, enabling the emergence of a self-concept. New possibilities for socioemotional behavior and understanding are generated by this core transition, as discussed by several of the authors.

Objective representation of oneself necessarily also entails explicit representations of others in relation to self, as Moore and Hobson both discuss. Thus, in the second year awareness begins to dawn that others, too, are agents of their own behavior and have feelings, wants, and intentions that are different from one's own and that have their own causes. As the toddler comes to understand that others can have the same or different mental states as the child himself, it becomes possible for the child to identify with others' psychological relations with the world, building on the implicit, bodily-based, emotional identification inherent in the social exchanges of infancy (Hobson). Experiencing self-in-relation-to-other at these multiple levels, the toddler can begin to share others' affect, goals, perceptions, and evaluations overtly and purposefully, in action and communication (Akhtar & Martinez-Sussman; Hay & Cook; Hobson; Hoffman; Mascolo & Fischer; Moore; Shatz). This then puts the toddler in position to communicate his own interests, experiences, intentions and goals explicitly to others and to attempt to change others' interests, experiences, and goals to correspond with or accommodate to his.

This fundamental transition in self- and other-understanding shapes a multitude of new social and emotional skills. As Mascolo and Fischer explain, self-reflection serves to coordinate cognitive, emotional, conative, and social elements of socioemotional functioning. They illustrate their larger point using the development of self-evaluative and sociomoral emotions, especially guilt, shame, and anger. These emotions are the result of self-reflection (e.g., I am naughty; I did a good thing) and the ability to represent explicitly one's own agency or causality in producing events, especially interpersonal events such as emotional distress or violation of others' expectations (see also Forman; Hay & Cook; Hobson; Hoffman); at the same time such emotions organize self-reflection and self-representation. All these processes take off in the latter part of the second year of life when children begin to represent what "ought" to be the case (i.e., to internalize standards for their own and others' behavior, and not only what they *want*) (Kagan, 1981). As both Mascolo and Fischer and Hay and Cook describe, this early moral representation of the toddler period ultimately transforms into moral norms and conventions. Thus, changes in the young child's emotional experiences and emotion expressions are a product, in part, of their ability to see themselves objectively through others' eyes and, correspondingly, their growing awareness of others' evaluations of themselves.

Forman characterizes the growth of autonomy in this period in terms of the toddler's increasing perception of choice and control as a function of the understanding of an internal locus of personal causality in both self and others (i.e., agency). The toddler can, perhaps even must, assert her own individuality (Forman; Nelson), her own distinct locus of control, thereby bringing the "private," unknowing, and uninterpretable infant (Nelson) into public—a sort of coming out for the implicit self. Successful assertions are rewarding, and thus contribute to the child's growing autonomy as well as to the child's interest in sharing perspectives and meanings through conversation (Mascolo & Fischer; Nelson; Shatz) and collaboration (Hay & Cook; Hughes & Dunn; Moore; Thompson & Goodvin). Insofar as young children's interests contribute to their exchanges with others and to what and how they learn about the world, including the meanings they share with others (Akhtar & Martínez-Sussman; Nelson; Shatz), their emerging ability to demand, defend, discuss, and negotiate their own interests (Forman) represents an important area for future research.

The blossoming of empathically motivated prosocial behavior over the second year further illustrates the centrality of developments in self- and other-understanding in the toddler period (Hay & Cook; Hobson; Hoffman; Mascolo & Fischer). Empathic prosocial behavior, while occasionally identified early in the second year, especially with parents in familiar settings, becomes reasonably reliable beginning in the second half of the second year, although it is by no means universal then (Zahn-Waxler & Radke-Yarrow, 1982; Zahn-Waxler, Radke-Yarrow, Wagner, & Chapman, 1992). To act prosocially to alleviate another's emotional distress, the child must understand that the other's behavioral and vocal cues index a subjective emotional state related to the other's experiences. The child must be able to think "what's wrong—why are you sad?" rather than "what's wrong with your face?" The prosocial toddler must also understand that an episode of distress has an identifiable cause or source, and that emotional states are under the control of the person experiencing them, at least to some extent, and that they can be modified by remedying the cause (e.g., removing the source of pain) or by comforting the distressed other. Just as important, the empathically prosocial child must be able to understand another's pain or distress as if it were his own, and yet at the same time to recognize it as not his own; the child must identify with the other's affective experience but also distinguish between his own and the other's emotion, regulating his own contagious arousal (Hoffman). This, in turn, requires conscious access to one's own feelings and the means to represent separately both one's own and another's affective experiences (Moore; Shatz). It should be no surprise, then, to learn that the development of empathic prosocial behavior is associated with growth in objective self-awareness (Hay & Cook; Hoffman; Mascolo & Fischer; Moore) and that prosocial behavior undergoes a variety of developmental changes over the toddler years, in part as a function of growing understanding of others' emotions and expectations (Hay & Cook; Hoffman).

If joint attention is the "first social-cognitive revolution," occurring at the end of the first year of life, setting the stage for cultural learning by providing the social and communicative context for sharing activity with others (Tomasello, 1999), then objective self-awareness is the second critical revolution. This qualitative shift over the second year in the child's representation of the world to include herself as a conscious object of thought and reflection is made possible by the social-cognitive revolution at the end of the first year of life. That is, the capacity for joint attention permits the child's own body and behavior to become a distinct and independent focus of shared attention and communication. Whereas the young infant may detect others' attention and social behavior focused toward self (Reddy, 2001), by the end of the first year of life the child's physical, behavioral, and psychological attributes and perspectives can become spotlighted as distinct entities of self via joint attention and activity (Mascolo & Fischer). We know of no research that has focused systematically on developments in how adults use joint attention to bring the child's own self explicitly into focus, or on developmental changes in which aspects of self are the focus of shared activity, attention, and reference. Interestingly, recent neuroscience work suggests that selective attention drives the formation of increased neural connectivity between early visual areas and higher-order cortical areas that process the object of attention (Bird, Catmur, Silani, Frith, & Frith, 2006). Thus, socially supported, joint attention with explicit focus on the child's own body, behavior, experiences, and attributes at the end of the first year of life may constitute an important mechanism in generating objective self-awareness in the second year of life. Being able to understand reference to self as an entity "external" to the dyad has its roots in the first social-cognitive revolution at the end of the first year, which then feeds development of the ability to locate the self in "representational space" (Butterworth, 1995), producing the second social-cognitive revolution in the second year of life.

Contributions of Inhibitory and Attentional Control

Rapid advances in effortful control of attention during the second and third years of life permit the child to maintain attention on a specific task, goal, or representation while ignoring, suppressing, or shutting out distracting, irrelevant information (Bell & Wolfe; Buss & Goldsmith; Calkins; Thompson & Goodvin). At the same time, toddlers' ability to control their own motor and emotional behavior by inhibiting it, modifying its intensity, or slowing it down as demanded by the social or physical environment increases, supporting the growth of self-regulation more generally (Calkins; Forman; Mascolo & Fischer; Thompson & Goodvin). These emerging capacities for executive attention and inhibitory control interface with developments in emotional expression (Calkins; Mascolo & Fischer; Thompson & Goodvin), autonomous action (Calkins; Forman), objective self-representation (Calkins; Bell & Wolfe; Hobson; Thompson & Goodvin), representation of others' psychological states (Hobson; Moore), and working memory (Bell & Wolfe). Growth in attentional and inhibitory control thus serves to link developments in social, cognitive, and emotion processes with toddlers' behavior during this period.

For example, developments in attention regulation converge with the development of objective self-awareness to enable the child to attend to and strategically monitor both his own and others' behavior in the service of coordinating his desires and intentions with those of others and generating mutually governed interactions around shared themes, events, or goals. The nature and quality of the child's engagement in cooperative social exchange changes as a result. Further, the ability to inhibit dominant emotional and behavioral responses, together with the ability to redirect attention flexibly between one's own and others' behavior and goals, is necessary to comply with standards of self-control and behavior as expected by others (Kopp, 1982; Forman). Thus, this core dimension of early socioemotional development enables young children to begin to regulate their own behavior and emotions autonomously, and to generate coordinated behavior and shared intentions with others across a variety of social interactional contexts from pretend play to prosocial behavior to compliance exchanges (Calkins; Hughes & Dunn; Lillard; Moore; Thompson & Goodvin).

Perhaps nowhere do these developments converge so clearly as in early developments in toddler peer interaction. Here, neither child can scaffold or support the social and emotional behavior of the other. Unlike children's interactions with skilled adults or older sibling partners, toddler peers must find a way themselves to generate mutually understood themes and goals. They must actively monitor and regulate their own behavior, attention, and understanding as well as that of the partner to maintain effective, mutually satisfying social play interactions. To generate a shared goal with a peer requires the young child to inhibit or ignore her own primary psychological perspective so that she can attend to and momentarily adopt the other's perspective on the world (including the partner's perspective on the child herself). It also requires the child to inhibit his individual goal-directed behavior to attend to and represent the other's behavior in relation both to the other's goal and to his own. Clearly, this calls the attentional and inhibitory control systems into play along with other components of yet rudimentary executive function, as the chapters by Hughes and Dunn and Hay and Cook discuss. Moreover, the growth of positive peer play also relies on children's developing abilities to regulate their emotions, especially their negative emotions (Buss & Goldsmith; Calkins; Hay & Cook; Thompson & Goodvin).

Toddlers' growing capacity for attentional and inhibitory control enters into the development of pretend, too, as Lillard explains. Self-regulatory and executive function abilities make it possible for children to bring relevant aspects of real objects and associated information into active attention, while at the same time inhibiting or ignoring other information about the current situation as reality is transformed into pretend. For example, in feeding a pretend banana (block) to a pretend monkey (sock), the child maintains active attention to multiple aspects of the current situation (i.e., that this is a long, yellow block, that bananas are long and yellow, and that monkeys eat bananas); at the same time the child inhibits attention to or ignores information or knowledge that the block is wooden, bananas are not wooden, and there are no actual monkeys here, only a sock. As Lillard further argues, the child must not only attend selectively to and inhibit attention selectively to relevant aspects of the current situation, she must also activate and maintain attention to mental representations about the absent stimuli, in this case monkeys and bananas. Thus, Bell and Wolfe's argument that developments in working memory are linked to growth in attention and inhibitory control during this period are relevant here as well (see also Moses, Carlson, & Sabbagh, 2005).

The chapters on self-regulation also provide excellent models for the integration of behavioral and biological methods and mechanisms in the study of early socioemotional development. Over two decades ago Kopp (1982, 1989) argued that development of self-regulation depends on growth in other codeveloping systems, from motor and locomotor systems to cognitive, representational, and linguistic systems. In the current chapters this argument is extended to developing physiological and neural systems. It is clear from these chapters that explanations of socioemotional development are incomplete without specifying the influences of the biological substrate. Several chapters detail developments in neuroendocrine and autonomic nervous systems that accompany the growth of physiological arousal and regulation in response to psychological events, and developments in prefrontal cortex that accompany the growth of conscious, planful, strategic control of behavior, attention, and emotion (Bell & Wolfe; Buss & Goldsmith; Calkins; Thompson & Goodvin). The chapters by Bell and Wolfe and Calkins explain how these systems are interconnected, in part via the anterior cingulate cortex, with connections to prefrontal and parietal areas on the one hand and connections to the limbic, autonomic, and neuroendocrine systems on the other. Bell and Wolfe argue further that developments in the anterior cingulate cortex and associated changes in executive attention link cognition and emotion during development. Thus, as these brain systems and their interconnections develop, self-regulatory processes also become more complex, flexible, intentional, reflective, and autonomous over the second and third years of life.

It is also clear that fuller understanding of developments in self-regulation will depend on specifying how the biological substrate is affected by the child's social experiences. For example, as Thompson and Goodvin explain, caregiving experiences contribute to maturationally governed decline in the lability of the HPA axis over the first 3 years of life. Calkins describes "hidden regulators" in maternal caregiving that are necessary for the development of adaptive regulatory responses. These are interesting and important examples of experience-expectant developmental change (Bertenthal & Campos, 1987; Greenough, Black, & Wallace, 1987). That is, universal age-related aspects of the human-specific environment are an integral part of biologically based, evolved developmental systems. Specific characteristics of the developing child's environments are as necessary to normal development as are characteristics of the child's underlying biology. In addition to mapping out more fully the biological substrate as it contributes to early socioemotional development, it is equally important to map out those features of the child's environments that support, drive, or fine-tune the activity and development of the biological substrate.

Interpersonal Processes

This point raises larger questions about the role of universal and pancultural social experience, as well as culture-specific and family-specific experience in socioemotional development. How does the structure of social experience vary developmentally, and how do particular social experiences help children acquire the skills and understanding that define socioemotional competence?

That all aspects of development occur within and are shaped by the social context has become a truism in recent years. Even for developments outside the socioemotional domain, investigators have turned to social processes as a key source of input to growth and change in the toddler period. This ranges from motor development (Campos et al., 2000; Tamis-LaMonda & Adolph, 2005) to memory development (Learmonth, Lamberth, & Rovee-Collier, 2005), problem solving and tool using (Goubet, Rochat, Marie-Leblond, & Poss, 2006), and other aspects of early cognitive development (Perez & Gauvain). Indeed, the once radical notion that human-specific cognitive skills are a product of evolutionary change in response to the social demands of group living (Humphrey, 1976) has gained widespread credence. Of course, explanations of socioemotional development have long appealed to the social context as a primary source of motivation and guidance in the growth of competence (Maccoby, 1984). The toddler years feature major transitions in the role of social context in children's development, as several of the chapters in the current volume attest.

The child's participation in socially shared behavior becomes more active in dyadic exchanges with adults over the first year, culminating in the ability to incorporate objects external to the dyad in episodes of joint attention by 9–12 months of age. This foundation gradually differentiates over the toddler years to include participation in and generation of collaborative activities in which self, others, objects, and their abstract, symbolic representations can be coordinated and manipulated to serve a wide variety of intrapersonal and interpersonal ends. These developments are served by continuous involvement in social exchange, including conversation and play, which supports, demands, and creates ever more advanced knowledge, reasoning, reflection, and behavior.

Intrapersonal Development Influences Interpersonal Processes of Change

Interpersonal processes drive socioemotional development, but they are also shaped, constrained, and motivated by developments in *intra*personal competence. Thus, to model and understand the nature of the interpersonal processes that influence development, we must also know about the child's socioemotional competence at particular ages. As many of the chapter authors describe, developments in infancy set the stage for the transitions of toddlerhood. However, we know relatively little about the details of such links, in part because of continuing disagreement and controversy over the nature of intrapersonal competence and change in infancy, as noted in the first part of this chapter. Consider, for example, the development of joint attention (Akhtar & Martínez-Sussman; Hobson; Moore)—that is, attending together with another person to a common event or object external to both individuals. This ability to follow others' looks and points to objects and events in the world and to draw others' attention to things in the world by pointing is often considered one of the crowning social achievements of late infancy along with the consolidation of primary attachments, together constituting the foundation for learning about the world from others. However, questions remain about what the child on the cusp of toddlerhood knows and understands about acts of joint attention. The answers are important not only for describing developmental change during toddlerhood but also for identifying and understanding the mechanisms involved.

With respect to joint attention, one interpretation of the data is that by 12 months of age infants understand others' actions and gaze as intentional—that is, that others have mental states that are influenced by their experiences in the world and that govern their behavior (e.g., Brooks & Meltzoff, 2002; Phillips, Wellman, & Spelke, 2002; Repacholi, 1998; Tomasello, 1999) This set of abilities, in turn, makes infants open to direct socialization as they comprehend and act on others' motives and intentions toward themselves. By implication, caregivers should be able to teach a wide variety of novel behavior to the 12-month-old as the child flexibly understands the caregiver's knowledge, intentions and expectations for the infant's own behavior and understanding. The infant can also contribute directly to the social learning process himself, by sharing information, emotions, and preferences, as well as by observing others, making inferences about their goals and intentions, and then appropriating relevant behavior for her own repertoire.

In contrast, a different interpretation holds that at 12 months of age infants have learned something general about goal-directed behavior, including the temporal and spatial relationships between one's own or others' bodily behavior (e.g., pointing, gazing, head turning, smiling, and frowning) and the objects and events in the world toward which it is directed. Likewise, they have come to appreciate that adults' language refers to what the adult is looking at (e.g., Perner & Ruffman, 2005). But this interpretation does not yet grant young toddlers the ability to understand or represent the mental states or social intentions that underlie and generate behavior, either their own or others' (e.g., Golinkoff & Hirsh-Pasek, 2006; Moore, 2006). This means that they must acquire this understanding over the course of toddlerhood, and furthermore, that the socialization process must take such limited understanding into account, in some cases perhaps teaching or demanding it and in others perhaps accommodating to the child's limitations. In this view both socialization processes and social learning processes change over the course of toddlerhood as the child becomes a more knowledgeable participant in social exchange and, thereby, a more active and autonomous contributor. This raises the intriguing possibility that the study of normative changes in socialization may offer an independent and unique window onto the development of young children's social understanding.

In Lillard's chapter on the development of pretend play, the social context is viewed as serving several necessary functions for young toddlers' participation in pretense. Lillard notes that when children are just starting to pretend, between 12 and 24 months of age, their ability to represent what is not there depends heavily on the support from a skilled partner and benefits from the use of familiar scripts and routines. Parents provide toddlers who are not yet skilled pretenders with specific, reliable behavioral cues signifying "this is play," thereby distinguishing pretend actions from real, goal-directed acts for the toddler who is not yet proficient in doing so independently. When pretend acts are components of familiar routines such as eating or grooming, the "not real" is more easily distinguished from the real. Moreover, parents' communications about the not real are more accessible and meaningful, further contributing to toddlers' comprehension of play signals. Interestingly, parents' use of the word *pretend* does not facilitate the very young child's pretense. Thus, according to Lillard, the earliest instances of pretending occur in the context of social play, with clear behavioral cues from more skilled social partners about how to interpret play actions and participate in the play.

Early pretense is thus action based, and young toddlers understand pretend in terms of play behaviors, not in terms of mental states. Even 2-year-olds have difficulty reading pretend actions as intentional pretending outside of the supportive context provided by a knowledgeable other. Development of pretending thus constitutes a gradual shift over the toddler years from the child's conceptualization and understanding of pretense as immediate, observable play actions to pretense as an underlying, unobservable mental state. As Lillard demonstrates in her chapter, this shift is partly driven by explicit socialization, with parents adapting the amount and nature of their behavioral support for the child's participation in and understanding of pretense as the child's skills and concepts change. No doubt, the parent's efforts also challenge the child's conceptualizations of the real and pretend worlds, facilitating the growth of pretense representations.

Mascolo and Fischer, in addressing the growth of moral emotions such as guilt and shame, argue that adults explicitly draw young children's attention to their own behavior and experiences, along with the effects of their behavior on others, thereby promoting children's representations of self and moral emotions. This socialization strategy emerges between 18 and 24 months, according to these authors, when children are first able to generate representations of self as an object of awareness (see also Forman; Hay & Cook). Thus, both what is socialized and how undergo dramatic change over the second year, with increasing parental expectations for the child's comprehension of the parent's behavior and expectations, and accompanying changes in standards for children's behavior.

Nelson's account of toddlers' early word learning also emphasizes changes in parental socialization with increasing child competence. Nelson argues that it is through participating in the "functional contexts" of social life such as going on a walk together, being taken to visit the doctor, reading a book together or eating a meal together, all with accompanying talk, often child centered, that children come to understand the meanings of words. In her view, children are continuously scaffolded and supported by adults as they become participants in everyday meaningful activities, including communicative activity. Children are motivated to learn language in order to participate in shared activities and meanings, a point that Akhtar and Martínez-Sussman make as well. As parents expand the toddler's world and their own expectations for the toddler's behavior, they also expand the meanings shared with the child and the language that marks shared meanings. Implicit in this argument is that toddlers' early words emerge, in part, out of caregivers' socialization of their children, not from socialization of language or communication per se but socialization of social and emotional competence more generally. This argument is well illustrated and given further credibility by the chapters that discuss the contributions to developing socioemotional competence of children's conversations about emotions with parents, siblings, and peers (Hay & Cook; Hughes & Dunn; Shatz; Thompson & Goodvin).

According to Nelson, the language that young children learn is at first idiosyncratic, not necessarily symbolic, learned mimetically, and not sharable outside the particular meanings established with familiar interlocutors in familiar action routines. This suggests that the 12-month-old's words and gestures are learned differently, mean different things, and serve different functions for the child, the parent, and others than the 24- or 36-month-olds' words. Hobson makes a similar point with respect to the language of children with autism. Lillard's suggestion that the word *pretend* signifies a way of behaving for 2-year-olds but a mental state for 4- and 5-year-olds provides a compelling example. Thus, it can be argued with respect to language, too, that what is socialized, and how, changes over toddlerhood as children's ability to understand and share meanings and activities develops and as parental expectations for children's skills and abilities change.

Onset of Explicit Socialization

Not only are shared meanings acquired through participating in ordinary, everyday interactions with others, but much of social and emotional competence in early childhood is shaped by such interactions as well. For example, toddlers' participation alongside parents in household tasks, engagement in parent–child or sibling play, and experiences of being helped and comforted all contribute to the development of prosocial behavior (Forman; Hay & Cook; Perez & Gauvain). These are examples of indirect socialization, as are those detailed above. But this is not the sole source of developments in social competence.

An especially noteworthy change in interpersonal influence processes during the toddler period is the inauguration of *explicit or direct socialization.* Via overt instruction, correction, and explanation parents begin to communicate specific expectations, standards, and rules for culturally appropriate behavior for the first time (Forman; Perez & Gauvain; Thompson & Goodvin). Parents, in addition, begin to communicate their evaluations of toddlers' behavior as good or bad, agreeable or disagreeable, normative or norm violating to the children themselves (Forman; Mascolo & Fischer). During this same period observational learning also emerges in its particularly human form (Moore). It is no accident that explicit socialization begins in the toddler years, coupled with children's emerging abilities to reflect on their own and others' behavior and goals, to regulate their behavior consciously and strategically, to understand others' expectations for their behavior, and to attend to and learn from verbally communicated instruction and from others' behavior. Explicit socialization processes are built on the communicative foundations laid down in infancy, but they begin in earnest during the second year even though language is still rudimentary. Prohibitions, encouragements, praise, and punishment require little language on the part of either parent or child, but they do rely on shared knowledge (Akhtar & Martínez-Sussman; Moore), shared emotions (Hobson; Mascolo & Fischer), and shared motivations (Forman; Perez & Gauvain). Interestingly, little attention has been paid to normative changes in the content of socialization over the toddler years; rather, most such research has focused on individual differences in socialization processes.

Conflict as an engine of developmental change emerges during this period as an inherent feature of explicit socialization. Emotionally charged social conflicts arise for the first time in toddlerhood as children contest parental restrictions and expectations that are discordant with the child's own goals or preferences (Forman). For "battles of will" to begin, the toddler must be able to infer the parent's goal or desire and to compare it with her own to recognize the mismatch. Toddlers must also understand that they themselves control their own experiences and behavior, as Forman explains. Thus, parent–child conflicts are normative, a vital component of explicit socialization, emerging out of the child's growing understanding of autonomous agency in self and others as it intersects with parents' efforts to encourage the child's adherence to culturally approved conduct. Importantly, such interpersonal conflicts provide the grist for further differentiation and growth of mental state understanding, self-concept and identity development, emotions and emotion understanding, language and communicative competence, self-regulation, and prosocial behavior. For example, when the child turns to a parent expecting to share positive affect while pointing out his newly created marks on the wall but instead encounters parental displeasure and negative affect because in the parent's mind it is a transgression (Mascolo & Fischer), or expects to engage a peer in joint play but instead encounters peer distress or parental displeasure over a misunderstood toy exchange (Hay & Cook), the child's own intentions and meanings are brought into stark and emotionally charged contrast with those of others.

There is as yet relatively little research concerning the role of interactional and emotional mismatches in generating normative developmental change in social understanding and behavior during the period when such mismatches first begin to occur. Although temper tantrums are perhaps the archetypal outcome and index of such mismatches, to our knowledge there is no contemporary research on the development of temper tantrums. Several of the chapters mention recent research on temper tantrums (Calkins; Forman; Mascolo & Fischer), but most such work addresses individual differences in anger reactivity and regulation. Yet, empirical research on the development of temper tantrums has the potential to shed light on a number of aspects of normative socioemotional competence in toddlerhood. Because such contests of will depend on developing competencies in the child, they could offer a window onto typical, age-related growth in social understanding, emotion expression, communication, and self-regulation. At the same time, they could also open a window onto age-related cultural universals in socialization. Across cultures, disagreement and conflict between parents and children increase normatively over toddlerhood in concert with universal changes in children's socioemotional competence. Perez and Gauvain describe, for example, a traditional Polynesian community in which toddlers' increasing expressions of anger, frustration, and sadness are not tolerated, yet emerging "willfulness" is considered an appropriate expression of personal autonomy. Universal developmental changes in parents' expectations for toddlers' behavior and their communications about children's behavior can provide a converging picture of the growth of social understanding and behavioral competence in this formative period.

Conversation as a "Bootstrapping" Mechanism

Several authors argue or imply that children's inherent motivation to share interests and emotions with others, and the corresponding motivation to express these shared experiences, generates universal developments in communicative and interactive competence (Akhtar & Martínez-Sussman; Hobson; Moore; Nelson; Shatz). Shatz takes this position still further, arguing that conversation provides a bootstrapping mechanism for many of the fundamental developments in social understanding and social skill in the toddler period. Children participate in social and emotional exchange in conversational contexts beginning in the second year of life before they themselves are skilled in the social and linguistic functions that give rise to mature conversation and discourse (Akhtar & Martínez-Sussman; Nelson; Shatz). It is in such conversational exchanges, Shatz maintains, that children build and practice skills of language, self-reflection, and mental state understanding. Moreover, conversation provides the mechanism for creating connections among these knowledge domains, which converge to define the emerging "person" of the toddler.

Words direct children's attentional states (Akhtar & Martínez-Sussman; Nelson). Parents' conversation with toddlers about themselves directs children's attention to themselves, causing them to reflect on themselves as originators of behavior and as objective beings with bodies, feelings, desires, and intentions (Akhtar & Martínez-Sussman; Mascolo & Fischer; Moore; Shatz; Thompson & Goodvin). Conversations with children about their own actions and their consequences also organize children's awareness of self in relation to others, contributing to the development of moral emotions such as guilt and shame, as well as empathy and prosocial behavior (Forman; Hay & Cook; Hoffman; Mascolo & Fischer). As detailed in several chapters (Hay & Cook;

Hughes & Dunn; Lillard; Mascolo & Fischer; Moore; Nelson; Shatz; Thompson & Goodvin), conversation also provides children with access to others' thoughts and emotions, and with the means for sharing thoughts and meanings with others, thereby producing opportunities to learn about others' mental states, about how the child is perceived and evaluated by others, and about others' expectations for the child, even for very young children (e.g., Taumoepeau & Ruffman, 2006). Conversation about norms, standards, and parental expectations provides a context for self-assertion and the development of autonomy as the child agrees or disagrees, conforms or defies, learns to negotiate, and observes the outcome of her own requests or directives (Forman; Thompson & Goodvin). Conversations about emotions help children understand and regulate their emotions and contribute to the development of self-regulatory strategies (Bell & Wolfe; Forman; Hughes & Dunn; Shatz; Thompson & Goodvin). Toddlers participate in conversations with siblings and peers as well (Hay & Cook; Hughes & Dunn), both conflictual and playful, and they attend to conversations of others (Akhtar & Martínez-Sussman), often those between siblings or between parents and siblings (Hay & Cook; Hughes & Dunn). These are frequently emotional and include talk about desires, preferences, and intentions, further contributing to the development of social understanding and social skill. Thus, conversation structures children's attention, emotions, cognitions, and self–other relations, as well as the relations among these domains of developing knowledge and functioning. Study of normative changes in conversational content in the toddler years holds promise for further elucidating these core developmental processes (e.g., Sperry & Smiley, 1995).

The World of Other Children

Research on early socialization processes emphasizes parental influences with good reason, as attachments to adults remain primary for much of the first 2 years of life. It is within emotionally stable and secure attachment relationships that children begin to learn about themselves and others; acquire initial communicative and interactive skills; develop early strategies for self-regulation; lay the foundations for empathy, altruism, and morality; and begin acquiring a symbol system and the shared meanings that motivate its use. It is within the predictable, scaffolded routines of adult–infant interaction that infants and toddlers begin to understand other people as people, whose behavior is motivated and governed by their unique feelings, perceptions, meanings, and intentions (Mascolo & Fischer; Moore; Nelson; Shatz).

However, the toddler years also feature the first real forays into the world of other children, a world whose importance will increase over the course of childhood for all dimensions of development, not just socioemotional competence (Gifford-Smith & Brownell, 2003). Although infants are certainly interested in their peers and may become attached to their older siblings, it is only in the latter part of the second year that children begin to share meanings and goals with peers in organized play and cooperative interaction (Brownell et al., 2006; Eckerman & Peterman, 2001; Smiley, 2001). Perez and Gauvain provide a number of fascinating glimpses into the early world of peer relations from research in different cultures. In nearly all of their examples, it is in the second year of life that children begin spending increasing amounts of time with peers and siblings, and when parents begin to expect children to do so, with corresponding reductions in the time that mothers spend with their young children. This apparently universal transition coincides with dramatic developments in toddlers' ability to sustain meaningful, thematic, playful exchanges with others (Hay & Cook; Hughes & Dunn), to regulate aggressive behavior and negative affect in interaction (Calkins; Mascolo & Fischer; Thompson & Goodvin), to behave prosocially (Hay & Cook; Hoffman; Thompson & Goodvin), to communicate about internal states (Akhtar & Martínez-Sussman), and to engage in social pretense (Lillard; Perez & Gauvain). It can be no coincidence that as toddlers begin to understand that others are individual agents with intentions, goals, desires, and emotions independent of the child's own and that others' behavior is governed by their internal states (Mascolo & Fischer; Moore), they also begin to see other children as playmates and interaction partners.

In some cultures, according to Perez and Gauvain, mothers and other adults rarely play with their young children; thus toddlers' primary companions are siblings or other children. It is especially noteworthy, then, that research shows that toddlers acquire social, communicative, and emotion regulation skills from playing with their siblings and peers (Hay & Cook; Hughes & Dunn; Perez & Gauvain). In many cultures toddlers begin to practice culture-specific skills in the context of pretend play, often organized and structured by older children (Hughes & Dunn; Perez & Gauvain). The skills learned with older siblings carry over into peer relationships and can even compensate for low levels of sociability or experience with peers (Hughes & Dunn). These experiences with other children, who vary in communicative and interactive skills, contribute to the growth of social understanding and social skill, as well as to language and cognitive skills (Hughes & Dunn; Perez & Gauvain; Shatz), and provide yet another entrée into human culture. Many unanswered questions remain about parallels between young children's understanding of and participation in the world of adults and the world of peers; about the contributions of parent–child interaction to toddlers' interactions with other children; about how the struggles and challenges of interacting with peers and siblings contribute to other developments in socioemotional skill, from social understanding to prosocial behavior, aggression, communication skills, and self-regulation; and about how developments in these various dimensions of social skill and understanding contribute to normative developments and individual differences in young children's competence in engaging and befriending other children.

INDIVIDUAL DIFFERENCES AND ATYPICAL DEVELOPMENT

How does the study of individual differences and/or atypical development inform our understanding of typical development in the toddler period (and vice versa), at both the intrapersonal and interpersonal levels? Because developing systems are so massively interconnected in toddlerhood, it is difficult to tease apart how each one develops, how they interconnect, and how the changes in one system influence changes in other systems. One cannot selectively "lesion" a developing system to identify its unique contributions to the growth of competence in other systems. And altering the experiential inputs to one system, a complementary approach, necessarily alters inputs to others. That is, if experiential differences alter the rate or trajectory of a developing system, is it because of the direct action of the environment on that system or are the effects of experience mediated by co-occurring changes in other systems? For example, Akhtar and Martínez-Sussman suggest that crawling and walking contribute to the development of joint attention; thus, if infants reared in socially depriving early environments are slow to develop joint attention, is it because of deficiencies in their social experiences or because of delays in the onset of independent locomotion? These kinds of research design problems make it especially challenging to identify the unique controls on or contributors to development, especially those that may be specific to particular systems.

We are left, then, with disorders in which the "lesion" has occurred naturalistically, if tragically. But such disorders, like autism or Down syndrome or cerebral palsy, very often have pervasive rather than specific effects on development. We can also look for instances in which the systems are "out of sync" naturally. How is variability expressed when one system is more or less advanced or engaged than another? As the child invests resources in one dominant system, how do others become disrupted or disorganized?

The chapter by Hobson offers a number of insights related to these kinds of questions. For example, he provides the intriguing observation that although children with autism recognize themselves in mirrors, thus can "see" themselves objectively, they are not upset or self-conscious about having a mark on their face. One implication is that autistic children do not infer that others evaluate self and thus do not evaluate themselves from another's perspective (or are significantly delayed in doing so); hence, they do not exhibit self-evaluative, moral emotions such as embarrassment, guilt, pride, or shame. The contrast with the toddler described by Mascolo and Fischer is striking. Their toddler is becoming sometimes painfully aware of the effects of his actions on others' emotions and evaluations, with the concomitant experiences of guilt, shame, or anxiety on the heels of wrongdoing or on being the cause of another's distress (see also Forman; Hay & Cook). Likewise, typical toddlers are eager to please, and begin to take pride in themselves in response to adults' positive evaluations of their behavior or appearance (Forman; Mascolo & Fischer). According to Moore's model, the child with autism has not fully integrated first- and third-person perspectives on herself. Such deficits, as Hobson points out, have the potential to reveal basic principles of normative development (e.g., that self-consciousness is constituted of dissociable components). Hobson further speculates that the inability of children with autism to connect socially and psychologically with others deprives them of the social experiences necessary to motivate and feed development of a self-evaluative stance; evaluations are fundamentally social and emotional, whereas self-recognition by itself, even if it depends on the social mirror, is perceptual and cognitive.

A number of the other chapters discuss individual differences in specific domains such as prosocial and moral behavior (Hay & Cook; Hoffman; Mascolo & Fischer), peer and sibling interaction (Hughes & Dunn), autonomy (Forman), self-regulation (Buss & Goldsmith; Calkins; Thompson & Goodvin), and word learning (Nelson). A focus on individual differences differs from the study of disorders such as autism. In the study of individual differences, interest lies in how relatively small differences early in childhood, often limited to one domain of functioning, become amplified and consolidated into different developmental trajectories that ultimately result in disorder. For example, children who experience difficulties in the fundamental regulation of physiology, attention, and emotion as these competencies are emerging in the toddler period are at risk of failure in mastering many of the other social and emotional developmental tasks of this period. Such early failures can cascade into problems with peer aggression, parent–child relationships, communication, attention and problem solving, and empathy and emotion understanding later in the preschool years and beyond (Calkins; Mascolo & Fischer). Thus, when one system is out of synchrony with codeveloping systems in the toddler period, the effects can be especially far reaching and often long lasting (Fitzgerald et al.).

To determine whether the effects of asynchronies in development are positive or negative it is necessary to study the child across multiple developing systems, at different points along the developmental trajectory, and in different contexts under varying demands (Wainwright & Colombo, 2006). Fitzgerald and his colleagues thus advocate for a systemic approach to assessment to capture the continuous transactions between toddlers and their environments at multiple levels of analysis, from biology to behavior to interaction to relationships to culture. Although this approach is clearly relevant from the perspective of atypical developments, these authors also argue that it will contribute to the discovery of "factors that regulate the organization of developmental pathways," including normative pathways and normal variation in them.

Thus, we have come full circle. What this chapter has argued the rest of the chapters in this volume articulate and explicate: namely, that to understand the development of any particular socioemotional competence in the toddler period requires the study and understanding of co-developing systems as they contribute to, control, and are affected by the system under investigation, particularly over time. We have pointed to important substrates for socioemotional development in other, often conserved, behavioral systems that emerge in the toddler period, in core aspects of frontal lobe development beginning in the second year, and in the onset of a conscious sense of personal agency. We have also argued, based on material in the chapters themselves, that several intrapersonal processes operate as domain-general organizers of development in the toddler years, specifically emotion, reflective self-awareness, and inhibitory and attentional control. Further, the *inter*personal processes that define toddlers' social experience and shape their behavior, feelings, and thought are themselves governed, in part, by the child's *intra*personal development. Again on the basis of the material presented in the chapters themselves, we suggest that several of these interpersonal processes, ascendant and nascent in the toddler years, are nevertheless particularly formative in this period: conversation, explicit socialization, and interactions with other children. We now invite the reader to explore these and other perspectives in the chapters that follow.

REFERENCES

Adolph, K. E. (2005). Learning to learn in the development of action. In J. J. Reiser, J. L. Lockman, & C. A. Nelson (Eds,), *Minnesota Symposia on Child Psychology: Vol. 33. Action as an organizer of learning and development* (pp. 91–122). Mahwah, NJ: Erlbaum.

Adolph, K. E., & Berger, S. E. (2006). Motor development. In W. Damon & R. Lerner (Series Eds.) & D. S. Kuhn & R. S. Siegler (Vol. Eds.), *Handbook of child psychology: Vol. 2: Cognition, perception, and language* (6th ed., pp. 161–213). New York: Wiley.

Adolph, K. E., Vereijken, B., & Shrout, P. E. (2003). What changes in infant walking and why. *Child Development, 74,* 475–497.

Amodio, D. M., & Frith, C. D. (2006). Meeting of minds: The medial frontal cortex and social cognition. *Nature Reviews Neuroscience, 7,* 268–277.

Ason, L., Bakeman, R., & Deckner, D. (2004). The development of symbol-infused joint engagement. *Child Development, 7,* 1171–1187.

Banyas, C. A. (1999). Evolution and phylogenetic history of the frontal lobes. In B. L. Miller & J. L. Cummings (Eds.), *The human frontal lobes: Functions and disorders* (pp. 83–106). New York: Guilford Press.

Baron-Cohen, S. (1995). *Mindblindness: An essay on autism and theory of mind.* Cambridge, MA: MIT Press.

Bauer, P. (2006). Constructing a past in infancy: A neuro-developmental account. *Trends in Cognitive Sciences, 10,* 175–181.

Bayley, N. (1965). Comparisons of mental and motor test scores for ages 1–15 months by sex, birth order, race, and geographical location. *Child Development, 36,* 379–411.

Bertenthal, B., & Campos, J. (1987). New directions in the study of early experience. *Child Development, 58,* 560–567.

Bird, G., Catmur, C., Silani, G., Frith, C., & Frith, U. (2006). Attention does not modulate neural responses to social stimuli in autism spectrum disorders. *NeuroImage, 31,* 1614–1624.

Bloom, L., & Tinker, E. (2001). The intentionality model and language acquisition. *Monographs of the Society for Research in Child Development, 66*(4, Serial No. 267).

Brooks, R., & Meltzoff, A. (2005). Development of gaze following and its relation to language. *Developmental Science, 8,* 535–543.

Brownell, C., Ramani, G., & Zerwas, S. (2006). Becoming a social partner with peers: Cooperation and social understanding in one- and two-year-olds. *Child Development, 77,* 804–821.

Bruner, J. (1990). *Acts of meaning: Four lectures on mind and culture.* Cambridge, MA: Harvard University Press.

Bullock, M., & Lütkenhaus, P. (1988). The development of volitional behavior in the toddler years. *Child Development, 59,* 664–674.

Butterworth, G. (1995). The self as an object of consciousness in infancy. In P. Rochat (Ed.), *The self in infancy: Theory and research* (pp. 35–51). Amsterdam: North Holland/Elsevier.

Calkins, S. D., & Fox, N. A. (2002). Self-regulatory processes in early personality development: A multilevel approach to the study of childhood social withdrawal and aggression. *Development and Psychopathology, 14,* 477–498.

Calkins, S., & Johnson, M. C. (1998). Toddler regulation of distress to frustrating events: Temperament and maternal correlates. *Infant Behavior and Development, 21,* 379–395.

Call, J. (2001). Object permanence in orangutans (*Pongo pygmaeus*), chimpanzees (Pan troglodytes), children (*Homo sapiens*). *Journal of Comparative Psychology, 115,* 159–171.

Campos, J., Anderson, D., Barbu-Roth, M., Hubbard, E., Hertenstein, M., & Witherington, D. (2000). Travel broadens the mind. *Infancy, 12,* 149–219.

Carlson, S. (2003). Executive function in context: Development, measurement, theory and experience. *Monographs of the Society for Research in Child Development, 68*(Serial No. 274), 138–151.

Carroll, S. B. (2005). *Endless forms most beautiful: The new science of Evo Devo.* New York: Norton.

Casey, B. J., Tottenham, N., Liston, C., & Durston, S. (2005). Imaging the developing brain: What have we learned about cognitive development? *Trends in Cognitive Sciences, 9,* 104–110.

Caspi, A., McClay, J., Moffitt, T., Mill, J., Martin, J., Craig, I. W., et al. (2002). Role of genotype in the cycle of violence in maltreated children. *Science, 297,* 851–854.

Chamberlain, S., Muller, U., Blackwell, A., Clark, L., Robbins, T., & Sahakian, B. (2006). Neurochemical modulation of response inhibition and probabilistic learning in humans. *Science, 311,* 861–863.

Collier-Baker, E., & Suddendorf, T. (2006). Do chimpanzees (Pan troglodytes) and 2–year-old children (*Homo sapiens*) understand double invisible displacement? *Journal of Comparative Psychology, 120,* 89–97.

Cook, D. T. (2004). *The commodification of childhood: The children's clothing industry and the rise of the child consumer.* Durham, NC: Duke University Press.

Davidov, M., & Grusec, J. (2006). Untangling the links of parental responsiveness to distress and warmth to child outcomes. *Child Development, 77,* 44–58.

Davidson, R. J., & Irwin, W. (1999). The functional neuroanatomy of emotion and affective style. *Trends in Cognitive Sciences, 3,* 11–21.

Decety, J., & Grezes, J. (2006). The power of simulation: Imagining one's own and others' behavior. *Brain Research, 1079,* 4–14.

Decety, J., & Jackson, P. (2006). A social neuroscience perspective on empathy. *Current Directions in Psychological Science, 15,* 54–58.

Decety, J., & Sommerville, J. (2003) Shared representations between self and others: A social cognitive neuroscience view. *Trends in Cognitive Science, 7,* 527–533.

DeLoache, J. S., Sugarman, S., & Brown, A. L. (1985). The development of error correction strategies in young children's manipulative play. *Child Development, 56,* 928–939.

Donald, M. (1991). *Origins of modern mind.* Cambridge, MA: Harvard University Press.

Donald, M. (2001). *A mind so rare: The evolution of human consciousness.* New York: Norton.

Eckerman, C. O., & Peterman, K. (2001). Peers and infant social/communicative development. In A. Fogel & G. Bremner (Eds.), *Blackwell handbook of infant development* (pp. 326–350). Malden, MA: Blackwell.

Eisenberg, N., Hofer, C., & Vaughan, J. (2007). Effortful control and its socioemotional consequences. In J. J. Gross (Ed.), *Handbook of emotion regulation* (pp. 287–306). New York: Guilford Press.

Fagot, B. (1984). The consequences of problem behavior in toddler children. *Journal of Abnormal Child Psychology, 12,* 385–395.

Flinn, M. V., & Ward, C. V. (2005). Ontogeny and evolution of the social child. In B. J. Ellis & D. F. Bjorklund (Eds.), *Origins of the social mind: Evolutionary psychology and child development* (pp. 19–44). New York: Guilford Press.

Frith, U., & Frith, C. (2001). The biological basis of social interaction. *Current Directions in Psychological Science,* 150–155.

Gifford-Smith, M., & Brownell, C. (2003). Childhood peer relationships: Social acceptance, friendships & peer networks. *Journal of School Psychology, 41,* 235–284.

Golinkoff, R. M., & Hirsh-Pasek, K. (2006). Baby wordsmith: From associationist to social sophisticate. *Current Directions in Psychological Science, 15,* 30–33.

Gopnik, A., & Meltzoff, A. (1984). Semantic and cognitive development in 15–21-month-old children. *Journal of Child Language, 11,* 495–513.

Goubet, N., Rochat, P., Maire-Leblond, C., & Poss, S. (2006). Learning from others in 9–18-month-old infants. *Infant and Child Development, 15,* 161–177.

Greenough, W., Black, J., & Wallace, C. (1987). Experience and brain development. *Child Development, 58,* 539–559.

Gunnar-VonGnechten, M. (1978). Changing a frightening toy into a pleasant toy by allowing the infant to control its own actions. *Developmental Psychology, 14,* 157–162.

Hartup, W. (2005). The development of aggression: Where do we stand? In R. Tremblay, W. Hartup, & J. Archer (Eds.), *Developmental origins of aggression* (pp. 3–22). New York: Guilford Press.

Hauf, P., & Prinz, W. (2005). Understanding of own and others' actions during infancy: You-like-me, or me-like-you? *Interaction Studies, 6,* 429–445.

Hay, D. (2006). Yours and mine: Toddlers' talk about possessions with familiar peers. *British Journal of Developmental Psychology, 24,* 39–52.

Hay, F. D. (2005). The beginnings of aggression in infancy. In R. E. Tremblay, W. W. Hartup, & J. Archer (Eds.), *Developmental origins of aggression* (pp. 107–132). New York: Guilford Press.

Humphrey, N. (1976). The social function of intellect. In P. Bateson & R. Hinde (Eds.), *Growing points in ethology* (pp. 303–317). Cambridge, UK: Cambridge University Press.

Izard, C. (1991). *The psychology of emotions.* New York: Plenum Press.

Johnson, M., & Munakata, Y. (2005). Processes of change in brain and cognitive development. *Trends in Cognitive Science, 9,* 152–158.

Kagan, J. (1981). *The second year: Emergence of self-awareness.* Cambridge, MA: Harvard University Press.

Keenan, K., & Shaw, D. (1994). The development of aggression in toddlers. *Journal of Abnormal Child Psychology, 22,* 53–78.

Kirschner, M. W., & Gerhart, J. C. (2005). *The plausibility of life: Resolving Darwin's dilemma.* New Haven, CT: Yale University Press.

Kochanska, G., Murray, K., & Coy, K. C. (1997). Inhibitory control as a contributor to conscience in childhood: From toddler to early school age. *Child Development, 68,* 263–277.

Koops, W., & Zuckerman, M. (2003). *Beyond the century of the child: Cultural history and Developmental Psychology.* Philadelphia: University of Pennsylvania Press.

Kopp, C. B. (1982) Antecedents of self-regulation: A developmental perspective. *Developmental Psychology, 18,* 199–214.

Kopp, C. B. (1989). Regulation of distress and negative emotions: A developmental view. *Developmental Psychology, 25,* 343–354.

Kopp, C. B. (2006). *The toddler years: Evolutionary, caregiving, and developmental considerations.* Paper presented at the International Society for the Study of Behavioral Development, Melbourne, Australia.

Kopp, C. B., Sigman, M., & Parmelee, A. H. (1974). Longitudinal development of sensorimotor development. *Developmental Psychology, 10,* 687–695.

Kuczynski, L. (2003). Beyond bidirectionality: Bilateral conceptual frameworks for understanding dynamics in parent–child relations. In L. Kuczynski (Ed.), *Handbook of dynamics in parent–child relations* (pp. 1–24). Thousand Oaks, CA: Sage.

Kuczynski, L., & Navara, G. S. (2005). Sources of innovation and change in socialization, internalization and acculturation. In M. Killen & J. Smetana (Eds.), *Handbook of moral development* (pp. 299–327). Mahwah, NJ: Erlbaum.

Langer, J. (2000). The descent of cognitive development. *Developmental Science, 3,* 361–378.

Learmonth, A. E., Lamberth, R., & Rovee-Collier, C. (2005). The social context of imitation in infancy. *Journal of Experimental Child Psychology, 91,* 297–314.

LeBar, K. S., & Cabeza, R. (2006). Cognitive neuroscience of emotional memory. *Nature Reviews Neurosciences, 7,* 54–64.

Lenroot, R., & Giedd, J. (2006). Brain development in children and adolescents. *Neuroscience and Biobehavioral Reviews, 30,* 718–729.

Leslie, A. M. (1994). Pretending and believing: Issues in the theory of ToMM. *Cognition, 50,* 211–238.

Lewis, M. (1994). The self. In S. T. Parker, R. Mitchell, & M. L. Boccia (Eds.), *Self awareness in animals and humans: Developmental perspectives* (pp. 20–34). Cambridge, UK: Cambridge University Press.

Lewis, M., & Brooks-Gunn, J. (1979). *Social cognition and the acquisition of self.* New York: Plenum Press.

Maccoby, E. (1984). Socialization and developmental change. *Child Development, 55,* 317–328.

Marcus, G. (2004). *The birth of the mind: How a tiny number of genes creates the complexities of human thought.* New York: Basic Books.

Martin, J. L., & Ross, H. S. (2005). Sibling aggression: Sex differences and parents' reactions. *International Journal of Behavioral Development, 29,* 129–138.

Meltzoff, A. (2002). Elements of a developmental theory of imitation. In A. Meltzoff & W. Prinz (Eds.), *The imitative mind: Development, evolution and brain bases* (pp. 19–40). Cambridge, UK: Cambridge University Press.

Meltzoff, A., Gopnik, A., & Repacholi, B. (1999). Toddlers' understanding of intentions, desires, and emotions: Explorations of the Dark Ages. In P. Zelazo, J. Astington, & D. Olson (Eds.), *Developing theories of intention: Social understanding and self-control* (pp. 17–42). Mahwah, NJ: Erlbaum.

Meltzoff, A., & Moore, K. (1995). A theory of the role of imitation in the emergence of self. In P. Rochat (Ed.), *The self in infancy: Theory and research* (pp. 73–93). Amsterdam: Elsevier.

Miller, E., & Cohen, J. (2001). An integrative theory of prefrontal cortex function. *Annual Review of Neuroscience, 24,* 167–202.

Moore, C. (2006) Understanding the directedness of gaze: Three ways of doing it. *Infant and Child Development, 15,* 191–193.

Moses, L., Carlson, S., & Sabbagh, M. (2005). On the specificity of the relation between executive function and children's theories of mind. In W. Schneider, R. Schumann-Hengsteler, & B. Sodian (Eds.), *Young children's cognitive development: Interrelationships among executive functioning, working memory, verbal ability, and theory of mind* (pp. 131–145). Mahwah, NJ: Erlbaum.

Nelson, K., & Fivush, R. (2004). The emergence of autobiographical memory: A social cultural developmental theory. *Psychological Review, 111,* 486–511.

NICHD Early Child Care Research Network. (2004). Trajectories of physical aggression from toddlerhood to middle childhood. *Monographs of the Society for Research in Child Development, 69*(4, Serial No. 278), vii–144.

Ochsner, K. N., & Gross, J. J. (2005). The cognitive control of emotion. *Trends in Cognitive Sciences, 9,* 242–249.

Onishi, K., & Baillargeon, R. (2005). Do 15–month-old infants understand false beliefs? *Science, 38,* 255–259.

Parker, S. T. (2000a). Comparative developmental evolutionary Biology, Anthropology, and Psychology: Convergences in the study of human biology ontogeny. In S. T. Parker, J. Langer, &

M. L. McKinney (Eds.), *Biology, brains, and behavior: The evolution of human development* (pp. 1–15). Santa Fe, NM: School of American Research Press.

Parker, S. T. (2000b). Homo erectus infancy and childhood. In S. T. Parker, J. Langer, & M. L. McKinney (Eds.), *Biology, brains, and behavior: The evolution of human development* (pp. 279–318). Santa Fe, NM: School of American Research Press.

Perner, J., & Ruffman, T. (2005). Infants' insight into the mind: How deep? *Science, 308,* 214–216.

Phillips, A., Wellman, H., & Spelke, E. (2002). Infants' ability to connect gaze and emotional expression to intentional actions. *Cognition, 85,* 53–78.

Piaget, J. (1952). *The origins of intelligence in the child.* New York: International Universities Press.

Piaget, J. (1954). *The construction of reality in the child.* New York: Basic Books.

Raz, A., & Buhle, J. (2006). Typologies of attentional networks. *Nature Reviews Neuroscience, 7,* 367–379.

Reddy, V. (2001). Mind knowledge in the first year: understanding attention and intention. In G. Bremner & A. Fogel (Eds.), *Blackwell handbook of infant development* (pp. 241–264). Malden, MA: Blackwell.

Repacholi, B. (1998). Infants use attentional cues to identify the reference of another person's emotion expression. *Developmental Psychology, 34,* 1017–1025.

Roth, G., & Dicke, U. (2005). Evolution of the brain and intelligence. *Trends in Cognitive Sciences, 9,* 250–257.

Rueda, M. R,. Posner, M. I., & Rothbart, M. K. (2004). Attentional control and self-regulation. In R. F. Baumeister & K. D. Vohs (Eds.), *Handbook of self-regulation: Research, theory, and applications* (pp. 283–300). New York: Guilford Press.

Ruff, H., & Rothbart, M. K. (1996). *Attention in early development.* New York: Oxford University Press.

Ruffman, T., & Perner, J. (2005). Do infants really understand false belief? *Trends in Cognitive Sciences, 9,* 462–463.

Sabbagh, M. A. (2006). Neurocognitive bases of preschoolers' theory-of-mind development: Integrating cognitive neuroscience and cognitive development. In P. J. Marshall & N. A. Fox (Eds.), *The development of social engagement: Neurobiological perspectives* (pp. 153–170). Oxford, UK: Oxford University Press.

Sacks. O. (2001). Forward. In E. Goldberg (Ed.), *The executive brain: Frontal lobes and the civilized mind* (pp. 1–6). Oxford, UK: Oxford University Press.

Saxe, R., Carey, R., & Kanwisher, N. (2004). Understanding other minds: Linking Developmental Psychology and functional neuroimaging. *Annual Review of Psychology, 55,* 87–124.

Seitz, R., Nickel, J., & Azari, N. (2006). Functional modularity of the medial prefrontal cortex: Involvement in human empathy. *Neuropsychology, 20,* 743–751.

Seth, A. K., Baars, B. J., & Edelman, D. B. (2005). Criteria for consciousness in humans and other mammals. *Consciousness and Cognition, 14,* 119–139.

Smiley, P. (2001). Intention understanding and partner-sensitive behaviors in young children's peer interactions. *Social Development, 10,* 330–354.

Sperry, L., & Smiley, P. (Eds.). (1995). *Exploring young children's concepts of self and other through conversation.* San Francisco: Jossey-Bass.

Tamis-LeMonda, C., & Adolph, K. (2005). Social referencing in infant motor action. In B. Horner & C. Tamis-LeMonda (Eds.), *The development of social cognition and communication* (pp. 145–164). Mahwah, NJ: Erlbaum.

Taumaoepeau, M., & Ruffman, T. (2006). Mother and infant talk about mental states relates to desire language and emotion understanding. *Child Development, 77,* 465–481.

Tomasello, M. (1999). *The cultural origins of human cognition.* Cambridge, MA: Harvard University Press.

Tomasello, M., Carpenter, M., Call, J., Behne, T., & Moll, H. (2005). Understanding and sharing intentions: The origins of cultural cognition. *Behavioral and Brain Sciences, 28,* 675–691.

Tremblay, R. E., & Nagin, D. S. (2005). The developmental origins of physical aggression in humans. In R. E. Tremblay, W. W. Hartup, & J. Archer (Eds.), *Developmental origins of aggression* (pp, 83–106). New York: Guilford Press.

Trevarthen, C. (1979). Communication and cooperation in early infancy: A description of primary intersubjectivity. In M. M. Bullowa (Ed.), *Before speech: The beginning of interpersonal communication*. New York: Cambridge University Press.

Wainwright, P., & Colombo, J. (2006). Nutrition and the development of cognitive functions: Interpretation of behavioral studies in animals and human infants. *American Journal of Clinical Nutrition, 84,* 961–970.

Warneken, F., Chen, F., & Tomasello, M. (2006). Cooperative activities in young children and chimpanzees. *Child Development, 77,* 640–663.

Wenar, C. (1976). Executive competence in toddlers. *Genetic Psychology Monographs, 92,* 189–295.

Wood, J. N., & Grafman, J. (2003). Human prefrontal cortex: Processing and representational perspectives. *Nature Reviews Neuroscience, 4,* 139–147.

Zahn-Waxler, C., & Radke-Yarrow, M. (1982). The development of altruism: Alternative research strategies. In N. Eisenberg (Ed.), *The development of prosocial behavior* (pp. 109–137). San Diego, CA: Academic Press.

Zahn-Waxler, C., Radke-Yarrow, M. Wagner, E., & Chapman, M. (1992). Development of concern for others. *Developmental Psychology, 28,* 126–136.

Zelazo, P. D. (2004). The development of conscious control in childhood. *Trends in Cognitive Science, 8,* 12–17.

Zelazo, P. D., & Müller, U. (2002). Executive function in typical and atypical development. In U. Goswami (Ed.), *Handbook of childhood cognitive development* (pp. 445–469). Malden, MA: Blackwell.

Part I

UNDERSTANDING SELF AND OTHERS

2

Understanding Self and Others in the Second Year

CHRIS MOORE

As with many aspects of development, the second year of life is a significant time for the development of social behavior. For parents there are both pleasures and challenges. On the positive side, toddlers are much better able to coordinate their behavior with that of others. They become capable of joint play and are able to interact with others on a more equal footing. They also become able to recognize and respond sensitively to others' emotional displays. At the same time, by 2 years, toddlers often start to show vigorous attempts to exert their independence. Two-year-olds regularly insist on doing things "by myself." "No" and "mine" become popular words to the extent of contrariness. This newfound independence of the "terrible twos" can lead to conflict because children's awareness of their independence from others is not yet accompanied by a recognition of their still rather comprehensive dependence on others. How should we make sense of these changes in social behavior? In this chapter I examine the developments in social understanding that accompany these behavioral changes. In particular, I review evidence that by the end of the second year, toddlers have acquired a level of social understanding that recognizes self and others as similar yet separate individuals who have different psychological orientations to objects or situations in the world. I argue that these complementary changes in the understanding of self and other are made possible in part by more general changes in cognitive development.

INTENTIONAL RELATIONS AND SOCIAL UNDERSTANDING IN THE SECOND YEAR

There is now good consensus that the development of social understanding entails a growing understanding of psychological or *intentional* relations (Barresi & Moore, 1996; Tomasello, Carpenter, Call, Behne, & Moll, 2005; Woodward, 2005). Intentional relations connect an agent to an object in virtue of the agent's sensorimotor, emotional, or cognitive capacities. As such they may be considered the core constructs of psychological knowledge. Some examples are listed here:

1. Columbus *sees* land.
2. The baby *wants* the rattle.
3. Betty *likes* broccoli.
4. Celia *wants* the chapter to be finished by March.
5. Chris *thinks* the chapter will be finished by July.

Note that in each case there is an agent who is engaged in some intentional activity (italicized) directed at an object. The large body of research in the "theory of mind" tradition has tended to focus on how young children conceptualize mental states—in particular, desires and beliefs—such as those represented in sentences 4 and 5 above. In such cases, an agent engages in an intentional relation to a representational object. However, a full account of the ontogenetic origins of social understanding requires that the understanding of such representational or mental relations be seen as developmentally homologous with the understanding of simpler forms of intentional relations. When we consider what infants and toddlers know about intentional relations we find that their understanding is limited to those relations that are directed at real objects, represented by sentences 1–3 above. Nevertheless, a broader characterization of social understanding reveals that a fundamental feature of all psychological activity is that such activity is directed at, or about, something.

Intentional relations come in different flavors. A convenient categorization is provided by a consideration of the types of psychological processes that have been the focus of psychological thinking throughout the history of the discipline (Hilgard, 1980). After all, the kind of social understanding being acquired in childhood is commonsense psychology (Moore, 2006). First, there are *epistemic* relations, which include the classical category of cognition or knowledge and also perception relations (e.g., sentences 1 and 4 above). Second, there are *affective* or emotional relations, such as 3 above. Finally, there are *conative* relations, which include acts of will and desires (e.g., sentences 2 and 4 above). We consider cases of all three types when we review toddlers' understanding of intentional relations later in the chapter.

It is important to note that the category of agents to whom we attribute intentional relations includes ourselves. Thus, I can talk about my own perceptions, feelings, and thoughts in the same way I can talk about yours. For adults, this is an obvious fact but on reflection can be seen to present something of a challenge to a naive observer of human psychological activity. The challenge arises because the experience a naive observer has of his or her own psychological activity (involving primarily *first-person experience*) is quite different from the experience gained from observing another person's psychological activity (*third-person experience*). First-person experience tends to emphasize the object of experience and involves subjective information about the agent's attitude toward the object as well as proprioceptive information about any action involved. It tends not to include information about the self as the agent. In contrast, third-person experience tends to be primarily about the agent and his or her behavior, and it tends not to include information about the object toward which the other's activity is directed, especially in those cases in which the object of the other person's intentional relation cannot be directly observed (such as when it is a mental representation or located at some distance spatially). As a result, a naive observer of human psychological activity would gain very different information about other agents' intentional relations than it would about its own intentional relations. To illustrate this problem consider the simple act of turning to look at an object. An agent who performs such an act experiences his or her own head and eye movements proprioceptively along with the visual percept of the attended object. The same agent observing another agent engage in the same act is directly aware of the other's action but has no direct information pertaining to the object of the other's gaze. Nevertheless, as adults we have no difficulty recognizing that these two forms of information represent tokens of the same type—in both cases a person is turning to look at something. Mature social understanding recognizes the equivalence of self and other for a wide range of psychological relations.

Along with self–other equivalence, however, mature social understanding also recognizes self–other diversity. We are in some sense the same as others in that we have objective status as actors in the world and we also have subjective experience of that world. But we are also all different. I am a different actor from you, and you may have different subjective experience from me. From its inception, the literature on theory of mind has considered the understanding of such diversity as criterial to the demonstration that children understand mental states at all (Wimmer & Perner, 1983). Indeed the rationale for the false-belief task is that in order to show that children understand the concept of belief, one has to demonstrate that children understand that beliefs can be false, or in other words that another person's belief may differ from what the child knows to be the case. Although it is less apparent, a similar logic applies to the demonstration that younger children understand simpler intentional relations to real objects. It is worth elaborating on this argument in a bit more detail because at first gloss some infant behavior looks very much as if it depends on understanding others' intentional relations.

It is now quite clear that by 12 months, infants can engage in rich object-centered interactions with others. Within such triadic interactions, infants respond to a wide range of intentional relations of others. They follow gaze to objects that are out of the immediate visual field and even behind barriers (Corkum & Moore, 1998; Moll & Tomasello, 2004). In social referencing, they use others' emotional displays toward novel objects to guide their own action in relation to those objects (Mumme, Fernald, & Herrera, 1996). They imitate others' goal-directed actions (Elsner & Aschersleben, 2003; Meltzoff, 1988). Infants will also direct others' intentional relations through the use of various communicative gestures such as pointing (Carpenter, Nagell, & Tomasello, 1998). However, in all these cases the result of the interactive event is that the infant's intentional relation becomes aligned with that of the interactive partner—they end up sharing attention, emotion, or action to an object. To achieve this result, the infant must be able to coordinate his or her own intentional activity with that of others. And for this the infant only has to coordinate the third-person characteristics of the other's intentional relation with the first-person characteristics of his or her own similar intentional relation (Barresi & Moore, 1996; Moore, 2006). Such coordination may be achieved in a variety of ways (e.g., attentional cuing and emotional contagion) but need not depend on any understanding of the independent intentional relations of self and other.

Understanding intentional relations as descriptive of independent individual agents requires children to be able to distinguish the intentional relations of self and other. There are two complementary sides to this level of social understanding. First, children must become aware of the objective nature of the self so that when they are experiencing the first-person or subjective side of an intentional relation, they are simultaneously aware of the self from a third-person point of view, as the agent of that intentional relation. To achieve this objective point of view on the self, children must be able to imagine themselves, as it were, from the outside, acting in the world. For example, to take the simple case of looking at or seeing an object, children must be aware that when they turn and see an object, they are also moving their head and eyes in the direction of the object. Or, similarly, children must recognize that when they act on a desire to obtain an object within reach, they are also extending their arm and grasping the object. In addition, becoming aware of the self as an objective agent involves recognizing the self's identity, just as children can recognize other people by their appearance.

The other side of this level of social understanding is that children must be able to attribute to another person a first-person perspective that is different from their own. They must recognize that when they observe another person acting in relation to an object, the other person also has a first-person experience. So, for example, the observation of someone turning and looking at an object corresponds to the first-person information of seeing the object. Similarly, seeing someone smiling, reaching, and grasping an object corresponds to that person experiencing a desire for the object.

In sum, to fully understand intentional relations to objects, children have to understand that they present third-person information like others do and that others experience first-person information like they do. In this way both self and other are understood in terms of integrated first- and third-person perspectives (Barresi & Moore, 1996). In what follows, we review evidence for each side of this level of social understanding. We start with children's developing understanding of the objective self and then move on to consider their developing understanding of the subjectivity of others.

THE OBJECTIVE SELF

The distinction between first-person and third-person perspectives on the self has a long history in psychology. William James (1890/1950) distinguished the pure ego, or "I," from the empirical self, or "Me." Similar distinctions have been made many times over the years (e.g., Allport, 1961; Lewis & Brooks-Gunn, 1979; Neisser, 1988). In general, the "I" represents the self that acts and has subjective experiences, whereas the "Me" represents the self that can be thought about objectively. For those authors concerned with early development, even infants in the first year can be said to have an "I," but a "Me" is considered not to be present until sometime during the second year.

Before moving on to reviewing the evidence from the second year, it is worth considering what kind of understanding of self is apparent during the first year. From studies of visual preference, we know that infants as young as 3 months will attend differently to live video images of their own movement compared to similar video images of another infant's movements (e.g., Bahrick & Watson, 1985). Thus, very young infants can already distinguish self from others in the sense of discriminating information derived from self and others. In this context, the perfect contingency between visual and proprioceptive information pertaining to the self's movements allows in principle the discrimination of self from not self. So, young infants are sensitive to the first-person information characterizing self. In addition, 3-month-old infants who are shown prerecorded videos of both themselves and another same-age infant spend more time looking at the other infant than they do at themselves (Bahrick, Moss, & Fadil, 1996). In this case, the infants are processing the third-person information characteristic of the self. Here, it is likely that regular exposure to mirrors in the first few months of life means that this visual stimulus has already become familiar within a few months of birth. In consequence, infants prefer the relative novelty provided by the face of another child. Clearly discriminating information, of either first- or third-person kind, derived from the self from that derived from others is not the same thing as recognizing information derived from the self *as* the self. There is not yet a sense of self as the same kind of thing as others.

A simple way of asking the question whether children recognize the self *as* the self is to show children pictures of themselves and other children and ask them, "Who is that?" Using this approach, toddlers sometimes differentiate the pictures, using their own name for the self picture only (e.g., Lewis & Brooks-Gunn, 1979). Acquisition of personal pronouns typically comes later, but by the end of the second year, toddlers will often refer to themselves as me (Lewis & Ramsay, 2004). Interpretation of this picture-naming approach is problematic, however. First, it is a verbal method and as such not useful for children much younger than about 18 months. Second, it is possible that children are able to use their name to label the picture of self in the same way that they can refer to any person or object they recognize—simply through having learned the verbal label for that entity. So the earliest reference using their own proper name may not indicate awareness of self. It is important to note that such a concern would not apply to the use of the personal pronoun, which changes its referent depending on who says it.

In recent years, the most popular approach to demonstrating awareness of self is mirror self-recognition. This approach was first developed by Gallup (e.g., 1970) as a nonverbal method to study self-awareness in chimpanzees. It was shortly afterwards developed independently for use with young children by Amsterdam (1972). Amsterdam used makeup to mark the cheeks of children from 3 to 24 months and then recorded their behavior in front of a mirror. Before abut 18 months, children's showed a combination of social behavior to the mirror image, searching for the image in or behind the mirror and observing the effects of their own movement in the mirror. After 18 months children started to show self-directed behavior, including touching their faces, thereby evidencing recognition that the image in the mirror corresponded to their own body.

This result has now been replicated many times (e.g., Bertenthal & Fischer, 1978; Johnson, 1982; Lewis & Brooks-Gunn, 1979; Nielsen, Dissanayake, & Kashima, 2003) and there is clear agreement on developmental changes in behavior in front of a mirror. However, the exact interpretation of the behavioral phenomena is still undecided. At one extreme it has been argued that mirror self-recognition tells us very little about self-awareness but rather reveals a developing understanding of the reflective properties of mirrors (e.g., Loveland, 1986, 1992). In contrast, most authors agree that mirror self-recognition does provide information relevant to the development of the objective self, although exactly what is involved is debated (see Mitchell, 1997).

One interpretation is that mirror self-recognition evidences the child's self-concept. An important component of this self-concept is facial appearance. As I mentioned earlier, younger infants can recognize their facial appearance. But what is different about mirror self-recognition is that the facial appearance observed in the mirror is understood by the toddler to be the same as the facial appearance that is part of the toddler's mental representation of him- or herself. When the toddler sees the mark on the face in the mirror, he or she recognizes the discrepancy between the observed image and the mental representation of self and thus explores his or her own face.

A second interpretation is that self-directed behavior in the mirror self-recognition task depends on the child's ability to compare the visual information provided by the mirror and the proprioceptive information provided by the child's movements while in front of the mirror. This matching is not simply a perceptual detection of the dynamic contingency between the visual and proprioceptive information. Infants are able to detect such contingency as early as 3–5 months of age (Bahrick & Watson, 1985). Rather, not only can the toddler detect the contingency, but he or she can also recognize that the perfect contingency between vision and proprioception afforded by mirror observation specifies the self (Mitchell, 1997; Povinelli, 1995). The specification of self in terms of perfect contingency allows the toddler to determine that what is true of the image in the mirror is also true of the self and therefore that the mark exists on his or her own face.

These two interpretations differ subtly in terms of emphasizing visual appearance alone versus contingency relations between vision and proprioception. Nevertheless, both interpretations are consistent with the idea that the child develops an objective self.

Whereas most research on the development of the objective self during the second year has focused on awareness of self-recognition, a number of other lines of research provide supportive evidence. An alternative approach is to examine children's understanding of self as a physical object. In *The Origin of Intelligence in the Child,* Piaget (1953/1977) recorded the following observation of his daughter Jacqueline at 18.5 months:

> . . . Jacqueline is standing on a rag (50 × 30 cm.) which she is trying to pick up. She pulls, is surprised at the resistance, but it does not occur to her to move. Finally she gives up. (p. 351, obs. 168)

Within a month Jacqueline was able to solve such a problem. Piaget interpreted this observation in terms of a developing awareness of self as an objective entity existing in, and interacting with, the world of objects. Following up on this observation, Geppert and Küster (1983) and Bullock and Lütkenhaus (1990) placed toddlers on a small blanket and then asked the children either simply to give the blanket to the experimenter or to retrieve an attractive object hidden underneath the blanket. Congruent with Piaget's observations, by 18 months, many toddlers were able to succeed on this task. However, this task presents to the children a situation that will have been a relatively common experience in their lives, so it is unclear to what extent success is the result of learning from similar situations that may have occurred in everyday life. Because of this concern, we decided to set up a novel situation in which the child would need to reflect on the self as an object (Moore, Mealiea, Garon, & Povinelli, in press; see also Brownell, Zerwas, & Ramani, in press). We took a toy shopping cart and modified it by attaching to the rear axle a small rug that extended for about 50 cm behind the cart. We then placed the children, one by one, behind the cart and encouraged them to push it to their mothers who were seated a short distance away. The rug was arranged so that if the children attempted to push the cart from the usual position they would have to step on the rug. In consequence their own weight would then prevent them from moving the cart forward. We tested toddlers of 15 and 21 months, all of whom were independently mobile, on this task. The 21-month-olds quickly realized that they had to get off the rug in order to move the cart forward. In contrast, the 15-month-olds made many more repeated, albeit unsuccessful, attempts to push the cart as they stood on the rug. This finding is consistent with the idea that toddlers begin to think about another objective property of the self—weight—around the middle of the second year. Interestingly this manifestation of the objective self coincides developmentally with the onset of mirror self-recognition. Performance on mirror self-recognition and the shopping cart task is significantly correlated (Moore et al., in press), supporting the idea that children are acquiring a more general ability to think of the self from an objective or third-person point of view about halfway through the second year.

The phenomena discussed so far reveal that toddlers can imagine themselves as objective entities with particular properties. There is also evidence that this understanding of self coincides with an awareness of self as a possible object of the intentional relations of others. In these cases, the self has to be imagined from a third-person point of view. A clear example comes from the emotional domain. In contrast to basic emotions such as joy, sadness, fear, and anger, which are evident in the first year, other emotions are not clearly evident until later in the second year. These social or self-conscious emotions, such as embarrassment and pride, depend on an awareness of self as the object of another person's intentional relation (e.g., Lewis, Sullivan, Stanger, & Weiss, 1989). Lewis and colleagues (1989) investigated this issue by examining toddlers' performance on mirror self-recognition and their expression of basic and social emotions. They used a variety of contexts to elicit different emotions. For example, fear or wariness was elicited by having a stranger approach the child. Embarrassment was elicited by overtly praising the child and asking the child to perform a dance for the parent and adult. Coding of the children's emotional reactions showed that fear or wariness was produced by children whether or not they passed the mirror self-recognition task. However, embarrassment was much more likely to be evidenced in children who showed mirror self-recognition than in those who did not. This result confirms that social emotions, such as embarrassment, that are elicited by being the focus of another's attention develop at about the same time as the other indices of the ability to think of the self from an objective point of view.

Two recent studies involving imitation also provide consistent evidence that 18-month-olds are able to imagine themselves as objective entities like others that can be the focus of another person's intentional relations. One valuable approach is to examine the ability of toddlers to engage in role-reversal imitation (Carpenter, Tomasello, & Striano, 2005). In one experiment, children of 12 and 18 months watched as an experimenter performed a series of 8 simple actions, such as patting the cheek or rolling a toy car on the arm. The actions were performed in turn on the child, on the experimenter herself or on another adult. After each demonstration the child was encouraged to perform the action as the experimenter said "it's your turn now," while offering the object if one was involved. No other guidance was provided to the child concerning on whom the action should be performed. Children's responses were coded in terms of whether they copied the demonstration and in terms of on whom the action was performed. The results revealed a clear difference between the age groups. The most common response for the 12-month-olds, when they copied the action demonstrated, was to perform the action on the same person as the experimenter had. Thus, if the experimenter performed the action on herself, then the child was most likely also to perform it on the experimenter. Similarly, if the experimenter performed the action on the child, then so did the child. These children were therefore capable of imitating the action but they tended not to reverse roles. In contrast, the 18-month-olds were most likely to perform the action on themselves in all demonstration conditions. This was particularly strongly indicated for the cases in which the experimenter demonstrated the action on the child and the cases in which the experimenter demonstrated the action on herself. This finding shows that only by 18 months did children start to become willing to substitute their own body for that of the experimenter, demonstrating an awareness of the equivalence of self and other as possible objects of the actions.

Finally, a study by Repacholi and Meltzoff (2005) drawing on the social referencing research tradition has also provided evidence through imitation that 18-month-olds can imagine themselves as the object of another person's emotional attitude. They presented toddlers with an adult demonstrating an action on a toy. After two demonstrations, another adult entered the room and a third demonstration was performed. At this point, the new adult either reacted angrily toward the first adult or made a neutral comment. The child was then given an opportunity to imitate the demonstrated action. During this response period, the second adult either remained looking at the child or was distracted from the child in one of various ways, including leaving the room, turning her back, or reading a magazine. Toddlers who had observed the second adult act neutrally were very likely to imitate the first adult's action. However, those toddlers who had observed the second adult react angrily to the first and then sat watching them were much less likely to imitate. Interestingly, when the angry adult was not watching during the response period, the children tended to imitate as much as in the neutral condition. These results are consistent with the idea that after viewing one adult react angrily to another, 18-month-olds can imagine themselves as the possible target of an angry outburst, but only if the adult can see them. To react in this way, the children must be thinking of themselves as equivalent to the first adult in the sense that they too might be an object toward which the second adult directs her anger.

In sum, there are now various lines of research including, but also going beyond the mirror self-recognition paradigm, that converge in revealing the development of the objective self around the middle of the second year. These studies show that toddlers acquire an understanding of the self as an objective entity with particular properties. At the same time, toddlers also come to appreciate that the self can be the focus of others' intentional relations. Together these studies show that at around 18 months, children can take a third person perspective on self. This third-person perspective cannot be directly perceived; rather, it has to be imagined.

THE SUBJECTIVITY OF OTHERS

As I argued earlier, social understanding in the second year involves both the development of an understanding of the self as an individual with third-person characteristics and also the development of an understanding of others as individual agents with first-person perspectives. The latter development is evidenced by a variety of situations in which children are able to respond to other people's intentional relations, even when they are different from their own. A sensitivity to others' independent intentional relations may be observed in various types of intentional relations, including epistemic, affective, and conative kinds. It is informative to look at examples of each.

As we have already mentioned, by the end of the first year infants are able to coordinate their own visual intentional relations with those of interactive partners. They can use another person's gaze and pointing gestures to locate interesting sights in the local environment, and they are able to use gestures such as pointing to direct another person's gaze to something that they are interested in (e.g., Carpenter et al., 1998). Infants have problems in dealing with situations in which self and other have different visual intentional relations. Only by about 2 years are children capable of engaging in level-I perspective taking, whereby they must recognize that another person may see something different from what they are currently seeing (e.g., Masangkay et al., 1974; Moll & Tomasello, 2006). They also have difficulty in showing something to another person if to do so would thereby remove the interesting sight from their own visual experience. In an early demonstration, Lempers, Flavell, and Flavell (1977) gave children from 12 to 36 months a variety of simple tasks in which they had to show a picture to an adult seated opposite at a table. In one task the picture was printed on one side of a card; in another it was fixed to the inside face of a hollow wooden cube, so that the picture was only visible by looking into the cube. All children were able to show the picture to the adult in some sense; however, younger toddlers appeared to need to maintain the picture in their own vision in order to show it. So in the card case, they would show the picture but position it flat on the table so that they could see it at the same time. In the cube case, many of the younger toddlers showed an interesting tendency to locate the cube open end up between the self and the adult and tilt it back and forth so that both could see in it. By 24 months, the majority of participants were quite able to show the picture even if to do so would mean they could no longer see it—they would turn the card so that it faced the other and orient the cube so that the other could see in it. This pattern shows that the younger toddlers needed to maintain their own visual relation to the picture in order to show it to another person—they did not appear to appreciate that the other person's visual relation could be independent of their own. In contrast, the older toddlers did seem to realize that the other person would see the picture even when they themselves did not. They therefore seemed to have a firmer grasp of the independence of their own and the other person's visual relation to the picture.

Over the same period of development, toddlers start to appreciate that what may be *interesting* to others may differ from what is interesting to self. Interest is an intriguing case of an intentional relation that sits somewhere between the epistemic and affective types. Tomasello and Haberl (2003) introduced a clever way of examining toddlers' understanding of others' interest. They showed 12- and 18-month-olds a series of three toys at a table. For two of the toys an experimenter played with it with the child, but for the third toy, the experimenter was away from the table. In one condition, the experimenter left the room and did not see the toy at all while the child played with it. In a second condition, the experimenter went a few feet away from the table and watched the child from there. After all the toys had been played with, they were returned to the table together on a tray. At this point the experimenter looked at the child and held out her hand as she said in an animated voice, "Oh wow! Look at that! Can you give it to me?" The results showed that in the experimenter absent condition, the children were more likely to give the toy that had been played with during the absence. This effect did not occur in the experimenter present condition.

This result suggests that toddlers recognize what may be interesting to another person based on relative novelty, but the design of the study did not allow an unambiguous assessment of the children's ability to differentiate their own interest from that of the experimenter—the children may have picked the target toy in the experimenter absent condition because they had not yet shared any experience in relation to that toy. So in a follow-up study, MacPherson and Moore (2004) arranged a similar task with 12- and 18-month-olds in which the children played with an experimenter while a series of toys were introduced. For two of the toys the experimenter left the play table and sat at a different table while she talked on the phone. In one of these cases, the child played with the toy without the adult and in the other case the adult played with the toy without the child. As in the Tomasello and Haberl (2003) procedure, after all the toys had been introduced, they were all presented on a tray to the child. The experimenter then requested a toy in the same manner as in the original study. Now, the large majority of 12-month-old children gave the toy that they had not yet played with, whereas 18-month-olds were more likely to give the toy that the experimenter had not yet played with. This result more clearly indicates that infants are more driven by their own first-person perspective and do not clearly distinguish what others may be interested in. In contrast, by the middle of the second year, children are starting to recognize that what is of interest to another person may not be what is of interest to themselves.

Sensitivity to other people's emotions also undergoes significant change in the second year and again these changes indicate a growing awareness of the independent first-person experience of others. In the first year of life, infants show obvious sensitivity to others' emotional expressions. From 2 months, infants engage in emotionally arousing interactions with familiar people (e.g., Brazelton, Koslowski, & Main, 1974). They discriminate and respond appropriately to facial and vocal expressions of emotions (Walker-Andrews, 1988). By about 9 to 10 months, they can use emotional expressions to guide their action toward novel objects or situations (Mumme et al., 1996). However, such responsivity to others' emotional expression is not yet evidence that they distinguish others' experience from their own. To evidence an understanding of the diversity of emotional experience, the child must respond appropriately to the other's emotional orientation even while they are experiencing a different orientation.

Although it is often interpreted as indicating an early understanding of desire, a well-known study by Repacholi and Gopnik (1997) provides relevant evidence. Repacholi and Gopnik presented children of 14 and 18 months with two bowls, one containing crackers and the other raw broccoli. Children were first asked which food they liked and they all chose the crackers. Another adult then sampled the two foods in turn. To the crackers she reacted with a clear expression of disgust, whereas to the broccoli she reacted with pleasure. The toddlers were then asked to give one of the foods to the same adult. In this situation a clear difference between the children's own preference and the adult's preference was set up and the children could react based either on their own preference or on the adult's expressed preference. The results showed a developmental difference with only the 18-month-olds reliably giving the adult the broccoli for which she had previously expressed a liking. The 14-month-olds, in contrast, were more likely to give the adult the snack that they themselves liked—the crackers. So only at 18 months did children appear to differentiate the preferences of self and other.

A significant social behavioral manifestation of this developing awareness of the independence of emotions in self and other and the subjectivity of others' emotions is seen in the development of empathic behavior (Hoffman, 1975; Zahn-Waxler & Radke-Yarrow, 1990). Empathy has its roots right at the beginning of infancy in that even neonates will respond with distress on hearing another baby's cry. Throughout infancy there is a natural sensitivity to the third-person information provided by another person's expression of distress. The effect of this sensitivity is that infants experience from a first-person perspective a similar emotional state. However, during the first year this empathic contagion of distress leads the infants to seek comfort for themselves and they show no obvious signs that they recognize that it is the other person who is experiencing a negative state. During the second year, on experiencing another person's expression of distress, toddlers will still empathically "catch" the emotion, but now they are more likely to attempt to comfort the other, either directly or by recruiting their mother's assistance. This development change has been shown in experimental contexts in which the child plays with an experimental confederate in a lab setting. During the session, the play partner either simulates an injury or "accidentally" breaks a toy and then feigns distress. During 12 to 18 months toddlers become gradually more likely to show concern under these conditions and they may try to help the distressed person. At the same time, children become less likely to show the pattern typical of young children whereby they simply become upset themselves and seek comfort from their own mothers (e.g., Zahn-Waxler, Radke-Yarrow, Wagner, & Chapman, 1992). This change in emotional responsivity is consistent with the interpretation that toddlers are becoming more able to distinguish between their own emotional state and that indicated by the expressions of distress by others. They recognize that it is the other person who is feeling unhappy and seek to react appropriately.

Turning to conative psychological relations, children become quite skilled at coordinating their own goal-directed action with that of others by the end of the first year. Developments in imitation and cooperative behavior provide perhaps the best insight into children's growing awareness of others' goals as independent of their own. Again, infants as young as 9 months can imitate goal-directed actions, such as actions on objects that result in interesting effects (Meltzoff, 1988; Piaget, 1962). However, the purpose of these early imitative acts is to reproduce the effect achieved by the observed action (Elsner & Aschersleben, 2003), and thus is perhaps better seen as "emulation" (e.g., Want & Harris, 2002). As infants gain more familiarity with actions on objects, they start to anticipate the effects that actions will have, and by early in the second year, imitation may be directed at achieving anticipated effects rather than effects that are actually observed. Research by Meltzoff (1995) illustrates this point. Meltzoff presented 18-month-olds with various manipulable objects in different experimental conditions. In the key condition, the experimenter demonstrated actions that appeared to be designed toward some goal but failed. For example, one object was a small dumbbell with removable blocks on the ends. The experimenter grasped the block on one end of the dumbbell and attempted to pull it off, but his fingers slipped away unsuccessfully. Comparison groups of children either saw successful actions (the experimenter succeeded in pulling the block off the dumbbell) or irrelevant actions (the experimenter manipulated the dumbbell without trying to pull the block off). Having observed these various demonstrations, the children were allowed to manipulate the objects and their actions on the objects were recorded. The children who had observed the adult successfully pull the block off the dumbbell tended to do likewise when given the opportunity; the children who had seen the irrelevant actions tended not to pull the block off. Of most importance however, the children who had observed the adult try but fail to remove the block were just as likely to pull the block off the dumbbell as those children who had seen the successful action. This finding shows that these toddlers were imitating the adult's action based on an expectation of the effects, not on the actual results. Using the same experimental procedure, it has been found that 15-month-olds, but not 12-month-olds, will also imitate goal-directed actions (Bellagamba & Tomasello, 1999; Meltzoff, 2002).

The research on imitation of goal-directed action is important because it shows that toddlers are not simply attempting to re-create observed effects but can process observed actions in terms of intended goals. However, this work does not provide clear evidence for recognizing the intentional relation of the other person independently of the self's own intention. In Meltzoff's (1995) paradigm the toddler is able to recognize and use the other's action directed at a goal to set up his or her own goal and then act toward it. Again, therefore, the result is the alignment of the two people's intentional relations rather than a differentiation. Goal-directed imitation is similar to the toddler being able to use another person's looking behavior toward an unseen object to guide his or her own search for the object. Thus to succeed in goal-directed imitation, the child does not have to understand the other person's goal as independent of his or her own.

Two types of imitation in which children coordinate their goal-directed action with others in imitative contexts provide clearer evidence of understanding the independence of conative intentional relations. First, toddlers start to engage in what has been called "synchronic imitation" (e.g., Asendorpf & Baudonnière, 1993). When placed in a play context with peers, even unfamiliar peers, toddlers often start spontaneously to copy each other's actions. Of particular significance is the fact that during synchronic imitative play, toddlers continuously monitor the actions of the other and start and stop different activities in close synchrony. As a result, extended bouts of imitative play may occur, with each participant aware of the other's activity and how it corresponds to their own. Asendorpf and Baudonnière argue that such imitation requires children to be aware of the reciprocity in their imitative play. The children not only copy their partner's action but also recognize that their partner is copying them. Synchronic imitation, therefore, reveals that toddlers recognize the equivalence between their own and others' intentional relations during play.

Second, and perhaps more tellingly, toddlers start to become capable of role-reversal imitation in interactive situations involving two complementary roles (e.g., Carpenter et al., 2005). Carpenter and colleagues (2005) used a simple task in which the experimenter hid a toy by covering it with a cloth. The child was then prompted to find the toy. This sequence was repeated three times. The experimenter then handed the toy and the cloth to the child and said, "It's your turn now." Successful role-reversal imitation was scored if the children proceeded to cover the toy with the cloth and look toward the experimenter. To succeed on this role reversal, the child has to be able to attend to the experimenter's action during the demonstration even while his or her role is to perform a different action, so that later the child can adopt the experimenter's role in anticipation of performing the experimenter's original role. Whereas only 1 of 23 12-month-olds were able to perform such a role-reversal imitation, about half of the 18-month-olds were able to do so. Again, therefore, it appears to be not until about 18 months of age that children are able to recognize the distinction between their own and a partner's separate actions directed toward a common goal.

In imitation, the actions of the participants are matched and so the understanding of the independent intentional relations of others may be less obvious. Many interactive situations, however, require the participants to take up separate and complementary roles in relation to shared goals. Such situations would seem more clearly to require recognition of the independence of others' intentional relations. It is interesting, therefore, that children from the middle of the second year start to take complementary roles when cooperation is required to achieve a goal. Brownell and Carriger (1990) tested 12- to 30-month-old children in age-matched pairs on various cooperation tasks that required one child to operate a handle or lever thereby releasing a toy from an apparatus for another child to retrieve. The working of the apparatus was initially demonstrated to each pair of children. The authors reported that the greatest improvement in performance on these tasks occurred between 18 and 24 months. By 24 months the children were able to adopt different but complementary roles in solving these cooperation problems.

More recent work by Warneken, Chen, and Tomasello (2006) examined 18- and 24-month-olds behavior in cooperative situations with an adult. They used tasks that involved a shared goal, which could either be functional (e.g., extracting an object from a tube) or just fun (e.g., bouncing a block on a trampoline). Half of the tasks involved complementary actions on the part of the two participants and half involved similar actions. The adult was initially fully cooperative but after a few trials stopped cooperating for a 15-second period. This design allowed the researchers to examine cooperative behavior under controlled conditions of both adult cooperation and noncooperation. They found that toddlers at both ages were able to engage in cooperative activity with the adult whether the roles were complementary or similar, although as in the Brownell and Carriger (1990) study there was significant improvement over this period. Perhaps of most interest, Warneken and colleagues found evidence of attempts to reengage the partner in both 18- and more commonly 24-month-olds. Even the 18-month-olds would on occasion actively try to get the adult to take up his or her role again by gesturing or showing the adult what to do.

In this section, I have reviewed research relevant to toddlers understanding of epistemic, affective, and conative intentional relations in others. These studies tell a quite consistent story. It is during the second year that children show a clear ability to respond to another person's psychological relation even if it contrasts with their own. They can show something to another person even when they cannot see it or are relatively uninterested in it. They can respond appropriately to another's emotional orientation even if they do not share that emotion. They can recognize the goal-directed nature of another person's action even if their own action is different. Together these findings support the general idea that during the second year, toddlers can be said to acquire an understanding of the *subjectivity* of others independently of themselves.

THE COGNITIVE BASIS OF SOCIAL UNDERSTANDING IN THE SECOND YEAR

Over the years, a number of authors have suggested that the various phenomena of social cognitive development during the second year depend on general changes in representational ability (e.g., Leslie, 1987; Perner, 1991; Piaget, 1962; Suddendorf & Whiten, 2001). Correlational studies of these phenomena have provided some support. For example, Bischof-Köhler (1991) tested a group of 16- to 24-month-olds on mirror self-recognition and on empathy. The mirror self-recognition task was conducted in the traditional manner and self-directed behaviors in front of the mirror were recorded. During the session, the children also participated in a play session with a familiar female adult who had teddy bear. While playing, the adult accidentally broke her teddy bear's arm and proceeded to drop the bear between the child and herself and start to sob. Bischof-Köhler reported that the children who helped or comforted the adult all showed evidence of self-recognition in the mirror test. In contrast, those who did not show self-recognition in front of the mirror appeared indifferent or uncertain in the empathy situation. These results and those from similar studies (e.g., Johnson, 1982; Zahn-Waxler et al., 1992) have provided support for an association between performance on the classic test of the objective self and performance in a situation requiring sensitivity to the first-person experience of another person.

As noted earlier, Asendorpf and colleagues (Asendorpf, 2002; Asendorpf & Baudonnière, 1993; Asendorpf, Warkentin, & Baudonnière, 1996) have argued that synchronic imitation reveals an awareness of others as independent psychological agents and they too claim that this understanding depends on the general changes in representational ability occurring in the second year. They (Asendorpf & Baudonnière, 1993) first assessed a sample of 19-month-olds on mirror self-recognition. They then constructed pairs of children who were either at the same level or a different level of self-recognition and allowed them to play together in a lab setting. Synchronic imitation was assessed by measuring the imitative turns that the pairs produced during play. They found that pairs of self-recognizers engaged in more extended bouts of mutual imitation than either recognizer–nonrecognizer pairs or pairs of nonrecognizers. Asendorpf and Baudonnière (1993) interpret this finding in support of the idea that an understanding of the objective self is developmentally linked to an understanding of subjectivity in others.

How might general changes in representational ability enable the social cognitive changes seen during the second year? During the second year children become capable of holding in imagination one representation of an object or event while simultaneously engaged perceptually with the world (Leslie, 1987; Olson, 1993; Perner, 1991; Suddendorf & Whiten, 2001). With this change, children are able not only to respond to perceptually available information but also to consider that information in relation to some other information held in imagination. As a result, the information from the perceptual and imaginative (or representational) sources can be combined into more complex representations. The most obvious manifestations of this developmental change in representational ability are the symbolic skills of pretense and language (Leslie, 1987; Olson, 1993).

It is likely that this advance in representational ability is critical to the acquisition of the level of social understanding we have been discussing in this chapter. The various aspects of social understanding reviewed earlier also appear to depend on the ability to hold in mind one piece of information while attending perceptually to something else. To understand the self in objective terms, children must be able to imagine the self from a third-person point of view even as they experience directly the first-person characteristics of their current activity. For example, to show mark-directed behavior in mirror self-recognition, children have to process the perceptual information available during observation of the mirror image and compare it to an image of the self, represented in imagination. Conversely, to understand others in subjective terms, children must be able to imagine those others' first-person points of view even as they experience directly the third-person manifestations of their activity. Thus, to show a concerned response to another person in distress, children must process the perceptual information produced by the other's emotional expression and also recognize that expression as an outward manifestation of subjective feelings.

Once children can consider both first-person and third-person forms of information for both self and other simultaneously, they will be able to construct representations of action that integrate these two forms of information. It is, therefore, no simple coincidence that understanding the objective nature of self and the subjectivity of others develops together. Both depend on having a concept of psychological agents for which first- and third-person forms of information are integrated. In the case of the self, first-person information that is available directly through perception is integrated with third-person information available via imagination or mental representation. In the case of others, it is the third-person information that is available directly through perception and the first-person information that must be imagined. Nevertheless, in the cases of both self and other, first- and third-person information are available and can be combined into representations that have both an objective and a subjective side (Barresi & Moore, 1996). In this way, both self and others become represented as individual agents with similar yet distinct subjective orientations to the world.

WHAT'S NEXT?

The achievement of a level of social understanding that involves self–other equivalence and self-other diversity is major accomplishment on the way to a mature form of commonsense psychology. But naturally, there is much more to be achieved and the social cognitive achievements of the second year also provide a foundation for further developments in social understanding. Much of the early research in the theory-of-mind tradition has explored in detail the developmental changes over the preschool period as children grapple with mental concepts such as belief and desire (e.g., Astington, Harris, & Olson, 1988; Wellman, 1990). These concepts depend fundamentally on an understanding of both self and other as independent agents. But too much has been written on these developments to allow a brief review here. Instead I concentrate on what I think is a new opportunity both in terms of children's social cognitive development and in terms of the research we can carry out in the early preschool period.

We have seen that in infancy and early toddlerhood, children are able to engage with others in a variety of ways, all of which result in an alignment of intentional relations of the self with the other. Epistemic intentional relations are shared in joint attention, affective intentional relations are shared in social referencing, and conative intentional relations are shared in goal-directed imitation. These are all ways in which children can start to participate in social interactions that provide the context through which children gain entry into a new world of cultural learning (Moore, 2006; Tomasello, Kruger, & Ratner, 1993). By participating in these social interactions, children learn about the social and nonsocial world through others because they can adopt their interactive partners' intentional relations to objects and events. So what more is gained from moving to a level of social understanding in which self–other equivalence and diversity are recognized?

My suggestion is that once the child has an individualistic notion of intentional agents, he or she can start to learn through what have been termed *third-party* interactions (e.g., Akhtar, 2005a). Third-party interactions are ones occurring between two or more participants not including the child, but for which the child is an observer. Although the social psychological tradition of observational learning has long recognized that children learn purely by observation, it has largely been assumed until recently that learning in very young children is particularly enhanced by interactive experiences such as joint attention and scaffolding (e.g., Bruner, 1983; Tomasello et al., 1993). However, there is a growing realization that it does not take long for children to become able to learn from others without direct participation or interaction with those others. Much of the impetus for this realization has come from a consideration of language learning. It is known that in some cultures children appear to acquire language with relatively little direct joint attentional experience (e.g., Schieffelin & Ochs, 1983; see also Akhtar, 2005a). There is now some direct evidence that by 24 months, children can easily learn novel labels through observation of third-party interactions (Akhtar, 2005b). Even 18-month-olds are starting to show some limited ability to learn novel words in overhearing contexts (Floor & Akhtar, 2006). These findings show that language learning can proceed from third-party interactions by the end of the second year. Although, the requisite studies have not been done to my knowledge, it is entirely plausible that skill learning through imitation may also be possible in third-party interactive situations at about the same time.

If there is indeed a rather general developmental transition from learning within interactions to learning from observation at about 18 to 24 months of age, there is the intriguing possibility that the changes in social understanding we have considered in this chapter may be involved. Once children can understand the third-person expressions of others' intentional relations in terms of integrated representations that involve both subjective and objective aspects, they can observe others' activity and immediately understand that activity from a first-person point of view. In effect, the actions of others are understood by adopting a first-person perspective on the actions. Seeing others' actions in terms of first-person information would immediately allow the child to relate to that action as if it was his or her own. In this way there is a sense in which the child becomes an imaginative interactive participant in third-party interactions. The others' actions are understood as if they were the child's own. This would be the basis for the understanding of intentional action through simulation (Harris, 1992).

This account makes a fairly straightforward prediction, but as yet I know of no relevant evidence. If learning from third-party interactions depends on an understanding of self and other as equivalent but diverse in the way I have considered in this chapter, there should be a clear developmental coordination between these achievements. Only toddlers who show evidence of having an objective self and of understanding the subjectivity of others should be able to learn in third-party interactions.

FINAL WORDS

I have argued in this chapter that the second year of life involves significant changes in social cognition whereby children gain a uniform understanding of self and other as independent intentional agents who can take diverse orientations to the world. This level of understanding involves a complementary ability to represent self as an objective entity and to represent others as subjective agents. Both sides of this advance depend on more general changes in representational ability whereby children become able to imagine or hold in mind certain information while attending perceptually to other information, in order for these two sources of information to be compared and integrated into more complex representations of intentional relations. With this new level of social understanding, children become much more aware of themselves and of how others may see them, feel about them, and respond to them. They become much more vigorous in asserting their individuality. At the same time they also become much more sensitive to the perspectives and feelings of others, and they become aware of how they might act to change those points of view. Together these changes enable the child to become at one and the same time both self-conscious and socially sensitive, and perhaps to be able to learn from others purely from observation.

ACKNOWLEDGMENTS

Writing of this chapter was supported by the Canada Research Chairs program. My thanks to Celia Brownell and Claire Kopp for their valuable guidance and their indulgence towards my tardiness. Thanks also to John Barresi for valuable comments on the manuscript.

REFERENCES

Akhtar, N. (2005a). Is joint attention necessary for early learning? In B. Homer & C. Tamis-LeMonda (Eds.), *The development of social cognition and communication* (pp. 165–179). Mahwah, NJ: Erlbaum.

Akhtar, N. (2005b). The robustness of learning through overhearing. *Developmental Science*, *8*, 199–209.

Allport, G. W. (1961). *Pattern and growth in personality.* New York: Holt, Rinehart & Winston.

Amsterdam, B. (1972). Mirror self-image reactions before age two. *Developmental Psychobiology*, *5*, 297–305.

Asendorpf, J. B. (2002). Self-awareness, other-awareness, and secondary representation. In A. Meltzoff & W. Prinz (Eds.), *The imitative mind: Development, evolution, and brain bases* (pp. 63–73). New York: Cambridge University Press.

Asendorpf, J. B., & Baudonnière, P. (1993). Self-awareness and other-awareness: Mirror self-recognition and synchronic imitation among unfamiliar peers. *Developmental Psychology*, *29*, 88–95.

Asendorpf, J. B., Warkentin, V., & Baudonnière, P. (1996). Self-awareness and other-awareness II: Mirror self-recognition, social contingency awareness, and synchronic imitation. *Developmental Psychology*, *32*, 313–321.

Astington, J. W., Harris, P. L., & Olson, D. R. (1988). *Developing theories of mind.* New York: Cambridge University Press.

Bahrick, L., Moss, L., & Fadil, C. (1996). Development of visual self-recognition in infancy. *Ecological Psychology*, *8*, 189–208.

Bahrick, L. E., & Watson, J. S. (1985). Detection of intermodal proprioceptive visual contingency as a potential basis of self-perception in infancy. *Developmental Psychology*, *21*, 963–973.

Barresi, J., & Moore, C. (1996). Intentional relations and social understanding. *Behavioral and Brain Sciences*, *19*, 107–122.

Bellagamba, F., & Tomasello, M. (1999). Re-enacting intended acts: Comparing 12- and 18-month-olds. *Infant Behavior and Development*, 22, 277–282.

Bertenthal, B., & Fischer, K. (1978). Development of self-recognition in the infant. *Developmental Psychology, 14*, 44–50.

Bischof-Köhler, D. (1991). The development of empathy in infants. In M. Lamb & H. Keller (Eds.), *Infant development: Perspectives from German-speaking countries* (pp. 1–33). Hillsdale, NJ: Erlbaum.

Brazelton, T. B., Koslowski, B., & Main, M. (1974). The origins of reciprocity: The early infant–mother interaction. In M. Lewis & L. A. Rosenblum (Eds.), *The effect of the infant on its caregiver* (pp. 49–76). New York: Wiley.

Brownell, C. A., & Carriger, M. S. (1990). Changes in cooperation and self–other differentiation during the second year. *Child Development, 61*, 1164–1174.

Brownell, C. A., Zerwas, S., & Ramani, G. B. (in press). "So big": The development of bodily self-awareness in toddlers. *Child Development.*

Bruner, J. S. (1983). *Child's talk. Learning to use language*. New York: Norton.

Bullock, M., & Lütkenhaus, P. (1990). Who am I?: Self-understanding in toddlers. *Merrill-Palmer Quarterly, 36*, 217–238.

Carpenter, M., Nagell, K., & Tomasello, M. (1998). Social cognition, joint attention, and communicative competence from 9 to 15 months of age. *Monographs of the Society for Research in Child Development, 63*(Serial No. 255), 1–143.

Carpenter, M., Tomasello, M., & Striano, T. (2005). Role reversal imitation and language in typically-developing infants and children with autism. *Infancy, 8*, 253–278.

Corkum, V., & Moore, C. (1998). Origins of joint visual attention in infants. *Developmental Psychology. 34*, 28–38.

Elsner, B., & Aschersleben, G. (2003). Do I get what you get? Learning about the effects of self-performed and observed actions in infancy. *Consciousness and Cognition, 12*, 732–751.

Floor, P., & Akhtar, N. (2006). Can 18-month-old infants learn words by listening in on conversations? *Infancy, 9*, 327–339.

Gallup, G. G. (1970). Chimpanzees: Self-recognition. *Science, 167*, 86–87.

Geppert, U., & Küster, U. (1983). The emergence of "wanting to do it oneself": A precursor of achievement motivation. *International Journal of Behavioral Development, 6*, 355–369.

Harris, P. L. (1992). From simulation to folk psychology. *Mind and Language, 7*, 120–144.

Hilgard, E. R. (1980). The trilogy of mind: Cognition, affection, and conation. *Journal of the History of the Behavioral Sciences, 16*, 107–117.

Hoffman, M. (1975). Developmental synthesis of affect and cognition and its implications for altruistic motivation. *Developmental Psychology, 11*, 607–622.

James, W. (1950). *The principles of psychology* (Vol. 1). New York: Dover. (Original work published 1890)

Johnson, D. (1982). Altruistic behavior and the development of the self in infants. *Merrill-Palmer Quarterly, 28*, 379–388.

Lempers, J. D., Flavell, E. R., & Flavell, J. H. (1977). The development in very young children of tacit knowledge concerning visual perception. *Genetic Psychology Monographs, 95*, 3–53.

Leslie, A. M. (1987). Pretense and representation: The origins of "theory of mind." *Psychological Review, 94*, 412–426.

Lewis, M., & Brooks-Gunn, J. (1979). *Social cognition and the acquisition of self*. New York: Plenum Press.

Lewis, M., & Ramsay, D. (2004). Development of self-recognition, personal pronoun use, and pretend play during the 2nd year. *Child Development, 75*, 1821–1831.

Lewis, M., Sullivan, M. W., Stanger, C., & Weiss, M. (1989). Self development and self-conscious emotions. *Child Development, 60*, 146–156.

Loveland, K. A. (1986). Discovering the properties of a reflecting surface. *Developmental Review, 6*, 1–24.

Loveland, K. A. (1992). Self-perception and self-conception. *Psychological Inquiry, 3*, 125–127.

MacPherson, A., & Moore, C. (2004). *New to me or new to you?: Determining objects of attention and desire on the basis of novelty.* Paper presented at International Conference on Infant Studies, Chicago.

Masangkay, Z., McCluskey, K., McIntyre, C., Sims-Knight, J., Vaughn, B., & Flavell, J. (1974). The early development of inferences about the visual percepts of others. *Child Development, 45*, 357–366.

Meltzoff, A. N. (1988). Infant imitation and memory: Nine-month-olds in immediate and deferred tests. *Child Development, 59*, 217–225.

Meltzoff, A. N. (1995). Understanding the intentions of others: Re-enactment of intended acts by 18-month-old children. *Developmental Psychology, 31*, 838–850.

Meltzoff, A. N. (2002). Imitation as a mechanism of social cognition: Origins of empathy, theory of mind, and the representation of action. In U. Goswami (Ed.), *Blackwell handbook of child cognitive development* (pp. 6–25). Oxford, UK: Blackwell.

Mitchell, R. (1997). Kinesthetic–visual matching and the self-concept as explanations of mirror self-recognition. *Journal for the Theory of Social Behavior, 27*, 17–39.

Moll, H., & Tomasello, M. (2004). 12- and 18-month-old infants follow gaze to spaces behind barriers. *Developmental Science, 7*, F1–F9.

Moll, H., & Tomasello, M. (2006). Level 1 perspective-taking at 24 months of age. *British Journal of Developmental Psychology, 24*, 603–613.

Moore, C. (2006). *The development of commonsense psychology in the first five years*. Mahwah, NJ: Erlbaum.

Moore, C., Mealiea, J., Garon, N., & Povinelli, D. (in press). The development of the bodily self. *Infancy*.

Mumme, D. L., Fernald, A., & Herrera, C. (1996). Infants' responses to facial and vocal emotional signals in a social referencing paradigm. *Child Development, 67*, 3219–3237.

Neisser, U. (1988). Five kinds of self-knowledge. *Philosophical Psychology, 1*, 35–59.

Nielsen, M., Dissanayake, C., & Kashima, Y. (2003). A longitudinal investigation of self-other discrimination and the emergence of minor self-recognition. *Infant Behavior and Development, 26*, 213–226.

Olson, D. R. (1993). The development of representations: The origins of mental life. *Canadian Psychology, 34*, 293–306.

Perner, J. (1991). *Understanding the representational mind*. Cambridge, MA: MIT Press.

Piaget, J. (1962). *Play, dreams, and imitation*. London: Routledge & Kegan Paul.

Piaget, J. (1977). *The origin of intelligence in the child*. Harmondsworth, UK: Penguin. (Original work published 1953)

Povinelli, D. P. (1995). The unduplicated self. In P. Rochat (Ed.), *The self in early infancy* (pp. 161–192). Amsterdam: North Holland-Elsevier.

Repacholi, B. M., & Gopnik, A. (1997). Early reasoning about desires: Evidence from 14- and 18-month-olds. *Developmental Psychology, 33*, 12–21.

Repacholi, B. M., & Meltzoff, A. N. (2005). *Other people's perceptual and emotional states influence infant imitation*. Paper presented at the biennial meeting of the Society for Research in Child Development, Atlanta, GA.

Schieffelin, B. B., & Ochs, E. (1983). A cultural perspective on the transition from prelinguistic to linguistic communication. In R. M. Golinkoff (Ed.), *The transition from prelinguistic to linguistic communication* (pp. 115–131). Hillsdale, NJ: Erlbaum.

Suddendorf, T., & Whiten, A. (2001). Mental evolution and development: Evidence for secondary representation in children, great apes, and other animals. *Psychological Bulletin, 127*, 629–650.

Tomasello, M., Carpenter, M., Call, J., Behne, T., & Moll, H. (2005). Understanding and sharing intentions: The origins of cultural cognition. *Behavioral and Brain Sciences, 28*, 675–691.

Tomasello, M., & Haberl, K. (2003). Understanding attention: 12- and 18-month-olds know what is new for other persons. *Developmental Psychology, 39*, 906–912.

Tomasello, M., Kruger, A. C., & Ratner, H. H. (1993). Cultural learning. *Behavioral and Brain Sciences, 16*, 495–511.

Walker-Andrews, A. S. (1988). Infants' perception of the affordances of expressive behaviors. In L. Lipsitt & C. Rovee-Collier (Eds.), *Advances in infancy research* (Vol. 5, pp. 173–221). Norwood, NJ: Ablex.

Want, S. C., & Harris, P. L. (2002). How do children ape?: Applying concepts from the study of non-human primates to the developmental study of "imitation" in children. *Developmental Science, 5*, 1–41.

Warneken, F., Chen, F., & Tomasello, M. (2006). Cooperative activities in young children and chimpanzees. *Child Development, 77*, 640–663.

Wellman, H. (1990). *The child's theory of mind.* Cambridge, MA: MIT Press.

Wimmer, H., & Perner, J. (1983). Beliefs about beliefs: Representation and constraining function of wrong beliefs in young children's understanding of deception. *Cognition, 13*, 103–128.

Woodward, A. L. (2005). The infant origins of intentional understanding. In R. V. Kail (Ed.), *Advances in child development and behavior* (Vol. 33, pp. 229–262). Oxford, UK: Elsevier.

Zahn-Waxler, C., & Radke-Yarrow (1990). The origins of empathic concern. *Motivation and Emotion, 14*, 107–130.

Zahn-Waxler, C., Radke-Yarrow, M., Wagner, E., & Chapman, M. (1992). Development of concern for others. *Developmental Psychology, 28*, 126–136.

3

The Codevelopment of Self and Sociomoral Emotions during the Toddler Years

MICHAEL F. MASCOLO
KURT W. FISCHER

Profound changes occur in self-awareness during the toddler years. During the second year, children begin to assert their own agency (Mascolo & Fischer, 1998), resist adult intervention, use the words "I" and "me" (Pipp, Fischer, & Jennings, 1987), show self-recognition when looking into a mirror (Bertenthal & Fischer, 1978; Lewis & Brooks-Gunn, 1979), and experience early forms of moral and self-conscious emotions (M. Lewis, 1993; Mascolo & Fischer, 1995; Zahn-Waxler, 1990). As self-awareness develops, the sense of self increasingly functions as a sociomoral guide to action (Tangney, 2002). The self is not simply a cognitive construction: Self-awareness is a type of *reflective activity* (Mead, 1934) that coordinates cognitive, emotional, conative, and social elements (Bertenthal & Fischer, 1978; Emde, 1983; Mayer, Chabot, & Carlsmith, 1997; Sarbin & Allen, 1968). Emotions—and particularly self-conscious and moral emotions—are important aspects of developing selves. Self-conscious emotions both *organize* and *are organized by* an individual's evolving capacity to evaluate the self within social contexts. For example, guilt arises in development as children gain the capacity to become aware of having committing a wrongdoing; however, feelings of guilt simultaneously organize and amplify children's sense of responsibility for moral infractions. In this way, self-conscious emotions function as building blocks for the construction of selves.

In this chapter, we examine the codevelopment of sociomoral, self-evaluative emotions and self as they develop in social interactions with parents and other socialization figures. We use dynamic skill theory (Fischer, 1980; Fischer & Bidell, 2006; Mascolo & Fischer, 1999, 2004) to chart the emergence and development of guilt, shame, and anger over the toddler years. We argue that (1) guilt, shame, and anger are sociomoral emotions that develop as children appropriate sociomoral standards from their joint activity with others; (2) experiences of guilt and shame take multiple forms over time; (3) partially internalized forms of guilt and shame can be identified by the third year of life; (4) similar socialization processes underlie the development of guilt, shame, and the regulation of anger; and (5) sociomoral and self-evaluative emotions in the toddler years provide a foundation for the construction of moral selves in development.

THE CONCEPT OF SELF IN SOCIAL CONTEXT

In what follows, we define *self* in terms of a child's developing awareness of *I*, *me*, or *mine*. From this view, the sense of self consists of a type of *reflective* experience, as expressed in the writings of George Herbert Mead (1934). According to him, the self is born when the process of awareness becomes "an object to itself." The experience of self consists of conscious activity that takes itself as an object. This model of self is depicted in Figure 3.1. The idea that self-awareness is a type of reflective activity implies the presence of a more primary level of activity that performs the requisite acts of reflection. This activity is represented by the bold arrow indicating primary conscious action operating on social objects. Self-awareness occurs as primary conscious activity loops back on itself and takes itself as a constructed object of awareness. Self-awareness is indicated in Figure 3.1 by the reflective looping-back of the base arrow on itself. The process by which this process occurs is a social one. In the example provided in Figure 3.1, a mother redirects her 27-month-old child after he angrily grabs a toy from his playmate. The darkened arrow represents the structure of the boy's primary goal-directed behavior. The dashed arrow on the right depicts the mother's disciplinary strategy. In this context, the mother's intervention fosters the development of self-awareness and self-control by *directing her child's conscious attention back on his own action and experience*. This process of externally regulated self-reflection is represented by the reflective looping back of a child's primary action onto his or her own ongoing activity and experience.

This notion of self-awareness directly implies a distinction between *agency* and *identity*, *subject* and *object*, "*I*" and "*me*." We generally experience conscious activity as a process through which we exert control over action (James, 1890). In this way, we experience a sense of *agency*, *subjectivity*, or "*I*" in our primary activity (Blasi & Glodis, 1995). When primary action loops back on itself, it constructs a representation of itself as an *object* of awareness (James, 1890; Mascolo, 2004; Mead, 1934). This reflective construction of the self as an object of awareness sets the stage for the social creation of self and identity. In the example provided in Figure 3.1, the mother's

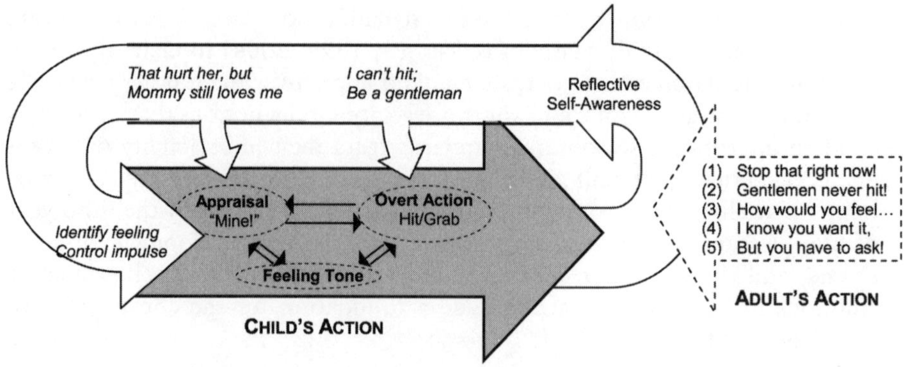

FIGURE 3.1. Self as a reflective process. The base gray arrow represents a child's primary action-on-objects. Emotional action is composed of an integration of appraisal, affective feeling, and overt action. In social contexts, self-awareness emerges as the actions and words of others function to direct constructive activity back onto the self's activities. In this way, self-awareness involves acts of reflecting consciousness back on itself. In development, self-awareness increasingly operates as a moral guide to action and experience.

words function to *organize* and *regulate* her child's awareness of "I" and "me" in socially meaningful ways. For example, the child is aware that his mother wants him to "stop hitting" and "be a gentleman." The development of the awareness that "I'm not being a *gentleman*" reflects the child's other-regulated construction of self-as-object. The other-regulated construction of the child's awareness that "*I* can stop hitting" organizes the child's sense of personal agency ("*I*").

What is the function of this constructed sense of self? Why is it important? The birth of the self brings with it the capacity of self-regulation and self-control (Kopp, 1982, 1989). When a child constructs a sense of *who she is* and *what she can do*, she can use this constructed sense to regulate her actions, thoughts, and feelings within social contexts (Carver & Scheier, 1998; Mascolo, Fischer, & Neimeyer, 1999). In this way, representations of self function as higher-order control structures that regulate action in social exchanges. In Figure 3.1, the mother's intervention directs an act of constructive reflection by her child. Over time, the child can use his jointly created representations of self to regulate his action and experience with others. This includes identifying and regulating his feelings of anger; acting in accordance with his image of "gentleman"; developing a sense of being able to interact with others, and so on. In this way, the development of self-awareness operates as a control system that drives social action.

SELF-EVALUATIVE MORAL EMOTIONS AND THE DEVELOPMENT OF SELF

In recent decades, researchers have proposed that emotion plays a central role in the organization of consciousness, action, and development (Fischer,

Shaver, & Carnochan, 1990; Freeman, 2002; Lewis & Douglas, 1998; Mascolo, Fischer, & Li, 2002; Tomkins, 1987). From this view, self-evaluative and moral emotions take on special significance. If the self functions as a moral guide in social action, it follows that sociomoral emotions must play a central role in the development of moral selves. Such emotions undergo profound changes throughout the toddler years (Barrett, 1998a; Mascolo & Fischer, 1995; Schore, 1994). Analysis of changes in these emotions provides a window to the development of self over the toddler years.

As indicated in Figure 3.1, emotional experiences are composed of at least three coacting classes of component processes (Mascolo et al., 2002). These include a motive-relevant *appraisal*, a characteristic affect or *feeling tone*, and a *motive–action tendency* (Frijda, 1986). Appraisal processes refer to ongoing assessments of the relation between perceived events and a person's goals, motives, and concerns (Lazarus, 1991). In any given context, ongoing motive-event appraisals continuously modulate the emotional *feeling tone*. In addition, any given form of emotional experience is organized with reference to particular classes of *motive–action tendencies*. An action tendency refers to emotion-typical actions that function to bring about changes in events that are consistent with one's goals, motives, and concerns. Action tendencies embody voluntary (i.e., instrumental actions) as well as involuntary motor–action systems (e.g., facial, postural, and vocal changes). In addition, in development, children develop strategies for regulating their emotional reactions (Garber & Dodge, 1991; Kopp, 1989, Kopp & Neufeld, 2003). Campos, Frankel, and Camras (2004) have convincingly argued that emotion regulation processes are not second-order strategies that are "added onto" primary emotions; instead, emotional regulation transforms the very nature of emotional experiences in development.

Table 3.1 provides a description of the anatomy of anger, guilt, and shame as they are experienced among adults in North American and Western European cultures. (The situation is different for adults in China, and presumably some other cultures; Marcus & Kitayama, 2003; Mascolo et al., 2002; Li, Wang, & Fischer, 2004.) Among adults, anger functions as a moral emotion. Anger involves appraisals that events are not only *unwanted* but also contrary to the way they *ought* to be (de Rivera, 1981; Mascolo & Griffin, 1998; Roseman, Spindel, & Jose, 1990). We call such morally tinged appraisals *ought violations*. In anger, this implies an attribution of blame to others (Lazarus, 1991). In describing the affective or feeling component of anger, individuals use metaphors such as "heat," "pressure," and "tension" (Davitz, 1969). de Rivera (1981) has suggested that the affective component of anger involves the experience of the *strengthening of will* to move against the other. The action tendencies involved in anger consist of actions directed toward *removing ought violations* (Mascolo & Griffin, 1998). Action tendencies include instrumental (verbal or physical attack, indirect or passive aggression, retribution, retaliation, etc.) as well as *facial* (e.g., furrowed brow and square mouth), *vocal* (e.g., increased volume and pace), and *bodily* (e.g., flailing arms) acts.

TABLE 3.1. The Anatomy of Anger, Guilt, and Shame

Emotion family	Appraisal: Motive ↔	Appraisal: Violation	Feeling tone/bodily transformation	Action tendencies
Anger	Maintain desired states and conditions that "ought" to exist.	Violation of sociomoral standards by blameworthy other.	Strengthening of will to move against other and remove the violation. The experience described with metaphors like "heat," "tension"; "pressure"; "feel like exploding"; etc.	Move against the other to remove the violation; physical, verbal or symbolic attack; indirect aggression or attack.
Guilt	Maintain sociomoral standards; maintain sense of self as moral person.	Self is responsible for sociomoral condition.	Sense of feeling "weighed down"; "heavy"; as if there is a "sinking" or "tugging" feeling in one's chest.	Remove sociomoral violation by making reparations; fixing the situation; apologizing; confessing wrongdoing.
Shame	Maintain positive social identity in eyes of other and self.	Self aware that other sees flawed self or identity.	Sense of self as feeing "small" or "this big"; face feels "exposed."	Desire to hide the self; hid the face; withdraw from social scrutiny; shame → anger cycle

Guilt and shame not only have strong sociomoral dimensions; they are also self-evaluative emotions. The experiences of guilt and shame are mediated by appraisals that one has departed from social standards for evaluating the self. At the same time, the experiences guilt and shame *motivate* acts of self-reflection and self-evaluation. As indicated in Table 3.1, experiences of guilt are mediated by appraisals that the self is responsible for a wrongdoing (Hoffman, 2000; Mascolo & Fischer, 1995; Zahn-Waxler, 1990). The experience of guilt is often described as "heavy," as if a person were "weighed down." Many people describe the experience as a "sinking" or "tugging" in the chest or torso (Davitz, 1969). In guilt, persons are motivated to correct the perceived wrongdoing (Baumeister, Stillwell, & Hetherton, 1994; Hoffman, 2000; Lindsay-Hartz, de Rivera, & Mascolo, 1995). Note that it is not always necessary for an individual to have committed an actual wrongdoing to feel guilt; it is merely necessary for individuals to *assume responsibility* for wrongful conditions. Examples of such experiences include the sense of survivor guilt, as well as feelings of guilt experienced by people (e.g., Mother Theresa) who assume responsibility for the plight of others (de Rivera, 1984).

Although they are strongly related, guilt and shame differ in fundamental ways in Western culture (Lindsay-Hartz et al., 1995; Tangney, Miller, Flicker, & Barlow, 1996). In guilt, a person's experience and action is focused on a wrongful act or condition; in shame, the focus is on a flaw in the self in the eyes of others (H. B. Lewis, 1971; M. Lewis, 1993; Scheff, 2000, 2003; Tangney & Dearing, 2002). In shame, one's entire identity or self is experienced as devalued in the eyes of others. This is embodied in Lindsay-Hartz's description of the "psychological situation" of shame: "upon viewing ourselves *through the eyes of another, we realize that we are in fact who we do not want to be and that we cannot now be otherwise*" (Lindsay-Hartz et al., 1995, p. 278, emphasis in original). Shame is embodied by a sense of being "small" or "exposed." In shame, people experience the desire to hide the face or hide the self. Thus, in guilt we focus on a wrongful act; in shame we reflect on a person's social identity in the eyes of self and other.

Scheff (2000, 2003) argues convincingly that shame operates as a quintessential *social* emotion. He differentiates among at least two meanings of shame. According to Scheff, these two senses are discriminated in non-English European languages. The first consists of the notion of shame as disgrace (*disgrace shame*; e.g., *schande* in German). The second refers to the more ubiquitous sense of everyday shame (*scham*). This more general conception of shame superordinates a family of emotions related to the social devaluation of self, including shame, embarrassment, shyness, humiliation, and so on. According to Scheff (2000), such everyday shame can arise from virtually any threat to a social bond. Because of its ubiquity, everyday shame functions as a "master emotion of everyday life"; it plays a central role in the regulation of social relations. In Chinese, this master emotion has been extensively elaborated, with a large vocabulary of shame words differentiated into six large families and more than a dozen subfamilies of shame (Li et al., 2004).

Because of a taboo placed on acknowledging shame in North American and Western European culture, people feel a strong need to hide their shame. As a result, much shame goes unacknowledged. For Scheff, such unacknowledged shame gives rise to feelings of anger and humiliated fury. One might suggest that these latter emotions function as ways to protect the self from social experience of shame. Evidence supports the proposition that shame can evoke anger not only in moment-by-moment social interaction (H. B. Lewis, 1971; Retzinger, 1991; Scheff & Retzinger, 1991) but also in studies that assess broad dispositions toward shame and anger (M. Lewis, 1992, 1993; Tangney, Wagner, & Gramzow, 1992; Tangney, Wagner, Hill-Barlow, Marschall, & Gramzow, 1996). In Chinese, with its elaborated vocabulary for shame, there is a substantial family of words for shame turning into anger (Li et al., 2004).

In toddlerhood, it is likely that guilt, shame, and anger develop through overlapping processes. Guilt, shame, and anger develop as children internalize sociomoral standards and use them to represent, evaluate, and regulate the self in social interaction (Mascolo & Fischer, 1995; Zahn-Waxler, 1990). Furthermore, as sociomoral emotions, anger, guilt, and shame are related in complex ways. Shame and guilt are structurally similar and are often experienced in similar contexts. Shame plays an important role in the evocation of anger and aggression in social interaction, and in some cultures such as China it plays a major role in socialization (Bedford & Hwang, 2003; Mascolo et al., 2003; Stipek et al., 1989). Furthermore, parental demands that children regulate their anger and conform to social rules figure in the development of guilt and shame as well. In what follows, we chart developmental transformations in multiple components of anger, guilt, and shame over the toddler years for children in American culture. In so doing, we examine social processes by which these experiences are formed as well as the ways in which they both organize and are organized by changes in the capacity to represent and regulate the self.

TRAJECTORIES OF SOCIOMORAL AND SELF-EVALUATIVE EMOTION

Sociomoral and self-evaluative emotions move through systematic developmental transformations in appraisal, action, and self-regulation. What changes in development is the particular *emergent structure* of an action and meaning as it is deployed within a particular context. We use Fischer's (1980; Fischer & Bidell, 2006) model of skill development to characterize these developmental trajectories, because it has been used successfully to predict emotional development in diverse domains. It specifies a series of 13 levels organized in four tiers in the development of particular skills from infancy through adulthood. For example, appraisal, action, and regulatory components of anger develop through the four broad tiers—*reflexes*, *sensorimotor actions*, *representations*, and *abstractions*. *Reflexes* (emerging near birth) consist of innate action elements (e.g., distress-related facial actions to painful stimuli). *Sensorimotor actions* (emerging around 4 months of age) consist of the proactive execution of actions directed toward persons or objects in one's immediate environs (e.g., pushing away an obstacle to a goal-directed action). *Representations* (emerging around 18–24 months of age) consist of symbolic meanings that symbolize concrete aspects of persons, objects, or internal states (e.g., "that dolly is mine!"). *Abstractions* (emerging around 10–11 years of age) consist of generalized meaning structures that represent intangible, abstract, or general aspects of persons, events, or experiences (e.g., "You don't care about me the way a father should").

Within each of these broad tiers, appraisal, action, and regulatory skills develop through four levels: single *sets*, *mappings*, *systems*, and *systems of systems*. Higher-level skill structures emerge from the successive differentiation and intercoordination of lower-level skills or skill components. For example, within the representational tier of development, skills develop through four levels. Beginning around 18–24 months, children are able to construct single representations, which consist of single concrete ideas about objects, events, or people. For example, a 2-year-old child can construct single representations of self, including concrete conceptions of "me," "my," or "mine" (e.g., "That is my doll!"). Beginning around 3½ to 4 years of age, children gain the capacity to coordinate the relation between two single concrete ideas into a representational mapping. Using representational mappings, children can represent concrete relations between ideas in terms of causality, temporality, part–whole, reciprocity, and so on. For example, a 4-year-old child can form a comparative representation such as "That doll is mine but that truck is yours," or "I want to be the first [rather than second] one to go upstairs!." Around 6–7 years old, children gain the capacity to coordinate two or more mappings into a representational system. For example, at this level, a child can construct a systems-based representation such as "I want to go upstairs first this time, but you can go upstairs first the next time!" Not only do skills develop through four levels within a given tier, but skill theory (Fischer, 1980) provides a series of transformation rules that allows specification of an indeterminate number of steps within any given level, depending on the skill in question. Below, drawing on skill theory, we trace developmental changes in the levels and steps of appraisal, action, and regulatory components through the sensory-motor and representational tiers of development. Figure 3.2 outlines strands in a developmental web describing structural changes in the development of guilt, anger, and shame. In the sections that follow, we outline developmental changes in these emotions and their relations through the toddler years.

The Development of Anger

Emerging around 2 months of age, anger develops gradually in a series of steps throughout the first year of life (Mascolo, Harkins, & Harakal, 2000; Mascolo & Mancuso, 1990; Mascolo, Mancuso, & Dukewich, in press; Sroufe, 1996). For our purposes, we begin analysis of the development of anger just prior to the onset of the toddler years. As depicted in step A1 in Figure 3.2, beginning around 7–8 months of age, an infant is capable of constructing *sensorimotor mappings,* coordinating the relation between two single sensorimotor acts (e.g., *removing* a cover in order to *retrieve* a hidden object). This level of skill underlies an infant's protest when a wanted adult leaves a child's field of vision. The parent's act of leaving his or her child's field of vision acts as a form of *cued recall* (Gerhardstein, Liu, & Rovee-Collier, 1998). The parent's leaving cues the wish to get him or her back, which creates a goal violation. The resulting anger state energizes the sensorimotor action of actively seeking the absent parent in order to reestablish contact.

Beginning around 12–13 months of age, toddlers gain the capacity to coordinate two or more sensorimotor mappings into a single sensorimotor system. At the level of sensorimotor systems, a child can deploy combinations of multiple sensorimotor actions to actively explore his or her physical and social world. Children's assurgent explorations inevitably begin to trespass parental boundaries. Soon after the onset of sensorimotor systems, toddlers begin to exhibit temper tantrums (Potegal & Davidson, 2003; Potegal, Kosorok, & Davidson, 1996). Tantrums often occur when an adult rejects a child's demand, especially in contexts involving the depletion of a toddler's physical or emotional resources (e.g., fatigue and hunger). Tantrums arise around this

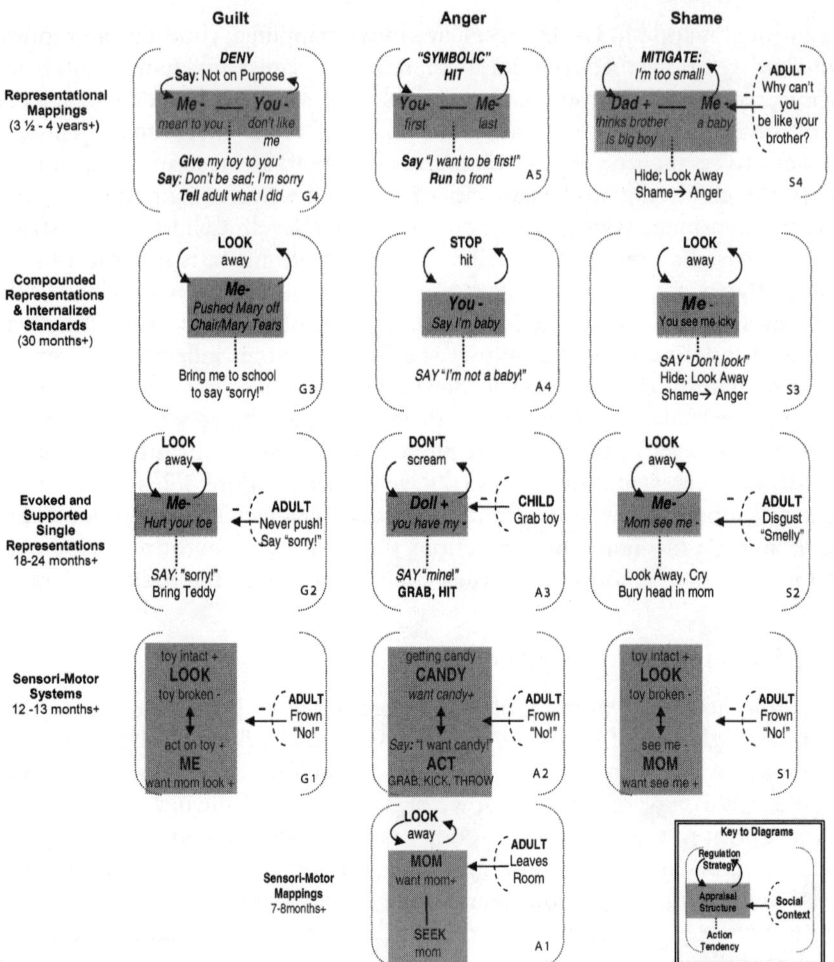

FIGURE 3.2. Developmental changes in the dynamic structure of anger, guilt, and shame. Emotional skill diagrams depicting changes in sociomoral emotions in development. The structure of the diagrams is depicted in the box in the lower lefthand corner of Figure 3.2. Using skill theory (Fischer, 1980), the shaded portion of the diagram reflects the structure of the child's appraisal activity. The lower (unshaded) portion, connected to appraisal structures with a dotted line, identifies the structure of emotion action-tendencies. The structure above the shaded portion of the diagram identities the structure of emotional control elements. The regulation function of control elements is indicated using bidirectional curved arrows. For some diagrams, the structure of adult action is provided to the right of the emotional skill diagram for the child. The arrow between the adult and child structures indicates the flow of action from the adult to the child. Plus and minus signs indicated the motivational valence (positive or negative) of the skill element in question. For emotions at the sensorimotor level, appraisal activity and action tendencies are represented together because, at this level, appraisal processes are embedded within sensorimotor action. The changes specified reflect changes typical of North American and Western European children. At any given age, the particular structure of emotional action varies with context, child, culture, affective state, and other important factors.

time as a product of a series of converging developmental conditions. First, at this level, in contexts that support their creation, toddlers can begin to construct more stable mental goals for wanted objects. While younger children are often able to be distracted from the wanted object, at the more advanced level of sensorimotor systems, a toddler can sometimes keep in mind the goal of the wanted object despite attempts to divert his or her attention. However, the prerepresentational capacities for delay of gratification and self-control remain limited, and children have not yet developed the capacity to control the emotional reactions that arise from unmet demands. In addition, they have not encountered the requisite social experiences needed to develop skills for delaying gratification. For these reasons also, the result is the temper tantrum.

How adults respond to a child's negative affect in contexts that involve tantrums is crucial in the development of anger-regulation strategies. Parental discipline in such contexts is important for promoting rule internalization and the development of effective social skills (Laible & Thompson, 2002). In North American and Western European societies, anger regulation is fostered by parenting styles that involve emotionally responsive but firm control of the enactment of anger (Dishion, Duncan, Eddy, Fagot, & Fetrow, 1994; Eisenberg et al., 2001; Granic & Patterson, 2006; Patterson, 1982) . In the context of a tantrum, this style involves providing both firm enforcement of the prohibition in question—not "giving in" to a child—while also providing a physically and emotionally safe environment for the child throughout the course of the tantrum (Patterson, 1982). After the tantrum, the parent is able to use inductive explanation (Hoffman, 1983, 2000; Mancuso & Handin, 1985) and provide alternative strategies for handling refusals in the future. Such practices not only enable children to develop strategies for bringing anger under control but also teach children that their anger enactments will not be successful.

Both punitive and permissive tantrum regulation strategies can put children at risk for emotional dysregulation. Given an angry episode, the parent may put forth efforts to terminate the outburst. Many parents find children's anger noxious. One way to terminate a child's unpleasant angry display is to yield to the child's demands. Such practices foster what Patterson (Patterson, Reid, & Dishion 1992) calls the *coercion cycle*. A child uses anger to advance his or her agenda; the parent gives in to the child's overture to eliminate the noxious display. The parent's yielding socially reinforces the child's anger, and the cycle escalates. Alternatively, parents may react to children's anger with hostile and punitive discipline. In some families, this may involve physical or hostile aggression. Research has consistently demonstrated that such forms of punishment do not forestall aggression in the long run but rather promote it (Grogan-Kaylor, 2005; Grusec & Goodnow, 1994; Watson, Fischer, & Andreas, 2004). Such extreme practices not only fail to promote the development of effective emotional regulation, but have the effect of perpetuating the use of aggression as a strategy for social problem solving.

Beginning around 18–24 months of age, children enter the *representational* tier of development. Representations consist of concrete symbolic meanings. The use of representations allows children to go beyond the here-and-now of sensorimotor experience and cued recall. Recall that with development, beliefs about what ought to happen play an increasing role: Experiences of anger become increasingly mediated by appraisals that events violate what a child believes *ought* to exist. As a sociomoral concept, an *ought* requires the capacity to compare what currently exists to some *preferred* or *idealized* way an event *should* be. In this way, the representation of "oughts" in appraisal activity requires the mediation of signs and symbols, which children develop the capacity to construct generally and effectively in the representational tier of development. Children begin to use moral language (Dunn & Munn, 1987) and to make accountability judgments to others soon during the second and third years of life (Schultz & Wells, 1985; Shultz, 1980).

At 18–24 months of age, children build many single representations by coordinating two or more skills at the sensorimotor system level. Using *single representations*, children can begin to construct single morally tinged social categories for representing self, others, social relations, and one's own desires. This includes the symbolic construct of a sense of *agency* (*I*), *identity* (*me*), and *possession* (*mine*) (Bullock & Lütkenhaus, 1990; Fasig, 2000; Mascolo & Fischer, 1998). As indicated in step A3 in Figure 3.2, the first genuine *ought violations* emerge as intrusions on a child's symbolic boundaries or concrete sense of agency or ownership. For example, at this level, a child can appraise a peer's actions as violating his or her concrete sense of *mine*. In anger, a child can construct an *appraisal* like "You took my doll!" At this level, although many children continue to exhibit various forms of physical aggression, verbal attacks (e.g., "I don't like you!") can begin to replace physical aggression in anger. In addition, using single representations, children can exhibit verbal protests accompanied by morally relevant justifications (e.g., "that's mine!"). At this age, anger regulation is often unstable; children can assuage strong emotion by looking away. They can often inhibit angry aggression in the presence of adults, but they are notably inconsistent.

The third year of life is an important time for sociomoral development and the further development of emotional regulation (Kopp, 1989; Vaughn, Kopp, & Krakow, 1984; Vaughn, Kopp, Krakow, Johnson, & Schwartz, 1986). The capacity to form signs and symbols allows children to represent increasingly sophisticated sociomoral–affective meanings—conceptions of the way the world *should* be, including their own wishes and goals. Over time, children appropriate and identify with such meanings (Tappan, 2000). As a result, the appraisals involved in anger states as well as other emotions become increasingly mediated by sociomoral standards. In addition, children use such sociomoral standards to regulate and control their enactments of anger. The construction of sociomoral meaning arises in everyday sign-mediated activity with socialization agents. Such meanings are constructed in everyday encounters with socialization agents.

This everyday process is represented in the mother–child interaction displayed in Figure 3.1. In this situation, a mother responds to her child's angry display with an inductive child-management strategy (Hoffman, 1983). The adult's disciplinary action serves multiple functions. It prompts her child to perform a *controlled act of inhibition* ("stop that right now!") and articulates the concrete *sociomoral rule* that was violated ("never hit!") and links that moral rule to the parent's desired image of the child's self (i.e., "gentleman"). It also directs the child's attention to the *internal state* of the hurt child ("how would you feel if . . . ?). Within the same exchange, the parent acknowledges the transgressor's emotional state ("I know you want the doll . . . ") while simultaneously providing directives that function to build social skills ("but you have to ask nicely"). These everyday interventions foster the development of moral meanings that come to mediate the regulation and experience of self and anger.

Kopp and her colleagues have identified the second and third year of life as an important period in the development of toddlers' understanding of parental rules and the capacity to regulate behavior in light of these rules. Early in the second year of life, in European American homes, parental regulation focuses largely on safety issues. Over time, parents begin to enforce compliance to requests (Vaughn et al., 1984), to encourage independent action, and to enforce family rules (Gralinski & Kopp, 1993). Children's capacity to follow adult rules changes as they gain the capacity to understand such requests, and as parents use inductive techniques (Hoffman, 1983; Grusec & Goodnow, 1994; Kalar & Kopp, 1990) to explain and induce moderate levels of emotional arousal in children (Eisenberg et al., 2005; Kochanska, 2002). Over time, such external regulation prompts transformation in and regulation of each component of a child's emotional processes (Kopp, 1989). Firm limits from parents instruct a child of the unacceptability of the anger display and place demands on him or her to develop strategies for regulating affect and action. Rule inductions stated by parents foster changes in the sociomoral appraisals that mediate experiences of anger (Hoffman, 1983). Strategy instruction and modeling provide the child with alternative strategies for negotiating social interaction. Strategy induction described by parents not only increases the likelihood that successful social relations will prevent future angry encounters but also promotes the development of conflict management and anger-regulation strategies (Kopp & Neufeld, 2003; Laible & Thompson, 2001). Acknowledgment of emotional reactions functions to maintain the affectively positive parent–child relationship within and beyond the context of a discipline encounter.

As a result of these social processes, throughout the third year of life, children become increasingly capable of exerting control over their experiences and enactments of anger. In addition, as children define themselves and their desires with reference to increasingly internalized sociomoral meanings (however concrete), the appraisals that mediate their experiences of anger become more complex. For example, by 30 to 36 months of age, many children in North American and Western European cultures begin to internalize a sense of the sociomoral value placed on being a "big boy" or a "big girl" (Mascolo &

Fischer, 1998). As a result, around this age, many children begin to resist being characterized as a "baby." The emotional shift is dramatic and abrupt (Pipp et al., 1987). As depicted in step A4 in Figure 3.2, children can begin to experience a sense of being "insulted" as they internalize and define the self in terms of single sociomoral categories (see Dunn & Munn's, 1985, 1987, work on teasing and moral justification among young children). At this level, a child who is called a baby by a peer or an adult is capable of verbally protesting the insult by asserting the opposite (e.g., "I'm not a baby!) or retaliating (e.g., "You are the baby!"). While instances of physical aggression remain common, children are increasingly able to limit and control aggressive impulses.

The mediation of anger by judgments that others have *insulted* the self highlights the relationship between the development of *anger* and *shame*. In her analysis of psychotherapy exchanges among adults, H. B. Lewis (1987) reported that verbal and nonverbal markers of anger were almost always preceded by markers of shame. Scheff (2000, 2003; Scheff & Retzinger, 1991) suggests that among adults, because of strong taboos against shame, unacknowledged or hidden shame gives rise to anger and rage, perhaps even as a strategy for hiding shame. Even in China, where there is no taboo on shame, the link between shame and anger is clear in the many words describing that link (Li et al., 2004). Toddlers have not yet developed the self-regulation strategies to hide their shame. We suggest that among most toddlers in North America, shame-relevant events (e.g., insults) lead directly to anger. We suggest that the ways in which adults respond to a child's shame are important in the development of the shame → anger cycle. This point is discussed further below.

Step A5 emerges at around 3½ to 4 years of age with the capacity to coordinate two single representations into a *representational mapping*. With this capacity, a child can understand different types of relations between two or more representations (cause and effect, sequential order, reciprocity, etc.). Using representational mappings, children can begin to construct motives based on social comparisons. For example, 4½-year-old Jack had developed a consistent desire to be the "first one" to go in or out of a door. This motive requires a capacity to *order* the actions of self and other. One day, an older girl raced Jack to the door. With an angry face and voice (*action*), Jack said "I want to be first" (motive-relevant *appraisal*) and forced himself in front of the girl (*action tendency*). In anger, the boy symbolically "hit" the girl by making a hitting gesture and pulling it just prior to contact. This act shows a continued capacity to *regulate* angry actions in a creative way. It will take several more years before children consolidate their social comparison skills to focus consistently on social comparisons in their interactions and motivations.

The Development of Shame

Shame and guilt are self-evaluative emotions, as we have emphasized; they require the dual capacity for self-awareness and the evaluation of self with social standards. Because self-awareness undergoes profound changes in the second year of life (Pipp et al., 1987; Lewis & Brooks-Gunn, 1979; Mascolo & Fischer, 1998), it is not surprising that the toddler years are important ones for the development of shame, guilt, and other self-evaluative emotions. Figure 3.2 contains representations of developmental changes in the structure of shame experiences over the toddler years.

A variety of emotion theorists (Schore, 1994; Tomkins, 1987) have suggested that shame emerges in the first quarter of the second year of life. Schore (1994) has suggested that shame has its origins in socioaffective interaction between adults and toddlers. Drawing on the work of Tomkins (1962), Schore suggests that shame functions as an inhibitor of positive and assurgent affect. Tomkins (1962) and Izard (1991) indicate that emotional experiences of interest–excitement and joy reflect states of heightened arousal. Shame occurs in interpersonal contexts in which an adult's negatively charged gaze inhibits a child's assurgent action, interest, and enjoyment. Over the first year of life, infants develop expectations that their adult companions will respond with contingent positive affect to their overtures. In the second year of life, with increases in exploratory behavior, children necessarily perform acts that bring about parental displeasure and even disgust (M. Lewis, 1992). When this occurs, adult facial and vocal behaviors function to inhibit a child's positive affect. The resulting shame for the child produces a precipitous decline in affective arousal, accompanied by negative feeling tone. In such contexts, infants avert their gaze from the disapproving adult. This is a precursor to or an early form of shame.

As with other emotions, shame develops gradually and takes on a series of different forms over time and in different interpersonal contexts. Shame-like behavior first emerges early in the second year of life. At step S1, with the onset of sensorimotor systems, a child is capable of experiencing shame-like *intersubjective misattunement* (Schore, 1994), as we have described. Figure 3.2 depicts a situation in which a toddler breaks a toy and is met with disapproving facial and vocal behavior on the part of a parent. At this level, the child is able to coordinate two sensorimotor mappings into a single sensorimotor system. Using the first mapping, the toddler is able to see a change in the toy from its initially intact state to a broken state (i.e., intact—broken). Using a second sensorimotor mapping, in the context of direct parental disapproval, the child is able to link the parent's disapproving affect to his own actions on the toy (e.g., unexpected adult affect—I act on toy). A shame-like state (e.g., gaze aversion) arises from the clash between the child's desired expectation of positive affect on the part of the adult and the sensorimotor experience of the parent's disapproving affect toward the child.

Although Schore (1994) and others (e.g., Tomkins, 1962) refer to such early emotional states as *shame*, we prefer to think of these reactions as precursors to shame. In shame, individuals are aware of the exposure of their flawed self in the eyes of others (Lindsay-Hartz et al., 1995). This is a complex self-evaluative and social appraisal. It not only requires the capacity for self-awareness but also the capacity to use sociomoral standards—however concrete and contextualized—to evaluate the self in the eyes of others. As such, we prefer to view early social distress in the context of a disapproving adult as but one early step in the continuous development of shame.

An important transformation in shame-like experiences occurs with the onset of single symbolic representations around 18–24 months of age. At this level, a toddler is capable of constructing single, concrete social categories, such as representing concrete aspects of his or her own sense of agency (i.e., "I"), identity (e.g., "me"), or ownership (e.g., "mine") (Fasig, 2000; Mascolo & Fischer, 1998). A toddler's sense of shame can be mediated by symbolic representations of how the self is seen in the eyes of others. However, at this early level of development, a child's representational capacities are still quite limited. An adult's affectively charged evaluative feedback provides a type of emotional scaffolding that helps to "put together" a symbolic sense of social devaluation in the toddler's experience. Among adults, shame can be experienced in terms of the differentiated and articulated sense that "I am a horrible person and everyone knows it." At this early level, a toddler's capacity to represent self through the eyes of others is rudimentary, concrete, and global. In the context of direct adult disapproval, a child can construct a concrete affect-laden awareness that "*mommy sees me—*" or "*mommy sees me bad,*" as depicted in step S2 in Figure 3.2.

Although shame and guilt have common elements, it is important to note the ways in which shame and guilt differ. In shame, the toddler has constructed an awareness of a flawed (bad) *self* in the eyes of the adult; in guilt, a toddler is aware of having *acted* in a way that hurts others or brings about adult disapproval. At this level, shame involves the self-conscious awareness of another's disapproving gaze; guilt involves the awareness that one's actions have caused disapproval or distress. It is tantamount to the difference between "mommy sees my badness" and "I did a bad thing."

Research on development of the experience of shame remains limited. A variety of studies have indicated that shame-like behavior emerges around 18–24 months of age, if not earlier, and continues to develop over the third year of life. In China, children develop words for shame at this age, but in the United States and England, these words appear several years later (Bretherton, Fritz, Zahn-Waxler, & Ridgeway, 1986; Shaver, Wu, & Schwartz, 1992). A common paradigm in the study of shame employs the broken-toy scenario (Barrett, Zahn-Waxler, & Cole, 1993; Kochanska, 2002). In this situation, an adult allows a child a valued toy that has been rigged to break upon casual use. The child's emotional reaction is observed upon breaking the toy and as adults question the child in a neutral fashion about the toy. Using this procedure, Barrett and colleagues (1993) found that toddlers between the ages of 25 and 36 months could be reliably distinguished into a shame-relevant and guilt-relevant group. The shame-relevant group—the avoiders—tended to avoid the adult after the mishap. They were also slow to attempt to fix the toy or admit the mishap. Toddlers in the guilt-relevant group—the amenders—were quick to admit and make reparations for the mishap.

Over the third year of life, toddlers' concrete self representations become organized with reference to increasingly internalized sociomoral content. By 36 months of age, many such concrete sociomoral meanings have been fully internalized. At step S3, a child can create more stable evaluations of self as viewed from the eyes of others. As a result, upon violating a rule, children can begin to *anticipate* an adult's opprobrium and begin to feel a more internalized sense of shame. At this level, a child's sense of shame can be mediated by concrete social categories. For example, given appropriate contextual support, a child can construct a motive-relevant representation such as "Mommy sees me a *baby*" or "Mommy thinks I'm *icky.*"

At this level, children's action tendencies in shame become both more deliberate and subtle. Children may run to another room and hide or verbally attempt to deflect attention from the self (e.g., "Don't see me!"). When confronted, a child may divert her gaze; when queried, a child remains silent, mumbles, or speaks in a halting or muted way. As indicated previously, at this level, as a child is able to represent the specific content of his or her socially or morally devalued self, a child can experience shame in the form of a rudimentary insult. As such, shame can motivate angry defiance or protest. Regulation of shame at this step is still quite limited. Actions exhibited in shame—both attempts to withdraw and hide the self as well as attempts to move against others in anger—function to defend the self against social scrutiny.

An alternative series of studies examines the development of shame in achievement rather than moral contexts (e.g., Lewis, Alessandri, & Sullivan, 1992; Mascolo & Harkins, 1998; Stipek, 1983; Stipek, Recchia, & McClintic, 1993). Lewis and colleagues (1992) identified clear evidence of shame (and pride) reactions in 3-year-old children upon failure (and success) in simple achievement tasks (e.g., a basketball toss). Lewis et al. defined shame as the simultaneous evocation of negative affect, negative self-evaluation (e.g., "I can't . . . ") and gaze aversion upon failure in goal-related tasks. Defined in this way, shame reactions in achievement contexts are clearly evident by 3 years of age. However, Stipek, Recchia, and McClintic (1992) and Mascolo and Harkins (1998) demonstrated that even prior to the third birthday, children in the second year of life often exhibit one or two elements of shame-like behavior (e.g., negative affect, gaze aversion, or, less frequently, negative self-evaluation) in contexts involving goal-related failure. In these studies, European American parents rarely offer criticism or negative evaluation in the context of goal failure. The emergence of more definitive and spontaneous shame reactions toward the third birthday seems mediated by changes in evaluative self-understanding. Around age 3, children are capable of understanding implications of goal failure for their fledgling evaluations of self.

Beginning around 3½ to 4 years of age, with the onset of the capacity to construct representational mappings, children can hold in mind relations between two representations. At this point, given contextual support, a child can compare the self and other on a variety of simple dimensions. At step S4, in the context of disapproving feedback, a child can construct a sense of comparative shame. For example, a child can construct a relational sense of shame in the context of receiving critical feedback such as a "What a tattletale! Why can't you be more like your sister? She never tattles on you!" or "Don't be a sissy—that boy over there can climb the bars!" Because these are emerging skills, children act inconsistently, sometimes using these shame skills and sometimes not.

Furthermore, having constructed internalized standards for representing the self in the eyes of others, a child can begin to represent more clearly the relation between his or her actions and their effects on others. For example, after a period of feeling proud of his capacity to use the bathroom successfully, one 4½-year-old boy, after having a bowel movement in the presence of his mother, said without provocation "What's that smell? No! Don't look at me!" Although this particular mother and child would often engage in mutually enjoyable games that centered on the theme of bad smells ("stinky feet," etc.), the mother reported that she was "open" and worked not to make her child feel ashamed of such matters. Still the negative valence of messing in his pants led to his shame reaction even in the absence of explicit shaming. Children play an active role in constructing their standards of self-evaluation.

The Development of Guilt

Although they are often experienced in similar social circumstances, guilt and shame are different experiences that serve different psychological and social functions (Barrett, 1998b; Lindsay-Hartz et al., 1995; Tangney, 1998, 2002). There are at least two salient occasions for the development of guilt in development: transgressions of social rules—violating the do's and don'ts of development (e.g., Emde & Buchsbaum, 1990; Gralinski & Kopp, 1993; Kaler & Kopp, 1990; Kochanska, 1993; Kopp, 1982), and taking responsibility for causing harm in others (Baumeister, Stillwell, & Heatherton, 1994; Zahn-Waxler, 1990). Figure 3.2 describes developmental changes in the structure of guilt-like states over the toddler years. At step G1, children in the first quarter of the second year of life exhibit (1) empathic concern for distress in others and (2) guilt-like reactions upon parental prohibition of action. (A skill at an earlier age relevant to guilt is the step shown for anger during the first year of life.) Zahn-Waxler and her colleagues (Zahn-Waxler, Radke-Yarrow, & King, 1979; Zahn-Waxler, Radke-Yarrow, Wagner, & Chapman, 1992) have shown convincingly that as young as the first quarter of the second year of life, infants show considerable empathic and sympathetic concern for the pain of others. At this level, children often have difficulty discriminating the source of another person's distress; many toddlers tend to show concern whether or not they have been the source of another person's pain. As indicated in Figure 3.2, children express their concern by showing signs of empathic or sympathetic distress for the other person's emotional state and/or attempting to comfort or help the person in distress. Such empathic and guilt-relevant action tendencies occur in both disciplinary encounters as well as in situations in which others experience pain.

It is important to stress the role of social context in producing empathic and guilt-like actions at this early level. Toddlers generally evince such reactions in richly affective social situations in which another person's pain or displeasure is abundantly evident. In this way, the other person's affective state helps to structure a child's empathic and guilt-like actions. Zahn-Waxler (1990) provided a series of representative descriptions of such empathic states in emerging toddlers. For example:

> Child is pounding with cup and accidentally hits father hard in the nose. (Father gives loud "ouch.") Child drops cup, looks very serious, leans forward to father for a kiss. (61 weeks; p. 247)
>
> Child repeatedly turns milk cup upside down. (Mother starts to hit child's hand but then takes the cup away and calls her a bad girl.) Child whines and calls herself "bad." (69 weeks; p. 247)
>
> Child bangs head against mother's face in excess of affection. (Mother restrains, verbally prohibits and explains, "that hurts.") Child says "kiss, kiss" and kisses mother. Then bangs head on mother again and says, "hurting, hurting." (Mother acknowledges and verbally prohibits.) (75 weeks; p. 248)

In these interactions, the children described evoke genuine emotional concern and reparative action in contexts of direct affective feedback and/or regulation on the part of a parent. The structure of such early empathic and guilt-like reactions is depicted in step G1 in Figure 3.2. Although there appears to be a vague awareness on the part of the parent of her child's role in producing negative affect, the child's awareness is highly and largely undifferentiated from her empathic concern for the other.

Step G2 emerges between 18 and 24 months of age with the capacity to form single symbolic representations. At this level, children begin to construct symbolic representations of their own agency in producing outcomes. As a result, children can begin to attribute causality to themselves for actions that cause distress in others or that bring about negatively charged reactions from others. This is an important step in the development of guilt experiences. In contexts in which children break parental rules or cause pain in others, a child can make an appraisal such as "I hurt your toe" or "I write on wall." In such contexts, as indicated in Figure 3.1, authoritative parents of North American and Western European children often use inductive discipline techniques to explain the nature of the violated rule, draw children's attention to the effects of their actions on others, and apologize to the offended party and make reparative actions (Hoffman, 2000). Although children increasingly internalize these prescriptions over the second and third years of life, their guilt-like reparative behavior is also motivated by their evolving sense of concern for the other. This involves both empathic concern and a continuing desire to please adults in their world. Zahn-Waxler (1990) provides descriptions of several such emotional reactions in children in the second year of life:

> Child writes on sofa with indelible pen. Mother and father express horror ("How could you? etc.) but do not yell. Child bursts into tears, starts screaming "I want Mommy," then throws arms around mother. He starts wiping at sofa with hands and says "I clean up pencil." (93 weeks; p. 248)
>
> Child throws tantrum. (Mother spanks her and sends her to her room.) Sibling tells child to "go give Mommy a kiss and tell her you're sorry." Child goes into room and says "sorry," then tries to cuddle with mother, sobbing profusely. (101 weeks; p. 249)
>
> Child pulls cousin's hair (Mother tells her not to.) Child crawls to cousin and says, "I hurt our hair; please don't cry," then gives her a kiss. (104 weeks; p. 249)

The structure of such guilt-like interactions is depicted in step G2 in Figure 3.2. In each of these states, the child is explicitly aware of his or her role in precipitating negative affect in another person (child or parent). In richly affective social interactions that often (but not always) involve direct parental intervention, the child expresses remorse, apologizes, or attempts to make reparations. At this age, children may use a variety of rudimentary strategies to regulate their guilt-like feelings, including looking away, emotional affiliation with adult, or self-soothing.

As children construct and internalize sociomoral meanings over the third year of life, they become increasingly capable of experiencing guilt feelings outside the context of direct intervention by parents. Children's guilt experiences are increasingly mediated by appraisals involving attributions of responsibility to the self for performing acts defined with reference to specific sociomoral content. In addition, although adult intervention is often needed to motivate prosocial activity, children become increasingly likely to apologize, make reparations, and confess misdeeds without direct intervention by adults. In some circumstances, children are able to experience guilt in circumstances that are removed from the initial transgression. Zahn-Waxler (1990) describes such a case of in a precocious 2-year-old:

> Child hurts friend at nursery school. (Teacher asks her if she can do something to make the friend feel better, and she brings other child toy.) The next day she points to her mother's eyes and says, "Tears, Mary had tears, I pushed Mary off chair, I sorry." Child wanted mother to take her to school that afternoon to say she was sorry (107 weeks). (Also, at 102 weeks, child verbalized regret; "Hurt—sorry—sorry Grandpa; hurt him," over having hurt her grandfather two weeks earlier. (p. 249)

The structure of such experiences is depicted in step G3 in Figure 3.2. The description provided above illustrates the case of a child whose assumption of explicit responsibility for the distress of another person is deferred in time; this suggests a degree of internalization of the capacity to experience guilt. Most likely, however, most experiences of guilt at this early age are evoked and supported by contextual cues (e.g., the sight of the mother's eyes in the aforementioned example). While we believe it is appropriate to begin to refer to such internalized experiences as interpersonal guilt, it is important to differentiate these early states as different from more ruminative experiences of guilt that are capable of structuring reparative action over longer periods of time later in childhood and in adulthood.

As children move beyond toddlerhood, they gain the capacity to construct more differentiated forms of guilt. Experiences of guilt are mediated by judgments that make reference to blameworthy actions in the self and the effect of those actions on others. With the onset of representational mappings around 3½ to 4 years of age, guilt experiences can become increasingly mediated by appraisals that explicitly embrace relations between concrete aspects of the self's actions and their effects on the internal states of others. The structure of such differentiated experiences of guilt is depicted in step G4 in Figure 3.2. For example, in social contexts that support their construction, a child is capable of making an appraisal such as "I took Mark's toy and now he is sad" or "I was mean to Sally and now she doesn't like me." Such other-oriented appraisals support the production of more complex guilt-relevant action tendencies. With the capacity to hold in mind both the self's misdeed and the other's internal state, children's attempts at reparations become less egocentric; although still quite limited, children are increasingly able to organize their reparations with reference to the internal state of the offended other. A child can link his apology directly to the victim's hurt feelings (e.g., "Don't be sad. I'm sorry I took your doll."). In addition, children's emerging powers to represent concrete relations between self and other bring forth new ways to regulate feelings of guilt. For example, in social interaction, children can begin to defend against their guilt feelings using social strategies such as prevarication (e.g., "I didn't take her doll!"), mitigation (e.g., "I didn't do it on purpose!"), and justification (e.g., "He hit me first!"). At this level, such strategies arise between individuals in social interaction, and because they are emerging skills, they are often not used consistently until a few years later. In general, the regulation of guilt experiences undergoes transformation in later childhood and even adulthood as individuals develop the capacity to direct such defensive strategies toward themselves within internal dialogue rather than using them to defray guilt in interactions with other persons.

The Role of Sociomoral Emotion in the Development of Self

The developmental progressions for self-evaluative and sociomoral emotions during the toddler years provide foundations for further development in self and social relations. Figure 3.3 describes a model for converging and diverging pathways in the development of self and socioemotional behavior that arise as a product of different patterns of child temperament and adult socialization. The model describes pathways toward three different developmental outcomes among North American and western European populations. Each pathway is defined with reference to relations between a child's temperamental dispositions and social experience. *Normative* pathways (Pathways A, B, and C) result in the development of self-regulated moral selves and interac-

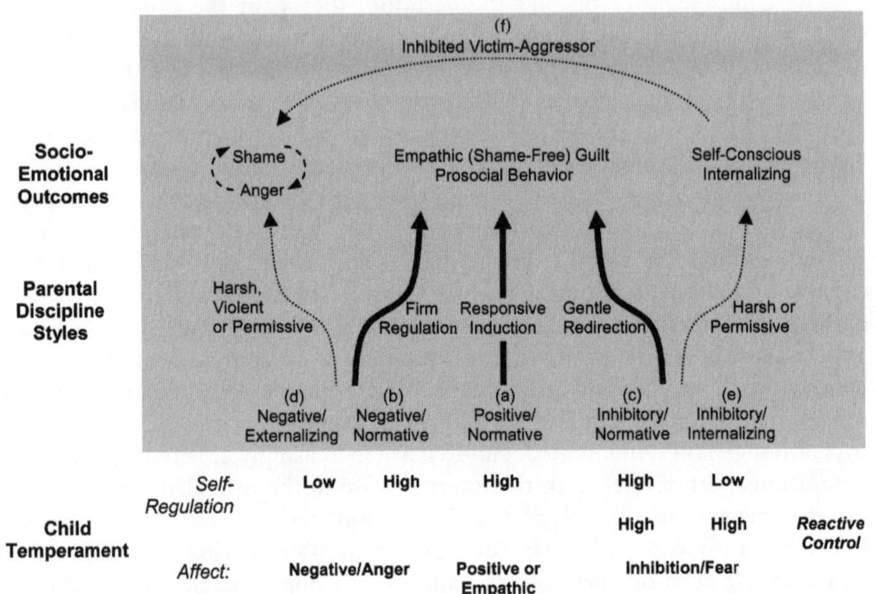

FIGURE 3.3. Pathways in the development of self-evaluative moral emotion. This figure depicts six pathways in self-conscious emotional development that occur as a product of different relations between children's temperamental dispositions (involving both affective and self-regulatory biases) and parenting practices. Pathways A, B, and C are normative pathways (bolded) in which self-conscious moral emotion develops in the direction of empathic, shame-free guilt and prosocial behavior. In the *positive affect/normative outcome* (Pathway A), among children who exhibit dispositions toward positive and/or empathic affect and high capacity for self-control, responsive and inductive discipline fosters prosocial development. In children who exhibit negative affect but high capacity for self-control, firm regulation can foster prosocial emotion (Pathway C). Contrastively, gentle redirection fosters sociality among inhibited or socially fearful children (Pathway B). Three nonnormative pathways are depicted. Among children who exhibit negative affect and low dispositional levels of effortful self-control, harsh, abusive, or permissive parenting fosters development in the direction of the shame–anger cycle (Pathway E). In contrast, self-conscious negative internalization can develop in reactively inhibited children with low dispositional levels of effortful self-control, especially under conditions of harsh or permissive discipline (Pathway D). Finally, in some circumstances, rejected-inhibited children can develop externalizing pathology, as exhibited among school-shooters and the inhibited victim-aggressor profile (Pathway F).

tions. Such modes of functioning are mediated by internalization of social rules, feelings of empathy, and experiences of "shame-free" guilt upon committing acts of wrongdoing toward others. The model identifies six pathways toward the development of three types of socioemotional moral selves. Pathway A (positive/normative) involves children who exhibit temperamental styles characterized by positive affect, capacity for high levels of effortful control, and/or a heightened capacity for empathy (Eisenberg et al., 1998; Rothbart & Ahadi, 1994; Valiente et al., 2004; Zahn-Waxler, 1990). Such children can readily profit from parents' use of inductive child-management strategies to regulate the children's behavior. Rule internalization is facilitated by children's empathic dispositions and capacity to regulate behavior in terms of parental standards (Hoffman, 1983, 2000). Pathway B (negative/normative) involves children with dispositions toward negative affect (irritability, frustration, etc.) and high capacity for self-regulation and attentional focus. Although such children enter social interactions with a disposition toward anger and aggression, in light of their capacity for self-regulation, such children can learn to regulate angry dispositions if they are provided with consistently firm but nonhostile parental discipline. Pathway C (inhibited/normative) is organized with reference to children who exhibit "fearful" (Kochanska, 1997), "inhibited" (Kagan & Saudino, 2001; Kagan, Snidman, & Zentner, 1999) affective biases. Many theorists have suggested that such affective dispositions predispose children to attend to and internalize parental rules and prohibitions. However, for such children, gentle discipline that functions to modulate fear reactions to subjectively tolerable levels is necessary to promote rule internalization.

The model also specifies three nonnormative developmental pathways. Pathway D (negative/externalizing) involves movement toward externalizing and antisocial behavior (Eisenberg et al., 2001, 2003; Eisenberg, Zhou, et al., 2005; Fagot & Leve, 1998; Loeber & Stouthamer-Loeber, 1998; Tremblay, 2000) as well as behavior reflecting the *shame–anger cycle* (M. Lewis, 1993; Scheff, 1987; Tangney et al., 1996). Children who are temperamentally disposed to *negative affect* and *poor self-regulation* are at risk for taking this development pathway. In light of their relative inability to control aggressive behavior, such children are more likely to engender harsh or extreme discipline strategies. Some adults are likely to respond to their children's aggression with hostile discipline. Such child-management strategies have the dual effects of precipitating shameful affect as well as aggressive reactions to shame experiences (the *shame–anger cycle*). Other parents respond by "giving in" to their child's aggressive behavior, perpetuating what Patterson calls the coercion cycle. In this cycle, a parent's "giving in" provides social reinforcement that perpetuates a child's aggression.

Pathway E (inhibited/internalizing) involves movement toward self-conscious and internalizing social interactions. We suggest that children who are temperamentally biased toward "fearful/inhibited" affect and who may be the recipients of harsh or affectively insensitive discipline will find it difficult to develop strategies for regulating fearful and self-conscious affect. Such children are at risk for the development of internalizing regulation strategies. However, recent research also shows that in some circumstances, temperamentally inhibited children may also develop toward the externalizing pathway and become highly aggressive. This is represented in Pathway F (victim-aggressor), which can occur in situations in which temperamentally inhibited children are raised in dysfunctional or violent families and/or are rejected by their peers (Watson et al., 2004).

This model is supported by the results of a series of different research programs addressing the development of self-conscious emotions, rule internalization, and aggression. In a series of elegant longitudinal studies, Kochanska and her colleagues (Kochanska, 1993, 1997, 2002; Kochanska, Gross, Lin, & Nichols, 2002; Kochanska & Murray, 2000) have identified different pathways in the development of conscience as a function of children's temperamental and parental socialization. Kochanska (1997) reported that for children who exhibit "fearful" or "inhibited" temperamental dispositions during toddlerhood, gentle parental discipline predicted the development of rule internalization and guilt-like emotion when children were 4 and 5 years of age. In contrast, among less fearful children, mutual responsiveness and secure attachment were more potent predictors of conscience. For both types of children, anxious or fearful arousal evoked by parental discipline seems to affect rule internalization for such children. For "fearful" children, negatively charged disciplinary strategies cause levels of emotional upset not conducive to rule internalization, apparently because they are generally fearful without any negative discipline. In contrast, parents of less fearful children must resort to other strategies to foster the development of conscience, because for such children, fear needs to be induced to create rule internalization. The attachment relationship provides a stable platform from which parents can evoke fear safely to promote the development of conscience (Kochanska, 2002; Kochanska & Murray, 2000).

Kochanska's distinction between fearful and less fearful socialization patterns provides empirical support differentiating normative Pathways A (positive/normative) and C (inhibited/ normative) depicted in Figure 3.3. In addition, it is likely that other affective states also bias development in the direction of guilt. Several theorists have suggested a strong role for empathy in the genesis of interpersonal guilt and prosocial behavior (Baumeister et al., 1994; Hoffman, 2000). These latter considerations suggest that experiences of empathy may mediate development along normative Pathway A (positive/normative). Finally, research that suggests that gentle discipline fosters the development of conscience in "fearful" children implies that the presence of harsh or emotionally intense discipline strategies may tilt development toward Pathway E (inhibited/internalizing).

Guilt has often been viewed as an important element of conscience. Using the broken-toy paradigm (Barrett et al., 1993), Kochanska (1997, 2002; Kochanska & Murray, 2000) observed that "fearful" toddlers exhibited higher levels of guilt-like affect than did less fearful toddlers. Consistent with the previous findings on the relationship between parental discipline and rule internalization (Hoffman, 1970, 2000; Radke-Yarrow & Zahn-Waxler, 1984), Kochanska (1997) found that parents who used power-assertive techniques had children who showed relatively low levels of guilt-like behavior and rule internalization. Although Kochanska concluded that fearful temperament biases children toward the development of guilt, in her studies, Kochanska defined "guilt" rather broadly to include indicators that are also typical of shame states (e.g., gaze aversion, covering the face, and bodily tension). As a result, it is difficult to identify the roles of guilt versus shame in the genesis of rule internalization in these studies. In Chinese and related cultures, socialization focuses heavily on shaming techniques, and shame and guilt seem to function differently from in North America (Fung & Chen, 2001; Li et al., 2004; Mascolo et al., 2002).

Research conducted by Tangney and her colleagues bears on this distinction (Tangney & Dearing, 2002). In a series of research studies using self-reports from children and adults, Tangney examined how guilt and shame differentially bias individuals toward specific social behaviors and experiences. Her research proceeds from the view that guilt and shame are distinguishable emotional states that modulate social behavior in different ways (Tangney & Dearing, 2002; Tangney, Miller, et al., 1996). In a variety of studies, Tangney has demonstrated relations between measures of shame-proneness and indices of poor responses to anger, indirect aggression and hostility, poor anger regulation, externalization of blame, and psychopathology (Tangney, Miller, et al., 1996; Tangney, Wagner, et al., 1996; Tangney et al., 1992). In contrast, measures of guilt-proneness are related to constructive anger management, willingness to make reparations in relationships, and other prosocial dispositions. Of particular importance, Tangney and colleagues (1992) reported that "shame-free" guilt was inversely related to measures of the externalization of blame and several indices of anger and hostility.

Although Tangney's studies were not performed with toddlers, they suggest the importance of differentiating shame- and guilt-proneness as important developmental biases, at least in Western cultures. As indicated earlier, Barrett and colleagues (1993) were able to differentiate toddlers into "avoiders" and "amenders" on the basis of their reactions in the broken-toy task. Taken together, these studies suggest the need to differentiate shame-mediated from guilt-mediated developmental pathways. Tangney's work suggests that the development of shame-free guilt may be important in the development of prosocial moral selves depicted in Pathway A.

A third line of research is related to the developmental roots of anger and aggression spurred by social cognitive models of anger. Research suggests that children as young as 3 years of age who display a tendency toward reactive aggression hold a *hostile attribution bias* (Crick & Dodge, 1994; Katsurada, & Sugawara, 1998). Such children are more likely to attribute hostile intent to a peer's negative or ambiguous social actions. Research suggests that relative to normative samples, children who display a tendency toward reactive aggression are more likely to exhibit difficult temperament organized around angry affect (Pettit, 1998); a history of punitive, hostile, or abusive parenting (Dodge, Pettit, Bates, & Valente, 1995); insecure attachment (Pettit, 1998); peer rejection (Yoon, Hughes, Cavell, & Thompson, 2000); and indiscriminant or enabling reactions to aggression in the home (Dumas, LaFreniere, & Serketich, 1996). This research, taken together with work that demonstrates a link between shame and anger (Li et al., 2004; Scheff, 1987; Tangney, Wagner, et al., 1996), provides empirical support for the distinction between Pathways A and C in Figure 3.3. Children with negative emotional biases who receive harsh or permissive discipline have difficulty developing effective social skills or regulatory skills for aggression (Mascolo & Margolis, 2005; Rubin, Bukowski, & Parker, 1998). Reactive anger in such children is likely to arise jointly as a reaction to both feelings of shame and poor self-regulation skills. Conversely, children whose aggressive impulses are consistently regulated using firm and responsive discipline can develop toward normative endpoints, especially in children exhibiting dispositions toward higher levels of self-control.

Finally, Pathway F (victim-aggressor) is supported by recent research showing that under certain circumstances, a temperamentally inhibited children can develop aggressive behavioral styles. In a longitudinal study, Watson and colleagues (2004) assessed children between the ages of 7 and 13 on a variety of parental-report measures of children's temperamental dispositions, aggressiveness, self-esteem, parental practices, and a variety of other variables. Families were culled from a multiracial sample that was representative of the entire community of Springfield, Massachusetts. This community-based sample differed from those used in many other studies in that it did not sample children who were explicitly at risk for the development of aggressive behavior. Watson and colleagues found that children who were inhibited, especially in combination with anxiety and other problems, showed a strong tendency to become aggressive, especially when they grew up in violent homes. These findings are consistent with those that address the origins of aggression exhibited by children who perpetrate school shootings, such as those that occurred in Columbine High School in Colorado. Several studies (Harter & Whitesell, 2001; McGee & DeBernardo, 1999) suggest that school shooters tend to be (1) withdrawn children, often described as "loners," who interact with others in a nonassertive fashion; who (2) have a history of being humiliated, teased or taunted by peers; (3) exhibit low and unstable levels of self-esteem; (4) come from dysfunctional families; and (5) exhibit high levels of aggressive and suicidal ideation and a high interest in and access to guns and related activities.

Eisenberg and her colleagues have conducted a series of well-designed studies that support the idea that the behavior of temperamentally inhibited children can develop in the direction of externalizing behavior (Eisenberg, Fabes, Guthrie, & Reiser, 2000; Eisenberg et al., 2001, 2003; Eisenberg,

Zhou, et al., 2005). Eisenberg has suggested a distinction between at least two forms of temperamentally based self-control: Effortful control and reactive control. Effortful control refers to a child's disposition to sustain attention to task activity and to regulate action and thought in a deliberate and methodical way (Rothbart, Ahadi, & Evans, 2000). In contrast, reactive control refers to a child's disposition toward impulsivity rather than moment-by-moment emotion regulation in particular contexts (Eisenberg et al., 2000, 2001, 2003; Eisenberg, Sadovsky, et al., 2005). In longitudinal studies tracking multiple cohorts of children from kindergarten through adolescence, Eisenberg and her colleagues assessed relations between, on the one hand, variations in parenting variables (e.g., warm, supporting parenting), children's temperamental dispositions toward negative emotionality, effortful control and reaction control, and, on the other hand, children's internalizing and externalizing behavior. Eisenberg's work shows that children's dispositional capacity for effortful control mediates the relation between supportive parenting and children's socially appropriate behavior. Furthermore, Eisenberg demonstrated that temperamentally inhibited children who exhibit high levels of *reactive* self-control but relatively low levels of *effortful* control are at risk for developing both *internalizing* and *externalizing* behavior later in development. In contexts of stress and novelty, the spontaneous inhibition of immediate impulses fosters the development of internalizing behavior. Conversely, the inability to exert effortful control over behavior is consistently related to externalizing behavior. These studies, along with the results of the Watson and colleagues (2004) study, suggest a pathway toward the development of a victim-aggressor behavior pattern in inhibited children. While the majority of this work has been conducted with children above the age of 5 years, to the extent that there exist relatively stable individual differences in children's temperamental dispositions that arise early in life (Rubin, Burgess, & Dwyer, 2003; Rubin, Burgess, & Hastings, 2002), there is reason to believe that the patterns described earlier have their origins early in development.

Taken together, the studies reviewed above suggest that self-evaluative and moral emotions emerge and undergo significant transformation during the toddler years. As indicated in Figure 3.3, the epigenetic development of emotions such as anger, shame, and guilt has important implications the development of children's social behavior and sense of self. Different pathways in the development of stable styles of social behavior emerge as products of relations between children's temperamental dispositions and social experiences. As such, there is no single pathway in the development of pro- or antisocial behavior. The development and regulation of emotions such as anger, guilt, and shame play a major role in mediating the development of normative and rule-violating modes of social behavior. In this way, the socialization of styles of emotional self-regulation and self-evaluation during the toddler years sets the stage for the development of social behavior and interpersonal relationships over the course of ontogenesis. Directive socialization experiences that are sensitive to a toddler's emerging self-evaluative and emotional dispositions tend to promote shame-free, prosocial development. In contrast, emotional dysregulation in the formative years can set the stage for the development of both internalizing and shame-mediated externalizing pathology in development.

FOUNDATIONS OF SELFHOOD THROUGH THE TODDLER YEARS

The toddler years are fundamental ones for the development of self. Building on profound changes that occur in the second year of life, the self arises in development as a form of reflective activity. The self emerges as conscious action gains the capacity to take itself as its own object, reflecting on itself (Mead, 1934). However, the self is not a solitary construction; it is a social product. Selves develop in interactions in which parents and other socialization agents use words and other communicative vehicles to direct a child's constructive processes to aspects of his or her own action and experience. The construction of a sense of self is a foundational achievement in development. The sense of self functions as a center for organizing experience. With development, valued images of self increasingly operate as social and moral guides to action.

Emotion plays a central role in organizing action, experience, and development. It follows that self-conscious and moral emotions are central organizers of the experience of self. Disciplinary encounters are salient occasions for the construction of moral rules and the social formation of emotions such as shame and guilt. Anger displays by young children are also situations for discipline. Emotions that arise in disciplinary and related encounters play an important role in the development and internalization of social standards that constitute moral selves. However, the emotions that arise in disciplinary encounters are not simply matters of socialization. Different pathways in the development of self and self-conscious emotion arise from coactions between the children's emotional biases and their socialization experiences. Through such encounters, selves and self-conscious emotions develop with reference to each other.

Shame, guilt, and anger develop; they do not emerge fully formed at a single point in ontogenesis. Figure 3.2 depicts *normative* pathways in the development of anger, guilt, and shame in toddlers in North American and Western European cultures. As self-evaluative and moral emotions, shame, guilt, and anger develop in different ways under different social and cultural contexts. For example, shame and guilt develop along different trajectories and through different processes in Asian cultures (Fung & Chen, 2001; Mascolo et al., 2002). In addition, as indicated in Figure 3.3, even within Western cultures, variations in the ways in which children's enactments of anger, shame, and guilt are socialized can prompt divergent pathways in children's self-evaluative, socioemotional and moral development. In this way, the emergence of self-evaluative and moral awareness during the toddler years sets the stage for the social and cultural development of self and social relations.

REFERENCES

Barrett, K. C. (1998a). A functionalist perspective to the development of emotion. In M. F. Mascolo & S. Griffin (Eds.), *What develops in emotional development?* (pp. 109–133) New York: Plenum Press.

Barrett, K. C. (1998b). The origins of guilt in early childhood. In J. Bybee (Ed.), *Guilt and children* (pp. 75–90). New York: Academic Press.

Barrett, K. C., Zahn-Waxler, C., & Cole, P. M. (1993). Avoiders vs. amenders: Implications for the investigation of guilt and shame during toddlerhood. *Cognition and Emotion*, *7*, 481–505.

Baumeister, R. F., Stillwell, A. M., & Heatherton, T. F. (1994). Guilt: An interpersonal approach. *Psychological Bulletin*, *115*, 243–267.

Bedford, O., & Hwang, K.-K. (2003). Guilt and shame in Chinese culture: A cross-cultural framework from the perspective of morality and identity. *Journal for the Theory of Social Behaviour*, *33*, 127–144.

Bertenthal, B. I., & Fischer, K. W. (1978). The development of self-recognition in infancy. *Developmental Psychology, 14*, 44–50.

Blasi, G., & Glodis, K. (1995). The development of identity: A critical analysis from the perspective of the self as subject. *Developmental Review, 15*, 404–433.

Bretherton, I., Fritz, J., Zahn-Waxler, C., & Ridgeway, D. (1986). Learning to talk about emotions: A functionalist perspective. *Child Development, 57*, 529–548.

Bullock, M., & Lütkenhaus, P. (1990). Who am I?: Self-understanding in toddlers. *Merrill-Palmer Quarterly, 36*, 217–238.

Campos, J. J., Frankel, C. B., & Camras, L. (2004). On the nature of emotion regulation. *Child Development*, *75*, 377–394.

Carver, C. S., & Scheier, M. F. (1998). *On the self-regulation of behavior.* New York: Cambridge University Press.

Cohen, P., & Brook, J. S. (1995) The reciprocal influence of punishment and child behaviour disorder. In J. McCord (Ed.), *Coercion and punishment in long-term perspectives* (pp. 154–164). Cambridge, UK: Cambridge University Press

Crick, N., & Dodge, K. A. (1994). A review and reformulation of social information-processing mechanisms in children's adjustment. *Psychological Bulletin*, *114*, 74–101.

Davitz, J. (1969). *The language of emotion.* New York: Academic Press.

de Rivera, J. (1981). The structure of anger. In J. H. de Rivera (Ed.), *Conceptual encounter* (pp. 35–82). Washington, DC: University Press of America.

de Rivera, J. (1984). The structure of emotional relationships. In P. Shaver (Ed.), *Review of personality and social psychology: Vol. 5. Emotions, relationships, and health* (pp. 116–145). Beverly Hills, CA: Sage.

Dishion, T. J., Duncan, T. E., Eddy, J. M., Fagot, B. I., & Fetrow, R. (1994). The world of parents and peers: coercive exchanges and children's social adaptation. *Social Development*, *3*, 255–268.

Dodge, K. A., Pettit, G. S., Bates, J. E., & Valente, E. (1995). Social information processing patterns partially mediate the effect of early physical abuse on later conduct problems. *Journal of Abnormal Psychology, 104*, 632–643.

Dumas, J. E., LaFreniere, P. J., & Serketich, W. J. (1996). "Balance of power": A transactional analysis of control in mother–child dyads involving socially competent, aggressive, and anxious children. *Journal of Abnormal Psychology, 104*, 104–113.

Dunn, J., & Munn, P. (1985). Becoming a family member: Family conflict and the development of social understanding in the second year. *Child Development*, *56*, 480–492.

Dunn, J., & Munn, P. (1987). Development of justification in disputes with mother and sibling *Developmental Psychology*, *23*, 791–798.

Eisenberg, N., Fabes, R. A., Guthrie, I. K., & Reiser, M. (2000). Dispositional emotionality and regulation: Their role in predicting quality of social functioning. *Journal of Personality and Social Psychology, 78*, 136–157.

Eisenberg, N., Fabes, R. A., Shepard, S. A., Murphy, B. C., Jones, S., & Guthrie, I. K. (1998). Contemporaneous and longitudinal prediction of children's sympathy from dispositional regulation and emotionality. *Developmental Psychology, 34*, 910–924.

Eisenberg, N., Losoya, S., Fabes, R. A., Guthrie, I. K., Reiser, M., Murphy, B. C., et al. (2001). Parental socialization of children's dysregulated expression of emotion and externalizing problems. *Journal of Family Psychology, 15*, 183–205.

Eisenberg, N., Sadovsky, A., Spinrad, T. L., Fabes, R. A., Losoya, S. H., Valiente, C., et al. (2005). The relations of problem behavior status to children's negative emotionality, effortful control, and impulsivity: Concurrent relations and prediction of change. *Developmental Psychology, 41*, 193–211.

Eisenberg, N., Valiente, C., Fabes, R. A., Smith, C. L., Reiser, M., Shepard, S. A., et al. (2003). The relations of effortful control and ego control to children's resiliency and social functioning. *Developmental Psychology, 39*, 761–776.

Eisenberg, N., Zhou, Q., Spinrad, T. L., Valiente, C., Fabes, R. A., & Liew, J. (2005). Relations among positive parenting, children's effortful control, and externalizing problems: A three-wave longitudinal study. *Child Development, 76*, 1055–1071.

Emde, R. N. (1983). The prerepresentational self and its affective core. *Psychoanalytic Study of the Child, 38*, 165–192.

Emde, R. N., & Buchsbaum, H. K. (1990). "Didn't you hear my mommy?": Autonomy with connectedness in moral self-emergence. In D. Cicchetti & M. Beeghly (Eds.), *The self in transition: Infancy to childhood* (pp. 35–60). Chicago: University of Chicago Press.

Fagot, B. I., & Leve, L. D. (1998). Teacher ratings of externalizing behavior at school entry for boys and girls: Similar early predictors and different correlates. *Journal of Child Psychology and Psychiatry, 39*, 555–566.

Fasig, L. G. (2000). Toddlers' understanding of ownership: Implications for self-concept development. *Social Development, 9*, 370–382.

Fischer, K. W. (1980). A theory of cognitive development: The control and construction of hierarchies of skills. *Psychological Review, 87*, 447–531.

Fischer, K. W., & Bidell, T. R. (1998). Dynamic development of psychological structures in action and thought. In W. Damon (Series Ed.) & R. Lerner (Vol. Ed.), *Handbook of child psychology: Vol. 1. Theory* (pp. 467–561). New York: Wiley.

Fischer, K. W., & Bidell, T. R. (2006). Dynamic development of action, thought, and emotion. In R. M. Lerner (Ed.), *Theoretical models of human development* (6th ed., Vol. 1, pp. 313–399). New York: Wiley.

Fischer, K. W., Shaver, P. R., & Carnochan, P. (1990). How emotions develop and how they organise development. *Cognition and Emotion, 4*, 81–127.

Freeman, W. (2002). Emotion is essential for all intentional behavior. In M. D. Lewis & I. Granic (Eds.), *Emotion, development and self-organization*. New York: Cambridge University Press.

Frijda, N. (1986). *The emotions*. New York: Cambridge University Press.

Fung, H., & Chen, E. C.-H. (2001). Across time and beyond skin: Self and transgression in the everyday socialization of shame among Taiwanese preschool children. *Social Development, 10*, 420–437.

Garber, J., & Dodge, K. A. (Eds.). (1991). *The development of emotional regulation and dysregulation*. New York: Cambridge University Press.

Gerhardstein, P., Liu, J., & Rovee-Collier, C. (1998). *Perceptual constraints on infant memory retrieval. Journal of Experimental Child Psychology, 69*, 109–131.

Gralinski, J. H., & Kopp, C. B. (1993). Everyday rules for behavior: Mothers' requests to young children. *Developmental Psychology, 29*, 573–584.

Granic, I., & Patterson, G. R. (2006). Toward a comprehensive model of antisocial development: A dynamic systems approach. *Psychological Review, 113*, 101–131.

Grogan-Kaylor, A. (2005). Corporal punishment and the growth trajectory of children's antisocial behavior. *Child Maltreatment, 10*, 283–292.

Grusec, J. E., & Goodnow, J. J. (1994). Impact of parental discipline methods on the child's internalization of values: A reconceptualization of current points of view. Developmental Psychology, 30, 4–19.

Harter, S., & Whitesell, N. (2001, April). *What we have learned from Columbine: The impact of self-esteem on suicidal and violent ideation among adolescents.* Paper presented at the annual meeting of the Society for Research in Child Development, Minneapolis.

Hoffman, M. (2000). *Empathy and moral development: Implications for caring and justice.* New York: Cambridge University Press.

Hoffman, M. L. (1970). Conscience, personality and socialization techniques. *Human Development, 13*, 90–126.

Hoffman, M. L. (1983). Affective and cognitive processes in moral internalization: An information processing approach. In E. T. Higgins, D. N. Ruble, & W. W. Hartup (Eds.), *Social cognition and social development: A sociocultural perspective* (pp. 236–274). Cambridge, UK: Cambridge University Press.

James, W. (1890). *The principles of psychology* (Vol. 1). New York: Henry Holt.

Izard, C. E. (1991). *The psychology of emotions.* New York: Plenum Press.

Kagan, J., & Saudino, K. J. (2001). Behavioral inhibition and related temperaments. In R. N. Emde & J. K. Hewitt (Eds.), *Infancy to early childhood: Genetic and environmental influences on developmental change* (pp. 111–119). New York: Oxford University Press.

Kagan, J., Snidman, N., & Zentner, M. (1999). Infant temperament and anxious symptoms in school age children. *Development and Psychopathology, 11*, 209–224.

Kaler, S. R., & Kopp, C. B. (1990). Compliance and comprehension in very young toddlers. *Child Development, 61*, 1997–2003.

Katsurada, E., & Sugawara, A. I. (1998). The relationship between hostile attributional bias and aggressive behaviors in preschoolers. *Early Childhood Research Quarterly, 13*, 623–636.

Kochanska, G. (1993). Toward a synthesis of parental socialization and child temperament in early development of conscience. *Child Development*, 64, 325–347.

Kochanska, G. (1997). Multiple pathways to conscience for children with different temperaments: From toddlerhood to age five. *Developmental Psychology, 33*, 228–240.

Kochanska, G. (2002). Committed compliance, moral self, and internalization: A mediational model. *Developmental Psychology, 38*, 339–351.

Kochanska, G., Gross, J. N., Lin, M.-H., & Nichols, K. E. (2002). Guilt in young children: Development, determinants, and relations with a broader system of standards. *Child Development, 73*, 461–482.

Kochanska, G., & Murray, K. T. (2000). Mother–child mutually responsive orientation and conscience development: From toddler to early school age. *Child Development, 71*, 417–431.

Kopp, C. B. (1982). Antecedents of self-regulation: A developmental perspective. *Developmental Psychology, 18,* 199–214.

Kopp, C. B. (1989). Regulation of distress and negative emotions: A developmental view. *Developmental Psychology, 25*, 343–354.

Kopp, C. B., & Neufeld, S. J. (2003). Emotional development during infancy. In R. J. Davidson, K. R. Scherer, & H. H. Goldsmith (Eds.), *Handbook of affective sciences* (pp. 295–408). New York: Oxford University Press.

Laible, D. J., & Thompson, R. A. (2002). Mother–child conflict in the toddler years: Lessons in emotion, morality, and relationships. *Child Development, 73*, 1187–1203.

Lazarus, R. S. (1991). *Emotion and adaptation.* New York: Oxford University Press.

Lewis, H. B. (1971). *Shame and guilt in neurosis.* New York: International Universities Press.

Lewis, H. B. (1987). *The role of shame in symptom formation.* Hillsdale, NJ: Erlbaum.

Lewis, M. (1992). *Shame, the exposed self.* New York: Free Press.

Lewis, M. (1993). The development of anger and rage. In R. A. Glick & S. P. Roose (Eds.), *Rage, power, and aggression* (pp. 148–168). New Haven, CT: Yale University Press.

Lewis, M., Alessandri, S., & Sullivan, M. W. (1990). Expectancy, loss of control and anger in young infants. *Developmental Psychology, 26*, 745–751.

Lewis, M., Alessandri, S., & Sullivan, M. W. (1992). Differences in shame and pride as a function of children's gender and task difficulty. *Child Development*, *63*, 630–638

Lewis, M., & Brooks-Gunn, J. (1979). *Social cognition and the acquisition of self*. New York: Plenum Press.

Lewis, M. D., & Douglas, L. (1998). A dynamic systems approach to cognitive–emotion interactions in development. In M. F. Mascolo & S. Griffin (Eds.), *What develops in emotional development?* (pp. 159–188). New York: Plenum Press.

Li, J., Wang, L., & Fischer, K. W. (2004). The organization of shame words in Chinese. *Cognition and Emotion, 18*, 767–797.

Lindsay-Hartz, J., de Rivera, J., & Mascolo, M. F. (1995). Differentiating guilt and shame and their effects on motivation. In J. P. Tangney & K. W. Fischer (Eds.), *Self-conscious emotions: The psychology of shame, guilt, embarrassment, and pride* (pp. 274–300). New York: Guilford Press.

Loeber, R., & Stouthamer-Loeber, M. (1998). Development of juvenile aggression and violence: Some common misconceptions and controversies. *American Psychologist, 53*, 242–259.

Mancuso, J. C., & Handin, K. (1985). Reprimand: Acting on one's implicit theory of behavior change. In I. Sigel (Ed.), *Parental belief systems* (pp. 143–176). Hillsdale, NJ: Erlbaum.

Markus, H. R., & Kitayama, S. (2003). Models of agency: Sociocultural diversity in the construction of action. In V. Murphy-Bergman & J. J. Berman (Eds.), *Cross-cultural differences in perspectives on the self* (pp. 18–74). Lincoln: University of Nebraska Press.

Mascolo, M. F. (2004). The coactive construction of selves in cultures. In M. F. Mascolo & J. Li (Eds.), *Culture and self: Beyond dichotomization* (pp. 79–90). San Francisco: Jossey-Bass.

Mascolo, M. F., & Fischer, K. W. (1995). Developmental transformations in appraisals for pride, guilt and shame. In K. W. Fischer & J. P. Tangney (Eds.), *Self-conscious emotions: Shame, guilt, embarrassment, and pride* (pp. 64–113). New York: Guilford Press.

Mascolo, M. F., & Fischer, K. W. (1998). The development of self through the coordination of component systems. In M. Ferrari & R. J. Sternberg (Eds.), *Self-awareness: Its nature and development* (pp. 332–384). New York: Guilford Press.

Mascolo, M. F., Fischer, K. W., & Neimeyer, R. (1999). The dynamic co-development of intentionality, self and social relations. In J. Brandstadter & R. M. Lerner (Eds.), *Action and development: Origins and functions of intentional self-development* (pp. 133–166). Thousand Oaks, CA: Sage.

Mascolo, M. F., & Fischer, K. W. (2004). Constructivist theories. In B. Hopkins, R. G. Barre, G. F. Michel, & P. Rochat (Eds.), *Cambridge encyclopedia of child development* (pp. 49–63). Cambridge, UK: Cambridge University Press.

Mascolo, M. F., Fischer, K. W., & Li, J. (2003). Dynamic development of component systems of emotions: Pride, shame, and guilt in China and the United States. In R. J. Davidson, K. Scherer, & H. H. Goldsmith (Eds.), *Handbook of affective sciences* (pp. 375–408). Oxford, UK: Oxford University Press.

Mascolo, M. F., & Griffin, S. (1998). Alternative trajectories in the development of anger. In M. F. Mascolo & S. Griffin (Eds.), *What develops in emotional development?* (pp. 219–249). New York: Plenum Press.

Mascolo, M. F., & Harkins, D. (1998). Toward a component systems approach to emotional development. In M. F. Mascolo & S. Griffin (Eds.), *What develops in emotional development?* (pp. 189–218). New York: Plenum Press.

Mascolo, M. F., Harkins, D., & Harakal, T. (2000). The dynamic construction of emotion: Varieties in anger. In M. Lewis & I. Granic (Eds.), *Emotion, self-organization and development* (pp. 124–152). New York: Cambridge University Press.

Mascolo. M. F., & Mancuso, J. C. (1990). The functioning of epigenetically-evolved emotion systems: A constructive analysis. *International Journal of Personal Construct Theory, 3*, 205–222.

Mascolo, M. F., & Mancuso, J. C., & Dukewich, T. (2006). Trajectories in the development of anger in development: Appraisal, action and regulation. In J. Cummins (Ed.), *Working with anger: A practical perspective* (pp. 159–172). New York: Wiley.

Mascolo, M. F., & Margolis, D. (2005). Social meanings as mediators of the development of adolescent experience and action: A coactive systems approach. *European Journal of Developmental Psychology, 1*, 289–302.

Mayer, J. D., Chabot, H. F., & Carlsmith, K. (1997). Conation, affect, and cognition in personality. In G. Matthews (Ed.), *Cognitive science perspectives on personality and emotion* (pp. 31–63). Amsterdam: Elsevier Science.

McGee, J. P., & DeBernardo, C. R. (1999). The classroom avenger: A behavioral profile of school-based shootings. *Forensic Examiner, 8*, 16–18.

Mead, G. H. (1934) *Mind, self and society.* Chicago: University of Chicago Press.

Patterson, G. R. (1982). *Coercive family processes.* Eugene, OR: Castalia.

Patterson, G. R., Reid, J., & Dishion, T. (1992). *Antisocial boys.* Eugene, OR: Castalia.

Pettit, G. S. (1998). The developmental course of violence and aggression: Mechanisms of family and peer influence. *Anger, Aggression and Violence*, 20, 283–299.

Pipp, S. L., Fischer, K. W., & Jennings, S. L. (1987). The acquisition of self and mother knowledge in infancy. *Developmental Psychology, 23*, 86–96.

Potegal, M., & Davidson, R. J. (2003). Temper tantrums in young children: 1. Behavioral composition. *Journal of Developmental and Behavioral Pediatrics, 24*, 140–147.

Potegal, M., Kosorok, M. R., & Davidson, R. J. (1996). The time course of angry behavior in the temper tantrums of young children. In C. F. Ferris & T. Grisso (Eds.), *Understanding aggressive behavior in children* (pp. 31–45). New York: Annals of the New York Academy of Sciences.

Radke-Yarrow, M., & Zahn-Waxler, C. (1984). Roots, motives, and patterning in children's prosocial behavior. In E. Staub, D. Bar-Tal, J. Karylowski, & J. Raykowski (Eds.), *The development and maintenance of prosocial behavior: International perspectives on positive morality* (pp. 81–99). New York: Plenum Press.

Retzinger, S. M. (1991). *Violent emotions.* Newbury Park, CA: Sage.

Roseman, I., Spindel, M. S., & Jose, P. E. (1990). Appraisals of emotion-eliciting events: Testing a theory of discrete emotions. *Journal of Personality and Social Psychology, 59*, 899-915.

Rothbart, M. K., & Ahadi, S. A. (1994). Temperament and the development of personality. *Journal of Abnormal Psychology, 103*, 55–66.

Rothbart, M. K., Ahadi, S. A., & Evans, D. E. (2000). Temperament and personality: Origins and outcomes. *Journal of Personality and Social Psychology, 78*, 122–135.

Rubin, K. H., Bukowski, W., & Parker, J. (1998). Peer interactions, relationships, and groups. In N. Eisenberg (Ed.), *Handbook of child psychology, 5th edition: Social, emotional and personality development* (pp. 619–700). New York: Wiley.

Rubin, K. H., Burgess, K. B., & Dwyer, K. M. (2003). preschoolers' externalizing behaviors from toddler temperament, conflict, and maternal negativity. *Developmental Psychology, 39*, 164–176.

Rubin, K. H., Burgess, K. B., & Hastings, P. D. (2002). Stability and social-behavioral consequences of toddlers' inhibited temperament and parenting behaviors. *Child Development, 73*, 483–495.

Sarbin, T., & Allen, V. L. (1968). Role theory. In G. Lindsey & E. Aronson (Eds.), *Handbook of social psychology* (Vol. 2, pp. 488–567). Boston: Addison Wesley.

Scheff, T. J. (1987). The shame-rage spiral: A case study of an interminable quarrel. In. H. B. Lewis (Ed.), *The role of shame in symptom formation* (pp. 109–149). Hillsdale, NJ: Erlbaum.

Scheff, T. J. (2000). Shame and the social bond: A sociological theory. *Sociological Theory, 18*, 84–99.

Scheff, T. J. (2003). Shame in self and society. *Symbolic Interaction*, 26, 239–262.

Scheff, T. J., & Retzinger, S. M. (1991). *Emotions and violence: Shame and rage in destructive conflicts.* Lexington, MA: Lexington Books.

Schore, A. (1994). *Affect regulation and the origin of the self: The neurobiology of emotional development.* Hillsdale, NJ: Erlbaum.

Schultz, T. R. (1980). Development of the concept of intention. *Minnesota Symposia on Child Psychology, 13*, 131–164.

Schultz, T. R., & Wells, D. (1985). Judging the intentionality of action-outcomes. *Developmental Psychology, 21*, 83–89.

Shaver, P. R., Wu, S., & Schwartz, J. C. (1992). Cross-cultural similarities and differences in emotion and its representation: A prototype approach. In M. S. Clark (Ed.), *Review of personality and social psychology* (Vol. 13, pp. 175–212). Newbury Park, CA: Sage.

Sroufe, L. A. (1996). *Emotional development: The organization of emotional life in the early years.* New York: Cambridge University Press.

Stipek, D. J. (1983). A developmental analysis of pride and shame. *Human Development, 26*, 42–54.

Stipek, D., Recchia, S., & McClintic, S. (1992). Self-evaluation in young children. *Monographs of the Society for Research in Child Development, 57*(1), 226.

Stipek, D., Recchia, S., & McClintic, S. (1993). Self-evaluation in young children. *Monographs of the Society for Research in Child Development, 57*, 1–98.

Stipek, D., Weiner, B., & Li, K. (1989). Testing some attribution–emotion relations in the People's Republic of China. *Journal of Personality and Social Psychology, 56*, 109–116.

Tangney, J., Wagner, P. E, Hill-Barlow, D., Marschall, D. E., & Gramzow, R. (1996). Relation of shame and guilt to constructive versus destructive responses to anger across the lifespan. *Journal of Personality and Social Psychology, 70*, 797–809.

Tangney, J. P. (1998). How does guilt differ from shame? In J. Bybee (Ed.), *Guilt and children* (pp. 1–18). New York: Academic Press.

Tangney, J. P. (2002). Self-conscious emotions: The self as a moral guide. In A. Tesser & D. A. Stapel (Eds.), *Self and motivation: Emerging psychological perspectives* (pp. 97–117). Washington, DC: American Psychological Association.

Tangney, J. P., & Dearing, R. L. (2002). *Shame and guilt.* New York: Guilford Press.

Tangney, J. P., Miller, R. S., Flicker, L., & Barlow, D. (1996). Are shame, guilt, and embarrassment distinct emotions? *Journal of Personality and Social Psychology, 70*, 1256–1269.

Tangney, J. P., Wagner, P. E., & Gramzow, R. (1992). Proneness to shame, proneness to guilt, and psychopathology. *Journal of Abnormal Psychology, 103*, 469–478.

Tappan, M. B. (2000). Autobiography, mediated action, and the development of moral identity. *Narrative Inquiry, 10*, 81–109.

Tomkins, S. (1962). *Affect, imagery and consciousness* (Vol. I). New York: Springer.

Tomkins, S. (1987). Shame. In D. L. Nathanson (Ed.), *The many faces of shame* (pp. 133–161). New York: Norton.

Tremblay, R. E. (2000). The development of aggressive behavior during childhood: What have we learned in the past century? *International Journal of Behavioral Development, 24*, 129–141.

Valiente, C., Eisenberg, N., Fabes, R. A., Shepard, S. A., Cumberland, A., & Losoya, S. H. (2004). Prediction of children's empathy-related responding from their effortful control and parents' expressivity. *Developmental Psychology, 40*, 911–926.

Vaughn, B. E., Kopp, C. B., & Krakow, J. B. (1984). The emergence and consolidation of self-control from eighteen to thirty months of age: Normative trends and individual differences. *Child Development, 55*, 990–1004.

Vaughn, B. E., Kopp, C. B., Krakow, J. B., Johnson, K., & Schwartz, S. S. (1986). Process analysis of the behavior of very young children in delay tasks. *Developmental Psychology, 22*, 752–759.

Watson, M. W., Fischer, K. W., & Andreas, J. B. (2004). Pathways to aggression in children and adolescents. *Harvard Educational Review, 74*, 404–430.

Yoon, J. S., Hughes, J. N., Cavell, T. A., & Thompson, B. (2000). Social cognitive differences between aggressive-rejected and aggressive-nonrejected children. *Journal of School Psychology, 38*, 551–570.

Zahn-Waxler, C. (1990). The origins of guilt. In R. A. Thompson (Ed.), *Socioemotional development: Nebraska symposium on motivation* (Vol. 36, pp. 183–258). Lincoln: University of Nebraska Press.

Zahn-Waxler, C., Radke-Yarrow, M., Wagner, E., & Chapman, M. (1992). Development of concern for others. *Developmental Psychology, 28,* 126–136.

Zahn-Waxler, C., Radke-Yarrow, M., & King, R. A. (1979). Child rearing and children's prosocial initiations towards victims of distress. *Child Development, 50,* 319–330.

4

The Transformation of Prosocial Behavior from Infancy to Childhood

Dale F. Hay
Kaye V. Cook

The aim of this chapter is to examine the transition from infancy to childhood in the quality of prosocial behavior, which can be defined as

> behaviors that are positively responsive to others' needs and welfare. . . . At a descriptive level, they are behaviors that are helpful and affiliative responses to others: responses to signs of suffering, need, or danger in another person or animal, such as assisting, sharing, being kind and considerate, comforting, cooperating, protecting someone from harm, rescuing someone from danger, and feeling empathy and sympathy. (Radke-Yarrow & Zahn-Waxler, 1986, p. 208)

In adopting this broad definition of prosocial activities, we seek not to conflate the terms *prosocial* and *altruistic*; rather, we see altruism as one example of the positive social behaviors that sustain society and create harmonious relations among members of any social group. When we examine the beginnings of prosocial behavior in the toddler years, we are not just looking for evidence for precursors to later self-sacrifice. We are trying to identify the roots of personal and civic virtue.

We propose that positive engagement in human society rests on the young human's basic interest in and emotional response to the social world, early developing tendencies to affiliate with others and work together in groups, and a growing understanding of the norms and moral principles that govern social relations in particular cultures. The prosocial behaviors of the very young thus attest to the early beginnings of the human capacities for affiliation, cooperation, altruism, enlightened self-interest, and understanding of social norms, all of which make civil society possible.

It might once have been thought that this transition from infancy to childhood was quite straightforward, with prosocial behavior being absent from the repertoire of the human infant and the toddler. In that traditional view, prosocial behavior might be expected to make its first appearance in the early childhood years, when children are first cared for together in groups and are exhorted by their parents and teachers to share with others. Nonetheless, the ability to engage in prosocial behavior is by no means absent in the toddler period (for reviews, see Hay, 1994; Hay, Castle, & Jewett, 1994; Hay & Rheingold, 1983; Radke-Yarrow, Zahn-Waxler, & Chapman, 1983; Rheingold & Hay, 1978). Thus the transition we need to examine is a qualitative change in the rules that govern prosocial behavior and the meaning it holds for young children and their companions, not its first occurrence in development.

Evidence bearing on the early development of prosocial behavior is somewhat limited, due to the fact that most studies have been based on very small, and not always representative, samples. The literature consists mainly of cross-sectional comparisons of relatively small samples of children of different ages, often tested in laboratory playrooms (e.g., Hay, 1979; Hay, Caplan, Castle, & Stimson, 1991; Rheingold, Hay, & West, 1976). Studies of larger samples report findings based on informants' ratings (e.g., NICHD Early Child Care Research Network, 2000) or concentrate attention on empathy and prosocial responses to distress (e.g., Zahn-Waxler, Robinson, & Emde, 1992). Thus many of the studies in this literature lack adequate statistical power to discern clear developmental trends in the full range of prosocial behavior. The available data are somewhat contradictory, with no general developmental trends evident across categories of prosocial behavior (see also Radke-Yarrow et al., 1983). This is largely because particular investigators have tended to concentrate on the study of particular forms of prosocial behavior.

In view of the absence of much longitudinal data in the literature, we make reference throughout this chapter to a short-term longitudinal study of social development in the second and third years of life, the South London Peer Study (SLPS—Demetriou & Hay, 2004; Hay, Castle, & Davies, 2000; Hay, Castle, Davies, Demetriou, & Stimson, 1999). In that study, focal toddlers recruited from the age and sex registers of two general medical practices in South London were observed at home with the mother (or, in a couple of cases, another primary caregiver), a familiar peer, and the peer's mother. The observations were made on two occasions, 6 months apart. In previously published work, analyses concentrated attention on the focal children, not the peers, who had been recruited by the focal children's mothers and on whom there was less background information. For the purposes of this chapter, however, we present some findings from a combined sample (n = 110) in which both the focal children and their peers are included, adjusting for statistical dependencies between members of the dyad (see Figures 4.1–4.3).

In the pages that follow we argue that toddlers' early prosocial tendencies may best be seen as a basic impulse to engage positively with other people that only gradually becomes *selective, socially appropriate*, *self-regulated*, and *morally informed* activity. Before considering these developments, however, we start with a consideration of three main strands in prosocial development that make their appearance in the first 2 years of life (Table 4.1).

DOMAINS OF EARLY PROSOCIAL BEHAVIOR

Spontaneous and Responsive Prosocial Behaviors

In the early years of infancy and childhood one can discern three general strands in prosocial development, which can be described as *feeling for another* (friendliness, affection, and empathic concern); *working with another* (cooperating to solve problems and meet mutual goals, sharing resources, and helping another accomplish tasks); and *ministering to another* (nurturing, comforting, providing resources that another person requires, and generally responding to another's needs or wishes). Because the development of empathy is being considered in detail elsewhere in this book (Hoffman, Chapter 5, this volume), we concentrate attention here on the latter two domains, infants' tendencies to *work with* and *minister to the needs* of other people. The first category comprises spontaneous activities that function as positive ways of engaging with other people in both serious and playful contexts. The second category comprises behavior that is responsive to the demands of a given situation, requiring some level of understanding of another person's circumstances, needs, and explicit requests. These two domains of prosocial behavior are similar in their positive social nature and are not orthogonal, but have different correlates, are ultimately governed by different sets of social norms, and may show different patterns of change from infancy to childhood.

Working (and Playing) with Others

Infants and toddlers commonly join with the people they know to explore the world and pursue mutual goals, displaying early forms of sharing, cooperation, and helpfulness. Toddlers enter into these mutual activities voluntarily, in the course of everyday experience with the people they know.

Sharing Interests and Resources

As soon as infants can crawl, their curiosity leads them to explore the physical environment (Rheingold & Eckerman, 1970), and they begin to share what

TABLE 4.1. Milestones in Early Prosocial Development

Year 1 ——————→	Year 2 ——————————→	Year 3+
	Ministering to others	
• Simple compliance	• Sharing in response to request • Attempts to comfort others • Cheerful compliance with requests	• Knowledge about caregiving • Knowledge about responses to distress • Responsibility norms • Reasoning about deservingness • Gender and individual differences
	Working and playing with others	
• Passive participation in social games • Sharing objects and food with others	• Cooperative games • Collaborative problem solving • Helping others with household tasks	• Mutual conversation • Reciprocity norms • Gender preferences • Reasoning about entitlement • Gender and individual differences
	Feeling for others	
• Crying when others cry	• Expressions of empathic concern • Individual differences	• Verbal references to emotion and expressions of sympathy

they see and find with their companions, showing and offering toys, food, and a variety of other objects (Eckerman, Whatley, & Kutz, 1975; Lewis, Young, Brooks, & Michalson, 1975; Rheingold, 1973; Rheingold et al., 1976). The early sharing behaviors have been discussed with reference to language development (Bates, 1979) and joint attention (Butterworth & Jarrett, 1991; Woodward, Sommerville, & Guajardo, 2001), and, as such, they are seen as precursors to the later skills needed for human interaction. Indeed, the absence of sharing behaviors is an early hallmark of autism (Sigman, Mundy, Sherman, & Ungerer, 1986).

Cooperative Games

Spontaneous bouts of cooperative interaction emerge in the first year of life, when infants play social games that are defined by mutual involvement of two people, repetition of defining actions, alternation of turns, and a consequent playful, nonliteral quality that distinguishes games from more literal interaction, such as interpersonal conflict. Infants and toddlers engage in such cooperative games with peers and unfamiliar adults (Ross & Goldman, 1977; Warneken, Chen, & Tomasello, 2006) as well as with parents (Hay, 1979).

In the second and third years of life, cooperation sometimes takes the form of collaborative problem solving as well as game playing (Brownell & Carriger, 1990; Camaioni, Baumgartner, & Perucchini, 1991; De Cooke & Brownell, 1995). Although early coordinated activities appear more coincidental than cooperative, during the second and third years of life, children become increasingly able to actively cooperate with unfamiliar adults and peers to meet a shared goal (Brownell, Ramani, & Zerwas, 2006; Warneken et al., 2006).

Helping with the Housework

In the course of their everyday activities, toddlers also spontaneously join in with their companions' tasks. For example, it has long been noted that toddlers try to help their parents do the housework (Church, 1966). In an experimental study, Rheingold (1982) increased the likelihood of these helpful tendencies being shown by setting up a simulated domestic environment in which groceries were to be unpacked, litter swept off the carpet, and the like. Without prompting, 18-month-olds spontaneously helped their mothers do the undone tasks.

Responsiveness to People's Needs and Wishes

During the second year of life, infants use instrumental actions to minister to the needs and accede to the wishes of other people. To respond to the needs of others, the toddler must first recognize the nature of the need, as inferred from the person's circumstances or explicit requests for assistance.

Comforting Others Who Are in Distress

Even young infants notice and sometimes cry when other infants cry (Hay, Nash, & Pedersen, 1981; see Hoffman, Chapter 5, this volume). Their early sensitivity to distress then translates into instrumental attempts to comfort or distract the distressed person, sometimes with items such as teddy bears that toddlers themselves find comforting (Demetriou & Hay, 2004; Hoffman, 1976; Lamb & Zakhireh, 1997; Murphy, 1937; Zahn-Waxler, Radke-Yarrow, & King, 1979; Zahn-Waxler, Radke-Yarrow, Wagner, & Chapman, 1992). By 3 years of age, children can explain how to help a distressed classmate (Caplan & Hay, 1989).

Nurturance and Care for Babies

In many societies, quite young children contribute to family life by caring for their infant siblings (Pelletier-Stiefel et al., 1986; Whiting, 1983). Even in Western cultures, very young children may minister to the needs of their siblings: for example, over half the 2- to 4-year-old British children observed at home with younger siblings at least occasionally comforted their siblings when they cried (Dunn, Kendrick, & McNamee, 1981).

Sharing in Response to Requests

Parents and, in particular, siblings and peers often request objects from infants. In the first year, it is easier for infants to offer objects to other people than to actually let them go into the other person's hand or lap; relinquishing an object may require inhibitory processes that develop later than the offering gesture. However, by 12 months of age, infants give objects in response to adults' outstretched hands and verbal requests (Hay & Murray, 1982; Rheingold et al., 1976) and release objects they have been holding, in response to the verbal and nonverbal demands of other children (Hay et al., 1991).

Obedience

In the post-Milgram era, many psychologists see obedience as a rather negative human tendency; however, the ability to respond positively to another's wishes often fosters harmony in personal relationships and allows members of a group to respond constructively to problems and emergencies. By the first birthday, infants comply with other people's verbal and nonverbal requests, particularly those pertaining to safety issues and the equitable use of particular possessions (Gralinski & Kopp, 1993). Most studies have explored compliance with parents' requests in particular (Gralinski & Kopp, 1993; Kaler & Kopp, 1990; Kuczynski, 1983; Kuczynski, Kochanska, Radke-Yarrow, & Girnius-Brown, 1987; Schneider-Rosen & Wenz-Gross, 1990; Smetana, 1989). However, it is sometimes necessary for infants and toddlers to acquiesce to an unfamiliar adult's requests; for example, compliance with the examiner's requests is required for developmental assessments and standard tests of vision and hearing administered in the first year of life.

The terms *obedience* and *compliance,* at least as applied to adults and older children, sometimes connote a grudging bowing to the will of others. However, toddlers often respond swiftly and with enthusiasm to the requests and commands of others and repeat the requested behavior again, without being asked to do so (Rheingold, Cook, & Kowlowitz, 1987). The pleasure children take in fitting their actions to the words of others is at the heart of "committed compliance" with the requests of others (Kochanska, 2002a).

THE UBIQUITY AND INTENTIONALITY OF EARLY PROSOCIAL BEHAVIOR

Prosocial Behavior Is Shown by Most Toddlers

Early tendencies to work or play with other people are shown by an overwhelming majority of toddlers (Hay et al., 1999; Rheingold et al., 1976;

Zahn-Waxler, Radke-Yarrow, et al., 1992). There is relatively little evidence for contextual influences on these spontaneous prosocial activities. For example, in a series of experiments on early sharing, all 18-month-olds shared, and did so at about the same rate, despite changes in the identity of the recipient, the recipient's behavior, and the toys and other resources that were available to be shared (Rheingold et al., 1976).

In contrast, toddlers do not always have the opportunity to respond to the needs or wishes of another person. For example, in the SLPS, when toddlers' responses to the distress of familiar peers were examined, only 60% of the focal children could be studied, because only those peers ever became distressed (Demetriou & Hay, 2004). However, when distress occurred, toddlers' rates of responding to distress compare favorably with adults. For example, the rate with which toddlers responded to peers' distress was about the same as that with which adults responded to simulated distress in airports (Darley & Latané, 1968; Demetriou & Hay, 2004).

On any given occasion, prosocial behavior does not occur at high rates. Toddlers spend much of their time in independent play, and they have relatively few opportunities to respond to other people's needs. Nonetheless, despite common beliefs to the contrary, prosocial behavior is no less common than aggression. In the SLPS (Hay et al., 2000), the toddlers initially shared objects with peers as often as they grabbed toys away from them. Six months later, on average, they shared significantly more often than they grabbed. More children shared with than hit or otherwise assaulted their peers (see also Lewis et al., 1975). In general, toddlers' prosocial actions and their aggressive behaviors are similar, in that each constitutes a unique category of social behavior that is deployed infrequently but is in the repertoire of virtually all normal children. Thus it is not the case that aggression is initially frequent and declines while prosocial behavior is initially uncommon and occurs only after aggression has declined. In the case of aggression, analyses for general trends are less informative than examination of individual trajectories (Tremblay & Nagin, 2005), and this may also be true for prosocial development.

Are the Early Prosocial Behaviors Truly Intentional?

Baldwin (1895) defined intentionality as "purposeful" or "deliberate" action. In very early infancy, parents attribute intentionality to their infants, an attribution that sometimes rests on observation of the infants' operations on objects (Vedeler, 1987). Goal-directed behavior toward objects can be discerned in the first months of life (Lewis, 1990). By the second year of life, toddlers have some understanding of intentionality, evincing surprise when an actor's behavior leads to an unintended result (Frye, 1993) and performing actions that meet the goals of modeled acts (Meltzoff, 1995). Toddlers' own intentional actions are seen in problem-solving contexts, when they repeat and vary their behavior and try to maneuver their way around problems until goals are reached (Chen & Siegler, 2000). This flexibility and use of alternative ways to achieve goals is clearly evident in early prosocial development. For example, toddlers will carry on trying to share objects or provide comfort or help their parents do the housework, even when their efforts are rebuffed because adults do not share their aesthetic tastes, or have no time to receive the type of help the toddler is providing (Rheingold, 1982; Rheingold et al., 1976). Toddlers' energetic attempts to encourage an adult experimenter to take a turn in a cooperative game also testify to the intentionality of early prosocial behavior (Ross & Lollis, 1987); 18-month-olds and 24-month-olds are equally likely to do this (Warneken et al., 2006).

The deliberate nature of prosocial behavior does not necessarily indicate exactly what intentions the toddler has, beyond the demands of the immediate social interaction. It is clear that the early prosocial behaviors are intentional, but it is not at all clear that they are directed to a single goal. We thus do not claim that they are motivated by altruistic impulses. Rather, the tendencies to work with others and to respond to the needs and wishes of others are common and deliberate ways in which toddlers engage in social life, which become further transformed over the next few years of life.

WHAT HAPPENS NEXT?

Does Prosocial Behavior Increase in a Linear Fashion from 12 to 36 Months?

We have seen that in the first 2 years of life prosocial activities are ubiquitous yet relatively infrequent. Prosocial behavior increases in frequency over childhood (e.g., Eisenberg & Fabes, 1998); however, it is not clear that there is an overall increase in the incidence of prosocial behavior from infancy to childhood. Different trends are observed for different types of prosocial behavior (Radke-Yarrow et al., 1983).

Working with Others

There is little cross-sectional or longitudinal evidence of change from 12 to 36 months in spontaneous sharing (Hay et al., 1991, 1999). In the combined sample of focal children and their peers from the SLPS, there was no evidence for a linear increase in sharing between 15 and 42 months; rather, for all but one age cohort, there was a small, nonsignificant decline in the rate of sharing with the familiar peer (Figure 4.1).

In contrast, ever since the classic observations of Parten (1932), there has been consistent evidence for an increased ability to engage in cooperative play as children grow older. An increase in cooperation in older age groups is found with mothers (Hay, 1979), experimenters (Warneken et al., 2006), and peers (Brownell et al., 2006; Camaioni et al., 1991). The age difference is as-

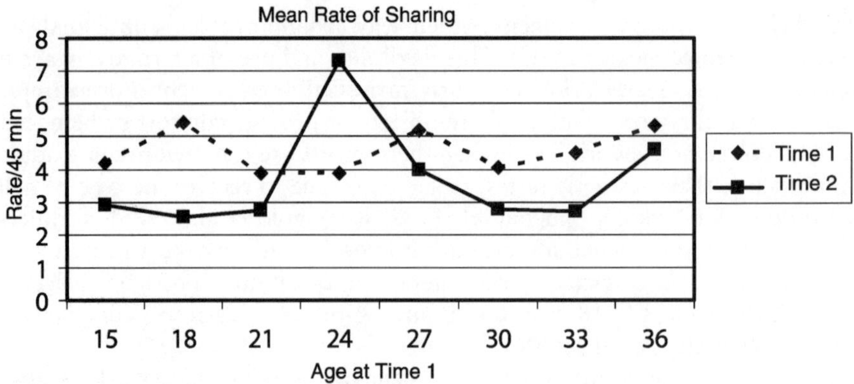

FIGURE 4.1. Age trends in spontaneous sharing. In the SLPS, spontaneous sharing occurred at slightly lower rates at the second time point, for all but one age cohort.

sociated with increases in toddlers' abilities to sustain joint attention and use language about self and others (Brownell et al., 2006).

Responding to the Needs and Wishes of Others

The available data are contradictory. Cross-sectional analyses of the sharing behaviors of 12- and 24-month-olds had suggested that sharing in response to unfamiliar peers' requests declines with age (Hay et al., 1991), but longitudinal observations of familiar peers showed no such trends (Hay et al., 1999). When adults simulate distress, there is evidence that toddlers' prosocial responses increase with age (Zahn-Waxler, Radke-Yarrow, et al., 1992). However, responsiveness to peers' distress in the SLPS showed no effect of age (Demetriou & Hay, 2004).

Quantitative versus Qualitative Change

In seeking to understand change in prosocial behavior from infancy to childhood, it is important to go beyond the initial assumption that there will be a universal increase with age. Rather, it appears that there are important qualitative changes in prosocial behavior from the second to the third and fourth years of life. Indeed, there may be two contradictory trends that result in relatively little change in rate of prosocial activity over this time period. As toddlers acquire new skills, their capacity for prosocial behavior increases; however, as they become more sensitive to context and social nuance, and thus more aware of the social conventions governing the display of prosocial behavior, their actions may become more selective. To the extent that both tendencies are at work, there may be only subtle changes in the rate with which 1-, 2-, and 3-year-olds actually show prosocial behavior.

Hence it is important to examine what qualitative changes do take place over the toddler years. We believe that, over these years, toddlers acquire more knowledge about how to be prosocial and skills to facilitate harmonious interaction; however, they simultaneously learn that prosocial behavior is not always necessary or desirable in a given situation.

Toddlers Acquire Domain-Specific Knowledge in Real and Playful Contexts

During the toddler years, children acquire a great deal of knowledge that promotes effective and socially appropriate prosocial behavior. In particular, by the time children are 3 or 4 years of age, they have acquired considerable knowledge about effective and culturally acceptable ways in which to minister to other people's needs. For example, when interviewed, preschoolers show that they know a great deal about how to respond to a peer's distress (Caplan & Hay, 1989) and how to resolve a dispute with a friend (Hay, Zahn-Waxler, Cummings, & Iannotti, 1992; Iskander, Laursen, Finkelstein, & Frederickson, 1995).

Oddly, much of this knowledge is revealed in the context of pretend play, which provides an opportunity for children to represent many details of their social worlds. Thus, just as early social play and exploration of the physical environment foster spontaneous forms of sharing and cooperation, so too does early pretend play. For example, toddlers are encouraged to tend to the "needs" of dolls and toy animals, and their play with such items reveals considerable knowledge about ways in which to care for babies and pets (Rheingold & Emery, 1986).

In some cultures, this knowledge would be deployed in service of the actual needs of younger siblings (Whiting, 1983). However, in Western cultures, children are not generally encouraged to take on responsibility for the care of other. Preschool teachers encourage their charges to pretend to provide care for distressed dolls and teddy bears but do not encourage prosocial responses to the distress of actual classmates (Caplan & Hay, 1989). It thus appears that, during the preschool years, children acquire a considerable amount of knowledge about how to respond positively to the needs of others but also learn more implicit lessons about reasons why they need not be prosocial all of the time (see Caplan, 1993).

Prosocial Behavior Becomes Increasingly Selective

As toddlers acquire knowledge about prosocial behavior, they learn that there are circumstances under which it is more or less appropriate. This means that their prosocial responses are shown more selectively.

Preferences for Particular Recipients

Even 12-month-olds make some distinctions between recipients of their prosocial actions, being more likely to share objects with their peers and with their own mothers than with the peers' mothers (Young & Lewis, 1979). Toddlers are generally more likely to share objects with their parents than with unfamiliar adults (Rheingold et al., 1976). In the preschool years, children are more likely to share food with friends than with acquaintances, although they are likely to offload unpalatable food on acquaintances (Birch & Billman, 1986). When interviewed, young children say that they will be more likely to sympathize with a friend's distress (Costin & Carlson Jones, 1992). As friendships consolidate over the preschool years, and some peers become more generally accepted than others, these preferences for particular recipients are likely to become quite marked.

Preferential Responsiveness to Same-Sex Peers

As children grow older, they are more likely to spend their time in gender-segregated activities (Maccoby, 1988), interacting with and making friends with members of their own sex. In the context of this general trend, it seems likely that prosocial behavior will be selectively displayed to same-sex peers. Analyses of data from the SLPS revealed that, over time, girls developed a preference for same-sex interaction; at the second visit, they shared more with other girls and never gave boys the food or toys they wanted (Hay et al., 1999). The sex of the recipient did not affect positive responses to peers' distress, but the toddlers were most likely to respond negatively to distress when they had caused the distress of an opposite-sex peer (Demetriou & Hay, 2004). Thus, an implicit display rule of preferential responsiveness to same-sex peers seems to emerge in the third year of life. It seems likely that, as children spend more and more time with same-sex peers, gender-specific norms governing prosocial activities emerge, possibly encouraging gendered specialization in different types of prosocial behavior.

Prosocial Behavior Becomes Increasingly Rule Governed

Toddlers are aware of the rules underpinning social interaction. For example, in an experimental study, adult experimenters engaged toddlers in a cooperative game and then systematically violated the turn-taking rule that was the basis of the game. The interruption demonstrated that infants knew the rules of the game and would use gestures and words to induce the experimenter to take her turn (Ross & Lollis, 1987; see also Warneken et al., 2006). As they grow older, toddlers become even more sensitive to social rules. The cultural norms that govern social interaction have been described as "display rules" (Masters, 1991; Underwood, Coie, & Herbsman, 1992). As the toddler turns into the young child, his or her display of prosocial behavior corresponds more precisely to the "display rules" of the particular culture (Kakavoulis, 1998; Miller & Bersoff, 1995).

The Reciprocity Norm

One of the principles thought to govern prosocial behavior in adulthood is the reciprocity norm (Gouldner, 1960), in which people respond positively to those who have been positive to them. There is some evidence for reciprocity in early sharing with peers (Levitt, Weber, Clark, & McDonnell, 1985). In the SLPS (Hay et al., 1999), we looked for evidence of reciprocity at both a macro level (computing intraclass correlations in rates of sharing between the focal children and their peers) and a more micro level (examining the extent to which a child reciprocated particular acts of sharing by the peer). At the macro level, for the sample as a whole, apparent reciprocity in sharing was no longer visible when the overall rate of interaction between the peers was taken into account; however, both micro- and macro-level analyses indicated that a reciprocity norm was emerging in boys' interactions with their peers.

In contrast, nursery school children's responses to the distress of their classmates did not show evidence of reciprocity; rather, children who responded actively to their peers' distress were significantly *less* likely than other classmates to be responded to when they became distressed themselves (Caplan & Hay, 1989). It is possible that reciprocity norms govern sharing and cooperation but not responsiveness to need.

Responsibility Norms

Adults' responses to persons in need are thought to be regulated by a general norm of *social responsibility* (Berkowitz, 1972). Such norms pertain both to responsibility for ministering to distress and responsibility as a function of causing distress.

Many experiments have shown that the sense of responsibility for helping someone in distress may be diluted if many other people are present to witness distress or more competent professionals are at hand (e.g., Darley & Latané, 1968). It is perhaps thus not surprising that, in our study, when interviewed and presented with a video of a classmate showing distress, 3- and 4-year-old children voiced many ideas about how to help but overwhelmingly expressed the view that it was the teacher's responsibility to do so (Caplan & Hay, 1989). Adults do not always encourage or respond positively to instances of prosocial behavior in practice (Eisenberg, Cameron, Tryon, & Dodez, 1981; Petersen & Reaven, 1984). Rather, in well-regulated social environments, adults respond swiftly to a young child's need, and rarely is there time enough for other children to try to help (Caplan & Hay, 1989). The adults' behavior promotes diffusion of responsibility and children's understanding of their own responsibilities vis-à-vis those of adults.

There are also cultural norms (and indeed laws) concerning personal responsibility for having caused other people's problems, so that the responsible party must either make reparations for the harm caused or justify his or her decisions not to do so. Investigators of toddlers' prosocial behavior have examined the importance of personal responsibility by comparing the experience of witnessing distress as a bystander and actually causing the distress through one's own actions. In studies of children's responses to distress, many of the incidents of distress that were recorded were actually caused by the children who were being observed (Demetriou & Hay, 2004; Murphy, 1937; Zahn-Waxler et al., 1979; Zahn-Waxler, Radke-Yarrow, et al., 1992). This situation may lead to negative as well as positive responses to the distress, particularly in the context of the sibling relationship (Dunn & Brown, 1994; Dunn & Munn, 1986). In the SLPS, negative responses were hardly ever shown if the toddler had merely witnessed and not actually caused the peer's distress (Demetriou & Hay, 2004). Rather, the toddlers were more likely to respond actively to distress they had caused and thus were more likely to show both negative and positive responses in that context. This finding stood in contrast to earlier reports that toddlers were more likely to respond positively if they had not caused the distress (Zahn-Waxler et al., 1979; Zahn-Waxler, Radke-Yarrow, et al., 1992).

In general, the evidence suggests that a norm of personal responsibility toward other people is not prominent in the toddler years, when toddlers do not always make reparations for their own behavior and have learned to expect adults to take responsibility for responding to other people's needs. Rather, attributions about personal responsibility become more linked to children's prosocial behavior in the preschool and middle childhood years (Chapman, Zahn-Waxler, Cooperman, & Iannotti, 1987).

Prosocial Behavior Becomes Embedded in a Sociomoral Framework

During the toddler years, the child becomes more aware of his or her behavior and its value as "good" or "naughty"; in other words, the child begins to make moral judgments about prosocial behavior, as shown by other people (e.g., siblings and peers) and by the self (Kelley & Brownell, 2000). The young child's growing understanding of social conventions and moral principles is attested to by a variety of evidence: 18-month-olds show a rudimentary moral sense when they mark mismatches between expectations and experience with such terms as "uh oh" (Dunn, 1988; Kagan, 1981; Lamb, 1993) and hesitate on the verge of wrongdoing (Lytton, 1980; Stayton, Hogan, & Ainsworth, 1971). Two-year-olds have some awareness of right and wrong (Barrett, 1995, cited in Eisenberg, 2000); 34-month-olds have some understanding of the difference between moral and social transgressions (Smetana & Braeges, 1990).

Moral emotions are one piece of this eventual organization in development whereby prosocial behavior becomes morally informed. Toward the end of the toddler period, children express the "moral emotions" of shame and guilt (Damon, 1988; Lewis et al., 1975). Feelings of guilt and personal responsibility may influence children's prosocial behavior as much as their feelings of empathy (Chapman et al., 1987).

Moral reasoning abilities in older children are related to empathic concern and to overt prosocial behavior (Miller, Eisenberg, Fabes, & Shell, 1996). Early reasoning abilities flower in emotionally charged situations in family life, when toddlers come to understand the need to justify their actions to parents, siblings, and peers (Dunn, 1988; Ross, 1996; Smetana & Braeges, 1990). Adults often refrain from trying to negotiate conflicts between siblings (Hay, Vespo, & Zahn-Waxler, 1998), which means that children must argue their positions and justify their actions, and they soon come to do so in terms of principles of justice (Ross, 1996). Thus, in their behavior as well as their words, young children show an understanding of such things as possession rights, entitlement, and fairness. This growing awareness of principles of justice converges with an understanding that one need not always be prosocial; for example, in the SLPS, toddlers who refuse to share with a familiar peer may do so while declaring "No! It's mine!" or indeed point out that the peer can use some toys but not others (Hay, 2006).

A child becomes a committed and morally engaged member of society when he or she accepts and advocates to others what might first be seen as arbitrary rules handed down by authority figures (Freud, 1938; Kohlberg, 1969; Miller & Dollard, 1941; Piaget, 1932; Sears, 1951). Kochanska (e.g., Kochanska, 2002b; Kochanska, Forman, Aksan, & Dunbar, 2005) argued that the older child's emerging "moral self" (as measured at 56 months of age by asking which puppet acting out each of two poles of nine moral dimensions such as guilt, empathy, and reparation was more "like them") is derived from the younger toddler's "wholehearted, willing, self-regulated compliance" (p. 339); however, this relationship may be more correlational than causal (Wahler, Herring, & Edwards, 2001).

The young child's growing understanding of the social conventions and moral framework surrounding prosocial behavior is evident in conversations with parents (Smetana, 1989) and siblings (Dunn, 1988; Ross, 1996). Indeed, one of the final achievements of this period is that 2- and 3-year-olds actually talk about and hold opinions about prosocial behavior, as shown (or not shown) by themselves and others.

Gender Differentiation

Another thing that happens between infancy and childhood is the emergence of gender differences in prosocial behavior, at the same point in early childhood that gender differences in aggression become more pronounced (Keenan & Shaw, 1997). In their classic review of the literature on sex differences, Maccoby and Jacklin (1974) concluded that there was relatively little evidence for psychological sex differences under the age of 2. Similarly, few of the studies of early prosocial behavior have reported significant differences between the sexes. For example, in a series of studies of early sharing, only one gender difference was apparent: Boys were more likely than girls to show objects to their mothers (Rheingold et al., 1976). One exception to this pattern is the finding from a study of twins (n = 184), which indicated that, by 14 months of age, girls show greater empathy and prosocial responses to another's distress than boys do (Zahn-Waxler, Robinson, et al., 1992).

Even when older children are studied, gender differences are not always evident in experimental or observational data. For example, no gender differences were found in a comparison of children between the ages of 3 and 7½ years (Yarrow et al., 1976). It is possible that gender differences emerge only gradually over the childhood years. For example, in a longitudinal study of British children, there were significant gender differences in the reports of prosocial behavior at age 11 given by mothers, teachers and the children themselves, but no gender differences in observed cooperation at age 4 (Hay & Pawlby, 2003).

It is, however, difficult to discern such trends in the absence of many longitudinal studies on samples with sufficient size to test such a hypothesis. The twin study in which gender differences were observed is one of the largest samples in which early prosocial behavior has been investigated (Zahn-Waxler, Robinson, et al., 1992). Most of the existing studies of early prosocial behavior have insufficient statistical power to test for gender differences in behaviors that in any case are expected to occur at low rates. To test the possibility that such trends might be detected in a sample of larger size, we again examined the combined data set from the SLPS, which contained both the focal children and their peers. Significant differences in the rate of sharing were found at the second but not the first visit (Figure 4.2); however, the difference

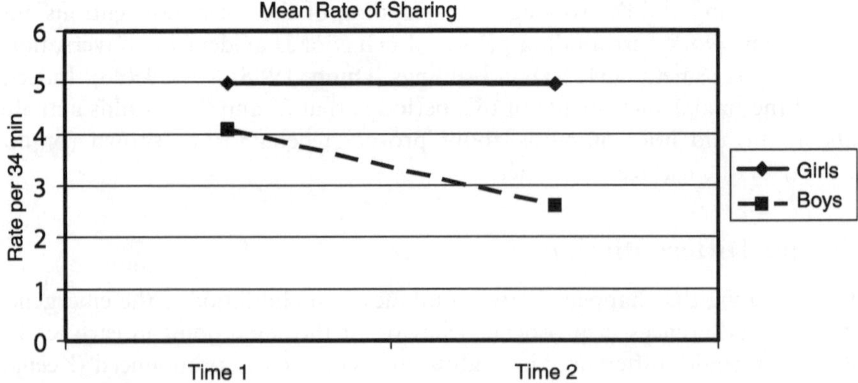

FIGURE 4.2. Gender differences in spontaneous sharing. In the SLPS, gender differences were no longer significant after controlling for the overall rate of interaction in dyads.

between the sexes became nonsignificant when the scores were adjusted for the dependencies in the data by using the peer's rate of sharing as a covariate. This may reflect the tendency of the focal girls to share significantly more often with same-sex peers, as described previously. Gender differentiation during the preschool years needs to be examined in larger and more representative samples.

The Construction of Individual Character

By the time children begin formal schooling, individual differences have consolidated, so that most children are fairly prosocial and generally socially competent, some are highly prosocial, and others show low rates of prosocial behavior and high rates of antisocial behavior. The individual differences in prosocial behavior that emerge in the preschool years are predictive of the child's later prosocial tendencies and general social adjustment. For example, sharing in the preschool years predicts prosocial behavior in adolescence (Eisenberg et al., 1999). Cooperation at age 4 predicts compliance and low rates of disruptive behavior at age 11 (Hay & Pawlby, 2003).

Our analyses suggest that these individual differences in prosocial behavior emerge in the third year of life. Stability coefficients in the rate of sharing from time 1 to time 2 for the combined sample of focal children and peers in the SLPS are presented in Figure 4.3. These analyses, as well as the original analyses reported for the focal children (Hay et al., 1999), suggest that individual differences in spontaneous sharing with peers consolidate between 30 and 36 months of age. Individual differences in sharing with the mother may emerge even earlier (Hay, 1979). Analysis of a large twin dataset suggests that

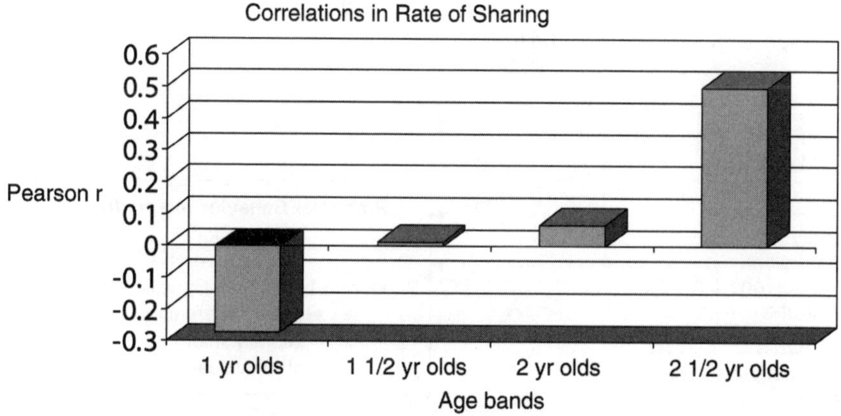

FIGURE 4.3. Stability of sharing over 6 months. In the SLPS, stable individual differences in prosocial behavior were apparent in the oldest cohort.

individual differences in empathic concern and prosocial responses to distress can be discerned as early as 14 months of age (Zahn-Waxler, Robinson, et al., 1992).

When individual differences emerge, they may be domain specific. In later childhood and adulthood, different categories of prosocial behavior do not necessarily correlate with each other, which provides further evidence for the validity of the distinction between domains of prosocial responses. For example, in young adults, prosocial behavior in emotionally fraught emergencies does not correlate with cooperative behavior under more ordinary conditions (Carlo, Knight, Eisenberg, & Rotenberg, 1991). Preschoolers' spontaneous sharing, but not sharing in response to request, is related to general sociability (Eisenberg, Pasternack, Cameron, & Tryon, 1984). Spontaneous sharing with the mother is correlated with the frequency of cooperative games (Hay, 1979). In contrast, sharing in response to peers' requests is positively associated with empathic and sensitive responses to peers' distress (Eisenberg-Berg & Lennon, 1980; Hay et al., 1999). Thus, during the toddler and preschool years, coherent individual differences emerge within each of the two domains of prosocial behavior.

PARALLEL DEVELOPMENTS

We have been arguing that, as children mature from infancy to childhood, the early prosocial impulse becomes transformed into more deliberate, selective, rule-governed, and morally informed choices. As this happens, gender differences emerge and individual differences consolidate. Several developmental processes underlie this transformation: the emergence of thought and language; the toddler's increasing understanding of other people's inner experience—their emotions, desires, and intentions; and the development of a more complex sense of self (Figure 4.4).

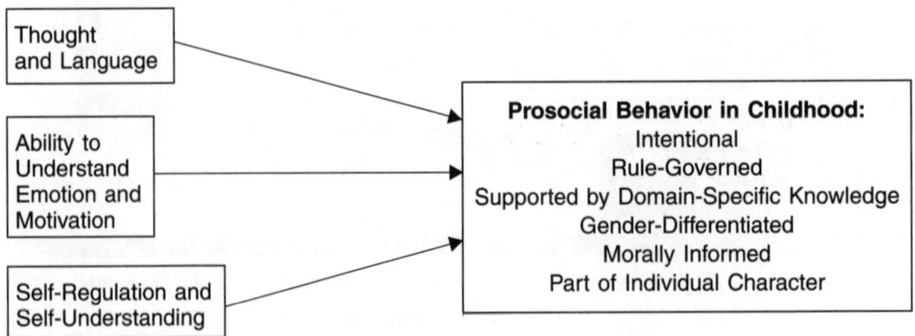

FIGURE 4.4. A model of the underlying developmental processes that transform prosocial behavior during the transition from infancy to childhood.

Thought and Language

Language emerges in a social context, in parallel with the early sharing behaviors, within episodes of joint engagement between infants and their caregivers. Longitudinal observations of the co-occurrence of language, pointing, and other symbolic behaviors during episodes of joint engagement documented that symbols increasingly "infuse" joint engagement between 18 and 30 months of age (Adamson, Bakeman, & Deckner, 2004). At about the same time, cooperative games and sharing incorporate verbal dimensions (Camaioni et al., 1991; Cook, 1977). Toddlers also begin to respond to other people's needs with words as well as deeds, providing verbal as well as physical comfort to persons in distress (Demetriou & Hay, 2004). Two-year-olds can also explain why they might choose not to share on particular occasions. For example, in the SLPS (Hay, 2006), one toddler explained to a familiar peer, "No, this is mine. That one is yours." Another finally gave in to repeated requests for an object by saying, "OK, have it!" Such speech reveals the thinking that goes on behind toddlers' prosocial acts and provides further evidence for the intentional quality of prosocial behavior in early childhood.

Increased Understanding of Other People's Inner Worlds

The years between the first and fourth birthdays are a time during which children develop a much more sophisticated understanding of the social world, and particularly the nature of human psychology. As they grow older, toddlers become more appreciative of the emotions, desires, and intentions of other people, finally developing the understanding of other people's mental states often described as a theory of mind (e.g., Baron-Cohen, 1994).

The understanding of the inner experience of other people fosters young children's abilities to work with other people and tend to their needs. Sensitivity to other people's emotions is clearly important if one is to provide care and comfort to people in need. An understanding of another person's desires and intentions is necessary if the child is to work alongside that person, sharing resources, cooperating to meet mutual goals, and helping the person meet his or her own personal goals.

Understanding of Emotion

To respond appropriately to a person in need of comfort or care, children must be able to recognize the need through the emotion expressed in the person's face and voice, the dangers or dilemmas in a given situation, and the possible assistance that might be offered by the other witnesses who are present. When toddlers are confronted with distress, they are highly likely to pay close attention and engage in hypothesis testing about the distressed person's behavior (e.g., Demetriou & Hay, 2004; Zahn-Waxler, Radke-Yarrow, et al., 1992); this attentional and cognitive response to distress, while not explicitly prosocial, promotes a more general understanding of emotion that may ultimately foster prosocial responsiveness.

Theoretical knowledge about emotion is clearly linked to children's prosocial responsiveness. Among 2- and 3-year-olds, affective knowledge is related to prosocial behavior. The ability to recognize facial expressions of different primary emotions, as measured in an experimental task, facilitates young children's prosocial responses to adults who pose those emotions (Denham & Couchoud, 1991). That study also suggested that increased knowledge of emotion influenced the selectivity of prosocial behavior; children with more knowledge about emotion were more likely to try to comfort the adult, particularly when the emotion being posed was sadness.

Responding prosocially seems also to require some understanding of the emotions accompanying prosocial behaviors, not just the emotions being expressed by persons in need (Hoffman, 1975; Denham, 1986). Children come to understand these emotions in part by producing prosocial behaviors and experiencing congruent emotions that over time appear to become attached to the behaviors (Eisenberg & Fabes, 1998). Four- and 5-year-old children recognize that the emotional consequences of situations in which people fail to act prosocially were unlike the emotional consequences of situations in which people initiate prosocial actions or, conversely, victimize others (Sy, DeMeis, & Scheinfeld, 2003).

Understanding Desires, Intentions, and Goals

Toddlers are capable of discerning other people's desires and intentions by the second year of life, and they start to anticipate other people's intentions. For example, when 18-month-olds saw adults attempting an act but not completing it (e.g., starting to put beads in a cylinder or activating a buzzer in a box), the toddlers reenacted the end result rather than the incomplete action (Meltzoff, 1995). When parallel actions were performed mechanically rather than by a person, infants did not reenact the end result of incomplete actions. The ability to understand another person's goals is likely to be related to infants' increased understanding of cause-and-effect relationships and their attainment of means–end reasoning (e.g., Woodward et al., 2001).

As children develop these capacities further, they acquire a greater understanding of the intentional nature of prosocial behavior that appears uniquely human. Young human children (ages 18–24 months) show episodes of joint engagement in problem solving but young chimpanzees do not (Warneken et al., 2006). The chimpanzees were not interested in the social games and, when problem solving was interrupted, human children but not chimpanzees recognized the intentionality of the game and tried to reengage their partner in shared problem solving.

Nevertheless, a full understanding of the motives and intentions that underlie prosocial activities takes some time to acquire. In a classic study

(Baldwin & Baldwin, 1970), children (ages 5–13) provided explanations of various acts of kindness, but their explanations, though clear and reasoned, did not necessarily match the explanations that adults gave. The adults tended to agree among themselves, which suggests that, over the course of development, members of a society attain some degree of consensus in their understanding of the psychological underpinnings of prosocial behavior.

Development of the Self

Toddlers' growing understanding of their own and other people's emotions and desires contributes to the consolidation of a sense of self, which in turn affects the toddlers' relations with others. Prosocial behaviors depend on the ability to regulate one's attention, emotions, and behavior to be able to share resources, take turns, and put one's own needs on hold while caring for or comforting another. Thus, developments in self-regulation during the toddler years allow the child to initiate and sustain prosocial behavior. More generally, the development of a more complex sense of self appears to facilitate prosocial activities.

Self-Regulation

Even before infants can recognize themselves in a mirror or refer to themselves by name, they have rudimentary ways of regulating their attention and emotion, by soothing themselves and turning toward or away from environmental stimuli. In early infancy, these two abilities are correlated (Bornstein & Suess, 2000). Individual differences in regulation of attention and emotion are at the heart of the construct of temperament (e.g., Rothbart & Bates, 1998). More complex ways of regulating behavior emerge at around 18 months of age (Kopp, 1982) and are consolidated during the second and third years of life (Vaughn, Kopp, & Krakow, 1984). The toddler's self-regulatory abilities depend at least in part on maternal scaffolding (Gralinski & Kopp, 1993); however, toddlers' attempts to regulate their own behavior also suggest that the toddlers themselves have some awareness that there are socially agreed standards of behavior (Kopp, 1991).

The toddler's capacity for self-regulation goes beyond the earlier homeostatic mechanisms of self-soothing and habituation and appears to be intentional; the intentionality of self-regulation is captured in the term *effortful control,* which is associated with prosocial behavior and social competence (Eisenberg et al., 2003; Zhou, Eisenberg, Wang, & Reiser, 2004) and with "committed compliance" and adherence to family rules (Kochanska, Coy, & Murray, 2001). Self-regulation itself varies from culture to culture (Zahn-Waxler, Friedman, Cole, Mizuta, & Hiruma, 1996), and self-regulatory abilities affect peer relationships in various cultures (see, e.g., Dunn & Hughes, 2001; Eisenberg & Guthrie, 1999; Zhou et al., 2004).

The Development of Self-Understanding

Social-cognitive changes in self-recognition between the ages of 1 and 2 are correlated with toddlers' increased tendencies to make prosocial responses to distress and to make reparations for distress they caused (Zahn-Waxler, Robinson, et al., 1992). Spontaneously emitted sharing behaviors (but not requested ones and not spontaneously emitted helping behaviors) are related to attributions about the self (Eisenberg et al., 1984). Development of a sense of the self as agent as well as object may be important; for example, children's understanding of agency promotes cooperation (Brownell & Carriger, 1990). Thus spontaneous prosocial overtures and responses to the needs and wishes of others depend on toddlers' growing understanding of themselves.

FACTORS THAT INFLUENCE PROSOCIAL DEVELOPMENT

The changes that take place in prosocial behavior over the toddler years are underpinned by biological maturation and socialization pressures. It is likely that some factors influence prosocial development directly, whereas others influence the parallel strands in early development that underlie overt prosocial behavior.

Biological Factors

Genes and Temperament

There is increasing evidence that children's social behavior, and prosocial behavior in particular, is influenced by genes (e.g., Knafo & Plomin, 2006; Scourfield, John, Martin, & McGuffin, 2004). Analyses of a large sample of toddler twins showed that empathic concern and prosocial responses to persons in distress were influenced by genetic factors (Zahn-Waxler, Robinson, et al., 1992). Thus, the differences in individual character that become increasingly apparent in the early childhood years are partly due to heritable tendencies. In particular, the child's temperament, which is influenced by genes (Auerbach, Faroy, Ebstein, Kahana, & Levine, 2001; Goldsmith, 1996), is linked to empathic concern and prosocial behavior (Young, Fox, & Zahn-Waxler, 1999). However, in contrast to prosocial behavior shown by older children, the prosocial activities of 2-year-olds are somewhat less influenced by genetic factors and more influenced by shared environmental factors (Knafo & Plomin, 2006).

Brain Development

Postnatal milestones in brain development underlie the development of the perceptual, emotional, and cognitive abilities that foster prosocial behavior. In particular, brain lateralization, which proceeds during the early childhood years, is related to the processing of emotional information and empathy (e.g., Preston & de Waal, 2002). The capacity to sustain joint attention, which underlies early sharing and cooperation, is influenced by the development of the frontal cortex (Mundy, Card, & Fox, 2000).

Neuroendocrine Development

As we have seen, prosocial development is influenced by parallel developments in self-regulatory processes. These in turn are partly underpinned by neuroendocrine development, with the emergence of stable individual differences in the secretion of cortisol in the second year of life (Gunnar, Brodersen, & Krueger, 1996). Toddlers with particular temperamental characteristics, and those who have been exposed to adverse rearing environments, may show hypo- or hypersecretion of cortisol (Gunnar, 1998). Hyposecretion of cortisol is associated with antisocial behavior and disregard for the needs of others (McBurnett, Lahey, Rathouz, & Loeber, 2000). In contrast, hypersecretion of cortisol is associated with emotional dysregulation and high levels of cortisol impact on hippocampal functioning and interfere with effortful control of behavior (Posner, 1990). Thus toddlers who show this type of neuroendocrine dysfunction may find it especially difficult to regulate their emotions and behavior when trying to deploy prosocial solutions to social dilemmas.

Parents

The early prosocial behaviors first emerge in the context of infants' relationships with their caregivers, growing out of joint attention and emotional synchrony. However, during the toddler years, parents themselves have to "multitask," providing love, comfort, and a secure base from which to explore, but also setting firm boundaries and providing age-appropriate discipline. Both the attachment functions and the socialization functions of the parent–child relationship influence prosocial development.

Attachment and Mutuality

Early prosocial development takes place in the context of infants' attachment relationships with familiar people. Early forms of sharing and cooperation emerge in this context of infants' interactions with their caregivers (Hay, 1979). The caregiver's own degree of "mind-mindedness," which promotes secure attachment (Meins, Fernyhough, Fradley, & Tuckey, 2001), is likely to foster the toddler's awareness of other people's emotions and mental states, which in turn promotes ministering to their needs and wishes. Furthermore, the development of a positive relationship between parent and child contributes to self-regulation and the development of conscience (Kochanska, 2002b).

Discipline

Nonetheless, in service of their long-term socialization goals, parents often object to their toddlers' behavior, and conflict ensues (Hay et al., 1998; Ross, 1996; Smetana & Braeges, 1990). Such disciplinary encounters serve as contexts for toddlers' moral education and internalization of parents' values (Grusec & Goodnow, 1994). It is not completely clear whether, in the course of such encounters with their toddlers, parents make special efforts to encourage prosocial behavior. The extensive social learning literature demonstrated the importance of reinforcement and modeling processes in the context of experimental studies of older children (for a review, see Radke-Yarrow et al., 1983). More recent work suggests that parents' values appear to influence children's prosocial behaviors indirectly, more through social styles than through direct transmission (Eisenberg & Wolchik, 1992). However, parents' acceptance of their toddlers' prosocial overtures, while keeping specific requests for compliance to a minimum, promotes the toddlers' general willingness to obey their parents (Wahler et al., 2001).

Gender-Role Socialization

In both the psychoanalytic and social learning traditions it is assumed that the family is the primary setting in which children learn critical lessons about gender roles. During the toddler years, parents appear to hold different goals and different standards of behavior for their sons and daughters, which may contribute to the gender differentiation over childhood. Girls are taught to pay attention to other people's feelings and needs. For example, mothers of 1- and 2-year-olds made more references to feeling states in conversation with daughters as opposed to sons (Dunn, Bretherton, & Munn, 1987). In disciplinary encounters, mothers respond differently to girls' and boys' moral transgressions (Smetana, 1989). When peers come to visit, mothers are more likely to encourage girls, as opposed to boys, to give in to the peers' demands for toys (Ross, Tesla, & Kenyon, 1990).

Parents' Mental Health Problems

Those children whose parents have clinically significant levels of depression and anxiety grow up in a family climate that is emotionally labile and where there may be occasions on which young children need to provide care for their ill parents. When observed under experimental conditions, toddlers whose mothers are depressed were more likely than other toddlers to try to comfort their mothers when the mothers simulated distress (Radke-Yarrow, Zahn-Waxler, Richardson, Susman, & Martinez, 1994). In that sample, toddlers were especially likely to care for their mothers if the mothers' depression was severe, if they were securely attached to their depressed mothers, and if they themselves had behavioral or emotional problems.

It should be noted that children of parents who have mental health problems are at genetic as well as environmental risk for problems of their own, and both factors may affect prosocial development. The children's own emotional and behavioral difficulties may affect their levels of prosocial responding. For example, there is an intergenerational link between anxiety disorders in parents and behavioral inhibition in toddlers; behavioral inhibition is negatively correlated with empathy (Young et al., 1999).

Siblings

Within family environments, sibling relationships are especially important for the development of moral reasoning skills (Ross, 1996) and social and emotional understanding (Dunn, 1988). Sibling conversations are replete with references to other people's emotions and mental states. Children with older siblings show accelerated development of a theory of mind (Ruffman, Perner, Naito, Parkin, & Clements, 1998). Nonetheless, these social cognitive advantages do not necessarily promote prosocial behavior. In the SLPS, children with older siblings were reliably less likely to share with peers (Hay et al., 1999) and reliably more likely than other toddlers to respond negatively to peers' distress (Demetriou & Hay, 2004).

Peers

Despite common beliefs to the contrary, infants and toddlers spend a great deal of time with peers, either in formal care arrangements or through informal visits to each other's homes (Hay et al., 1999). Young peers bring their individual proclivities to dyadic interaction, which influence their relationships (Brownell & Carriger, 1991). Within encounters with peers, the peers' shared emotions shape cooperative play (Brownell, Zerwas, & Balaram, 2002).

Does the experience of being cared for with peers affect prosocial development? A large study of the impact of child care demonstrated that the amount of time spent being cared for by someone other than the mother had a modest but significant effect on externalizing problems (NICHD Early Child Care Research Network, 2003); as children grow older, their externalizing problems become significantly and negatively related to prosocial behavior (e.g., Hay & Pawlby, 2003). However, it is not clear that toddlers who spend their days with peers are any less prosocial than children who do not experience child care. In the SLPS, children's experience being cared for with peers was indeed associated with higher rates of instrumental aggression but was not associated with sharing or responses to peers' distress (Demetriou & Hay, 2004; Hay et al., 1999, 2000).

The Broader Culture

There are remarkable universals in prosocial development. For example, infants' early sharing behaviors have been remarked on across the centuries

(Rheingold & Hay, 1978), and forms of empathy are identified across cultures and even species (Preston & de Waal, 2002). Nevertheless, there is also cross-cultural variation in both the quantity and quality of prosocial behavior (e.g., Eckerman & Whitehead, 1999).

Different cultures require different things of their children; for example, the extent to which young children provide care to siblings varies across cultures and is related to the types of work done by men and women in particular cultures (Whiting, 1983). Some cultures promote cooperation, others competition, and cultures differ in the extent to which they expect girls and boys to be cooperative (Sparkes, 1991). The norms governing children's behavior differ across cultures; in some cases, lower expectations for children may promote cooperative behavior (Mosier & Rogoff, 2003).

CONCLUSIONS

Prosocial behaviors emerge in the first 2 years of life, and subsequently become regulated in accordance with societal expectations. There is no clear evidence for an increase in prosocial behavior with increasing age; the age trends observed differ for different forms of prosocial behavior. Qualitative changes in prosocial behavior are likely to be influenced by parallel changes in cognitive and emotional development. An array of biological and social influences affect the initial emergence of prosocial behavior and the way it changes over the first years of childhood. It is a challenge for researchers to identify the ways in which these biological and social influences work together to influence prosocial development. There is a fundamental paradox in that, as the toddler becomes a child, prosocial actions become more social, in their convergence with cultural norms, and more individual, becoming freely chosen acts motivated by personal preferences and individual conscience. We believe that this paradox best sums up the fundamental change that takes place between infancy and childhood.

ACKNOWLEDGMENTS

The South London Peer Study was supported by the Bethlem-Maudsley Fund and the Medical Research Council, United Kingdom. Our thinking about prosocial development has been profoundly influenced by our teacher, the late Professor Harriet Rheingold.

REFERENCES

Adamson, L. B., Bakeman, R., & Deckner, D. F. (2004). The development of symbol-infused joint engagement. *Child Development*, *75*, 1171–1188.

Auerbach, J. G., Faroy, M., Ebstein, R., Kahana, M., & Levine, J. (2001). The association of the dopamine D4 receptor gene (DRD4) and the serotonin transporter promoter gene (5-HTTLPR) with temperament in 12-month-old infants. *Journal of Child Psychology and Psychiatry*, *42*, 777–783.

Baldwin, C. P., & Baldwin, A. L. (1970). Children's judgments of kindness. *Child Development*, *41*, 29–47.

Baldwin, J. M. (1895). *Mental development in the child and the race*. New York: MacMillan.

Baron-Cohen, S. (1994). Development of a theory of mind: Where would we be without the intentional stance? In M. Rutter & D. F. Hay (Eds.), *Development through life: A handbook for clinicians* (pp. 303–349). Oxford, UK: Blackwell.

Bates, E. (1979). *The emergence of symbols: Cognition and communication in infancy*. New York: Academic Press.

Berkowitz, L. (1972). Social norms, feelings, and other factors affecting helping and altruism. In L. Berkowitz (Ed.), *Advances in experimental social psychology* (Vol. 6, pp. 63–108). New York: Academic Press.

Birch, L. L., & Billman, J. (1986). Preschool children's food sharing with friends and acquaintances. *Child Development*, *57*, 387–395.

Bornstein, M. H., & Suess, P. E. (2000). Physiological self-regulation and information-processing in infancy: Cardiac vagal tone and habituation. *Child Development*, *71*, 273–287.

Brownell, C. A., & Carriger, M. S. (1990). Changes in cooperation and self-other differentiation during the second year. *Child Development*, *61*, 1164–1174.

Brownell, C. A., & Carriger, M. S. (1991). Collaborations among toddler peers: Individual contributions to social contexts. In L. B. Resnick, J. M. Levine, & S. D. Behrend (Eds.), *Perspectives on socially shared cognition* (pp. 365–383). Washington DC: American Psychological Association.

Brownell, C. A., Ramani, G. B., & Zerwas, S. (2006). Becoming a social partner with peers: Cooperation and social understanding in one- and two-year-olds. *Child Development*, *77*(4), 803–821.

Brownell, C., Zerwas, S., & Balaraman, G. (2002). Peers, cooperative play, and the development of empathy in children. *Behavioral and Brain Sciences, 25*, 28–30.

Butterworth, G. E., & Jarrett, N. I. M. (1991). What minds have in common is space: Spatial mechanisms for perspective taking in infancy. *British Journal of Developmental Psychology*, *9*, 55–72.

Camaioni, L., Baumgartner, E., & Perucchini, P. (1991). Content and structure in toddlers' social competence with peers from 12 to 36 months of age. *Early Child Development and Care*, *67*, 17–27.

Caplan, M. Z. (1993). Inhibitory influences in development: The case of prosocial behavior. In D. F. Hay & A. Angold (Eds.), *Precursors and causes in development and psychopathology* (pp. 169–198). Chichester, UK: Wiley.

Caplan, M. Z., & Hay, D. F. (1989). Preschoolers' responses to peers' distress and beliefs about bystander intervention. *Journal of Child Psychology and Psychiatry*, *30*(2), 231–243.

Carlo, G., Knight, G. P., Eisenberg, N., & Rotenberg, K. J. (1991). Cognitive processes and prosocial behaviours among children: The role of affective attributions and reconciliations. *Developmental Psychology*, *27*, 456–461.

Chapman, M., Zahn-Waxler, C., Cooperman, G., & Iannotti, R. (1987). Empathy and responsibility in the motivation of children's helping. *Developmental Psychology*, *23*, 140–145.

Chen, Z., & Siegler, R. S. (2000). Overview of toddlers' problem solving. *Monographs of the Society for Research in Child Development*, *65*, 32–43.

Church, J. (1966). *Three babies: Biographies of cognitive development*. New York: Random House.

Cook, K. V. (1977). *The verbal and nonverbal sharing of 2- and 3-year-olds*. Unpublished master's thesis, University of North Carolina, Chapel Hill.

Costin, S. E., & Carlson Jones, D. (1992). Friendship as a facilitator of emotional responsiveness and prosocial interventions among young children. *Developmental Psychology*, *28*, 941–947.

Damon, W. (1988). *The moral child: Nurturing children's natural moral growth*. New York: Free Press.

Darley, J. M., & Latané, B. (1968). Bystander intervention in emergencies: Diffusion of responsibility. *Journal of Personality and Social Psychology*, *8*, 377–383.

De Cooke, P. A., & Brownell, C. A. (1995). Young children's help-seeking in mastery-oriented contexts. *Merrill–Palmer Quarterly, 42*, 229–246.

Demetriou, H., & Hay, D. F. (2004). Toddlers' reactions to the distress of familiar peers: The importance of context. *Infancy, 6*, 299–319.

Denham, S. A. (1986). Social cognition, prosocial behavior, and emotion in preschoolers: Contextual validation. *Child Development, 57*, 194–201.

Denham, S. A., & Couchoud, E. A. (1991). Social-emotional predictors of preschoolers' responses to adult negative emotion. *Journal of Child Psychology and Psychiatry, 32*, 595–608.

Dunn, J. (1988). *The beginnings of social understanding*. Cambridge, MA: Harvard University Press.

Dunn, J., Bretherton, I., & Munn P. (1987). Conversations about feeling states between mothers and their young children. *Developmental Psychology, 23*, 132–139.

Dunn, J., & Brown, J. (1994). Affect expression in the family, children's understanding of emotion and their interactions with others. *Merrill–Palmer Quarterly, 40*, 120–137.

Dunn, J., & Hughes, C. (2001). "I got some swords and you're dead!": Violent fantasy, antisocial behavior, friendship, and moral sensibility in young children. *Child Development, 72*, 491–505.

Dunn, J., Kendrick, C., & McNamee, R. (1981). The reactions of children to the birth of a sibling: Mothers' reports. *Journal of Child Psychology and Psychiatry, 22*, 1–18.

Dunn, J., & Munn, P. (1986). Siblings and the development of prosocial behavior. *International Journal of Behavioural Development, 9*, 265–284.

Eckerman, C. O., Whatley, J. L., & Kutz, S. L. (1975). Growth of social play with peers during the second year of life. *Developmental Psychology, 11*, 42–49.

Eckerman, C. O., & Whitehead, H. (1999). How toddler peers generate co-ordinated action: A cross-cultural exploration. *Early Education and Development, 10*, 226–241.

Eisenberg, N. (2000). Emotion, regulation, and moral development. *Annual Review of Psychology, 51*, 665–697.

Eisenberg, N., Cameron, E., Tryon, K., & Dodez, R. (1981). Socialization of prosocial behavior in the preschool classroom. *Developmental Psychology, 17*, 723–729.

Eisenberg, N., & Fabes, R. A. (1998). Prosocial development. In W. Damon (Series Ed.) & N. Eisenberg (Vol. Ed.), *Handbook of child psychology: Vol. 3. Social, emotional, and personality development* (5th ed., pp. 701–778). New York: Wiley.

Eisenberg, N., & Guthrie, I. K. (1999). *The role of emotionality and regulation in children's social competence*. Paper presented at the Society for Research in Child Development, Albuquerque, NM.

Eisenberg, N., Guthrie, I. K., Murphy, B. C., Shepard, S. A., Cumberland, A., & Carlo, G. (1999). Consistency and development of prosocial dispositions: A longitudinal study. *Child Development, 70*, 1360–1372.

Eisenberg, N., Pasternack, J. F., Cameron, E., & Tryon, K. (1984). The relation of quantity and mode of prosocial behavior to moral cognitions and social style. *Child Development, 55*, 1479–1485.

Eisenberg, N., & Wolchik, S. A. (1992). Parental values, reinforcement, and young children's prosocial behaviour: A longitudinal study. *Journal of Genetic Psychology, 153*(1), 19–37.

Eisenberg, N., Zhou, Q., Losoya, S. H., Fabes, R. A., Shepard, S. A., Murphy, B. C., et al. (2003). The relations of parenting, effortful control, and ego control to children's emotional expressivity. *Child Development, 74*, 875–895.

Eisenberg-Berg, N., & Lennon. R. (1980). Altruism and the assessment of empathy in the preschool years. *Child Development, 51*, 552–558.

Freud, S. (1938). *An outline of psychoanalysis*. London: Hogarth Press.

Frye, D. (1993). Causes and precursors of children's theories of mind. In D. F. Hay & A. Angold (Eds.), *Precursors and causes in development and psychopathology* (pp. 145–168). Chichester, UK: Wiley.

Goldsmith, H. (1996). Studying temperament via construction of the Toddler Behavior Assessment Questionnaire. *Child Development, 67*, 218–235.

Gouldner, A. J. (1960). The norm of reciprocity: A preliminary statement. *American Sociological Review*, *25*, 161–178.

Gralinski, J. H., & Kopp, C. B. (1993). Everyday rules for behavior: Mothers' requests to young children. *Developmental Psychology*, *29*, 573–584.

Grusec, J. E., & Goodnow, J. J. (1994). Impact of parental discipline methods on the child's internalization of values: A reconceptualization of current points of view. *Developmental Psychology*, *30*(1), 4–19.

Gunnar, M. R. (1998). Quality of early care and buffering of neuroendocrine stress reactions: potential effects on the developing human brain. *Preventative Medicine*, *27*, 208–211.

Gunnar, M. R., Brodersen, L., & Krueger, K. (1996). Dampening of adrenocortical responses during infancy: Normative changes and individual differences. *Child Development*, *67*, 877–889.

Hay, D. F. (1979). Cooperative interactions and sharing between very young children and their parents. *Developmental Psychology*, *15*, 647–655.

Hay, D. F. (1994). Prosocial development. *Journal of Child Psychology and Psychiatry*, *33*, 29–71.

Hay, D. F. (2006). Yours and mine: Toddlers talk about possessions with familiar peers. *British Journal of Developmental Psychology*, *24*, 39–52.

Hay, D. F., Caplan, M., Castle, J., & Stimson, C. A. (1991). Does sharing become increasingly "rational" in the second year of life? *Developmental Psychology*, *27*, 987–994.

Hay, D. F., Castle, J., & Davies, L. (2000). Toddlers' use of force against familiar peers: A precursor of serious aggression? *Child Development*, *71*, 457–467.

Hay, D. F., Castle, J., Davies, L., Demetriou, H., & Stimson, C. (1999). Prosocial action in very early childhood. *Journal of Child Psychology and Psychiatry*, *40*, 905–916.

Hay, D. F., Castle, J., & Jewett, J. (1994). Character development. In M. Rutter & D. F. Hay (Eds.), *Development through life: A handbook for clinicians* (pp. 319–349). Oxford, UK: Blackwell Scientific.

Hay, D. F., & Murray, P. (1982). Giving and requesting: Social facilitation of infants' offers to adults. *Infant Behavior and Development*, *5*, 301–310.

Hay, D. F., Nash, A., & Pedersen, J. (1981). Responses of six-month-olds to the distress of their peers. *Child Development*, *52*, 1071–1076.

Hay, D. F., & Pawlby, S. (2003). Prosocial development in relation to children's and mothers' psychological problems. *Child Development*, *74*, 1314–1327.

Hay, D. F., & Rheingold, H. L. (1983). The early appearance of some valued behaviours. In D. L. Bridgeman (Ed.), *The nature of prosocial development: Interdisciplinary theories and strategies* (pp. 73–94). New York: Academic Press.

Hay, D. F., Vespo, J. E., & Zahn-Waxler, C. (1998). Young children's quarrels with their siblings and mothers: Links with maternal depression and bipolar illness. *British Journal of Developmental Psychology*, *16*, 519–538.

Hay, D. F., Zahn-Waxler, C., Cummings, E. M., & Iannotti, R. J. (1992). Young children's views about conflict with peers: A comparison of the daughters and sons of depressed and well women. *Journal of Child Psychology and Psychiatry*, *33*, 669–684.

Hoffman, M. L. (1975). Developmental synthesis of affect and cognition and its interplay for altruistic motivation. *Developmental Psychology*, *11*, 607–622.

Hoffman, M. L. (1976). Empathy, role taking, guilt, and the development of altruistic motives. In T. Lickona (Ed.), *Moral development and behaviour: Theory, research, and social issues* (pp. 124–143). New York: Holt, Rinehart & Winston.

Iskander, N., Laursen, B., Finkelstein, B., & Fredrickson, L. (1995). Conflict resolution among preschool children: The appeal of negotiation in hypothetical disputes. *Early Education and Development*, *6*, 359–376.

Kagan, J. (1981). *The second year.* Cambridge, MA: Harvard University Press.

Kakavoulis, A. (1998). Aggressive and prosocial behaviour in young Greek children. *International Journal of Early Years Education*, *6*, pp. 343–351.

Kaler, S. R., & Kopp, C. B. (1990). Compliance and comprehension in very young toddlers. *Child Development*, *61*, 1997–2003.

Keenan, K., & Shaw, D. (1997). Developmental and social influences on young girls' early problem behavior. *Psychological Bulletin*, *121*, 95–113.

Kelley, S. A., & Brownell, C. A. (2000). Mastery motivation and self-evaluative affect in toddlers: Longitudinal relations with maternal behavior. *Child Development*, *71*, 1061–1072.

Knafo, A., & Plomin, R. (2006). Prosocial behaviour from early to middle childhood: Genetic and environmental influences on stability and change. *Developmental Psychology*, *42*, 771–786.

Kochanska, G. (2002a). Committed compliance, moral self, and internalization: A mediational model. *Developmental Psychology*, *38*, 339–351.

Kochanska, G. (2002b). Mutually responsive orientation between mothers and their young children: A context for the early development of conscience. *Current Directions in Psychological Science*, *11*, 191–195.

Kochanska, G., Coy, K. C., & Murray, K. T. (2001). The development of self-regulation in the first four years of life. *Child Development*, *72*, 1091–1111.

Kochanska, G., Forman, D. R., Aksan, N., & Dunbar, S. B. (2005). Pathways to conscience: Early mother-child mutually responsive orientation and children's moral emotion, conduct, and cognition. *Journal of Child Psychology and Psychiatry*, *46*, 19–34.

Kohlberg, L. (1969). Stage and sequence: The cognitive-developmental approach to socialization. In D. A. Goslin (Eds.), *Handbook of socialization theory and research* (pp. 347–480). Chicago: Rand-McNally.

Kopp, C. B. (1982). Antecedents of self-regulation: A developmental perspective. *Developmental Psychology*, *18*, 199–214.

Kopp, C. B. (1991). Young children's progression to self-regulation. In M. Bullock (Ed.), *Development of intentional action: Cognitive, motivational, and interactive processes. Contributions to human development* (Vol. 22, pp. 38–54). Basel, Switzerland: S. Karger AG.

Kuczynski, L. (1983). Reasoning, prohibitions, and motivations for compliance. *Developmental Psychology*, *19*, 126–134.

Kuczynski, L., Kochanska, G., Radke-Yarrow, M., & Girnius-Brown, O. (1987). A developmental interpretation of young children's noncompliance. *Developmental Psychology*, *23*, 799–806.

Lamb, S. (1993). First moral sense: An examination of the appearance of morally related behaviours in the second year of life. *Journal of Moral Education*, *22*, 97–110.

Lamb, S., & Zakhireh, B. (1997). Toddlers' attention to the distress of peers in a day care setting. *Early Education and Development*, *8*, 105–118.

Levitt, M. J., Weber, R. A., Clark, M. C., & McDonnell, P. (1985). Reciprocity of exchange in toddler sharing behavior. *Developmental Psychology*, *21*, 122–123.

Lewis, M. (1990). The development of intentionality and the role of consciousness. *Psychological Inquiry*, *1*, 231–247.

Lewis, M., Young, G., Brooks, J., & Michalson, L. (1975). The beginning of friendship. In M. Lewis & G. Rosenblum (Eds.), *The origins of behaviour: Vol. 4. Friendship and peer relations* (pp. 27–65). New York: Wiley.

Lytton, H. (1980). *Parent–child interaction: The socialization process observed in twin and singleton families*. New York: Plenum Press.

Maccoby, E. E. (1988). Gender as a social category. *Developmental Psychology*, *24*, 735–765.

Maccoby, E. E., & Jacklin, C. N. (1974). *The psychology of sex differences*. Stanford, CA: Stanford University Press.

Masters, J. C. (1991). Strategies and mechanisms for the personal and social control of emotion. In J. Garber & K. A. Dodge (Eds.), *The development of emotion regulation and dysregulation* (pp. 182–207). Cambridge, UK: Cambridge University Press.

McBurnett, K., Lahey, B., Rathouz, P. J., & Loeber, R. (2000). Low salivary cortisol and persistent aggression in boys referred for disruptive behavior. *Archives of General Psychiatry*, *57*, 38–43.

Meins, E., Fernyhough, C., Fradley, E., & Tuckey, M. (2001). Rethinking maternal sensitivity: Mothers' comments on infants' mental processes predict security of attachment at 12 months. *Journal of Child Psychology and Psychiatry*, *42*, 637–658.

Meltzoff, A. N. (1995). Understanding the intentions of others: Re-enactment of intended acts by 18-month-old children. *Developmental Psychology, 31*, 838–850.

Miller, J. G., & Bersoff, D. M. (1995). Development in the context of everyday family relationships: Culture, interpersonal morality, and adaptation. In M. Killen & D. Hart (Eds.), *Morality in everyday life: Developmental perspectives* (pp. 259–282). Cambridge, UK: Cambridge University Press.

Miller, N. E., & Dollard, J. (1941). *Social learning and imitation.* New Haven, CT: Yale University Press.

Miller, P. A., Eisenberg, N., Fabes, R. A., & Shell, R. (1996). Relations of moral reasoning and vicarious emotion to young children's prosocial behavior toward peers and adults. *Developmental Psychology, 32*, 210–219.

Mosier, C. E., & Rogoff, B. (2003). Privileged treatment of toddlers: Cultural aspects of individual choice and responsibility. *Developmental Psychology, 39*, 1047–1060.

Mundy, P., Card, J., & Fox, N. (2000). EEG correlates of the development of infant joint attention skills. *Developmental Psychobiology, 36*, 325–338.

Murphy, L. (1937). *Social behavior and child personality.* New York: Columbia University Press.

NICHD Early Child Care Research Network. (2000). The interaction of child care and family risk in relation to child development at 24 and 36 months. *Applied Developmental Science, 6*, 144–156.

NICHD Early Child Care Research Network. (2003). Does amount of time spent in child care predict socioemotional adjustment during the transition to kindergarten? *Child Development, 74*, 976–1005.

Parten, M. B. (1932). Social participation among preschool children. *Journal of Abnormal and Social Psychology, 27*, 243–269.

Pelletier-Stiefel, J., Pepler, D., Crozier, K., Stanhope, L., Corter, C., & Abramovitch, R. (1986). Nurturance in the home: A longitudinal study of sibling interaction. In A. Fogel & G. E. Melson (Eds.), *Origins of nurturance* (pp. 3–24). Hillsdale, NJ: Erlbaum.

Petersen, I., & Reaven, N. (1984). Limitations imposed by parents on children's altruism. *Merrill–Palmer Quarterly, 30*, 269–286.

Piaget, J. (1932). *The moral judgment of the child.* New York: Harcourt, Brace.

Posner, M. (1990). The attention system of the human brain. *Annual Review of Neuroscience, 13*, 25–42.

Preston, S., & De Waal, F. B. M. (2002). Empathy: Its ultimate and proximate bases. *Behavioral and Brain Sciences, 25*, 1–72.

Radke-Yarrow, M., & Zahn-Waxler, C. (1986). The role of familial factors in the development of prosocial behavior: Research findings and questions. In D. Olweus, J. Block, & M. Radke-Yarrow (Eds.), *Development of antisocial and prosocial behavior: Research theories, and issues* (pp. 207–233). New York: Academic Press.

Radke-Yarrow, M., Zahn-Waxler, C., & Chapman, M. (1983). Children's prosocial dispositions and behavior. In P. Mussen (Series Ed.) & E. M. Hetherington (Vol. Ed.), *Handbook of child psychology: Vol. 4. Socialization, personality and social development* (4th ed., pp. 469–545). New York: Wiley.

Radke-Yarrow, M., Zahn-Waxler, C., Richardson, D. T., Susman, E., & Martinez, P. (1994). Caring behavior in children of clinically depressed and well mothers. *Child Development, 65*, 1405–1414.

Rheingold, H. L. (1973). Independent behavior of the human infant. In A. D. Pick (Ed.), *Minnesota Symposia on Child Psychology* (Vol. 7, pp. 178–203). Minneapolis: University of Minnesota Press.

Rheingold, H. L. (1982). Little children's participation in the work of adults, a nascent prosocial behavior. *Child Development, 53*, 114–126.

Rheingold, H. L., Cook, K. V., & Kolowitz, V. (1987). Commands activate the behavior and pleasure of 2-year-old children. *Developmental Psychology, 23*, 146–151.

Rheingold, H. L., & Eckerman, C. O. (1970). The infant separates himself from his mother. *Science, 168*, 78–83.

Rheingold, H. L., & Emery, G. (1986). The nurturant acts of very young children. In D. Olweus, J. Block, & M. Radke-Yarrow (Eds.), *The development of antisocial and prosocial behavior: Research, theories, and issues* (pp. 75–96). New York: Academic Press.

Rheingold, H. L., & Hay, D. F. (1978). Prosocial behavior of the very young. In G. Stent (Ed.), *Morality as a biological phenomenon*. Berlin: Dahlem Konferenzen.

Rheingold, H. L., Hay, D. F., & West, M. (1976). Sharing in the second year of life. *Child Development*, *47*, 1148–1159.

Ross, H. L. (1996). Negotiating principles of entitlement in sibling property disputes. *Developmental Psychology*, *32*, 90–101.

Ross, H. S., & Goldman, B. D. (1977). Infants' sociability toward strangers. *Child Development*, *48*, 638–643.

Ross, H. S., & Lollis, S. P. (1987). Communication within infant social games. *Developmental Psychology*, *23*, 241–248.

Ross, H. S., Tesla, C., & Kenyon, B. (1990). Maternal intervention in toddler peer conflict: The socialization of principles of justice. *Developmental Psychology*, *26*, 994–1003.

Rothbart, M. K., & Bates, J. E. (1998). Temperament. In W. Damon (Series Ed.) & N. Eisenberg (Vol. Ed.), *Handbook of child psychology: Vol. 3. Social, emotional, and personality development* (pp. 105–176). New York: Wiley.

Ruffman, T., Perner, J., Naito, M., Parkin, L., & Clements, W. A. (1998). Older (but not younger) siblings facilitate false belief understanding. *Developmental Psychology*, *34*, 161–174.

Schneider-Rosen, K., & Wenz-Gross, M. (1990). Patterns of compliance from eighteen to thirty months of age. *Child Development*, *61*, 104–112.

Scourfield, J., John, B., Martin, N., & McGuffin, P. (2004). The development of prosocial behaviour in children and adolescents: A twin study. *Journal of Child Psychology and Psychiatry*, *45*, 927–936.

Sears, R. R. (1951). A theoretical framework for personality and social behavior. *American Psychologist*, *6*, 476–483.

Sigman, M., Mundy, P., Sherman, T., & Ungerer, J. (1986). Social interactions of autistic, mentally retarded and normal children and their caregivers. *Journal of Child Psychology and Psychiatry*, *27*, 647–656.

Smetana, J. G. (1989). Toddlers' social interactions in the context of moral and conventional transgressions in the home. *Developmental Psychology*, *25*, 499–508.

Smetana, J. G., & Braeges, J. L. (1990). The development of toddlers' moral and conventional judgments. *Merrill–Palmer Quarterly*, *36*, 329–346.

Sparkes, K. M. (1991). Cooperative and competitive behavior in dyadic game playing: A comparison of Anglo-American and Chinese children. *Early Child Development and Care*, *68*, 37–47.

Stayton, D. J., Hogan, R., & Ainsworth, M. D. S. (1971). Infant obedience and maternal behavior: The origins of socialization reconsidered. *Child Development*, *42*, 1057–1069.

Sy, S. R., DeMeis, D. K., & Scheinfield, R. E. (2003). Pre-school children's understanding of the emotional consequences for failures to act prosocially. *British Journal of Developmental Psychology*, *21*, 259–273.

Tremblay, R. E., & Nagin, D. (2005). Physical aggression in humans. In R. E. Tremblay, W. W. Hartup, & J. Archer (Eds.), *Developmental origins of aggression* (pp. 83–106). New York: Guilford Press.

Underwood, M. K., Coie, J. D., & Herbsman, C. R. (1992). Display rules for anger and aggression in school-age children. *Child Development*, *63*, 366–380.

Vaughn, B. E., Kopp, C. B., & Krakow, J. B. (1984). The emergence and consolidation of self-control from eighteen to thirty months of age: Normative trends and individual differences. *Child Development*, *55*, 990–1005.

Vedeler, D. (1987). Infant intentionality and the attribution of intentions to infants. *Human Development*, *30*, 1–17.

Wahler, R. G., Herring, M., & Edwards, M. (2001). Coregulation of balance between children's prosocial approaches and acts of compliance: A pathway to mother-child cooperation? *Journal of Clinical Child Psychology*, *30*, 473–478.

Warneken, F., Chen, F., & Tomasello, M. (2006). Cooperative activities in young children and chimpanzees. *Child Development*, *77*(3), 640–663.

Whiting, B. B. (1983). The genesis of prosocial behavior. In D. Bridgeman (Ed.), *The nature of prosocial development: Interdisciplinary theories and strategies* (pp. 221–242). London: Academic Press.

Woodward, A. L., Sommerville, J. A., & Guajardo, J. J. (2001). How infants make sense of intentional action. In B. F. Malle, L. J. Moses, & D. A. Baldwin, *Intentions and intentionality: Foundations of social cognition* (pp. 149–169). Cambridge, MA: MIT Press.

Yarrow, M. R., Waxler, C. Z., Barrett, D., Darby, J., King, R., Pickett, M., et al. (1976). Dimensions and correlates of prosocial behavior in young children. *Child Development*, *47*, 118–126.

Young, G., & Lewis, M. (1979). Effects of familiarity and maternal attention on infant peer relations. *Merrill–Palmer Quarterly*, *25*, 105–119.

Young, S. K., Fox, N. A, & Zahn-Waxler, C. (1999). The relations between temperament and empathy in 2-year-olds. *Developmental Psychology*, *35*, 1189–1197.

Zahn-Waxler, C., Friedman, R. J., Cole, P. M., Mizuta, I., & Hiruma, N. (1996). Japanese and United States preschool children's responses to conflict and distress. *Child Development*, *67*, 2462–2477.

Zahn-Waxler, C., Radke-Yarrow, M., & King, R. (1979). Child rearing and children's prosocial initiations toward victims of distress. *Child Development*, *50*, 319–330.

Zahn-Waxler, C., Radke-Yarrow, M., Wagner, E., & Chapman, M. (1992). Development of concern for others. *Developmental Psychology*, *28*, 126–136.

Zahn-Waxler, C., Robinson, J. L., & Emde, R. N. (1992). The development of empathy in twins. *Developmental Psychology*, *28*, 1038–1047.

Zhou, Q., Eisenberg, N., Wang, Y., & Reiser, M. (2004). Chinese children's effortful control and dispositional anger/frustration: Relations to parenting styles and children's social functioning. *Developmental Psychology*, *40*, 352–366.

5

The Origins of Empathic Morality in Toddlerhood

MARTIN L. HOFFMAN

Empathic morality is based on the human tendency to empathize with others in need or distress (i.e., to feel empathic distress). Empathic distress refers to the involuntary, at times, forceful experiencing of another person's painful emotional state. It may be elicited by expressive cues that directly reflect the other's feelings or situational cues that convey the impact of external stimuli on him (Hoffman, 1975). Thus in experiencing empathic distress one responds at least in part to the other's circumstance rather than one's own, feeling the other's pain or distress regardless of one's own condition at the time. I have over the years (from Hoffman, 1975, to Hoffman, 2000) elaborated a theory of the development of empathic morality, which assumes a nonconscious preverbal empathy in infants and suggests that a mature level of empathy emerges, through several stages, as a result of social-cognitive development. Specifically, empathic affect is shaped by and develops in accord with the child's cognitive sense of others as separate from him- or herself. I suggested further that each stage results from the synthesis of empathic affect and the cognitive sense of the other. The theory in broad outline is now widely accepted. What is more problematic is my hypothesis that early in toddlerhood empathic distress is transformed into sympathetic distress or compassion for the other, and this constitutes the beginning of a prosocial moral system. My aim here is to pull together the argument and probe more deeply into the processes underlying the transformation.

EMPATHY AS A MORAL MOTIVE

There is a great deal of empirical evidence for the following: empathic distress motivates helping behavior; observers have more intense empathic distress and are quicker to help when the victim shows more pain and when their own empathic distress is higher; observers' empathic distress tends to decrease more quickly and they feel better when they engage in helping behavior than when they do not (see reviews by Eisenberg & Miller, 1987; Hoffman, 1978). There are also evolutionary grounds for empathy's having been necessary for human survival (Hoffman, 1981), brain-scan experiments and clinical studies showing empathy's neural basis (Gallese, 2003), laboratory research suggesting empathy's presence in primates (Brothers, 1989), identical-twin evidence for a hereditary component (Zahn-Waxler, Robinson, Emde, & Plomin, 1992), and evidence for empathy's, or at least a precursor of empathy's, presence at birth (Sagi & Hoffman, 1976; Simner, 1971). It thus seems reasonable to consider empathic distress a moral motive and conclude that human nature is not just egoistic, as long assumed in Western psychology, but includes a prosocial empathic moral base as well.

MODES OF EMPATHIC AROUSAL

To survive the pressures of natural selection, empathy must have always been a multidetermined response, and indeed I have found five modes of empathic arousal (Hoffman, 1978). Three are preverbal: mimicry, conditioning, association.

Mimicry

This is a two-step process: One spontaneously imitates a victim's facial, vocal, or postural expression of distress, and the resulting change in one's facial and postural musculature results in afferent feedback from the brain that makes one feel distressed. The recent discovery of mirror neurons suggests a simpler neural substrate: The same neural pattern is involved in feeling an emotion and observing someone else feeling it; therefore, observing another's emotional expression is all it takes to feel it (Iacoboni & Lenzi, 2002; Iacoboni et al., 2005). Either way, mimicry is by definition the quintessential empathy mode. Mimicry research has involved adult subjects (see Hoffman, 2000) but there is suggestive evidence that it occurs in infants: the original work of Meltzoff and Moore (1983), replicated in laboratories worldwide, shows that newborns are capable of selective imitation of facial and manual gestures. That research does not deal with infants' emotional responses to the stimuli they imitate, but there is research that does, namely, the research on synchronicity of emotional exchanges between mothers and their babies, in which each responds to the affect exhibited by the other (e.g., Jaffe, Beebe, Feldstein, Crown, & Jasnow, 2001; Stern, Hofer, Haft, & Dore, 1985). The babies in these studies are responding to their mothers as well as imitating them, but it seems reasonable that the continued mingling of shared mother-and-infant affect is ideal for promoting or reinforcing any preexisting, innate mimicry. It is also possible that part of the affect infants exhibit in these exchanges is due to feedback from imitating the mother's facial expressions and postural movements.

The other two preverbal modes—conditioning and association—are not peculiar to empathy but contribute to its arousal.

Classical Conditioning

Contrary to previous belief, conditioning is possible in newborns: the sucking response of 1-day-olds, for example, can be conditioned to stroking their forehead (Blass, Ganchrow, & Steiner, 1984). Conditioning empathic distress requires that infants' actual distress be paired with expressive cues of another's distress. Such pairing is inevitable in mother–infant interactions, occurring whenever mothers' feelings are transferred to infants in the course of physical handling. Thus, when a mother feels anxiety or tension, her body may stiffen, transmitting her distress to the infant. The infant gets distressed and the mother's stiffening is the unconditioned stimulus. Her accompanying facial expressions and sounds of distress then become conditioned stimuli, which can later evoke distress in the child even in the absence of physical contact. This mechanism can explain Escalona's (1945) finding, in a woman's reformatory where mothers cared for their own infants, that the infants were most upset when their mothers were waiting to appear before a parole board. Furthermore, through generalization of the conditioned stimulus, facial and other signs of distress from anyone can make the infant feel distressed.

Direct Association

A variant of conditioning, described by Humphrey (1922), is direct association of cues in a victim's situation that remind one of similar experiences in one's past and evoke feelings fitting the victim's situation. We have a distressing experience; later, seeing someone in a similar situation, his or her facial expression, voice, posture, or other situational cue similar to that past experience evokes empathic distress in us. Children who experience short or prolonged separation from their mother might empathize with another child whose mother leaves or dies. Association does not require pairing actual distress with another's expression of distress, only a previously a painful experience that has things in common with distress cues from victims or their situation.

Mimicry, conditioning, and direct association are important mechanisms of empathic arousal for several reasons: (1) they are automatic, quick acting, and involuntary; (2) they enable infants and preverbal children to empathize with others in distress; (3) they produce early pairings of children's empathic distress with other people's actual distress, which contributes to children's expecting to feel distress whenever they are exposed to another's distress; (4) they contribute an involuntary dimension to children's (and adults') future empathy experiences and operate through life as an empathy-enhancing force even when empathy is initially aroused by cognitively more advanced modes.

The question may be raised whether conditioning and direct association are really empathy-arousing processes when triggered by a victim's situation rather than his or her expression of distress. I define them as empathy-arousing processes when they are put into play and cause one to feel distress, *because the distress fits the victim's situation rather than one's own*, whether the processes are triggered by the victim's expression of distress, the victim's situation, or both. This potential confusion does not exist in face-to-face encounters, where mimicry clearly defines one's distress as empathic, and conditioning and association serve mainly to add to its intensity.

The empathy aroused by the combination of mimicry, conditioning, and association is a passive, involuntary response based on the pull of surface cues and requires only the shallowest level of cognitive processing (sensory registration). It is a potentially powerful empathy-arousing package, nonetheless, because it shows that humans are built in such a way as to involuntarily and forcefully experience another's emotion: One's distress is contingent upon someone else's painful experience. It also signifies, crucially for present purposes, that a primitive level of empathy exists in infants before toddlerhood. This is why I give it so much space here, as my task is to explain how this primitive empathy begins to develop into a mature, prosocial moral motive early in the toddler period.

Having mentioned all these positive qualities, I must also note that it is a limited empathy-arousing package, with minimal involvement of language and cognition, thus requiring a victim's being present and enabling one to empathize only with simple emotions. It makes little if any contribution to mature empathy's meta-cognitive dimension: awareness that one's distress feeling is a response to another's distress. These limitations are overcome by language and cognitive development, which are central to the advanced empathy-arousing modes. I mention these modes here only briefly because they are prominent after the toddler period. *Mediated association* is like direct association except that language makes the connection between the victim's distress and one's own painful past experience. *Perspective taking* involves imagining how the victim feels or how one would feel in the victim's situation. These modes may be voluntary and drawn out over time, although if one is observing the victim closely perspective taking may kick in right away. They both contribute to enlarging empathy's scope to include subtle types of distress (e.g., disappointment, guilt, and loss) and enable one to empathize with victims who are absent.

Together with the preverbal modes, which while necessary for empathic arousal in infancy do continue through life, the advanced modes enable observers to respond empathically to whatever distress cues are available. Cues from a victim's face, voice, or posture can be picked up through mimicry; situational cues, through conditioning or association. When victims express distress verbally or in writing, or someone else describes their situation, observers can be empathically aroused through mediated association or perspective taking.

Now for the main argument, beginning with empathy's early development.

EARLY STAGES OF EMPATHY DEVELOPMENT

Mature observers are aware of their empathic feelings: They feel distressed, but they know this is a response to another's misfortune and have an idea of how that person feels. They have a sense of how they would feel in the victim's situation and they know that the victim's outward behavior and facial expression may not reflect how he or she feels inside. Furthermore, they are likely to make spontaneous inferences about the cause of the victim's plight based on available information. All this requires having a cognitive sense of themselves and others as separate beings with independent inner states, personal identities, and life conditions.

When can children empathize in this metacognitive way? My hypothesis is that empathic distress develops along with children's acquisition of a cognitive sense of others, in five developmental stages.

Global Empathic Distress: Reactive Newborn Cry

The well-known cry in response to the sound of another's cry by alert, content newborns is not simply imitation of the cry sound or a painful reaction to the cry as a noxious stimulus. It is vigorous, intense, and identical to spontaneous cries of infants in actual distress (Sagi & Hoffman, 1976; Simner, 1971). Martin and Clark (1982) replicated these findings and also showed that infants do not cry as much on hearing the cry of a chimpanzee (which adults find more aversive than infant cries) or even the sound of their own cry. A possible explanation for the cry is that it is an innate, isomorphic response to the cry of a conspecific, which survived natural selection and is adaptive. The underlying mechanism could be mimicry: Newborns automatically imitate the sound of a human cry, and the sound of their own cry and its accompanying facial muscle movements trigger a feedback process that throws them into an agitated state.[1] Conditioning and association could also be involved: If the sucking re-

---

[1] It is interesting that Charles Darwin (1862/1965), who carefully observed his son's facial and emotional responses from birth, reported something similar: "Empathy was clearly shown at 6 months and 11 days by his melancholy face, with the corners of his mouth well depressed, when his nurse pretended to cry."

sponse can be conditioned to stroking foreheads in 1-day-olds, it seems likely that reactive crying can be a conditioned distress response to the sound of another's cry, which resembles the infant's own cries that are associated with his previous pain and discomfort (perhaps beginning with birth).

Regardless of the cause, the newborn is responding to a cue of distress in others by feeling distressed him- or herself. The newborn reactive cry may thus be considered an early, global empathic distress of the type mentioned earlier: empathizing without awareness of empathizing. From the hypothesis that empathy development is shaped by self–other differentiation we would expect this cry to begin to disappear at around 6 months with the dawning awareness of self and other as separate beings, because this awareness should interfere with, or at least slow down, their mimicry and conditioned responses to other's cries. There is evidence for this decline: Hay, Nash, and Pedersen (1981) found that 6-month-olds generally looked at a crying child without immediately crying or showing signs of distress. There was a cumulative effect, however: In response to prolonged cries they looked sad and puckered up their lips before starting to cry.

My interpretation is that self–other differentiation undermines the basis of global empathic distress. By 6 months, infants stop responding to another's cry automatically, because the other is becoming more of a true "other" who is, at least dimly, perceived as physically separate from themselves. As a result they require more prolonged signs of another's distress before feeling distressed themselves.

"Egocentric Empathic Distress"

By 11–12 months, infants continue to do the same thing, but they also whimper and silently watch the victim (Radke-Yarrow & Zahn-Waxler, 1984). Some are more active, but their actions seem designed to reduce their own distress. A 1-year-old saw a friend fall and cry, stared at her friend, began to cry, then put her thumb in her mouth and buried her head in her mother's lap, just as she does when she hurts herself. A parsimonious explanation is that she, like most infants her age, still has not fully graduated from the global level of empathic distress and remains unclear about the difference between something happening to another and to herself.[2] As before, distress cues from others elicit global empathic distress—a fusion of unpleasant feelings and stimuli from the dimly perceived other, from her own body, and from the situation. She is thus unclear about who is experiencing any distress that she witnesses and often behaves as though what is happening to the other is happening to

[2] Other factors may be involved as well: Infants that age have other interests and may therefore require the more salient stimulus of a prolonged cry to shift their attention from what they are doing. Also looking sad and puckering their lips before crying, as they do when in actual distress, may reflect the beginnings of emotional control.

her. Cues associated with another's distress produce an upset state in her and she seeks comfort for herself.

This may seem to contradict Stern's (1985) research showing that infants have a "core self" by 7 months. There is no contradiction: Stern's core self is a sense of being a coherent, physically bounded continuous entity, but an entity that is tied together by the kinesthetic sensations infants receive from their muscles, bones, and joints every time they move—not a representational, reflective self. This core self is also very likely a fragile self whose boundaries may temporarily break down when its constituent bodily sensations are mingled with the bodily sensations associated with empathic distress (presumably from preverbal empathy-arousal modes). As a result the infant is confused about the source of his or her distress: The infant cannot tell the difference between another's distress and his or her own actual or empathic distress and responds the same way to another's distress as to his or her own. This temporary breakdown of boundaries could explain the 6-month-old's looking sad, whimpering, and bursting into tears, as well as our I-year-old's confusion about the origin of her empathic distress. In any case, the response to one's own and another's distress is essentially the same, so I call it egocentric empathic distress, an oxymoron to be sure, but it is both egocentric (a motive to reduce own distress) and prosocial (contingent on another's distress). *It is this being contingent upon another's distress that makes it a precursor of empathic morality.*

Quasi-Egocentric Empathic Distress

About a month or two later, children's empathic cry, whimpering, and staring become less frequent and they begin making helpful advances toward a victim. The earliest advances (tentative physical contact such as patting and touching) soon give way to more differentiated positive interventions (kissing, hugging, getting someone else to help, giving physical assistance, advising, reassuring), as reported by Radke-Yarrow and Zahn-Waxler (1984). These actions show that while the infants are still confined largely to preverbal empathy-arousal modes and still lack a sense of their body as an object that can be represented outside their subjective self (cannot recognize their mirror image), they are more cognitively anchored in external reality; that is, they realize it is the other who is in pain or discomfort and their actions are clearly designed to help the other.

Despite the advance, these same actions reveal an important cognitive limitation: Children have inner states but they do not realize that others have their own independent inner states. They do not know that their own desires influence how they perceive the world, and they assume others sees things the same way they do. They know the other is in distress but are still egocentric enough to use helping strategies that they themselves find comforting. A 14-month-old boy responded to a crying friend with a sad look, then gently took the friend's hand and brought him to his own mother, although the friend's mother was also present (Hoffman, 1978). This behavior clearly shows empathic distress functioning as a prosocial motive, but at the same time it reveals the child's egocentric confusion between his friend's and his own needs. Similar behavior by a 15-month-old girl was reported by a mother in Radke-Yarrow and Zahn-Waxler's (1984) longitudinal sample: "Mary watches a visiting baby who is crying: she watched him carefully. She followed him around, and kept handing him toys and also other items that were valuable to her, like her bottle or this string of beads which she's so fond of."

To summarize, children at this stage are aware that others are physically separate from themselves and know when another is in distress. Though still probably confined to preverbal empathy-arousal modes, they no longer confuse their empathic distress with the victim's or their own actual distress. *Empathic distress is clearly a prosocial motive at this stage—the child tries to help, although his actions are misguided because he lacks insight into the inner states of others and assumes that what helps him will help others.* This assumption is often valid (adults make it too but are not limited to it), but when it is not valid its underlying cognitive limitations are clearly evident.

Veridical Empathy for Another's Distress

Major developments in the sense of self occur toward the end of the second year and continue into the third. Children that age can recognize themselves in a mirror (Lewis & Brooks-Gunn, 1979), which signifies that they have a clear sense of their body as a physical entity that exists outside their subjective, kinesthetically based self, and they may have a sense of their body as an entity that can be seen by others. A little later, and even more significantly, they begin to show awareness that others have inner states (thoughts, feelings, desires) and that another's inner states may at times differ from their own. This awareness enables them to empathize more accurately with another's feelings and needs in different situations, and their efforts to help become more effective.

The transition from quasi-egocentric to veridical empathic distress is illustrated by 2-year-old David who brought his own teddy bear to comfort a crying friend. When it did not work, David paused, then ran to the next room and returned with the friend's teddy bear; the friend hugged it and stopped crying. David's bringing his own teddy is a typical example of quasi-egocentric empathy, but in this case he was able to profit from corrective feedback (his friend kept crying). I assume this means that David was cognitively advanced enough to wonder why his teddy bear did not stop his friend's crying, and thinking about it made him realize that he would want his own teddy bear in a similar situation, so his friend might want his own teddy bear as well. Corrective feedback in other words may have triggered perspective taking (aided by David's memory both of his friend's playing happily with his own teddy bear and his friend's teddy being in the next room). In sum, this toddler's behavior pattern illustrates both "quasi-egocentric" and veridical empathy in the service of helping another, and it also suggests that the process of transition from one to the other might be as follows: When children are cognitively ready they can profit from their quasi-egocentric mistakes, learn from corrective feedback that another's feelings in a situation may differ from their own, and move on to veridical empathy. Eventually, the feedback becomes unnecessary, although even adults need it at times.

In a similar incident, described by Blum (1987), which did not involve corrective feedback but revealed a toddler's ability to bridge time in the service of helping another, Sarah, 2 years and 3 months old, was riding in a car with her cousin. The cousin became upset when he could not find his teddy bear. Someone said it was in the trunk and could be retrieved when they get home. Ten or 15 minutes passed and as the car approached the house Sarah said, "Now you can get your bear." The same Sarah, at 3 years, showed an even more impressive ability to bridge time in a helping context when she gave her friend her Donald Duck hat to keep "forever"; the hat was to replace the Boston Celtics cap that her friend had lost several days earlier.

At the veridical stage, then, not only can children empathize accurately with another's distress, but they can also assume the other's perspective, reflect on the others particular needs in the situation, and guide their helpful acts more effectively. Veridical empathy, unlike the preceding, short-lived stages, has most of the basic features of mature empathy and continues to develop through life. With increased understanding of causes, consequences, and correlates, of emotions, children can empathize not only with simple distress feelings like those in our teddy bear examples but also with increasingly subtle and complex ones. I discuss these further developments more fully elsewhere (Hoffman, 2000) but present a few examples here to place the toddler period in its proper developmental context: Thus, preschoolers can empathize with another's feeling disappointed in his own performance; older children can empathize with another's feelings of ambivalence about something; adolescents, with another's fear of losing face if one accepts help; adults' empathic distress can at times be more intense than the victim's actual pain; therapists may delay expressing empathic grief so a patient can express negative feeling toward the one who died. More generally, between toddlerhood and adolescence children begin to realize that their inner self has a reflective component, an "I" that thinks, feels, plans, remembers, and that everyone else also has such an inner self; their empathic responses also begin to be influenced by knowing that people can control their emotional expression, that displayed emotions are not always felt, and that felt emotions are not always acted on. Empathy also acquires a metacognitive component: Children become aware of empathizing. And, finally, their empathy is affected by knowing that others have a life and an identity that may contradict their behavior in the immediate situation.

Returning to the toddler period, I now continue and dig a little deeper into the processes underlying empathy's becoming a prosocial motive.

TRANSFORMATION OF EMPATHIC INTO SYMPATHIC DISTRESS

Thus far I have suggested that empathic distress includes both an affective component and a cognitive component based on one's cognitive sense of others as distinct from oneself. This development of the cognitive sense of others drives the development of empathic distress by modifying and shaping empathic affect into increasingly complex forms. What lies behind this hypothesis? It begins with theorists in the 1960s who noted that how a person experiences an affect is heavily influenced by pertinent cognition: "One identifies this stirred-up state in terms of the characteristics of the situation and one's apperceptive mass" (Schachter & Singer, 1962, p. 380). These writers were explaining how we distinguish among specific affects (anger, joy, fear) aroused *directly,* and they started a still-ongoing debate about how important cognition is for feeling specific emotions. Quite apart from this debate about direct emotion (reviewed by Hoffman, 1986), the cognitive sense of oneself and others as separate, independent entities is so obviously intrinsic to *empathic* emotion that it must alter the very quality of the observer's feeling: Once children have a sense of others as separate from oneself, the quality of their empathic distress changes. They might, for example, once they discover that the pain or discomfort is someone else's and not their own, simply feel relieved, turn away, and forget about it. Some children may do that, but turning away is not an effective way to reduce empathic distress, because with the capacity to represent others, the image of the victim that remains is likely to feed their empathic distress. They might try distracting themselves, but this is not efficient because it requires expending cognitive energy and it might not succeed in dispelling the image of the victim anyway. In any case the weight of the evidence cited earlier, especially research connecting empathic distress to helping, is that most children do not turn away but respond with at least as much empathic distress as they did when they were younger, and, in addition, they are now motivated to help the victim.

There is a possibly more fundamental explanation that may account for their not turning away, which I suggested some time ago:

> It seems reasonable to suppose that along with the gradual emergence of a sense of the other as distinct from oneself, the affective portion of the child's global empathic distress—the feeling of distress and desire that it would end—is extended to the separate self and other that emerge from the global self. Early in this process, when the child is only vaguely and momentarily aware of the other as distinct from himself, the image of the other may often be transitory and slip in and out of focus. Consequently, he probably reacts to another's distress as though his dimly perceived self and dimly perceived other were somehow simultaneously, or alternately, in distress. Consider this child whose typical response to his own distress, beginning late in the first year, was to suck his thumb with one hand and pull his ear with the other. At 12 months, on seeing a sad look on his father's face, he proceeded to look sad

> and suck his thumb while pulling on his father's ear. This co-occurrence of distress in the emerging self and emerging other may be an important factor in the transition from empathic to sympathetic distress, which includes an affective response, awareness that another person is the victim, and the desire to terminate the victim's distress.
>
> The child's response may continue to have a purely empathic component—desire to terminate "own" (global) distress. The important thing, however, is that the "quasi-egoistic" concern for his "own" discomfort gives way, at least in part, to a feeling of concern for another person. This is a new addition to the child's repertoire which enables him for the first time to behave in what appears to be a truly altruistic manner, that is, to attempt to relieve the distress of another person who is perceptually separate from himself. The response of this 20-month-old boy is illustrative: when a visiting friend who was about to leave burst into tears, complaining that her parents were not home (they were away for 2 weeks), his immediate response was to look sad, but then he offered her his beloved teddy-bear to take home. His parents said he would miss his teddy but he insisted—presumably because his sympathetic distress was greater than the anticipated unpleasantness of not having his teddy, which seems indicative of the strong motivational potential of sympathetic distress. (Hoffman, 1975, p. 615)

My hypothesis, then, is that once children have separate images of self and others their own empathic distress, which is a parallel response (a more or less exact replication of the victim's actual or presumed feeling of distress), may be transformed at least in part into a more reciprocal feeling of concern for the victim, and the motive to comfort themselves is correspondingly transformed into a motive to help the victim. This developmental transformation fits with how older children and adults report feeling when observing someone in distress: They continue to respond in a partly egoistic manner—to feel uncomfortable and highly distressed themselves—but they also experience a feeling of compassion or what I call sympathetic distress for the victim, along with a conscious desire to help the victim.

In other words, the same advance in self–other differentiation that moves children from "egocentric" to "quasi-egocentric" empathy, discussed earlier, produces a *qualitative transformation of empathic distress into sympathetic distress.* From then on and continuing through life, children's empathic distress always includes a sympathetic component and, insofar as it does, children want to help the victim because they feel sorry for the victim, not just to relieve their own empathic distress. *The sympathetic distress component of empathic distress is thus the child's first truly prosocial motive.*

It is difficult to test hypotheses about qualitative developmental shifts in inner states. When I first advanced the foregoing hypothesis (Hoffman, 1975) the only supportive evidence consisted of anecdotes like those described here and several studies showing that children in the aggregate generally progress from responding to another's distress by seeking comfort for themselves to trying to comfort the victim. Since then, three independent groups of investigators have tested the hypothesis by predicting that advances in self–other differentiation predate children's shift from empathic to sympathetic distress (Bischoff-Kohler, 1991; Johnson, 1992; Zahn-Waxler, Radke-Yarrow, & King, 1979). All three found, as expected, that mirror-self-image recognition predicts later sympathetic distress and helping behavior. If one recognizes oneself in the mirror it may not be too much of a stretch to assume that one would realize that someone else in the mirror (or in the world) is not the self but another person. In other words, mirror self-recognition may be an indirect index of awareness of others as physically entities. These studies may thus be taken as partial confirmation of my hypothesis. They say nothing, however, about the processes underlying a qualitative shift in inner states (i.e., the transition from empathic to sympathetic distress). To ferret out these underlying processes in the absence of research the best we can do is look carefully at anecdotal details, which I now attempt to do.

My process hypothesis is that infants begin with a "global self" in which self and other are fused and their response to another's distress is felt as a fused self–other distress, which I call global empathic distress. With the gradual emergence of a sense of the other as separate from oneself, the affective portion of one's global empathic distress (the feeling of distress and desire to end it) is extended to the separate self and other that emerge. At first the child is only vaguely and momentarily aware of the other as distinct from self, and the image of the other is transitory and may slip in and out of focus. *He therefore reacts to another's distress as though his dimly perceived self and dimly perceived other were simultaneously, or alternately, in distress.* If we take this co-occurrence of distress in the emerging self and other as a step in the transition from empathic to sympathetic distress, then there is anecdotal evidence for it. A prime example is the child described earlier whose typical response to his own distress, beginning late in the first year, was to suck his thumb with one hand and pull his ear with the other, and at 12 months, on seeing a sad look on his father's face, proceeded to look sad and suck his thumb while pulling on his father's ear. Three similar anecdotes were reported by Radke-Yarrow and Zahn-Waxler (1984): One child's first prosocial act alternated between gently touching the victim and gently touching himself; another child comforted his crying mother by wiping her tears while wiping his own eyes although there were no tears in his eyes; and a third child, who, on seeing his mother bump her elbow, did the following: rubbed her elbow, rubbed his own elbow, said "ow," and grimaced as though in pain. Also, in a study by Main, Westen, and Wakeling (1979), a child who observed an adult "clown" pretending to cry said "man crying" very sadly, went to his father's lap, and from there with a sad expression repeatedly addressed the clown as if to comfort or distract him. These anecdotes support the idea of a step in the transition from empathic to sympathetic distress, a step in which only part of the empathic distress appears to be transformed into sympathetic distress, which I suggest may be the affective basis of empathic morality.

With further advances in social cognition and a sharpened sense of the other, the transformation of empathic into sympathetic distress becomes more complete. However, as noted earlier, a purely empathic component may remain even in adulthood. This is exemplified by the observation that nurses in training may experience a conflict between sympathetic distress (intense desire to help their terminally ill patients) and pure empathic distress, which makes it difficult to stay in the same room with them (Stotland, Mathews, Sherman, Hansson, & Richardson, 1978), and by the phenomenon of "vicarious traumatization," which includes intense feelings of both empathic and sympathetic distress in trauma therapists (Hoffman, 2002; Pearlman & Saakvitne, 1995).

REFERENCES

Bischoff-Kohler, D. (1991). The development of empathy in infants. In M. Lamb & M. Keller (Eds.), *Infant development: Perspectives from German-speaking countries* (pp. 245–273). Hillsdale, NJ: Erlbaum.

Blass, E. M., Ganchrow, J. R., & Steiner, J. E. (1984). Classical conditioning in newborn humans 2–48 hours of age. *Infant Behavior and Development, 7,* 223–235.

Blum, L. (1987). Particularity and responsiveness. In J. Kagan & S. Lamb (Eds.), *The emergence of morality in young children.* Chicago: University of Chicago Press.

Brothers, L. (1989). A biological perspective on empathy. *American Journal of Psychiatry, 146,* 1–19.

Darwin, C. (1965). *The expression of the emotions in man and animals.* Chicago: University of Chicago Press. (Original work published 1862)

Eisenberg, N., & Miller, P. (1987). Relation of empathy to prosocial behavior. *Psychological Bulletin, 101,* 91–119.

Escalona, S. K. (1945). Feeding disturbances in very young children. *American Journal of Orthopsychiatry, 15,* 76–80.

Gallese, V. (2003). The roots of empathy: The shared manifold hypothesis and the neural basis of intersubjectivity. *Psychopathology, 36,* 171–180.

Hay, D. F., Nash, A., & Pedersen, J. (1981). Responses of six-month-olds to the distress of their peers. *Child Development, 52,* 1071–1075.

Hoffman, M. L. (1975). Developmental synthesis of affect and cognition and its implications for altruistic motivation. *Developmental Psychology, 11,* 607–622.

Hoffman, M. L. (1978). Empathy, its development and prosocial implications. *Nebraska Symposium on Motivation, 25,* 169–218.

Hoffman, M. L. (1981). Is altruism part of human nature? *Journal of Personality and Social Psychology, 40,* 121–137.

Hoffman, M. L. (1985). Affect, motivation, and cognition. In R. M. Sorrentino & E. T. Higgins (Eds.), *Handbook of motivation and cognition: Foundations of social behavior* (pp. 244–280). New York: Guilford Press.

Hoffman, M. L. (2000). *Empathy and moral development: Implications for caring and justice.* New York: Cambridge University Press.

Hoffman, M. L. (2002). *Empathy and vicarious traumatization in therapists.* Unpublished manuscript.

Humphrey, G. (1922). The conditioned reflex and the elementary social reaction. *Journal of Abnormal and Social Psychology, 17,* 113–119.

Iacoboni, M., & Lenzi, G. L. (2002). Mirror neurons, the insula, and empathy. *Behavioral and Brain Sciences, 25,* 39–40.

Iacoboni, M., Molnar-Szakacs, I., Gallese, V., Buccino, G., Mazziotta, J. C., & Rizzolatti, G. (2005). Grasping the intentions of others with one's own mirror neuron system. *PLOS Biology, 3,* 529–535.

Jaffe, J., Beebe, B., Feldstein, S., Crown, C. L., & Jasnow, M. D. (2001). Rhythms of dialogue in infancy. *Monographs of the Society for Research in Child Development, 66.*

Johnson, D. B. (1992). Altruistic behavior and the development of the self in infants. *Merrill–Palmer Quarterly, 28,* 379–388.

Kessen, W., Haith, M. M., & Salapatek, P. H. (1970). Infancy. In P. Mussen (Ed.), *Carmichael's manual of child psychology* (Vol. 1, pp. 287–446). New York; Wiley.

Lewis, M., & Brooks-Gunn, J. (1979). *Social cognition and the acquisition of self.* New York: Plenum Press.

Main, M., Weston, D., & Wakeling, S. (1979). *Concerned attention to the crying of an adult actor in infancy.* Paper presented at the biennial meeting of the Society for Research in Child Development, San Francisco.

Martin, G. B., & Clark, R. D. (1982). Distress crying in infants: Species and peer specificity. *Developmental Psychology, 18,* 3–9.

Meltzoff, A. N., & Moore, N. K. (1983). Newborn infants imitate adult's facial gestures. *Child Development, 14,* 702–709.

Pearlman, L. A., & Saakvitne, K. W. (1995). *Trauma and the therapist.* New York: Norton.

Radke-Yarrow, M., & Zahn-Waxler, C. (1984). Roots, motives, and patterns in children's prosocial behavior. In E. Staub, D. Bar-Tal, J. Karylowski, & J. Reykowski (Eds.), *Development and maintenance of prosocial behavior* (pp. 81–99). New York: Plenum Press.

Sagi, A., & Hoffman, M. L. (1976). Empathic distress in the newborn. *Developmental Psychology, 12,* 175–176.

Schachter, S., & Singer, J. E. (1962). Cognitive, social, and physiological determinants of emotional state. *Psychological Review, 69,* 379–399.

Simner, M. L. (1971). Newborn's response to the cry of another infant. *Developmental Psychology, 5,* 136–150.

Stern, D. N. (1985). *The interpersonal world of the infant.* New York: Basic Books.

Stern, D. N., Hofer, L., Haft, W., & Dore, J. (1985). Affect attunement: The sharing of feeling states between mother and infant by means of inter-modal fluency. In T. M. Field & N. A. Fox (Eds.), *Social perception in infants* (pp. 249–268). Norwood, NJ: Ablex.

Stotland, E., Matthews, K., Sherman, S., Hansson, R., & Richardson, B. (1978). *Empathy, fantasy, and helping.* Beverly Hills, CA: Sage.

Zahn-Waxler, C., Radke-Yarrow, M., & King, R. (1979). Childrearing and children's prosocial initiations toward victims of distress. *Child Development, 50,* 319–330.

Zahn-Waxler, C., Robinson, J. L., Emde, N. E., & Plomin, R. (1992). The development of empathy in twins. *Developmental Psychology, 28,* 1038–1047.

Part II

PLAY AND COMMUNICATION

6

Pretend Play in Toddlers

ANGELINE LILLARD

Pretend play is a ubiquitous activity of early childhood. Although of long-standing interest to researchers, it has proved somewhat elusive to research as compared to, say, language. Since the seminal work of Parten (1932, 1933) and Piaget (1962), two waves of research have made good progress, the first in the late 1970s, and the second beginning in the 1990s and continuing today. In this chapter I review what pretending is and discuss its importance and its emergence, including developing use of the word *pretend.* In the second part of the chapter, I discuss some crucial outstanding issues regarding pretense in toddlerhood. One set of issues concerns understanding pretending, both as a mental state and as an activity. I end with the important issue of how pretend events are cognitively represented.

THE DEFINITION OF PRETEND PLAY

Pretend play has been defined as the transformation of the here and now (Garvey & Berndt, 1975) for purposes of recreation (Lillard, 1993a). For example, a child might pretend that a stick is a horse, and gallop it around, or that he himself is a king, or that a group of friends are various family members engaged in going to a pretend fair. Pretending can involve the substitution of one object for another, the attribution of pretend properties, and even the conjuring up of imaginary objects (Leslie, 1987) and friends (Taylor, 1999). It always involves the intentional projection of a mental representation on to some reality (Lillard, 1993a).

Because pretense involves creating and acting out of mentally constructed worlds, it can be seen as a progenitor of several outstanding cognitive features of the human species. The philosopher Walton (1990) holds that pretend play is at the root of all human art forms. To create and appreciate art, drama, music, and so on, one suspends the here and now. In this same way, pretending is also linked to counterfactual reasoning: One temporarily suspends the present situation to imagine and partake in a different one (Byrne, 2002, 2005; Harris, 2000). Pretending also bears important similarities to engaging in discourse (Harris, 2000). Both pretending and discourse involve the creation and updating of mental models (Johnson-Laird, 1983), complete with realistic causal chains (Harris, 2000). Our ability to engage in conversations, sharing information about nonpresent realities and following them out to their logical conclusions, seems analogous to our early ability to pretend.

THE UNIVERSALITY OF PRETEND PLAY

Pretend play has been found in every culture in which it has been sought (Eibl-Eibesfeldt, 1989; Roopnarine, Johnson, & Hooper, 1994; Schwartzman, 1978), and it emerges on a similar timetable (Bates, 1979; Fenson, Kagan, Kearsley, & Zelazo, 1976; Kagan, Kearsley, & Zelazo, 1978). This makes symbolic play an important addition to Brown's (1991) list of human universals, which includes the broader *play* but not *pretend play.* Although the content (e.g., the scripts) and style of children's play can vary (Farver, 1992; Farver & Shin, 1997; Farver & Wimbarti, 1995; Goncu, Mistry, & Mosier, 2000; Haight, Wang, Fung, Williams, & Mintz, 1999), its very existence is robust, even in the face of adult discouragement. Menonite and some fundamentalist Christian families discourage pretending (Carlson, Taylor, & Levin, 1998; Taylor & Carlson, 2000) as (traditionally) have the Mopan Maya (Danziger, 1999), and under such circumstances children are still observed to pretend on the sly. Furthermore, although delayed, pretend play occurs even in blind children (Lewis, Norgate, Collis, & Reynolds, 2000), deaf children (Spencer, 1996), and children with mental retardation (Baron-Cohen, 1987; Li, 1985). The only children who do not spontaneously engage in pretend play are those with autism (Baron-Cohen, 1987; Jarrold, Boucher, & Smith, 1996), and absence of pretend play at 18 months is one of the major prognostic signs of this disorder (Baird et al., 2000) and a defining feature (Kanner, 1943). The other prognostic signs of autism concern joint attention—showing an adult an object, and producing and following finger points for the purpose of sharing. As discussed later, joint attention may also be very important to early pretense. Pretending also is entwined with early language, and language is also impaired in autism, with half of autistics never speaking, and virtually all being delayed in their speech (DSM-IV-TR; American Psychiatric Association, 2000). In sum, excepting autistic children, pretend play is a universal of early childhood.

THE UNIQUENESS OF HUMAN PLAY

The manner and extent to which humans pretend are unique among animals. It is the case that some human-reared sign-trained apes have been noted to occasionally do something that would be considered pretending were a child to do it. One famous example is the Gardners' observation of Washoe, a chimpanzee they raised in their home, bathing a doll (Gardner, Harris, Ohmoto, & Hamazaki, 1988). In unenculturated primates in the wild, actions are harder to interpret—for example, a rhesus monkey carrying a coconut shell in a manner similar to how its mother carried her new infant (Breuggeman, 1973) (for full discussion, see Mitchell, 2002). Regardless, these are isolated incidents. When one enters a group of young humans at leisure, pretend play, replete with object substitutions and assumed identities, is very likely to be a prominent activity. This does not appear to be the case for a group of young chimpanzees.

Deception appears to occur with some frequency in nonhuman primates, and there is a sense in which deception is pretending (without the play)—one creates an alternative view over reality. Isolated incidents of deception in primates and other species (e.g., an animal "pretending" not to know there is food at a given source until its companions go away) have been documented (Byrne & Whiten, 1991). These deceptive acts can be explained as evolved or learned responses, and regardless they are unlike human pretend play in that they serve obvious instrumental purposes like protecting one's food source. Pretend play in human children rarely serves any obvious immediate purpose.

Play fighting is sometimes noted for its similarity to pretending (Bateson, 1972; Bekoff, 1999), but although a play "bite" does not mean the same thing as a real "bite" and this may be a precursor to pretense, clearly the routine use of substitute objects and the frequent reenactment of multiple themes (not just fighting) that we see in human pretend play are absent in other animals; in the animal world we see nothing that is really akin to human pretend play (Tomasello & Call, 1997; Tomasello & Rakoczy, 2003).

THE IMPORTANCE OF PRETEND PLAY

Pretending is widely recognized to be important. One reason for this is its relationship to language, and the assumption that both tap a symbolic capacity (Piaget, 1962; Vygotsky, 1978; Werner & Kaplan, 1963). Many studies have shown relations between the emergence of pretend play and the emergence of language (Bates, 1979; Tamis-LeMonda & Bornstein, 1994). Robert Kavanaugh and I (2007) have also found a relation between frequency of early pretending and success on a scale model task (DeLoache, 1991) believed to assess symbolic understanding in young children. We have also found a strong relation between passing the scale model task and some aspects of language and observed the long-respected relations between language and pretend play.

Another reason for pretending's importance is its apparent relationship to social cognition. Many people have noted that in pretend play, children seem to have an advanced theory of mind. The fact that children with autism do not pretend or show normal development of a theory of mind adds to the view that the two activities are linked (Baron-Cohen, 1987). The issue of how pretending and theory of mind are related is taken up in depth later in the chapter.

THE CONTEXT AND DEVELOPMENTAL COURSE OF PRETENDING

Pretending begins in early childhood, with its first appearance around 12 months and full-fledged engagement beginning around 24 to 30 months (Bates, 1979; Haight & Miller, 1993; Piaget, 1962). Even very young children spend up to 20% of their free time pretending, and during the preschool years this percentage of time doubles (Dunn & Dale, 1984; Haight & Miller, 1993). Following Piaget, many have thought that pretending declines after age 6, to be replaced by games with rules (Fein, 1981), a claim currently being studied in my laboratory. However, adults' engagement in books, movies, and other symbolic media (Harris, 2000; Walton, 1990) and our ability to engage in counterfactual thought (Byrne, 2005) can be seen as an outgrowth of our ability to pretend: to intentionally take an imagined scenario as if it were for real (Lillard, 1998a).

Very young children's pretending usually occurs in the context of strong social support (Smolucha & Smolucha, 1998), often provided by their parents (Fein & Fryer, 1995; Haight & Miller, 1993). When children pretend with their mothers, their pretending is more advanced than it is when they pretend alone (DeLoache & Plaetzer, 1985; Miller & Garvey, 1984; O'Connell & Betherton, 1984).

Recent research suggests that one crucial reason pretending advances when mothers and children pretend together is that mothers help young children through contexts of joint attention. Recent research in my laboratory, described later, has shown that mothers' looking at children is associated with children seeming to "get" pretense because they smile more and produce more pretend actions when mothers look at them more (Lillard & Witherington, 2004; Lillard et al., 2007), but only in pretend contexts, not in real ones (Nishida & Lillard, 2007). When a mother looks frequently at her child, she can assist the child to jointly attend to her pretend activities, scaffolding the child's understanding with well-timed actions, familiar scripts, and language which can then help the child to represent and partake in the pretense scenario. Other research has coded joint attention in a more global way and found that 30-month-olds are more apt to be engaged in all kinds of symbolic activities (including pretense) when engaged in joint attention with the mother (Adamson, Bakeman, & Deckner, 2004) and that the more joint attention that

1-year-olds and their mothers achieve during pretense, the higher the level of the child's play (Bigelow, MacLean, & Proctor, 2004).

One central pretend act is object substitution, as when a child picks up a shoe and begins to treat it as a telephone. Such acts usually seem like clear examples of pretending, projecting one's mental representation of one object onto some other object. Generally speaking, younger children's substitute objects are perceptually more similar to the object they represent (for pretend) and are less likely to have some alternative function than are the substitute objects of older children. Young children are most apt to pretend with objects that visually resemble that which they are supposed to represent, like miniatures (Sutton-Smith, 1983). For example, in one study half of 18-month-olds spontaneously pretended with highly similar objects (e.g., drank from a teacup), but just a handful pretended with nonsimilar objects (e.g., drank from a block). At 34 months, almost all children pretended with highly similar objects, and close to half pretended with nonsimilar objects (Ungerer, Zelazo, Kearsley, & O'Leary, 1981; see also Watson & Fischer, 1977).

Young children are also limited in terms of the number of object substitutions they can enact in one pretense episode and this varies depending on perceptual similarity. For example, having watched an experimenter feed a pretend horse (made of wire) with a pretend bucket (a half clam shell), only a third of 21-month-olds repeated the action. When the wire horse was replaced by a realistic-looking plastic horse and the shell by a plastic egg half (making the substitute objects perceptually more similar to what they represent), almost all 21-month-olds could reenact these two object substitutions (Fein, 1975; see also Jackowitz & Watson, 1980). When just one of the substitutes was involved (feeding the plastic horse with the clam shell) just over half of children were successful.

In sum, research on early pretending shows that young children's ability to internally represent what is not really there is tenuous and heavily dependent on external support. The more perceptually similar are the real substitute objects to the pretend objects for which they stand, the more capable is the child of carrying out the pretend actions. As children get older, they can enact more substitutions with more dissimilar objects (Fein, 1975). They need less perceptual support from those objects, perhaps because their mental schemas representing the pretense objects are stronger, and can be activated with less external stimulation.

Developing script knowledge also appears important in pretense development (Nelson & Seidman, 1984). Young children clearly reenact the scripts of everyday life in their pretense, and early on young children's pretending is limited to everyday themes like house, going to bed, and tea party (Haight & Miller, 1992; Harris & Kavanaugh, 1993). Young children's pretend play is also most advanced (e.g., involves more object substitutions) when they are pretending familiar scripts rather than more novel ones (Lucariello, 1987). As children get older, their pretending becomes increasingly expansive, often involving emotional, exciting, and somewhat dangerous scripts they might have not personally experienced firsthand, like divorce, witches, and spies (Opie & Opie, 1969; Sorenson & Lillard, 2007; Sutton-Smith, 1997).

Children also develop in predictable ways in terms of the attribution of agency in pretend. Pretending begins with self-directed acts (Piaget, 1962). Around age 2, children begin to act on other objects, including replicas of animates, attributing passive agency to them. By age 4, they make the objects into active agents and attribute mental states and emotions to them (McCune, 1995; Nicolich, 1977; Wolf, 1982; Wolf, Rygh, & Altshuler, 1984).

Another important issue in the development of pretending is the use of pretend language. Some studies have looked at how children's language changes when they pretend. It has been noted that in the end of preschool, children begin to use special forms of speech when they pretend—for example, the subjective tense ("Let's say I was a dog and you were a cat and . . . ") (Garvey & Kramer, 1989; Marjanovic-Shane, 1989; Musatti, Veneziano, & Mayer, 1998). A few studies have also examined use of the word *pretend,* which would seem to indicate acquisition of an explicit concept of pretending.

LEARNING THE WORD *PRETEND*

It is important to address how children understand *pretend*. One reason is that many experiments about pretending ask children to pretend or discuss someone else's pretending (Gottfried, Hickling, Totten, Mkroyan, & Reisz, 2003; Joseph, 1998; Lillard, 1998b; Rakoczy, Tomasello, & Striano, 2004; Taylor, Lussier, & Maring, 2003). If we really want to understand what children know about pretending, it is crucial that we examine how they construe the word in our experiments.

A second reason is that in natural interaction, the word *pretend* could be very useful for helping children to know when to quarantine pretense from real, keeping the representations separate. If children did not correctly quarantine pretense from real, their real-world representations could be very confused by pretense, an issue taken up in the end of the chapter.

Evidence from studies of mother–toddler snacks in our laboratory suggests that toddlers are not helped by the word *pretend*: many mothers pretending with 15- to 24-month-olds never use the word, and when mothers do, it does not appear to encourage pretense behavior in children (Lillard & Witherington, 2004). However, the word might clarify understanding for somewhat older children, given that by ages 4–5 many children use the word themselves in apparent effort to engage their playmates in pretense (Lloyd & Goodwin, 1995).

Two studies have looked at children's use of the word *pretend* on school playgrounds and found an increase in the use of the word around 4 to 5 years (Hall, Frank, & Ellison, 1995; Lloyd & Goodwin, 1995). Hall et al. also believed they had evidence that *mentalistic* use of the term *pretend* developed late. This supports an "acting-as-if" definition of pretend (Harris, Lillard, &

Perner, 1994; Lillard, 1993b, 2001). In this view, children initially think about pretending as acting in a given way, but they do not think of it as involving mental representations. Although surely children have mental representations when they pretend (this is required by definition), they are not metacognitively aware of those representations.

The playground studies are interesting but are limited both in terms of the ages sampled and the situations in which "pretend" is used. A third study looking at the emergence of mental state talk included "pretend," and found that 30% of children used the word at 28 months. However, it did not explore children's meaning for the word (Bretherton & Beeghly, 1982). A fuller view can be obtained from the CHILDES database (MacWhinney, 1990), the web-based corpus of hundreds of children's speech taped in home and/or preschool settings that others have successfully used to learn about children's mental state talk (Bartsch & Wellman, 1995). The word *pretend* in the CHILDES corpus has been examined only in a small (three-child) study that was particularly concerned with real/mental state contrasts (Shatz, Wellman, & Silber, 1983).

Recently, Ashley Pinkham has examined natural language transcripts of children sampled 20 or more times over at least two of three ages: 2, 3, and 4–5 years (Pinkham & Lillard, 2007). Ten children, 7 boys and 3 girls, met these criteria. Transcripts were searched for child uses of *pretend* or *make-believe* (including derivatives), resulting in 227 spontaneous uses. Each use was then sorted into one of three mutually exclusive categories. *Directing the interaction* utterances are used to persuade a play partner to accept some element as the basis for current or future play ("Pretend this [washcloth] is a blanket"). These uses are related to the physical activity of pretending. *Clarification of reality* utterances are attempts to clarify a discrepancy between the pretend frame and reality ("I'm not going anywhere; I'm just pretending I'm going"). These uses are comparable to contrastives in other research (Bartsch & Wellman, 1995). *Other* utterances did not fall into the previous two categories.

Multinomial regression indicated an interaction between age and type of "pretend" usage ($p < .05$). The proportion of "pretend" uses directing the interaction remained relatively constant across ages 2–3, but declined significantly by ages 4–5. By comparison, clarification of reality uses increased across all three age groups, accounting for a larger proportion of uses than did directing the interaction by ages 4–5.

These findings suggest that productive use of "pretend" transitions from action oriented to mentalistic between the ages of 2 and 4–5. Such a transition supports an early "acting-as-if" definition of pretense: Young children first conceptualize pretending as behavioral and do not achieve a sophisticated mentalistic understanding of pretense until age 4 or later (Lillard, 1993b). The present study suggests that such a transition is gradual, occurring over the course of three or more years. Learning the word *pretend* signals a conceptual advance in understanding pretending, first as an activity and then as a mental state.

PRETENDING AND UNDERSTANDING THE MIND

Even with language abilities controlled for, children who pretend more pass theory of mind tasks earlier (Astington & Jenkins, 1995; Lalonde & Chandler, 1995; Taylor & Carlson, 1997; Taylor, Carlson, Maring, Gerow, & Charley, 2004; Youngblade & Dunn, 1995). Many studies suggest that pretend play training enhances social cognitive skills such as perspective taking and role taking (Rakoczy, Tomasello, & Striano, 2005; Rubin, 1980; Rubin, Fein, & Vandenberg, 1983). Children also reason about mental states better when the mental states are embedded in a fantasy context (Hickling, Wellman, & Gottfried, 1997; Lillard, 1996; Sobel & Lillard, 2001). Interestingly, these benefits of pretense contexts even extend outside the social realm: When children are provided with a pretend context, they are better at solving even nonsocial problems like those involving logical syllogisms (Dias & Harris, 1988, 1990; Hawkins, Pea, Glick, & Scribner, 1984; Kuczaj, 1981; Scott, Baron-Cohen, & Leslie, 1999). But the relation between pretending and understanding others' minds seems deeper and this has led to an interesting body of research. My theoretical model overlaying this work is called the Twin Earth Model of Pretend (Lillard, 2001; see Figure 6.1). This model, referred to in discussions of studies that follow, addresses potential paths of relations between understanding minds and pretend play. The first set of studies discussed here concerns the question of whether children understand that pretending involves mental representation. The second concerns pretense and understanding intentions.

Pretense and Mental Representation

In the late 1980s, as theory of mind research was gaining prominence, a going assumption was that pretend play was an arena of advanced competence for understanding mental representation (Flavell, Flavell, & Green, 1987; Forguson & Gopnik, 1988; Leslie, 1987; Moses & Chandler, 1992). Clearly, pretending involves mentally representing one thing as something else; young children engage in pretending; and it seemed logical to many people that the only way to understand pretending—in oneself or in another—was to mentally represent the others' pretend mental representations (metarepresentation), and to represent them *as such*. This made pretending a very interesting issue for theory of mind researchers, because children pretend at least 2 years before they begin to understand false belief!

A study I conducted with John Flavell led me to question the assumption that pretending entails metarepresentation (Lillard & Flavell, 1992). Our aim was to test whether children understand desire and pretense earlier than belief, or whether contextual factors in the presentations of some mental states made them appear easier to understand. To test this, I presented young children with a two-room dollhouse with a doll in one room. I told children that the doll had a particular desire, pretense, or belief about what

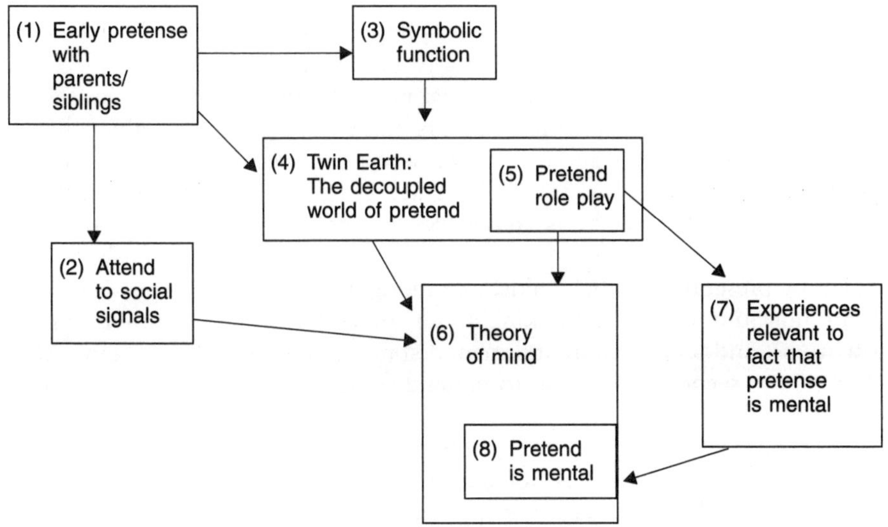

FIGURE 6.1. The Twin Earth model of pretend theory of mind relations.

was in different locations in the other room, and after the child confirmed the doll's mental state and content, I showed them that reality was discrepant with the doll's mental state content and asked again about the desire, pretense, or belief. For example, I told children, "She's pretending there's juice in the cupboard" (or for other children, she wants there to be juice, or she thinks there's juice). I then showed a teddy bear in the cupboard and asked what was really there and what she was pretending (or wanted, or thought) was there. When presented in this way, 3-year-olds did fairly well on desire (saying that she wanted one thing, when in fact another was there) but were at about chance on pretend and think (claiming the mental state content corresponded to reality). The important finding emerged from a cross-condition. Half the time, for each mental state, the doll was engaged in some action consistent with her desire, pretense, or thought, like getting a cup (for juice). The action made no difference to performance on desire and thought, but it made a significant difference for pretending. Thus, children seemed to get that pretense can differ from reality when it involves an action but not when it is purely mental projection.

This inspired a focused test of whether children might only understand pretending as action, not as a mental representational state as had been assumed. To test this, I presented children with a troll doll named Moe, who I explained was from a faraway place called the Land of the Trolls, where there were no kangaroos (Lillard, 1993b). As a result, Moe knew nothing about kangaroos, he had never even heard of a kangaroo, and did not know that they hopped. However, I showed them that Moe happened to be hopping very much like a kangaroo hops. I confirmed their understanding that he did not know kangaroos hopped but that he was hopping like one, and then asked the crucial question: Was Moe pretending to be a kangaroo?

If one has a mental representational understanding of pretending, clearly not, and indeed that is what most adults and even 8-year-olds claim (Lillard, 1998b). However, only about 30% of 4-year-olds seem to understand this; most 4-year-olds will consistently claim, across four trials, that the troll is pretending to be whatever he is acting like, regardless of his mental state (see Lillard, 2001, for a review). Some researchers have been able to push this age down by presenting artificial aids, like thought bubbles above the character's head indicating that he is thinking about something else, but in more typical situations, and when action and mental state do not correspond, young children do not seem to "get" that to pretend something, one must mentally represent it.

This line of work suggests that the link between theory of mind and pretending in young children is not due to children coming to an early understanding mental representation in pretending. The same children who failed the Moe task passed a basic false-belief task. Another possible reason for the link could be that children understand other aspects of pretending that provide a link into mental states.

Pretense and Understanding Intention

One candidate aspect is intention. An early test of this aspect (Lillard, 1998b) suggested intention is not understood earlier in pretense: When shown a character who was described as not wanting to be like a bird but nonetheless flying like one, 4-year-olds also tended to describe the character as pretending to be a bird. However, two experiments using more subtle methods in which action and mental state were consistent convincingly demonstrate some early understanding of intention in pretense. First, Joseph (1998) showed that 4-year-olds know that if one child has a cold and is really sneezing and the other is pretending to sneeze, the latter child but not the former is trying to sneeze. Lillard (2002) reports a replication of this study controlling for the negativity of the event. Four-year-olds could reason from pretense to intention, even if they could not reason from lack of intention to lack of pretense.

More recently, Rakoczy and colleagues (2004) presented children with live actors who were engaged in pretend or attempted activities. For example, one was pretending to write with a pen, and another was trying to write with a pen but failing because the pen had a cap on. The pretend actor acted silly, whereas the trying actor acted frustrated. Children at 3 imitated the pretend actor faithfully but "corrected" the trying actor by removing the cap and really writing. In other words, for both pretending and trying, they saw through to the actor intent. Two-year-olds, in contrast, really wrote in both instances, suggesting that young children are less apt at reading pretend intentions as pretense than young children are at reading true intentions for what they are. Clearly by age 3, however, children seem to understand that someone who is pretending is pretending on purpose. Not until age 4 can children understand that people pretend what they intend to pretend, regardless of outcome.

The latter understanding might hinge on understanding mental representation. To know someone is doing something on purpose entails an understanding of will; to know that they might pretend one thing when in fact something else occurs requires an understanding of how mind relates to action and world. This suggests a parallel in pretense understanding to Wellman's (1990) belief–desire psychology and Flavell's (1988) cognitive connections-to-mental representations theory, each of which addressed understanding minds more generally.

One might speculate that there is a role for pretend play in pushing children from one level of understanding minds to the other. For example, a child who is pretending to be someone else clearly is willing their behavior to be like that someone else's and is therefore cognitively connected to their idea of how that person behaves. However, when assigned by another child a role whose content the child does not know, the child might then need to confront that he or she lacked a mental representation of what he or she was being asked to do. This personal experience with pretend role play might help shift a child's understanding of the mind more generally from a connections to a representation level of understanding. Supporting this, children do pass Moe-like tasks with reference to the self earlier than they pass them with reference to others (Mitchell & Neal, 2005). On the other hand, the fact that children generally pass false belief tasks before the Moe task suggests that pretending does not lead the way for understanding mental representation.

Other Links between Understanding Pretend and Mind

The statistical association between pretending and theory of mind might stem from an early intentional understanding of pretending. Yet the association might be due to more than one factor. The Twin Earth Model of Pretending presents many possible links between pretending and early understanding of the mind. The name of this model derives from pretending being posed as in some ways akin to a device Hillary Putnam originally used to explore philosophical problems (Pessin & Goldberg, 1996). Philosophers imagine a place called Twin Earth where everything is exactly as it is on our earth except some crucial variables. Twin Earth retains most relationships and causal chains one finds on real earth, and thus one can explore how the world would be if one just changed one or two factors; this allows for consideration of many important philosophical issues. I believe pretending is similar for children: It is a place where they work through scripts and issues that arise in their daily lives but can experiment with changing a few parameters (identities, occurrences) to examine how the world would unfurl were those revisions manifest.

Understanding intention and mental representation are only a small part of the Twin Earth model (see Figure 6.1). Specifically, they are part of #8, understanding that pretending is mental. In more recent work we have explored other aspects of the model, or potential reasons for the statistical association between pretending and understanding minds. One link is sensitivity to social signals (#2), conceivably heightened by pretense.

The Social Signaling of Pretense

Pretending might also be linked to theory of mind because early pretending with parents and siblings might heighten children's sensitivity to social signals. When parents pretend with young children, they need to signal to children not to take the activity seriously. If children did take pretense activities seriously, then pretending could confuse their real world understandings. For example, if a child watches his mother pretend to eat off a pen (which she is pretending is a spoon), the child might assume that this is a normal real-world activity and might classify pens as a kind of eating device. The child would then try to really eat with pens. How do parents signal to children not to interpret pretense activities as real ones?

We have recently been examining this issue by asking mothers to pretend and engage in activities for real with their young children. We have microanalyzed mothers' behavior when pretending and contrasted it with their behavior when doing the same activities for real. Our paradigmatic activity has been pretend snacks, because it is very common in the lives of young children, but we have also studied the less common activity of personal grooming (Lillard, 2004; Lillard & Witherington, 2004; Lillard et al., 2005). Below I report results from a series of studies of pretend snacking with children from 15 to 24 months of age and note divergences for grooming where they existed in our single study with 18-month-olds. These ages were chosen because across this period of pretend emergence, it should be particularly important for parents to signal pretense to children.

When mothers pretend with young children, they tend to look at them much more than when they engage in activities for real. When they snack, but not when they groom, mothers smile more frequently and each smile lasts for longer on average. For both snacking and grooming, smiles are placed more often at particular points in the behavior stream: namely, right after a pretend activity. It is as though mothers smile to comment on the activity, to say, "Don't take this seriously now."

In this way, we believe that we have identified a new use of social referencing in pretending (Nishida & Lillard, 2007). The sequence of activities in which a child looks at the mother, the mother acts, then smiles, and then the child engages in a pretend behavior or smiles herself occurs significantly more often in pretend than in real snacks, and significantly more often than chance, whereas during real snacks, the sequence occurs no more often than one would expect by chance (given the overall frequency of each activity during real snacks).

The evidence that mothers' well-placed smiles are assisting children's correct interpretations of the activity as pretense is also gleaned from the grooming experiment. In the grooming scenario, even though mothers did not smile more when pretending to groom themselves than when really grooming themselves, children whose mothers did smile more were more likely to evidence understanding of the pretense by pretending to groom themselves and/or smiling at the mother. Other work suggests that such smiling is not mere mirroring. For example, children do not smile more in real conditions when their mothers smile more (Lillard et al., 2007; Nishida & Lillard, 2007). In sum, pretending appears to involve social signaling, which is known to underlie early theory of mind understandings. Because of this, pretending might heighten children's sensitivity to social cues involving the interpretation of mental states, thereby assisting the relationship between pretending and theory of mind.

Mothers also talk more when they are pretending to have snacks, a finding that did not obtain in our single grooming study. However, across experiments including the grooming study, the more mothers talked while pretending, the more children appeared to understand pretending. This does not seem to be because mothers directly explain pretending—mothers rarely use the word *pretend,* and they do not tend to label the pretend objects' substitute identities (e.g., claiming there are Cheerios where there are none). What they do tend to label is the real objects and the action forms they engage in: the bowls and cups and drinking and eating. Perhaps this labeling is part of the joint attention maintenance that seems to assist early pretense, and that in turn might link pretending to theory of mind.

In sum, part of the reason why pretending is linked to understanding minds might be because early pretending with parents tends to involve partic ular signals on the part of parents, signals that also serve theory of mind (like joint attention and social referencing). Although probably not intentionally (because parents do not adjust their pretense behaviors to the age of child, at least within this range), parents might effectively "teach" young children pretending by presenting this conflux of social signals indicating "this is pretend." Children whose parents pretend more with them might be more sensitive to a subset of those social signals that also feed theory of mind (the path from #1 to #2 to #6 in the model).

We have seen other behavioral variations in pretend—mothers move faster, exaggerate some actions, and engage in more actions overall when pretending. They also issue many more sound effects. Although these changes appear to assist older children and adults in interpreting pretense as pretense (Richert & Lillard, 2004), they do not seem to assist younger children. Interestingly, both older children and adults are aware of what cues they use to decipher pretense, and their coherent theories predict their success in pretense judgments (Ma & Lillard, 2007).

Decoupling as a Link between Pretending and Understanding Minds

In the Twin Earth model, other paths from early pretense to theory of mind are via the symbolic function (#3) and what is termed *decoupling* (#4), and also directly from pretense to decoupling (as a child need not always understand the symbolic nature of pretense to appreciate its decoupled aspect). In decoupling with the symbolic function, the child "decouples" her mental representation of an object, like a "spoon," from its usual referent (a real spoon) and applies to it momentarily to another object (like a pen). At a lower level, the child might simply carry out activities that are typical of a mother but not see herself as a symbol for a mother. She has decoupled herself from her usual behaviors and temporarily taken on those of a mother.

A crucial issue for this route to the statistical association between pretending and theory of mind is children's understanding of pretense episodes. In the recent studies of mother–child pretend behavior in our laboratory, we assume that when a child smiles and engages in pretend behaviors the child understands that the situation is pretend. But that is clearly a questionable assumption. A child might smile and lift a glass to his or her mouth for other reasons, besides understanding pretense (but see Lillard & Witherington, 2004, for discussion). In other work, Lili Ma and I (2006) examine just what young children do understand about pretending and when. In particular, we examine children's ability to symbolize pretense content in its absence, based purely on behavioral cues of the pretender. This work follows on issues recently raised by Harris and Kavanaugh (1993).

Early Understanding of Pretense

In 1993 Harris and Kavanaugh authored a seminal monograph on children's ability to follow pretense sequences. The first four experiments involved a child's ability to make pretend stipulations with substitute objects. The paradigm is a straightforward one: The child watches as an experimenter carries out a pretend action with substitute objects, then the child is asked to carry it out as well. If the child does so, the child appears to understand pretense. For example, in their first study, an animal was described as wanting tea or cereal, props that were present on the table. Children were scored according to whether they performed a correct action with the correct set of props. At 22 months, children had mean scores of 5.1 of 8, and at 27 months, of 7.1, earned by almost always pretend-feeding the animals, and by often correctly pouring before feeding.

In their next experiment Harris and Kavanaugh examined pretend extrapolation. The experimenter implied that a curved yellow brick was a banana and a red brick was cake. By 28 months, most children correctly extrapolated these identities to other "bananas" and "cake," and feeding the right shapes to animals who were claimed to desire them. At 21 months, performance was less strong but still respectable. Children could accept a pretense stipulation provided verbally by an experimenter and extend the identity to other perceptually identical objects.

A third experiment examined children's ability to follow pretense scripts with substitute objects. For example, in a breakfast script, children were given a popsicle stick and asked to "Show how you stir Teddy's tea with the spoon." In a later script, the same object had to be put to a different use (e.g., as a toothbrush). Twenty-one-month-olds had considerable difficulty with this task, but 28-month-olds did reasonably well, with 9 of 12 children correctly using two or three of the objects for the two different actions.

Another experiment concerned pretend transformations: understanding that if I pretend to pour water on something, for example, it becomes pretend "wet." The test was to ask children to dry (of two choices) "the one who is all wet." About half of younger children (20 months) chose the correct one, whereas almost all of the 28-month-olds did so (see also Walker-Andrews & Harris, 1993; Walker-Andrews & Kahana-Kalman, 1999).

Taken together, these studies suggest that around 2 years of age, children become able to make pretend stipulations and follow two-step pretend transformations when they are clearly presented by an adult. What I think they leave open is the extent to which children are really imagining the pretend transformations, versus carrying out instructions for an experimenter. When the experimenter says, "This is Teddy's sandwich. Show me what Teddy does with his sandwich" (in another of the Harris and Kavanaugh experiments), it is not clear to me that the child is fully imagining a sandwich, as opposed to accepting that the object (a yellow block) is to stand in for a sandwich in this episode (see Perner, 1991). In other words, the child appears to be decoupling (#4) the substitute object from its usual role and carrying out sandwich activities with it, but not necessarily symbolizing it (#3) as a sandwich.

Lili Ma and I (2006) have examined this in a set of studies in which the child needs to extrapolate pretend substance from pretend activity and real substance from real activity. In our paradigm,[1] a child watches as one person really eats and another merely pretends to eat. In both cases, the food is never visible. It is eaten from covered bowls, and the actor's hand is cupped so one cannot tell if a real object is in the hand. The pretender, however, exhibits the full range of pretend behaviors (as discovered in our earlier work), looking intently at the child, smiling after her own actions, making sound effects, and so on. After watching the pretend eater pretend to eat and the real eater really eat, the child is asked to "get the [real food]." The response measure is whether the child indicates the bowl containing the real food or mistakenly chooses to uncover the pretender's bowl. The child must extrapolate based solely on behavior, as the content (real food or the absence of it) is not visible.

We began the study with 18-month-olds, expecting they would easily select the real eater, and we could begin to explore which of the set of pretend behaviors that we presented was most useful to children. However, 18-month-

[1] This paradigm was developed in discussions with Bekah Richert, Hannes Rakoczy, Tricia Striano, and Mike Tomasello at the Max Planck Institute in Leipzig. We are grateful for the hospitality and inspiration.

olds were at chance, as were 21-month-olds, and 24-month-olds, in selecting which person was really eating! This was very surprising, as it is completely obvious to adults, and even 5-year-olds succeed easily on the task. Finally at 30 months, we found reliably good performance in selecting the real eater, but only on the first of four trials, and when pointing to the pretender rather than uncovering the bowls. We have now conducted several experiments with this paradigm, and the finding has replicated repeatedly: not until 2½ years of age do children correctly infer that a person who is really eating is more likely to have real food than a person who is pretending to eat. And this they grasp only on the first trial; after the first trial, they revert to chance performance.

I believe the first trial finding suggests that it is an implicit understanding of pretense, and that after the issue is raised to an explicit level (by the first trial), the child is at sea, because the child does not know consciously what enabled him or her to identify pretense in the first place. This unconscious knowledge fuels behavior in the mother–child snack scenarios described earlier. In addition, in that earlier work, both pretense content and pretense behaviors were available to children. Young children do not seem to be able to assign pretense content based on behaviors alone. Children clearly know the pretender is silly, and sometimes they even say so during the procedure, but they seem to think that the pretend eating behavior is as likely to signify the presence of real food as real eating behavior is.

Another fascinating result in this study is that if one looks at implicit signs of knowing which one has real food, children appear to understand a full 6 months earlier: They smack their lips and swallow more when they are watching real eating (even though the pretend eater's eating movements are more exaggerated, so if children were mirroring behavior they would gesture in these ways more when observing the pretender), and they reach toward the bowl more often while watching the real eater than the pretend one. They seem to have the knowledge across trials but are unable to access it in response to an explicit question.

This raises the issue of what children are doing in the paradigms so cleverly used by Harris and Kavanaugh. We believe that further research should more carefully examine whether the children are really projecting pretend mental representations on to the elements, or whether they are merely following scripts, able to use the designated props as stand-ins but not appreciate that one is mentally projecting absent content on to props. Such research will help clarify how children construe pretend.

THE COGNITIVE REPRESENTATION OF PRETENSE

The work reviewed in this chapter so far indicates that there is an expanding base of knowledge about pretense in toddlerhood. However, we know very little about one deeply important and fascinating issue: How does one (adult or child) cognitively represent pretense? When one pretends, say, that a patty of mud is a pie, what is happening cognitively? The pretender must be representing "pie": he or she calls it "pie," serves it like pie, and stores it like pie. None of these behaviors is normally directed at mud, and it seems clear that the child pretender is acting based largely on his or her mental representation of pie. On the other hand, clearly the pretender also is representing the mud as "mud" because the child does not actually eat the mud! One possibility is that certain features of mud remain active in one's mind throughout the "mud = pie" episode, and certain features of pie (like "edible") must be at least partially inhibited. Some aspects of the "mud" representation appear to be inhibited as well, like its verbal label. How does a young child, absorbed in developing conceptual knowledge of the real world (Mandler, 2004), manage the cognitive feat of coordinating pretense and real representations of one and the same object? In addition, how (and how well) does the pretender keep the representational links established during the pretense scenario (such as that mud = pie) from interfering with real-world representations once the pretend episode is over (Leslie, 1987)? Having established that mud = pie for this moment, why isn't mud forever "pie" in the future? Is there some sense in which it is?

Extant models of pretending pay little heed to what happens to one's representations of what is real while one is engaged in pretense. Three important models are those of Harris (2000), Leslie (1987), and Nichols and Stich (2000). Others exist, but all are similarly vague about how what is real is represented while one pretends (Currie & Revenscroft, 2002; Perner, 1991), and thus they miss the important issue of how pretense and real representations are coordinated.

Models of How Pretense Representations Are Managed

Harris (2000) claims that when people pretend, they *suspend* processing of the real situation. "Children compose mental 'flags' or reminders, encoding information implied in the [pretend play] partner's various stipulations" (p. 22). Each "flag" is encoded with the note that the stipulation is in effect only for the pretend episode at hand. In Harris's model, real-world processing is simply suspended while one engages in the world of flagged stipulations. In contrast, I think the real situation and objects continue to be represented *at least in part*: They constrain some of the pretender's actions, among other things. However, many aspects of the real are inhibited, so they will not impinge on the pretense episode any more than is necessitated by such constraints. The degree to which some aspects are activated yet inhibited, versus simply not represented, is currently being tested in our laboratory with semantic priming methods described later.

In the second model, Leslie (1987) has argued that to represent pretense, a child represents a single proposition, like "Mother pretends [of the banana] 'it is a telephone.' " An "expression raiser" decouples and raises the telephone representation from its usual referent (real telephones) and applies it to the substitute object (a banana). The real representation ("telephone") is "quarantined" or kept separate during this exercise, so pretending has no effect on real-world representation; telephones and bananas will not be confused in the future. In Leslie's model, like that of Harris, the real is apparently irrelevant during pretense.

Nichols and Stich (2000), authors of the third model, argue for the existence of a metaphorical "possible world box" in the human mind, in which people can process pretend representations and engage in hypothetical reasoning. This "box" is part of the architecture of the human mind, along with a "desire box" and a "belief box." Pretense representations, by their claim, are isomorphic to belief representations but simply occur in a different mental "box." Representations in this pretend mental space are handled and updated just as they would be if they were representations of the real, but they are quarantined from the real, just as they are in Leslie's model. Nichols and Stich make this claim in part because the contents of pretense representations are often the same as the contents of real representations. For example, in a tea party scenario, a child might represent a cup as empty or full, just as one might in the real world. They also note that pretense representations are updated by the same inferential processes by which beliefs are updated, so if the pretend cup turns over, one represents its contents as having spilled—even if the cup were *really* empty to begin with. What they say distinguishes pretense from belief (and desire) is the function of the pretense representation—although they are vague about what this function is. As in the other models, these theorists are silent on the issue of how pretense and real representations are coordinated during pretense, opting to focus entirely on the pretense as though the real scenario onto which the pretense is projected were immaterial.

An Inhibition/Activation Model

I believe that during pretense, overall there is inhibition of the real objects and scenarios and activation of the pretend ones. Although real and pretense representations must to some degree be quarantined, there is also some crosstalk. Furthermore, some aspects of one's representation of what is real are still active during pretense, and some aspects of what is pretend are inhibited.

By "representation," I mean at some level the collection of neurons or nodes that fire to create a mental enactment of an object or event. Given our current knowledge and crude measurement abilities, this has to be viewed as a metaphor for representation, but it is a metaphor that is consistent with our knowledge of brain function and it is useful to guiding research. The use of "representation" in this model aligns with spreading-activation theories of memory (Collins & Loftus, 1975; McNamara & Holbrook, 2003; Plaut & Booth, 2000) and distributed network models of concept representation (McClelland & Rogers, 2003; McClelland & Rumelhart, 1985). In these approaches, when one considers a pencil, a collection of neurons or nodes is activated that together bear on pencils as one knows them: their color, what they feel like to hold, their material, what one does with them, and so on. If one is using a pencil as if it were an airplane, one's representation of a pencil is activated (because one must perceive the pencil, in order to grasp the object in a appropriate manner, etc.), but a select subset of features subserving one's representation of pencils, although activated, is also inhibited (so one will not refer to it as a pencil, or begin to write with it while it is an airplane). Which aspects of one's pencil or real-object representation are activated probably varies across objects and pretense; developing a taxonomy of this is a worthy goal for research.

Regarding the pretend representation, I believe that much of the circuitry that represents "airplane" is activated during the pencil = airplane pretense. Many (but not all) of the actions and expectations indicated by the activated components of that representation are directed at the pencil. For example, the sound made by an airplane is activated, enabling me to render a similar sound. The fact that an airplane flies above the ground, rather than along tracks, is activated, making me fly the pencil up in the air. On the other hand, I am not looking at this airplane from afar and am not boarding it as I might a real airplane; instead, I am holding it between my fingers. Therefore, information about an airplane's *size* seems to be inhibited in this situation, with information about the *pencil's* size controlling my actions instead. The activated and inhibited features sum to a net effect of inhibition of the real and activation of the pretend when one engages in pretense, either by observing or by enacting pretense scenarios.

Jennifer Van Reet and I (2007) have conducted preliminary tests of this model using observation of filmed pretense or real episodes as treatments. Briefly, we have presented a film of someone pretending various objects are other objects to undergraduates, in effect priming their semantic representations (McNamara & Holbrook, 2003). After viewing the film, participants engaged in a lexical decision task, viewing words and deciding whether each word was related to real or pretend objects in the films, or control items not featured in the films. It is well established that people are faster to make lexical decisions (like whether something is a word) about primed concepts (McNamara & Holbrook, 2003). Thus the speed with which participants make lexical decisions about the real and pretend objects, relative to control items, can provide information about the activation and inhibition of pretend and real concepts. Faster decision times (relative to controls) would reflect activated representations (or aspects of them) and slower times would reflect inhibited representations.

For example, if one of the object substitutions viewed in the film were that a banana is a telephone (the actor pretended to make a telephone call with a banana) then those who viewed the pretend film one would see slower reaction times to banana-related words than to telephone-related words, whereas people who had not viewed the pretend films showed the opposite pattern similar reaction times to both kinds of words. However, this is not what we have found. Instead, real and pretend are equally activated. One possibility is that the real object was inhibited during pretense, but a "White Bear" (Wegner, 1989, 2002) effect is leading to its activation at test. Another possibility is that real objects are also activated and not inhibited during pretense. Further research is needed to resolve this issue.

The Cognitive Representation of Pretending and Development

As stated earlier, pretending emerges between 12 and 24 months of age, and from 2 to 3 years it becomes well established (Haight & Miller, 1993). According to my activation-inhibition model of pretend, very young children have two limitations that are responsible for pretense not emerging earlier. One difficulty is activating the pretense representation in the absence of some real perceived stimulator. In fact, young children's first pretending is often with real or real-looking objects, like a miniature teacup to simulate a tea party pretense, or a spoon to simulate feeding a toy duck. In one study, 3-year-olds were able to pretend a ball was a comb, but few 2-year-olds could do so (Elder & Pederson, 1978); younger children need objects that are more similar in function and appearance to serve as substitutes. Other evidence for an early deficit in mental activation of absent stimuli was also presented earlier: young children are greatly assisted in pretense by adults who work to create pretense scenarios in contexts of joint attention, and children's earliest pretend scripts are ones that are well rehearsed in real life and thereby easier to conjure up. The development of pretending therefore appears to be led by factors that aid in activating mental representations.

Besides requiring activation of a representation of an absent stimulus, pretending requires inhibition of a representation of a present stimulus. This is the second difficulty. It is well established that very young children are lacking in inhibitory control. For example, children between about 8 and 12 months of age fail the Piagetian A-Not-B Object Permanence task: When an object has been repeatedly hidden at A, and then is moved to B, young children persist in searching for it at A. Diamond (2001) has provided strong evidence that maturation of inhibitory control is responsible for their eventual ability to pass this task: They must inhibit the prepotent response of repeating the previously successful motion (of searching at A) and opt instead to search at B. Inhibitory control increases rapidly from 2 to 3 years of age (Kochanska, Murray, & Harlan, 2000), and its development in individual children is correlated with their proficiency in pretense across this same age range (Carlson, Mandell, & Williams, 2004). Two-year-olds' ability to accept and use a substitute object, obliquely presented as part of a pretend script, was correlated with three tests of executive function: a modified A-not-B search task, a shape Stroop task, and a test of delayed gratification (Carlson et al., 2004). At age 3, these same children's ability to name the real and pretend identity of several substitute objects was also related to several measures of executive function. These results also support the hypothesis that pretending involves inhibitory control, perhaps of real-world representations and related actions.

According to the model, pretending begins to flourish around age 3 in part because of increases in inhibitory control (thus the correlation detected by Carlson and her colleagues would be causal). This increase also permits children to pretend with more different objects. Pretending also begins to flourish at this age because children become more able to call alternatives to mind in the absence of structural support, to activate and let run representations of realities. Ongoing work in our laboratory is directed at these issues.

SUMMARY

Pretending is an important development in young children, linked to developing symbolic understanding. It is a uniquely human activity, and a human universal. Research on pretense is active, with many important questions and issues remaining to be resolved.

In this chapter I reviewed research on the predictable developmental timetable or pretend play and discussed its relationship to theory of mind. Initially researchers saw the connection as being due to pretending requiring appreciation of others' mental representations. Although there is still some controversy about this, a good deal of research suggests that in ordinary situations of life, most 4-year-olds, most of the time, do not see pretense as involving mental representations of the pretense reality; they instead construe it as action. However, 3-year-olds seem to understand that pretending is done on purpose, and that pretenders have intentions. This parallels the cognitive-connections-to-mental-representations pattern that has been discussed for belief–desire psychology (Flavell, 1988).

Lillard (2001) laid out other potential reasons for the link between theory of mind and pretend play in children. In particular, the Twin Earth model posed sensitivity to social signals in pretend as also contributing to the development of theory of mind. In several studies we have shown that parents do behave in particular ways when they pretend, but only a subset of those ways actually encourages young children to smile at and begin to participate in pretense episodes—behaviors that we consider indicative of understanding pretense. Those parent behaviors are smiling, particularly right after their own behaviors (social referencing smiles) and looking intently at the child. Several laboratories have converged on noting the joint attention connection for pretense, and joint attention is thought to be an important theory of mind precursor (Wellman, 1993). Social referencing is also thought to be a building block of theory of mind.

An issue that arises is the extent to which children use such social signals to construe the pretend world. A surprising set of results in our laboratory suggests that children decipher pretense in strangers rather late, when the pretense is presented only as behavior, not supported by content. The cues of pretense are very obvious even to 5-year-olds, but younger children, although implicitly aware of the pretend–real distinction, are quite a bit weaker when it comes to making an explicit judgment about who has pretend food. This research in conjunction with the research on how parents signal pretense raises many interesting issues for further research. Harris and Kavanaugh's (1993) line of studies can be seen as the base of this: What do children understand about pretense and when? Added to this by our later work is the question of why: How do parents' and others' behaviors and pretense content or its absence interact to facilitate knowledge about pretense in the toddler years? In addition, the issue of understanding at an implicit versus an explicit level should be explored. This same distinction has been raised with the pretend–mental representation issues discussed earlier. Perhaps children's appreciation of intention in pretense appears to be earlier than their understanding of mental representation in part because the methods employed have tapped different levels of knowing.

Another interesting point of connection between theory of mind and pretend play is over the supposed decoupling mechanism that allows children to think of one object as not playing its usual role but playing some other one instead. In mature pretense, it plays this role as a symbol for that other object. Leslie (1987) pointed out that this seems structurally analogous to thinking of one person's mental representation of a situation as different from one's own. Currently, research in my laboratory is examining how pretend and real representations are negotiated across development, with a going theory being that in pretense, several aspects of the real are inhibited, while others are activated. Little research to date has addressed this issue, but it is central to how the human brain can manage pretend play. Toddlers are just learning about the real world but somehow manage to cast it aside to engage in unreal exploits. Exactly how they manage to do this should be a productive area of research in the coming years.

REFERENCES

Adamson, L. B., Bakeman, R., & Deckner, D. F. (2004). The development of symbol-infused joint engagement. *Child Development, 75*(4), 1171–1187.

American Psychiatric Association. (2000). *Diagnostic and statistical manual of mental disorders* (4th ed., text rev.). Washington, DC: Author.

Astington, J. W., & Jenkins, J. M. (1995). Theory of mind development and social understanding. *Cognition and Emotion, 9*, 151–165.

Baird, G., Charman, T., Baron-Cohen, S., Cox, A., Swettenham, J., Wheelwright, S., et al. (2000). A screening instrument for autism at 18 months of age: A 6-year follow-up study. *Journal of the American Academy of Child and Adolescent Psychiatry, 39*(6), 694–702.

Baron-Cohen, S. (1987). Autism and symbolic play. *British Journal of Developmental Psychology, 5*, 139–148.

Bartsch, K., & Wellman, H. M. (1995). *Children talk about the mind.* Oxford, UK: Oxford University Press.

Bates, E. (1979). *The emergence of symbols: Cognition and communication in infancy.* New York: Academic Press.

Bateson, G. A. (1972). A theory of play and fantasy. In G. A. Bateson (Ed.), *Steps to an ecology of mind* (pp. 177–193). New York: Chandler.

Bekoff, M. (1999). Social cognition: Exchanging and sharing information on the run. *Evolution and Cognition, 5*, 128–136.

Bigelow, A. E., MacLean, K., & Proctor, J. (2004). The role of joint attention in the development of infants' play with objects. *Developmental Science, 7*(5), 518–526.

Bretherton, I., & Beeghly, M. (1982). Talking about internal states: The acquisition of an explicit theory of mind. *Developmental Psychology, 18*, 906–921.

Breuggeman, J. A. (1973). Parental care in a group of free-ranging rhesus monkeys (Macaca mulatto). *Folia Primatologica, 20*, 196.

Brown, D. (1991). *Human universals.* New York: McGraw-Hill.

Byrne, R. (2005). *The rational imagination: How people create alternatives to reality.* Cambridge, MA: MIT Press.

Byrne, R. M. J. (2002). Mental models and counterfacutal thoughts about what might have been. *Trends in Cognitive Sciences, 6*(10), 426–431.

Byrne, R. W., & Whiten, A. (1991). Computation and mindreading in primate tactical deception. In A. Whiten (Ed.), *Natural theories of mind* (pp. 127–141). Oxford, UK: Basil Blackwell.

Carlson, S. M., Mandell, D. J., & Williams, L. (2004). Executive function and theory of mind: stability and prediction from ages 2 to 3. *Developmental Psychology, 40*(6), 1105–1122.

Carlson, S. M., Taylor, M., & Levin, G. (1998). The influence of culture on pretend play: The case of Mennonite children. *Merrill–Palmer Quarterly, 44*, 538–565.

Collins, A. M., & Loftus, E. F. (1975). A spreading-activation theory of semantic processing. *Psychological Review, 82*(6), 407–428.

Currie, G., & Revenscroft, I. (2002). *Recreative minds.* Oxford, UK: Oxford University Press.

Danziger, E. (1999). *To play a speaking part.* Unpublished manuscript, University of Virginia.

DeLoache, J. S. (1991). Symbolic functioning in very young children: Understanding of pictures and models. *Child Development, 62*, 736–752.

DeLoache, J. S., & Plaetzer, B. (1985). *Tea for two: Joint mother–child symbolic play.* Paper presented at the bienniel meeting for the Society for Research in Child Development, Toronto.

Diamond, A. (2001). A model system for studying the role of dopamine in prefrontal cortex during early development in humans. In C. Nelson & M. Luciana (Eds.), *Handbook of developmental cognitive neuroscience* (pp. 433–472). Cambridge, MA: MIT Press.

Dias, M. G., & Harris, P. L. (1988). The effect of make-believe play on deductive reasoning. *British Journal of Developmental Psychology, 6*, 207–221.

Dias, M. G., & Harris, P. L. (1990). The influence of the imagination on reasoning by young children. *British Journal of Developmental Psychology, 8*, 305–318.

Dunn, J., & Dale, N. (1984). I a daddy: 2-year-olds collaboration in joint pretend play with sibling and with mother. In I. Bretherton (Ed.), *Symbolic play* (pp. 131–158). London: Academic Press.

Eibl-Eibesfeldt, I. (1989). *Human ethology.* New York: Aldine de Gruyter.

Elder, J. L., & Pederson, D. R. (1978). Preschool children's use of objects in symbolic play. *Child Development, 49*, 500–504.

Farver, J. (1992). An analysis of young Mexican and American children's play dialogues. In C. Howes, O. A. Unger, & C. C. Matheson (Eds.), *The collaborative construction of pretend: Social pretend play functions* (pp. 55–66). Albany: State University of New York Press.

Farver, J. A., & Wimbarti, S. (1995). Indonesian children's play with their mothers and older siblings. *Child Development, 66*, 1493–1503.

Farver, J. A. M., & Shin, Y. L. (1997). Social pretend play in Korean- and Anglo-American preschoolers. *Child Development, 68*, 544–556.

Fein, G. G. (1975). A transformational analysis of pretending. *Developmental Psychology, 11*, 291–296.

Fein, G. G. (1981). Pretend play in childhood: An integrative review. *Child Development, 52*, 1095–1118.

Fein, G. G., & Fryer, M. G. (1995). Maternal contributions to early symbolic play competence. *Developmental Review, 15*, 367–381.

Fenson, L., Kagan, J., Kearsley, R. B., & Zelazo, P. R. (1976). The developmental progression of manipulative play in the first two years. *Child Development, 47*, 232–236.

Flavell, J. H. (1988). The development of children's knowledge about the mind: From cognitive connections to mental representations. In J. W. Astington, P. L. Harris, & D. R. Olson (Eds.), *Developing theories of mind* (pp. 244–271). Cambridge, UK: Cambridge University Press.

Flavell, J. H., Flavell, E. R., & Green, F. L. (1987). Young children's knowledge about the apparent-real and pretend-real distinctions. *Developmental Psychology, 23*, 816–822.

Forguson, L., & Gopnik, A. (1988). The ontogeny of common sense. In J. W. Astington, P. L. Harris, & D. R. Olson (Eds.), *Developing theories of mind* (pp. 226–243). Cambridge, UK: Cambridge University Press.

Gardner, D., Harris, P. L., Ohmoto, M., & Hamazaki, T. (1988). Japanese children's understanding of the distinction between real and apparent emotion. *International Journal of Behavioral Development, 11*, 203–218.

Goncu, A., Mistry, J., & Mosier, C. (2000). Cultural variations in the play of toddlers. *International Journal of Behavioral Development, 24*(3), 321–329.

Gottfried, G. M., Hickling, A. K., Totten, L. R., Mkroyan, A., & Reisz, A. (2003). To be or not to be a galaprock: Preschoolers' intuitions about the importance of knowledge and action for pretending. *British Journal of Developmental Psychology, 21*(3), 397–414.

Haight, W., & Miller, P. J. (1992). The development of everyday pretend play: A longitudinal study of mothers' participation. *Merrill–Palmer Quarterly, 38*(3), 331–349.

Haight, W. L., & Miller, P. J. (1993). *Pretending at home*. Albany: State University of New York Press.

Haight, W. L., Wang, X.-L., Fung, H. H.-T., Williams, K., & Mintz, J. (1999). Universal, developmental, and variable aspects of young children's play: A cross-cultural comparison of pretending at home. *Child Development, 70*(6), 1477–1488.

Hall, W. S., Frank, R., & Ellison, C. (1995). The development of pretend language: Toward an understanding of the child's theory of mind. *Journal of Psycholinguistic Research, 24*, 231–254.

Harris, P. L. (2000). *The work of the imagination*. Oxford, UK: Blackwell.

Harris, P. L., & Kavanaugh, R. D. (1993). Young children's understanding of pretense. *Monographs of the Society for Research in Child Development, 58*(1, Serial No. 231).

Harris, P. L., Lillard, A., & Perner, J. (1994). Commentary: Triangulating pretence and belief. In C. Lewis & P. Mitchell (Eds.), *Children's early understanding of mind: Origins and development* (pp. 287–293). Hillsdale, NJ: Erlbaum.

Hawkins, J., Pea, R. D., Glick, J., & Scribner, S. (1984). Merds that don't like mushrooms: Evidence for deductive reasoning by preschoolers. *Developmental Psychology, 20*, 584–589.

Hickling, A., Wellman, H. M., & Gottfried, G. M. (1997). Preschoolers' understanding of others' mental attitudes toward pretend happenings. *British Journal of Developmental Psychology, 15*, 339–354.

Jackowitz, E. R., & Watson, M. W. (1980). The development of object transformations in early pretend play. *Developmental Psychology, 16*, 543–549.

Jarrold, C., Boucher, J., & Smith, P. (1996). Generativity deficits in pretend play in autism. *British Journal of Developmental Psychology, 14*, 275–300.

Johnson-Laird, P. N. (1983). *Mental models*. Cambridge, MA: Havard University Press.

Joseph, R. M. (1998). Intention and knowledge in preschoolers' conception of pretend. *Child Development, 69*, 979–990.

Kagan, J., Kearsley, R. B., & Zelazo, P. R. (1978). *Infancy: Its place in human development*. Cambridge, MA: Harvard University Press.

Kanner, L. (1943). Autistic disturbances of affective contact. *Nervous Child, 2*, 217–250.

Kavanaugh, R., & Lillard, A. S. (2007). [Longitudinal study of symbolism]. Unpublished raw data, Williams College.

Kochanska, G., Murray, K. T., & Harlan, E. T. (2000). Effortful control in early childhood: Continuity and change, antecedents, and implications for social development. *Developmental Psychology, 36*(2), 220–232.

Kuczaj, S. A. (1981). Factors influencing children's hypothetical reference. *Journal of Child Language, 8*, 131–137.

Lalonde, C. E., & Chandler, M. J. (1995). False belief understanding goes to school: On the social-emotional consequences of coming early or late to a first theory of mind. *Cognition and Emotion, 9*, 167–185.

Leslie, A. M. (1987). Pretense and representation: The origins of "theory of mind." *Psychological Review, 94*, 412–426.

Lewis, V., Norgate, S., Collis, G., & Reynolds, R. (2000). The consequences of visual impairment for children's symbolic and functional play. *British Journal of Developmental Psychology, 18*(3), 449–464.

Li, A. K. (1985). Toward more elaborate pretend play. *Mental Retardation, 23*(3), 131–136.

Lillard, A. S. (1993a). Pretend play skills and the child's theory of mind. *Child Development, 64*, 348–371.

Lillard, A. S. (1993b). Young children's conceptualization of pretense: Action or mental representational state? *Child Development, 64*, 372–386.

Lillard, A. S. (1996). Body or mind: Children's categorizing of pretense. *Child Development, 67*, 1717–1734.

Lillard, A. S. (1998a). Playing with a theory of mind. In O. N. Saracho & B. Spodek (Eds.), *Multiple perspectives on play in early childhood education* (pp. 11–33). Albany: State University of New York Press.

Lillard, A. S. (1998b). Wanting to be it: Children's understanding of intentions underlying pretense. *Child Development, 69*, 979–991.

Lillard, A. S. (2001). Pretend play as Twin Earth. *Developmental Review, 21*, 1–33.

Lillard, A. S. (2002). Just through the looking glass: Children's understanding of pretense. In R. Mitchell (Ed.), *Pretending in animals and children* (pp. 102–114). Cambridge, UK: Cambridge University Press.

Lillard, A. S. (2004). Discriminating real and pretend snacks: A fundamental problem in early social cognition. *Developmental Psychology Forum of the British Psychological Society, 62*, 9–17.

Lillard, A. S., & Flavell, J. H. (1992). Young children's understanding of different mental states. *Developmental Psychology, 28*, 626–634.

Lillard, A. S., Nishida, T., Massaro, D., Vaish, A., Ma, L., & McRoberts, J. (2007). Signs of pretense across age and scenario. *Infancy, 11*(1), 1–30.

Lillard, A. S., & Witherington, D. (2004). Mothers' behavior modifications during pretense snacks and their possible signal value for toddlers. *Developmental Psychology, 40*(1), 95–113.

Lloyd, B., & Goodwin, R. (1995). Let's pretend: Casting the characters and setting the scene. *British Journal of Developmental Psychology, 13*, 261–270.

Lucariello, J. (1987). Spinning fantasy: Themes, structures, and the knowledge base. *Child Development, 58*, 434–442.

Ma, L., & Lillard, A. S. (2006). Where is the real cheese?: Young children's understanding of pretense. *Child Development, 77*(6), 1762–1777.

Ma, L., & Lillard, A. S. (2007). *Naive theories that guide pretense interpretations*. Manuscript submitted for publication.

MacWhinney, B. (1990). *The childes project: Computational tools for analyzing talk* (Vol. 12). Philadelphia: Carnegie Mellon University Press.

Mandler, J. M. (2004). *Foundations of mind: Origins of conceptual thought*. New York: Oxford University Press.

Marjanovic-Shane, A. (1989). "You are a pig": For real or just pretend? Different orientations in play and metaphor. *Play and Culture, 2*, 225–234.

McClelland, J. L., & Rogers, T. T. (2003). The parallel distributed processing approach to semantic cognition. *Nature Reviews Neuroscience, 4*(4), 310–322.

McClelland, J. L., & Rumelhart, D. E. (1985). Distributed memory and the representation of general and specific information. *Journal of Experimental Psychology: General, 114*(2), 159–188.

McCune, L. (1995). A normative study of representational play in the transition to language. *Developmental Psychology, 31*(2), 198–206.

McNamara, T. P., & Holbrook, J. B. (2003). Semantic memory and priming. In A. F. Healy & R. W. Proctor (Eds.), *Handbook of psychology: Experimental psychology* (Vol. 4, pp. 447–474). New York: Wiley.

Miller, P., & Garvey, C. (1984). Mother–baby role play: Its origins in social support. In I. Bretherton (Ed.), *Symbolic play* (pp. 101–158). London: Academic Press.

Mitchell, R. W. (Ed.). (2002). *Pretending and imagination in animals and children.* Cambridge, UK: Cambridge University Press.

Mitchell, R. W., & Neal, M. R. (2005). Children's understanding of their own and others' mental states. Part A. Self-understanding precedes understanding of others in pretense. *British Journal of Developmental Psychology, 23*, 175–200.

Moses, L. J., & Chandler, M. J. (1992). Traveler's guide to children's theories of mind. *Psychological Inquiry, 3*, 286–301.

Musatti, T., Veneziano, E., & Mayer, S. (1998). Contributions of language to early pretend play. *Cahiers de Psychologie Cognitive, 17*(2), 155–184.

Nelson, K., & Seidman, S. (1984). Playing with scripts. In I. Bretherton (Ed.), *Symbolic play* (pp. 45–72). London: Academic Press.

Nichols, S., & Stich, S. (2000). A cognitive theory of pretense. *Cognition*, *74*, 115–147.

Nicolich, L. M. (1977). Beyond sensorimotor intelligence: Assessment of symbolic maturity through analysis of pretend play. *Merrill–Palmer Quarterly, 23*, 89–99.

Nishida, T., & Lillard, A. S. (2007). The informative value of emotional expressions: Social referencing behavior in mother–infant pretense. *Developmental Science, 10*(2), 205–212.

O'Connell, B., & Bretherton, I. (1984). Toddler's play, alone and with mother: the role of maternal guidance. In I. Bretherton (Ed.), *Symbolic play* (pp. 337–368). London: Academic Press.

Opie, I., & Opie, P. (1969). *Children's games in street and playground.* Oxford, UK: Clarendon Press.

Parten, M. B. (1932). Social participation among preschool children. *Child Development, 27*, 243–269.

Parten, M. B. (1933). Social play among preschool children. *Journal of Abnormal and Social Psychology, 28*, 136–147.

Perner, J. (1991). *Understanding the representational mind.* Cambridge, MA: MIT Press.

Pessin, A., & Goldberg, S. (Eds.). (1996). *The Twin Earth chronicles.* London: M. E. Sharpe.

Piaget, J. (1962). *Play, dreams, and imitation in childhood* (G. Gattegno & F. M. Hodgson, Trans.). New York: Norton.

Pinkham, A., & Lillard, A. (2007). *Children's everyday use of the word "pretend."* Manuscript under review.

Plaut, D. C., & Booth, J. R. (2000). Individual and developmental differences in semantic priming: Empirical and computational support for a single-mechanism account of lexical processing. *Psychological Review, 107*(4), 786–823.

Rakoczy, H., Tomasello, M., & Striano, T. (2004). Young children know that trying is not pretending: A test of the "behaving as if" construcal of children's understanding of "pretense." *Developmental Psychology, 40*(3), 388–399.

Rakoczy, H., Tomasello, M., & Striano, T. (2005). *The role of experience and discourse in children's developing understanding of pretend play actions.* Unpublished manuscript, Max Planck Institute for Cognition and Culture, Liepzig, Germany.

Richert, R., & Lillard, A. S. (2004). Observers' proficiency at identifying pretense acts based on behavioral cues. *Cognitive Development, 19*, 223–240.

Roopnarine, J. L., Johnson, J. E., & Hooper, F. H. (Eds.). (1994). *Children's play in diverse cultures.* Albany: State University of New York Press.

Rubin, K. H. (1980). Fantasy play: Its role in the development of social skills and social cognition. In K. H. Rubin (Ed.), *Children's play: New directions for child development* (Vol. 9, pp. 69–84). San Francisco: Jossey-Bass.

Rubin, K. H., Fein, G. G., & Vandenberg, B. (1983). Play. In E. M. Hetherington (Ed.), *Handbook of child psychology: Socialization, personality, and social development* (Vol. 4, 4th ed., pp. 693–774). New York: Wiley.

Schwartzman, H. B. (1978). *Transformations: The anthropology of children's play.* New York: Plenum Press.

Scott, F. J., Baron-Cohen, S., & Leslie, A. (1999). "If pigs could fly": A test of counterfactual reasoning and pretence in children with autism. *British Journal of Developmental Psychology, 17*, 349–362.

Shatz, M., Wellman, H. M., & Silber, S. (1983). The acquisition of mental verbs: A systematic investigation of the first reference to mental states. *Cognition, 14*, 301–321.

Smolucha, L., & Smolucha, F. (1998). The social origins of mind: Post-Piagetian perspectives on pretend play. In O. N. Saracho & S. Bernard (Eds.), *Multiple perspectives on play in early childhood education* (pp. 34–58). Albany: State University of New York Press.

Sobel, D., & Lillard, A. S. (2001). The impact of fantasy and action on young children's understanding of pretense. *British Journal of Developmental Psychology, 19*, 85–98.

Sorenson, L., & Lillard, A. S. (2007). *Pretending in middle childhood.* Unpublished manuscript, University of Virginia.

Spencer, P. E. (1996). The association between language and symbolic play at two years: Evidence from deaf toddlers. *Child Development, 67*(3), 867–876.

Sutton-Smith, B. (1983). Piaget, play, and cognition, revisited. In W. F. Overton (Ed.), *The relationship between social and cognitive development* (pp. 229–250). Hillsdale, NJ: Erlbaum.

Sutton-Smith, B. (1997). *The ambiguity of play.* Cambridge, MA: Harvard University Press.

Tamis-LeMonda, C., & Bornstein, M. (1994). Specificity in mother-toddler language-play relations across the second year. *Developmental Psychology, 30*, 283–292.

Taylor, M. (1999). *Imaginary companions and the children who create them.* Oxford, UK: Oxford University Press.

Taylor, M., & Carlson, S. M. (1997). The relation between individual differences in fantasy and theory of mind. *Child Development, 68*, 436–455.

Taylor, M., & Carlson, S. (2000). The influence of religious beliefs on parent's attitudes about children's fantasy behavior. In K. S. Rosengren, C. N. Johnson, & P. L. Harris (Eds.), *Imagining the impossible: Magical, scientific, and religious thinking in children* (pp. 247–268). Cambridge, UK: Cambridge University Press.

Taylor, M., Carlson, S. M., Maring, B. L., Gerow, L., & Charley, C. M. (2004). The characteristics and correlates of fantasy in school-age children: Imaginary companions, impersonation, and social understanding. *Developmental Psychology, 40*(6), 1173–1187.

Taylor, M., Lussier, G. L., & Maring, B. L. (2003). The distinction between lying and pretending. *Journal of Cognition and Development, 4*(3), 299–323.

Tomasello, M., & Call, J. (1997). *Primate cognition.* New York: Oxford University Press.

Tomasello, M., & Rakoczy, H. (2003). What makes human cognition unique? From individual to shared to collective intentionality. *Mind and Language, 18*(2), 121–147.

Ungerer, J., Zelazo, P. R., Kearsley, R. B., & O'Leary, K. (1981). Developmental changes in the representation of objects in symbolic play from 18 to 34 months of age. *Child Development, 52*, 186–195.

Van Reet, J., & Lillard, A. S. (2007, March). *The inhibition/activation theory of pretense representation.* Paper presented at the biennial meeting of the Society for Research in Child Development, Boston.

Vygotsky, L. S. (1978). *Mind in society.* Cambridge, MA: Harvard University Press.

Walker-Andrews, A., & Harris, P. (1993). Young children's comprehension of pretend causal sequences. *Developmental Psychology, 29*, 915–921.

Walker-Andrews, A., & Kahana-Kalman, R. (1999). The understanding of pretense across the second year of life. *British Journal of Developmental Psychology, 17*, 523–536.

Walton, K. L. (1990). *Mimesis as make-believe*. Cambridge, MA: Harvard University Press.

Watson, M. W., & Fischer, K. W. (1977). A developmental sequence of agent use in late infancy. *Child Development, 48*, 828–836.

Wegner, D. M. (1989). *White bears and other unwanted thoughts: Suppression, obsession, and the psychology of mental control*. New York: Viking.

Wegner, D. M. (2002). *The illusion of conscious will*. Cambridge, MA: MIT Press.

Wellman, H. M. (1990). *The child's theory of mind*. Cambridge, MA: Bradford Books/MIT Press.

Wellman, H. M. (1993). Early understanding of mind: The normal case. In S. Baron-Cohen, H. Tager-Flusberg, & D. Cohen (Eds.), *Understanding other minds: Perspectives from autism* (pp. 21–49). Oxford, UK: Oxford University Press.

Werner, H., & Kaplan, B. (1963). *Symbol formation*. New York: Wiley.

Wolf, D. (1982). Understanding others: A longitudinal case study of the concept of independent agency. In G. E. Forman (Ed.), *Action and thought* (pp. 297–327). New York: Academic Press.

Wolf, D. P., Rygh, J., & Altshuler, J. (1984). Agency and experience: Actions and states in play narratives. In I. Bretherton (Ed.), *Symbolic play* (pp. 195–218). Cambridge, MA: Academic Press.

Youngblade, L. M., & Dunn, J. (1995). Individual differences in young children's pretend play with mother and sibling: Links to relationships and understanding of other people's feelings and beliefs. *Child Development, 66*, 1472–1492.

7

Children's Relationships with Other Children

CLAIRE HUGHES
JUDY DUNN

Children's relationships with other children have attracted a surge of research interest over the past 25 years; much of this work has already received scholarly reviews (e.g., Dunn & McGuire, 1992; Rubin, Hastings, Stewart, Henderson, & Chen, 1997). As these reviews note, a key source of interest in this field is the special significance child–child relationships hold for social, cognitive, and moral development. That is, children's interactions with peers and sibs are increasingly recognized as contexts in which children make intellectual advances and which provide windows on (1) children's understanding of themselves and others and (2) the nature of children's relationships. Despite the progress made on each of these fronts, a few striking gaps remain in the field. This chapter addresses two such neglected areas: child–child relationships in very young children and the relationship between individual differences in the quality of children's interactions with peers and with siblings. We begin with the premise that very young children have meaningful relationships with other children (familiar and unfamiliar), which illuminate the nature of their social understanding and may contribute to their development in this domain and are therefore worthy of study. Next we review the literature on developmental change and individual differences in sibling relationships and note that much less is known about the links between these aspects of sibling relationships and children's early peer relationships. In the final section of this chapter we return to the themes arising from this review in relation to recent findings from an ongoing study with a socially diverse British sample of 2-year-olds.

As a background to this consideration of child–child relationships during the toddler and preschool years, it is important to recognize the increasing powers of children's communication and of their understanding of other people over this period, which transform their relationships in key ways (Dunn, 1993). Shared pretend, for instance is a core feature of early friendships, as Gottman (1983) pointed out, and this clearly depends on the cognitive changes of the second year. These new powers of understanding do not mean, however, that their relationships necessarily become more harmonious. Longitudinal research has shown, for example, that between 33 and 47 months, children became more likely to use reasoned argument when in conflict with their mothers and siblings, but these powers of argument were *less* likely to be used for conciliatory purposes and more likely to be used toward gaining their own immediate goals. The children did not use their developing social-cognitive skills toward increasing harmony in their relationships with mother or sibling. Rather, as they became more cognitively sophisticated they chiefly applied their skills in argument for their own self-interest, with their family worlds in which competing self-interests were common (Tesla & Dunn, 1992). These results support the hypothesis that young children's developing autonomy during the toddler and preschool years is often expressed through their refusal of parental requests and their increased use of reasoning to defend their own needs and desires (Kochanska, Kuczynski, & Radke-Yarrow, 1989). It is worth noting too that both mothers and siblings also became less likely to compromise or conciliate with children over this period. The complexity of relations between cognitive milestones and social harmony is also apparent in more recent work involving pairs of familiar 18- to 24-month olds followed up over a year (Hay, 2006). Specifically, frequent use of possessive pronouns (e.g., saying "mine") was associated concurrently with elevated levels of aggression, but predicted elevated rates of sharing and prosocial behavior at later time points.

The foregoing findings have clear implications for our understanding of early development in social skills. In particular, they make clear that cognitive milestones in children's social understanding are affectively neutral—how children apply their social understanding will depend on both the identity and the quality of the relationship in question. For example, while children have a clear motivation to sustain harmonious interactions with friends, this motivation does not necessarily exist in their relationships with siblings. As a result, siblings provide a particularly interesting context for examining children's social behavior. More generally, individual differences in social understanding may relate to children's social skills in quite different ways across distinct relationships. For example, in a study of 4-year-olds observed interacting with mothers, siblings, and friends, false-belief performance showed significant correlations with the use of (1) more advanced strategies in conflict situations and (2) shared pretend play in all three relationships. Nevertheless, these social measures showed no correlations across relationships. The frequency of shared pretend with siblings, for instance, was not correlated with the frequency of shared pretend with mothers. Similarly, no significant correlations across relationships were found for the frequency with which children took into account the other person's perspective in conflict, and for the frequency of causal conversations. We return to this issue later in the chapter in our discussion of recent findings from 2-year-olds.

EARLY CHILD–CHILD RELATIONSHIPS

Detailed observational accounts of friendships between very young children extend back more than 50 years. For example, Dorothy Burlingham and Anna Freud, both psychoanalysts, documented close friendships in the second year of life between children attending a residential nursery in Hampstead for children made homeless, destitute, or orphaned in World War II. They comment: "We observe many instances of friendship among infants which lasts days, weeks, or even months. Playmates are certainly not chosen indiscriminately; in playing together the partners often seem no less important than the game" (Burlingham & Freud, 1944, p. 41). Despite this early evidence to the contrary, psychologists have traditionally resisted the idea that very young children are capable of forming friendships. Three separate axes are pivotal for this skeptical view.

The first is that the foregoing observations derive from an atypical group and so cannot be extrapolated to ordinary children. Indeed, Anna Freud attributed the attachments found between these very young children to their unusual experiences in the war, without their families. Within ordinary families, she suggested, relationships with other children develop "only after the child–mother relationship has been firmly established" (p. 41). This principle of monotropism (in which attachments to the primary caregiver precede and exceed other attachments) is central to orthodox attachment theory but has been challenged by robust evidence that from a very early age, infants form multiple secure attachments, for example, to fathers (Lamb, 1982; Schaffer & Emerson, 1964) and siblings (Stewart, 1983). Finally, recent work by Lynne Jones (2004) on children growing up in wartime Bosnia provides compelling evidence that exposure to potentially traumatic experiences of war rarely impedes healthy psychological development. Together, these points suggest that the close friendships between the residents of the Hampstead nursery were not extraordinary but rather demonstrate very young children's capacities for forming close relationships with other children.

The second axis derives from the influence of Mildred Parten's (1933) account of age-related increases in the frequency and complexity of peer interactions. She described children's social maturation in terms of the unfolding of six categories of social participation: unoccupied behavior, solitary play, onlooker behavior, parallel play, associative play, and cooperative play. From the age of 2 to 5 years, Parten concluded that children show steadily increasing frequencies of associative and cooperative play, coupled with steadily decreasing frequencies of unoccupied, solitary and onlooker behavior. The legacy of this very simple developmental account is that 3-year-olds have commonly been characterized as solitary or parallel players, while 5-year-olds are typically referred to as spending much of their time in associative or cooperative play. However, this view is simply not supported by evidence from other studies. For example, the frequency of parallel play appears to show *no* developmental change across this period (e.g., Howes & Matheson, 1992; Rubin, Watson, & Jambor, 1978) and in general it is the *form* that solitary or parallel or social activity takes that is developmentally significant (Rubin et al., 1978). The picture is also made more complex by findings that apparently simple forms of play can have relatively advanced *functions*. For example, parallel play can provide a smooth entry into cooperative play (Bakeman & Brownlee, 1980). The clear conclusion from these more recent studies is that Parton's classic and influential account of social development seriously underestimated the social interaction skills shown by very young children.

The third axis impeding recognition of early child–child relationships stems from the classical view—developed from the ideas of Piaget—that children under the age of 7 have real difficulty in understanding the feelings and perspectives of others. Over the past 25 years, however, this view has undergone radical change, as researchers have charted *when* and *what* children understand about others' thoughts, feelings, beliefs, and intentions, and how young children's understanding of why people behave the way they do develops. While most of this research has centered on improvements between the ages of 3 and 5 in children's understanding of mistaken beliefs, recent studies have begun to chart earlier milestones. For example 2-year-olds can recognize diverse desires (Wellman, Phillips, & Rodriguez, 2000) and are skilled in predicting the emotional consequences of simple events (Denham, McKinley, Couchoud, & Holt, 1990). Two-year-olds are also adept at distinguishing pretense from reality (Harris, 1991; Taylor, 1996).

Support for the sophistication of very young children's social understanding comes from the detailed observational work conducted independently by Carollee Howes (1988, 1996) and Hildy Ross (Ross, 1982; Ross & Lollis, 1989). In these studies 2-year-olds often cooperated with their friends, demonstrating both their understanding of their friends' intentions and their ability to share an imaginary world. These striking skills are likely to be as important for both the formation and the maintenance of early friendships. Howes's elegant longitudinal studies demonstrate that although friendships between toddlers are typically viewed as fleeting, in fact 50–70% of friendships were maintained from one year to the next (Howes, Hamilton, & Phillipsen, 1998). Similar patterns of stable friendships have been documented in our own studies of preschoolers (Dunn, 2004). At the same time it is worth noting that, as Ross and Lollis (1989) argue, the sophistication of young friends' interactions is an emergent property of their *relationship*; in their study individual children did not show similar behaviors toward peers in general.

Ross and colleagues have also demonstrated reciprocal patterns in *conflict*. Interestingly, the same social partners often elicit elevated rates of both conflict and friendly play (see Hartup, 1996, for similar findings among older children). That is, conflict often arises in the course of play between "fighting friends"; such conflict is typically less hostile and more likely to be resolved than conflict between nonfriends. Theoretically, these findings are consistent with recent rapprochements between Piagetian and Vygotskian perspectives on the links between peer interaction and cognitive development, which traditionally highlight peer conflict versus cooperation (respectively) as evoking change. More recent work with older children shows that these views can be reconciled: Conflicting ideas can stimulate cooperation (e.g., Damon & Killen, 1982; Doise & Mugny, 1984; Roy & Howe, 1990; Wertsch, 1984), especially between friends (e.g., Azmitia & Hesser, 1993). The finding that, in the context of friendship, very young children are able to resolve disagreements is further evidence of their striking social competence. If only adults were equally able and willing to "bury the hatchet" following disagreements!

In summary, the documentation of fledgling theory of mind skills in very young children has implications for how we should characterize developmental changes in social understanding and the factors likely to underlie change. Specifically, these early skills support a model of gradual development (rather the "watershed" model that characterized early research in this field). Empirical evidence from older children also points to developmental continuities. For example, a longitudinal study in London reports that the quality of preschool friendships predicts a variety of aspects of social understanding in the school years—including insights into friends and moral sensitivity. Moreover, the preschool friends' social-cognitive characteristics predicted unique variance in the children's later social understanding (Dunn, Cutting, & Fisher, 2002). From this we can conclude that individual differences are developmental stable across the transition to school, and that developmental trajectories are influenced by friends' characteristics from a very early age. Whether similar conclusions apply even earlier in development is a question for future research.

A second implication of the growing evidence that children can display a relatively sophisticated understanding of other minds even though they fail classical false-belief tasks (e.g., Newton, Reddy, & Bull, 2000) concerns the importance of the particular methods and contexts used to investigate early social understanding. Further more, relationship-specific findings and links between social understanding and relationship quality indicate that the development of social understanding is not solely a matter of cognitive maturation but also reflects participation in fruitful social interactions—for example, conversations about mental states, especially those that are relevant and connected to the child's interests, or those that have an elaborated form, or that include a discussion of causes (the interested reader is referred to a recent special issue on conversations and childhood—Hughes & de Rosnay, 2006).

SIBLING RELATIONSHIPS

Thus far, we have only discussed very young children's friendships and peer interactions. We turn now to early child–child relationships within the family: to the special case of sibling relationships. Several features make sibling relationships unique. These include their longevity and temporally dynamic nature; the inextricable link between parent–child and sibling relationships; the combination of horizontal and vertical elements that results in "diagonal" relationships between siblings; and, last but by no means least, the magnitude and complexity of individual differences in the quality of sibling relationships. For middle childhood and adolescence, the research on each of these features has been comprehensively reviewed elsewhere (see Dunn & McGuire, 1992). Here, we restrict our discussion to studies of sibling relationships that involve children in their first few years of life. Four key findings emerge from this research. First, the birth of a sibling can pose an enormous challenge to young children, with the constellation of changes to family life that accompany the new sibling's arrival. Second, the younger sibling's progression through developmental milestones drives developmental changes in the sibling relationship—for example, ignoring a younger sib becomes much harder once he or she can crawl and topple over one's toys—and the cognitive changes of the second year, which make possible the sharing of an imaginative world with another child make young siblings dramatically more rewarding companions for their older siblings (Dunn, 1988). Third, maternal differential treatment is associated with increased conflict between siblings. Fourth, destructive sibling conflict predicts later conduct problems, but only for young children who also experience difficult relationships with their caregivers. We review each of these findings briefly, in turn.

Recognition of the impact of a sibling's arrival is relatively recent, leading to marked changes in parental practices: Examples include the recent abundance of picture books designed to help children understand and accept the changes to family life that a new baby brings and the new custom of inviting friends to send presents to the older child as well as to the new baby. Despite these positive changes, the arrival of a new baby in the family is often a time of emotional upheaval that can jeopardize the security of children's attachment to caregivers (Teti, Sakin, Kucera, Corns, & Eiden, 1996) and adversely affect caregivers' sensitivity toward the older children (Dunn & Kendrick, 1982). Does this dual damage also have an adverse effect on the children's relationships with their new siblings? Here, striking individual differences in the involvement of older children appear critical. In particular, two separate studies (Dunn & Kendrick, 1982; Howe & Ross, 1990) have documented links between the way mothers *talk* to their young children at the time of the sibling's birth and the quality of the relationship that develops between the siblings over time. In families in which the mothers discussed the feelings and needs of the baby, friendly child–child interactions were more common, both for the older sibling and, over time, for the younger sibling. This suggests that older children's attributions are important for establishing good foundations for the sibling relationship.

Whatever their foundation, sibling relationships are developmentally dynamic, and research suggests that changes in the younger sibling's competencies, as well as those of the older sibling, are a driving force in this change (e.g., Munn & Dunn, 1989). This perhaps is unsurprising, given the remarkable speed at which babies develop. As illustrated previously, clear changes in sibling interactions are brought about by motoric milestones such as the ability to crawl; milestones in younger siblings' conversational skills and capacities for shared pretend play are also crucial and result in heightened interest from older siblings between the younger children's second and fourth birthdays (Brown & Dunn, 1991). In contrast, younger siblings appear fascinated by their older siblings from a very early age. For example, in an early Cambridge longitudinal study of siblings (Dunn & Kendrick, 1982), when asked how much their 8- to 14-month-old babies missed the older sibling when the two children were apart, replies from two mothers were typical:

> "She thinks he's marvelous. Hero-worships him. If he plays with her foot, she kills herself laughing. She doesn't cry till he goes out of the room."

> "She misses him a great deal if he isn't there. Shouts till she hears him in the morning. Fusses till she can see him. I'm not enough."

The vividness of these comments is strong enough to warrant the speculation that influences may also be found in the opposite direction; that is, young children may be so determined to be with and like their older siblings that they tackle both physical and social developmental milestones at the earliest opportunity. While young firstborns appear advantaged in vocabulary development, perhaps reflecting the greater parental attention they receive (Hoff-Ginsberg, 1998), later-born children understand mistaken beliefs at an earlier age than either firstborns or only children (Ruffman, Perner, Naito, Parkin, & Clements, 1998); this social-cognitive milestone is important for all kinds of social situations, including avoiding blame, sharing jokes, teasing, and taunting. Toddlers in two further Cambridge studies showed remarkable capacities for understanding exactly what would upset their older sibling. Two examples from 15- to 23-month-olds include leaving a fight to destroy an object cherished by the older sibling and fetching a toy spider and pushing it in the face of an older sibling who was afraid of spiders (Dunn, 1988).

Juxtaposed with the very positive comments from mothers noted earlier, these examples testify to the love–hate quality that often characterizes early sibling relationships. As noted earlier, however, individual differences in the quality of sibling relationships are striking, and the third clear finding to emerge from the literature is that sibling conflict is associated with maternal differential treatment (Boer & Dunn, 1990; Brody, Stoneman, McCoy, & Forehand, 1992; Stocker, Dunn, & Plomin, 1989). Marked individual differences can be found in the magnitude, persistence, and form of maternal differential treatment (for a review, see Boyle et al., 2004). As many parents will have noticed, young children are often finely tuned to the minor injustices that are part and parcel of family life. Social comparisons are therefore a plausible mechanism underpinning the link between differential parenting and sibling conflict. That is, less favored children may come to view themselves as less worthy of love than their siblings.

Note, however, that differential parenting predicts increased hostility from both more- and less-favored siblings (Boer & Dunn, 1990). Several factors may contribute to this rather puzzling finding. First, differential treatment that is not clearly justified or predictable may cause favored children to worry about possible loss of status; this point is especially pertinent for very young children who can have only a very limited understanding of the factors leading to differential treatment. Second, favored children's experience of raised parental support may be more than offset by reduced support from the less-favored sibling. Third, differential parenting is likely to covary with other forms of negative parenting that are associated with maternal stress (Jenkins, Dunn, Rasbash, O'Connor, & Simpson, 2005). It is also worth noting that the links between caregiver–child and sibling interactions show complex moderation effects. For example, attachment status appears to moderate the effect of differential parenting on sibling conflict, such that securely attached firstborns exposed to differential parenting did not show elevated rates of sibling conflict (Volling & Belsky, 1991).

The aforementioned points lead to the fourth finding from studies of early sibling relationships: Destructive sibling conflict predicts later conduct problems, but only for young children who also experience negative relationships with caregivers (e.g., Garcia, Shaw, Winslow, & Yaggi, 2000). That is, for many families, fights between brothers and sisters are "horribly normal"—that is, horrible, but normal. However, for children who experience rejection from caregivers, exposure to intense sibling conflict doubles the likelihood (in early school years) of displaying problems of behavior that are sufficiently serious and persistent to warrant a diagnosis of conduct disorder. This finding echoes the challenges to monotropism noted earlier, in that the impact of one negative family relationship is moderated by the quality of other family relationships. That is, as first noted by Robert Hinde (1979), relationships cannot be understood in isolation, as they are formed and maintained within a complex network of other relationships. Observational research has shown that in their second year of life younger siblings show intense interest in what happens between their older siblings and their mothers (Dunn, 1988; Dunn & Munn, 1985). They respond to disputes, for instance, in the great majority of conflicts between mother and sibling, and their reaction varies according to the *emotion* expressed by the other family members and to the *topic* of the disputes. Building on this point, in the next section we consider the links between children's relationships with siblings and with peers.

LINKS BETWEEN CHILDREN'S RELATIONSHIPS WITH SIBLINGS AND WITH PEERS

Traditionally, children's interactions with peers and with sibs have been studied independently. However, children's relationships with their siblings may well influence (and be influenced by) their relationships with children outside the family. It is therefore surprising how little systematic research there is concerning relations between young children's interactions with peers and with sibs. Furthermore, findings to date suggest a divided picture. While some studies of preschoolers suggest very few associations between interactions with siblings and with peers (e.g., Berndt & Bulleit, 1985; Stocker & Dunn, 1991), other studies indicate quite specific links between interactions with these two social partners. For example, in one study, preschoolers who were close to their friends at the time of the birth of a sibling had more friendly relations with their infant siblings than did other children (Kramer & Gottman, 1992), while individual differences in the frequency of preschoolers' talk about thoughts and ideas also appear stable across conversations with siblings and friends (Hughes, Lecce, & Wilson, 2007).

Theoretically, the arguments are equally divided. At least three distinct theoretical perspectives provide grounds for proposing a link between the quality of the relationships that children form with their siblings and with peers and friends. For example, within attachment theory, internal working models of relationships with caregivers, once consolidated, are thought to carry forward to relationships with siblings and other children (Bretherton, 1985). Likewise, from the perspective of social learning theory, behaviors learned within family relationships become generalized to children's interactions with others (e.g., Parke, MacDonald, Bietel, & Bhavnagri, 1988; Putallaz, 1983, 1987). Links between relationships are also proposed from the rather different perspective of personality theory; here, children's personality characteristics are thought to elicit similar responses from different social partners (Caspi & Elder, 1988). Similarly, children's temperamental characteristics have been linked to features of relationships within and outside the family (e.g., Stevenson-Hinde & Shouldice, 1993; Stocker & Dunn, 1991).

At the same time theorists have also argued for contrasts rather than continuities between children's relationships with siblings and with peers. Perhaps surprisingly (given the point raised earlier about internal working models shaping relationships), one such argument comes from attachment research. Specifically, it is argued that children with an insecure avoidant pattern of attachment learn to suppress anger around the caregiver but are often very aggressive in settings outside the home and with peers (e.g., Crowell, O'Connor, Wollmers, Sprafkin, & Rao, 1991). Other arguments for contrasts are largely founded on the differences in the quality, structure, and context of these two types of relationship. For example, as noted earlier, sibling relationships vary enormously in quality and may lack the affection and trust that is a key element of children's friendships. Conversely, the age gap that is typically found between siblings allows interactions between siblings to be scaffolded by the older child; siblings also often know each other very well and are uninhibited in their communications with each other, which may also enhance the effectiveness of "tutoring" within sibling relationships.

In support of this view, numerous studies have shown that young children do better when learning new tasks with a sibling than with a peer (Azmitia & Hesser, 1993). Of course, the age gap between siblings also means that these relationships are typically less egalitarian than peer relationships. This is important, as behavioral homophyly is a key factor in drawing children together (Rubin, Lynch, Coplan, Rose-Krasnor, & Booth, 1994). This point relates to a further contrast between peer and sibling relationships, namely, that only the former show striking gender segregation. This is apparent from a very early age and has been argued to reflect the importance of behavioral compatibilities (Maccoby, 1998). Finally, while young friends may see each other relatively infrequently and usually in positive contexts, siblings typically share the same home environment and so come to know each other "warts and all."

The variety of predictions that can be made concerning the relationship between children's interactions with peers and with siblings is in striking contrast with the paucity of empirical research aimed at illuminating this relationship. We address this gap later in this chapter.

THE TODDLERS UP PROJECT

At the start of this chapter we cast a critical eye on three axes of skepticism regarding very young children's abilities to form and maintain close relationships with other children. The first of these was the presumed atypicality of the wartime sample of nursery friends observed by Burlingham and Freud (1944). The second was Parten's early model of developmental change in child–child interactions as a gradual shift from solitary to social play. The third was a research emphasis on young children's difficulties in understanding subjectivity, resulting from Piaget's work on children's conceptual development. As reviewed earlier, these ideas were challenged by later evidence that many young children engage in quite sophisticated social interactions with friends and siblings and, when questioned in a developmentally appropriate manner, can attribute inner states to themselves and others. The second section in this chapter reviewed findings from studies of early sibling relationships and noted three emerging themes: (1) the combination of love and hate that appears as a particular feature of sibling relations; (2) the connections between family relationships, such that differential parenting is associated with increased sibling conflict; and (3) the question of whether continuities and contrasts are found across sibling and peer relationships.

In the remainder of this chapter we aim to extend this work by capitalizing on data from the first time point of a recent longitudinal study of early social development (the Toddlers Up Project). Of the 140 children in this study,

109 (61 boys and 48 girls, mean age = 2.36 years *SD* = 0.32) had an older sibling under 10 years of age who could be filmed playing with the target child (the sibling sample included 52 boys and 56 girls; mean age = 5.06 years, *SD* = 1.60). Our peer play analyses are based on data from the 102 of these children who were also filmed in the lab playing with a (same-sex, same-age) unfamiliar peer. Key feature of this study included the social diversity of the sample and the availability of a wealth of observational data, including video-based coding of the children's interactions with both siblings and peers. Our summary of the study findings is framed by the axes and themes noted earlier.

The first two axes concerned the nature of age-related changes in child–child interactions and the extent to which existing observational findings from specific samples can be generalized to the wider population. Carollee Howes has conducted pioneering work in this field and so her developmental coding scheme (Howes et al., 1998; Howes & Matheson, 1992) was applied to the child–child observations carried out in the Toddlers Up Project. This coding scheme focuses on children's abilities to engage in progressively more complex play interactions. For example, role reversals and exchanges have long been recognized as requiring greater competence than either parallel play or simple imitative or turn-taking exchanges (e.g., Brownell, 1986). Howes and colleagues (1988) identified four levels of play that can be rated reliably (with a test–retest reliability of .91 over 4 weeks):

1. *Parallel play*—children are within 3 feet of each other and engage in similar activity but do not acknowledge each other.
2. *Parallel aware play*—parallel play with eye contact.
3. *Simple social play*—children engage in same or similar activity and show social interaction (e.g., talk, smile, and offer or receive toys).
4. *Complementary and reciprocal play*—children show action-based role reversals in social games such as chase or peekaboo.

At a descriptive level, the results from the Toddlers Up Project (see Table 7.1) suggest two clear conclusions. First, average play ratings showed that these young 2-year-olds engaged in simple social play (e.g., offering a toy) equally frequently with peers and siblings. Second, there were nevertheless striking individual differences in both play and conversational quality: Maximum levels of play ranged from "eye contact but no social overture" to "repeated role reversal in joint play." (It is also worth noting that boys and girls showed similar mean scores for play, as well as similar patterns of correlates; our results are therefore reported for the sample as a whole [see Table 7.2].)

With regard to age-related changes in child–child social interactions, Howes and Matheson (1992) found no significant changes in the frequency of parallel play from infancy to preschool (15 months to 47 months). In contrast, each of the other forms of play shows age-related changes. Specifically, while "parallel aware play" appears more frequent in 24- to 41-month-olds than in older children, "simple social play" appears more frequent from 36 to 47

TABLE 7.1. Descriptive Statistics for All Study Measures

Measure	Mean	*SD*	Range
Sociability (CCTI)	17.26	3.75	0 to 40
Verbal ability (BAS)	19.97	10.11	0 to 36
Theory of mind	13.25	8.15	0 to 32
Differential parenting[a]	–3.72	8.36	–34 to 14
C–S play			
Average	1.66	0.36	1.03 to 2.63
Maximum	2.92	0.45	2 to 4
C–P play			
Average	2.07	0.38	1.00 to 3.19
Maximum	2.75	0.68	1 to 4

Note. $n = 109$, except for child–peer play, for which $n = 102$. C, target child; S, older sibling; P, peer. Sibling dyads included 33 boy–boy pairs, 28 girl–girl pairs, and 47 boy–girl pairs.

[a]Positive Parenting scores for sibling minus Positive Parenting scores for child.

months than in younger children. Alongside this increase in the relative proportion of simple social play is a steady increase in complementary and reciprocal play from the youngest ages to 42–47 months. These findings demonstrate the developmental sensitivity of Howes's coding scheme. Note that these observations involved familiar playmates in child-care centers. Our findings from the Toddlers Up Project allow us to extend this picture, as a similar pattern of age-related changes in form rather than frequency emerged for social interactions between *unfamiliar* peers. Thus, age was unrelated to average rat-

TABLE 7.2. Correlations between Observational Measures of Play with Siblings and Peers

	C–P play average	C–P play max.	C–S play average	C–S play max.
C–P play				
Average	—	.72** (.66**)	.19† (.27**)	.05 .05
Maximum		—	.15 (.20†)	.21* (.20†)
C–S play				
Average			—	.53** (.52**)
Maximum				—

Note. C, Child; S, sibling; P, peer (partial correlations with verbal ability controlled shown in parentheses).

** $p < .01$; * $p < .05$; † $p < .10$.

ings for social interactions with peers, but was significantly related to maximum ratings on the Howes coding scheme (see Table 7.3).

The second axis concerned the generalizability of early findings. To address this point, we capitalized on the social diversity of the Toddlers Up Project sample. Following the procedures developed by Moffitt and E-Risk Team (2002), information about seven binary markers of social disadvantage were collected during home-based interviews with mothers: no parental educational qualifications, no paid employment, no access to car, family income < £10,000, family receiving noncontributory benefits, family living in Council (government) accommodation, family living in very poor neighborhood. The distribution of total markers of disadvantage was skewed, and so families were categorized as showing low disadvantage (i.e., zero markers), moderate disadvantage (1–3 markers), or high disadvantage (4+ markers). Of the 109 target children for the current analyses, 42 were from "low disadvantage" families, 48 were from "moderately disadvantaged" families, and 19 were from "highly disadvantaged" families.

In a previous study, Howes and Matheson (1992) compared the play shown by children attending minimally adequate versus model child-care centers in order to investigate whether individual differences in the complexity of very young children's play are related to contrasts in the quality of their social environments. To avoid ceiling effects, Howes added a further category of *cooperative social pretend play* (i.e., social pretend play that includes clear but not necessarily explicit complementary roles) to her scale, in order to index the frequencies of pretend play. The findings from Howes and Matheson's study indicated that children enrolled in minimally adequate care showed a 3-month lag for complementary and reciprocal play at 18 months, and a 12-month lag in cooperative social pretend play at age 4. That is, in addition to being sensitive to developmental changes within children, the complexity of peer play appears to be influenced by the quality of children's social environments. However, the complexity of the literature reviewed earlier in this chapter indicates that multiple factors contribute to individual differences in young children's social interactions. The results from

TABLE 7.3. Correlations between Observational Measures and Child Characteristics

	Social disadvantage	Age	Verbal ability	Theory of mind	Sociability
C–P play (n = 102)					
Average	–.04	.09	.30**	.32**	.21**
Maximum	–.07	.23*	.34**	.28*	.22*
C–S play (n = 109)					
Average	–.04	–.03	.06	.03	.20*
Maximum	.03	.17	.14	.06	.03

** $p < .01$; * $p < .05$.

the Toddlers Up Project confirm this view. In particular, the rich dataset provided by this project allowed us to test the hypothesis that the quality of children's relationships with siblings may moderate the influence of social disadvantage on peer play. For example, the scaffolding afforded by supportive relationships with an older sibling may be especially valuable for 2-year-olds exposed to social disadvantage. Conversely, negative sibling relationships may counteract the benefits typically shown by children from more advantaged social backgrounds.

Although there was no overall association between social disadvantage and peer play (see Table 7.3), a hierarchical regression analysis with standardized maternal ratings of positive sibling relationships and social disadvantage entered at step 1 explained no significant variance in average ratings of peer play ($R^2 = .00$, $F(2,96) = 0.09$, *n's*), but the interaction term (positive sib × disadvantage) entered at step 2 accounted for a marginally significant 3% of the variance in peer play ($R^2 = .03$, $F(1,95) = 2.96$, $p < .10$). To explore this effect further, we calculated correlations between peer play and social disadvantage separately for the subgroups of children with low, medium, or high maternal ratings of positive sibling relationships. The expected inverse relationship between social disadvantage and peer play was found for children with medium ratings of positive sibling relationships ($r = -.36$, $p < .05$), but social disadvantage was unrelated to peer play for children with either low ($r = .07$, *n's*) or high ($r = -.02$, *n's*) ratings of positive sibling relationships. Although only marginally significant ($z \geq 1.74$, $p = .08$, $2t$), these group differences are consistent with the view that effects of social disadvantage on young children's peer play are attenuated in the context of either very negative or very positive sibling relationships.

The third axis for skepticism regarding children's early social competencies with other children concerned their limited cognitive capacities for appreciating subjective states. Here, the Toddlers Up Project extends the scope of Howes's detailed observational work by including cognitive measures—specifically, three experimental tasks designed to tap very young children's understanding of mind. Elsewhere (Hughes & Ensor, 2005) we describe how individual differences in the 2-year-olds' overall performance on these tasks related to individual differences in other cognitive abilities (executive functions and language skills) and in family relationships; again, sibling relationships figured prominently here. As a complement to this work, here we summarize the children's performances on individual tasks. First, given a mix of prototypical and junk objects (e.g., duplo horse and hay), more than two-thirds of the 2-year-olds were able to engage in pretend play with very little prompting from the experimenter. Second, just over half the 2-year-olds were at least partially successful in their attempts to deceive the experimenter in a "penny hiding" game (Charman & Baron-Cohen, 1997); this finding is consistent with recent observational studies of deception (Newton et al., 2000). Third, almost half the 2-year-olds showed at least some understanding of false belief, when the standard false-belief questions were presented within a supportive storytelling format (an engaging book involving pop-up pictures, peep-through holes, and a simple repeating narrative to maximize the salience of the child's false belief when faced with a deceptive picture on the penultimate page). These findings are all the more striking given the large proportion of children from disadvantaged families in the study, many of whom had rather limited language skills. The external validity of these findings are, however, supported by clear correlations between children's aggregate theory of mind scores and both the frequency and complexity of their interactions with unfamiliar peers (see Table 7.3). Together, these findings support our earlier expressed view that children can display a relatively sophisticated understanding of other minds even though they fail classical false-belief tasks. In addition, the particular methods and contexts used to investigate early social understanding are very important—a point that echoes recent conclusions regarding the importance of careful and developmentally appropriate methods of interviewing children in a forensic context (Lamb & Brown, 2006).

We turn now to the themes arising in our earlier review of young children's sibling relationships: their love–hate quality, their interconnectedness with other family relationships; and continuities and contrasts with peer relationships. To investigate the first of these themes, episodes of angry conflict were coded from transcripts of the sibling play sessions. Just over half the sample (66%) showed at least some conflict during the play sessions, while a quarter showed high levels of angry conflict (4+ angry turns per hour). However, these conflict ratings were unrelated to either the average or maximum scores on Howes' coding scheme. In other words, conflict and cooperation appeared as independent dimensions of the children's interactions with their siblings.

The second theme in our review concerned the links between different family relationships. Specifically, the evidence from previous studies suggests that high levels of sibling conflict are associated with high levels of differential treatment from parents. To address this hypothesis we compared maternal responses to an interview about parenting strategies used with the older sibling and the target child in order to construct a "differential parenting" scale. As shown in Table 7.1, on average mothers reported themselves as being more positive with their 2-year-old than with their older child, but there was considerable variation in scores on this differential parenting measure: 53% of mothers reported themselves as more positive with their 2-year-olds than with the older sib; 33% as equally positive with both children; and 14% as more positive toward the older sib. As hypothesized, individual differences in maternal reports of differential parenting were correlated with the frequency of angry conflict between siblings, coded from transcripts of the sib-play sessions ($r(96) = .21, p < .05$). In other words, consistent with the predictions of family systems theory, interactions within specific family relationships are associated with each other, highlighting the importance of gathering information about multiple relationships, even for very young children. Inferences about the direction of causality are, of course, not appropriate from these correlations across relationships.

The third theme in our review concerned contrasts and continuities in young children's interactions with sibs and with peers. Here, our first question concerned the *stability* of individual differences in the frequency and complexity of children's social interactions with these two social partners. Previous observational studies (Dunn, 1993) have highlighted the relationship-specific nature of children's social behaviors. In contrast, our results show modest but significant stability of individual differences in play ratings across contexts and social partners. That is, children who displayed more frequent or advanced interactions in their play at home with older siblings also received higher ratings for their play in a lab setting with an unfamiliar peer. When verbal ability was partialed, the across-partner correlation remained significant for average play ratings ($r(99) = .27$, $p < .01$) and was marginally significant for maximum play ratings ($r(99) = .20$, $p < .10$). When maternal ratings of child sociability were also partialed, the correlation across social partners became nonsignificant for average scores ($r(99) = .14$, *n's*) and remained marginal for maximum scores ($r(99) = .19$, $p < .10$). Thus the across-partner stability of individual differences in children's average levels of play appears to reflect individual differences in temperamental sociability.

Next, we asked whether there were any differences in the mean levels of complexity of children's play with older siblings and with peers, or in the correlates of individual differences in these two arenas? Here, two competing hypotheses stand out. From the Vygotskian construct of a "zone of proximal development," one would predict that 2-year-olds would show more advanced play with older sibs because these more competent social partners can scaffold social interactions. The second derives from the evidence for the importance of behavioral homophyly; according to this view, children should show more frequent interactions with same-sex, same-age peers than with older siblings. That is, 2-year-olds may be relegated to rather passive roles in their interactions with older siblings (e.g., playing the part of baby, or of "audience") but enjoy an equal status with peers and so be motivated to "make friends" by initiating or responding to social overtures. As stated here, these two views are not mutually exclusive: Indeed, our prediction was that 2-year-olds should show more *advanced* play with older siblings but more *frequent* play with peers. Our results offer some support for each of these predictions. Specifically, the 2-year-olds' *maximum* ratings were higher in sib play ($t(1,99) = 2.47$, $p < .02$) while their *average* ratings were higher in peer play ($t(1,99) = 8.46$, $p < .001$). That is, there was some support for both the "zone of proximal development" view (older sibs appeared to facilitate higher levels of play) and the "making friends" argument (2-year-olds made more frequent overtures toward peers than toward sibs). Note also that individual differences in children's play with sibs and with peers showed somewhat distinct correlates. In particular, individual differences in children's verbal ability and early theory of mind skills were significantly related to both the frequency and form of children's social interactions with unfamiliar peers but were unrelated to children's interactions with older sibs, presumably because these were typically led by the older child.

Finally, we asked whether the quality of sibling relationships moderate the influence of sociability on peer play? Interactions with older siblings can provide a valuable means of developing very young children's play skills (Dunn, 1988, 1993). However, this depends on the quality of children's sibling relationships: Only 2-year-olds who enjoy positive relationships with their older siblings are likely to be at an advantage in initiating and maintaining social interactions with their peers. For 2-year-olds with less positive sibling relationships, temperamental sociability is likely to be the key predictor of individual differences in interactions with peers. Table 7.3 shows that overall, temperamental sociability was modestly but significantly associated with both average and maximum ratings of peer play ($r(99) = .21$, .22 respectively, $p < .05$). Did the strength of this association depend on the quality of 2-year-olds' relationships with their older siblings?

We investigated this proposed moderation effect in two ways. First, we used a hierarchical regression analysis with average peer play ratings as the dependent variable. Standardized maternal ratings of positive sibling relationships and temperamental sociability were entered at step 1 and jointly explained just 5% of the variance in peer play ($R^2 = .05$, $F(2,94) = 2.37$, $p < .10$). The interaction term (positive sib x sociability) was entered at step 2, and accounted for a significant additional 13% of the variance in peer play ($R^2 = .13$, $F(1,93) = 14.31$, $p < .001$). Second, we divided the sample into three groups according to whether maternal ratings of a positive sibling relationship were low ($n = 35$), medium ($n = 32$) or high ($n = 32$). As predicted, the correlation between peer play and temperamental sociability was especially strong for children with low ratings of positive sibling relationships ($r(35) = .61$, $p < .01$), compared with children with either medium ($r(32) = -.17$, *n's*) or high ($r(32) = -.04$, *n's*) ratings of a positive sibling relationship (these group contrasts were all significant: $z \geq 2.92$, $p < .01$, $2t$). Together, these results suggest that positive sibling relationships may compensate for lower levels of temperamental sociability and so attenuate the relationship between sociability and peer play.

SUMMARY OF RESULTS

Several sets of findings emerged from this study. With regard to the peer interactions, it is worth emphasizing that the 2-year-olds showed equally frequent social overtures toward these unfamiliar peers as toward their older siblings. While individual differences in the complexity but not the frequency of social overtures with peers were related to age, both complexity and frequency were related to verbal ability and to performances on simple theory of mind tasks.

With regard to the sibling interactions, our findings provide some support for both a "zone of proximal development" view (older sibs appeared to facilitate higher levels of play) and a "making friends" view (2-year-olds made more frequent overtures toward peers than toward sibs). Our results also support the view that many sibling relationships have a love–hate quality: Individual differences in observed angry conflict between sibs were unrelated to individual differences in either the frequency or complexity of positive social interactions. In contrast, higher levels of angry conflict were associated with maternal reports of differential parenting, highlighting the value of multiple sources of information and of studying interactions in the context of other relationships.

The foregoing point leads us nicely to our findings of an interesting interplay between children's interactions with peers and with sibs. First, children who displayed more frequent or advanced interactions in their play at home with older siblings also received higher ratings for their play in a lab setting with peers. Second, effects of temperamental sociability appeared to underpin the stability of these individual differences in complexity of play but were moderated by the quality of children's relationships with older sibs. In particular, positive sibling relationships appeared to compensate for lower levels of temperamental sociability and so attenuate the relationship between sociability and peer play. Third, effects of social disadvantage on young children's peer play were also moderated by the quality of children's relationships with older sibs. More specifically, effects of social disadvantage were attenuated in the context of either very negative or very positive sibling relationships.

CONCLUSIONS

Children's relationships with their siblings and friends during the second and third years offer an illuminating window on the nature of their understanding and on how this develops. We see their growing grasp of how to tease effectively, to anticipate the behavior of another, how to cooperate in sharing a pretend world, how to "win" in arguments, as well as how to conciliate and to comfort. Individual differences in the quality of sibling relationships are marked and these show some stability over time; so too do close friendships, which are evident among some children younger than 3 years old (Dunn, 2004). The emotional intensity and the *interest* children show in their childhood companions as they make the transition to the preschool years highlight how important a topic this is for us to take seriously and learn more about. Observations of how these relationships change, and of the links between cognitive developments and such relationship changes, will provide key evidence if we are to make progress in understanding the transitions of the second and third years.

APPENDIX 7.1. Study Measures

Direct Observational Ratings for Complexity of Play

During each home visit, the target child was filmed playing with an older sibling for approximately 20 minutes ($X = 23.15$, $SD = 4.45$), using a big bag of toys provided by the research team. About a month later, pairs of mothers and target children visited a university lab-playroom. During this visit, 15-minute peer-play sessions were filmed following the procedures developed by Rubin and colleagues (1998). This was followed by a 10-minute snack break, at the end of which a double-size trampoline was placed in the center of the room, and the children were invited to play on the trampoline for the final 5 minutes of the visit. To maximize the comparability of the two play sessions, coding of the peer play was restricted to the two 5-minute episodes that least involved mothers: when the children were alone in the room before snacktime, and the trampoline session at the end of the visit. Coding was made from videotape, which was divided into 30-second segments before applying Howes's coding scheme (Howes & Matheson, 1992), described in the introduction. That is, for each 30-second segment, each child was rated according to the most complex form of play displayed (parallel, parallel aware, simple social, complementary, and reciprocal). Across all segments (for peer play, $X = 14.27$, $SD = 4.47$; for sib play, $X = 40.50$, $SD = 8.61$), children were then assigned two scores for complexity of play: the overall average and the maximum rating. In total, 42 children (21 2-year-olds and 21 sibs) were independently double-coded by two trained researchers. Interrater reliability was confirmed using intraclass correlation coefficients ($r_{\text{c-s av}} = .84$; $r_{\text{c-s max}} = .85$; $r_{\text{c-p av}} = .97$; $r_{\text{c-p max}} = .98$).

Maternal Questionnaire Measures

During the home visit, mothers completed a semistructured interview that included a variety of questionnaires. Two of these are relevant to the present study. The first of these is the Colorado Childhood Temperament Inventory (CCTI; Rowe & Plomin, 1977), which has been validated against observed behavioral measures of temperament (Saudino & Cherny, 2001). For our analyses, the five-item sociability subscale was used; this scale had good internal consistency (Cronbach's $\alpha = .81$) and a possible range of 0–20 points. The second instrument is the Sibling Relationship Interview, developed in the Colorado Adoption Project (Stocker et al., 1989), which yields two factors. Here, our interest lies with the first, main factor, which includes 16 items that index individual differences in positive aspects of the sibling relationship (e.g., affection and willingness to share). Cronbach's alpha for this scale was .73, showing reasonable internal consistency for this scale.

Verbal Ability

The Naming and Comprehension Subtests of the British Abilities Scale (Elliott, Murray, & Pearson, 1983) were individually administered during lab visits and summed to give a single index of verbal ability, with a possible range of 0–36 points. The mean score on this verbal ability was 19.97 ($SD = 10.12$).

Theory of Mind

Each child completed three tasks. The first of these was a penny-hiding game that has been used in previous studies of preschoolers (Hughes, Dunn, & White, 1998) and children with autism (Baron-Cohen, 1992). The experimenter hid a coin behind her back and, bringing both hands forward with the coin concealed in one hand, asked the child to guess which hand held the coin. This was repeated three times, after which the experimenter announced that it was now the child's turn to hide the coin. For each of the following three test trials, the experimenter gave 1 point for each of the following: hiding both hands behind back, bringing both hands forward, keeping hand closed, and keeping coin hidden. (Note that this is a considerably more lenient scoring system than that used with preschoolers, for whom *all four* criteria had to be met to receive credit on a trial.)

The second task (Charman & Baron Cohen, 1997; Fein, 1975) involved elicited pretend play. First, the child was shown four objects: two realistic (toy horse and plastic grass) and two less realistic (Duplo models of a horse and hay). In the baseline condition the child was shown the realistic objects only. In the "single substitution" condition the child was shown the prototypical horse and the junk hay. In the "double substitution," the child was shown the junk horse and the junk hay. Three trials were coded for each condition: display, modeling, and suggestion. In the "display" trials the child was asked simply, "Show me how you can play with these," and given 10 seconds to respond. In the "modeling" trials, the experimenter pretended to feed the horse, saying "yum yum" and clicking tongue before allowing 10 seconds for the child to respond. In the "suggestion" trials the experimenter said, "Let's pretend he's still hungry. You give him something to drink," and then waited 10 seconds for the child to respond. For each trial, 1 point was awarded for any pretend play actions (e.g., making the horse walk and feeding the horse).

The third task was a deceptive-identity task (also used by Hughes, 1998) that involved a pop-up picture book. The first five pages of this book showed an eye peeping through a hole in the page. On the final page, what had initially appeared to be an eye was revealed to be a spot on a snake's tail. After turning back to the penultimate page, the child was asked a test question *"Before we turned the page, what did you think this would be, an eye or a spot?"* and a reality question *"What is it really, an eye or a spot?"* Next, the researcher showed the child a puppet and said, "Look, this is Charlie. Charlie has never seen this book before. If we show him this picture, what will he think it is, an eye or a spot?" and a second reality control question *"What is it really, an eye or a spot?"* The order of the alternatives was counterbalanced across children, who were credited with success on the memory-for-own-false-belief and predicting-other's-false-belief questions only if they also passed the corresponding reality control question.

Note that the range of scores on each theory of mind task varied widely (0–2 for the most difficult deceptive identity task; 0–9 points for the elicited pretense task; 0–12 for the penny-hiding game). Scores from each task were therefore weighted so that each task had an (equivalent) range of 0–12 points.

REFERENCES

Azmitia, M. M., & Hesser, J. (1993). Why siblings are important agents of cognitive development: A comparison of siblings and peers. *Child Development, 64*, 430–444.

Bakeman, R., & Brownlee, J. R. (1980). The strategic use of parallel play: A sequential analysis. *Child Development, 51.*

Baron-Cohen, S. (1992). Out of sight or out of mind?: Another look at deception in autism. *Journal of Child Psychology and Psychiatry, 33*, 1141–1155.

Berndt, T., & Bulleit, T. (1985). Effects of sibling relationships on preschoolers' behavior at home and at school. *Developmental Psychology, 21*, 761–767.

Boer, F., & Dunn, J. (1990). *Children's sibling relationships: Developmental and clinical issues.* Hillsdale, NJ: Erlbaum.

Boyle, M., Jenkins, J., Georgiades, K., Cairney, J., Duku, E., & Racine, Y. (2004). Differential–maternal parenting behavior: Estimating within- and between-family effects on children. *Child Development, 75*, 1457–1476.

Bretherton, I. (1985). Attachment theory: Retrospect and prospect. *Monographs of the Society for Research in Child Development, 50*(1–2, Serial No. 209), 3–35.

Brody, G., Stoneman, Z., McCoy, J. K., & Forehand, R. (1992). Contemporaneous and longitudinal associations of sibling conflict with family relationship assessments and family discussions about sibling problems. *Child Development, 63*, 391–400.

Brown, J. R., & Dunn, J. (1991). "You can cry, mum": The social and developmental implications of talk about internal states. Special Issue: Perspectives on the child's theory of mind: II. *British Journal of Developmental Psychology, 9*, 237–256.

Brownell, C. (1986). Convergent developments: Cognitive-developmental correlates of growth in infant/toddler peer skills. *Child Development, 57*, 275–286.

Burlingham, D., & Freud, A. (1944). *Infants without families.* London: Allen & Unwin.

Caspi, A., & Elder, G. H., Jr. (1988). Emergent family patterns: The intergenerational construction of problem behaviour and relationships. In R. Hinde & J. Stevenson-Hinde (Eds.), *Relationships within families: Mutual influences* (pp. 218–240). Oxford, UK: Clarendon.

Charman, A., & Baron-Cohen, S. (1997). Brief report: Prompted pretend play in autism. *Journal of Autism and Developmental Disorders, 27, 325–332.*

Crowell, J. A., O'Connor, E., Wollmers, G., Sprafkin, J., & Rao, U. (1991). Mothers' conceptualizations of parent–child relationships: Relation to mother–child interaction and child behavior problems. *Developmental and Psychopathology, 3*, 431–444.

Damon, W., & Killen, M. (1982). Peer interaction and the process of change in children's moral reasoning. *Merrill–Palmer Quarterly, 28*, 347–367.

Denham, S. A., McKinley, M., Couchoud, E. A., & Holt, R. (1990). Emotional and behavioral predictors of preschool peer ratings. *Child Development, 61*, 1145–1152.

Doise, W., & Mugny, G. (1984). *The social development of the intellect.* Oxford, UK: Pergamon Press.

Dunn, J. (1988). *The beginnings of social understanding.* Cambridge, MA: Harvard University Press.

Dunn, J. (1993). *Young children's close relationships: Beyond attachment* (Vol. 4). Newbury Park, CA: Sage.

Dunn, J. (2004). *Children's friendships: The beginnings of intimacy.* Oxford, UK: Blackwell.

Dunn, J., Cutting, A., & Fisher, N. (2002). Old friends, new friends: Predictors of children's perspective on their friends at school. *Child Development, 73*, 621–635.

Dunn, J., & Kendrick, C. (1982). *Siblings: Love, envy and understanding.* London: Grant McIntyre.

Dunn, J., & McGuire, S. (1992). Sibling and peer relationships in childhood. *Journal of Child Psychology and Psychiatry and Allied Disciplines, 33*, 67–105.

Dunn, J., & Munn, P. (1985). Becoming a family member: Family conflict and the development of social understanding in the second year. *Child Development, 56*, 764–774.

Elliott, C., Murray, D., & Pearson, L. (1983). *British Abilities Scales.* Windsor, UK: NFER-Nelson.

Fein, G. (1975). A transformational analysis of pretending. *Developmental Psychology, 11*, 291–296.

Garcia, M. M., Shaw, D. S., Winslow, E. B., & Yaggi, K. E. (2000). Destructive sibling conflict and the development of conduct problems in young boys. *Developmental Psychology, 36*, 44–53.

Gottman, J. M. (1983). How children become friends. *Monographs of the Society for Research in Child Development, 48*(3, Serial No. 201), S87–S97.

Harris, P. L. (1991). The work of the imagination. In A. Whiten (Ed.), *Natural theories of mind: The evolution, development, and simulation of everyday mindreading* (pp. 283–304). Oxford, UK: Blackwell.

Hartup, W. W. (1996). The company they keep: Friendships and their developmental significance. *Child Development, 67*, 1–13.

Hay, D. F. (2006). Yours and mine: Toddlers' talk about possessions with familiar peers. *British Journal of Developmental Psychology, 24*, 39–52.

Hinde, R. A. (1979). *Towards understanding relationships*. London: Academic Press.

Hoff-Ginsberg, E. (1998). The relation of birth order and socioeconomic status to children's language experience and language development. *Applied Psycholinguistics, 19*, 603–629.

Howe, N., & Ross, H. (1990). Socialization, perspective-taking, and the sibling relationship. *Developmental Psychology, 26*, 160–165.

Howes, C. (1988). Peer interaction of young children. *Monographs of the Society for Research in Child Development, 53*(1, Serial No. 217), 94.

Howes, C. (1996). The earliest friendships. In W. M. Bukowski, A. F. Newcomb, & W. W. Hartup (Eds.), *The company they keep: Friendship in childhood and adolescence* (pp. 66–86). New York: Cambridge University Press.

Howes, C., Hamilton, C., & Phillipsen, L. (1998). Stability and continuity of a child–caregiver and child–peer relationships. *Child Development, 69*, 418–426.

Howes, C., & Matheson, C. (1992). Sequences in the development of competent play with peers: Social and social pretend play. *Developmental Psychology, 28*, 961–974.

Hughes, C., & de Rosnay, M. (2006). Conversations and childhood [Special issue]. *British Journal of Developmental Psychology, 24*.

Hughes, C., Dunn, J., & White, A. (1998). Trick or treat?: Uneven understanding of mind and emotion and executive function among "hard to manage" preschoolers. *Journal of Child Psychology and Psychiatry, 39*, 981–994.

Hughes, C., & Ensor, R. (2005). Theory of mind and executive function: A family affair? *Developmental Neuropsychology, 28*, 645–668.

Hughes, C., Lecce, S., & Wilson, C. (2007). "Do you know what I want?": Preschoolers' talk about desires, thoughts and feelings in their conversations with sibs and friends. *Cognition and Emotion, 21*, 330–350.

Jenkins, J. M., Dunn, J., Rasbash, J., O'Connor, T. G., & Simpson, A. (2005). Mutual influence of marital conflict and children's behavior problems: shared and non-shared family risks. *Child Development, 76*, 24–39.

Jones, L. (2004). *Then they started shooting: Growing up in wartime Bosnia*. Cambridge, MA: Harvard University Press.

Kochanska, G., Kuczynski, L., & Radke-Yarrow, M. (1989). Correspondence between mother's self-reported and observed child-rearing practices. *Child Development, 60*, 56–63.

Kramer, L., & Gottman, J. M. (1992). Becoming a sibling: "With a little help from my friends." *Developmental Psychology, 28*, 685–699.

Lamb, M. (1982). Paternal influences on early socio-emotional development. *Journal of Child Psychology and Psychiatry, 23*, 185–190.

Lamb, M., & Brown, D.A. (2006) Conversational apprentices: Helping children become competent informants about their own experiences. *British Journal of Developmental Psychology, 24*, 215–234.

Maccoby, E. E. (1998). *The two sexes: Growing up apart, coming together.* Cambridge, MA: Bellknap.

Moffitt, T., & E-Risk Team. (2002). Contemporary teen aged mothers in Britain. *Journal of Child Psychology and Psychiatry, 43*, 727–742.

Munn, P., & Dunn, J. (1989). Temperament and the developing relationship between siblings. *International Journal of Behavioral Development, 12*, 433–451.

Newton, P., Reddy, V., & Bull, R (2000). Children's everyday deception and performance on false-belief tasks. *British Journal of Developmental Psychology, 18*, 297–317.

Parke, R. D., MacDonald, K. B., Bietel, A., & Bhavnagri, N. (1988). The role of the family in the development of peer relationships. In R. D. Peters & R. J. McMahon (Eds.), *Social learning and systems approaches to marriage and the family* (pp. 17–44). New York: Brunner/Mazel.

Parten, M. B. (1933). Social participation among pre-school children. *Journal of Abnormal and Social Psychology, 28*, 136–147.

Putallaz, M. (1983). Predicting children's sociometric status from their behavior. *Child Development, 54*, 1417–1426.

Putallaz, M. (1987). Maternal behavior and children's sociometric status. *Child Development, 58*, 324–340.

Ross, H. S. (1982). Establishment of social games amongst toddlers. *Developmental Psychology, 18*, 509–518.

Ross, H. S., & Lollis, S. P. (1989). A social relations analysis of toddler peer relationships. *Child Development, 60*, 1082–1091.

Rowe, D. C., & Plomin, R. (1977). Temperament in early childhood. *Journal of Personality Assessment, 41*, 150–156.

Roy, A. W., & Howe, C. (1990). Effects of cognitive conflict, socio-conflict and imitation on children 's socio-legal thinking. *European Journal of Social Psychology, 20*, 241–252.

Rubin, K. H., Hastings, P. D., Stewart, S. L., Henderson, H. A., & Chen, X. (1997). The consistency and concomitants of inhibition: some of the children, all of the time. *Child Development, 68*, 467–483.

Rubin, K. H., Lynch, D., Coplan, R., Rose-Krasnor, L., & Booth, C. L. (1994). "Birds of a feather . . . ": Behavioral concordance and preferential personal attraction in children. *Child Development, 65*, 1778–1785.

Rubin, K. H., Watson, K. S., & Jambor, T. W. (1978). Free-play behavior in preschool and kindergarten children. *Child Development, 48*, 534–536.

Ruffman, T., Perner, J., Naito, M., Parkin, L., & Clements, W. (1998). Older but not younger siblings facilitate false belief understanding. *Developmental Psychology, 34*, 161–174.

Saudino, K., & Cherny, S. (2001). Parental ratings of temperament in twins. In R. N. Emde & J. K. Hewitt (Eds.), *Infancy to early childhood: Genetic and environmental influences on developmental change* (pp. 73–88). London: Oxford University Press.

Schaffer, H., & Emerson, P. (1964). The development of social attachments in infancy. *Monographs of the Society for Research in Child Development, 29*.

Stevenson-Hinde, J., & Shouldice, A. (1993). Wariness to strangers: A behavior systems perspective revisited. In K. H. Rubin & J. Asendorpf (Eds.), *Social withdrawal, inhibition, and shyness in childhood* (pp. 101–116). Hillsdale, NJ: Erlbaum.

Stewart, R. B. (1983). Sibling attachment relationships: Child–infant interaction in the Strange Situation. *Developmental Psychology, 19*, 192–199.

Stocker, C., & Dunn, J. (1991). Sibling relationships in adolescence. In A. Peterson, R. Lerner, & J. Brookes-Gunn (Eds.), *Encyclopedia of adolescence* (pp. 1046–1048). New York: Garland Press.

Stocker, C., Dunn, J., & Plomin, R. (1989). Sibling relationships: Links with child temperament, maternal behavior, and family structure. *Child Development, 60*, 715–727.

Taylor, M. (1996). A theory of mind perspective on social cognitive development. In R. Gelman & T. Kit-Fong Au (Eds.), *Handbook of perception and cognition: Vol. 13. Perceptual and cognitive development* (pp. 282–329). San Diego, CA: Academic Press.

Tesla, C., & Dunn, J. (1992). Getting along or getting your own way: The development of young children's use of argument in conflicts with mother and sibling. *Social Development, 1*, 107–121.

Teti, D. M., Sakin, J. W., Kucera, E., Corns, K. M., & Eiden, R. D. (1996). And baby makes four: Predictors of attachment security among preschool-age firstborns during the transition to siblinghood. *Child Development, 67*, 579–96.

Volling, B. L., & Belsky, J. (1991). Multiple determinants of father involvement during infancy in dual-earner and single-earner families. *Journal of Marriage and the Family, 53*, 461–474.

Wellman, H. M., Phillips, A. T., & Rodriguez, T. (2000). Young children's understanding of perception, desire, and emotion. *Child Development, 71*, 895–912.

Wertsch, J. (Ed.). (1984). *The zone of proximal development: Some conceptual issues*. San Francisco: Jossey-Bass.

8

Intentional Communication

NAMEERA AKHTAR
CARMEN MARTÍNEZ-SUSSMANN

The period between 1 and 3 years of age is one in which tremendous interrelated changes take place in social cognition, emotion, and communication (Brownell, 1989; Kopp, 1989). At the end of the first year, children start to express themselves through gestures and words, and they begin to understand others in new ways. The ability to communicate intentionally parallels the more general ability to behave intentionally (both have their origins in Piaget's sensorimotor stage 5), but it also involves the construction of a social-cognitive understanding of others as intentional beings like themselves (Tomasello, 1999b; Tomasello, Kruger, & Ratner, 1993). Children learn language "in and for conversations" (Bloom, 1998, p. 348); however, their goal in those conversations is not to learn language but to understand and be understood by their interlocutors. Achieving this understanding requires social-cognitive skills of intention reading, but, we would like to stress, it also requires the motivation to achieve a "meeting of minds" (Golinkoff, 1993).

Although we have been given the charge of discussing intentional communication during the toddler years, we would be remiss if we did not begin our review of communicative development with a description of the changes that occur in the latter part of the first year. Nine to 12 months is widely recognized as the period when both the ability to produce intentional communicative acts and the ability to comprehend the intentions of others really take off. In this chapter, we provide a description of the most notable developments in infants' comprehension and production of communicative acts, beginning with their preverbal communicative acts (i.e., gestures) in the first year. We then examine toddlers' learning and use of conventional symbols (words) in the second year and their production of multiword speech in the third year. In each section we describe some of the major communicative milestones of the period (preverbal, one-word, multiword) and discuss the factors that may underlie attainment of these milestones. Finally, we end the chapter with some speculations about what kinds of early experiences and developments might contribute to the emergence of infants' and toddlers' impressive social-cognitive skills of intention reading.

YEAR 1: INTENTIONAL COMMUNICATION IN THE PREVERBAL PERIOD

In a classic paper, Bates, Camaioni, and Volterra (1975) distinguished between the perlocutionary (preintentional) stage in which babies behave in ways that have communicative effects and are interpreted by adults as communicative (e.g., crying, smiling, and vocalizing) and the illocutionary (intentional) stage in which infants can control their (nonverbal) communicative behaviors and can establish and maintain attention on a shared "topic." The illocutionary stage begins around 9–10 months, and in this stage babies primarily use deictic gestures (sometimes in combination with vocalizations) such as pointing, showing, and giving to communicate. A variety of behaviors have been used to establish the communicative intent of these gestures: use only or primarily when the infant has an attentive audience (O'Neill, 1996), gaze alternation between addressee and event or object of interest (Bates, 1979; Franco & Butterworth, 1996), and attempts to repair failed messages (i.e., repeating and/or elaborating the message when misunderstood—Bates, 1979; Golinkoff, 1986).

Repairing failed messages is a particularly good indication that preverbal infants can communicate intentionally as it shows that babies recognize when their communicative goals are not achieved, and they are able to, and motivated to, adjust their behavior (e.g., to elaborate or substitute new means of communicating the same message) to achieve their goals. Golinkoff (1986) showed that when a mother misunderstood or ignored her 1-year-old infant's communicative signals, the infant was likely to repeat the original signal, to augment it in some way (e.g., with additional vocal emphasis or the addition of a gesture), or to substitute another signal for the original one. It is important to note that infants produced repairs of failed messages even when they had no instrumental goal to speak of, for example, when they were simply pointing something out to their mother to share their interest in it (Golinkoff, 1993). Older toddlers will repair failed messages even when they have achieved their instrumental goal (Shwe & Markman, 1997). These findings support Bloom and Beckwith's (1989) contention that, in addition to using language as an instrument to get things done, infants and toddlers are also motivated to acquire language to express themselves and share their interests with others.

Language is used for both instrumental and sharing functions—by both children and adults—and so are early gestures. Perhaps the most studied gesture is the point—the extension of the index finger to an object or event—that emerges at the end of the first year. Early studies (e.g., Bates et al., 1975) described two distinct functions of 1-year-old infants' points: imperative (instrumental pointing to request the object pointed at) and declarative (pointing to share interest in the object or event pointed to). More recent work has confirmed this distinction and has emphasized that imperative points involve using a person as a means to obtaining an object (the goal), whereas declarative points involve using an object as a means to obtaining adult attention (Camaioni, 1997). Declarative pointing is therefore seen as involving a deeper understanding of others as beings with attentional states that can be manipulated. Indeed, the claim is that the use of declarative pointing implies an attribution of an internal psychological state (as opposed to mere agency) to the addressee (Liszkowski, Carpenter, Henning, Striano, & Tomasello, 2004; Tomasello & Camaioni, 1997). While some studies have shown a nearly simultaneous emergence of the two types of points (see Franco, 2005), recent research (Camaioni, Perucchini, Bellagamba, & Colonnesi, 2004) indicates that declarative points may develop a few months later than imperative points. Camaioni and colleagues (2004) also demonstrated that it is only the declarative point that is linked to intention understanding (as measured by a modification of Meltzoff's, 1995, task assessing imitation of failed attempts), supporting the view that declarative points rely on a more complex social-cognitive understanding of people as intentional agents.

Some researchers (e.g., Moore & Corkum, 1994) argue for attributing less social sophistication to 1-year-old infants on the basis of these and other communicative behaviors. While it is certainly the case that intentional understanding is not complete at 12 months and develops in complexity over the first 3 years of life, there is considerable evidence to support the view that it is present in nascent form at the end of the first year of life. In this regard, it is interesting that autistic children (Baron-Cohen, 1989; Camaioni, Perucchini, Muratori, Parrini, & Cesari, 2003) and human-reared apes (Call & Tomasello, 1994) show a dissociation between the two types of points—both populations appear to have difficulty with declarative pointing (both comprehension and production) but not with imperative pointing. This dissociation provides additional support for the conclusion that declarative points index a deeper understanding of others' minds than imperative points. While this is one possible interpretation, it is also possible that the dissociation seen in these two populations is due to motivational differences rather than an inability to detect others' mental states; for example, apes may simply have little interest in sharing sights and sounds with others (Tomasello, 2006; Tomasello, Carpenter, Call, Behne, & Moll, 2005). We know of no studies that have attempted to tease apart the motivational versus social-cognitive explanations, but recent research by Liszkowski and colleagues may lead in that direction.

These researchers have described a third function of prelinguistic pointing: to provide information (Liszkowski, Carpenter, Striano, & Tomasello, 2006). In their study, they found that 12- and 18-month-olds spontaneously pointed to an object they inferred the experimenter needed to complete a task. This type of point is particularly interesting because it clearly involves both the cognitive ability to understand the experimenter's need for information and the motivation to cooperate with and help the experimenter. It would be interesting to conduct a similar study with human-reared apes to see if they are motivated to engage in this type of pointing. Finding that they do not point to inform would not be very instructive on its own; however, if apes, for example, looked to the object the experimenter needed but did not point to it, that might provide evidence that they possess the social-cognitive capacity to determine what the experimenter needs but lack the motivation to provide that information. For present purposes, however, it is sufficient to note that all three types of pointing in which toddlers engage are examples of intentional communication that involve directing the attention and/or behavior of others.

While there is considerable research on infants' production and comprehension of pointing (for reviews, see Butterworth, 2003, and other chapters in Kita, 2003; see also Franco, 2005), it is also important to examine infants' ability to follow others' gaze as gaze may often be used without pointing in communicative situations (Butterworth, 2001). By 12 months babies can reliably follow an experimenter's gaze to an object and will spend more time inspecting that object than if the experimenter had turned toward it with her eyes closed (Brooks & Meltzoff, 2002), indicating that they understand the object-directedness of looking. This is important for word learning because the most likely target of what an adult is talking about is what he or she is looking at; toddlers seem to realize this and, when they hear a novel object label, will look up from what they themselves are focused on to determine what the speaker is looking at (Baldwin, 1993).

It is widely agreed that preverbal infants use intentional vocalizations and gestures to communicate, but there is less consensus on the number and variety of specific meanings or communicative intentions their vocalizations and gestures express. As discussed previously, pointing is used for imperative (instrumental) as well as declarative (sharing, commenting) purposes, but prelinguistic infants also produce requests for actions, they greet their social partners, and they sometimes protest or reject the actions of others (Ninio & Snow, 1999). Eventually they begin to use words for these and other communicative functions.

Before they start using words, however, infants and toddlers produce symbolic gestures in interactions with their caregivers—for example, sniffing to label a flower (Acredolo & Goodwyn, 1988). These gestures appear to be used for the same communicative functions as early words; that is, to request, comment on, and label objects and to describe children's experiences (Acredolo, Goodwyn, Horobin, & Emmons, 1999). Some of these gestures are learned within interactive routines, but some seem to be spontaneously generated by children themselves. Regardless of how they originate, these gestures are generalized and used in a contextually flexible way (i.e., in different contexts for multiple communicative functions), much as early words are, and so their acquisition probably relies on the same social-cognitive skills that word learning does (see next section). The production of symbolic gestures emerges earlier than word production probably because toddlers have better control over the larger muscles used in forming a gesture compared to the many tiny muscles used to articulate words (Acredolo et al., 1999). One interesting finding, however, is that children who are encouraged (trained) to use multiple symbolic gestures actually seem to have an advantage in subsequent verbal comprehension and production (Goodwyn, Acredolo, & Brown, 2000). The question of course is, "Why?" Why would training babies to use symbolic gestures lead them to develop verbal language faster? Goodwyn and colleagues (2000) offer the following suggestions.

One possibility is that once babies start producing some symbolic gestures, the adults around them start to treat them differently—they may talk to them more because there is more to communicate about. So, infants who produce many symbolic gestures may receive more verbal input than infants who produce few or none. A related possibility is that once babies start producing gestures, it is easier to read their minds and figure out what they are focused on—so that makes it easier to establish joint attention with them and determine their specific communicative intentions. If the baby makes the sign for HUNGRY, for example, the parent might respond with "Oh, you're hungry," thereby providing a verbal label for what the child was feeling at the time. In this way the children might receive more *relevant* verbal input. Finally, another possibility is that by using symbolic gestures and being understood children might become even more motivated to talk and be even better understood. Indeed, one of the main benefits reported by parents of children trained to sign is that it makes communication with their toddlers easier and interactions more positive overall. Request gestures help children get their needs met without whining or crying; symbols for specific foods help clarify what they want when they are hungry; and in some cases a gesture for an emotional state can let their parents know what they are feeling. Gestures can even help parents figure out what the child is trying to say verbally. One child produced the phonological form "tata" and no one knew what it meant until she learned the gesture for turtle and said "tata" while making this gesture, enabling her parents to figure out that "tata" meant turtle. Thus, it appears that encouraging the use of symbolic gestures can have multiple potential benefits for subsequent language learning in particular and for intentional communication more generally.

It is important to note that almost all of the developments in preverbal intentional communication reviewed earlier have also been demonstrated by nonhuman primates in captivity—for example, pointing (Leavens & Hopkins, 1998), gaze following (Tomasello, Hare, & Agnetta, 1999), gaze alternation (Leavens & Hopkins, 1998), and even communicative repairs (Leavens, Russell, & Hopkins, 2005). There are a few important differences, however. One is that apes tend to use their communicative gestures for imperative purposes only. Second, to our knowledge, they do not invent novel symbolic gestures as young human infants do. Finally, the apes in these studies do not appear to use their human-like communicative behaviors in communication with conspecifics, suggesting that these are behaviors that they learn only through training and that the learning does not transfer to their interactions with one another (Tomasello, 2006). These differences between apes and children suggest that apes' understanding of communicative signals may be qualitatively different from the understanding of human toddlers; that is, the apes may only appreciate the impact of their gestures on the overt behaviors of the humans who interact with them and not any impact on their mental states. Alternatively, human-reared apes may have the same cognitive level of understanding of internal states as young children, but they may, in sharp contrast to human infants, lack the motivation to share these states with others (Tomasello, 2006; Tomasello et al., 2005). Again, we know of no research that has directly examined the issue of interspecies motivational differences in intentional communication.

By the end of the first year of life, a variety of preverbal behaviors (gaze following, gaze alternation, communicative repairs, pointing, vocalizations, and symbolic gestures) demonstrate not only that infants have the ability to communicate intentionally but also that they have come to understand others as intentional beings. Although nonhuman primates in captivity also engage in some of these behaviors, they seem to do so in qualitatively different ways from human infants (e.g., using pointing only for instrumental purposes, and not using it to communicate with conspecifics). Future research will need to explore the role of motivation in the development of intentional communication.

YEAR 2: EARLY WORD LEARNING AND USE

Before beginning to use conventional symbols (words), some children produce transitional forms known variously as phonetically consistent forms (Dore, Franklin, Miller, & Ramer, 1976) or protowords (Vihman, 1996; Zinober & Martlew, 1985). These forms function as words in that they are intentionally used for consistent communicative functions but are unlike words in that they are not fully conventional symbols in the adult linguistic system. Use of protowords is a significant development because it indicates very clearly that toddlers understand that specific sound patterns can be used for specific communicative intentions, a necessary precursor for word learning.

Infants typically demonstrate the first signs of word comprehension at approximately 9 months of age but do not start to spontaneously produce words until around 12 months (Dale & Fenson, 1996; Fenson et al., 1994). This lag between comprehension and production is probably due in large part to the difficulties associated with coordinating the many nerves and muscles involved in speech production (Acredolo et al., 1999; Vihman, 1996). Indeed, early difficulties with articulation may also explain why toddlers' first words tend to include the same phonemes they used most frequently in earlier babbling (Vihman, Ferguson, & Elbert, 1986). Toddlers' earliest words also tend to be used for similar communicative intentions as their preverbal gestures and vocalizations (Dore, 1974, 1975; Ninio, 1993), but as children acquire more words, they learn to use those words in new ways. That is, the variety of communicative intents expressed increases at the same time as the intelligibility of children's productions improves (Ninio, 1995; Snow, Pan, Imbens-Bailey, & Herman, 1996). Children also gradually develop the capacity to take into account multiple aspects of the interaction context in producing different speech acts (Ryckebusch & Marcos, 2004). And, as in the prelinguistic stage, they continue to negotiate communicative breakdowns with their caregivers, but, not surprisingly, they are more adept at tailoring the reformulations of their initial utterances to the type of feedback provided by their interlocutor (Marcos, 1991; Shwe & Markman, 1997; Tomasello, Conti-Ramsden, & Ewert, 1990). For example, they respond differently to specific versus general queries of their utterances ("What does he need?" vs. "What?") and they are able to monitor their own speech for errors and respond appropriately when queried (Levy, 1999).

Following Bruner (1983), many researchers now view children's ability to discern others' communicative intentions as playing a critical role in early word learning (also see Ninio & Snow, 1988). In brief, the view is that words are used primarily to direct the attentional states of addressees, and that children match the sound patterns they hear to their interpretations of what the speaker is trying to get them to attend to. In Bruner's words, "The problem of how reference develops can . . . be restated as the problem of how people manage and direct each other's attention by linguistic means" (p. 68). If words are used by speakers to direct the attentional states of their listeners, then the child listener's goal in communicative contexts must be to try to understand what a speaker is directing their attention to with a given word (Akhtar & Tomasello, 2000)—that is, to achieve word learning the child must achieve joint focus with the speaker. Indeed Tomasello (1998b) argues that an act of reference is actually an intention to invite the listener to engage in joint attention.

Many experimental studies have shown that 18- and 24-month-old toddlers can use a variety of cues and skills to establish joint focus with their interlocutors and thereby determine their communicative intentions. These include gaze direction (Baldwin, 1993), facial expressions (Tomasello & Barton, 1994), and event or script knowledge (Akhtar & Tomasello, 1996), as well as sensitivity to the prior discourse topic (Akhtar, 2002; Akhtar, Carpenter, & Tomasello, 1996; Diesendruck, Markson, Akhtar, & Reudor, 2004; for reviews, see Akhtar, 2004; Sabbagh & Baldwin, 2005; Tomasello, 2003). These skills enable young children to attend to the appropriate referents and learn the words their interlocutors use, but they also index a motivation to establish joint attention with others. In all these studies, the onus was on the child participant to establish joint attention with the adult in order to learn the word the adult used; thus, joint attention in the second year and beyond may be a special form of what Lang, Bradley, and Cuthbert (1997) call motivated attention.

It is also important to note, however, that in all these studies the children were engaged in a dyadic interaction with the experimenter. One interesting question is whether toddlers are also able to tune in to the communicative intentions of a person who is *not* interacting with them. This is an important question because anthropologists suggest that in many communities young children do not experience as many one-on-one interactions with adults as the children we typically study, yet children in those communities do not appear to be greatly delayed in language learning (Akhtar, 2005a). Indeed, children growing up in these contexts seem to be quite good at monitoring others' interactions, which leads to the hypothesis that they may learn a great deal of language by listening in on the conversations of others (Rogoff, 2003; Rogoff, Paradise, Mejia Arauz, Correa-Chavez, & Angelillo, 2003). Indeed, children in all cultural contexts probably learn a great deal of language from third-party interactions. So more recently we have begun to examine young children's ability to learn new words through overhearing—that is, through monitoring third-party interactions.

In an initial series of studies (Akhtar, Jipson, & Callanan, 2001) we compared toddlers' ability to learn a new word through overhearing to their ability to learn from a direct interaction with an adult experimenter. It is important to note that in these studies the children never got to see the objects (or actions) being labeled as they heard the novel words—rather, they heard the adult say, for example, "I'm going to show you the *toma*" before extracting an object from a hiding place—so they had to continue to monitor the experimenter's actions in order to link the word with the object or action being labeled. The main findings were that toddlers aged 25 months and 30 months were equally good at learning a new object label through overhearing as when they were directly addressed and the older 2-year-olds were able to learn a verb through overhearing as well. Finally, 18-month-olds are also able to learn a new object label through overhearing, but they seem to need additional familiarity with the experimental setting and procedure in order to do so (Floor & Akhtar, 2006).

These are interesting findings, but it is not clear to what extent the experimental context that we constructed approximates the everyday contexts in which children overhear new words. In these studies, the children in the overhearing condition were seated as onlookers to the adults' interaction, but there was nothing to really distract them from that interaction. There was nothing else that was particularly interesting going on; certainly, the most interesting thing in the room was the interaction between the two adults who were playing with fun toys. But in real life children do not just sit down and pay attention to others' conversations. There are generally other things going on that compete for their attention. If children are truly motivated to attend to others' communicative intentions, they should do so even when they are not addressed and even when they are engaged in an interesting activity themselves. So, in two recent studies (Akhtar, 2005b) we examined learning through overhearing in the presence of a distracting activity. Both of these studies looked at 2-year-olds' learning of novel object labels and both had two overhearing conditions—one with a distracter and one without. The no-distracter condition was essentially a replication of the overhearing condition from prior studies—children simply watched as two adults played with four novel objects and labeled one of them. In the distracter condition, children were given an engaging toy to play with while the adults interacted. In study 1, the novel word was introduced in an explicit labeling utterance directed to the confederate ("I'm going to show you the *toma*"). In study 2, the word was embedded in a directive aimed at the confederate ("Put the *toma* in there"). One question was, given that the children were interested in playing with the distracter toy, would they disengage from it to monitor the third-party conversation? Another question was would they show learning of the novel word?

The main findings were that children in both studies monitored the third-party interaction and were able to learn a new word from it, even when they were engaged in another fun activity. Although they attended less overall in the distracter condition, clearly they were attending enough—or at the appropriate times—to learn the new word. In fact, one of the interesting findings that emerged from attention analyses was that the children were most likely to disengage from the distracter when the experimenter used the novel word. Thus, they seemed to be strategically monitoring the third-party interaction (also see Martínez-Sussmann, Akhtar, Markson, & Diesendruck, 2005). These experimental studies of word learning through overhearing along with natu ralistic observations of children's attention to third-party conversations (Barton & Tomasello, 1991; Dunn & Shatz, 1989) demonstrate that toddlers can monitor the attention and communicative intentions of people who are not even interacting with them, giving them multiple sources from whom to learn words.

It is probably true that many (if not most) children spend a significant amount of time in multispeaker environments (Blum-Kulka & Snow, 2002) in which they are not always directly addressed; therefore, overhearing contexts may represent a vital part of young children's early learning experiences. The vast majority of studies of early language learning focus on dyadic contexts; only a few relatively recent studies have systematically examined children's learning through overhearing (see relevant work by Au, Knightly, Jun, & Oh, 2002; Forrester, 1988; Oshima-Takane, 1988; Oshima-Takane, Goodz, & Derevensky, 1996). Future studies should assess the various strategies that children use in monitoring third-party interactions, and the aspects of these interactions that may contribute to the development of intentional communication.

YEAR 3: MULTIWORD SPEECH

Before toddlers begin to combine words, they first combine gestures with words—for example, pointing to a book and saying "mommy" to indicate something like "that book belongs to my mom" (Greenfield & Smith, 1976). These gesture-plus-word combinations appear to "pave the way" for two-word combinations as children who are first to produce gesture-plus-word combinations are also first to produce word–word combinations (Iverson & Goldin-Meadow, 2005). One way in which gesture–word combinations may facilitate the production of word–word combinations is that they may lead parents to "translate" the communicative intents children express with gesture–word combinations into word–word combinations, providing an appropriate models for children on how to verbally express their communicative intents.

Early word combinations allow children to begin to rely somewhat less on the nonlinguistic context to get their communicative intentions across (Snow, 1999). In the one-word stage, their holophrastic utterances can only be interpreted with heavy reliance on context, and even then the child's intent may be ambiguous. Although two-word utterances can also be ambiguous, they provide a bit more information about what the child has in mind. In a wide variety of languages, children's early word combinations tend to be used for a similar range of communicative functions. For instance, toddlers make requests, reject and negate others' assertions, describe and comment on actions and locations, talk about possessions, and so on (Clark, 2003). They also ask questions, often *yes–no* questions that are marked with rising intonation, but *where* questions are also frequent. In their two-word utterances, toddlers tend to mark new information with stress (Wieman, 1976), suggesting that they may take the context (and perhaps the listener's perspective) into account when formulating their utterances.

There is not as much known about the communicative intentions of children in the later stages of linguistic development when they start producing full-length sentences because the emphasis (of most researchers) appears to shift to matters of form (morphology and syntax) rather than function (pragmatics) when children start speaking in longer sentences. Indeed, most of the research on children's developing syntactic abilities is not framed in terms of communicative intentions as grammar has been considered by many theorists and researchers to be a completely autonomous linguistic module. An early exception was Bruner (1974/1975) who said that "one cannot understand the transition from prelinguistic to linguistic communication without taking into account the uses of communication as speech acts" (p. 283). More recent functional approaches to grammar (Goldberg, 1995; Tomasello, 1998a) are promising, but it remains true that most of the research on the early development of syntax and morphology does not explicitly examine the communicative functions of the various constructions children are learning to comprehend and produce.

It is noteworthy, however, that Snow and colleagues (1996) found positive correlations between measures of pragmatic development and grammatical development in their longitudinal study, and Snow (1999) suggests that "being able to achieve joint attention may . . . be a prerequisite to making progress in grammar" (p. 266). This is consonant with Tomasello's (2003) view that "learning words and learning grammatical constructions are both part of the same overall process" (p. 93), the process being reading the communicative intentions of the people speaking those words and constructions. The process is slightly different in the case of grammatical constructions because the child has to pay attention to (and abstract) a *pattern* of symbols and link that pattern to the speaker's communicative intent. In this view, constructions are essentially pairings of form and function (or communicative intent; Goldberg, 1999). It is certainly the case that different syntactic constructions can provide different perspectives on the same scene or event (e.g., the passive vs. the active transitive construction in English), and children and adults do use different syntactic constructions to convey different communicative intentions. We know of no empirical research, however, that has directly addressed whether children learn syntactic constructions in the same way as they learn words—that is, through "pragmatic bootstrapping" (Snow, 1999) or attention to the speaker's intentions.

Some suggestive evidence is provided, however, by Ochs and Schieffelin's (1995) description of the language socialization of Kaluli children. They found that there are several grammatical forms that are frequent in input to Kaluli children but that the children themselves do not use because it is not culturally appropriate for them to do so (e.g., command forms of a verb that the society's rules dictate can only be used by adults to children and not vice versa). The children show comprehension of these verb forms at a young age (by 19 months), but they do not use them themselves. Similarly, there are grammatical forms that are relatively infrequent in the input that children do pick up and use. In discussing these findings, Ochs and Schieffelin conclude that "children's use of particular grammatical forms at particular moments of their language development is profoundly linked to social and cultural norms, expectations, and preferences which may not be explicit and are not easily counted or detected" (p. 88).

Finally, in another major advance in intentional communication, toward the end of the third year, some children begin to tell stories and engage in extended discourse on a given topic (Ninio & Snow, 1999). To do so effectively, they need to adapt to their audience and use linguistic devices such as ellipsis, pronouns, and various causal connectives to maintain coherence and cohesion across utterances (Shapiro & Hudson, 1991). They need to monitor their listener's comprehension and in general use social perspective taking and their developing linguistic skills to ensure this comprehension.

In summary, children's early ability to combine gestures with words facilitates their ability to combine words with each other. As children move from two-word combinations to multiword utterances, they rely less on the communicative context and more on linguistic means for expressing their communicative intentions. The ability to produce complex constructions ultimately allows young toddlers to engage in extended discourse, which requires both linguistic skills and social-cognitive skills of perspective taking. Engaging in extended discourse with multiple partners in turn probably provides children with even more opportunities for further developing these skills.

Our review of developments in intentional communication suggests that the new social-cognitive skills 9-month-old infants have to establish joint attention and read others' intentions play a critical role in communicative development. While we now know a great deal about the "nine-month revolution" (Tomasello, 1999a) and its impact on developments in multiple domains (social referencing, communication, imitative learning, emotion understanding, etc.), we know considerably less about how infants arrive at this social-cognitive revolution. In concluding our chapter, we turn to a discussion of several factors that may contribute to infants' emerging abilities to understand others' intentions in the first year. While this is certainly not an exhaustive list, we consider neonatal imitation, early interactions in which the infant is the object of others' attention, self-produced locomotion, emotion regulation, and an intrinsic motivation to connect with conspecifics.

POTENTIAL PRECURSORS TO DEVELOPING AN UNDERSTANDING OF OTHERS' INTENTIONS

Beginning at birth, according to Meltzoff (2002), human infants are able to imitate others' bodily acts because they have an innate ability to detect self–other correspondences—in particular, cross-modal correspondences between what they perceive themselves doing and what they perceive others doing. In combination with infants' experiences of their own mental and bodily states, and their experience of seeing others behave "like me," this innate ability can provide the starting point for infants' developing understanding of others. The ability to see the self as similar to others probably plays an important role in developing an understanding of others' intentions, as it is most likely through analogy with their own experiences (especially experiences of their own intentional behavior) that infants first begin to attribute intentions to others (Meltzoff & Brooks, 2001). From quite early in ontogeny infants differentiate between objects and humans, and by viewing the latter as "like me," infants can engage in an implicit (i.e., not conscious) simulation of others' intentional states on analogy with their own (Tomasello, 1999a).

Human infants also from very early on participate in face-to-face reciprocal interactions with their caregivers, and these and other interactions in which the infant is the focus of another person's attention have been posited to play a critical role in infants' understanding of the directedness of attention. Indeed, Reddy (2001, 2003, 2005) argues that in early social interactions, there are multiple ways in which young infants manifest an awareness of the self as an object of attention—what she calls affective self-consciousness. For example, they smile more in response to eye contact, they "show off" in order to gain attention, and they sometimes act coy. Babies' sensitivity to others' attention to the self may partly explain why they get upset when gaze directed at them is still-faced or if the interaction is not contingent upon their behaviors (Muir & Hains, 1999; Nadel & Tremblay-Leveau, 1999). While the young infant may not yet have a conceptual or representational understanding of either the self or of others' attention, Reddy (2003) claims that "the other person's attending is perceived rather than represented and the self's objecthood is experienced rather than conceived" (p. 400). The important point of course is that early face-to-face interactions in which the self is the object of attention may contribute to the more sophisticated understanding of others' attention and intentions that emerges at the end of the first year.

It is important to bear in mind that the frequency of face-to-face interactions that babies participate in varies considerably across cultural contexts, and we do not want to be interpreted as implying that babies who experience fewer of these types of interactions may be slower to develop intentional understandings. First, it is important to consider the potential role of witnessing third-party interactions in which the infant can note the attentional focus and intentional actions of others who are not interacting with her (deLeon, 1998). Second, presumably in all cultures babies are the objects of others' attention even if they do not experience a lot of face-to-face interactions—they could not survive otherwise. Attention is not solely visual and can be manifested in multiple modalities—including touch and posture—and in many contexts other than face-to-face interactions. It should also be noted that even infants who do experience a lot of face-to-face interactions are sensitive to a variety of social behaviors that indicate attention: gaze, touch, vocalizations, and so on (Muir & Hains, 1999). It is possible that we may see more sophisticated understanding of others in the contexts that infants are most familiar with. In support of this notion, Woodward and her colleagues contend that babies can show understanding of intentional action much earlier in the first year if one focuses on actions (e.g., grasping) with which infants have a great deal of firsthand experience (Sommerville, Woodward, & Needham, 2005; Woodward, Sommerville, & Guajardo, 2001).

Self-produced locomotion provides infants with additional firsthand experience of intentional actions. While self-produced locomotion may not at first seem an obvious candidate contributor to the understanding of others' minds, Campos and colleagues argue that there are at least two ways in which changes associated with the onset of crawling may indirectly contribute to the development of joint attention (Campos, Kermoian, Witherington, Chen, & Dong, 1997). First, locomotor experience facilitates infants' ability to relate two points in space, a necessary prerequisite for joint attention. Second, when an infant begins to move around on his or her own, changes in the parent–infant interaction follow—for instance, there may be more emotional and regulatory messages from parent to infant and greater exposure to referential gestures and words (Campos et al., 2000; Campos, Kermoian, & Zumbahlen, 1992). Campos and colleagues (1997) tested infants with varying degrees of locomotor experience on their ability to follow an experimenter's gaze and found a strong link between locomotor experience and infants' tendency to shift attention in the appropriate direction. Acredolo and Goodwyn (1997) provide indirect support for Campos and colleagues' second claim: They found that in children slow to learn conventional words, earlier onset of crawling was related to a larger gesture vocabulary. It is possible that locomotor experience may provide infants with more exposure to gestures and words as well as more experiences to communicate about. Many of these experiences will likely be emotional ones (e.g., falling and discovering new things).

Emotions play a particularly important role in early communication and intention understanding (Meltzoff, Gopnik, & Repacholi, 1999; Moses, Baldwin, Rosicky, & Tidball, 2001); for example, toddlers' one-word utterances (e.g., "mine!" and "no!") are often very emotion-laden communications. The phenomenon of social referencing that emerges at the end of the first year (the same time that intentional use of communicative gestures emerges) suggests that infants attend to and use emotional signals from their caregivers. More specifically, Moses et al. (2001) have shown that infants as young as 12 months of age understand the referential intent of emotional expressions. These babies clearly responded differently (and appropriately) to objects toward which an experimenter had previously displayed a positive versus negative emotion, indicating that they understood the referential significance of the experimenter's emotional signals. Recently, Adamson and Russell (1999; see also Kopp, 2002; Reddy, 2005) have highlighted the affective aspects of joint attention in an attempt to understand the role that emotion regulation might play in the emergence of joint attention. In particular, they posit that to achieve joint attention, infants must coordinate their *interest* in objects with their *interest* in people; rather than refer to this phenomenon as joint attention, it may be more appropriate to speak of "joint interest" (see also Hobson, 2005).

Finally, as we have stressed throughout this review, human infants' intrinsic motivation to connect with others is probably a necessary component in the development of intention understanding and intentional communication. Trevarthen (1982) claims that "cooperative intentionality" or an "intrinsic motive for companionship" (Trevarthen, 2001, p. 95) is an innate characteristic of typically developing human infants. There is, of course, development in how this motive is manifested: while 1-year-old infants use gestures to communicate with caregivers, older toddlers are able to use conventional symbols and eventually syntactic rules to express themselves in ever more complex ways. In addition, the variety of communicative intents expressed increases, as does the intelligibility of children's productions. While an innate motive to connect with others may provide the initial foundation for intentional communication, it is quite likely that development in infants' and toddlers' ability to communicate also contributes to an increased motivation to share knowledge, experiences, and emotions with others.

ACKNOWLEDGMENTS

Many thanks to Celia Brownell, Maureen Callanan, Kate Herold, Claire Kopp, Michael Tomasello, and Su-hua Wang for their comments on earlier drafts of this chapter.

REFERENCES

Acredolo, L., & Goodwyn, S. (1988). Symbolic gesturing in normal infants. *Child Development, 59*, 450–466.

Acredolo, L., & Goodwyn, S. (1997). Furthering our understanding of what humans understand. *Human Development, 40*, 25–31.

Acredolo, L. P., Goodwyn, S. W., Horobin, K. D., & Emmons, Y. D. (1999). The signs and sounds of early language development. In L. Balter & C. S. Tamis-LeMonda (Eds.), *Child psychology: A handbook of contemporary issues* (pp. 116–139). Philadelphia: Psychology Press.

Adamson, L. B., & Russell, C. L. (1999). Emotion regulation and the emergence of joint attention. In P. Rochat (Ed.), *Early social cognition: Understanding others in the first months of life* (pp. 281–297). Mahwah, NJ: Erlbaum.

Akhtar, N. (2002). Relevance and early word learning. *Journal of Child Language, 29*, 677–686.

Akhtar, N. (2004). Contexts of early word learning. In D. G. Hall & S. R. Waxman (Eds.), *Weaving a lexicon* (pp. 485–507). Cambridge, MA: MIT Press.

Akhtar, N. (2005a). Is joint attention necessary for early word learning? In B. D. Homer & C. Tamis-LeMonda (Eds.), *The development of social cognition and communication* (pp. 165–179). Mahwah, NJ: Erlbaum.

Akhtar, N. (2005b). The robustness of learning through overhearing. *Developmental Science, 8*, 199–209.

Akhtar, N., Carpenter, M., & Tomasello, M. (1996). The role of discourse novelty in early word learning. *Child Development, 67*, 635–645.

Akhtar, N., Jipson, J., & Callanan, M. (2001). Learning words through overhearing. *Child Development, 72*, 416–430.

Akhtar, N., & Tomasello, M. (1996). Two-year-olds learn words for absent objects and actions. *British Journal of Developmental Psychology, 14*, 79–93.

Akhtar, N., & Tomasello, M. (2000). The social nature of words and word learning. In R. M. Golinkoff & K. Hirsh-Pasek (Eds.), *Becoming a word learner: A debate on lexical acquisition* (pp. 114–135). Oxford, UK: Oxford University Press.

Au, T. K., Knightly, L. M., Jun, S., & Oh, J. S. (2002). Overhearing a language during childhood. *Psychological Science, 13*, 238–243.

Baldwin, D. A. (1993). Infants' ability to consult the speaker for clues to word reference. *Journal of Child Language, 20*, 395–418.

Baron-Cohen, S. (1989). Perceptual role taking and protodeclarative pointing in autism. *British Journal of Developmental Psychology, 7*, 113–127.

Barton, M. E., & Tomasello, M. (1991). Joint attention and conversation in mother–infant–sibling triads. *Child Development, 62*, 517–529.

Bates, E. (1979). Intentions, conventions, and symbols. In E. Bates, L. Benigni, I. Bretherton, L. Camaioni, & V. Volterra, *The emergence of symbols: Cognition and communication in infancy* (pp. 33–42). New York: Academic Press.

Bates, E., Camaioni, L., & Volterra, V. (1975). The acquisition of performatives prior to speech. *Merrill–Palmer Quarterly, 21*, 205–226.

Bloom, L. (1998). Language acquisition in its developmental context. In D. Kuhn & R. S. Siegler (Eds.), *Handbook of child psychology: Vol. 2. Cognition, perception, and language* (pp. 309–370). New York: Wiley.

Bloom, L., & Beckwith, R. (1989). Talking with feeling: Integrating affective and linguistic expression in early language development. *Cognition and Emotion*, *3*, 313–342.

Blum-Kulka, S., & Snow, C. E. (2002). *Talking to adults: The contribution of multiparty discourse to language acquisition*. Mahwah, NJ: Erlbaum.

Brooks, R., & Meltzoff, A. N. (2002). The importance of eyes: How infants interpret adult looking behavior. *Developmental Psychology*, *38*, 958–966.

Brownell, C. A. (1989). Socially-shared cognition: The role of social context in the construction of knowledge. In L. T. Winegar (Ed.), *Social interaction and the development of children's understanding* (pp. 173–205). Norwood, NJ: Ablex.

Bruner, J. S. (1974/1975). From communication to language: A psychological perspective. *Cognition*, *3*, 255–287.

Bruner, J. S. (1983). *Child's talk: Learning to use language*. New York: Norton.

Butterworth, G. (2001). Joint visual attention in infancy. In G. Bremner & A. Fogel (Eds.), *Blackwell handbook of infant development* (pp. 213–240). Oxford, UK: Blackwell.

Butterworth, G. (2003). Pointing is the royal road to language for babies. In S. Kita (Ed.), *Pointing: Where language, culture, and cognition meet* (pp. 9–33). Mahwah, NJ: Erlbaum.

Call, J., & Tomasello, M. (1994). Production and comprehension of referential pointing by orangutans (*Pongo pygmaeus*). *Journal of Comparative Psychology*, *108*, 307–317.

Camaioni, L. (1997). The emergence of intentional communication in ontogeny, phylogeny, and pathology. *European Psychologist*, *2*, 216–225.

Camaioni, L., Perucchini, P., Bellagamba, F., & Colonnesi, C. (2004). The role of declarative pointing in developing a theory of mind. *Infancy*, *5*, 291–308.

Camaioni, L., Perucchini, P., Muratori, F., Parrini, B., & Cesari, A. (2003). The communicative use of pointing in autism: Developmental profile and factors related to change. *European Psychiatry*, *18*, 6–12.

Campos, J. J., Anderson, D. I., Barbu-Roth, M. A., Hubbard, E. M., Hertenstein, M. J., & Witherington, D. (2000). Travel broadens the mind. *Infancy*, *1*, 149–219.

Campos, J. J., Kermoian, R., Witherington, D., Chen, H., & Dong, Q. (1997). Activity, attention, and developmental transitions in infancy. In P. J. Lang, R. F. Simons, & M. T. Balaban (Eds.), *Attention and orienting: Sensory and motivational processes* (pp. 393–415). Mahwah, NJ: Erlbaum.

Campos, J. J., Kermoian, R., & Zumbahlen, M. R. (1992). Socioemotional transformations in the family system following infant crawling onset. In N. Eisenberg & R. A. Fabes (Eds.), *Emotion and its regulation in early development* (pp. 25–40). San Francisco: Jossey-Bass.

Clark, E. V. (2003). *First language acquisition*. Cambridge, UK: Cambridge University Press.

Dale, P. S., & Fenson, L. (1996). Lexical development norms for young children. *Behavior Research Methods, Instruments and Computers*, *28*, 125–127.

deLeon, L. (1998). The emergent participant: Interactive patterns in the socialization of Tzotzil (Mayan) infants. *Journal of Linguistic Anthropology*, *8*, 131–161.

Diesendruck, G., Markson, L., Akhtar, N., & Reudor, A. (2004). Two-year-olds' sensitivity to speakers' intent: An alternative account of Samuelson and Smith. *Developmental Science*, *7*, 33–41.

Dore, J. (1974). A pragmatic description of early language development. *Journal of Psycholinguistic Research*, *3*, 343–350.

Dore, J. (1975). Holophrases, speech acts and language universals. *Journal of Child Language*, *2*, 21–40.

Dore, J., Franklin, M. B., Miller, R. T., & Ramer, A. L. H. (1976). Transitional phenomena in early language acquisition. *Journal of Child Language*, *3*, 13–28.

Dunn, J., & Shatz, M. (1989). Becoming a conversationalist despite (or because of) having an older sibling. *Child Development*, *60*, 399–410.

Fenson, L., Dale, P., Reznick, J. S., Bates, E., Thal, D., & Pethick, S. J. (1994). Variability in early communicative development. *Monographs of the Society for Research in Child Development*. *59*(5, Serial No. 242), v–173.

Floor, P., & Akhtar, N. (2006). Can 18-month-old-infants learn words by listening in on conversations? *Infancy, 9*, 327–339.

Forrester, M. A. (1988). Young children's polyadic conversation monitoring skills. *First Language, 8*, 201–226.

Franco, F. (2005). Infant pointing: Harlequin, servant of two masters. In N. Eilan, C. Hoerl, T. McCormack, & J. Roessler (Eds.), *Joint attention: Communication and other minds* (pp. 129–164). Oxford, UK: Oxford University Press.

Franco, F., & Butterworth, G. (1996). Pointing and social awareness: Declaring and requesting in the second year. *Journal of Child Language, 23*, 307–336.

Goldberg, A. E. (1995). *Constructions: A construction grammar approach to argument structure.* Chicago: University of Chicago Press.

Goldberg, A. E. (1999). The emergence of the semantics of argument structure constructions. In B. MacWhinney (Ed.), *The emergence of language* (pp. 197–212). Mahwah, NJ: Erlbaum.

Golinkoff, R. M. (1986). "I beg your pardon?": The preverbal negotiation of failed messages. *Journal of Child Language, 13*, 455–476.

Golinkoff, R. M. (1993). When is communication a "meeting of minds"? *Journal of Child Language, 20*, 199–207.

Goodwyn, S. W., Acredolo, L. P., & Brown, C. A. (2000). Impact of symbolic gesturing on early language development. *Journal of Nonverbal Behavior, 24*, 81–103.

Greenfield, P., & Smith, J. (1976). *The structure of communication in early language development.* New York: Academic Press.

Hobson, R. P. (2005). What puts the jointness into joint attention? In N. Eilan, C. Hoerl, T. McCormack, & J. Roessler (Eds.), *Joint attention: Communication and other minds* (pp. 185–204). Oxford, UK: Oxford University Press.

Iverson, J. M., & Goldin-Meadow, S. (2005). Gesture paves the way for language development. *Psychological Science, 16*, 367–371.

Kita, S. (2003). *Pointing: Where language, culture, and cognition meet.* Mahwah, NJ: Erlbaum.

Kopp, C. B. (1989). Regulation of distress and negative emotions: A developmental view. *Developmental Psychology, 25*, 343–354.

Kopp, C. B. (2002). Commentary: The codevelopments of attention and emotion regulation. *Infancy, 3*, 199–208.

Lang, P. J., Bradley, M. M., & Cuthbert, B. N. (1997). Motivated attention: Affect, activation, and action. In P. J. Lang, R. F. Simons, & M. T. Balaban (Eds.), *Attention and orienting: Sensory and motivational processes* (pp. 97–135). Mahwah, NJ: Erlbaum.

Leavens, D. A., & Hopkins, W. D. (1998). Intentional communication by chimpanzees: A cross-sectional study of the use of referential gestures. *Developmental Psychology, 34*, 813–822.

Leavens, D. A., Russell, J. L., & Hopkins, W. D. (2005). Intentionality as measured in the persistence and elaboration of communication by chimpanzees (*Pan troglodytes*). *Child Development, 76*, 291–306.

Levy, Y. (1999). Early metalinguistic competence: Speech monitoring and repair behavior. *Developmental Psychology, 35*, 822–834.

Liszkowski, U., Carpenter, M., Henning, A., Striano, T., & Tomasello, M. (2004). Twelve-month-olds point to share attention and interest. *Developmental Science, 7*, 297–307.

Liszkowski, U., Carpenter, M., Striano, T., & Tomasello, M. (2006). 12– and 18-month-olds point to provide information for others. *Journal of Cognition and Development, 7*, 173–187.

Marcos, H. (1991). Reformulating requests at 18 months: Gestures, vocalizations, and words. *First Language, 11*, 361–375.

Martínez-Sussmann, C., Akhtar, N., Markson, L., & Diesendruck, G. (2005, April). *Orienting to third-party conversations.* Poster presented at the biennial meeting of the Society for Research in Child Development, Atlanta, GA.

Meltzoff, A. N. (1995). Understanding the intentions of others: Re-enactment of intended acts by 18-month-old children. *Developmental Psychology, 31*, 838–850.

Meltzoff, A. N. (2002). Imitation as a mechanism of social cognition: Origins of empathy, theory of mind, and the representation of action. In U. Goswami (Ed.), *Blackwell handbook of childhood cognitive development* (pp. 6–25). Malden, MA: Blackwell.

Meltzoff, A. N., & Brooks, R. (2001). "Like me" as a building block for understanding other minds: Bodily acts, attention, and intention. In B. F. Malle, L. J. Moses, & D. A. Baldwin (Eds.), *Intentions and intentionality: Foundations of social cognition* (pp. 171–191). Cambridge, MA: MIT Press.

Meltzoff, A. N., Gopnik, A., & Repacholi, B. M. (1999). Toddlers' understanding of intentions, desires, and emotions: Explorations of the dark ages. In P. D. Zelazo, J. W. Astington, & D. R. Olson (Eds.), *Developing theories of intention: Social understanding and self-control* (pp. 17–41). Mahwah, NJ: Erlbaum.

Moore, C., & Corkum, V. (1994). Social understanding at the end of the first year of life. *Developmental Review*, *14*, 349–372.

Moses, L. J., Baldwin, D. A., Rosicky, J. G., & Tidball, G. (2001). Evidence for referential understanding in the emotions domain at twelve and eighteen months. *Child Development*, *72*, 718–735.

Muir, D., & Hains, S. (1999). Young infants' perception of adult intentionality: Contingency and eye direction. In P. Rochat (Ed.), *Early social cognition: Understanding others in the first months of life* (pp. 155–187). Mahwah, NJ: Erlbaum.

Nadel, J., & Tremblay-Leveau, H. (1999). Early perception of social contingencies and interpersonal intentionality: Dyadic and triadic paradigms. In P. Rochat (Ed.), *Early social cognition: Understanding others in the first months of life* (pp. 189–212). Mahwah, NJ: Erlbaum.

Ninio, A. (1993). Is early speech situational?: An examination of some current theories about the relation of early utterances to the context. In D. J. Messer & G. J. Turner (Eds.), *Critical influences on child language acquisition and development* (pp. 23–39). New York: St Martin's Press.

Ninio, A. (1995). Expression of communicative intents in the single-word period and the vocabulary spurt. In K. E. Nelson & Z. Reger (Eds.), *Children's language* (Vol. 8, pp. 103–124). Hillsdale, NJ: Erlbaum.

Ninio, A., & Snow, C. E. (1988). Language acquisition through language use: The functional sources of children's early utterances. In Y. Levy, I. M. Schlesinger, & M. D. S. Braine (Eds.), *Categories and processes in language acquisition* (pp. 11–30). Hillsdale, NJ: Erlbaum.

Ninio, A., & Snow, C. E. (1999). The development of pragmatics: Learning to use language appropriately. In W. C. Ritchie & T. K. Bhatia (Eds.), *Handbook of child language acquisition* (pp. 347–383). San Diego, CA: Academic Press.

Ochs, E., & Schieffelin, B. (1995). The impact of language socialization on grammatical development. In P. Fletcher & B. MacWhinney (Eds.), *The handbook of child language* (pp. 73–94). Oxford, UK: Blackwell.

O'Neill, D. K. (1996). Two-year-old children's sensitivity to a parent's knowledge state when making requests. *Child Development*, *67*, 659–677.

Oshima-Takane, Y. (1988). Children learn from speech not addressed to them: The case of personal pronouns. *Journal of Child Language*, *15*, 95–108.

Oshima-Takane, Y., Goodz, E., & Derevensky, J. L. (1996). Birth order effects on early language development: Do secondborn children learn from overheard speech? *Child Development*, *67*, 621–634.

Reddy, V. (2001). Mind knowledge in the first year: Understanding attention and intention. In G. Bremner & A. Fogel (Eds.), *Blackwell handbook of infant development* (pp. 241–264). Oxford, UK: Blackwell.

Reddy, V. (2003). On being the object of attention: Implications for self–other consciousness. *Trends in Cognitive Sciences*, *7*, 397–402.

Reddy, V. (2005). Before the "third element": Understanding attention to self. In N. Eilan, C. Hoerl, T. McCormack, & J. Roessler (Eds.), *Joint attention: Communication and other minds* (pp. 85–109). Oxford, UK: Oxford University Press.

Rogoff, B. (2003). *The cultural nature of human development*. New York: Oxford University Press.

Rogoff, B., Paradise, R., Mejia Arauz, R., Correa-Chavez, M., & Angelillo, C. (2003). Firsthand learning through intent participation. *Annual Review of Psychology, 54*, 175–203.

Ryckebusch, C., & Marcos, H. (2004). Speech acts, social context and parent–toddler play between the ages of 1;5 and 2;3. *Journal of Pragmatics, 36*, 883–897.

Sabbagh, M. A., & Baldwin, D. (2005). Understanding the role of communicative intentions in word learning. In N. Eilan, C. Hoerl, T. McCormack, & J. Roessler (Eds.), *Joint attention: Communication and other minds* (pp. 165–184). Oxford, UK: Oxford University Press.

Shapiro, L. R., & Hudson, J. H. (1991). Tell me a make-believe story: Coherence and cohesion and young children's picture-elicited narratives. *Developmental Psychology, 27*, 960–974.

Shwe, H. I., & Markman, E. M. (1997). Young children's appreciation of the mental impact of their communicative signals. *Developmental Psychology, 33*, 630–636.

Snow, C., Pan, B. A., Imbens-Bailey, A., & Herman, J. (1996). Learning how to say what one means: A longitudinal study of children's speech act use. *Social Development, 5*, 56–84.

Snow, C. E. (1999). Social perspectives on the emergence of language. In B. MacWhinney (Ed.), *The emergence of language* (pp. 257–276). Mahwah, NJ: Erlbaum.

Sommerville, J. A., Woodward, A. L., & Needham, A. (2005). Action experience alters 3-month-old infants' perception of others' actions. *Cognition, 96*, B1–B11.

Tomasello, M. (1998a). *The new psychology of language: Cognitive and functional approaches to language structure*. Mahwah, NJ: Erlbaum.

Tomasello, M. (1998b). Reference: Intending that others jointly attend. *Pragmatics and Cognition, 6*, 229–243.

Tomasello, M. (1999a). *The cultural origins of human cognition*. Cambridge, MA: Harvard University Press.

Tomasello, M. (1999b). Having intentions, understanding intentions, and understanding communicative intentions. In P. D. Zelazo, J. W. Astington, & D. R. Olson (Eds.), *Developing theories of intention: Social understanding and self-control* (pp. 63–75). Mahwah, NJ: Erlbaum.

Tomasello, M. (2003). *Constructing a language: A usage-based theory of language acquisition*. Cambridge, MA: Harvard University Press.

Tomasello, M. (2006). Why don't apes point? In N. J. Endfield & S. C. Levinson (Eds.), *Roots of human sociality: Culture, cognition and interaction* (pp. 506–524). Oxford, UK: Berg.

Tomasello, M., & Barton, M. E. (1994). Learning words in nonostensive contexts. *Developmental Psychology, 30*, 639–650.

Tomasello, M., & Camaioni, L. (1997). A comparison of the gestural communication of apes and human infants. *Human Development, 40*, 7–24.

Tomasello, M., Carpenter, M., Call, J., Behne, T., & Moll, H. (2005). Understanding and sharing intentions: The origins of cultural cognition. *Behavioral and Brain Sciences, 28*, 675–735.

Tomasello, M., Conti-Ramsden, G., & Ewert, B. (1990). Young children's conversations with their mothers and fathers: Differences in breakdown and repair. *Journal of Child Language, 17*, 115–130.

Tomasello, M., Hare, B., & Agnetta, B. (1999). Chimpanzees, *Pan troglodytes*, follow eye gaze geometrically. *Animal Behavior, 58*, 769–777.

Tomasello, M., Kruger, A. C., & Ratner, H. H. (1993). Cultural learning. *Behavioral and Brain Sciences, 16*, 495–552.

Trevarthen, C. (1982). The primary motives for cooperative understanding. In G. Butterworth & P. Light (Eds.), *Social cognition: Studies of the development of understanding* (pp. 77–109). Chicago: University of Chicago Press.

Trevarthen, C. (2001). Intrinsic motives for companionship in understanding: Their origin, development, and significance for infant mental health. *Infant Mental Health Journal, 22*, 95–131.

Vihman, M. (1996). *Phonological development: The origins of language in the child*. Cambridge, MA: Blackwell.

Vihman, M. M., Ferguson, C. A., & Elbert, M. (1986). Phonological development from babbling to speech: Common tendencies and individual differences. *Applied Psycholinguistics*, *7*, 3–40.

Wieman, L. A. (1976). Stress patterns of early child language. *Journal of Child Language*, *3*, 283–286.

Woodward, A. L., Sommerville, J. A., & Guajardo, J. J. (2001). How infants make sense of intentional action. In B. F. Malle, L. J. Moses, & D. A. Baldwin (Eds.), *Intentions and intentionality: Foundations of social cognition* (pp. 157–169). Cambridge, MA: MIT Press.

Zinober, B., & Martlew, M. (1985). Developmental changes in four types of gesture in relation to acts and vocalizations from 10 to 21 months. *British Journal of Developmental Psychology*, *3*, 293–306.

9

Becoming a Language User

Entering a Symbolic World

KATHERINE NELSON

Unlike the young of other species each human child develops within a specific cultural milieu, where meanings are embedded in symbols, including language, auditory and visual displays, and artifacts of all kinds. By these varying symbolic means the child unknowingly is taking part in the cultural world—the "community of minds"—from birth (Nelson, 2005). Yet, making sense of that world—entering into its shared meanings—remains a private endeavor for most of the child's first 3 years, albeit scaffolded, guided, and promoted by caregivers. Parents and others envelop the young in cultural narratives, projecting messages about how children should develop, behave, believe, and grow up within their version of an idealized world (Hendriks-Jansen, 1996). The baby's parents often project their own cultural expectations onto a future life that has barely begun through cultural artifacts (toys and furnishings) and symbols, including songs, stories, and protoconversations (Cole, 1996). Although the symbolic forms may be accessible to perceptual and conceptual processes, their meanings at the outset are not interpretable by the infant, whose limited consciousness informs a private, unshareable experience.

The questions of when and how infants or young children may awake to the cultural meanings that surround them is relevant to many developments of the toddler years and later, but for the most part the answers are not at hand. For example, the soft toys in the child's crib are recognized as representations of different kinds of wild animals by the adult but not by the child, although they often have strong personal meanings for the child. The baby dressed in a pink and white dress is not aware of the cultural symbolism of pink dresses, although over time she will no doubt implicitly learn its significance, as children's early awareness of gender markers indicates. Thus far those who have dealt with the questions of symbolic understanding (Bates, 1979; Tomasello, 1999) have barely touched the edges of these complexities.

The question of when the young acquire symbolic functions is of course relevant to the process of acquiring language, specifically of learning first words. The question is often posed as a cognitive one (e.g., Piaget, 1962). What is overlooked in that perspective is that symbols, including linguistic symbols, are quintessentially social constructions—abstract arbitrary forms that have no natural association with the referent or meaning. It follows that learning to use words is at base a social endeavor, although it also calls on cognitive capacities as well as some specifically linguistic skills such as phonemic productions. In this chapter I consider the process of entering the symbolic world by becoming a language user from the perspective of its social foundations and in some degree contrast it with other views that consider the process as primarily a cognitive one.

It is widely agreed that a major transition in social functioning on the intersubjective plane takes place during the latter part of the first year that sets the stage for language learning during the second and third years. During this period the infant appears to awaken to a new sense of self and other with an implicit understanding of self agency and the intentionality of others. This transitional period includes sharing attention to objects, people, and scenes, together with the infant's monitoring of the caregiver's emotional reactions to them (Carpendale & Lewis, 2004; Moore, 1999), developments that lead into the child's acquisition of first words (Carpenter, Nagell, & Tomasello, 1998). Specifically, Tomasello (2003) claims that around the first birthday infants are able to

- establish with adults various *joint attentional frames* that create a common intersubjective ground for communication;
- within these frames, *understand communicative intentions* as they are expressed in utterances; and
- engage in role reversal imitation *to acquire symbolic conventions* first used toward them in these frames. (p. 41)

Tomasello argues that the social practices of mother–child interactions in late infancy establish the conditions within which children are able to use their capacities for imitation and inference to acquire words, that is, conventional symbols that may be used to refer and to affect action within established frames of activity. This argument is in line with that of other theorists who view the developments during the last half of the first year and into the second in terms of the emergence of the symbolic function from the triadic relation of mother, child and object, emphasizing the social more than the cognitive aspect of this construction (Fogel, 1993; Hobson, 1993; Werner & Kaplan, 1963).

Views of the process of word learning reflect to some extent different perspectives on the interpretation of symbols and symbolic development. Cognitive theories of word learning view symbolic functioning as an individual development, whereas social cultural theories view symbol systems as cultural constructions that must be entered into through the support offered by social partners. The latter theorists see the acquisition of language (and words in particular) as both the product of social cultural engagement and the pathway to its further enrichment. The two approaches, not surprisingly, differ broadly in the process that they envision as necessary and sufficient for word learning to take place. These differences help to illuminate what is at stake in understanding development as a social and cultural process.

FIRST WORDS: COGNITIVE AND SOCIAL EXPLANATIONS

Word learning begins and typically gains traction during the early toddler period, roughly from 1 to 2 years of age. As Bates and Goodman (1999) documented, the subsequent acquisition of grammar is closely related to the acquisition of words and uses similar processes (Tomasello, 2003). Thus developments in word learning are central to the questions of language and symbolic development during the toddler and early childhood years, and the differences between a cognitive individualist approach and a sociocultural pragmatic approach are relevant to understanding this critical area of development.

The theoretical framework termed here *cognitivist* incorporates a model of lexical acquisition that requires mapping between a well-defined system of linguistic meaning–form relationships and cognitive concepts that are assumed to be held by people in general (based on the assumption of a real world of things and events that is the same for everyone). Thus the problem for the child is framed as that of acquiring a predefined and narrowly bounded meaning of a word—its correct reference—determined by its place in lexical semantics. What is in question is the accuracy of the child in attaining correct reference. Clearly this end will be most easily achieved if the child has the same set of underlying concepts as that in the language to be learned. Then the process can be thought of as a simple mapping of the particular form onto the available concept or meaning.

The social contextual framework rests on very different assumptions about the problem and the framework for solutions than the individualist cognitive theories (Akhtar & Tomasello, 2000; Bruner, 1983; Nelson, 1973, 1974, 1985, 1996). The social case rests on empirical evidence from studies of children's acquisition of words in everyday settings, emphasizing individual differences in the process and challenging the universality of the learning sequence that is generally assumed. A deeper problem concerns the meaning of the word in relation to its use. This problem appears first in children's "errors" in word use and again the two frameworks view the data from different perspectives. The following discussion aims to illuminate these perspectives.

The Naming Game Pro and Con

One dominant word learning paradigm was outlined by Roger Brown in his 1958 book *Words and Things*, calling it the Original Word Game (OWG) as follows:

> The tutor names things in accordance with the semantic customs of his community. The player forms hypotheses by trying to name new things correctly. The tutor . . . checks the accuracy of fit between his own categories and those of the player. He improves the fit by correction. . . . We play this game as long as we continue to extend our vocabularies and that may be as long as we live. (p. 194)

Notice that in this account the "game" has more than one trial or round, and the tutor and player play equal roles; the player is not dependent solely on his own guesses or inferences as implied in current research paradigms that provide only one opportunity or trial. The game incorporates both social exchange and cognitive processes (hypothesis testing).

Bruner (1983) improved on the OWG by emphasizing the changing role of the tutor (usually assumed to be the mother) as the player (the child) gained skill in identifying and naming objects in picture books. He elaborated this idea in terms of LASS (language acquisition support system), named to contrast with Chomsky's (1965) proposed modular LAD (language acquisition device), the internal black box that was assumed to hold all the necessary cognitive equipment for solving the problems of universal grammar. In contrast, Bruner established the ground for the claim that the role of the tutor (e.g., the mother) was as critical as that of the player (e.g., the child).

Nonetheless, there are several fatal weaknesses in the assumptions of the naming game as a description of the general process of word learning. Most important, a tutor is assumed to clearly point out what is to be named—a thing, an object in the world—and no ambiguity is assumed to exist with respect to the reference of the word. This assumption was challenged in the light of W. V. O. Quine's (1960) philosophical analysis of the indeterminacy of reference. Quine framed this issue through a scenario in which a native speaker points to a rabbit running by and utters a term *gavagai* in his language (unknown to the accompanying stranger to the language and culture). The listener's assumption that *gavagai* means *rabbit* is held to be unwarranted in this account as the term might apply to any number of other aspects of the scene, such as running, rabbit parts, the color brown, and so on. In light of this problem, developmental psychologists proposed that there must be specific constraints on the child's assumptions about the meaning of a word (Markman & Hutchinson, 1984; see Nelson, 1988, for comment.

An extensive research literature has grown up addressed to the question, "how can the child know that the word refers to the whole object and not to one of its parts or a function or feature of the object?" The initial proposals were in terms of specific linguistic constraints on word meaning that would guide the child to the correct reference, specifically the "whole object constraint." After much research and debate along these lines, innate constraints on word learning mutated toward biases and principles assumed to be held by the child learner. Most recently, different researchers have proposed a sequence of principles that emerge during the course of word learning in the second year that are presumed to guide the child's decisions about the meaning of a word used by an adult (Hirsh-Pasek, Golinkoff, & Hollich, 2000; Hollich, Hirsh-Pasek, & Golinkoff, 2000). An alternative approach considers the child as simply employing associative strategies, such as relying on the shape of an object for making decisions about the object's name (Smith, 2000).

Experiments based on the OWG paradigm typically present a child with a novel word for a novel object and then test the child's assumption of the word's reference with a set of objects that vary in terms of their similarity to or categorical relation to the original object. Note that in the experimental naming game paradigm the burden of learning is put on the child; the experimenter's role is simply to point and name. However, in the real-world version taking place in the context of joint activity of the "tutor" and child, the sensitivity of the parent (or other adult) to the child's mistaken assumptions is given expression. Under these conditions the Quinnean dilemma loses its force. When word learning is viewed as (at least) a two-person game, with more than one round, taking place within a situation of shared action and understanding, its ultimate communicative success is less mysterious than Quine suggested, as social context theorists have pointed out (Akhtar & Tomasello, 2000; Nelson, 1985, 1988; Tomasello, 1992b).

A corollary to the general assumptions behind the naming game is that if the game gets off on the right foot, words that refer to things other than objects (e.g., actions, or attributes of things) will be readily learned in analogy to names for things. For example, there are demonstrations that if a child knows a word for an object, then when a new word is used in relation to that object the child will infer that it refers to an attribute or part of the object. However, these general assumptions are challenged by evidence that the naming game is *not* in fact a preeminent beginning point for word learning (see below).

In a comprehensive and influential book, *How Children Learn the Meanings of Words*, Paul Bloom (2000) reviewed many issues and data that have emerged over the past 20 years from research on how children acquire words, with a particular emphasis on the constraints and principles literature and its problems. Bloom argues against constraint theories and their variants in the form of principles or biases but does not abandon the basic "naming game" approach to word learning, placing weight instead on children's general cognitive problem-solving capacities for inferring correct meaning from the adult's naming of objects. Indeed, in Bloom's view word learning is a task to be solved by the child's problem-solving resources, regardless of social context. Among these available resources are capacities for inferring the intentions of others. For example, after reviewing the claims and evidence for the influence of adults' teaching on children's acquisition of words, Bloom states: "adults' attempts to teach children words might help speed up the word-learning process. But they are not necessary for word learning and, even when they are present, do not substitute for the *child's own ability* to infer the referential intentions of others" (p. 84, emphasis added). Thus Bloom assumes that the primary burden of word learning rests on the child's own cognitive ability to interpret the adult's intention in referring to something with a particular word. But, of course, the adult's behavior—whether pointing, looking, or engaging in play or demonstration—is an integral part of the interaction that becomes the toddler's basis for making inferences. The two are not easily separable.

Many other researchers have reached conclusions similar to Bloom's, and indeed, many studies have shown that 2-year-olds are quite good at inferring referential intentions, at least under the assumption that referring to an object (present or absent from view) is the point of the exercise (Tomasello & Kruger, 1992). However, the issue here is not whether 2-year-olds are capable of making such inferences; as the vast amount of literature on social cognition has now affirmed, they are and do. The issue here is what it is about the social communicative contexts that leads children toward this outcome during the toddler years.

Evidence from Word Learning in Natural Contexts

Some comprehension of a surprising amount of language use is common among toddlers, and it is generally assumed that this leads naturally to the production of first words. But this start, and much else about early words, turns out to be highly variable among children, raising the question of what motivates a child to begin producing words. The extreme variability among children in beginning to talk and in the rate of word production shows up in different measures. Although traditionally parents and others have focused on the "first word" that a baby produces, this word is often difficult to identify with confidence, as it tends to be used irregularly in regard to a referent and mixed with uninterpretable babble. Two benchmarks have been used in contemporary work: age of the first 10 words, a mark that is more confidently noted than the first word, and the first 50 words, a benchmark often closely followed by two-word constructions (Nelson, 1973). The latter mark is usually associated with a notable increase in numbers of words learned and used daily, often referred to as the vocabulary spurt (Bloom, 1993). There is some doubt, however, as to whether every child experiences a vocabulary spurt of the kind indicated (Goldfield & Reznick, 1990) and whether it indicates a new level of word awareness (Bates & Carnevale, 1993).

Mean ages of achievement of these benchmarks are often treated as norms, but this practice overlooks the very wide range in age of achievement by typically developing children from similar family backgrounds. In my (Nelson, 1973) sample of 18 children the mean age of producing 10 words was 15 months with a range of 13–19 months. Lois Bloom traced language achievements in this period in terms of number of words used in monthly laboratory play sessions. Although the database was slightly different (i.e., words used in the observation session) the range in age of achievement was very similar (see L. Bloom, 1993, Fig. 7.7, p. 149). On average the age that children from English-speaking middle-class socioeconomic backgrounds achieve 50 words is generally reported between 18 and 20 months. In my 1973 sample it was 19.6 months, with a range from 14 months to 24 months; moreover, individual children achieved this level within 4 to as many as 13 months from first word to 50th. In the fastest cases the two children were clearly "verbal" during most of the second year, while in the slowest, the child was "nonverbal" throughout this period. It is noteworthy that the more recent large-scale studies of children's word learning, largely based on parental reports using the MacArthur checklist across different languages and subgroups, have not significantly changed this picture (Fenson et al., 1994). What might account for such wide differences in such an obviously critical social-cognitive ability?

Why are some children moved to talk before their first birthdays while others remain virtually speechless throughout the second year? Differences in expressive language are not strongly associated with concurrent cognitive abilities; many late talkers score high on both infant and child intelligence scales. Most people are familiar with the tale that Einstein did not talk until he was 4 years old; whether this is true or not, it reflects a reality that the age of beginning to talk varies widely among the bright as well as the dull. The relation of infant intelligence with receptive language (comprehension of words in the first half of the second year) is stronger, with receptive language accounting for the largest proportion of the variance in the Mental Development Index (MDI) at each age and across ages in the analysis of longitudinal twin data in the second year (Reznick, Corley, & Robinson, 1997).

Lois Bloom (1993) emphasized the child's interest in expressing her ideas in the use of first productive words. Her evidence comes in part from a study of 14 children videotaped at regular intervals over the second year whose utterances were tracked closely in temporal relation to their actions and emotional expressions. A major finding was that emotional expression and expression in words were complementary, not unified, suggesting that words were being used cognitively, not emotionally, at least to begin with. However, the emphasis on expressing ideas by itself does not account adequately for the wide variations found among children in their use of words during the early toddler period, unless one assumes that some children have ideas to express and others do not, which seems unlikely. Other researchers have emphasized temperamental variables, suggesting that more sociable children may talk more readily. I return to this question later in regard to differences in meaning of words.

Clues to Motivation and Learning from Words Learned

Most research on early word learning takes for granted that beginning vocabularies are largely comprised of nouns, and specifically names of objects. Therefore, we might assume that toddlers are focused on objects and are motivated to learn their names, but why? To share reference with others? To request? To comment or classify? To display knowledge? Halliday's (1975) analysis (based on one child) suggested that pragmatic uses dominated early word productions. Close analysis of how words are used is required to assess these possibilities.

Although Nelson (1973) is often cited as a major source in support of the predominance of object names, in actuality that study, while finding that 51% of the first 50 words learned by all the children in the sample were "general nominals," it also reported considerable variability among children on this point that is generally hidden from view and not often considered today. Instead, the focus has turned largely to explain object name learning and, later in the process, at the end of the second year, verb learning. Yet longitudinal studies of the word learning process in natural home environments (Bates, Bretherton, & Snyder, 1988; Bloom, 1973; Bloom, Tinker, & Margulis, 1993; Nelson, 1973; Nelson, Hampson, & Kessler Shaw, 1993) have consistently emphasized the variation in vocabulary content among first-word learners, as well as in the rate of learning. These variations suggest the different foci of meanings that infants bring to the word learning process, as well as the social context in which they begin to use words.

In contrast to the first assumption of the naming paradigm, the words that children learn, even at the outset of learning a first vocabulary, are not all—or in most cases not even the majority—names of things, that is, terms for basic-level object categories (BLOCs) as those were defined by Rosch, Mervis, Gray, Johnson, and Boyes-Braem (1976). The related assumption about early word learning—that it relies on a tutor who is available to point to objects whose names are to be learned—is equally fallacious. The empirical evidence that it is not the names of things that need to be explained in word learning but rather words signifying a variety of ontological kinds and relations has led to different conceptions of the cognitive problems children must solve and the kinds of support they receive from social interactors (Nelson, 1985).

Individual differences in the interactions of parents and children during the period of early word learning are striking, even within the restricted samples of middle-income parents from suburban and urban English-speaking communities. Variations across ethnic groups and national cultures are even more diverse (Choi & Gopnik, 1995; Heath, 1983; Ochs & Schieffelin, 1984). Some parents appear to focus on teaching children the names of things by looking at picture books and announcing the names of the things pictured. Others spend time conversing with children (often with older siblings as well) and spend little or no time directly teaching specific words (Nelson, 1973). In spite of the skepticism expressed by Paul Bloom (2000) and others, it seems likely that such differences are reflected not only in the rate of word acquisition, but in the kinds of words learned. Indeed, research supports this assumption. Nelson (1973) identified different styles of acquisition by children in terms of noun learners (referential) versus expressive language learners and in qualitative analyses related these to different parental styles of interaction. Hampson and Nelson (1993) reported quantitative analyses indicating convergence of mothers and children in styles of interaction during the second year. It is clear from these and other studies that a simple application of principles of the "naming game," or of scaffolding principles to all children and all words in the same way is inappropriate. Differences among children must be taken into account in evaluating the effects of parental interactions. Not all styles fit all minds.

Meanings of Nouns and Other Words

What meanings do children intend to verbalize? Part of the discrepancy between observed use and the current experimental research on learning in this domain comes from the claim that children learn mainly nouns in their first forays into word learning and the inherent ambiguity of the designation *noun*. This issue is somewhat complex but is basic to the enterprise of understanding the process of word learning. Given that the early words are used alone with no apparent sentential relations and not in sentences, it is technically incorrect to attribute grammatical class status such as noun and verb to them, but this practice is widely accepted.

Contrary to general claims, the first 10 words are quite variable among presumed nouns, verbs and other classes (Bloom et al., 1993; Caselli et al., 1995; Nelson, 1973). As examples, the most common words among the first 10 in the 1973 sample were *Mommy*, *Daddy*, *dog*, *hi*, and *ball*. Names of people familiar to the child tended to be produced by most children among their earliest words. Action words, those used as verbs and in relation to action, such as *Hi* when someone appears or is attended to, were quite frequent in the early words, as they were in comprehension vocabularies. Names of favorite animals and toys—*dog*, *ball*, and *car*—appear as well. The latter types are considered general classes, but as Barrett's (1986) analysis of his son's use of the word *duck* indicated, often these are used initially for single items in specific contexts (e.g., the yellow duck accompanying the bath) and are only later generalized to whole classes. (See Fenson et al., 1994, for complete frequency counts of words produced by their large sample of children at 16 months and later as reported on maternal checklists.)

The noun class itself is diverse, including proper nouns that name a single individual and common nouns (class names), the latter distinguishing count nouns (countable things) from mass nouns (generally substances). The largest and most studied type are count nouns, specifically names of objects. The diversity of noun reference was revealed in an analysis of words learned by 45 toddlers at 20 months (Nelson et al., 1993). This analysis showed that object names represented only a bit more that half of all the nouns learned in the second year, and just over a third of all the words learned by the children by 20 months. Thus, even among a child's first 50 words, not all nouns are BLOCs. Many are proper nouns, names of individuals, places, brand names, and so on. Others are terms for substances such as water sand, glue, shampoo, and so on. These can also be pointed to and named, but the inferences to be drawn with regard to what is named are quite different from either the proper or common name situation. When writers comment on the commonality of nouns in early vocabularies it is well to keep in mind this diversity of reference, especially when explanations are offered that apply primarily to objects that can be pointed to or held in the hand. Because only about a third of all the words that children acquire even in the first year of learning can be accurately interpreted as names of concrete object categories at the basic level, the "naming game" paradigm must necessarily fail for *most* of the words that these children begin using.

Consider those words we call XBLOCs, nouns that stand for constructs such as temporally organized events like *lunch* or *party*, or places such as *park* or *basement*, or role designations such as *brother* or *doctor*. Other nouns designate natural phenomena like *wind*, *noise*, or *snow*, and some early learned nouns are superordinate category terms like *animal* and *food*. Moreover, some early words are used as both noun and verb in the same form, such as *drink, kiss,* and *walk* (Nelson, 1995). It may be argued that some (or even all) of these words can be learned in an ostensive (i.e., point and name) paradigm; at least they might be acquired in the course of daily activities in which the child can infer at least roughly what the adult is talking about. However, although these inferences may allow common reference they cannot address the possible differences in meanings that an adult may imply in his or her use of a term like *doctor* and the child's understanding, for example, of doctor as a specific person. The lesson to be drawn from these and other analyses is that toddlers learn to use words that occur in their contexts of interest, regardless of their role in sentences.

The following was written more than 30 years ago:

> Frequency of personal experience, exposure to words, strength of need or desire cannot apparently explain the selection of these words. They are personal, selective, and for the most part action related. . . . Children learn the names of the things they can act on, whether they are toys, shoes, scissors, money, keys, blankets, or bottles as well as things that act themselves such as dogs and cars. They do not learn the names of things in the house or outside that are simply "there" whether these are tables, plates, towels, grass, or stores. With very few exceptions all the [object name] words . . . are terms applying to manipulable or movable objects. (Nelson, 1973, p. 31)

This statement (which still represents the empirical data) holds the clue to understanding the learning of words: the child's world of interactions, interwoven with the activities of those around him or her and the talk with those and others, is laden with social and emotional meaning. The child's interest in and understanding of the world is highly restricted in place and activity and reflects the social and cultural choices made by the child's particular family and community. This particularity places constraints on research. Individual pathways are negotiated jointly with parental participation through the initial landscapes of symbol and reference, sometimes giving priority to children's interests but often in benign neglect of those interests, parents preferring the priorities of cultural expectations of how word learning takes place.

In brief, the point-and-name "mapping" paradigm works with objects because we can assume that adults and children have roughly the same category structure for concrete objects that they are using together, although they may have different meanings, such as typical characteristics of dogs, whether friendly or threatening. That this does not work for many objects or for many other entities is well illustrated by the word *doctor*, which the toddler may apply to a single person with an evolving concept of doctor quite different from that of the adult's. In short, "mapping" works in some cases for reference but very poorly for meaning. This outcome reflects the situation of growing up in a cultural and symbolic world; its symbolism must be decoded, learned with the help of the adult community.

Returning to the Quinean dilemma of the ambiguity of reference to ask, "How can the child know what the adult means by the use of a word?" I suggest that we need to leave the problem of reference altogether. Reference allows words to point to something in the world whether present or absent (when both the hearer and the speaker share the same understanding of the reference of the word). But many words (e.g., the XBLOCs that children learn) do not allow reference of this kind; rather they relate to other words within a system of semantic and conceptual relations,[1] and they may have many different uses, which depend on context to determine. Indeed, philosophers have long grappled with the unreliability of reference as a guide to meaning (Frege, 1892/1960; Putnam, 1975). Fortunately, children do not appear to be greatly misled by the problem of reference. They appear to pay more attention to what adults seem to be about and the way they use their words in ongoing activities and topics. In this they are guided by what they know as well as by what they are engaged in with the other speaker.

A SOCIAL GAME, A COGNITIVE PUZZLE

The kernel of truth in Brown's (1958) original naming game lies in the "game" part. However, the different conception of language games put forth

[1]Quine's point, in fact.

by (Wittgenstein, 1953) provides a better fit to the child's experience. Wittgenstein began his metaphoric account of word learning with a kind of naming game, but one that took place in the joint activity of building where naming was functional within the activity (asking for slabs of different sizes) and its use indicated its signification. Among the many points that Wittgenstein brought out, two are significant to the present account. First, he emphasized that there are many different "language games," each relevant to a different activity context or discourse. For example, philosophical discussion calls on one kind of language use, gossip among friends a different kind, and the talk that takes place among the workers involved in navigating a ship a much different one (see Hutchins, 1996). We can extrapolate this idea of different language games to those contexts in which children learn to use their words, such as playing or caretaking activities. Children are often sensitive to the context of use of words (especially nonobject words), and appear to be conservative with respect to crossing over from one miniature language game to another (Nelson & Shaw, 2002).

The second point of interest is Wittgenstein's emphasis on the indefiniteness of reference of familiar words. This point is a bit different from Quine's. Quine (1960) asked how one could know to which of innumerable possible real-world referents a given word was meant to apply. Once reference was established, however, application to a given class of items would not be in doubt; when hearing the word *rabbit* one would bring to mind the whole animal. Wittgenstein noted that the same word can be used for different kinds of referents. He cited the example of "game," asking what all games had in common, and concluding that the answer was "nothing," nothing that is, except the common word. The word in itself (its meaning component) would not predict its reference. He proposed the idea of "family resemblances" among the instances of games, which exhibit overlapping characteristics (e.g., board games, team games, athletic contexts, hide and seek, and peekaboo), but without any essential "core" that all have in common. This idea contradicts the traditional philosophical and psychological concept of "concept" or "meaning" of a word, which classically was held to be a logical construct of necessary and sufficient features. Beginning in the 1970s under the influence of Rosch's (1975) pioneering studies, psychologists have revised their concepts of concept, incorporating the idea of family resemblances as part of the theory of concept structure.

Thus, from Wittgenstein we can take two lessons relevant to children's acquisition of the meaning of words: that they are learned in the course of activities where words are used by others in functional contexts; and that words do not have definite single meanings, based on reference, but rather meanings that are derived from, and are displayed in, use in functional discourse contexts. To acquire the meanings of words children must note their use by language speakers in relevant contexts. For example, object names may be used to refer to single prototypical objects (e.g., "dog" for the small terrier next door), but they may also be used in many others ways, for cartoon characters, wild dogs, kinds of things related and unrelated to dogs (dog dish, dog days), as well as in derogatory reference to other things ("it's a dog"). Not all of these uses are "natural" extensions of the concept of dog.

Wittgenstein (1953, p. 23) famously noted that to learn a language is to enter a "form of life." The social context and conditions of children's lives toward the end of the first year set the stage for entering a different "form of life": where infant and parents share in joint activities, interpreting each other within familiar contexts, sharing attention to objects in play, in caretaking, in "reading" together, or in other kinds of experiences, familiar and novel, such as shopping or visiting the doctor. This everyday largely child-centered form of life includes talk by adults on many different topics, sometimes directed toward the child and his or her actions, but not always.[2] Studies of word learning in the laboratory usually lose the essential social contextedness of the use of words by children in the natural environment, particularly during the early stages of learning to talk (Barrett, 1986; Nelson, 1985; Tomasello, 1992a). It is only within this contextual framework that we can understand certain aspects about the process of early word learning, such as the great variability in both the pace and the composition of vocabulary development over the second year (Nelson, 1973, 1981).

A Child's Perspective

During the first year infants sometimes seem to have an "infatuation" with objects (Rochat, 2001), but their experiences with objects are typically embedded in socially shared activities such as eating, bathing, going for a walk, visiting friends, and so on. Through these experiences children build up knowledge of the things and events of their world from a unique child-based perspective. They then come to word learning with concepts and categories based on their own direct experience of the world and use these preexisting frames to bootstrap the interpretation of words that are used by parents and other caregivers in their daily lives. For example, the child's concept of "dog" may include many functional and perceptual characteristics (Nelson, 1974) and may overlap only somewhat with the concept that an adult has of the category. Both child and adult may include only some of the characteristics that a complete expert or folk account would require (Putnam, 1975). Nonetheless, when the child learns to say "dah" in the context of dogs, he or she will be able to share with the other the "same" label for instances of dog in books and on the street. In addition, as is often observed, a 1-year-old may extend the word to other four-legged creatures, indicating either that the category is not bounded in the same way that the

[2]Of course, not all cultures are child centered in the way that middle-class American society tends to be; they may be more child centered in different ways, or less. In fact, there are many different ways to learn language in different cultural milieus. See Ochs and Schieffelin (1984).

adult's is or that the way words are used to bind categories is not yet well understood.

Typically, parents do not make the assumption made by many theorists that first-word learning is exclusively about the names of objects. Rather, they embed word learning in ongoing activities relevant to the child (e.g., in caregiving). They do not typically point to a glass and say "juice" but rather ask, "Do you want some juice?" before pouring it into the glass and handing it on, and then find that before long the child is saying "jus, jus" in this context (Nelson, Engel, & Kyratzis, 1985). They also point out a great deal of information about the word, some of which young word learners cannot absorb because of limitations on vocabulary and background knowledge. Parents typically themselves find it more interesting to converse than to point and name, and they expect the child to find these activities of interest as well. It is not surprising that among the very first words many children learn to say indicate actions such as "peek" (for "peekaboo") or "bye-bye" because these are fun games to play with sociable partners.

What Are Children Learning When They Learn Words?

The assumption of learning from use exposes the difference between a strictly cognitive view of word learning and a social pragmatic view in terms of what it is assumed that children are learning. In the cognitive view the assumption is that children are learning a language, where language is thought of as a linguistic system of grammar, semantics, phonology, and so forth, as studied in linguistic theory. In theory a lexicon is specified as part of the grammar (and indeed in some theories it carries a good deal of grammatical specification with it) and is associated with the phonological component so that every lexical item has a phonological representation as well as a meaning representation and a specification as to whether it is a noun, verb, or other grammatical kind. Acquiring words to fit into these structures requires some precision, and it is clear that having the right concepts as well as a grammar onto which to map the word forms would be very helpful. Thus the assumption that concepts must be in place before words are acquired for them appears reasonable from this perspective. As Paul Bloom asserts, concepts are not acquired from language; rather, language is "a tool for the communication of ideas. It is not a mechanism that gives rise to the capacity to generate and appreciate those ideas in the first place" (2000, p. 258).

The social pragmatic view assumes that the child is not engaged in "learning a language" but rather is learning words to enable understanding and active participation in situations in which words are used. Words may be fitted into "discourse slots" that is, places in the ongoing conversations that fulfill a discourse function. That children eventually acquire a large number of words and the grammatical structures to employ them in sentences and thus to engage in conversations is evidence that they have become native speakers of a language; it does not mean that they "know" the language in the linguistic sense. One of the well-kept secrets of language acquisition is that children do not have intuitions about nouns, verbs, and so on, a fact revealed when they are asked to learn and classify the parts of speech late in the primary school years (Anglin, 1970). Although they do not "acquire a language" children learn to *use* language, both communicatively and cognitively, and that makes a great difference to their capacity for engaging in the cultural world and entering its "community of minds" (Nelson, 2005; Nelson, Henseler, & Plesa, 2000; Nelson et al., 2003).

The social pragmatic position does not deny that children construct concepts independently of language on the basis of their experience and that these may match those of adults and be reflected in language in use. However, it assumes that what children are learning are not lexical items but bits of language that are used in shared activity contexts, some of which are conventional words, while others are phrases or oddments. In many cases the child's experience does not suggest a concept that matches the vocal element but rather its *use* in a specific context. Such a process has been traced for many abstract concepts that preschoolers may begin to talk about with their parents and others, such as concepts of time (e.g., *today, tomorrow,* and *yesterday*) (Budwig, 1995; Nelson, 1996). The earlier words that children learn to use in context during the toddler period may equally serve functions of filling in patterns or accomplishing verbal acts (Budwig, 1995; Tomasello, 2003). Using these bits of language sometimes provides the framework for formulating concepts about evanescent understandings that stabilize, generalize, and make sharable the ideas involved.

Learning the words for concepts that the child has implicitly formed on her own (e.g., concepts such as *ball, dog*, or *give*) provides those concepts with a stability and generality that they do not necessarily achieve independently of a common language. Under the influence of how the words they adopt are used by other speakers the original concepts may be differentiated or integrated into new structures, or provided with boundaries that they did not originally possess. Thus learning the words both complexifies and systematizes the child's cognitive space. In addition, as words are learned that signify concepts that have not already been formulated the child's conceptual space is enriched and broadened, becoming in the process more conventionalized and less idiosyncratic. These are cognitive consequences resulting simply from coming into the acquisition of words. From the social-pragmatic perspective, children of 2 years of age have learned many things about how different words are used and are in the process of honing their initial fuzzy concepts to those reflected in speech uses by older speakers.

What Does Becoming a Language User Do for the Child?

Once in command of a common language the child can communicate with anyone else in the community who speaks the language, about a range of things, including novel creations that the child has never seen, heard, or otherwise experienced. The words the child learns and uses are used in the same conventional ways by all others who share the same cultural/linguistic world. The child's uses of words are constrained by the uses of these others, but by the same token, they take her into a "social network of minds." As Goody (1997) put it: "Once a lexicon has been established a speaker hears the same word as does his listener [which] may [be] the crucial factor in escaping from the private worlds of thought into the shared social world of spoken language" (p. 391). But reciprocally, the child can begin to express his or her own individuality in this shared world by expressing his or her ideas and feelings in conventionally understood language. Realizing these possibilities begins in the second year with learning words but increases in pace during the third and fourth years as the child enters the conversational and narrative worlds of discourse (Nelson, 1996). Rochat (2001) makes a claim similar to Goody's:

> When the symbolic gateway is opened at the end of infancy, a whole new universe of cognitive and learning opportunities opens up . . . the child . . . can . . . contemplate the world, reenact past events, imagine virtual realities, and generate logical inferences about future outcomes. She can exchange abstract ideas with others within conventional symbolic systems using words, gestures, drawings, or mathematical formulas, or express love, hate, bliss, boredom, or blues via songs, poems, movies, symphonies, dance, books, drumming, or a simple eye exchange. (p. 193)

As emphasized at the outset of this chapter, symbols are not individual creations, or at least not only individual creations. From a neurocognitive standpoint, Deacon's (1997) theory of the "symbolic species" asserts that symbols are very special cultural signs that exist only in abstract relational systems made possible by specifically human brain adaptations. This view implies that children's first words are not yet symbols; rather, they serve other sign functions indicating indexical or iconic relations to things in the world. Donald (1991) took a slightly different view: that cultural symbols emerged as mimetic functions in pre-*Homo sapiens* evolution and that symbolic systems, specifically languages, were human social-cultural inventions. In both views, individual brain adaptations enabled the emergence of cultural-level symbolic language systems, which in turn have revolutionized the mentality of the human species across phylogenetic time and within each generation of childhood (see also Tomasello, 1999, 2003). A symbolic system that enriches, enlarges, and changes social, cultural, and individual life must be used conventionally with groups for purposes constituted within the group. The symbolic system of a natural language evolves over historical time within the cultural groups that use it. The evolving system reveals relationships that are not apparent when symbols are considered on their own. A person, or a child, only grasps that portion of it that is useful within the particular language games in which he or she engages within different sectors of the culture. Within these contexts, abstractions from the experienced world come into focus, ideas that can only be expressed in language and do not exist without it, such as temporal systems or ideas of justice or patriotism.

The riches that Rochat (1997) articulated so well as benefits of symbolic functioning require a great deal of cultural learning on the part of the child, learning that takes place in social contexts that involve three essential parts: conceptual structures and cognitive processes of the child; social interactions displaying symbolic structures by a variety of others, parents, other adults, and peers; and cultural complexes that represent aspects of the world in specific cultural perspectives. In the absence of such learning, the child would continue to experience the surface structures of the cultural world but understand it only from his or her own private perspective, missing its symbolic interpretations. From this perspective it is clear that theories that assume a simple mapping between words and the child's concepts miss the significance of the entire structure of cultural interpretations imparted through everyday social interactions.

How then do symbols become part of the child's understanding of the world? It is usually not until the age of 3 or 4 years or even later that children begin to rely on language as a major system of interpretation, communication, and cognitive representation. Before then, during the toddler period and a bit later, children continue to rely on mimetic functioning as a major tool for understanding the world, as well as a bootstrap into the more complex world of symbolic relations (Nelson, 1996, 2007). The complication is that the adult works within a symbolic system of language and uses that system in communicating with the very young child who has just begun to understand and use a few of its vocal parts, bits that are not clearly symbolic, as they do not fit into a larger system of symbols, nor are they sharable with a larger community. The process of working through language as a system takes place slowly during the toddler years as the child adapts more and more parts of the language for his or her own use in talking with parents and others about shared interests. The system allows communication with anyone who speaks the language, and its meanings are honed to those of the symbolic community. This process is described more fully from the linguistic side by Tomasello (2003) and from the individual social-cognitive side by Nelson (2007).

CONCLUSION

This chapter has presented the view of early word learning as a social and cultural contexted process taking place in natural environments in which the child is engaged in activities with adults who use language relevant to ongoing experience. This places language learning within the context of other developments during the same period and does not isolate it as a singular problem or task. Indeed, it is reasonable to assume that many aspects of social experience and social-cognitive development, as well as physical, cognitive, and emotional development may influence the way in which a child may approach, understand, and begin to use productive language during the second year. The proposal here is two-faced: On the one hand, learning language is not divorced from everyday life as an isolated problem. On the other hand, achieving command of language, even in the beginning stages, leads the child into new communicative and cognitive spaces in the cultural world, increasingly wider in prospect. The successful transformation from infant through toddler to childhood rests to a surprising extent on this transition into becoming a full-fledged native language speaker.

ACKNOWLEDGMENTS

Portions of this chapter (now revised) were originally presented at the Social-Cultural Developmental Workshop held at Cambridge University, September 2002. I thank the participants in that workshop for their interest and comments on that version.

REFERENCES

Akhtar, N., & Tomasello, M. (2000). The social nature of words and word learning. In R. M. Golinkoff, K. Hirsh-Pasek, L. Bloom, L. B. Smith, A. L. Woodward, N. Akhtar, et al. (Eds.), *Becoming a word learner: A debate on lexical acquisition* (pp. 115–135). New York: Oxford University Press.

Anglin, J. M. (1970). *The growth of word meaning*. Cambridge, MA: MIT Press.

Barrett, M. D. (1986). Early semantic representations and early word-usage. In I. S. A. Kuczaj & M. D. Barrett (Eds.), *The development of word meaning: Progress in cognitive development research* (pp. 39–68). New York: Springer-Verlag.

Bates, E. (1979). *The emergence of symbols*. New York: Academic Press.

Bates, E., Bretherton, I., & Snyder, L. (1988). *From first words to grammar: Individual differences and dissociable mechanisms*. New York: Cambridge University Press.

Bates, E., & Carnevale, G. F. (1993). New directions in research on language development. *Developmental Review, 13*, 436–470.

Bates, E., & Goodman, J. C. (1999). On the emergence of grammar from the lexicon. In B. MacWhinney (Ed.), *The emergence of language* (pp. 29–80). Mahwah NJ: Erlbaum.

Bloom, L. (1973). *One word at a time*. The Hague, The Netherlands: Mouton.

Bloom, L. (1993). *The transitions from infancy to language: acquiring the power of expression*. New York: Cambridge University Press.

Bloom, L., Tinker, E., & Margulis, C. (1993). The words children learn: Evidence against a noun bias in children's vocabularies. *Cognitive Development, 8*, 431–450.

Bloom, P. (2000). *How children learn the meaning of words*. Cambridge, MA: MIT Press.

Brown, R. (1958). *Words and things*. New York: Free Press.

Bruner, J. S. (1983). *Child's talk: Learning to use language*. New York: Norton.

Carpendale, J. I. M., & Lewis, C. (2004). Constructing an understanding of mind: The development of children's social understanding and social interaction. *Behavioral and Brain Sciences, 27*, 79–151.

Budwig, N. (1995). *A developmemtal-functiomalist approach to child language*. Mahwah, NJ: Erlbaum.

Carpenter, M., Nagell, K., & Tomasello, M. (1998). Social cognition, joint attention, and communicative competence from 9 to 15 months of age. *Monographs of the Society for Research in Child Development, 63*(4, Serial No. 255), 1–176.

Caselli, M. C., Bates, E., Casadio, P., Fenson, J., Fenson, L., & Sanderl, L. (1995). A cross-linguistic study of early lexical development. *Cognitive Development, 10*, 159–199.

Choi, S., & Gopnik, A. (1995). Early acquisition of verbs in Korean: A cross-linguistic study. *Journal of Child Language, 22*, 497–529.

Chomsky, N. (1965). *Aspects of a theory of syntax*. Cambridge, MA: MIT Press.

Cole, M. (1996). *Cultural psychology: A once and future discipline*. Cambridge, MA: Harvard University Press.

Deacon, T. W. (1997). *The symbolic species: Coevolution of language and the brain*. New York: Norton.

Donald, M. (1991). *Origins of the modern mind*. Cambridge, MA: Harvard University Press.

Fenson, L., Dale, P. S., Reznick, J. S., Bates, E., Thal, D. J., & Pethick, S. J. (1994). Variability in early communicative development. *Monographs of the Society for Research in Child Development, 59*(5).

Fogel, A. (1993). *Developing through relationships: Origins of communication, self, and culture*. Chicago: University of Chicago Press.

Frege, G. (1960). On sense and reference. In P. Geach & M. Black (Eds.), *Translations from the philosophical writings of Gottlob Frege*. Oxford, UK: Blackwell. (Original work published 1892)

Goldfield, B., & Reznick, J. S. (1990). Early lexical acquisition: Rate, content, and the vocabulary spurt. *Journal of Child Language, 17*, 171–183.

Goody, E. N. (1997). Social intelligence and language: Another Rubicon. In A. Whiten & R. W. Byrne (Eds.), *Machiavellian Intelligence II: Extensions and evaluations* (pp. 365–377). Cambridge, UK: Cambridge University Press.

Halliday, M. A. K. (1975). *Learning how to mean*. London: Edwin Arnold.

Hampson, J., & Nelson, K. (1993). The relation of maternal language to variation in rate and style of language acquisition. *Journal of Child Language, 20*, 313–342.

Heath, S. B. (1983). *Ways with words*. Cambridge, UK: Cambridge University Press.

Hendriks-Jansen, H. (1996). *Catching ourselves in the act: Situated activity, interactive emergence, evolution, and human thought*. Cambridge, MA: MIT Press.

Hirsh-Pasek, K., Golinkoff, R. M., & Hollich, G. (2000). An emergentist coalition model for word learning: Mapping words to objects is a product of the interaction of multiple cues. In R. M. Golinkoff, K. Hirsh-Pasek, L. Bloom, L. B. Smith, A. L. Woodward, N. Akhtar, et al. (Eds.), *Becoming a word learner: A debate on lexical acquisition* (pp. 136–164). New York: Oxford University Press.

Hobson, R. P. (1993). *Autism and the development of mind*. Hillsdale, NJ: Erlbaum.

Hollich, G. J., Hirsh-Pasek, K., & Golinkoff, R. M. (2000). Breaking the language Barrier: An emergentist coalition model for the origins of word learning. *Monographs of the Society for Research in Child Development, 65*(3), 1–123.

Hutchins, E. (1996). *Cognition in the wild*. Cambridge, MA: MIT Press.

Markman, E. M., & Hutchinson, J. E. (1984). Children's sensitivity to constraints on word meaning: Taxonomic vs. thematic relations. *Cognitive Psychology, 16*, 1–27.

Moore, C. (1999). Intentional relations and triadic relations. In P. D. Zelazo, J. W. Astington, & D. R. Olson (Eds.), *Developing theories of intention* (pp. 43–62). Mahwah, NJ: Erlbaum.

Nelson, K. (1973). Structure and strategy in learning to talk. *Monographs of the Society for Research in Child Development, 38*(1–2, Serial No. 149).

Nelson, K. (1974). Concept, word, and sentence: Interrelations in acquisition and development. *Psychological Review, 81*, 267–285.

Nelson, K. (1981). Individual differences in language development: Implications for development and language. *Developmental Psychology, 17*, 170–187.

Nelson, K. (1985). *Making sense: The acquisition of shared meaning*. New York: Academic Press.

Nelson, K. (1988). Constraints on word learning? *Cognitive Development, 3*, 221–246.
Nelson, K. (1995). The dual category problem in lexical acquisition. In W. Merriman & M. Tomasello (Eds.), *Beyond names for things* (pp. 223–250). Hillsdale, NJ: Erlbaum.
Nelson, K. (1996). *Language in cognitive development: The emergence of the mediated mind*. New York: Cambridge University Press.
Nelson, K. (2005). Language pathways to the community of minds. In J. W. Astington & J. Baird (Eds.), *Why language matters to theory of mind* (pp. 26–49). New York: Oxford University Press.
Nelson, K. (2007). *Young minds in social worlds: Experience, meaning and memory.* Cambridge, MA: Harvard University Press.
Nelson, K., Engel, S., & Kyratzis, A. (1985). The evolution of meaning in context. *Journal of Pragamatics, 9*, 453–474.
Nelson, K., Hampson, J., & Kessler Shaw, L. (1993). Nouns in early lexicons: Evidence, explanations, and implications. *Journal of Child Language, 20*, 61–84.
Nelson, K., Henseler, S., & Plesa, D. (2000). Entering a community of minds: A feminist perspective on theory of mind development. In P. Miller & E. S. Scholnick (Eds.), *Toward a feminist developmental psychology* (pp. 61–84). New York: Routlege.
Nelson, K., Plesa, D., Goldman, S., Henseler, S., Presler, N., & Walkenfeld, F. F. (2003). Entering a community of minds: An experiential approach to theory of minds. *Human Development, 46*, 24–46.
Nelson, K., & Shaw, L. K. (2002). Acquiring a socially shared symbolic system. In E. Amsel & J. Byrnes (Eds.), *Language and literacy* (pp. 27–58). Mahwah, NJ: Erlbaum.
Ochs, E., & Schieffelin, B. (1984). Language acquisition and socialization: Three developmental stories. In R. Schweder & R. LeVine (Eds.), *Culture theory: Essays on mind, self and emotion* (pp. 276–320). Cambridge, UK: Cambridge University Press.
Piaget, J. (1962). *Play, dreams, and imitation in childhood.* New York: Norton.
Putnam, H. (1975). The meaning of meaning. In H. Putnam (Ed.), *Philosophical papers: Vol. 2. Mind, language and reality* (pp. 215–271). Cambridge, UK: Cambridge University Press.
Quine, W. V. O. (1960). *Word and object*. Cambridge, MA: MIT Press.
Reznick, J. S., Corley, R., & Robinson, J. (1997). A longitudinal twin study of intelligence in the second year. *Monographs of the Society for Research in Child Development, 62*(1), 1–154.
Rochat, P. (2001). *The infant's world.* Cambridge, MA: Harvard University Press.
Rosch, E. (1975). Cognitive representation of semantic categories. *Journal of Experimental Psychology: General, 104*, 192–233.
Rosch, E., Mervis, C., Gray, W., Johnson, D., & Boyes-Braem, P. (1976). Basic objects in natural categories. *Cognitive Psychology, 8*, 382–439.
Smith, L. B. (2000). Learning how to learn words: An associative crane. In R. M. Golinkoff, K. Hirsh-Pasek, L. Bloom, L. B. Smith, A. L. Woodward, N. Akhtar, et al. (Eds.), *Becoming a word learner: A debate on lexical acquisition* (pp. 51–80). New York: Oxford University Press.
Tomasello, M. (1992a). *First verbs: A case study of early grammatical development.* New York: Cambridge University Press.
Tomasello, M. (1992b). The social bases of language acquisition. *Social Development, 1*, 67–87.
Tomasello, M. (1999). *The cultural origins of human cognitions*. Cambridge, MA: Harvard University Press.
Tomasello, M. (2003). *Constructing a language: A usage-based theory of language acquisition.* Cambridge, MA: Harvard University Press.
Tomasello, M., & Kruger, A. C. (1992). Joint attention on actions: Acquiring words in ostensive and non-ostensive contexts. *Journal of Child Language, 19*, 313–333.
Werner, H., & Kaplan, B. (1963). *Symbol formation: An organismic-developmental approach to language and the expression of thought*. New York: Wiley.
Wittgenstein, L. (1953). *Philosophical investigations*. New York: Macmillan.

10

Revisiting *A Toddler's Life* for *The Toddler Years*

Conversational Participation as a Tool for Learning across Knowledge Domains

MARILYN SHATZ

Minds of their own: Birds gain respect
Smarter than anyone thought
—BLAKESLEE (2005, p. F1)

"Not my sister—she wouldn't be surprised," I mused, as I read the headline on that Tuesday's "Science Times," recalling the anecdote with which I began the preface to *A Toddler's Life*, the book I had written more than a decade earlier. In that preface, I had recounted how my sister had extolled the cleverness of her pet cockatiel, Wafu, comparing him favorably to a 2-year-old, and how that had caused me to consider what was special about young children. What I had argued then was that I had evidence from the close observation of my young grandson during his toddler years that by age 3 he had developed at least basic competencies in three critical domains, complex language, self-reflection, and the ability to think about mental states, which built on his uniquely human capability to become a person. Now, here was an article describing the remarkable capacities of birds that purportedly could solve problems creatively and practice deception. "Clark nutcrackers can hide up to 30,000 seeds and recover them up to six months later. Nutcrackers also hide and steal. If they see another bird watching them as they cache food, they return later, alone, to hide the food again. Some scientists believe this shows a rudimentary theory of mind—understanding that another bird has intentions and beliefs" (Blakeslee, 2005, p. F1). The article even reported on a parrot who "can sound out letters the same way a child does" (p. F1). So, it seemed a good time to revisit my arguments for the human capacities that crucially develop during the toddler years and that make possible the unique expression of what I had labeled *personhood.*

This chapter is the result of that reassessment. Starting with the skeptical perspective of one who is less impressed with Science Times articles the more I know about their particular scientific topic, I was biased to hold to my original thesis. Despite my bias, I was a scholar, curious to learn more about bird and animal behavior; and so, with the help of online resources and advice from colleagues, I delved into some of the recent animal literature, focusing, though not exclusively, on corvids, a family of songbirds that includes more than 120 species thought to be particularly intelligent (Clayton & Emery, 2005). Among the data I found were that cacheing food is a common practice among a wide variety of animals; over many generations, cacheing has evolved an array of rather impressive species-specific characteristics. For example, some cachers store food in one site while others scatter-hoard, some species create many more caches than others, and the kind of cacheing done can depend for some species on the presence of conspecifics; also, the cache sites depend on climatic conditions (e.g., nutcrackers prefer south-facing sites that have less snow in winter). Some species are cachers, some are pilferers, stealing food others have cached, and some are both. And, nutcrackers repeatedly go back to sites where they have cached food even after the sites are empty.

Such facts suggest some important caveats regarding the interpretations of particular animal behaviors. Every species occupies an ecological niche that supports evolving behavior patterns. A bird that witnesses cacheing in another bird might very well dig up that cache not because it has a penchant to steal but because its species has evolved simply to recover food where it sees it stored. Similarly, cachers revisiting cache sites even when empty and/or digging up and reburying food may constitute practice or perseverative behavior, with the fortuitous, rather than intended, consequence of making the pilferers' task harder. Yet, whether a bird has itself had the experience of digging up others' caches is critical for changing its own cacheing behavior when another bird is watching it (Clayton & Emery, 2005).[1] Thus, corvids demonstrate skills of both memory and learning. As with chimpanzees (e.g., Tomasello, Call, & Hare, 2003), it remains to be seen how closely sophisticated behaviors like these are tied to competitive food-gathering or -protecting situations.

---

[1]The full story is more complicated. Clayton (2006) reports that both amount of experience cacheing and dominance relations between observer and cacher influence behavior.

Given the current state of research, even on higher-order primates—although the hours I spent reading had made me no expert—I maintained my belief that anthropomorphic explanations of animal behavior are at best premature. Although nutcrackers may hide food with apparent cleverness from other nutcrackers, and they may even be taught, utilizing a variant of that behavior, to hide pennies or buttons if trained with reinforcements, one can still ask whether they *intended to deceive* another or could do so in the natural world in anything but a competitive-food situation. Sophisticated behavior requiring memory and learning need not require representations of others as beings with minds (see Dennett, 1978; Povinelli & Vonk, 2004). Birds may be "smarter" than was previously believed, and their brains may even be morphologically more like mammals than previously thought (but see Emery & Clayton, 2004, for an alternative proposal). Still, immense behavioral consequences can be wrought by seemingly small morphological changes in brain structure or genetic expression. Witness, for example, the linguistic or cognitive performances of some stroke victims or the differences between chimpanzees and humans (Povinelli, 2004).

Still, my reading and what I knew of human development—how the infant, prepared to utilize experience, becomes a person by participating in the social life around her—encouraged more thinking about mechanisms of development. The song a baby bird learns to sing depends both on the bird's type and on the songs it hears, confirming the roles of both nature and nurture in development. But a baby bird uses its considerable learning capacities to become an adult bird, whereas a human infant uses hers to become a person. The essence of different natural kinds may include differences in types of learning. What type of human learning is central to personhood?

NAVIGATING AMONG KNOWLEDGE DOMAINS: CONVERSATIONS AS A TOOL FOR LEARNING

I argued in my book that, for the toddler, human language is a powerful tool for learning when combined with the abilities to self-reflect and to attend to internal states. Interacting across their respective domains of knowledge, these abilities allow for learning "in new ways about new things. She [the child] can get from others information not based on immediate experience, and she can compare her own experience of feelings and thoughts with the statements of others about theirs. Thus, the world becomes many-faceted, beyond immediate experience and limited perspectives" (p. 191). (See Harris, 2002, for the related notion of learning from testimony.) But, regardless of the degree or nature of their preparedness for language, infants must acquire specific languages in the social contexts of particular language communities. I argued that they do so by bootstrapping their nascent knowledge of language, self-reflection, and understanding of mind.

Implicit in my book was my understanding of the means by which knowledge in the domains of language, self-reflection, and mind understanding can be bootstrapped by communication among them. There, the examples themselves of conversational interactions between Ricky, the central participant in my book, and his family members illustrated opportunities for cross-domain learning. Here, I state explictly the means fostering such bootstrapping: Conversations with parents, peers, teachers, and others in the community are vital not only to learning without personal experience but to learning among domains. The immense power of human conversation comes not only from its utilization among knowledgeable language users of a complex, recursive, symbol system but also from its function, even at the child's earliest level of conversational participation, as a common medium of social interaction, where practice, teaching, information sharing, and feedback all take place. Now, as then, I maintain that a toddler becomes a person as he or she builds the skills of language, self-reflection, and internal-state knowledge by continually exercising them in mutually interactive ways within a language community.

In the years since the publication of the book, there has been much research that has supported the view that the toddler years are a time of great accomplishment in the realms of language, self-reflection, and understanding of others. Much of that work is reviewed in other chapters in this book. In this chapter, I consider whether and how some of the recent work supports and elaborates my position. I also expand on my discussion of conversations as a means by which bootstrapping among knowledge domains can be accomplished. Finally, as I write, I briefly address methodological questions that have been recurrent concerns of developmentalists, such as how to interpret a behavior, when to say a particular skill or piece of knowledge has been acquired, and whether development is best considered as continuous—seen as essentially seamless, with underlying mechanisms for change remaining constant over time—or as discontinuous—seen as a series of steps or stages accounted for by major reorganizations based on various underlying mechanisms.

LANGUAGE INFLUENCES ON UNDERSTANDING OF MIND AND ON SELF-REFLECTION

Conversations and the Development of Mind Understanding

I recounted in my book the steps that Ricky took during his toddler years as he developed an understanding of mind. At 1 year, 3 months, he delighted in playing "where's Ricky" but believed that covering his face was all that was necessary to hide from his interlocutors. By 1 year, 5 months, he recognized when he had failed to communicate his own actions successfully by phone but he did not understand the visual limitations the telephone imposed on his phone partner. At 1 year, 9 months, he showed he knew the difference between his knowledge and someone else's ignorance, and a few months later, he began justifying his own behavior when he thought it was not expected by others. By 2 years, 6 months, he questioned others about their desires and preferences and the sources of their knowledge, and by 2 years, 9 months, Ricky could make appropriate inferences about others' perceptions and beliefs, even when they were false and different from his. Thus, the development of mental state understanding was gradual, and progressed not only from a focus on desires to one on beliefs (Wellman & Woolley, 1990) but also through an extended period of what I called a knowledge psychology, a concern with knowing and ignorance, sources of knowledge, and eventually, false beliefs.

In light of recent work, more can be added to this story. For one, there has been ongoing controversy over whether an understanding of mind is due to conceptual change (Wellman, Cross, & Watson, 2001) or has an innate, possibly modular basis (Scholl & Leslie, 2001). However, regardless of one's stance on that theoretical debate or on the possible mechanisms for continued development of understanding of mind throughout the preschool years and beyond (see Wellman, 2002, for a review), there is little doubt about two points: First, there is some preverbal understanding of intention in infants. Second, conversations are an important means to development of mind understanding beyond that early level, not least of all because sophisticated mind understanding utilizes so many other kinds of knowledge, and conversations are useful in acquiring them.

More particularly, the changes that have been documented over a period of less than 2 years, from 1 year, 3 months, to 3 years, are remarkable when one considers how much is involved in the sophisticated cognition displayed in recognizing and reporting, as Ricky did, on others' false beliefs. Understandings about perceptual constraints, reality, pretense, knowledge, imagination, internal states, actions, expectations, social conventions, and artifacts like telephones all increase during this period. (See, e.g., Lillard, 2002, on pretend play, and Yaniv & Shatz, 1988, on perceptibility.) Some of these new understandings surely come from immediate experiences with both the natural and the artifactual world, but some undoubtedly come from linguistic interactions with more knowledgeable others. There are many examples in *A Toddler's Life* of conversations about percepts, knowledge, artifacts, ownership, and acceptable behavior. Talk about reality and "make-believe" is frequent during the third year of life, with numerous researchers reporting anecdotes of children asking for confirmation of whether or not something is real, and parents reporting how many times they assuage their child's fears about fantasy characters like the Wicked Witch of the West in *The Wizard of Oz* by saying, "She's not real." Although a 3-year-old still reveals incomplete understandings about at least some of these topics, that fact does not diminish the varied accomplishments of the toddler that derive at least in part from conversations; nor does it detract from the argument that these increased understandings contribute to improved mental state reasoning that may be especially evident in natural settings.

In addition, it is now well documented that talk within the family about internal states relates to preschoolers' understandings of others (e.g., Dunn, Brown, Slomkowski, Tesla, & Youngblade, 1991). Indeed, the amount of mothers' talk about cognitive states around a child age 2 years is related to children's awareness of inner states at both 2 years and 3 years, even for moderately disadvantaged children (Hughes, Ensor, Fujisawa, & Lecce, 2005). And, child lexical and grammatical development at age 2 is predictive of performance on false-belief tasks at age 4 (Farrar & Maag, 2002; Watson, Painter, & Bornstein, 2001), although even the method of correlating factors measured at different time points does not suffice to establish unequivocally a direct causal relation between the two. Rather, there may be a third factor underlying one or both of the two factors (e.g., participation in conversations or some other aspect of cognitive development). In any case, the mechanism of conversation influences the understanding of mind both indirectly—as in conversations about the multiple kinds of knowledge like perceptual understandings that affect the quality of mental state reasoning—and directly—as in conversations about cognitive states themselves.

Conversations and the Development of Self-Understanding

Language is also a tool for learning more about oneself (Budwig, 2000). Employing the framework of language socialization, Budwig argues that language is the mechanism by which the self is constructed in culturally acceptable ways, via linguistic interactions between caregiver and child that offer the child culturally appropriate perspectives on the self. Whether or not one accepts radical cultural relativism, some version of the argument for social-linguistic influences on the construction of self seems indisputable. An example from Ricky's life reveals how social-linguistic experiences can encourage even the child's construction of a body image. At the zoo, as we watched a Siberian tiger flick his tongue, Ricky stuck out his tongue and then asked to see ours. When the tiger flicked his tail and his mother said, "Look at the tiger's long tail," Ricky turned to check his own backside.

The ability to self-reflect, that is, the ability to compare oneself to others' bodies, behaviors, mental states, and standards, is important to the process of adjusting one's behavior and/or self-image to interface appropriately with one's social community. Although the precise nature of what has been called emotion regulation in the literature is still controversial, it is very likely often implicated in the adjustment process that takes as input self-reflection. Language has been suggested to have a role in the development of emotion regulation (Kopp, 1982), but whether talk about emotions facilitates the development of self-regulation of emotions requires further research (Campos, Frankel, & Camras, 2004), However, we already have some suggestive findings regarding relations between language and emotion: family talk about emotions facilitates the understanding of others' emotions (Dunn, Brown, & Beardsall, 1991) and facial expressions of sadness are related to toddlers' scores on the MacArthur vocabulary checklist, and this relation is mediated by degree of caregiver-reported self-regulation (Bolnick et al., 2005). Moreover, difficulties in language development measured at age 2 years, coupled with a parenting style that does not use language to help the child structure experience, relate to serious behavior problems (Cole, Bender, Radzioch, Bender, & Yetter, 2005). (See also Chambers, 1999, on family talk and learning to cope.)

Important as it is, the construction of self involves, of course, more than just emotion regulation. One concept of self concerns the "categorical self," the representation of physical and personality characteristics constructed at least in part from experiencing (often linguistic) evaluations of self by others. (See Harter, 1999, for a review.) This can be distinguished from that of "self as mental agent," an intentional actor with desires and beliefs. (See Gergely, 2002, on this distinction and for a review of the literature on self as agent and how it develops from infancy through the preschool years, as mental state understanding grows.) As the work on Ricky, and much other research, has shown, language impacts the development of both aspects of self-concepts. Thus, there are likely multiple influences of language experience on the development of self-understanding, again some direct and some indirect. More research will be needed to elaborate the kinds and extent of these influences.

Language Use and/or Conversation as Method

As a companion to language as mechanism, Budwig (2000) offers language as method, the use of language as a tool for researchers "that aids in tapping underlying thoughts" (p. 195). Indeed, language as method was what enabled me, by using conversations (i.e., Ricky's linguistic interactions with family members), to document Ricky's development. His language rather readily revealed the progress he had made in understanding others, as well as in many other domains. For example, when he reported that his teacher had unzipped his jacket at school and added, "Her thought me was warm" (Shatz, 1994, p. 160), he left little doubt that he could think about what thoughts might have motivated another's actions. Thus, when there are many such examples, language as method can be a powerful tool for assessing competence, in particular, competence in representing others as beings capable of internal states.

Both language use in a social context as mechanism and language as method are important, then, for understanding the developing skills of toddlers, the former for its explanatory value and the latter for its evidential value. Conversation as mechanism is a tool for acquiring all sorts of knowledge, including learning more about others, even as it is a tool for learning more about language itself. As the toddler bootstraps his or her way into language use, the toddler can engage his or her caregivers in more conversations and hence learn from them as well as from immediate experience (Shatz, 1987, 1994). And, with the use of language as method, the child's linguistic interactions can provide evidence of both growing social-linguistic competence and of conversations as a source of information for learning still more.

It is important to reiterate clearly what aspects of "language" are especially relevant here. Rather than rely solely on the word *conversation*, I have sometimes used the word *language* in part to include evidence for influences that occasionally involve measures of language development like vocabulary. But much of the most convincing evidence in fact depends on language use in conversation. This fact stands in contrast to the to-date less compelling evidence for the influence of differences in linguistic form, at least with regard to understanding of mind (see, e.g., Shatz, Diesendruck, Martinez-Beck, & Akar, 2003; So, Tardif, & Karciroti, 2005). Moreover, research on bilinguals (Goetz, 2003) and twins (Hughes, Jaffee, et al., 2005) suggests that neither formal differences between languages nor genetic similarities between children have as much impact on progress in understanding of mind as do environmental factors such as experiences with different kinds of listeners. This is not to say that the correlations between measures of language development like vocabulary size and various aspects of social cognition like the understanding of mind are spurious. Rather, such correlations suggest that the more language the child has to contribute to conversations, the more likely those conversations are to be of the sort that are facilitative of social cognitive development.

Interpreting Nonverbal Behavior

When children (and animals) do not give evidence of competence by their use of language, there are several alternatives left to the scientist. One is to observe nonverbal behavior that occurs either with language or without language to examine it for a possible lack of full understanding. When a 1-year-old puts a towel over his head and calls, "Where's Ricky?," it is a reasonable inference that he is unsophisticated about visual perceptibility, and considerable research has confirmed that accruing knowledge about perceptual capacities is an extended process (Yaniv & Shatz, 1988). A second strategy is to do cleverly designed experimentation, for example, examining infants' understandings of others. Recent research of this sort has revealed nascent abilities to interpret other humans' actions in terms of their intentions. However, there is considerable evidence that children's skills in this arena continue to develop throughout the preverbal and into the postverbal period (see Poulin-Dubois & Graham, 2007, for a review). Nonetheless, the question of just what to call a precursor to mental state understanding and what to take as evidence of actual mental state understanding requires not only careful experimentation but careful theorizing as well (see, e.g., Gergely & Csibra, 2003).

Third, the behavioral data available need to be interpreted conservatively, and in light of other relevant research. My sister recently reported that her (now much older) cockatiel kept his head swiveled toward her as he walked to get behind the curtains where she hides the cable wires on which he likes to chew. Her story reminded me of how Ricky's mom and I sat at the kitchen table watching his younger brother, Max, when he was about 1 year, 6 months, walk backwards into the bathroom to get to the forbidden toilet paper that he liked to unroll. At the time I thought, "how cute. Max thinks that by facing us he will fool us into thinking he is not intending to do a forbidden act." Then I believed Max had an understanding of mind, however unsophisticated. Now one can ask whether my everyday naive psychology applied not only to Max but to Wafu as well. The professional answer is "no," at least not on the basis of current research.

Although both Max at age 1 year, 6 months, and the mature Wafu may have produced similar orienting behaviors, that alone is insufficient to assume a common explanation for the inadequacy of their thinking. The recent literature suggests that what each lacked in reasoning may be different, and the application of naive psychology to explain Max's behavior but not Wafu's is appropriate. There is considerable evidence that, sometime during the second year of life, toddlers exhibit some awareness of others' mental states (see Gergely, 2002; Moore, Chapter 2, this volume; Wellman, 2002). A positive answer to the question whether Wafu and his kind do as well awaits further research, but given the limitations on human infants' abilities already noted, I am not sanguine about birds. In Max's case, he was old enough for me to infer he was trying to conceal his intentions from others, even though he did not yet know that others could perceive direction of motion regardless of facing behavior or how sophisticated adults could be when judging others' motives. That is, by his age, he very likely had an awareness of mental states in others, however naive and inaccurate his understanding of adults. In contrast, Wafu's thinking may have involved no notion of mental states at all; he may have had the intention to go behind the curtain, but as long as he moved to it while facing my sister, he may have thought he would not incur a negative reaction from her (see also Povinelli & Vonk, 2004, on the importance of facing behavior for chimpanzees). The anecdote, then, suggests that Wafu can behave on the basis of learning from past experience, but it does not require us to grant him an understanding of mind equivalent to Max's. As Povinelli (2004) notes with regard to chimpanzee–human comparisons, what look like identical units of observable behavior may still require different explanations regarding the nature of the thinking underlying them.

UNDERSTANDING OF MIND AND SELF-REFLECTION INFLUENCES ON LANGUAGE DEVELOPMENT

The relations among language, self-reflection, and the ability to think about mental states are not unidirectional. As I noted in the introduction to my book (Shatz, 1994), despite formal differences among domains of knowledge, "learning in one area can still influence learning in another" (p. 5). "Ricky uses what understanding he has of language to increase his knowledge about others, and . . . his developing social knowledge enhances his learning of language" (p. 6.) The bootstrapping involves reciprocal relationships.

Mind Understanding and Vocabulary Development

Given the idea that children use whatever they have to learn more, even across disparate domains like social and linguistic knowledge, it should come as no surprise that there is increasing evidence for how preschoolers use their early understandings of mental states to acquire vocabulary. Even toddlers aged 1 year, 6 months, at early stages of mental state awareness, use cues like eye gaze to help them map labels to referents (Baldwin, 1993). And, by 2 years, 3 months, toddlers can use a variety of behavioral cues to actors' intentions to learn new verbs (Poulin-Dubois & Forbes, 2002).

Nonetheless, we need more research documenting just when and how much children under age 3 use their burgeoning mental state understandings to learn language, as well as what kinds of understandings they can use for that purpose. Recent findings raise the question of just how readily toddlers can apply their understandings to vocabulary learning. For example, although a 1½-year-old can offer food items to others based on their desires that differ from his or her own (Repacholi & Gopnik, 1997), even toddlers a year older fail to use others' verbal testimony about their desires in a word-learning task (Saylor & Troseth, 2005). Possibly, nonverbal information about desires, like intentions in action (Poulin-Dubois & Forbes, 2002), would be easier to integrate into the job of word learning. Indeed, other research suggests that the more specific verbal information the child has to deal with (such as incorrect labels as opposed to general statements of ignorance), the less able even a 3-year-old is to use source information (whether a speaker is trustworthy or not) to learn words (Koenig, Clement, & Harris, 2005).

Paradoxically, then, when information relevant to the analysis of another's mental state is made available in verbal form, that information itself may require enough processing from the child to leave too few resources to apply the result to the word-learning task at hand. Thus, one implication of a limited-resources approach is that information provided in conversational interactions has to be within the child's ability to use it (i.e., within his or her "zone of proximal development") (see Valsiner, 1998, for a discussion of this notion). For example, if a child's developing language skills require much in the way of resources to extract information about another's desires, the child may not be able to use that information efficiently to impact additional cognitive activities like word learning that would call simultaneously on processing resources. This limited-resources explanation contrasts with one based on cognitive deficits: The naturalistic data revealing false-belief understanding in toddlers like Ricky suggest that failures at experimental tasks requiring 3-year-olds to think about false beliefs signaled by verbal information may not be due to their inability to think about false beliefs in such contexts but to their inability to do so and to apply that knowledge at the same time to word learning (Shatz, 2005).

The limited-resource explanation suggests that older children and adults should also exhibit failures of mental state reasoning in computationally taxing situations. There is much evidence for such failures, with alternative explanations for such behavior across the lifespan (for reviews, see Birch, 2005; Royzman, Cassidy, & Baron, 2003). Future research should distinguish among them.

Self-Reflection and the Development of "Me"

As for self-reflection, already at 1 year, 4 months, toddlers look longer at a human speaker who uses true labels for common objects than they do at speakers using false labels (Koenig & Echols, 2003), although such a finding does not indicate that the infants have metaknowledge (i.e., that they know what they know). Rather, they may only know—or expect—other humans to use the correct labels they have regularly experienced, and they may not do a comparative evaluation of the knowledge of self and other. Similarly, children under age 2 years do not show enhanced performance in the presence of others as predicted by Zajonc's social facilitation hypothesis (Wanshaffe, 2002).

By age 2, or shortly thereafter, there is some evidence, from Ricky and elsewhere (see Kagan, 1981), that toddlers are beginning to self-evaluate via comparisons to others. Physical self-recognition behaviors are undoubtedly prerequisite to such comparisons, and 18-month-olds demonstrate such behavior, but chimpanzees can also self-recognize (Gallup, 1970). Stipek, Gralinski, and Kopp (1990) proposed the following sequence of development based on an analysis of 25 behaviors related to self-concept: (1) physical self recognition, (2) neutral and evaluative self-description, and (3) emotional responses to wrongdoing. More recently, Lewis and Ramsay (2004) found that children reaching the milestone of physical self-recognition at ages 15–21 months were more likely to exhibit more personal pronoun use and more advanced pretend play than children of comparable ages who had not reached that milestone. They argue that the concomitance of these accomplishments indicates that a metarepresentation of self—which they define as having an idea of "me" or "I know that I know"—emerges sometime during the second half of the second year of life.

Whether metarepresentation of self develops as early as 1 year, 8 months or by 2 years, 6 months, various capacities—and more than just physical self-recognition—feed into it. One such ability may be the ability to do recursive thinking (see Premack, 2004). Another may be some early ability to represent mental states. Again, more research is needed, not only to assess whether conversational experience facilitates progress toward a metalevel of self-reflection but to address whether the observed increase in linguistic self-reference is a consequence of it. There is also a need to clarify how comparisons between self and other relate to metarepresentation of self, or self-reflection. I favor a bootstrapping model: Some primitive metarepresentational ability—possibly the ability to do recursive thinking coupled with the propensity to be social (see Gelman, 1990)—is likely necessary for self–other comparisons, but such comparisons enhance the quality of metarepresentations of self. Moreover, the more elaborated the metarepresentations, the more valuable they become as tools in social cognition and social-linguistic interactions. For example, we know that the process of self-comparison to others in terms of both knowledge and ability is well established in preschoolers; 3-year-olds evaluate others' testimony against their own experience to assess the trustworthiness of their informants (Clément, Koenig, & Harris, 2004). And one 3-year-old declined to try her hand at an activity her grandfather had just done by saying, "I just a little girl."

WILL THE REAL TODDLER PLEASE STAND UP?

As a scientist, I appreciate the analytic method, the stripping away of variables that can interfere with the propounding of more compelling causal theories of particular phenomena. For example, our understanding of gravity ignores the role of friction, and our knowledge of grammatical universals is greatly enhanced by ignoring phonological differences among languages (see Baker, 2001). Any introductory textbook in child development can attest to the great strides in our understanding of child development that have been made using analytic methods to study categorization, memory, attachment, and a host of other topics in cognitive and social development. Toddlers as subjects have participated, along with chimpanzees and humans of other ages, in experimental studies that have enhanced our understanding of particular human capacities and abilities at different ages. Moreover, a focus on particular phenomena has helped to establish that different domains of knowledge can have different structural descriptions and be based on different skeletal principles (see, e.g., Gelman & Williams, 1998; Hirschfeld & Gelman, 1994; Keil & Wilson, 2000).

There is, however, another aspect of toddlers not to be ignored: Examining toddlers in the context of their everyday lives emphasizes the whole child and how various aspects of their knowledge seem to interact. It is the toddler as whole child who is becoming a person by using what he or she knows to learn more, not just in one domain at a time but across domains. This does not mean the same thing as that there are domain-general mechanisms of learning. Others have proposed domain-general tools such as frequency-counting computational devices that help account for development within multiple domains (see Gelman & Lucariello, 2002, for an enlightening discussion of the explanatory limitations of such tools). Rather, a consideration of the whole child suggests that there is at least one other sort of mechanism relevant to human learning that operates not just within a variety of domains but—importantly—among them. Such a mechanism allows communication among knowledge domains; it already functions in toddlerhood and is a powerful tool for bootstrapping among domains. Recently, several researchers have offered candidates for developing skills that may play similar domain-permeating executive functions, for example, inhibitory control and working memory (Moses, Carlson, & Sabbagh, 2005) and language (Spelke, 2003), though the details of the candidate mechanisms (such as the combinatorial power of language) are often not well enough specified to assess how much they can account for as executive operators. There is little reason at this point to believe there is only one such mechanism.

My candidate for a domain-permeating mechanism is the capacity to engage in "conversations." The mechanism builds on the child's abilities to attend to and analyze a human language, to see the world in social terms, and to relate self and other—three capacities that Mead (1934) had proposed long ago were interrelated. Moreover, it entails the child's ability to engage others in conversations and to take up and to utilize the information available therein. (See Shatz, 1987, on the elicitation, entry, and expansion operations available for language development.) From the time infants as young as 2 months of age respond to caregivers with cooing and smiling, they are encouraging caregiver engagement, and caregivers typically are delighted to continue to interact, thereby offering input for the child. This early "conversational" reciprocal behavior gradually becomes more sophisticated as the child uses the input to develop more language and understanding of self and others, and as interlocutors readily elaborate their roles as teachers. As within-domain knowledge structures grow, the opportunity for more learning from increasingly sophisticated conversational interactions does as well. Thus, this mechanism has the advantage of accounting for gradual development in a variety of domains over time as well as among domains. And it suggests that at least some deficits in development can be traced to disruptions (for either biological or environmental reasons) in conversational symbiosis, which prohibit the child's access to the information needed to become a fully functioning person in a speech community.

However, neither studies of the toddler as subject nor studies of the toddler as whole child in themselves constrain the theoretical issue of whether development is best conceived of as seamless (continuous development) or as a series of reorganizations (discontinuous development). On the surface, some candidates for a mechanism for across-domain learning such as language (as suggested by Spelke, 2003) may seem more compatible with a reorganization approach and, hence, discontinuous development. A close look at language development itself, however, suggests that it may be virtually impossible to pinpoint when "enough" language has been learned to generate reorganizations. The same criticism may be applicable to the mechanism of working memory. A more productive approach may be to abandon major reorganization theories for dynamic systems theories that favor a more continuous approach and allow for increasingly sophisticated organizations to emerge without postulating broad executive mechanisms (see, e.g., Courage & Howe,

2002). Yet, dynamic systems theory, as applied to human development is still in its infancy, and its enduring usefulness is an open question. In any event, it may even be productive for developmental theorists to eschew the continuity–discontinuity debate altogether in favor of an across-domain bootstrapping approach. (See Shatz, 1983, for a discussion of the questionable value of the continuity–discontinuity dichotomy.)

In sum, there is more compelling evidence than there was even 15 years ago that language development, mental state understandings, and self-reflection are related, and that toddlers are well on their way to fulfilling the promise of their humanity by bootstrapping their knowledge among these domains to learn more. I have suggested that conversations are the mechanism undergirding such bootstrapping. Toddlers' lives are busy ones: They are busy learning about the natural and artifactual world, about themselves, and about others. And, they are using their growing social-linguistic knowledge to participate more fully in their language community as they transition from infancy to childhood. In short, the toddler years are crucial ones for becoming a person.

When has personhood been achieved? A lifespan perspective would undoubtedy argue against any single benchmark time. The influences beyond toddlerhood of peers, schooling, and changing family circumstances all have their impact, and sometimes it is hard even now to find in Ricky as a young adult the person I described in my book as emerging from toddlerhood years ago. As he experiences the college years and beyond, he will undoubtedly continue to develop. What long-term effects the experiences in the toddler years have on the adult person is yet another topic for continued research, and one that of necessity will involve much more than the efforts of a single investigator.

ACKNOWLEDGMENTS

Thanks to Karen Ebeling, Rochel Gelman, Richard Feingold, and the editors for comments on an earlier version of this chapter and to Dolores Jardine and Michael Tomasello for discussions of behavior in nonhumans. Of course, all points of controversy and errors are my own.

REFERENCES

Baker, M. C. (2001). *The atoms of language*. New York: Basic Books.

Baldwin, D. (1993). Infants' ability to consult the speaker for clues to word reference. *Journal of Child Language, 20*, 395–419.

Birch, S. A. J. (2005). When knowledge is a curse: Children's and adults' reasoning about mental states. *Current Directions in Psychological Science, 14*, 25–29.

Blakeslee, S. (2005, February 1). Minds of their own: Birds gain respect. *New York Times*, p. F1.

Bolnick, R., Spinrad, T., Eisenberg, N., Champion C., Greving, K., & Kupfer, A. (2005, April). *Toddlers' negative emotionality and language development: moderating effects of self-regulation.*

Poster presented at the biennial meeting of the Society for Research in Child Development, Atlanta.

Budwig, N. (2000). Language and the construction of self. In N. Budwig, I. Užgiris, & J. Wertsch (Eds.), *Communication: An arena of development* (pp. 195–214). Stamford, CT: Ablex.

Campos, J. J., Frankel, C. B., & Camras, L. (2004). On the nature of emotion regulation. *Child Development, 74*, 377–394.

Chambers, S. M. (1999). The effect of family talk on young children's development and coping. In E. Freydenberg (Ed.), *Learning to cope: Developing as a person in complex societies* (pp. 130–149). London: Oxford University Press.

Clayton, N. (2006, November). *Corvid cognition: What do birds know about other minds and other times?* Biopsychology colloquium, University of Michigan, Ann Arbor.

Clayton, N., & Emery, N. (2005). Corvid cognition. *Current Biology, 15*, R80–R81.

Clément, F., Koenig, M. A., & Harris, P. L. (2004). The ontogenesis of trust. *Mind and Language, 19*, 360–379.

Cole, P. M., Bender, S. E., Radzioch, A. M., & Yetter, E. (2005, April). A toddler's talk: Relations to parenting and early behavior problems. In Hans M. Koot (Chair), *Early parent–child interaction and the development of externalizing problems.* Symposium conducted at the biennial meeting of the Society for Research in Child Development, Atlanta.

Courage, M. L., & Howe, M. L. (2002). From infant to child: The dynamics of cognitive change in the second year of life. *Psychological Bulletin, 128*, 250–277.

Dennett, D. C. (1978). *Brainstorms*. Cambridge, MA: Bradford Books.

Dunn, J., Brown, J., & Beardsall, L. (1991). Family talk about feeling states and children's later understanding of others' emotions. *Developmental Psychology, 27*, 448–455.

Dunn, J., Brown, J., Slomkowski, C., Tesla, C., & Youngblade, L. (1991). Young children's understanding of other people's feelings and beliefs: Individual differences and their antecedents. *Child Development, 62*, 1352–1366.

Emery, N., & Clayton, N. (2004).The mentality of crows: Convergent evolution of intelligence in corvids and apes. *Science, 306*, 1903–1907.

Farrar, J. M., & Maag, L. (2002). Early language development and the emergence of theory of mind. *First Language, 22*, 197–213.

Gallup, G. G. (1970). Chimpanzees: Self-recognition. *Science, 167*, 86–87.

Gelman, R. (1990). First principles organize attention to and learning about relevant data: Number and the animate-inanimate distinction as examples. *Cognitive Science, 14*, 79–106.

Gelman, R., & Lucariello, J. (2002). Role of learning in cognitive development. *Stevens' handbook of experimental psychology* (3rd ed.,Vol. 3, pp. 395–443). New York: Wiley.

Gelman, R., & Williams, E. (1998). Enabling constraints for cognitive development and learning: Domain specificity and epigenesis. In W. Damon (Series Ed.), D. Kuhn & R. S. Siegler (Volume Eds.), *Handbook of child psychology, Vol. 2: Cognition, perception, and language* (pp. 575–630). New York: Wiley.

Gergely, G. (2002). The development of understanding self and agency. In U. Goswami (Ed.), *Blackwell handbook of childhood cognitive development* (pp. 26–46). Oxford, UK: Blackwell.

Gergely, G., & Csibra, G. (2003). Teleological reasoning in infancy: The naïve theory of rational action. *Trends in Cognitive Sciences, 7*, 287–292.

Goetz, P. (2003). The effects of bilingualism on theory of mind development. *Bilingualism: Language and Cognition, 6*, 1–15.

Harris, P. (2002). What do children learn from testimony? In P. Carruthers, S. Stich, & M. Siegal (Eds.), *The cognitive basis of science*, (pp. 316–334). Cambridge, UK: Cambridge University Press.

Harter, S. (1999). *The construction of the self: A developmental perspective*. New York: Guilford Press.

Hirschfeld, L. A., & Gelman, S. A. (Eds.). (1994). *Mapping the mind: Domain specificity in cognition and culture*. New York: Cambridge University Press.

Hughes, C., Ensor, R., Fujisawa, K., & Lecce, S. (2005, April). *Links between early inner state awareness and quantity, content and connectedness of maternal talk*. Paper presented at the biennial meeting of the Society for Research in Child Development, Atlanta.

Hughes, C., Jaffee, S. R., Happé, F., Taylor, A., Caspi, A., & Moffitt, T. E. (2005). Origins of individual differences in theory of mind: From nature to nurture? *Child Development, 76*, 356–370.

Kagan, J. (1981). *The second year: The emergence of self-awareness*. Cambridge, MA: Harvard University Press.

Keil, F. C., & Wilson, R. A. (Eds.). (2000). *Explanation and cognition*. Cambridge, MA: MIT Press.

Koenig, M. A., & Echols, C. H. (2003). Infants' understanding of false labeling events: The referential roles of words and the speakers who use them. *Cognition, 87*, 179–208.

Koenig, M. A., Harris, P. L., & Clément, F. (2005, April). *Children's epistemic trust when learning object names and functions*. In Melissa A. Koenig (Chair), *What makes good labeling: Children's use of epistemic and non-epistemic mental state information during word learning*. Symposium conducted at the biennial meeting of the Society for Research in Child Development, Atlanta.

Kopp, C. (1982). Antecedents of self-regulation: A developmental perspective. *Developmental Psychology, 28*, 199–214.

Lewis, M., & Ramsay, D. (2004). Development of self-recognition, personal pronoun use, and pretend play during the 2nd year. *Child Development, 75*, 1821–1831.

Lillard, A. (2002). Pretend play and cognitive development. In U. Goswami (Ed.), *Blackwell handbook of childhood cognitive development* (pp. 188–205). Oxford, UK: Blackwell.

Mead, G. H. (1934). *Mind, self, and society*. Chicago: University of Chicago Press.

Moses, L. J., Carlson, S. M., & Sabbagh, M. A. (2005). On the specificity of the relation between executive function and children's theories of mind. In W. Schneider, R. Schumann-Hengsteler, & B. Sodian (Eds.), *Young children's cognitive development: Interrelationships among executive functioning, working memory, verbal ability, and theory of mind* (pp. 131–145). Mahwah, NJ: Erlbaum.

Poulin-Dubois, D., & Forbes, J. N. (2002). Toddlers attention to intentions-in-action in learning novel action words. *Developmental Psychology, 38*, 104–114.

Poulin-Dubois, D., & Graham, S. A. (2007). In E. Hoff & M. Shatz (Eds.), *Blackwell handbook of language development* (pp. 191–211). Oxford, UK: Blackwell.

Povinelli, D. J. (2004). Behind the ape's appearance: Escaping anthropocentrism in the study of other minds. *Daedalus, 133*, 29–41.

Povinelli, D. J., & Vonk, J. (2004). We don't need a microscope to explore the chimpanzee's mind. *Mind and Language, 19*, 1–28.

Premack, D. (2004, January). Is language the key to human intelligence? *Science, 16*, 318–320.

Repacholi, B. M., & Gopnik, A. (1997). Early reasoning about desires: Evidence from 14- and 18-month olds. *Developmental Psychology, 33*, 12–21.

Royzman, E. B., Cassidy, K. W., & Baron, J. (2003). "I know, you know": Epistemic egocentrism in children and adults. *Review of General Psychology, 7*, 38–65.

Saylor, M. M., & Troseth, G. L. (2005, April). Using desires to learn words. In Douglas A. Behrend & Megan M. Saylor (Chairs), *What makes good labeling: Children's use of epistemic and non-epistemic mental state information during word learning*. Symposium conducted at the biennial meeting of the Society for Research in Child Development, Atlanta.

Scholl, B. J., & Leslie, A. M. (2001). Minds, modules, and meta-analysis. *Child Development, 72*, 696–701.

Shatz, M. (1983). On transition, continuity, and coupling: An alternative approach to communicative development. In R. M. Golinkoff (Ed.), *The transition from prelinguistic to linguistic communication* (pp. 43–55). Hillsdale, NJ: Erlbaum.

Shatz, M. (1987). Bootstrapping operations in child language. In K. E. Nelson & A. van Kleek (Eds.), *Children's language* (Vol. 6, pp. 1–22). Hillsdale, NJ: Erlbaum.

Shatz, M. (1994). *A toddler's life: Becoming a person*. New York: Oxford University Press.

Shatz, M. (2005, April). Commentary. In D. A. Douglas & M. M. Saylor (Chairs), *What makes good labeling: Children's use of epistemic and non-epistemic mental state information during word learning*. Symposium conducted at the biennial meeting of the Society for Research in Child Development, Atlanta.

Shatz, M., Diesendruck, G., Martinez-Beck, I., & Akar, D. (2003). The influence of language and socioeconomic status on children's understanding of false belief. *Developmental Psychology, 39*, 717–729.

So, W. C., Tardif, T., & Karciroti, N. (2005, April). *Achieving false belief understanding in Cantonese: Mastery of syntactic competence or general language abilities?* Poster presented at the biennial meeting of the Society for Research in Child Development, Atlanta.

Spelke, E. (2003). What makes us smart? Core knowledge and natural language. In D. Gentner & S. Goldin-Meadow (Eds.), *Language in mind: Advances in the study of language and thought* (pp. 277–311). Cambridge, MA: MIT Press.

Stipek, D. J., Garalinski, J. H., & Kopp, C. B. (1990). Self-concept development in the toddler years. *Developmental Psychology, 26*, 972–977.

Tomasello, M., Call, J., & Hare, B. (2003). Chimpanzees understand psychological states – the question is which ones and to what extent. *Trends in Cognitive Science*, 7, 153–156.

Valsiner, J. (1998). The development of the concept of development: Historical and epistemological perspectives. In W. Damon (Series Ed.) & R. M. Lerner (Volume Ed.), *Handbook of child psychology: Vol. 1. Theoretical models of human development* (pp. 189–232). New York: Wiley.

Wanshaffe, K. R. (2002). Social facilitation in young toddlers. *US: Psychological Reports, 90*, 349–350.

Watson, A. C., Painter, K. M., & Bornstein, M. H. (2001). Longitudinal relations between 2-year-olds' language and 4-year-olds' theory of mind. *Journal of Cognition and Development, 2*, 449–457.

Wellman, H. M. (2002). Understanding the psychological world: Developing a theory of mind. In U. Goswami (Ed.), *Blackwell handbook of childhood cognitive development* (pp. 167–187). Oxford, UK: Blackwell.

Wellman, H. M., Cross, D., & Watson, J. (2001). Meta-analysis of theory-of-mind development: The truth about false beliefs. *Child Development, 72*, 655–684.

Wellman, H. M., & Woolley, J. D. (1990). From simple desires to ordinary beliefs: The early development of everyday psychology. *Cognition, 35*, 245–275.

Yaniv, I., & Shatz, M. (1988). Children's understanding of perceptibility. In J. Astington, P. Harris, & D. Olson (Eds.), *Developing theories of mind* (pp. 93–108). Cambridge, UK: Cambridge University Press.

Part III

SELF-REGULATION

11

The Emergence of Self-Regulation

Biological and Behavioral Control Mechanisms Supporting Toddler Competencies

SUSAN D. CALKINS

OVERVIEW

In this chapter, I argue that the marked developments in a broad range of adaptive skills that are characteristic of toddlerhood, including self-control, autonomy, and compliance, are a function of foundational regulatory developments that occur across a number of domains of functioning. These developments are likely to be hierarchically organized, with basic biological processes contributing to developments in emotional and cognitive functioning (Calkins, in press; Calkins, Graziano, & Keane, 2007). From this perspective, the transition through toddlerhood to preschool and the subsequent transition to school is marked by the acquisition of an integrated set of domain-specific control mechanisms, broadly referred to as *self-regulation*. I note the central role played by the control of physiological arousal, which is achieved during early infancy and eventually becomes integrated into the processes of attentional engagement and disengagement (Porges, 1996; Richards, 1985, 1987), emotional regulation, and the behavioral regulation and executive cognitive control processes characteristic of early childhood (Belsky, Friedman, & Hsieh, 2001; Rothbart, Posner, & Boylan, 1990; Sethi, Mischel, Aber, Shoda, & Rodriguez, 2000). Individual differences in these processes likely are implicated in both personality and behavioral adjustment during the early childhood years when the self-regulation of emotion and behavior becomes a core indice of successful adaptation. I present data from ongoing research with a sample of toddlers displaying early behavioral difficulties that illustrate the foundational role of biological, attentional, and affective regulation in early development. Finally, I offer some suggestions on how multiple measures of self-regulation may be studied from within a developmental framework emphasizing diverse pathways to adaptation and maladaptation.

A SELF-REGULATION FRAMEWORK FOR STUDYING TODDLER COMPETENCIES

Toddlerhood is a developmental period marked by an emerging self-concept that allows children to see themselves as capable of independent action, and by linguistic and motor developments that support the production of such action. These changes in the way children see themselves and the accompanying skills that support autonomous behavior are a function of fundamental changes in self-regulatory abilities that occur at both a biological and a behavioral level. During infancy and early childhood, children gradually acquire the necessary self-regulation skills and strategies that enable them to cope with a variety of developmental challenges (Bronson, 2000; Cicchetti, Ganiban, & Barnett, 1991; Kopp, 1982, 1989; Tronick, 1989). In infancy, the child's success at regulation depends heavily on the parent's awareness, flexibility, and responsivity to emotional expression and the child's need for intervention. During toddlerhood, the ability to initiate use of a greater repertoire of self-regulating behaviors becomes critical as the child is gaining independence, control, and an identity separate from the caregiver. Moreover, failures of early self-regulation are considered to be both core features of childhood psychological problems and factors that constrain subsequent development and the child's response to later developmental challenges (Calkins & Fox, 2002; Keenan, 2000).

Despite general agreement within the discipline of developmental psychology that self-regulation skills emerge and support competent functioning during toddlerhood and early childhood (Bronson, 2000), there has been considerable conceptual ambiguity, as well as a lack of specificity, with regard to the processes that comprise the construct of self-regulation (Calkins & Fox, 2002). Recently, the field of child temperament has offered an explanation of how the toddler's emerging repertoire of self-initiated and independent behavior is supported by a class of control mechanisms that are observed across multiple levels of analysis (Posner & Rothbart, 1998; Rothbart & Bates, 1998; Rothbart & Derryberry, 1981). In this approach, self-regulation is defined as the child's ability to modulate behavior according to the cognitive, emotional, and social demands of a particular situation (Derryberry & Reed, 1996; Rothbart & Posner, 1985).

Regulatory processes begin to develop prenatally and evolve into more sophisticated and self-initiated processes over the course of the toddler, preschool, and school years (Posner & Rothbart, 2000; Rothbart & Jones, 1998). So, for example, infants may differ initially in their threshold to respond to visual or auditory stimuli of a certain intensity (e.g., Calkins, Fox, & Marshall, 1996). This reactivity is thought to be present at birth and to reflect a relatively stable characteristic of the infant (Rothbart, Derryberry, & Hershey, 2000). Over the course of development, the child's increasing capacity to regulate his or her motoric and affective behavior, first as a result of a supportive caregiving context and later as a function of voluntary and effortful control, moderates these initial reactive responses.

Thus, much of the development of self-regulation is a result of increasing control over attentional processes and emotional reactivity, as well as enhanced inhibitory control over motor behavior (Eisenberg, Smith, Sadovsky, & Spinrad, 2004; Kochanska, Coy, & Murray, 2001; Rueda, Posner, & Rothbart, 2004; Ruff & Rothbart, 1996). During the second and third years of life, children begin to gain control over impulses and actions that are activated primarily by the situation and become capable of behavioral compliance and the delay of gratification. During the preschool years, children become aware of the factors that affect their attention such as motivation and noise (Miller & Zalenski, 1982) and begin to engage in more executive or cognitive control of thoughts and actions. Importantly, each of these discrete skills will support the emergence of the kind of independent and adaptive behavioral functioning that is necessary for the child to transition successfully to the school and peer environment. It is important to note, however, that these normative developments do not preclude the possibility that both reactivity and self-regulation may be influenced by environmental events that alter the trajectory of a child's development (Calkins, 2004; Cicchetti & Rogosch, 1996).

A key construct in Rothbart's theory of temperament is effortful control, defined as the ability to inhibit responses to stimuli in the immediate environment while pursuing a cognitively represented goal (Rothbart & Posner, 1985). As a temperamental dimension, effortful control refers to a special class of self-regulatory processes that develop with the maturation of attentional mechanisms, particularly the anterior attention system (Posner & Rothbart, 1992). Although it is believed that effortful control begins to emerge at the end of the first year of life, its development continues at least through the preschool years (Eisenberg et al., 2004). Thus, the system of self-regulation that emerges over time becomes more differentiated, more voluntary, and more systematically deployed. Nevertheless, this system is relatively slow to develop, and its development, while influenced by temperamental reactivity, is likely a function of a number of internal and external factors as well (Calkins, 1994).

Inherent in Posner and Rothbart's (2000) theory is the idea that neurobiological systems underlie the developments in behavioral regulation. Thus, one comprehensive way to conceptualize the self-regulatory system is to describe it as adaptive control that may be observed at the level of physiological, attentional, emotional, behavioral, cognitive, and interpersonal or social processes (Calkins & Fox, 2002). And, control at these various levels emerges, at least in primitive form, across the prenatal, infancy, toddler, and early-childhood periods of development. Importantly, though, the mastery of earlier regulatory tasks becomes an important component of later competencies (Calkins, in press; Calkins et al., 2007; Eisenberg et al., 2004).

One rationale for examining the development and integration of these domain-specific regulatory processes emanates from recent work in the area of developmental neuroscience that has identified specific brain regions that may play a functional role in the deployment of attention and in the processing and regulation of emotion, cognition, and behavior (Posner & Rothbart, 1994, 1998). This work has identified areas of the prefrontal cortex as central to the effortful regulation of behavior via the anterior attention system. This system is guided by the anterior cingulate cortex (ACC), which includes two major subdivisions. One subdivision governs cognitive and attentional processes and has connections to the prefrontal cortex. A second subdivision governs emotional processes and has connections with the limbic system and peripheral autonomic, visceromotor, and endocrine systems (Lane & McRae, 2004; Luu & Tucker, 2004). Recent research suggests that these subdivisions have a reciprocal relation (Davidson, Putnam, & Larson, 2000; Davis, Bruce, & Gunnar, 2002). Moreover, the functional relation between these two areas of the cortex provides a biological mechanism for the developmental integration of specific types of self-regulatory processes in childhood. These discrete self-regulatory processes are described later with clear acknowledgment that once integration across levels occurs in support of more complex skills and behaviors, it is often difficult to parse these complex behavioral responses into independent types of control. Nevertheless, from a developmental point of view, it is useful to describe explicit types of control and how they emerge, as this specification may provide insight into nonnormative developments and problems that emerge as a result of deficits in specific components of self-regulation at particular points in development (Calkins, in press; Calkins et al., 2007).

CHARACTERIZING NORMATIVE SELF-REGULATORY PROCESSES IN EARLY DEVELOPMENT

Recent developmental neuroscience work suggests that because of its dependence on the maturation of prefrontal–limbic connections, the development of self-regulatory processes are relatively protracted (Beauregard, Levesque, & Paquette, 2004), from the development of basic and automatic regulation of physiology in infancy and toddlerhood to the more self-conscious and intentional regulation of cognition emerging in middle childhood (Ochsner &

Gross, 2004). From a developmental perspective then, opportunities for success and failure of self-regulation are numerous over the course of toddlerhood, particularly given the potential of environmental factors such as parenting to facilitate or disrupt development in these domains (Calkins, Smith, Gill, & Johnson, 1998). Below, I describe early normative processes in each of these domains, with a brief reference to the nature of the general problems that might be associated with the failure to acquire basic regulatory skills in particular domains. Greater emphasis is placed on those component processes that are emerging early in development (physiological, attentional, and emotional self-regulation) and supporting toddler competencies than those that emerge in preschool and early childhood (behavioral and cognitive control).

Physiological Regulation

Recent developmental psychophysiological work emphasizes that certain underlying physiological processes and functioning may play an important role in the etiology of early regulatory behaviors (Fox, 1994; Fox & Card, 1999; Porges, 1991, 1996). Researchers have also been drawn to physiological measures of regulation as a function of the growing interest in the critical role of emotion regulation in child functioning. Theories of emotion regulation that focus on underlying biological components of regulation assume that maturation of different biological support systems lays the foundation for increasingly sophisticated emotional and behavioral regulation that is observed across childhood. Fox (1989, 1994), for example, has noted that the frontal lobes of the brain are differentially specialized for approach versus avoidance and that these tendencies influence the behaviors in which children engage when emotionally and behaviorally aroused. He further notes that maturation of the frontal cortex provides a mechanism for the more sophisticated and planful regulatory behaviors of older children versus infants. Other researchers have emphasized the role of biological stress responses (Stansbury & Gunnar, 1994) and physiological regulation as processes that support behavioral manifestations of regulation (Calkins, 1997; Calkins & Dedmon, 2000).

In terms of the empirical work investigating these theoretical formulations, it is clear that heart rate (HR) measures have been of particular interest to researchers studying self-regulation because of the potential to index arousal, and control of arousal, with such measures. However, Porges (Porges, 1996; Porges, Doussard-Roosevelt, & Maita, 1994) argues that isolating parasympathetic from sympathetic autonomic processes is needed in order to interpret the nature of the physiological and behavioral responses. He notes that maturation of the parasympathetic nervous system in particular plays a key role in the regulation of state, motor activity, and emotion, and that such functioning may be indexed by measures of HR variability. Although there are multiple ways to measure HR variability, Porges (1991, 1996) and colleagues developed a method that measures the amplitude and period of the oscillations associated with inhalation and exhalation (U.S. Patent No. 4520944). This measure refers to the variability in heart rate that occurs at the frequency of breathing (respiratory sinus arrhythmia [RSA]) and is thought to reflect the parasympathetic influence on HR variability via the vagus nerve. High resting RSA, or greater HR variability under conditions of little environmental challenge, supports a greater physiological and behavioral response, or reactivity, when a response to an environmental event is needed. Several studies have linked high RSA in newborns and children with good developmental outcomes, suggesting that it may be an important physiological component of appropriate engagement with the environment (Hofheimer, Wood, Porges, Pearson, & Lawson, 1995; Richards, 1985, 1987; Richards & Cameron, 1989; Stifter & Fox, 1990; Suess, Porges, & Plude, 1994).

Porges's theory further suggests that one particular measure of cardiac activity that may be more directly related to the kinds of regulatory behaviors children begin to display in toddlerhood and early childhood is *vagal regulation* of the heart, which is indexed by a decrease (suppression) in RSA during situations in which coping or emotional and behavioral regulation is required. Vagal regulation in the form of suppression of RSA during demanding tasks may reflect physiological processes that allow the child to shift focus from internal homeostatic demands to demands that require internal processing or the generation of coping strategies to control affective or behavioral arousal. Thus, suppression of RSA is thought to be a physiological strategy that permits sustained attention and behaviors indicative of active coping that are mediated by the parasympathetic nervous system (Porges, 1991, 1996; Wilson & Gottman, 1996), and that results in greater cardiac output in the form of HR acceleration.

Numerous studies document that RSA does change under conditions in which the individual must generate a response to emotional, cognitive, and behavioral challenges (Blair, Peters, & Granger, 2004; Calkins, 1997; Calkins et al., 1998; Calkins & Dedmon, 2000; Calkins & Keane, 2004; Calkins et al., 2007; Donzella, Gunnar, Krueger, & Alwin, 2000; Moore & Calkins, 2004). Moreover, the RSA suppression measure does seem to be an indicator of both the degree of challenge the task imposes on the child's regulatory ability and the extent to which the child can generate a coping response independently versus with environmental support. That is, across task comparisons of children's physiological response to a task that taxes the child's attention versus one that taxes the child's cognitive ability or emotion regulation skills indicate that cognitive and emotional challenges typically elicit a larger physiological response. And, a child's physiological response to challenge has been shown to be augmented when the caregiver is involved in helping the child manage the task versus when the child must deal with the challenge alone (Calkins & Dedmon, 2000; Calkins & Keane, 2004). Finally, data clearly indicate that this response is observable in early infancy and differs across infants with differing levels of attentional and emotional regulation abilities (Calkins, Dedmon, Gill, Lomax, & Johnson, 2002). Given its early appearance in the child's repertoire, and that it is influenced by caregiver support, physiological regulation is very likely to provide a foundation for later-appearing regulatory competencies.

Attentional Regulation

Early efforts at attentional self-regulation, those occurring prior to about 3 months of age, are thought to be controlled largely by physiological mechanisms driven by posterior orienting systems that are innate (Derryberry & Rothbart, 1997; Kopp, 1982; Posner & Rothbart, 1998). By 3 months of age, primitive and more reactive attentional self-regulatory mechanisms of orienting and attentional persistence assist in simple control of behavioral state and emotional reactivity (Eisenberg et al., 2004).

The period between 3 and 6 months of age marks a major transition in infant development generally. First, sleep–wake cycles and eating and elimination processes have become more predictable, signaling an important biological transition. Second, the ability of the infant to *voluntarily* control arousal levels begins to emerge. This control depends largely on attentional control mechanisms and simple motor skills (Rothbart, Ziaie, & O'Boyle, 1992; Ruff & Rothbart, 1996) and leads to coordinated use of attention engagement and disengagement, particularly in contexts that evoke negative affect. Infants are now capable of engaging in self-initiated distraction and of moving attention away from the source of negative arousal to more neutral nonsocial stimuli.

The emergence of voluntary control of attention occurring during the infant's first year coincides with the development of three related but anatomically distinct attentional systems. The first attentional system of importance is the reticular activating system ascending from the brainstem to the cortex and thought to be involved in maintaining and adjusting general alertness. It is believed that this system focuses attention on important aspects of the environment and prevents distraction, thus facilitating defensive behavior (Derryberry & Rothbart, 1997). The second attentional system maturing during the end of the first year of life is the posterior attentional system. Neurologically, this system is distributed across the brain's superior colliculus, the pulvinar nucleus of the thalamus, and the parietal lobe within the cortex. The operations of this system allow attention to move from one location to another through engagement and disengagement of attention. In addition, this system allows for the adjustment of the breadth of attention to closely focus on the details or to give a broader, more general picture of the information to be processed (Posner & Rothbart, 1992). The third system, which develops later than the other attentional systems and is proposed to be the most important to the development of effortful control, is the anterior attentional system. This system is located within the frontal cortex and is viewed as an executive system that regulates sensory information (Rothbart, Derryberry, & Posner, 1994). Furthermore, Posner and Rothbart (1992) suggest that this system underlies the conscious, willful, or *effortful* control of behavior through which the individual can regulate more reactive motivational functions. Although aspects of effortful control can be seen at the end of the first year, this system is relatively late to develop with the most rapid maturation occurring during toddlerhood and preschool (Derryberry & Rothbart, 1997).

The development and integration of the three attentional systems provide the young child with the neural mechanisms necessary to regulate reactivity through orienting, redirecting, and maintaining attentional focus. And, effortful control of attention will permit the young child to engage in a broader array of cognitive tasks as well (Eisenberg et al., 2004; Rothbart & Bates, 1998). However, not all children will be able to engage in these behaviors successfully to control reactivity, to inhibit a behavioral response, or to carry out a planned activity. For example, for some children, the inability to shift their attention from a negative event (such as something frightening) to a positive distracter may lead to increases in the experience of negative affect. Thus, there are clear individual differences in the ability to utilize attention skills of engagement, disengagement, and maintenance successfully to control emotion, cognition, and behavior.

By toddlerhood, effortful control of attention plays a key role in delay behavior and in suppressing and slowing down behavior (Kochanska, Murray, & Harlan, 2000), each of which is a component of the behavioral regulation necessary for successful social and academic functioning. In addition, the vulnerabilities in attention control implicated in attention-deficit/hyperactivity disorder (ADHD) may lead to problems with emotion and behavioral self-regulation (Nigg & Huang-Pollock, 2003; Sethi et al., 2000) as the child gets older. In this way, problems such as ADHD may act to constrain the normal development of self-regulation (Barkley, 2004).

Emotion Regulation

Emotion regulatory processes refer to skills and strategies that serve to manage, modulate, inhibit, and enhance emotions and support adaptive social and nonsocial responses (Calkins, 1994; Kopp, 1982, 1989; Thompson, 1994). Recent research on the self-regulation of emotion demonstrates that the display of affect and affect regulation are powerful mediators of interpersonal relationships and socioemotional adjustment, including behavioral self-control, in the first few years of life (Calkins, 1994; Cicchetti et al., 1991; Malatesta, Culver, Tesman, & Shephard, 1989; Rothbart, 1989; Thompson, 1994). Dramatic developments are observed during the infancy and toddler periods of development in terms of emotional self-regulation skills and abilities. The process may be broadly described as one in which the relatively passive and reactive neonate becomes a child capable of self-initiated behaviors that serve a regulatory function (Calkins, 1994; Kopp, 1982; Sroufe, 1996). In addition, this process has also been described as one in which the infant progresses from near complete reliance on caregivers for regulation to independent self-regulation. As the infant makes this transition, the use of specific strategies and behaviors becomes organized into the infant's repertoire of emotional self-regulation that may be used in a variety of contexts.

Kopp (1982) provides an excellent overview of the early developments in emotional self-regulation. This description has been verified by studies of both normative development (Buss & Goldsmith, 1998; Rothbart et al., 1992) and studies of individual differences (Stifter & Braungart, 1995). These descriptions provide an explanation of how infants develop and use a rich behavioral repertoire of strategies in the service of reducing, inhibiting, amplifying, and balancing different affective responses. Moreover, it is also clear from these descriptions that functioning in a variety of nonemotional domains, including motor, language and cognition, and social development, is implicated in these changes (Kopp, 1989, 1992). For example, increases in motor ability facilitate the use of strategies such as withdrawal from a source of negative arousal. The emergence of language facilitates verbal expressions of distress. And, increases in problem-solving skills enhance the range of alternative coping strategies a child may use in an emotionally evocative situation. In this way, the regulation of emotional reactivity in the service of adaptive functioning is linked in important ways to developments that are often viewed as independent of emotional functioning.

By the end of the first year of life, infants become much more active and purposeful in their attempts to control affective arousal (Kopp, 1982). First, they begin to employ organized sequences of motor behavior that enable them to reach, retreat, redirect, and self-soothe in a flexible manner that suggests they are responsive to environmental cues. Second, their signaling and redirection become explicitly social as they recognize that caregivers and others may behave in a way that will assist them in the regulation of affective states (Rothbart et al., 1992).

During the second year of life, the transition from passive to active methods of emotional self-regulation is complete (Rothbart et al., 1992). Although infants are not entirely capable of controlling their own affective states by this age, they are capable of using specific strategies to attempt to manage different affective states, albeit sometimes unsuccessfully (Calkins & Dedmon, 2000; Calkins et al., 1998). Moreover, during this period, infants begin to respond to caregiver directives, and as a consequence of this responsivity, compliance and behavioral self-control begin to emerge (Kopp, 1989). This shift is supported by developments in the motor domain, as well as changes in representational ability and the development of language skills. The capacity for upright locomotion, gains in memory and problem-solving abilities, and the use of private or internalized speech to guide behavior all contribute to the child's increased capacity for managing emotions.

Recent research on the regulation of specific types of negative affect suggests processes through which this regulation affects behavioral control later in development. In one study, Stifter and Braungart (1995) examined changes in the types of regulatory behaviors infants use to manage emotional reactivity and observed that there were relations between these behaviors and changes in negative affect. Stifter also found that emotional regulation in response to frustration in infancy was related to compliance in toddlerhood (Stifter, Spinrad, & Braungart-Rieker, 1999). Grolnick, Bridges, and Connell (1996) described the relations between emotion regulation strategies and distress among a sample of 2-year-olds observed in a delay of gratification paradigm and a separation situation. They observed that the strategy of visual reorienting during these tasks was the most commonly used form of emotion regulation, and the one that was most predictive of decreases in distress. Eisenberg and colleagues (Eisenberg et al., 1993, 1994, 1995) found relations among emotionality, emotion regulation, and peer competence in early childhood. Rothbart and colleagues (1990) observed that at least one specific emotion regulation behavior, that of attentional control, is related to decreases in negative emotionality in infancy. Buss and Goldsmith (1998) and Diener, Manglesdorf, McHale, and Frosch (2002) also observed that a number of different behaviors that infants display when observed in frustrating or constraining situations appear to reduce negative affect. Taken together, these studies demonstrate that there are individual differences in the use of particular emotion regulation behaviors that are observable by toddlerhood, that some behaviors are more effective than others for reducing negative affect, that the use of particular emotion regulation behaviors changes over time, and that certain behaviors affect the development of social competence.

Deficits in emotion regulation may manifest in different ways. For example, Shipman, Schneider, and Brown (2004) hypothesize that while problems with emotion regulation may be broadly related to externalizing behavior problems characterized by aggression (Calkins, Gill, & Williford, 1999), they may differentially predict children who are prone to oppositional defiant disorder in particular. Moreover, problems with undercontrolled emotion regulation may distinguish children who display reactive aggression from those who display proactive aggression, which may differentiate behavioral outcomes characterized by oppositiomal defiant disorder from those with early indicators of conduct disorder (Keenan & Shaw, 2003). In addition, the overcontrol of emotion may characterize children with anxiety and depression, which are indicators of internalizing spectrum problems (Eisenberg et al., 2004). Thus, patterns of emotion regulation that children acquire early in development influence the nature of their subsequent psychological functioning in important ways (Fox & Calkins, 2003).

Behavioral Regulation

Examples of behavioral management or control include compliance to adult directives and the ability to control impulsive responses (Kopp, 1982; Kuczynski & Kochanska, 1995). Increasingly, these kinds of demands are placed on children during toddlerhood and early childhood; the task for the child is to overcome impulsive reactions or to suspend desired activity to meet external demands. Behavioral self-control is demonstrated when a child is able to comply with demands, delay specific activities, and monitor his or her own behavior. And, it is likely that earlier-acquired physiological, attentional, and emotional control processes are integral to the regulation of behavior. Compliance to external directives is often achieved in situations in which the child must cease or initiate an undesirable (from the child's point of view) activity. The regulation of arousal is necessary to meet such demands. To the extent that children have successfully achieved a level of control of physiological and emotional arousal, compliance with such demands is greater.

Behavioral regulation is critical to the child's transition into the social and school environment. Importantly, these skills will support the development of internally driven standards of behavior and conduct that the child will need to function independently in the school and peer domain. For example, effortful control, a construct that Kochanska and others have identified as incorporating both attentional and behavioral demands, has also been implicated in the development of conscience and the internalization of standards of conduct (Eisenberg et al., 2004; Kochanska, Murray, & Coy, 1997; Kochanska et al., 2000), suggesting that the absence of such behavioral control skills may be implicated in behavioral outcomes characterized by a lack of empathy and conscience.

Failures of behavioral self-regulation also characterize profiles of behavior problems in early childhood. For example, clear evidence exists for a negative relation between the child's success at behavioral regulation (compliance, control of impulsivity, and delay of gratification ability) and externalizing problem behavior. Eisenberg and colleagues have examined the relation between behavioral regulation and externalizing behaviors among older children. In one study, Eisenberg found that teacher and parent ratings of children's problem behavior were related to children's persistence on a behavioral regulation task. In addition, parent ratings of impulsivity, inhibition control, and global self-control predicted parent ratings of later problem behavior and teacher ratings of children's social competence (Eisenberg et al., 1997). In a separate sample of 214 children (ages 4½–8), Eisenberg and colleagues (2001) found a negative correlation between child persistence and mother report of externalizing behavior. Thus, behavioral control processes support the development of adaptive functioning in childhood and failures of such regulation are a marker of poor outcomes.

Executive or Cognitive Control

Executive functioning encompasses a number of cognitive factors including working memory and inhibitory control. Executive functions enable the child to focus his or her behavior toward achieving a goal and adjust behavior to meet situational demands (Pennington & Ozonoff, 1996). Paris and Newman (1990) define this type of self-regulation as involving planfulness, control, reflection, competence, and independence. Importantly, this more sophisticated level of self-regulation is likely supported by earlier forms of self-regulation. In fact, Kuhl and Kraska (1993) argue that children's early school performance, which requires executive processes, is influenced not only by behavioral self-regulation but also by attentional and emotional control. To the extent that children can utilize effective strategies for monitoring and maintaining attention, and to the extent that they are able to control frustration to challenging cognitive tasks, they will be more successful at completing such tasks. For example, in a follow-up study of toddlers assessed for early behavior problems, earlier deficits in emotion regulation were mediated by behavioral regulation in the classroom, which predicted academic performance (Howse, Calkins, Anastopoulos, Keane, & Shelton 2003).

It should be noted, however, that there is debate as to the fundamental competencies underlying the development of executive function skills (Zelazo & Reznick, 1991; Zelazo, Reznick, & Pinon, 1995). A number of researchers have suggested that increases in working memory (another "frontal" function) may account for the development of these skills (Zelazo et al., 1995) while others have argued for the importance of an inhibitory component toward understanding executive control (e.g., Diamond, 1991).

A number of recent studies have linked executive functioning deficits in children to a range of early behavioral difficulties. For example, immature executive functioning is common in children with attention problems (Hinshaw, 1994; Nigg, Hinshaw, Carte, & Treuting, 1998), but executive function deficits have also been linked to conduct problems and learning-style differences (Moffitt, 1993; Pennington & Ozonoff, 1996). Moreover, the frequently reported association between executive function and disruptive behavior is independent of IQ (Moffitt, 1993). While the causal role of executive functioning deficits has not been examined in longitudinal studies (Nigg et al., 1998), Rutter (1987) proposes that executive functions mediate the development of psychopathology in children. However, the majority of research highlighting the relation between executive functioning and behavioral difficulties has been cross-sectional or conducted with clinical versus normative between-groups designs where the effects of executive functioning, independent of behavioral functioning, are difficult to identify.

Summary of Self-Regulatory Processes

This brief review of the self-regulatory processes that become functional during early development highlights the central role these processes play in many dimensions of emerging toddler competence. This review also suggests that there may be expected trajectories of skills in the subdomains of self-regulation, and that patterns of regulatory deficits are related to patterns of behavioral adjustment versus maladjustment. Such a framework has implications for an understanding of both normative and compromised development and clearly contributes to the identification of *mechanisms* of development that have largely been neglected in the behavior problem literature. An important goal of this framework is to specify the role that different levels of self-regulation may play in constraining subsequent development. To illustrate, in the next section, I discuss the challenges to the acquisition of self-regulatory skills and explore in greater depth one measure of physiological regulation, cardiac vagal tone, and research supporting its role in emerging self-regulation across multiple levels.

CHALLENGES TO TODDLER SELF-REGULATION

Although there are clearly identifiable normative achievements in a number of domains of self-regulation that may be observed by the toddler period, there are also individual differences in whether and how such achievements are made. Indeed, such individual differences create opportunities for a range of outcomes to emerge out of the challenges of the toddler period of development. In fact, the challenge of the toddler period can be described in terms of both the normative developmental processes of mastering the competencies of emotional and behavioral regulation, processes that often result in expressed frustration, willful noncompliance, and tantrumming, and in terms of the ongoing failures of some children to become competent at managing their own behavior. And, although the challenging and difficult behavior of toddlerhood can be highly stable across development and predictive of later difficulties (Campbell, Pierce, Moore, & Marakovitz, 1996; Cohen & Bromet, 1992; Heller, Baker, Henker, & Hinshaw, 1996), increases in language development, cognitive abilities, and specific self-regulation skills during toddlerhood should allow most children to learn to control early normative noncompliant, aggressive, and impulsive tendencies, leading to a decline in problem behavior (Campbell, 2002). In fact, the majority of studies on childhood aggression have demonstrated that aggressive behavior decreases across toddlerhood and preschool (e.g., Cummings, Ianotti, & Zahn-Waxler, 1989; Parke & Slaby, 1983; Rubin, Burgess, Dwyer, & Hastings, 2003). Nevertheless, there is clearly a subset of children for whom continuing difficulties managing emotion and behavior contribute to stable and increasing trajectories of problem behavior (NICHD Early Child Care Research Network, 2004). When these continuing difficulties are examined from within a self-regulatory framework, the failure to achieve control in one or more domains of functioning may be viewed as a mechanism that maintains the difficult behavior of toddlerhood.

A self-regulatory perspective on the stability of problem behavior from toddlerhood to early childhood may begin to answer the question of *how* known risk factors such as compromised parent functioning work in conjunction with child characteristics in defining the trajectories of problem behavior or normative functioning. In our work, we have attempted to examine the child's behavior in contexts and situations that may provide insight into the proximal mechanisms whereby children engage in aggressive, impulsive, disruptive, or oppositional behavior versus adaptive behavior. In early work

(Calkins, 1994, 1997; Calkins, Gill, Johnson, & Smith, 1999), I hypothesized that the regulation of affect was a proximal mechanism for such behavior, in that the failure to regulate affect could lead directly to aggressive behavior. Here, and in more recent work (Calkins & Dedmon, 2000; Calkins & Fox, 2002; Calkins & Howse, 2004), I argue that emotion regulation should be viewed as one component process of self-regulation, and that the capacity to self-regulate across a number of levels influences the toddler's adaptive functioning and capacity to learn from experiences. Clearly, the early processes of physiological, attentional, and emotional regulation are integral to the emergence of toddler competence. When these processes are not functional, the child's success at managing the challenges of toddlerhood is compromised. Moreover, failures of these basic regulatory processes have cascading consequences. First, they contribute directly to behaviors that are disruptive to the child's functioning in the situations in which they occur. Second, because the child is unable to control negative affect, these failures limit opportunities to learn adaptive skills in social–interactional contexts with parents and peers. From this perspective, then, understanding the contribution of self-regulation to behavior problems versus adaptive behavior of childhood is enhanced by an examination of the component processes of self-regulation that emerge over this developmental period. Thus, a central focus of our recent research has been to examine the role of these early foundational processes in subsequent behavioral adaptation.

Earlier, I noted the central role played by the regulation of physiological processes in the emergence of adaptive control at multiple behavioral levels. One cardiac measure, RSA, seems to capture the efforts on the part of the child to generate an organized coping response under conditions of emotional, behavioral, or cognitive challenge (Calkins, 1997; Calkins et al., 1998; Calkins & Dedmon, 2000; Calkins & Keane, 2004). The extension of these research findings is that while the ability to suppress RSA may be related to complex responses involving the regulation of attention and behavior, a deficiency in this ability may be related to early behavior problems, particularly problems characterized by a limited repertoire of behavioral and emotional control skills (Calkins & Dedmon, 2000; Porges, 1996; Wilson & Gottman, 1996).

In general, recent research on the physiological characteristics of older children with behavior problems supports the notion that deficits in the regulation of physiological arousal underlie the behavioral characteristics of these children. For example, HR variability is reduced in children with conduct disorder (Pine et al., 1996, 1998). Eisenberg and colleagues (1995) found that greater HR variability was also related to better social competence. Such relations may occur because of parasympathetic links to regulatory abilities involving attentional and behavioral control. For example, control of physiological arousal eventually becomes integrated into the processes of attention engagement and disengagement, which provides a mechanism for emotional and behavioral control (Porges, 1996; Richards, 1985, 1987). One question that may be asked is whether children with conduct problems display a pattern of physiological dysregulation that impairs their ability to generate and engage appropriate regulatory strategies in situations that are emotionally or behaviorally challenging.

Many of the studies of RSA and externalizing or conduct problems are limited in their focus on adolescent male samples. Our recent work has addressed the question whether such findings may be observed in samples of younger girls and boys. In one study, children at high risk for the development of aggressive behavior problems were identified at age 2 and assessed in a number of challenging tasks (Calkins & Dedmon, 2000). These children displayed significantly lower RSA suppression across these tasks than did children at low risk for behavior problems. In a follow-up of these same children, continued behavioral difficulties, including social problems and difficulties with emotion regulation, were characteristic of the children who displayed, across the preschool period, a stable pattern of physiological dysregulation, in the form of lower RSA suppression to challenge (Calkins & Keane, 2004). Interestingly, children who displayed a pattern of lower suppression at age 2 but who were observed to suppress RSA at age 4 showed continued difficulties, suggesting that the early pattern of cardiac vagal regulation may have constrained the acquisition of regulatory skills that affected behavior later in the preschool period.

These limited findings suggest that there may be a physiological profile of poorer vagal regulation of HR activity that may be characteristic of children with early externalizing problems, and that contributes to the development of other forms of regulation that are needed for social and academic functioning. However, one challenge to the study of physiological regulation among children with behavior problems characterized by aggression is that these problems often present with comorbid internalizing symptoms (anxiety, withdrawal) (Achenbach, Howell, Quay, & Connors, 1991; Gilliom & Shaw, 2004). These comorbid problems are often ignored, either because they are thought to be a consequence of single-reporter bias or because the sample sizes in most studies of children's behavior problems are too small to allow for separate consideration of pure versus comorbid problems (Calkins & Dedmon, 2000). However, in a recent large-scale study of early externalizing behavior problems, researchers identified differential behavioral and environmental correlates and predictors of pure versus mixed patterns of externalizing behavior problems (Keiley, Lofthouse, Bates, Dodge, & Pettit, 2003). Clearly, it is important to examine whether these different behavioral patterns may be distinguished by cardiac vagal regulation in the form of RSA suppression to emotional and behavioral challenges. One hypothesis is that the comorbid anxiety symptoms, which are often associated with overcontrol of emotion, may indicate less severe behavior problems (Lillienfield, 2003) and may reflect greater cardiac vagal regulation compared to children with pure externalizing problems. A second possibility is that comorbid problems may be considered more severe than pure problems (Hinshaw, Lahey, & Hart, 1993) and may result in significantly poorer cardiac vagal regulation compared to children with pure externalizing problems.

We explored these questions in a large sample of 5-year-old children, some of whom were at high risk for externalizing problems, others of whom displayed early externalizing problems with comorbid internalizing problems, and a third group of children with no behavioral problems (Calkins et al., 2007). The children were assessed in a battery of tasks that were emotionally and behaviorally challenging. We found that children displaying a mixed profile of externalizing and internalizing behavior problems displayed the greatest cardiac vagal regulation whereas children with a pure externalizing profile displayed the least cardiac vagal regulation. These data suggest that either the pattern of greater vagal regulation leads to anxiety symptoms or that children with emergent anxiety become more, or perhaps over-, regulated physiologically. The question as to why these seemingly well regulated children also display concurrent externalizing problem behaviors remains unanswered. It would be important for future research to identify which behavior problems emerge first. Perhaps a child's initial internalizing symptoms impact his or her ability to cffectively communicate with parents and/or peers, which may lead a child to feel more frustrated during social interactions and, eventually, to react in a more impulsive, blunt, and aggressive manner. On the other hand, a child's initial externalizing symptoms may also impact his or her ability to effectively communicate with parents and/or peers, which may lead that child to being rejected at school and potentially to experience internalizing symptoms. The cross-sectional nature of this dataset precludes answering these questions.

The data from this study and our prior work suggest that children with different patterns of behavior problems, patterns that may reflect lack of control of emotion and aggression versus overcontrol of emotion and aggression, also display a distinct pattern of parasympathetic nervous system functioning that has been linked in past research to the regulation of attention, affect cognition, and behavior (Calkins, 1997; Calkins & Dedmon, 2000; Calkins & Keane, 2004). Differentiating among subtypes at the behavioral as well as physiological level is critical, as such differentiation may suggest sources of these behavioral differences as well as factors that influence the outcomes of these behavioral patterns. Future research with these kinds of populations must determine whether the parasympathetic processes precede the behavioral pattern or are a consequence of it. Moreover, future research should also examine whether the greater cardiac vagal regulation of the anxious/aggressive group might serve as a protective factor against later and more severe conduct problems.

SUMMARY AND IMPLICATIONS

In this chapter, I have outlined a general theoretical framework for addressing questions about the processes and mechanisms that may be implicated in the development of independent and competent behavior in toddlerhood. I have argued that early behavioral competencies necessary for the successful transition to the peer and school environment are a function of an emergent self-regulatory system that integrates control mechanisms across multiple domains of functioning. As these control mechanisms emerge and begin to function in an integrated way, it is often difficult to view them as separate processes. I noted that, indeed, research investigating the cortical networks and brain regions supporting these processes provides a biological mechanism for their integration. Nevertheless, clear developments in physiological, attentional, and emotional regulation can be observed during the infancy and toddler period, and these developments support the behavioral competencies of toddlerhood that require independent, autonomous, and self-initiated action. Moreover, I have presented evidence that suggests that failure to acquire regulatory skills across these levels of functioning can impede children's development in ways that influence their success in the peer and school environment. I focused on the central role of physiological regulation of arousal in constraining the development of more sophisticated regulatory achievements of toddlerhood, achievements that are critical for successful school, family, and peer functioning. Finally, I highlighted findings from several studies with infants and young children demonstrating the associations between behavior and one measure of physiological regulation, vagal regulation of cardiac output, which we have found differentiates children with different behavior problem profiles.

While the notion that physiological regulation may be foundational to adaptive functioning across a number of subdomains of regulation has been generally supported by our work, many more issues clearly need to be addressed before we can fully appreciate the role this type of regulation, and other foundational regulatory processes, plays in the normative developments of toddlerhood or in the failures of such development that contribute to childhood disruptive behavior problems or other forms of childhood psychopathology. For example, although discussed only briefly here, implicit in this framework is that the developments that take place in the domains of self-regulation and the relations between self-regulation and the trajectories of competent versus problematic behavior will be moderated by numerous environmental factors. Considerable empirical evidence supports the theoretical notion that both biological and innate dispositions and environmental experiences contribute to emerging emotional self-regulation (Calkins et al., 2002; Calkins & Johnson, 1998; Stifter & Braungart, 1995). Clearly, though, self-regulatory processes begin to develop in the context of dyadic interactions (Sroufe, 1996). Such interactions both contribute to normative developments in multiple domains of self-regulation and create opportunities for individual variability in such skills and abilities to emerge (Cassidy, 1994).

One important direction for future research is the study of *how* early caregiving experiences influence the development of physiological regulation, a question that has been addressed primarily in the animal literature but not in studies of humans. For example, Hofer (1994; Polan & Hofer, 1999) addresses the multiple psychobiological roles that the caregiver plays in regulating infant's behavior and physiology early in life. Based on his research with infant rat pups, he describes these "hidden regulators" as operating at multiple sensory levels (e.g., olfactory, tactile, and oral) and influencing multiple levels of behavioral and physiological functioning in the infant. So, for example, maternal tactile stimulation may have the effect of lowering the infant's heart rate during a stressful situation, which may in turn, support a more adaptive behavioral response. Moreover, removal of these regulators, during separation, for example, disrupts the infant's functioning at multiple levels as well. Clearly, then, opportunities for individual differences in the development of emotional self-regulation may emerge from differential rearing conditions providing more or less psychobiological regulation. More comprehensive study is needed of the effects of the environment on the development of infant and child self-regulation.

Finally, it is important to continue to address the question of self-regulation and its role in both normative and nonnormative psychological functioning from a developmental psychopathology perspective. Such a perspective suggests that (1) there are multiple contributors to maladaptive and adaptive outcomes, (2) these contributors may interact in various ways within different individuals, and (3) the consequences for development are multiple pathways to disordered behavior and/or multiple variants of outcome from individual causative factors (Cicchetti, 1984, 1993; Cicchetti & Rogosch, 1996; Sroufe & Rutter, 1984). A developmental psychopathology perspective on the differentiated self-regulatory processes described here may illuminate the mechanisms implicated in the different pathways and outcomes that have been observed among children with disruptive behavior disorders, as well as those mechanisms implicated in other early-childhood difficulties.

ACKNOWLEDGMENTS

The writing of this chapter was supported by National Institute of Health Grant Nos. MH 55584 and MH 74077 to Susan D. Calkins.

REFERENCES

Achenbach, T. M., Howell, C. T., Quay, H. C., & Connors, C. K. (1991). National survey of problems and competencies among four-to-sixteen-year-olds: Parents' reports for normative and clinical samples. *Monographs of the Society for Research in Child Development*, *56*(Serial No. 225).

Barkley, R. A. (2004). Attention-deficit/hyperactivity disorder and self-regulation: Taking an evolutionary perspective on executive functioning. In R. F. Baumeister & K. D. Vohs (Eds.), *Handbook of self-regulation: Research, theory and applications* (pp. 301–323). New York: Guilford Press.

Beauregard, M., Levesque, J., & Paquette, V. (2004). Neural basis of conscious and voluntary self-regulation of emotion. In M. Beauregard (Ed.), *Consciousness, emotional self-regulation and the brain* (pp. 163–194). Philadelphia: John Benjamins.

Belsky, J., Friedman, S., & Hsieh, K. (2001). Testing a core emotion-regulation prediction: Does early attentional persistence moderate the effect of infant negative emotionality on later development? *Child Development, 72,* 123–133.

Blair, C., Peters, R., & Granger, D. (2004). Physiological and neuropsychological correlates of approach/withdrawal tendencies in preschool: Further examination of the behavioral inhibition system/behavioral activation system scales for young children. *Developmental-Psychobiology, 45*(3), pp. 113–124.

Bronson, M. B. (2001). *Self-regulation in early childhood: Nature and nurture.* New York: Guilford Press.

Buss, K. A., & Goldsmith, H. H. (1998). Fear and anger regulation in infancy: Effects on the temporal dynamics of affective expression. *Child Development, 69*(2), 359–374.

Calkins, S. D. (1994). Origins and outcomes of individual differences in emotional regulation. In N. A. Fox (Ed.), Emotion regulation: Behavioral and biological considerations. *Monographs of the Society for Research in Child Development, 59*(2–3, Serial No. 240).

Calkins, S. D. (1997). Cardiac vagal tone indices of temperamental reactivity and behavioral regulation in young children. *Developmental Psychobiology, 31,* 125–135.

Calkins, S. D. (2004). Early attachment process and the development of emotional self-regulation. In R. F. Baumeister & K. D. Vohs (Eds.), *Handbook of self-regulation: Research, theory, and applications* (pp. 324–339). New York: Guilford Press.

Calkins, S. D. (in press). Regulatory competence and early disruptive behavior problems: The role of physiological regulation. In S. Olson & A. Sameroff (Eds.), *Regulatory processes in the development of behavior problems: Biological, behavioral, and social-ecological interactions.* New York: Cambridge University Press.

Calkins, S. D., & Dedmon, S. E. (2000). Physiological and behavioral regulation in two-year-old children with aggressive/destructive behavior problems. *Journal of Abnormal Child Psychology, 28,* 103–118.

Calkins, S. D., Dedmon, S., Gill, K., Lomax, L., & Johnson, L. (2002). Frustration in infancy: Implications for emotion regulation, physiological processes, and temperament. *Infancy, 3,* 175–198.

Calkins, S. D., & Fox, N. A. (2002). Self-regulatory processes in early personality development: A multilevel approach to the study of childhood social withdrawal and aggression. *Development and Psychopathology, 14,* 477–498.

Calkins, S. D., Fox, N. A., & Marshall, T. R. (1996). Behavioral and physiological antecedents of inhibited and uninhibited behavior. *Child Development, 67*(2), 523–540.

Calkins, S. D., Gill, K. A., & Williford, A. (1999). Externalizing problems in two-year-olds: Implications for patterns of social behavior and peers' responses to aggression. *Early Education and Development, 10,* 266–288.

Calkins, S. D., Gill, K. L., Johnson, M. C., & Smith, C. L. (1999). Emotional reactivity and emotional regulation strategies as predictors of social behavior with peers during toddlerhood. *Social Development, 8,* 310–334.

Calkins, S. D., Graziano, P. A., & Keane, S. P. (2007). Cardiac vagal regulation differentiates children at risk for behavior problems. *Biological Psychology, 74*(2), 144–153.

Calkins, S. D., & Howse, R. (2004). Individual differences in self-regulation: Implications for childhood adjustment. In P. Philipot & R. S. Feldman (Eds.), *The regulation of emotion* (pp. 324–339). Hillsdale, NJ: Erlbaum.

Calkins, S. D., & Johnson, M. C. (1998). Toddler regulation of distress to frustrating events: Temperamental and maternal correlates. *Infant Behavior and Development, 21*(3), 379–395.

Calkins, S. D., & Keane, S. P. (2004). Cardiac vagal regulation across the preschool period: Stability, continuity, and implications for childhood adjustment. *Developmental Psychobiology, 45,* 101–112.

Calkins, S. D., Smith, C. L., Gill, K., & Johnson, M. C. (1998). Maternal interactive style across contexts: Relations to emotional, behavioral and physiological regulation during toddlerhood. *Social Development*, *7*, 350–369.

Campbell, S. B. (2002). *Behavior problems in preschool children: Clinical and developmental issues* (2nd ed.). New York: Guilford Press.

Campbell, S. B., Pierce, E. W., Moore, G., & Marakovitz, S. (1996). Boys' externalizing problems at elementary school age: Pathways from early behavior problems, maternal control, and family stress. *Development and Psychopathology*, *8*, 701–719.

Cassidy, J. (1994). Emotion regulation: Influences of attachment relationships. In N. A. Fox (Ed.), Emotion regulation: Behavioral and biological considerations. *Monographs of the Society of Research in Child Development*, *59*(2–3, Serial No. 240).

Cicchetti, D. (1984). The emergence of developmental psychopathology. *Child Development*, *55*, 1–7.

Cicchetti, D. (1993). Developmental psychopathology: Reactions, reflections, projections. *Developmental Review*, *13*, 471–502.

Cicchetti, D., Ganiban, J., & Barnett, D. (1991). Contributions from the study of high-risk populations to understanding the development of emotion regulation. In J. Garber & K. A. Dodge (Eds.), *The development of emotion regulation and dysregulation* (pp. 69–88). Cambridge, UK: Cambridge University Press.

Cicchetti, D., & Rogosh, F. (1996). Equifinality and multifinality in developmental psychopathology. *Development and Psychopathology*, *4*, 597–600.

Cohen, S., & Bromet, E. J. (1992). Maternal predictors of behavioral disturbance in preschool children: A research note. *Journal of Child Psychology and Psychiatry and Allied Disciplines*, *33*, 941–946.

Cummings, M., Ianotti, R. J., & Zahn-Waxler, C. (1989). Aggression between peers in early childhood: Individual continuity and developmental change. *Child Development*, *60*, 887–895.

Davidson, R. J., Putnam, K. M., & Larson, C. L. (2000). Dysfunction in the neural circuitry of emotion regulation—A possible prelude to violence. *Science*, *289*, 591–594.

Davis, E. P., Bruce, J., & Gunnar, M. R. (2002). The anterior attention network: Associations with temperament and neuroendocrine activity in 6–year-old children. *Developmental Psychobiology*, *40*, 43–65.

Derryberry, D., & Reed, M. A. (1996). Regulatory processes and the development of cognitive representations. *Development and Psychopathology*, *8*(1), 215–234.

Derryberry, D., & Rothbart, M. K. (1997). Reactive and effortful processes in the organization of temperament. *Development and Psychopathology*, *9*(4), 633–652.

Diamond, A. (1991). Frontal lobe involvement in cognitive changes during the first year of life. In A. C. Petersen & K. R. Gibson (Eds.), *Brain maturation and cognitive development: Comparative and cross-cultural perspectives* (pp. 127–180). Hawthorne, NY: Aldine de Gruyter.

Diener, M. L., Mengelsdorf, S. C., McHale, J. L., & Frosch, C. A. (2002). Infants' behavioral strategies for emotion regulation with fathers and mothers: Associations with emotional expressions and attachment quality. *Infancy*, *3*(2), 153–174.

Donzella, B., Gunnar, M. R., Krueger, W. K., & Alwin, J. (2000). Cortisol and vagal tone responses to competitive challenge in preschoolers: Associations with temperament. *Developmental Psychobiology*, *37*(4), 209–220.

Eisenberg, N., Cumberland, A., Spinrad, T. L., Fabes, R. A., Shepard, S. A., Reiser, M., et al. (2001). The relations of regulation and emotionality to children's externalizing and internalizing problem behavior. *Child Development*, *72*(4), 1112–1134.

Eisenberg, N., Fabes, R. A., Bernzweig, J., Karbon, M., Poulin, R., & Hanish, L. (1993). The relations of emotionality and regulation to preschoolers' social skills and sociometric status. *Child Development*, *64*, 1418–1438.

Eisenberg, N., Fabes, R., Murphy, B., Maszk, P., Smith, M., & Karbon, M. (1995). The role of emotionality and regulation in children's social functioning: A longitudinal study. *Child Development*, *66*, 1360–1384.

Eisenberg, N., Fabes, R. A., Richard, A., Nyman, M., Bernzweig, J., Bernzweig, J., et al. (1994). The relations of emotionality and regulation to children's anger-related reactions. *Child Development, 65*, 109–128.

Eisenberg, N., Fabes, R. A., Shephard, S. A., Murphy, B. C., Gutherie, I. K., Jones, S., et al. (1997). Contemporaneous and longitudinal prediction of children's social functioning from regulation and emotionality. *Child Development, 68*, 642–664.

Eisenberg, N., Smith, C. L., Sadovsky, A., & Spinrad, T. L. (2004). Effortful control: Relations with emotion regulation, adjustment, and socialization in childhood. In R. R. Baumeister & K. D. Vohs (Eds.), *Handbook of self-regulation: Research, theory and applications* (pp. 259–282). New York: Guilford Press.

Fox, N. A. (1989). Psychophysiological correlates of emotional reactivity during the first year of life. *Developmental Psychology, 25*, 364–372.

Fox, N. A. (1994). Dynamic cerebral processes underlying emotion regulation. In N. A. Fox (Ed.), Emotion regulation: Behavioral and biological considerations. *Monographs of the Society for Research in Child Development*, (2–3, Serial No. 240), 152–166.

Fox, N. A., & Calkins, S. D. (2003). The development of self-control of emotion: Intrinsic and extrinsic influences. *Motivation and Emotion, 27*, 7–26.

Fox, N. A., & Card, J. A. (1999). Psychophysiological measures in the study of attachment. In J. Cassidy & P. R. Shaver (Eds.), *Handbook of attachment: Theory, research, and clinical applications* (pp. 226–245). New York: Guilford Press.

Gilliom, M., & Shaw, D. S. (2004). Codevelopment of externalizing and internalizing problems in early childhood. *Development and Psychopathology, 16*, 313–333.

Grolnick, W. S., Bridges, L. J., & Connell, J. P. (1996). Emotion regulation in two-year-olds: Strategies and emotional expression in four contexts. *Child Development, 67*(3), 928–941.

Heller, T. L., Baker, B. L., Henker, B., & Hinshaw, S. P. (1996). Externalizing behavior and cognitive functioning from preschool to first grade: Stability and predictors. *Journal of Clinical Child Psychology, 25*, 376–387.

Hinshaw, S. P. (1994). *Attention deficits and hyperactivity in children.* Newbury Park, CA: Sage.

Hinshaw, S. P., Lahey, B. B., & Hart, E. (1993). Issues of taxonomy and comorbidity in the development of conduct disorder. *Development and Psychopathology, 5*, 31–49.

Hofer, M. (1994). Hidden regulators in attachment, separation, and loss. In N. A. Fox (Ed.), Emotion regulation: Behavioral and biological considerations. *Monographs of the Society for Research in Child Development, 59*(2–3, Serial No. 240), 192–207.

Hofheimer, J. A., Wood, B. R., Porges, S. W., Pearson, E., & Lawson, E. (1995). Respiratory sinus arrhthymia and social interaction patterns in preterm newborns. *Infant Behavior and Development, 18*, 233–245.

Howse, R., Calkins, S. D., Anastopoulos, A., Keane, S., & Shelton, T. (2003). Regulatory contributors to children's kindergarten achievement. *Early Education and Development, 14*, 101–119.

Keenan, K. (2000). Emotion dysregulation as a risk factor for child psychopathology. *Clinical Psychology: Science and Practice, 7*, 418–434.

Keenan, K., & Shaw, D. S. (2003). Starting at the beginning: Exploring the etiology of antisocial behavior in the first years of life. In B. B. Lahey, T. E. Moffitt, & A. Caspi (Eds.), *Causes of conduct disorder and juvenile delinquency* (pp. 153–181). New York: Guilford Press.

Keiley, M. K., Lofthouse, N., Bates, J. E., Dodge, K. A., & Pettit, G. S. (2003). Differential risks of covarying and pure components in mother and teacher reports of externalizing and internalizing behavior across ages 5 to 14. *Journal of Abnormal Child Psychology, 31*, 267–283.

Kochanska, G., Coy, K. C., & Murray, K. Y. (2001). The development of self-regulation in the first four years of life. *Child Development, 72*(4), 1091–1111.

Kochanska, G., Murray, K., & Coy, K. C. (1997). Inhibitory control as a contributor to conscience in childhood: From toddler to early school age. *Child Development, 68*, 264–277.

Kochanska, G., Murray, K. T., & Harlan, E. T. (2000). Effortful control in early childhood: Continuity and change, antecedents, and implications for social development. *Developmental Psychology, 36*, 220–232.

Kopp, C. (1982). Antecedents of self-regulation: A developmental perspective. *Developmental Psychology, 18*, 199–214.

Kopp, C. (1989). Regulation of distress and negative emotions: A developmental view. *Developmental Psychology, 25*(3), 343–354.

Kopp, C. (1992). Emotional distress and control in young children. In N. Eisenberg & R. Fabes, (Eds.), *Emotion and its regulation in early development* (New directions for child development, No. 55, pp. 7–23). San Francisco: Jossey-Bass/Pfeiffer.

Kuczynski, L., & Kochanska, G. (1995). Function and content of maternal demands: Developmental significance of early demands for competent action. *Child Development, 66,* 616–628.

Kuhl, J., & Kraska, K. (1993). Self-regulation: Psychometric properties of a computer-aided instrument. *German Journal of Psychology, 17,* 11–24.

Lane, R. D., & McRae, K. (2004) Neural substrates of conscious emotional experience. In M. Beauregard (Ed.), *Consciousness, emotional self-regulation and the brain* (pp. 87–122). Philadelphia: John Benjamins.

Lilienfeld, S. O. (2003). Comorbidity between and within childhood externalizing and internalizing disorders: Reflections and directions. *Journal of Abnormal Child Psychology, 31,* 285–291.

Luu, P., & Tucker, D. M. (2004). Self-regulation by the medial frontal cortex: Limbic representation of motive set-points. In M. Beauregard (Ed.), *Consciousness, emotional self-regulation and the brain* (pp. 123–162). Philadelphia: John Benjamins.

Malatesta, C. Z., Culver, C., Tesman, J. R., & Shepard, B. (1989). The development of emotion expression during the first two years of life. *Monographs of the Society for Research in Child Development, 54,* 1–104.

Miller, P. H., & Zalenski, R. (1982). Preschoolers' knowledge about attention. *Developmental Psychology, 18*(6), 871–875.

Moffitt, T. E. (1993). Adolescence-limited and life-course-persistent antisocial behavior: A developmental taxonomy. *Psychological Review, 100*(4), 674–701.

Moore, G. A., & Calkins, S. D. (2004). Infants' vagal regulation in the Still-Face Paradigm is related to dyadic coordination of mother–infant interaction. *Developmental Psychology, 40*(6), 1068–1080.

NICHD Early Child Care Research Network. (2004). Trajectories of physical aggression from toddlerhood to middle childhood: Predictors, correlates, and outcomes. *Monographs for the Society for Research on Child Development, 69*(4, Serial No. 278).

Nigg, J. T., Hinshaw, S. P., Carte, E. T., & Treuting, J. J. (1998). Neuropsychological correlates of childhood attention-deficit/hyperactivity disorder: Explainable by comorbid disruptive behavior or reading problems? *Journal of Abnormal Psychology, 107*(3), 468–480.

Nigg, J. T., & Huang-Pollock, C. L. (2003). An early-onset model of the role of executive functions and intelligence in conduct disorder/delinquency. In B. B. Lahey, T. E. Moffit, & A. Caspi (Eds.), *Causes of conduct disorder and juvenile delinquency* (pp. 227–253). New York: Guilford Press.

Ochsner, K. N., & Gross, J. J. (2004). Thinking makes it so: A social cognitive neuroscience approach to emotion regulation. In R. F. Baumeister & K. D. Vohs (Eds.), *Handbook of self-regulation: Research, theory, and applications* (pp. 229–258). New York: Guilford Press.

Paris, S. G., & Newman, R. S. (1990). Developmental aspects of self-regulated learning. *Educational Psychologist, 25,* 87–102.

Parke, R. D., & Slaby, R. G. (1983). The development of aggression. In P. H. Mussen (Ed.), *Handbook of child psychology* (Vol. 4, pp. 547–641). New York: Wiley.

Pennington, B. F., & Ozonoff, S. (1996). Executive functions and developmental psychopathology. *Journal of Child Psychology and Psychiatry and Allied Disciplines, 37*(1), 51–87.

Pine, D. S., Wasserman, G. A., Coplan, J. D., Staghezza-Jaramillo, B., Davies, M., Fried, J. E., et al. (1996). Cardiac profile and disruptive behavior in boys at risk for delinquency. *Psychosomatic Medicine, 58,* 342–353.

Pine, D., Wasserman, G., Miller, L., Coplan, J., Bagiella, E., Kovelenku, P., et al. (1998). Heart period variability and psychopathology in urban boys at risk for delinquency. *Psychophysiology, 35,* 521–529.

Polan, A., & Hofer, M. A. (1999). Psychobiological origins of infants attachment and separation responses. In J. Cassidy & P. R. Shaver (Eds.), *Handbook of attachment: Theory, research, and clinical applications* (pp. 162–180). New York: Guilford Press.

Porges, S. W. (1991). Vagal tone: An autonomic mediator of affect. In J. Garber & K. A. Dodge (Eds.), *The development of emotional regulation and dysregulation* (pp. 111–128). Cambridge, UK: Cambridge University Press.

Porges, S. W. (1996). Physiological regulation in high-risk infants: A model for assessment and potential intervention. *Development and Psychopathology, 8,* 43–58.

Porges, S. W., Doussard-Roosevelt, J., & Maita, A. K. (1994). Vagal tone and the physiological regulation of emotion. *Monographs of the Society for Research in Child Development, 59*(2–3, Serial No. 240), 167–186.

Posner, M. I., & Rothbart, M. K. (1992). Attentional mechanisms and the conscious experience. In M. D. Rugg & A. D. Milner (Eds.), *The neuropsychology of consciousness* (pp. 91–111). San Diego, CA: Academic Press.

Posner, M. I., & Rothbart, M. K. (1994). Attentional regulation: From mechanism to culture. In P. Bertelson & P. Eelen (Eds.), *International perspectives on psychological science: Vol. 1. Leading themes* (pp. 41–55). Hillsdale, NJ: Erlbaum.

Posner, M. I., & Rothbart, M. K. (1998). Summary and commentary: Developing attentional skills. In J. Richards (Ed), *Cognitive neuroscience of attention: A developmental perspective* (pp. 317–323). Mahwah, NJ: Erlbaum.

Posner, M. I., & Rothbart, M. K. (2000). Developing mechanisms of self-regulation. *Development and Psychopathology, 12,* 427–441.

Richards, J. E. (1985). Respiratory sinus arrhythmia predicts heart rate and visual responses during visual attention in 14– and 20–week-old infants. *Psychophysiology, 22,* 101–109.

Richards, J. E. (1987). Infant visual sustained attention and respiratory sinus arrhythmia. *Child Development, 58,* 488–496.

Richards, J. E., & Cameron, D. (1989). Infant heart rate variability and behavioral developmental status. *Infant Behavior and Development, 12,* 45–58.

Rothbart, M. K. (1989). Temperament and development. In G. Kohnstamm, J. Bates, & M. K. Rothbart (Eds.), *Temperament in childhood* (pp. 187–248). Chichester, UK: Wiley.

Rothbart, M. K., & Bates, J. E. (1998). Temperament. In W. Damon (Series Ed.) & N. Eisenberg (Vol. Ed.), *Handbook of child psychology: Vol 3. Social, emotional, and personality development* (5th ed., pp. 105–176). New York: Wiley.

Rothbart, M. K., & Derryberry, D. (1981). Development of individual differences in temperament. In M. E. Lamb & A. L. Brown (Eds.), *The neuropsychology of individual differences: A developmental perspective* (pp. 93–123). New York: Plenum Press.

Rothbart, M. K., Derryberry, D., & Hershey, K. (2000). Stability of temperament in childhood: Laboratory infant assessment to parent report at seven years. In D. L. Molfese & V. J. Molfese (Eds.), *Temperament and personality development across the life span* (pp. 85–119). Mahwah, NJ: Erlbaum.

Rothbart, M. K., Derryberry, D., & Posner, M. I. (1994). A psychobiological approach to the development of temperament. In T. D. Wachs & J. E. Bates (Eds.), *Temperament: Individual differences at the interface of biology and behavior* (pp. 83–116). Washington, DC: American Psychological Association.

Rothbart, M. K., & Jones, L. B. (1998). Temperament, self-regulation and education. *School Psychology Review, 27*(4), 479–491.

Rothbart, M. K., Posner, M. I., & Boylan, A. (1990). Regulatory mechanisms in infant development. In J. Enns (Ed.), *The development of attention: Research and theory* (pp. 139–160). Amsterdam: Elsevier.

Rothbart, M. K., Ziaie, H., & O'Boyle, C. G. (1992). Self-regulation and emotion in infancy. In N. Eisenberg & R. Fabes (Eds.), *Emotion and its regulation in early development* (New directions for child development, No. 55, pp. 7–23). San Francisco: Jossey-Bass/Pfeiffer.

Rubin, K. H., Burgess, K. B., Dwyer, K. M., & Hastings, P. D. (2003). Predicting preschoolers' externalizing behaviors from toddler temperament, conflict, and maternal negativity. *Developmental Psychology, 39,* 164–176.

Rueda, M. R., Posner, M. I., & Rothbart, M. K. (2004). Attentional control and self-regulation. In R. F. Baumeister & K. D. Vohs (Eds.), *Handbook of self-regulation: Research, theory and applications* (pp. 283–300). New York: Guilford Press.

Ruff, H. A., & Rothbart, M. K. (1996). *Attention in early development: Themes and variations.* London: Oxford University Press.

Rutter, M. (1987). Psychosocial resilience and protective factors. *American Journal of Orthopsychiatry, 57*, 316–331.

Sethi, A., Mischel, W., Aber, J. L., Shoda, Y., & Rodriguez, M. L. (2000). The role of strategic attention deployment in development of self-regulation: Predicting preschoolers' delay of gratification from mother-toddler interactions. *Developmental Psychology, 36*, 767–777.

Shipman, K., Schneider, R., & Brown, A. (2004). Emotion dysregulation and psychopathology. In M. Beauregard (Ed.), *Consciousness, emotional self-regulation and the brain* (pp. 61–85). Philadelphia: John Benjamins.

Sroufe, A. L. (1996). *Emotional development: The organization of emotional life in the early years.* New York: Cambridge University Press.

Sroufe, L., & Rutter, M. (1984). The domain of developmental psychopathology. *Child Development, 55*, 17–29.

Stansbury, K., & Gunnar, M. R. (1994). Adrenocortical activity and emotion regulation. In N. A. Fox (Ed.), The development of emotion regulation: Biological and behavioral considerations. *Monographs of the Society for Research in Child Development, 59*(2–3, Serial No. 240), 108–134.

Stifter, C. A., & Braungart, J. M. (1995). The regulation of negative reactivity in infancy: Function and development. *Developmental Psychology, 31*, 448–455.

Stifter, C. A., & Fox, N. A. (1990). Infant reactivity: Physiological correlates of newborn and 5-month temperament. *Developmental Psychology, 26*, 582–588.

Stifter, C. A., Spinrad, T. L., & Braungart-Rieker, J. M. (1999). Toward a developmental model of child compliance: The role of emotion regulation in infancy. *Child Development, 70*, 21–32.

Suess, P. E., Porges, S. W., & Plude, D. J. (1994). Cardiac vagal tone and sustained attention in school-age children. *Psychophysiology, 31*, 17–22.

Thompson, R. A. (1994). Emotion regulation: A theme in search of a definition. In N. A. Fox (Ed.), Emotion regulation: Behavioral and biological considerations. *Monographs of the Society for Research in Child Development, 57*(Nos. 2–3, Serial No. 240), 25–52.

Tronick, E. Z. (1989). Emotions and emotional communication in infants. *American Psychologist, 44*, 112–119.

Wilson, B., & Gottman, J. (1996). Attention—The shuttle between emotion and cognition: Risk, resiliency, and physiological bases. In E. Hetherington & E. Blechman (Eds.), *Stress, coping and resiliency in children and families* (pp. 189–228). Mahwah, NJ: Erlbaum.

Zelazo, P. D., & Reznick, J. S. (1991). Age-related asynchrony of knowledge and action. *Child Development, 62*(4), 719–735.

Zelazo, P. D., Reznick, J. S., & Pinon, D. E. (1995). Response control and the execution of verbal rules. *Developmental Psychology 31*(3), 508–517.

12

Autonomy, Compliance, and Internalization

David R. Forman

When a toddler says, "I want to do it myself!," nearly everyone recognizes it as a sign of the child's developing autonomy (Geppert & Küstner, 1983). Fewer people understand the equally vehement, "I want to do it with you!" whether directly stated or implied, as another aspect of the same development. Similarly, psychoanalytic theorists have long described the toddler's emphatic use of the word *no*, when refusing to cooperate as a milestone of autonomy development (Spitz, 1965). The equally emphatic *yes*, which the toddler can use in proud and eager cooperation, has only more recently been appreciated.

Child compliance or noncompliance begins with a demand or suggestion from another person, conveying his or her intention or preference that the child act in a certain way. Internalization is a process by which these preferences, or social standards for right behavior, eventually are transformed into self-endorsed individual standards for behavior. That self-endorsement, or commitment, can be understood as a freely chosen "yes," which is the hallmark of an autonomous moral agent (Emde, Biringen, Clyman, & Oppenheim, 1991). From this perspective, internalization is one form of autonomy development in which the child comes to freely choose to act in accord with society's values. An understanding of both autonomy development and internalization should therefore help inform each other. However, older understandings that equate autonomy with resistance to control persist.

This chapter begins with an argument that autonomy development should be viewed not in terms of increasing independence, self-reliance, or resistance to control but rather as an increase in the child's range of effective choices. Rapid changes in a variety of developmental capacities in the toddler period are then reviewed. These changes affect both children's preferred actions and parents' limit setting. There is, however, variability in parents' proximal and developmental goals for their children, and this also influences what areas become "hot topics" in a given parent–toddler relationship at a given time. Therefore, one must consider the extent to which compliance, autonomy striving, and internalization are situation specific or generalize across activities. Theory and research on the development of both positive and negative reciprocities support the idea that, over time, young children do begin to develop a general sense of their parents' and their own goals as compatible or incompatible. Internalization is more likely when autonomy and connectedness are mutually supporting. Future research and theory are needed to extend and integrate our understanding of compliance and autonomy on two levels. The first level concerns forces that support or constrain toddlers' effective and socially approved choice making in individual contexts. The second level concerns processes through which relationships develop over time so that closeness and autonomy are compatible or mutually exclusive goals.

AUTONOMY IN THE TODDLER PERIOD: PROBLEMS OF DEFINITION

Research on autonomy in toddlerhood has recently been at something of a low ebb, particularly when contrasted with research on autonomy development in adolescence (Zimmer-Gembeck & Collins, 2003). Historical trends in social development have contributed to the problem. The rise of attachment theory and research overturned traditional definitions of autonomy. Following this rethinking of autonomy, more current perspectives have typically relied on self-report measures of autonomy and have not often been applied to toddlers. One useful way to think about autonomy is to consider the range of effective choices available to the child.

Overturning the Traditional Understanding of Autonomy: Independence, Self-Reliance, and Freedom from Control

Historically, autonomy has been seen as independence, self-reliance, or freedom from external control. When secondary drive theory and other social learning theories were dominant in developmental psychology, autonomy was understood to be the opposite of dependency. Dependency, in turn was described as a broad motive system focused around the need for closeness, nurturance, or instrumental help and measured as nearly all behavior directed toward the caregiver (Sears, 1972; Sears, Maccoby, & Levin, 1957). Therefore, autonomy was the lack of need for closeness (independence), or the lack of a need for instrumental help (self-reliance). A third common view of autonomy with deep historical roots is that autonomy is freedom from external control.

Independence

The social learning definition of dependency comprised nearly all socially directed behavior. As Hartup (1963) put it, "Whenever the individual gives evidence that people, as people, are satisfying and rewarding, it may be said that the individual is behaving dependently." (p. 333). By contrast, autonomy was viewed as independence. However, this definition was found to be developmentally inappropriate in the toddler period. Observations of young toddlers' behavior showed that the caregiver's proximity and emotional availability enable children to explore more effectively and independently (Ainsworth & Wittig, 1969; Mahler, Pine, & Bergman, 1975; Sorce & Emde, 1981). Furthermore, attachment research showed that infants and toddlers who are more securely attached show more independent behavior later in preschool (Sroufe, Fox, & Pancake, 1983).

Self-Reliance

Another traditional indicator of autonomy is self-reliance, or lack of the need for instrumental help. This definition is also not appropriate in the toddler period. Theoretical progress and empirical research over the past two decades have revealed the extent to which skill development in a wide variety of areas is supported by adults, who simplify problems, provide access to cultural tools for learning, and provide a broad range of other supports (Rogoff, 1990, 1998; Vygotsky, 1978). Developmentally appropriate openness to the receipt of help is therefore promotive of later self-reliance.

Attachment research provides evidence against the utility of self-reliance as a measure of autonomy in toddlerhood. Faced with separation from the primary caregiver in an unfamiliar situation, the young toddler normally draws on his or her caregiver's help in regulating that distress. While securely attached children seek this help directly, 1-year-olds classified as avoidant appear self-reliant, not displaying any distress, or regulating their unease independently by turning their attention to toys. Attachment researchers claim that the pattern of premature self-reliance displayed by avoidantly attached infants does not fully succeed in regulating the stress of separation (Spangler & Grossman, 1993). Longitudinal follow-up studies of securely attached infants also describe the competent toddler as open to help when a task is beyond the child's capacity (Matas, Arend, & Sroufe, 1978). The pattern of apparent self-reliance in infancy, however, leads not to later self-reliance but rather to immature and ineffective forms of help seeking (Sroufe et al., 1983).

Resistance to Control

Finally, a third classic approach to autonomy is to define it as freedom from, or resistance to, the control of others. Viewing autonomy as freedom from influence, or resistance to external control, assumes that social values are imposed on children. This, in turn, is based on a view of children as individualistic by nature, and as being driven by impulses that must be brought into line with social expectations (Freud, 1930). More recent views describe a socially fitted infant who has a motivation to learn cultural skills and values as part of his or her natural equipment (Emde & Clyman, 1997; Trevarthan, 1988). Some processes of socialization are not conflict driven. Children can view the taking on of adult values as an individual accomplishment, with learning the "right way" to do something as an important and intrinsic goal (Emde & Buchsbaum, 1990). According to this view, the earliest form of moral conduct emerges from the learning of correct procedures for what to do and what not to do, and some of this learning is eagerly absorbed and proudly demonstrated. It is possible for both of these perspectives to be correct. Children may be both eager to learn from their elders and moved by impulses that are often unacceptable by adult standards.

Recent research confirms that compliance and noncompliance have both autonomous and heteronomous forms. Kochanska and her colleagues have argued that the quality of child-compliant behavior can reveal the child's underlying motivational stance. Committed compliance, which is self-sustaining and affectively positive, is an autonomous form of compliance that reflects the eager commitment to the parent's agenda (Kochanska & Aksan, 1995). Situational compliance, which appears motivationally "shaky" and depends on an adult's ongoing support for its maintenance, is a less autonomous form. Support for this distinction comes from the fact that the committed form of compliance is associated with low levels of parent control and predicts the child's continued rule-abiding conduct in the absence of the caregiver (e.g., Kochanska, Tjebkes, & Forman, 1998). In addition, a pattern described as compulsive compliance has been observed in children of abusive parents (Crittenden & DiLalla, 1988). Obviously, obedience that is coerced under threat of harm cannot be viewed as autonomous, by any definition. Again, the observed quality of a toddler's compliant behavior can reveal whether it is experienced as freely chosen.

Behaviors that resist others also vary in quality. Some resistant behaviors, including ignoring and defiance (doing the opposite of a directive, or emotion-laden refusals), are experienced as aversive by caregivers. These aversive forms tend to decrease developmentally in the toddler period, while simple verbal refusals (self-assertion) and negotiation increase (Kuczynski, Kochanska, Radke-Yarrow, & Girnius Brown, 1987; Vaughn, Kopp, & Krakow, 1984). Moreover, self-assertion is associated with autonomy-supportive parenting (Crockenberg & Littman, 1990). Parents who are low in coercion also have children who can later negotiate conflict with their peers in more socially competent ways (Crockenberg, Jackson, & Langrock, 1996). Because autonomy-supportive parenting is associated with more mature, more socially effective, and less emotionally negative forms of resistance to control, it makes sense to labels these forms of negotiation and direct self-assertion as *autonomous* (Crockenberg & Littman, 1990).

Despite their association with power-assertive parenting, it is less clear at first that other forms of resistance should be labeled as *heteronomous*, unless there is other evidence that the behavior is compulsive or anxious, or experienced by toddlers as obligatory, or out of their conscious control in some way. Toddlers, however, are necessarily dependant on their primary caregivers both instrumentally and emotionally, and relationship closeness can promote competence which, in turn, enables further autonomy development. One may therefore speculate that aversive forms of child resistance, if they function to erode reciprocity in the parent–child relationship, will limit the toddler's effective choices and put the child's later autonomy striving at risk. In families with antisocial children, for example, coercive exchanges forestall other positive development-promoting interactions (Patterson, 1982). Unfortunately, the study of noncompliance is still too often relegated to clinical research (Kuczynski & Hildebrandt, 1997). For example, little or no recent nonclinical research deals with the parenting correlates, the social functions, or the consequences of normal toddler temper tantrums (for an exception, see Weinfeld & Ogawa, 2005). Research including the full range of typically developing children could yield insight into whether frequent tantrums portend later coercive exchanges, and into how some children learn to substitute more effective and appropriate resistance strategies while others do not.

Summary

Rather than viewing autonomy as action taken away from people (independence), without help from other people (self-reliance), or in opposition to other people (resistance), many contemporary scholars agree that relationship closeness is compatible with autonomy development (Emde & Buchsbaum, 1990; Hill & Holmbeck, 1986; Kağitçibaşi, 2005; Ryan & Lynch, 1989). That is, given a supportive relationship context, there are at least some autonomous forms of action that are socially directed, open to the receipt of help when necessary, and cooperative. This is especially true in the toddler period when the child's exploration of, and effective action in, the world is still very much tied to the caregiver's presence and support (Mahler et al., 1975; Murphy, 1962). This requires a different definition of autonomy.

A Description of Autonomy as Self-Government in Toddlers

Provisional Definition

I use as a provisional definition of autonomy *the potential to choose and to act effectively on that choice*. This is a deliberately broad and integrative definition. Because potential includes ability as well as permission, this description incorporates capacity and choice. To the extent that effectively carrying out a given choice (without, for example, becoming distracted or frustrated) requires self-regulation, this is necessary as well. Note that this definition admits internal as well as external limits to early autonomy development. At first, toddlers are still relatively helpless, constrained as much by their behavioral repertoires, their emotional reactivity, and their limited understanding, as they are by the imposition of rules by adults. Under such circumstances, parent support for competence development is as important as other more direct forms of autonomy support (choice granting, providing explanations for rules, and avoiding coercive control) because it leads to social and behavioral skills that in turn will enable a greater range of choices for the child.

Self-Determination Theory: Autonomy as Perceived Choice

Choice is central to self-determination theory, which defines autonomy as perceived internal locus of causality or perceived choice (Deci & Ryan, 1987). This approach to autonomy can include connected as well as independent forms of autonomy striving. One can choose to act toward or away from people, one can choose to seek help or to attempt an action without help, and one can choose to act in accord with, or against, other people's goals. It therefore avoids the problems of the older assumptions of autonomy as a nonsocial, or antisocial, characteristic. However, there are also challenges to a straightforward application of this definition to the study of toddlers.

The first challenge is due to toddlers' cognitive and language ability. Perceived causality is phenomenological, based on the individual's felt experience, and is typically measured by self-report. Toddlers cannot reflect and report on why they do what they do. Still, as Kochanska's distinction between situational and committed compliance demonstrates, something of the toddler's motivation can be inferred from the quality of the child's behavior. When a behavior is pursued "wholeheartedly," in a flexible, self-sustaining, and affectively positive manner, we may infer that the child experiences the act as something they want to, rather than having to, do.

The second challenge is that self-determination theorists have traditionally drawn a sharp distinction between efficacy or agency and self-determination. However, capacity is necessary for meaningful choice. It is no benefit to be permitted an activity of which one is incapable. In addition, children prefer (choose) to do what makes them feel effective (Bandura, 1997; White, 1959). This is particularly important in the toddler period when capacities for action are rapidly changing. Newly emerging capacities carry their own motive force (Piaget, 1952) and create the subject matter for negotiation of choice. For these reasons the definition has been expanded to emphasize choice that leads to effective action.

The third challenge in applying the self-determination definition to toddler behavior is that very young children change rapidly in their preferences or choices, both developmentally and temporally. Developmentally, children are motivated to exercise emerging capacities, while remaining in close connection to their caregivers. Temporally, toddlers are still impulsive and distractible.

The temporal changes mean that a certain degree of regulation is required in the translation from choice to effective action, and this regulation is at first supported by the caregiver. Moreover, choices that are initially imposed can come to be "endorsed" or freely chosen even during the activity itself. For example, Kochanska's committed compliance is not simply either present or absent during a full 5-minute clean-up task, but it may be shown half the time for one child and three-quarters of the time for another (Kochanska, Coy, & Murray, 2001).

Despite these challenges, the perspective here is broadly compatible with self-determination theory. The difference is largely in emphasis. Motivation at this age is not viewed as due to a process of mature self-reflection about the causes of behavior. It cannot be measured through self-report but must be inferred from the dynamic affect quality of behavior. Choices are enabled or constrained by ability as well as by external control, and parental control is sometimes necessary in order to support those capacities that will enable effective choices later in development. Insight into the ground on which autonomy is negotiated can be therefore gained by studying the normative development of related capacities, and by viewing compliance development in the light of these normative changes.

COMPLIANCE DEVELOPMENT IN TODDLERHOOD

Normative Development in Related Skills

Compliance and noncompliance begin with a parent directive or suggestion that is not initially the child's goal. Both the direction of the toddler's motivated behavior and the parent's desire to limit it follow from the multiple rapid changes in capacity seen in this developmental period. These rapid changes include transformations in locomotion, language, memory, self-control, emotional expressions, and social understanding. New abilities emerge, bearing their own motive force (they are the "activities of choice"). They may be celebrated and the child may be proud of them. But children also extend and test the limits of these new abilities, often using them in ways that are considered socially inappropriate. This leads to new parental expectations for right conduct, with accompanying instructions as to how and when to judiciously, or appropriately, or effectively employ the new skill, as well as how and when not to do so. These lead to increasing child self-control, to negotiation, and to conflict. Furthermore, the child's skills in anticipating the parent's point of view and in navigating these disagreements also increase.

Walking and Other Physical Skills

Children's early shaky attempts to walk may give the "toddler" period its English name, but they do not "toddle" for long, gaining rapidly in coordination and speed. Upright locomotion changes the ecology of childhood, as children get into new places, encounter new objects, and are harder to monitor. This mobility, initially a source of pride for parent and child alike, also leads directly to compliance concerns about where the child is permitted to go and what he or she is allowed to handle, especially when safety issues are concerned. With competent locomotion, the child also becomes extremely active in regulating distance or proximity to the caregiver, often by following, and by protesting separation, to the point where some parents of toddlers complain of not being able to go to the bathroom alone without a struggle.

Toward the end of the toddler period, children are often physically able to dress themselves, to use a toilet or potty, and to perform other self-help skills. Again, the initial achievement of these skills may be a source of pride, but achievements also lead to demands. Demands that the child get dressed, for example, are a frequent subject for compliance among older toddlers (Gralinski & Kopp, 1993; Kuczynski & Kochanska, 1995). Toilet training in middle-class North American families occurs later in development than it did a generation ago, but even though many parents may prefer not to force the issue, successful toilet training is often a requirement for preschool entry (Blum, Taubman, & Nemeth, 2004).

Language

Among the many ways in which language relates to compliance and internalization are comprehension of requests, internalization of parents' speech for self-regulation, and discourse about standards of conduct. Later, language itself may become the subject of cooperation and conflict. First, children's understanding necessarily limits what they can be asked to do and not to do (Kaler & Kopp, 1990). Parents sensitively adjust their demands to the rapid development of children's receptive language in the second year, as nonverbal "suggestions," such as handing a child an object, occur in free play with 15-month-olds more often than with 24-month-olds (Shaffer & Crook, 1979). Parents use linguistic categories to label prohibited objects, and children internalize these labels. In our study of toddler compliance (Kochanksa et al., 1998), it was not uncommon for mothers to point to the toys that were designated off limits and use the word *hot,* which was then dutifully repeated by the child. Children commonly imitate parents' discipline language and gestures, directing their words to themselves but also to others, including pets, siblings, parents, and dolls (Kuczynski, Zahn-Waxler, & Radke-Yarrow, 1987). The importance of language in promoting compliance and internalization is underscored by the fact that language-delayed toddlers tend to show lower rates of compliance than do typically developing children (Irwin, Carter, & Briggs-Gowan, 2002).

Later in the toddler period, parents and children directly talk about values, especially in conversations about transgressions and parent–child conflicts (Thompson, Laible, & Ontai 2003). Characteristics of parents' talk, both during conflict and concerning past conflicts, can predict their children's later internalized conduct (Laible & Thompson, 2002). Discourse, however, is not a top-down but a collaborative process. In conversing about the past, even very young children have their own version of what happened, and so they also learn in this venue to assert themselves in the face of opposition and to negotiate (Wiley, Rose, Burger, & Miller, 1998). Negotiation has been described earlier as an autonomous form of noncompliance, partly because it attempts to influence the parent in a manner that is more flexible and less aversive than defiance or ignoring. Clearly, language skills are a prerequisite for negotiation, and vocabulary and social understanding are both important for effective persuasion. Finally, language itself is a form of conduct directly regulated by parents when they judge the child's words to be incorrect or inappropriate.

Though this chapter focuses on child compliance and autonomy development, the shared quality of discourse may also serve as a reminder that socialization is bidirectional. With their increased communication abilities, children also frequently issue directives and make requests of their parents (Ryckebusch & Marcos, 2004). How and when parents respond with compliance, refusal, and negotiation can serve as models for the children's own responses. They also can help the children actively learn which of their attempted influence tactics are effective and under what circumstances (Kuczynski, 2003).

Memory

The ability of very young children to remember events is much better than had been understood until recently. Rapid advances in memory in the second year enable toddlers to learn new procedures and even to carry out multistep actions, as shown by Patricia Bauer's series of studies using elicited imitation tasks (Bauer, Wenner, Dropik, & Wewerka, 2000). Rheingold and her colleagues argue that this new skill is a source of intrinsic pleasure for children (Rheingold, Cook, & Kolowitz, 1987). They show that in the second half of the second year, parental demands for specific actions on objects generally elicit positive affect, as well as cooperation. They explicitly link children's motivation to comply with the moderate challenge inherent in understanding, remembering, and enacting the demand, claiming that "for children at 18 and 24 months of age, the carrying out of verbally directed tasks of some complexity represents a newly gained achievement" (Rheingold et al., 1987, p. 146). In other words, increases in memory can increase the child's motivation to comply in "do" tasks, if the action to be carried out is at the newly mastered level of complexity.

Self-Control

The child's rapid increases in self-regulation, including attention regulation, emotion regulation, and behavioral self-control, are the subject of another chapter and thus are only briefly touched on here. With increasing child ability, parents may expect more in these domains, for example, by being requiring their toddlers to pay attention to the parent, to wait, or to moderate their displays of negative affect. When all goes well, expectations match the shaky and scaffolded nature of these early abilities.

Most parental commands or prohibitions require the child to inhibit or shift ongoing actions. Variations in children's abilities to shift their ongoing behavior in this manner have historically described by constructs such as ego control, executive control, inhibitory control, and effortful control (Kochanska, Murray, & Harlan, 2000). Effortful control has an important influence on compliance and internalization (Kochanska et al., 2000). Again, one must be capable of something before one can be required to do it, and ability is a powerful contributor to motivation. Effortful control ability increases throughout the toddler period. However, indices of individual abilities (motor slowing, delay of gratification) cohere only loosely at first, become more correlated from the third into the fourth year (Murray & Kochanska, 2002).

The three aspects of self-regulation—attention regulation, emotion regulation, and behavioral self-control—are also linked. Several theorists have claimed that attentional control develops earlier and underlies both emotional regulation and behavioral self-control (Kopp, 2002; Ruff & Rothbart 1996; Sethi, Mischel, Aber, Shoda, & Rodriguez, 2000). It makes sense, then, that characteristics of infant attention and maternal guidance of infant attention are associated with differences in compliance ability and delay of gratification early on (Vaughn et al., 1984). In the extreme, inability to control attention is a core dimension of hyperactivity, along with the inability to inhibit inappropriate behavior (American Psychiatric Association, 2000).

Self-Conscious Emotions

The emergence of self-awareness and the appearance of self-conscious emotions, pride, guilt, and shame are also treated in detail elsewhere in this volume, so I confine myself here to three points regarding their joint role in autonomy development and internalization. First, consistent with the importance of competence in both compliance and autonomy development, pride and shame form a motivational link between competence promotion, or the teaching of skills, and moral socialization, or the teaching of values. Skill development and moral development share the theme of the child meeting or failing to meet standards for behavior. Two-year-old children react with pride to both success at a cognitive task and right conduct, and with shame to both failure and wrongdoing (Stipek, Recchia, & McClintic, 1992).

Second, individual differences in self-conscious emotions are anticipated by earlier child characteristics and parenting. Self-conscious emotions appear late in development compared with other emotions, because their existence depends on the appreciation of social standards, as they relate to the self (Jennings, 2004; Lewis & Brooks-Gunn, 1979). However, there is meaningful continuity from both earlier infant characteristics and parenting to individual differences in self-conscious emotions. Other developments already presage the child's likely later attitude toward social standards for conduct, even before such standards are understood by the child. For example, children's responsive imitation at 14 months predicts guilt during the preschool period, even though guilt per se does not yet exist at 14 months (Forman, Aksan, & Kochanska, 2004; see also Belsky, Domitrovich, & Crnic, 1997; Kochanska, Forman, & Coy, 1999, for other infancy predictors of self-conscious emotions). For many adults, guilt might mark the earliest sign of conscience, proper, but it is not the starting point for the study of internalization. As theory emphasizes, the emergence of the "moral self" draws on earlier emotional underpinnings and procedural knowledge about what to do and what not to do (Emde et al., 1991; Kochanska, 1994).

Third, though pride, guilt, and shame are responses to meeting or failing to meet social standards, these emotions do not always serve the aim of bringing the child into line with parental standards of conduct. Shame, for example, is associated with avoidance. A shame response therefore might motivate a child's avoidance of potential responsibility for a mishap, or for avoidance of challenge in cognitive tasks, both of which have been observed in 2-year-olds (Barrett & Morgan, 1995; Barrett, Zahn-Waxler, & Cole, 1994).

Pride can be attached to resistance, and this may be especially likely in cases in which the child has received mixed signals. Parents may be ambivalent about their own authority or about their socialization goals, possibly because they place a high value on their own freedom from social control. Theory and research on culture and parenting suggest that many European Americans see resistance to control as a positive, or at least normal, sign of their child's emerging autonomy, whereas traditionally noncompliance has been viewed as immaturity in Japan (Rothbaum, Pott, Azuma, Miyake, & Weisz, 2000). It would follow that Japanese parents are unlikely to feel proud of, or reassured by, their toddler's disobedience (Ujiie, 1997).

Social Understanding I: Understanding Emotions

At age 1, children already use others' emotions to guide their behavior. Social referencing studies show that adults' directed facial expressions of fear, anger, or disgust make toddlers less likely to interact with an object, while signals of pleasure make that contact more likely (e.g., Klinnert, Emde, Butterfield, & Campos, 1986; Sorce, Emde, Campos, & Klinnert, 1985). With more experience, in cases in which an adult's emotional reaction does not appear to fit the situation, toddlers are capable of "testing" or negotiating over that reaction. For example, in a social referencing study at age 2, toddlers reacted to their parents' fear faces by smiling and touching a toy more than they did when parental fear was absent (Walden & Ogan, 1988). This testing reaction may have occurred because parents showed exaggerated fear to a toy that appeared harmless to the child, or because a fear face did not make sense in the absence of any vocalization or behavioral intervention. Perhaps because marked facial expressions are used in play, more subtle fear faces are actually more effective in regulating child behavior (Rosen, Adamson, & Bakeman, 1992).

Children also test their emerging emotion knowledge using imitation. Kuczynski and his colleagues report that children's imitations of affect in third year, compared to second year, are more likely to be perceived by parents as "fake," or instrumental, or to appear contrived, such as when they imitate crying followed by a smile (Kuczynski, Zahn-Waxler, & Radke-Yarrow, 1987). In other words, children are not just expressing emotions but using them in conscious representation of how emotions function interpersonally. One may speculate that following such demonstrations, children may now begin to be held accountable for their facial affect, for example, in displaying situationally appropriate gratitude, or in being required not just to say "sorry" but also to include the matching facial expression. In addition, after empathy emerges, effective parents utilize it in their teaching of right conduct (Hoffmann, 2001).

Social Understanding II: Understanding Intentions and Goals

To understand a parent's directive is to understand something about their intention or goal. "She wants me to do this." This early aspect of desire understanding must be present early in the second year, as children demonstrably comply with directives and suggestions. Recent studies using imitation confirm that, by 14 months, children are more likely to imitate intended actions than accidental ones (Carpenter, Akhtar, & Tomasello, 1998; Gergely, Bekkering, & Kiraly, 2002). Because cooperation and conflict are early and salient venues in which children regularly encounter parent goals and intentions that differ from their own, aspects of compliance, discipline, negotiation, and conflict may promote social cognitive development.

However, the reverse is not necessarily the case. Understanding goals or intentions does not immediately lead either to prosocial conduct or to moral knowledge (Astington, 2004). Though it has not been tested, theorists have suggested that children's newfound understanding of intentions can lead to social expectations that cause frustration when they are violated, and that this frustration may be a cause of negativism and temper tantrums (Rothbaum & Weisz, 1989). To cite a different example, though children tell lies early, before they are able to articulate the role deception plays in changing others' goals, lying increases from the toddler through the preschool period (Talwar & Lee, 2002; Wilson, Smith, & Ross, 2003). Increased social understanding does not lead automatically to increasing cooperation. New forms of cooperation may be possible as well as new forms of resistance and manipulation.

Apart from a recent suggestion by Happé and Frith (1996) that what antisocial children have is a "theory of nasty minds," very little theory of mind research has paid attention to what children think about the *content* of others' intentions, as they relate to the child him- or herself. However, this may be a very important way in which relationships influence internalization. To a toddler, more important than the knowledge structure underlying mother's goal (the belief–intention link) are the questions, "Does mother wish me well or ill?" and "Do I want what she wants?" In mutually responsive relationships, each partner wishes to please the other and help the partner to obtain his or her goals (Maccoby, 1992). On the other hand, in coercive relationships, where one partner wins, the other usually loses (Bugental & Happaney, 2000). An important developmental issue is when and how individual interactions begin to generalize to cognitions such as these expectations of shared or conflicting goals. In turn, these expectations likely bear on the child's motivation to identify with the parent, and eventually on the perceived legitimacy of the parent's authority (Grusec & Goodnow, 1984).

Integration of Individual Skills

At the intersection of language, memory, and the understanding of others' intentions in general and standards for behavior in particular, the child begins to construct explicit moral knowledge. While Freud (1966) and Piaget (1965) were both skeptical about the status of very young children's moral development, the quality of a 30-month-old's moral life is clearly very different from that of an 18-month-old. By their third year, toddlers have the ability to understand what someone else wants of them, and can remember and talk about salient discipline events. They can comply with simple rules, show some self-control ability, and express pride and shame. The three broad aspects of moral development—moral understanding, moral conduct, and moral affect—are all present in some form.

At this point, parents may begin to hold children more accountable not only for proximal obedience but also for remembering rules and continuing to follow them. It may be more difficult for parents to understand that the consolidation and integration of multiple individual skills takes time. Self-control in the parent's absence may appear to be present but suddenly disappear in the presence of some strong stimulus, as in the case in which a child knows not to run into the street, has shown the ability to refrain, but suddenly forgets everything when a ball rolls out (Kopp, 1982). Evidence for a consolidation process comes from data showing that individual differences in moral affect and moral conduct are at first loosely related but that the link grows stronger from the third to the fourth year (Aksan & Kochanska, 2005).

Summary

For each type of behavioral or cognitive skill, developmental level determines the child's range of possible choices, the child's understanding of the parent's preferences, and the tools the child has for navigating between the two. Because of the number of skills and domains involved, this process requires continual adjustment both on the parent's part, as the child rapidly develops new ways of cooperating and causing trouble, and on the child's part, as behaviors celebrated and rewarded yesterday are today subject to new demands for self-regulation, leading to new potential for conflict and for internalization.

From this point of view, transition is not an event but is a characteristic of the toddler period as a whole. Some skill is always emerging, while some other skill may be being extended or consolidated. On the one hand, the child's developmental level may strongly influence what the "hot topics" are, including which kinds of behaviors are being celebrated and which are the subject of restriction or redirection. On the other hand, the content of parenting is not causally determined by the child's developmental level but depends on how the parent reacts to the child's behavior. What demands are made will be influenced by what the caregiver's values are and by what he or she is trying to do in a given situation. In addition, the same new skills or new parental demands can either bring the parent's and child's goals closer together, if they result in committed compliance or negotiation, or underline their separateness, when the child submits involuntarily, ignores the parent, or shows defiance. I discuss these two issues next, first illustrating how parenting goals interact with toddlers' development and then (after an aside on the specificity or generality of child cooperation) discussing individual differences in relationships and their associations with compliance and autonomy development.

The Content of Early Compliance: Parenting Goals

Compliance or noncompliance begins when the parent and child goals differ, and when the parent attempts to limit or guide the child's action. While the emergence of individual skills in the young child exerts a strong influence on the child's intrinsic goals, the specific values and rules governing right conduct come from the parent. This joint contribution of parenting and child goals can be seen throughout the toddler period, as different "hot topics" arise in parent–child interactions.

Compliance often becomes a salient issue in parent–child relationships following the onset of child locomotion (Campos et al., 2000). Based on parents' responses to open-ended questions, safety is by far the most frequent issue around which parents attempt to elicit compliance from young toddlers, eclipsing all other compliance categories combined in the second year (Gralinski & Kopp, 1993). The salience of safety issues for compliance decreases significantly over development, while demands for self-care and for respecting others' property increase. In still older toddlers, there may be an increase of demands to adhere to norms for interpersonally appropriate conduct (Kuczynski & Kochanksa, 1995). This appears to be an extremely gradual process. Data from the parents' free responses in the fourth year show that safety remains the most frequently mentioned category (Gralinski & Kopp, 1993). However, despite these regularities, parents vary and their goals are multifaceted. The examples of two common issues in early compliance development, safety and property, are used to illustrate this complexity.

Safety and Injury Prevention

Ensuring a child's survival has long been regarded as a universal function of the parent's role across cultures (LeVine, 1970). It can be viewed as *disordered* to place on the child a responsibility for which he or she is not ready. Peterson (1994) argues that permitting injuries to occur is continuous with the concept of child neglect. From this point of view, ensuring the young child's safety is solely the parent's moral and practical responsibility. In support of this perspective, Morrongiello and her colleagues present data that show that preemptive strategies for 2- and 3 year-olds are far more effective than the child-based strategy of teaching safety rules (Morrongiello, Ondejko, & Littlejohn, 2004b).

On the other hand, some parents (particularly fathers) endorse comments implying that there are potential developmental benefits of minor childhood injuries (Lewis, DiLillo, & Peterson, 2004). These perceived benefits include the possibility of "toughening up" the child, and of allowing the child to learn lessons from minor injuries that may prevent more serious ones later on. Furthermore, parents vary across cultures in the age at which they begin to teach their child not only how to avoid hazards but also how to interact safely with potentially hazardous objects (Rogoff, 1990).

Thus, even in an extreme case, where choice granting could be viewed as pathological, there are grounds for viewing parents as making trade-offs between two conflicting goals of ensuring their child's immediate safety and of promoting development. This leads to an interesting general point about preemptive parenting tactics. A tactic that prevents a child's mistake or a parent–child conflict may promote development by preserving harmony in the relationship (Gardner, Sonuga-Barke, & Sayal, 1999; Holden, 1983). At the same time, such tactics also necessarily have the secondary effect of forestalling any learning that might happen as a result of the mistake, or in the course of that conflict (Laible & Thompson, 2002). One way to compensate for this loss is to combine preemptive parenting tactics with teaching the child about safety issues (Power, Olvera, & Hays, 2002)

Another aspect of injury prevention, documented mostly with older children, is that child factors contribute to the likelihood of injuries. For example, both impulsive temperament and risk-related spatial cognition ("Can I jump over this gap?") are associated with child injuries (Schwebel & Plumert, 1999). In toddlers, ease of behavior management (compliance) and risk taking are also related to injury (Morrongiello, Ondejko, & Littlejohn, 2004a). Consistent with the literature on internalization in other domains, parenting and child factors interact in their effects on the likelihood of injury (Schwebel, Brezausek, Ramey, & Ramey, 2004).

Property Disputes

Parents generally do not apply a consistent principle of fairness when intervening in property disputes, either in sibling disputes (Ross, 1996) or in disputes among toddler peers (Ross, Tesla, Kenyon, & Lollis, 1990). Again, more than one parenting goal is implicated in this problem. Principles of property ownership vie with the desire to keep objects from breaking and with the desire to teach children to share. Furthermore, when at a play date, parents most often intervene in property disputes to rule in favor of the child who is not their own. This may be to teach their child to share, to keep the peace, or to model the social role of being a good host or guest (Ross et al., 1990). Cultural beliefs may determine which parenting goals are most salient. For example, in Mayan culture, older siblings are expected to routinely defer to their toddler siblings in property disputes (Mosier & Rogoff, 2003). Naturally, toddlers are also active and able contributors to the process of arguing over property. For very young children, ownership status may be more salient than sharing, protecting objects from harm, or fulfilling social roles, and this principle may hold sway even despite parental intervention to the contrary (Ross, 1996).

Situational Sources of Variation in Parenting Goals

It appears from the two foregoing examples that parenting goals are idiosyncratic and not always closely matched with the child's concerns, or even with the child's developmental level. Why are parenting goals so variable? First, parents as a group have many, often conflicting, goals among which to choose. Second, there are many influences on parenting goals apart from the developmental needs of the child.

Parents must choose among the sometimes overlapping and sometimes diverging goals of obtaining immediate and long-term compliance, teaching the child values, satisfying their own needs of the moment, including convenience and projecting a public image as a good parent, promoting competence development, making the child happy, building their relationship with the child, and helping the child to learn cooperation and self-discipline. The relative salience of these goals may influence the choice of parenting strategy (Hastings & Grusec, 1998). Although stable aspects of culture and personality undoubtedly exert important influences on parenting goals and on discipline behavior, parenting goals also change from one situation to another (Grusec, Goodnow, & Kuczynski, 2000).

One well-investigated aspect of situations is the domain, or type of compliance rule at issue (Smetana, Kochanska, & Chuang, 2000; Turiel, 1998). Different kinds of compliance rules, because they involve harm, pragmatic considerations, or relatively arbitrary cultural norms, are associated with different parenting cognitions and different choice of tactics (Smetana et al., 2000). What is included in the domains changes with development. In adolescence, changes in children's capacity for autonomy may, as part of a more general readjustment of goals and expectations, alter what parents consider to be pragmatic and what is a matter for the child's personal domain (Collins, 1995; Smetana, Campione-Barr, & Daddis, 2004). It has been suggested that parenting goals must adjust in a similar way when the family as a system must cope with toddlers' growing autonomy (Emery, 1992).

Another aspect of situations is being in public versus in one's home (Hastings & Grusec, 1998). Public self-consciousness has not been studied systematically as it relates to the activation of parenting goals and the choice of tactics. However, it is not likely a coincidence that one of the first well-known studies of preventive parenting tactics and child compliance was conducted in a supermarket! (Holden, 1983). In this type of public setting, avoiding conflict may take precedence over teaching the child long-term self-control. Situations also partly determine what is prohibited or permitted. Lytton (1980) has noted that many prohibited acts are simple behaviors, such as playing with objects or talking, that may be generally permitted, but unacceptable in a particular situation or at a particular time.

Summary

The child's developmental level is only one of many factors influencing a parent's proximal goal in a given situation. A combination of the child's and the parent's goals will determine the subject matter of compliance. Because parents vary even in the case in which their goals might be assumed to be obvious (as in child safety), individual observed compliance episodes or tasks may hold different meanings for different dyads. In addition, because multiple competing goals must be balanced or reconciled adaptively in changing situations, it is also important to consider the strength of the parent's commitment to individual goals (Goodnow, 1997), as well as her ability to appropriately select and flexibly regulate goals to fit a changing situation (Dix & Branca, 2003). By their third year, toddlers, too, are balancing goals, with one eye on what they want and another on how best to maintain closeness with the parent (Emde & Buchsbaum, 1990). Given these pervasive sources of variability, it is necessary to ask whether child compliance and nascent internalization have any general trait-like features, or whether changes from one moment to the next are the rule.

Specificity and Generality of Compliance Development and Internalization

Recent research on individual differences in compliance defies a simple answer to whether child compliance generalizes across different types of tasks. On the one hand, individual differences in child behavior sometimes cohere only weakly, or not at all, across different compliance tasks. On the other hand, children's eagerness to cooperate with the caregiver in compliance tasks has been found to cohere with a similarly eager responsive stance even in tasks not typically classified as compliance. One good example each of specificity and generality follows.

On the Specificity of Effects: Dos and Don'ts

One of the best documented examples of specificity is that compliance develops differently in demands and prohibitions, or "do" and "don't" tasks. The content of parental prohibitions and demands differ (Gralinski & Kopp, 1993; Kuczynski & Kochanska, 1995). They have different developmental trajectories, with don'ts being mastered earlier. Individual differences are stable over time within task types but cohere only weakly between do and don't contexts (Kochanska et al., 2001). They also have different temperamental underpinnings. Toddlers' behavioral inhibition and effortful control, the two early "systems of inhibition," chiefly contribute to child committed compliance and internalization in the don't contexts (Aksan & Kochanska, 2004; Kochanska et al., 2001). Other work shows that compliance in the do and don't contexts may have different parenting correlates as well. A highly involved and directive style of parenting may be useful in a clean-up (do) task, where the child's attention and energy must be maintained, but may backfire in a prohibition, where a directive style may call attention to the object a child would be better off ignoring (Feldman & Sarnat, 1986).

This clear divergence poses a challenge to a central claim made for committed compliance—that it reflects a general, not context-specific, willingness to cooperate (Kochanska & Aksan, 1995). One possible explanation is that there are suppressor effects. Children may actually have similar motivations across these different tasks, but that similarity may be masked by the diverging influences of temperament and parenting tactics. However, it may simply be that individual children choose to cooperate first at tasks that they enjoy and are good at. Effortful control or temperamental anxiety, for example, might increase the likelihood that a child takes pride in his or her ability to avoid trouble. It is possible that moral development diverges from the beginning across these two broad categories of "Thou Shalt" and "Thou Shalt Not" (Emde, Johnson, & Easterbrooks, 1987). Even late into adulthood, regret over commissions and omissions (some of which do and some do not involve matters of conscience) apparently operate according to different rules (Gilovich & Medvec, 1995). Theory is needed to guide further exploration of the developmental differences between these two strands of internalization.

On the Generality of Effects: Teaching and Control

An example of the generality of child cooperation, beyond the tasks usually considered in studies of compliance, is consistency in child receptiveness to parent teaching and control. Cognitive skill development and the development of right conduct have historically been studied by different researchers. However, there are parallels in adult guidance and child motivation across teaching and moral socialization tasks. Theorists have pointed out that value socialization involves the teaching of complex information about social norms (Grusec & Goodnow, 1984) and skilled procedures for right conduct (Emde et al., 1991). In addition, the cultural transmission of cognitive skills depends on child cooperation. It also includes value judgments about what is worth knowing, by whom and when, and about the right way to learn (Goodnow, 1990).

Parallels between teaching and control have been found in studies of parenting tactics. Shaffer and Crook, in their study of parents' compliance-eliciting behavior in free play with 15- and 24-month-olds, found a developmental increase in complexity of parent demands. Simple requests for "attentional compliance" decrease from 15 to 24 months, while requests to perform specific actions on objects increase. At both ages, parents were most successful in obtaining compliance when they timed their demands to make sure that the child first was attending, then was in contact with the object, and finally executed the action on the object (Shaffer & Crook, 1979, 1980). This matches exactly the description of how parents of toddlers provide problem-solving support to their children in a puzzle task (Wertsch, McNamee, McLane, & Budwig, 1980). Variation among parents, described earlier regarding commitment to specific compliance goals, is also characteristic of commitment to teaching activities. For example, parents who believe children should learn to draw on their own offer toddlers less help in a structured drawing task and less information about shapes in an unstructured drawing activity, than do parents without such a belief (Braswell & Rosengren, 2005).

Children's emotions and motivation are also similar across the themes of skill learning and right conduct. Children's displays of pride and shame have already been discussed. Child responsiveness also has been found to cohere across discipline and teaching contexts. For example, committed compliance (responsiveness to control) is associated with children's eagerness to learn through imitation (responsiveness to teaching) at 14 and 22 months (Forman & Kochanska, 2001). This coherence of child motivation provides support for Maccoby's assertion that children develop a general receptive stance to socialization (Maccoby, 1992; Maccoby & Martin, 1983). The generality of child motivation has implications for development in both cognitive socialization and moral socialization domains. For example, children's eagerness to learn through imitation predicts their later conscience development (Forman et al., 2004).

INTERNALIZATION: THE ROLE OF PARENT–CHILD RELATIONSHIPS

Another aspect of generality is the question whether broad features of the toddler's relationship with the primary caregiver play an important role in fostering child internalization of parental values. Internalization is one type of autonomy development, in which extrinsic goals and choices become freely held internal ones. Because committed compliance, the autonomous form of cooperation, predicts child internalization, and because the same relationship processes are held to promote both (Kochanska, 2002), this issue addresses what autonomy development and compliance development have in common. The normative negotiations of conflicting goals, described earlier, can have a positive or negative impact on relationship development, while the quality of the relationship with the caregiver will have an impact on the convergence or divergence of these goals over time (Maccoby, 1992). This means that over time, parent–child dyads come to differ on whether cooperation and autonomy development are seen as mutually reinforcing or mutually exclusive.

Individuals and Relationships

A focus on relationships is not intended to deny that those relationships are composed of individuals. Parents are affectionate or controlling, or both, and this behavior influences child outcomes (Maccoby & Martin, 1983). In addition, the general tone set by these broad parenting dimensions can influence children's receptiveness to more specific, or proximal, parenting tactics (Darling & Steinberg, 1993). Parents also have beliefs about children, and goals that they strive toward, that guide their behavior and organize the structure of parent–child interactions (Bugental & Goodnow, 1998; Hastings & Grusec, 1998; Kuczynski, 1984). Parent behavior serves as a model for the child to imitate, and parents talk directly about moral values. Parents also structure their children's environments in various ways and interact with others who have influence on their children (Parke & Buriel, 1998). Parent behavior predicts changes in child behavior over time (Kochanska, Forman, Aksan, & Dunbar, 2005; see also Grusec et al., 2000, for suggestions about ways to broaden parenting research).

In turn, children contribute to their own socialization in many ways. Main effects of temperament on compliance, internalization, or both have been shown for reactive aspects of temperament, such as fearfulness and anger-prone reactivity, as well as for regulatory aspects of temperament, such as emotion regulation and effortful control (Kochanska et al., 2000; Stifter, Spinrad, & Braungart-Rieker, 1999). Child temperament and proximal child behavior also influence parent discipline tactics (Bell & Chapman, 1986; Kochanska, 1995; Rubin, Nelson, Hastings, & Asendorpf, 1999) and parenting goals (Hastings & Rubin, 1999). Temperament also moderates the impact of specific aspects of parenting (Bates, Petit, Dodge, & Ridge, 1998; Kochanska, 1995). For example, gentle discipline is particularly effective in promoting internalization among relatively fearful children (Kochanska, 1995). Not all child effects are due to temperament. As the second part of this chapter emphasizes, the timing of children's development of a wide variety of abilities can strongly influence the subject matter of compliance and conflict. To summarize, both parents and toddlers influence each other in multiple ways. This fact of mutual influence suggests the technical difficulty of determining which partner is responsible for the other's behavior. Other recent approaches have emphasized more global characteristics of the relationship including attachment and mutuality.

Security of Attachment

Attachment poses something of a puzzle in internalization research. Mary Ainsworth made an early argument that attachment security should be associated with eager child cooperation (Ainsworth, Bell, & Stayton, 1974; Stayton, Hogan, & Ainsworth, 1971). This was also supported a decade later by Londerville and Main (1981), showing that attachment measured in the Strange Situation at 12 months predicts child cooperation 9 months later. However, despite other studies that include measures of both attachment and child compliance or internalization, this main effect has not often been replicated. For example, the Minnesota group found attachment security to predict child cooperation in a challenging cognitive task, but not in a clean-up task (Matas et al., 1978). Sroufe warns against the expectation that all socially valued characteristics should cohere and argues for a narrower, ethologically based definition of attachment, focused on issues of security, vulnerability, and trust. He explicitly describes the discipline relationship as distinct from attachment security (Sroufe, 1988). Kochanska (1995) also argued that attachment security promotes conscience development in some cases, but not others, depending on child temperament.

Several theoretical possibilities for the lack of a robust main effect remain to be systematically tested. It is possible that attachment promotes autonomy generally, but because autonomy can have cooperative and resistant forms, attachment may promote committed compliance only when the demand makes sense according to the child's developmental goals (Matas et al., 1978). It is possible that attachment security promotes child emotion regulation (Cassidy, 1994), which predicts compliance best under stressful situations. Recent data, however, suggest a third possibility—that attachment moderates the impact of parenting by promoting sensitivity to maternal discipline and teaching style (Kochanska, Aksan, Knaack, & Rhines, 2004). From this point of view, attachment may amplify both positive *and negative* effects of parenting in other domains, because the securely attached child is more identified with the caregiver and more responsive to the caregiver's behavior than an insecurely attached child (Waters, Kondo-Ikemura, Posada, & Richters, 1991).

Finally, the focus of compliance studies may be responsible for the lack of a strong link. Most compliance studies have focused, in one way or another, on parental standards for child behavior and on power. This emphasizes only the first of two broad classes of interpersonal conflict that have been identified and distinguished—power conflicts and intimacy conflicts (Emery, 1992). An example of the latter might be compliance and noncompliance with bedtime in the toddler period. When North American parents insist that their child go to bed and provide a routine to support their child's compliance, they are doing so in the context of cultural patterns of separate sleeping (Morelli, Rogoff, Oppenheim, & Goldsmith, 1992). An "intimacy conflict" may arise because these parents have a goal of developing child independence, while children have a goal of maintaining closeness. Perhaps the quality of child compliance and noncompliance may be more strongly linked to attachment in this context. Marvin describes negotiation over the parent's intention to separate, in the late toddler period, as the beginning of what Bowlby called a goal-corrected partnership and as resulting from the child's improved understanding of parents' goals (Marvin, 1977).

Mutually Responsive or Coercive Relationships

Positive Mutuality

Positive cycles exist when the cooperation of each partner increases that of the other over time. Committed compliance predicts decreases in maternal power assertion, while maternal gentle discipline and responsiveness predict increases in child committed compliance (Kochanska, 1997). In addition, when the mother and child are observed together, their mutually responsive orientation (MRO), a combination of maternal responsiveness and the harmonious and positive affective quality of mother–child interactions, consistently predicts later child internalization (Kochanska & Murray, 2000; Kochanska, 2002). This orientation also predicts converging positive cycles of responsiveness—higher levels of MRO in the second year predict increasingly positive child mood in mother's company, increasing levels of child committed compliance and decreasing maternal power assertion (Kochanska et al., 2005).

Mutual Coercion

Unfortunately, mutual reinforcement works the other way as well. Patterson has demonstrated coercive cycles in which child antisocial behavior grows out of the transaction between temperamentally difficult child behavior and inept, unresponsive, or explosive parenting, which both inadvertently reinforces escalating child noncompliance and serves as a model for child aggression (Patterson, 1982; Patterson & Fisher, 2002). Others have confirmed in a low socioeconomic status sample that child noncompliance predicts increases in maternal control, while maternal control, in turn, predicts increases in child noncompliance from ages 2 to 4 (Smith, Calkins, Keane, Anastopoulos, & Shelton, 2004). Coercive cycles are also associated with the erosion of social and academic competence (Patterson, 1986). This means that children who participate in high levels of mutual coercion eventually end up with fewer effective choices outside the parent–child dyad.

Some studies have found that negative cycles are more likely with boys and their caregivers. Calkins (2002) found that angry, frustrated child behavior predicted increases in negative parenting from 18 months, but only for boys. Some studies with older children have also found coercive parenting to predict externalizing behavior for boys but not girls (e.g., Kerr, Lopez, Olson, & Sameroff, 2004; McFadyen-Ketchum, Bates, Dodge, & Petit, 1996). Perhaps the greater likelihood of coercive cycles for boys and their parents explains why, for boys, high maternal rejection *or* high child noncompliance predicts increases in externalizing problems from age 2 to 3, while for girls, only high rejection *and* high noncompliance predict such increases (Shaw et al, 1998).

Mechanisms

Mutually reinforcing positive cycles and negative cycles exist in the toddler period, and they predict moral internalization and antisocial behavior later on. The logical next question involves the mechanism through which these relationships exert their effects. Two candidates are suggested. First, mutually responsive relationships may lead to positive affect in both partners, while mutually coercive relationships amplify negative affect. Second, mutual responsiveness may influence autonomy development via general expectations of whether the interaction partners' goals are shared or conflicting.

Momentum in parent–child interactions, or the tendency for compliance to lead to compliance and opposition to opposition, is mediated by mood (Strand, Wahler, & Herring, 2000). Not only does parent responsiveness induce a short-term improvement in child mood (Lay, Waters, & Park, 1989), mutually responsive orientation predicts increasing child pleasure in the mothers' company over development (Kochanska et al., 2005). This is a mechanism that can drive further cooperation. Children's pleasure in mother's company predicts increasing internalized moral conduct into the preschool years, as well as predicting a later measure of moral cognition (Kochanska et al., 2005). On the other side of the coin, Scaramella and Leve (2004) describe child emotion dysregulation as an engine of negative reciprocities. Also, for the parent, negative mood influences the parent's interpretation of child opposition as deliberate; induces parent-centered, rather than child-centered, goals; and affects the parent's evaluation of likely effective ways of dealing with the child's misbehavior (Dix, 1991; Dix, Gershoff, Meunier, & Miller, 2004). The importance of mood explains how parent personality and child temperament can moderate the stability of mutually reinforcing interaction sequences (Kochanska, Friesenborg, Lange, & Martel, 2004). Some partners are more likely to get pulled into negative affect or to sustain positive affect than are others.

A second possible mechanism through which positive and negative reciprocities lead to internalization is the through the child's view of parent and child goals as shared and mutually reinforcing or conflicting. As Kochanska (2002) puts it, "The parent child relationship influences the child's conscience mainly through a gradually evolving shared working model of the relationship as a mutually cooperative enterprise" (p. 193). Such a global sense of consonant versus conflicting goals has important ramifications for autonomy development more generally. If the child develops a general expectation that cooperating with the parent will result in the child's own intrinsic goals being met, then autonomy and relatedness are mutually reinforcing. If, on the other hand, the child perceives that parent and child goals are mutually exclusive, then the child must choose between autonomy and connectedness.

A recent discussion of dyadic synchrony by Harrist and Waugh (2002) argues that promotion of autonomy is a core function of synchrony in the toddler period. While toddlers are becoming more active in initiating behaviors designed to please the caregiver, the relationship is still asymmetrical in the toddler period (Maccoby, 1999). Therefore, the review states that the best way to promote dyadic synchrony is for the parent to follow the child's lead (Harrist & Waugh, 2002). Just as parent attunement in infancy starts with the parent matching the child's current emotion state and then guiding it to another (Stern, 1985), in toddlerhood synchrony will often start by the parent's matching or reflecting the goal toward which the child's activity is directed, and then varying the goal or adding another (e.g., Parpal & Maccoby, 1985; Rocissano, Slade, & Lynch, 1987). Child cooperation that results from this synchrony, because it is not in response to parental power assertion, is experienced as freely chosen (see Hoffman, 1983; Lepper, 1981) and helps to promote both autonomy and increasingly internalized self-control (Harrist & Waugh, 2002).

CONCLUSION: WHERE TO LOOK FOR TRANSITIONS

The discussion up to this point has several implications for what to look for when considering transitions. Where stage-like global and qualitative changes are the object of interest in understanding development, the evidence sought pertains to discontinuity. Discontinuities may be indicated by the shape of developmental change, by changes in the coherence of variables said to tap a common construct, or by changes in the external correlates of a variable or variables (Hinde & Bateson, 1984). However, based on the argument up to this point, if we ask whether compliance and internalization change in their developmental trajectories, in their relations with one another, or in their external correlates at some specific point during the toddler period, we are unlikely to obtain a simple answer.

Changes in compliance can best be understood against a backdrop that includes rapid changes in several child capacities. These changes in available actions, along with the desire for mastery, increase the goal-directed quality of child behavior and make choice making salient. Whether the child's proximal choices are supported, channeled into socially accepted forms of expression, or directly opposed depends on the parent's multifaceted and dynamic childrearing goals. Nevertheless, individual differences research makes it clear that parent–child dyads vary distinctly in their overall levels of mutuality, and that these variations have a profound impact on the child's developing autonomous connectedness.

A search for transitions should therefore be conducted at two different levels at the very least. The first is in changes in the subject matter of compliance and autonomy striving. The second is in the relationship processes that relate to the child's internalization of parent goals. Finally, theory and research are needed to understand how the views of development at these two levels relate to each other.

Changes in "Hot Topics"

One model for the study of coherence or divergence across different subject matters is Kochanska's work on "do's" and "don'ts" (Kochanska et al., 2001). Children were studied at multiple time points to see whether the different forms of compliance differ in their developmental trajectories, in their external correlates, and in their implications for internalization of a similar task over time. Unfortunately, a very limited number of compliance tasks have been studied in this intensive way. This work should be used as a model and extended to a broader range of compliance tasks, including some that have not often been simulated in laboratories but are important to parents and children. These include separation conflicts, misbehavior in public, and the many specific subject matters, such as socially appropriate use of language, described previously in the study of normative development.

Another fruitful way to understand more about change in whether something is a hot topic would be to observe children in natural settings. A focus of these observations would be whether toddler striving toward some particular goal is particularly time consuming or affect laden at a particular developmental level but not at another. We would also want to know about correlated changes in parents' goals, and in the frequency or intensity of communicating rules, as well as other efforts at changing or adapting to child behavior. To do this we need to augment observations with parent reports of their goals, and of their cognitive and affective reactions to child misbehavior. In addition to confirming the pattern of how development leads to changes in the content of parent–toddler interactions, there are two other central questions to be addressed. First, how do child behavior and parenting interact to determine whether a particular issue is resolved within a given relationship, or whether the hot topic continues to generate conflict or negotiation for an extended period of time? Second, how does the nature of the resolution contribute to the toddler's ongoing development?

Changes in Process

A different set of questions about transitions focuses on the process of development through which patterns of parent–child interaction predict individual differences in internalization. We first need to know whether specific child characteristics, parenting behaviors, or relationship qualities are particularly important at one time in development but not another. That is, are there age-specific effects on the trajectory of internalization or some other element of autonomy development? If so, this will be a good starting point for theory as to how developmental processes change in the toddler period. Here a few speculations will be ventured. Though they rest on an inadequate empirical base, they can serve as illustrations of how such theory building and testing need to be done.

First, is early eager imitation a particularly potent predictor of later internalization? The effects of responsive imitation at 14 months add independent variance to 22-month variables in predicting conscience during the preschool period (Forman et al., 2004). It could be that early imitation is particularly important because procedural knowledge forms the core of early learning about moral rules (Emde et al., 1991), or because these physical enactments of similarity help empathic emotion and social cognitions to develop (Meltzoff, 2002). Early imitation also evokes pleasure from the caregiver, potentially adding to the development of interactive harmony and mutual understanding (Užgiris, 1984). Unfortunately, little work has been done on whether imitation continues to contribute to socialization at older ages.

Second, is child fearfulness particularly important in the second half of the second year? One pattern of findings in Kochanska's work seems to suggest this, as the predictive effects of behavioral inhibition seem particularly strong at this age (Kochanska et al., 2001). It might be that this is a time when the behavioral inhibition has a particularly strong impact on the child's emerging effortful control ability, which is just beginning to form a coherent personality characteristic at this age (Kochanska et al., 2000). One plausible reason could be that fearful children can begin developing expertise at avoiding trouble and may (implicitly) take this as a positive goal. That is, the link between these two "systems of inhibition" (Aksan & Kochanska, 2004) may be strengthened by the general tendencies of children to practice emerging skills, and to prefer choosing goals that they are good at accomplishing. In addition, child inhibition contributes to the relationship by evoking gentler parenting and by influencing parenting goals.

Third, does power assertion backfire increasingly with development? The experiences of self-assertion and choice making, described earlier, may be iterative, with children's expectations of an active role in negotiating rules more likely with increasing age. Further, the child's understanding of the parent's goals as distinct from their own and increasing ability to remember and integrate information from one encounter to the next make discipline encounters more cumulative. Therefore, direct tactics that emphasize the difference between parent and child goals may now feed into a general sense that closeness and effective choice are incompatible. On the other hand, methods that include acknowledgement of the child's goal state as legitimate, and that grant the child some sense of agency through the negotiation process, increase the general sense of the parent and child as being "on the same side." There is some evidence for increasing links between power-assertive parenting and child opposition over development, not only in toddlerhood but also later (Kochanska et al., 2001; Rothbaum & Weisz, 1994). This, however, addresses the issue of process only indirectly. Any test for a developmental increase in the self-defeating nature of parental power assertion would have to take into account the fact that power assertion is also a *product of* earlier child behavior in discipline encounters.

These suggestions are admittedly preliminary and speculative. The point is that to understand developmental process better, we need research on how different specific relationship features promote autonomy and internalization at different times. To be most diagnostic, such work would control for other correlated aspects of behavior, and for the effects of continuity in both predictor and outcome variables (see Collins, 2006). If successful, such research might enable greater understanding of how implicit habits of cooperation or self-assertion develop over time into explicit cognitions about autonomy, connectedness, and moral responsibility.

Integration

A final important future direction for theory is to integrate the picture of development given at these two different levels. The central question here is how children come to differ in the direction of their autonomy striving or internalization, based on context-specific child factors or on variations in parent–child cooperation across different situations. Specific developmental goals have differing importance to individual children and individual parents. The description of relationship development has assumed that some children come to believe that their goals are incompatible with those of their parents, while others are able to pursue both autonomy and connectedness together. It seems more than likely, however, that these cognitions are at least somewhat specific to various hot topics within families, or even within dyads.

For example, one toddler may have pitched battles with his parents over winter clothing, while language learning is eagerly pursued by the child and flexibly promoted by the parents. A different child might be unhappy with her bedtime routine but feel powerless to change it. Thus, autonomy, or its absence, may come to mean different things for different children. Or, children may be supported in a context-specific form of autonomy striving (such as negotiating about choice of food) in one significant relationship but not another. A complete picture of how compliance and autonomy codevelop may eventually require understanding the experience of autonomy-connectedness relations with specific adults in specific domains.

The other way to think about integration across these two levels is to ask how and when global attitudes are generalized from, and feed back to, the specific developmental domains. This issue is, of course, a central one in the study of relationships. What are the dynamics between development at the level of relationships and at the level of the interactions that comprise them

(Hinde & Stevenson-Hinde, 1987)? One such question raised in this discussion was how the resolution of a given hot topic, or the absence of such a resolution, subsequently makes the different partners more or less responsive in other situations. Development will condition the answer to this question, as younger toddlers have shorter memories. Clearly, other such questions can be raised from both the parent and child side of the relationship.

REFERENCES

Ainsworth, M. D. S., Bell, S. M., & Stayton, D. J. (1974). Infant–mother attachment in social development: 'Socialization' as a product of reciprocal responsiveness to signals. In M. P. M. Richards (Ed.), *The integration of a child into the social world* (pp. 99–135). London: Cambridge University Press.

Ainsworth, M. D. S., & Wittig, B. A. (1969). Attachment and exploratory behavior of one year old children in a strange situation. In B. M. Foss (Ed.), *Determinants of infant behavior* (Vol. 4, pp. 111–136). New York: Academic Press.

Aksan, N., & Kochanska, G. (2004). Links between systems of inhibition from infancy to preschool years. *Child Development, 75*, 1477–1490.

Aksan, N., & Kochanska, G. (2005). Conscience in childhood: Old questions, New answers. *Developmental Psychology, 41*, 506–516.

American Psychiatric Association. (2000). *Diagnostic and statistical manual of mental disorders* (4th ed., text rev.). Washington, DC: Author.

Astington, J. (2004). Bridging the gap between theory of mind and moral reasoning. *New Directions for Child and Adolescent Development, 103*, 63–72.

Bandura, A. (1997). *Self-efficacy: The exercise of control.* New York: Freeman.

Barrett, K. C., & Morgan, G. A. (1995). Continuities and discontinuities in mastery motivation during infancy and toddlerhood: A conceptualization and review. In R. H. MAcTurk & G. A. Morgan (Eds.), *Mastery motivation: Origins, conceptualizations, and applications. Advances in applied developmental psychology* (Vol. 12, pp. 57–93). Norwood, NJ: Ablex.

Barrett, K. C., Zahn-Waxler, C., & Cole, P. M. (1994). Avoiders vs. amenders: Implications for the investigation of guilt and shame during toddlerhood? *Cognition and Emotion, 7*, 481–505.

Bates, J. E., Pettit, G. S., Dodge, K. A., & Ridge, B. (1998). Interaction of temperamental resistance to control and restrictive parenting in the development of externalizing behavior. *Developmental Psychology, 34*, 982–995.

Bauer, P. J., Wenner, J. A., Dropik, P. L., & Wewerka, S. S. (2000). Parameters of remembering and forgetting in the transition from infancy to early childhood. *Monographs of the Society for Research in Child Development, 65*(4).

Bell, R. Q., & Chapman, M. (1986). Child effects in studies using experimental or brief longitudinal approaches to socialization. *Developmental Psychology, 22*, 595–603.

Belsky, J., Domitrovich, C., & Crnic, K. (1997). Temperament and parenting antecedents of individual differences in three-year-old boys' pride and shame reactions. *Child Development, 68*, 456–466.

Blum, N. J., Taubman, B., & Nemeth, N. (2004) Why is toilet training occurring at older ages? A study of factors associated with later training. *Journal of Pediatrics, 145*, 107–111.

Braswell, G. S., & Rosengren, K. S. (2005). Children and mothers drawing together: Learning graphic conventions during social interactions. *British Journal of Developmental Psychology, 23*, 299–315.

Bugental, D. B., & Goodnow, J. J. (1998). Socialization processes. In N. Eisenberg (Ed.) & D. William (Vol. Ed.), *Handbook of child psychology* (5th ed., pp. 389–462). New York: Wiley.

Bugental, D. B., & Happaney, K. (2000). Parent–child interaction as a power contest. *Journal of Applied Developmental Psychology, 21*, 267–282.

Calkins, S. D. (2002). Does aversive behavior during toddlerhood matter?: The effects of difficult temperament on maternal perceptions and behavior. *Infant Mental Health Journal, 23*, 381–402.

Campos, J. J., Anderson, D. I., Barbu-Roth, M. A., Hubbard, E. M., Hertenstein, M. J., & Witherington, D. (2000). Travel broadens the mind. *Infancy, 1*, 149–219.

Carpenter, M., Akhtar, N., & Tomasello, M. (1998). Fourteen- through 18-month-old infants differentially imitate intentional and accidental actions. *Infant Behavior and Development, 21*, 315–330.

Cassidy, J. (1994). Emotion regulation: Influences of attachment relationships. In N. A. Fox (Ed.), The development of emotion regulation. *Monographs of the Society for Research in Child Development, 59*(2–3, Serial No. 240), 228–249.

Collins, W. A. (1995). Relationships and development: Family adaptation to individual change. In S. Shulman (Ed.), *Close relationships and socioemotional development* (pp. 216–241). New York: Cambridge University Press.

Collins, W. A. (2006). Commentary: Parsing parenting. In B. K. Barber, H. E. Stolz, & J. A. Olsen (Eds.), Parental support, psychological control, and behavioral control. *Monographs of the Society for Research in Child Development, 70*(4), 138–145.

Crittenden, P. M., & DiLalla, D. L. (1988). Compulsive compliance: The development of an inhibitory coping strategy in infancy. *Journal of Abnormal Child Psychology, 15*, 585–599.

Crockenberg, S., Jackson, S., & Langrock, A. M. (1996). Autonomy and goal attainment: Parenting, gender, and children's social competence. In M. Killen (Ed.), *Children's autonomy, social competence, and interactions with adults and other children* (pp. 41–56). San Francisco: Jossey-Bass.

Crockenberg, S., & Littman, C. (1990). Autonomy as a competence in 2-year-olds: Maternal correlates of child defiance, compliance, and self-assertion. *Developmental Psychology, 26*, 961–971.

Darling, N., & Steinberg, L. (1993). Parenting style as context: An integrative model. *Psychological Bulletin, 113*, 487–496.

Deci, E. L., & Ryan, R. M. (1987). The support of autonomy and the control of behavior. *Journal of Personality and Social Psychology, 53*, 1024–1037.

Dix, T. (1991). The affective organization of parenting: Adaptive and maladaptative processes. *Psychological Bulletin, 110*, 3–25.

Dix, T., & Branca, S. H. (2003). Parenting as a goal-regulation process. In L. Kuczynski (Ed.), *Handbook of dynamics in parent–child relations* (pp. 167–187). Thousand Oaks, CA: Sage.

Dix, T., Gershoff, E. T., Meunier, L. N., & Miller, P. C. (2004). The affective structure of supportive parenting: Depressive symptoms, immediate emotions, and child-oriented motivation. *Developmental Psychology, 40*, 1212–1227.

Emde, R. N., Biringen, Z., Clyman, R. B., & Oppenheim, D. (1991). The moral self of infancy: Affective core and procedural knowledge. *Developmental Review, 11*, 251–270.

Emde, R. N., & Buchsbaum, H. (1990). "Didn't you hear my mommy?": Autonomy with connectedness in moral self-emergence. In D. Cicchetti & M. Beeghly (Eds.), *The self in transition: Infancy to childhood* (pp. 35–60). Chicago: University of Chicago.

Emde, R. N., & Clyman, R. B. (1997). "We hold these truths to be self-evident": The origins of moral motives in individual activity and shared experience. In J. D. Noshpitz (Series Ed.) & S. Greenspan, S. Wieder, & J. Osofsky (Vol. Eds.), *Handbook of child and adolescent psychiatry: Vol. 1. Infants and preschoolers: Development and syndromes* (pp. 320–339). New York: Wiley.

Emde, R. N., Johnson, W. F., & Easterbrooks, A. (1987). The do's and don'ts of early moral development: Psychoanalytic tradition and current research. In J. Kagan & S. Lamb (Eds.), *The emergence of morality in young children* (pp. 245–276). Chicago: University of Chicago Press.

Emery, R. E. (1992). Family conflict and its developmental implications: A conceptual analysis of deep meanings and systemic processes. In C. U. Shantz & W. W. Hartup (Eds.), *Conflict in child and adolescent development* (pp. 270–298). London: Cambridge University Press.

Feldman, S. S., & Sarnat, L. (1986). Israeli town and kibbutz toddlers' compliance and adults' control attempts. *Merrill-Palmer Quarterly, 32*, 365–382.

Forman, D. R., Aksan, N., & Kochanska, G. (2004). Toddlers' responsive imitation predicts preschool-age conscience. *Psychological Science, 15*, 699–704.

Forman, D. R., & Kochanska, G. (2001). Viewing imitation as child responsiveness: A link between teaching and discipline domains of socialization. *Developmental Psychology, 37*, 198–206.

Freud, A. (1966). *The ego and the mechanisms of defense* (rev. ed.) (C. M. Baines, Trans.). New York: International Universities Press. (Original work published 1936).

Freud, S. (1930). *Civilization and its discontents.* Chicago: University of Chicago.

Gardner, R. E. M., Sonuga-Barke, E. J. S., & Sayal, K. (1999). Parents anticipating misbehaviour: An observational study of strategies parents use to prevent conflict with behaviour problem children. *Journal of Child Psychology and Psychiatry, 40*, 1185–1196.

Geppert, U., & Küstner, U. (1983). The emergence of "wanting to do it oneself": A precursor of achievement motivation. *International Journal of Behavioral Development, 6*, 355–369.

Gergely, G., Bekkering, H., & Kiraly, I. (2002). Rational imitation in preverbal infants. *Nature, 416*, 755.

Gilovich, T., & Medvec, V. H. (1995). The experience of regret: What, when, and why. *Psychological Review, 102*, 379–395.

Goodnow, J. (1990). The socialization of cognition: What's involved? In J. W. Stigler, R. A. Shweder, & G. H. Herdt (Eds.), *Cultural psychology: Essays on comparative human development* (pp. 259–286). New York: Cambridge University Press.

Goodnow, J. (1997). Parenting and the transmission and internalization of values: From social-cultural perspectives to within-family analyses. In J. E. Grusec & L. Kuczynski (Eds.), *Parenting and children's internalization of values* (pp. 333–361). New York: Wiley.

Gralinski, J. H., & Kopp, C. B. (1993). Everyday rules for behavior: Mothers' requests to young children. *Developmental Psychology, 29*, 573–584.

Grusec, J., & Goodnow, J. J. (1984). Impact of parental discipline methods on the child's internalization of values: A reconceptualization of current points of view. *Developmental Psychology, 30*, 4–19.

Grusec, J. E., Goodnow, J. J., & Kuczynski, L. (2000). New directions in analyses of parenting contributions to children's acquisition to values. *Child Development, 11*, 307–331.

Happé, F. G. E., & Frith, U. (1996). Theory of mind and social impairment in children with conduct disorder. *British Journal of Developmental Psychology, 14*, 385–398.

Harrist, A. W., & Waugh, R. M. (2002). Dyadic synchrony: Its structure and function in children's interactions. *Developmental Review, 22*, 555–592.

Hartup, W. W. (1963). Dependence and independence. In H. W. Stevenson (Ed.), *Child psychology: The sixty-second yearbook of the National Society for the Study of Education* (pp. 333–363). Chicago: University of Chicago Press.

Hastings, P. D., & Grusec, J. E. (1998). Parenting goals as organizers of responses to parent–child disagreement. *Developmental Psychology, 34*, 465–479.

Hastings, P. D., & Rubin, K. H. (1999). Predicting mothers' beliefs about preschool-aged children's social behavior: Evidence for maternal attitudes moderating child effects. *Child Development, 70*, 722–741.

Hill, J. P., & Holmbeck, G. N. (1986). Attachment and autonomy during adolescence. In G. Whitehurst (Ed.), *Annals of child development* (Vol. 3, pp. 145–189). Greenwich, CT: JAI Press.

Hinde, R., & Bateson, P. (1984) Discontinuities versus continuities in behavioural development and the neglect of process. *International Journal of Behavioural Development, 7*, 129–143.

Hinde, R. A., & Stevenson-Hinde, J. (1987). Interpersonal relationships and child development. *Developmental Review, 7*, 1–21.

Hoffman, M. L. (1983). Affective and cognitive processes in moral internalization. In E. T. Higgins, D. Ruble, & W. W. Hartup (Eds.), *Social cognition and social development* (pp. 236–274). New York: Cambridge University Press.

Hoffmann, M. L. (2001). *Empathy and moral development.* New York: Cambridge University Press.

Holden, G. W. (1983). Avoiding conflict: Mothers as tacticians in the supermarket. *Child Development, 54,* 233–240.

Irwin, J. R., Carter, A. S., & Briggs-Gowan, M. (2002). The social-emotional development of late-talking toddlers. *Journal of the American Academy of Child and Adolescent Psychiatry, 41,* 1324–1332.

Jennings, K. D. (2004). Development of goal-directed behaviour and related self-processes in toddlers. *International Journal of Behavioral Development, 28,* 319–327.

Kağitçibaşi, C. (2005). Autonomy/relatedness in cultural context. *Journal of Cross-Cultural Psychology, 36,* 403–422.

Kaler, S. R., & Kopp, C. B. (1990). Compliance and comprehension in very young toddlers. *Child Development, 61,* 1997–2003.

Kerr, D. C., Lopez, N. L., Olson, S. L., & Sameroff, A. J. (2004). Parental discipline and externalizing behavior problems in early childhood: The roles of moral regulation and child gender. *Journal of Abnormal Child Psychology, 32,* 369–383.

Klinnert, M. D., Emde, R. N., Butterfield, P., & Campos, J. J. (1986). Social referencing: The infant's use of emotional signals from a friendly adult with mother present. *Developmental Psychology, 22,* 427–432.

Kochanska, G. (1994). Beyond cognition: Expanding the search for the early roots of internalization and conscience. *Developmental Psychology, 30,* 20–22.

Kochanska, G. (1995). Children's temperament, mothers' discipline, and security of attachment: Multiple pathways to emerging internalization. *Child Development, 66,* 597–615.

Kochanska, G. (1997). Mutually responsive orientation between mothers and their young children: Implications for early socialization. *Child Development, 67,* 94–112.

Kochanska, G. (2002). Mutually responsive orientation between mothers and their young children: A context for the early development of conscience. *Current Directions in Psychological Science, 11,* 191–195.

Kochanska, G., & Aksan, N. (1995). Mother–child mutually positive affect, the quality of child compliance to requests and prohibitions, and maternal control as correlates of early internalization. *Child Development, 66,* 236–254.

Kochanska, G., Aksan, N., Knaack, A., & Rhines, H. M. (2004). Maternal parenting and children's conscience: Early security as moderator. *Child Development, 75,* 1229–1242.

Kochanska, G., Coy, K. C., & Murray, K. T. (2001). The development of self-regulation in the first four years of life. *Child Development, 72,* 1091–1111.

Kochanska, G., Forman, D. R., Aksan, N., & Dunbar, S. B. (2005). Pathways to conscience: Early mother–child mutually responsive orientation and children's moral emotion, conduct, and cognition. *Journal of Child Psychology and Psychiatry, 46,* 19–34.

Kochanska, G., Forman, D. R., & Coy, K. C. (1999). Implications of the mother-child relationship in infancy for socialization in the second year of life. *Infant Behavior and Development, 22,* 249–265.

Kochanska, G., Friesenborg, A. E., Lange, L. A., & Martel, M. M. (2004). Parents' personality, and infants' temperament as contributors to their emerging relationship. *Journal of Personality and Social Psychology, 86,* 744–759.

Kochanska, G., & Murray, K. T. (2000). Mother–child mutually responsive orientation and conscience development: From toddler to early school age. *Child Development, 71,* 417–431.

Kochanska, G., Murray, K. T., & Harlan, E. (2000). Effortful control in early childhood: Continuity and change, antecedents, and implications for social development. *Developmental Psychology, 36,* 220–232.

Kochanska, G., Tjebkes, T. L., & Forman, D. R. (1998). Children's emerging regulation of conduct: Restraint, compliance, and internalization from infancy to the second year. *Child Development, 69,* 1378–1389.

Kopp, C. B. (1982). Antecedents of self-regulation: A developmental perspective. *Developmental Psychology, 18,* 199–214.

Kopp, C. B. (2002). Commentary: The codevelopments of attention and emotion regulation. *Infancy, 3*, 199–208.

Kuczynski, L. (1984). Socialization goals and mother–child interaction: Strategies for long-term and short-term compliance. *Developmental Psychology, 20*, 1061–1073.

Kuczynski, L. (2003). Beyond bidirectionality: Bilateral conceptual frameworks for understanding dynamics in parent–child relations. In L. Kuczynski (Ed.) *Handbook of dynamics in parent–child relations* (pp. 3–24). Thousand Oaks, CA: Sage.

Kuczynski, L., & Hildebrandt, N. (1997). Models of conformity and resistance in socialization theory. In J. E. Grusec & L. Kuczynski (Eds.), *Parenting and children's internalization of values: A handbook of contemporary theory* (pp. 227–256). New York: Wiley.

Kuczynski, L., & Kochanska, G. (1995). Function and content of maternal demands: Developmental significance of early demands for competent action. *Child Development, 66*, 616–628.

Kuczynski, L., Kochanska, G., Radke-Yarrow, M., & Girnius Brown, O. (1987). A developmental interpretation of young children's noncompliance. *Developmental Psychology, 23*, 799–806.

Kuczynski, L., Zahn-Waxler, C., & Radke-Yarrow, M. (1987). Development and content of imitation in the second and third years of life: A socialization perspective. *Developmental Psychology, 23*, 276–282.

Laible, D. J., & Thompson, R. A. (2002). Mother–child conflict in the toddler years: Lessons in emotion, morality, and relationships. *Child Development, 73*, 1187–1203.

Lay, K. L., Waters, E., & Park, K. A. (1989). Maternal responsiveness and child compliance: The role of mood as mediator. *Child Development, 60*, 1405–1411.

Lepper, M. R. (1981). Intrinsic and extrinsic motivation in children: Detrimental effects of superfluous social controls. In W. A. Collins (Ed.), *Minnesota Symposia on Child Psychology* (Vol. 14, pp. 155–214). Minneapolis: University of Minnesota Press.

LeVine, R. A. (1970). Cross-cultural study in child psychology. In P. H. Mussen (Ed.), *Carmichael's manual of child psychology* (3rd ed., Vol 2, pp. 539–612). New York: Wiley.

Lewis, M., & Brooks-Gunn, J. (1979). *Social cognition and the acquisition of self*. New York: Plenum Press.

Lewis, T., DiLillo, D., & Peterson, L. (2004). Parental beliefs regarding developmental benefits of childhood injuries. *American Journal of Health Behavior, 28*, 485–494.

Londerville, S., & Main, M. (1981). Security of attachment, compliance, and maternal training methods in the second year of life. *Developmental Psychology, 17*, 289–299.

Lytton, H. (1980). *Parent–child interaction: The socialization process observed in twin and singleton families*. New York: Plenum Press.

Maccoby, E. E. (1992). The role of parents in socialization of children: An historical overview. *Developmental Psychology, 28*, 1006–1017.

Maccoby, E. E. (1999). The uniqueness of the parent–child relationship. In W. A. Collins & B. Laursen (Eds.), *Minnesota Symposia on Child Psychology: Vol. 29. Relationships as developmental contexts* (pp. 157–176). Mahwah, NJ: Erlbaum.

Maccoby, E. E., & Martin, J. A. (1983). Socialization in the context of the family: Parent–child interaction. In E. M. Heatherington (Ed.), *Manual of child psychology: Vol. 4. Socialization, personality and social development* (pp. 1–101). New York: Wiley.

Mahler, M. S., Pine, F., & Bergman, A. (1975). *The psychological birth of the human infant: Symbiosis and individuation*. New York: Basic Books.

Marvin, R. S. (1977). An ethological–cognitive model of the attenuation of mother–child attachment behavior. In T. Alloway, L. Krames, & P. Pilner (Eds.), *Advances in the study of communication and affect: Vol 3. Attachment behavior* (pp. 25–60). New York: Plenum Press.

Matas, L., Arend, R. A., & Sroufe, L. A. (1978). Continuity of adaptation in the second year: The relationship between quality of attachment and later competence. *Child Development, 49*, 547–556.

McFadyen-Ketchum, S. A., Bates, J. E., Dodge, K. A., & Pettit, G. S. (1996). Patterns of change in early childhood aggressive–disruptive behavior: Gender differences in predictions from early coercive and affectionate mother–child interactions. *Child Development, 67*, 2417–2433.

Meltzoff, A. N. (2002). Elements of a developmental theory of imitation. In A. N. Meltzoff & W.

Prinz (Eds.), *The imitative mind: Development, evolution, and brain bases* (pp. 19–41). Cambridge, UK: Cambridge University Press.

Morelli, G. A., Rogoff, B., Oppenheim, D., & Goldsmith, D. (1992). Cultural variation in infants' sleeping arrangements: Questions of independence. *Developmental Psychology, 28*, 604–613.

Morrongiello, B. A., Ondejko, L., & Littlejohn, A. (2004a). Understanding toddlers' in-home injuries: I. Context, correlates, and determinants. *Journal of Pediatric Psychology, 29*, 415–431.

Morrongiello, B. A., Ondejko, L., & Littlejohn, A. (2004b). Understanding toddlers' in-home injuries: II. Examining parental strategies, and their efficacy, for managing child injury risk. *Journal of Pediatric Psychology, 29*, 433–446.

Mosier, C. E., & Rogoff, B. (2003). Privileged treatment of toddlers: Cultural aspects of individual choice and responsibility. *Developmental Psychology, 39*, 1047–1060.

Murphy, L. B. (1962). *The widening world of childhood.* New York: Basic Books.

Murray, K. T., & Kochanska, G. (2002). Effortful control: Relation to externalizing and internalizing behaviors and factor structure. *Journal of Abnormal Child Psychology, 30,* 503–514.

Parke, R. D., & Buriel, R. (1998). Socialization in the family: Ethic and ecological perspectives. In N. Eisenberg (Ed.) & D. William (Vol. Ed.), *Handbook of child psychology* (5th ed., pp. 463–552). New York: Wiley.

Parpal, M., & Maccoby, E. E. (1985). Maternal responsiveness and subsequent child compliance. *Child Development, 56*, 1326–1334.

Patterson, G. R. (1982). *Coercive family process*. Eugene, OR: Castalia.

Patterson, G. R. (1986). Performance models for antisocial boys. *American Psychologist, 41*, 432–444.

Patterson, G. R., & Fisher, P. A. (2002). Recent developments in our understanding of parenting: Bidirectional effects, causal models, and the search for parsimony. In M. Bornstein (Ed.), *Handbook of parenting: Practical and applied parenting* (2nd ed., Vol. 5, pp. 59–88). Mahwah, NJ: Erlbaum.

Peterson, L. (1994). Child injury and abuse-neglect: Common etiologies, challenges, and courses toward prevention. *Current Directions in Psychological Science, 3*, 116–120.

Piaget, J. (1952). *The origins of intelligence in children* (M. Cook, Trans.). New York: International Universities Press.

Piaget, J. (1965). *The moral judgment of the child.* New York: Free Press.

Power, T. G., Olvera, N., & Hays, J. (2002). Maternal socialization of safety practices among Mexican American children. *Journal of Applied Developmental Psychology, 23*, 83–97.

Rheingold, H. L., Cook, K., & Kolowitz, V. (1987). Commands activate the behavior and pleasure of two-year-old children. *Developmental Psychology, 23*, 146–151.

Rocissano, L., Slade, A., & Lynch, V. (1987). Dyadic synchrony and toddler compliance. *Developmental Psychology, 23*, 698–704.

Rogoff, B. (1990). *Apprenticeship in thinking.* New York: Oxford University Press.

Rogoff, B. (1998). Cognition as a collaborative process. In W. Damon (Series Ed.), D. Kuhn, & R. S. Siegler (Vol. Eds.), *Handbook of child psychology: Vol. 2. Cognition, perception, and language*, (pp. 679–744). New York: Wiley.

Rosen, W. D., Adamson, L. B., & Bakeman, R. (1992). An experimental investigation of infant social referencing: Mothers' messages and gender differences. *Developmental Psychology, 28*, 1172–1178.

Ross, H. S. (1996). Negotiating principles of entitlement in sibling property disputes. *Developmental Psychology, 32*, 90–101.

Ross, H., Tesla, C., Kenyon, B., & Lollis, S. (1990). Maternal intervention in toddler peer conflict: The socialization of principles of justice. *Developmental Psychology, 26*, 994–1003.

Rothbaum, F., Pott, M., Azuma, H., Miyake, K., & Weisz, J. (2000). The development of close relationships in Japan and the United States: Paths of symbiotic harmony and generative tension. *Child Development, 71*, 1121–1142.

Rothbaum, F., & Weisz, J. R. (1989). *Child psychopathology and the quest for control.* Newbury Park: Sage.

Rothbaum, F., & Weisz, J. R. (1994). Parental caregiving and child externalizing behavior in nonclinical samples: A meta-analysis. *Psychological Bulletin, 116*, 55–74.

Rubin, K. H., Nelson, L. J., Hastings, P., & Asendorpf, J. (1999). The transaction between parents' perceptions of their children's shyness and their parenting styles. *International Journal of Behavioral Development, 23*, 937–957.

Ruff, H. A., & Rothbart, M. K. (1996). *Attention in early development*. New York: Oxford University Press.

Ryan, R. M., & Lynch, J. H. (1989). Emotional autonomy versus detachment: Revisiting the vicissitudes of adolescence and young adulthood. *Child Development, 60*, 340–356.

Ryckebusch, C., & Marcos, H. (2004). Speech acts, social context and parent–toddler play between the ages of 1;5 and 2;3. *Journal of Pragmatics, 36*, 883–897.

Scaramella, L. V., & Leve, L. D. (2004). Clarifying parent–child reciprocities during early childhood: The early childhood coercion model. *Clinical Child and Family Psychology Review, 7*, 89 – 107.

Schwebel, D. C., Brezausek, C. M., Ramey, S. L., & Ramey, C. T. (2004). Interactions between child behavior patterns and parenting: Implications for children's unintentional injury risk. *Journal of Pediatric Psychology 29*, 93–104.

Schwebel, D. C., & Plumert, J. M. (1999). Longitudinal and concurrent relations among temperament, ability estimation, and injury proneness. *Child Development, 70*, 700–712.

Sears, R. R. (1972). Attachment, dependency, and frustration. In J. L. Gewirtz (Ed.), *Attachment and dependency* (pp. 1–27). Washington, DC: Winston.

Sears, R. R., Maccoby, E. E., & Levin, H. (1957). *Patterns of child rearing*. Evanston, IL: Row Peterson.

Sethi, A., Mischel, W., Aber, J. L., Shoda, Y., & Rodriguez, M. L. (2000). The role of strategic attention deployment in development of self-regulation: Predicting preschoolers' delay of gratification from mother-toddler interactions. *Developmental Psychology, 36*, 767–777.

Shaffer, H. R., & Crook, C. K. (1979). Maternal control techniques in a directed play situation. *Child Development, 50*, 989–996.

Shaffer, H. R., & Crook, C. K. (1980). Child compliance and maternal control techniques. *Developmental Psychology, 16*, 54–61.

Shaw, D. S., Winslow, E. B., Owens, E. B., Vondra, J. I., Cohn, J. F., & Bell, R. Q. (1998). The development of early externalizing problems among children from low income families: A transformational perspective. *Journal of Abnormal Child Psychology, 26*, 95–107.

Smetana, J. G., Campione-Barr, N., & Daddis, C. (2004). Longitudinal development of family decision making: Defining healthy behavioral autonomy for middle-class African American adolescents. *Child Development, 75*, 1418–1424.

Smetana, J. G., Kochanska, G., & Chuang, S. (2000). Mothers' conceptions of everyday rules for young toddlers: A longitudinal investigation. *Merrill-Palmer Quarterly, 46*, 391–416.

Smith, C. L., Calkins, S. D., Keane, S. P., Anastopoulos, A. D., & Shelton, T. L. (2004). Predicting stability and change in toddler behavior problems: Contributions of maternal behavior and child gender. *Developmental Psychology, 40*, 29–42.

Sorce, J. F., & Emde, R. N. (1981). Mother's presence is not enough: Effect of emotional availability on infant exploration. *Developmental Psychology, 17*, 737–745.

Sorce, J. F., Emde, R. N., Campos, J., & Klinnert, M. D. (1985). Maternal emotional signaling: Its effect on the visual cliff behavior of 1-year-olds. *Developmental Psychology, 21*, 195–200.

Spangler, G., & Grossman, K. E. (1993). Biobehavioral organization in securely and insecurely attached infants. *Child Development, 64*, 1439–1450.

Spitz, R. A. (1965). *The first year of life: A psychoanalytic study of normal and deviant development of object relations*. New York: International University Press.

Sroufe, L. A. (1988). The role of infant–caregiver attachment in development. In T. Nezworski & J. Belsky (Eds.), *Clinical implications of attachment* (pp. 18–38). Hillsdale, NJ: Erlbaum.

Sroufe, L. A., Fox, N., & Pancake, V. (1983). Attachment and dependency in developmental perspective. *Child Development, 54*, 1615–1627.

Stayton, D. J., Hogan, R., & Ainsworth, M. D. (1971). Infant obedience and maternal behavior: The origins of socialization reconsidered. *Child Development, 42*, 1057–1069.

Stern, D. (1985). *The interpersonal world of the infant: A view from psychoanalysis and developmental psychology.* New York: Basic Books.

Stifter, C. A., Spinrad, T. L., & Braungart-Rieker, J. M. (1999). Toward a developmental model of child compliance: The role of emotion regulation in infancy. *Child Development, 70,* 21–32.

Stipek, D., Recchia, S., & McClintic, S. (1992). Self-evaluation in young children. *Monographs of the Society for Research in Child Development, 57*(1).

Strand, P. S., Wahler, R. G., & Herring, M. (2000). Momentum in child compliance and opposition. *Journal of Child and Family Studies, 9,* 363–375.

Talwar, V., & Lee, K. (2002). Development of lying to conceal a transgression: Children's control of expressive behaviour during verbal deception. *International Journal of Behavioral Development, 26,* 436–444.

Thompson, R. A., Laible, D. J., & Ontai, L. L. (2003). Early understandings of emotion, morality, and self: Developing a working model. *Advances in Child Development and Behavior, 31,* 137–172.

Trevarthan, C. (1988). Universal co-operative motives: How infants begin to know the language and culture of their parents. In G. Jahoda & I. M. Lewis (Eds.), *Acquiring culture: Cross-cultural studies in child development* (pp. 37–90). London: Croon Helm.

Turiel, E. (1998). Moral development. In W. Damon (Series Ed.) & N. Eisenberg (Vol. Ed.), *Handbook of child psychology: Vol. 3. Social, emotional, and personality development* (5th ed., pp. 863–932). New York: Wiley.

Ujiie, T. (1997). How do Japanese mothers treat children's negativism? *Journal of Applied Developmental Psychology, 18,* 467–483.

Užgiris, I. (1984). Imitation in infancy: Its interpersonal aspects. In M. Perlmutter (Ed.), *Minnesota Symposia on Child Psychology: Vol. 17. Parent–child interactions and parent–child relations in child development* (pp. 1–32). Hillsdale, NJ: Erlbaum.

Vaughn, L. S., Kopp, C., & Krakow, J. B. (1984). Emergence and consolidation of self-control from eighteen to thirty months of age: Normative trends and individual differences. *Child Development, 55,* 990–1004.

Vygotsky, L. S. (1978). *Mind in society: The development of higher psychological process.* Cambridge, MA: Harvard University Press.

Walden, T. A., & Ogan, T. A. (1988). The development of social referencing. *Child Development, 59,* 1230–1240.

Waters, E., Kondo-Ikemura, K., Posada, G., & Richters, J. E. (1991). In M. R. Gunnar & L. A. Sroufe (Eds.), *Minnesota Symposia on Child Development: Vol. 23. Self processes and development* (pp. 217–255). Hillsdale, NJ: Erlbaum.

Weinfeld, N. S., & Ogawa, J. R. (2005, April). *More than a feeling: Parental attachment and toddler emotion regulation.* Poster presented at the 2005 biennial meeting of the Society for Research in Child Development. Atlanta, GA.

Wertsch, J. V., McNamee, G. D., McLane, J. B., & Budwig, N. A. (1980).The adult–child dyad as a problem-solving system. *Child Development, 51,* 1215–1221.

White, R. W. (1959). Motivation reconsidered: The concept of competence. *Psychological Review, 66,* 297–333.

Wiley, A. R., Rose, A. J., Burger, L. K., & Miller, P. J. (1998). Constucting autonomous selves through narrative practices: A comparative study of working-class and middle-class families. *Child Development, 69,* 833–847.

Wilson, A. E., Smith, M. D., & Ross, H. D. (2003). The nature and effects of young children's lies. *Social Development, 12,* 21–45.

Zimmer-Gembeck, M. J., & Collins, W. A. (2003). Autonomy development during adolescence. In G. R. Adams & M. D. Berzonsky (Eds.), *Blackwell handbook of adolescence* (pp. 175–204). Oxford, UK: Blackwell.

13

Taming the Tempest in the Teapot

Emotion Regulation in Toddlers

Ross A. Thompson
Rebecca Goodvin

The toddler years can be viewed as a period of major achievement, and significant limitations, in managing emotions. A parent witnessing a 2-year-old's temper tantrum is painfully aware that the child has much to learn about emotional self-control and the strategies involved in anticipating, regulating, and enlisting emotional expressions into competent social functioning. That parent is likely to agree with the popular culture's characterization of this period as the "terrible twos." But the same 2-year-old is significantly more capable of emotional self-regulation than when she was a newborn, having mastered (but inconsistently applying) simple strategies such as attentional redirection, comfort seeking, self-soothing, and withdrawal to manage her feelings. Developing capacities for emotion regulation at this age are also shaping young children's social tendencies, including cooperative behavior with peers and compliance with adults. In many respects, therefore, the toddler years are an important transitional period from the dependence of the infant on others for emotion management to the more competently self-regulatory capacities of the preschooler.

This chapter is concerned with the development of emotion regulation between the ages of 1 and 3 years. Because emotion regulation is a complex and multifaceted developmental process, we begin by defining emotion regulation and the implications of this conceptualization for how emotion management occurs and its effects. We outline the major features of this developmental process and profile the importance of emotion regulation for competent social and personality functioning, even in very young children. In the next section, we consider the development of emotion regulation in toddlerhood, particularly the contributions of temperamental individuality, neurobiological growth, and cognitive development. We also highlight the importance of caregiving influences for the direct and indirect ways that parents guide the growth of emotion regulation in the early years. In doing so, we argue that although emotion regulation is typically viewed as if it was a single, coherent developmental phenomenon, emotional self-control is actually based on a network of loosely-allied developmental processes arising from within and outside the child. This makes the growth of emotion regulation an integrative developmental process, but one that is challenging to study. In the final section, we discuss future directions of research on emotion regulation in toddlers.

WHAT IS EMOTION REGULATION? WHY IS IT IMPORTANT?

It is easy to see emotion regulation in an 18-month-old who grasps a special blanket or stuffed toy to help calm himself or who turns to a child-care teacher to be picked up when distressed. But does emotion regulation occur when parents provide soothing during a painful inoculation, or when a toddler's crying during peer conflict increases when the teacher arrives, or when a 3-year-old is coached by parents on how to calm down and go to sleep the night before her birthday? Defining emotion regulation relies on basic conceptualizations of emotion and the goals and functions for managing them. Our definition of emotion regulation addresses these issues:

> Emotion regulation consists of the extrinsic and intrinsic processes responsible for monitoring, evaluating, and modifying emotional reactions, especially their intensive and temporal features, to accomplish one's goals. (Thompson, 1994, pp. 27–28)

Incorporated within this definition are several assumptions about emotion and its management.

First, emotion regulation targets positive as well as negative emotions and can include diminishing, heightening, or simply maintaining current levels of emotional arousal. Viewed in this manner, emotion regulation usually alters the *dynamics* of emotion rather than changing its valence. In other words, emotion regulation commonly alters the intensity, escalation (i.e., latency and rise time), or duration of an emotional response, or speeds its recovery, or reduces or enhances the lability or range of emotional responding in particular situations, depending on the individual's emotional goals in that situation (Thompson, 1990). Children who are emotionally well regulated are capable of altering how long or how deeply they feel as they do, or can manage fluctuations in their emotions rather than directly changing negative feelings into happiness. Positive and negative emotions are each the targets of emotion regulatory efforts. Even young children learn, for example, how to blunt their exuberance when necessary in formal social situations, or how to accentuate feelings of sadness to elicit nurturance.

Second, consistent with a functionalist approach to emotion, strategies of emotion regulation are rarely inherently optimal or maladaptive. Rather, the efficacy of emotion regulation strategies must be evaluated in the context of the individual's goals for the situation. This functionalist orientation is especially important for developmental analysis because a young child's goals for managing emotions may be very different from those of an adult. When a toddler cries petulantly in the supermarket after being denied candy but ceases immediately after the parent accedes, does this reflect poor emotion self-regulation (as the parent may intuitively assume) or strategic use of emotion to accomplish a desired goal? In these and similar instances, young children can be emotional tacticians in ways that reflect capable, not deficient, capacities for emotion management, even though their emotional behavior appears unregulated—because it is undesirable—to adults. A functionalist approach to emotion regulation is also important for understanding individual differences in emotionality in the early years. Temperamental individuality means that young children experience different thresholds for the arousal of distress, anxiety, anger, and other negative emotions in everyday situations, and their behavior in those situations (such as social withdrawal from peers) must be interpreted in the context of their efforts to manage aversive feelings that other children may not share. One young child's withdrawal in the presence of gregarious peers may reflect the goal of managing the anxiety of this social encounter (even though doing so diminishes the opportunity for sociability), while another child engages in cooperative social play. Each child's behavior reflects emotionally regulatory efforts.

Third, emotion regulation arises not only from developing *self*-regulatory capacities but also from the management of emotions by other people. Although this is most apparent early in life when young infants depend on caregivers for controlling their arousal, the social management of emotion is a lifelong phenomenon, with adults relying on others for comfort, emotion coaching, and a sympathetic ear. Social influences are thus an important feature of developmental growth in emotion regulation by which capacities for emotion management are socialized, cultural values are appropriated, and gender differences in emotionality are fostered (Thompson & Meyer, 2007).

Finally, modifying emotional reactions is the central feature of emotion regulation, but it is not the only important process. Consistent with a functionalist orientation, young children's developing capacities for *emotional self-monitoring* and for *evaluating* their feelings in light of personal and social standards for emotional behavior are also core features of emotion management (Saarni, 1999). For this reason, emotion regulation emerges in concert with children's developing understanding of emotion and its meaning. During the toddler years, for example, young children begin to comprehend the subjectivity of emotional experience and how emotions are related to other mental events like satisfied or frustrated desires (Thompson & Lagattuta, 2006). Toddlers are also beginning to talk about their feelings with others, and from these conversations they learn further about the causes and consequences of emotion. These developing conceptual and linguistic capacities contribute significantly to the growth of emotion regulation because they enable young children to better understand why they feel as they do, the social contexts warranting emotional self-control, and how to manage their emotions.

Taken together, these elements of our definition of emotion regulation highlight the surprisingly multifaceted contributions to developing capacities for emotion self-control. It underscores how emerging strategies of emotion management are deeply influenced by social experience and culture and unfold with psychological understanding, language, and emotional self-awareness. These influences also contribute to young children's developing capacities to manage their emotional *displays* in social situations, although this is not the same as emotion regulation. Emotion regulation is focused on managing emotional arousal, whereas display rules can be enlisted without changing one's feelings at all (e.g., expressing delight in a gift that one does not like). This is developmentally important because skills for managing emotional displays do not typically emerge until late in the preschool years, while capacities for emotion regulation begin to develop much earlier (Thompson & Lagattuta, 2006).

The development of emotion regulation extends into early adulthood as individuals acquire more psychologically sophisticated, contextually sensitive means of achieving emotional self-efficacy (i.e., feeling the way one wishes to feel) (Saarni, 1999). Throughout this period, and especially during infancy and childhood, the growth of emotion regulation is characterized by several developmental progressions (for reviews, see Eisenberg & Morris, 2002; Fox & Calkins, 2003; Kopp, 1989; Thompson, 1990, 1994), including:

- Growth from regulation by other people to increasingly self-initiated emotion regulation, as children assume growing responsibility for managing their own feelings.
- Increasing breadth, sophistication, and flexibility in the use of emotion regulatory strategies: Children become more capable of using strategies in contextually-appropriate ways, of substituting effective for ineffective strategies, and of using multiple strategies as needed for managing their feelings.
- Increasing use of emotion-specific regulatory strategies (e.g., managing fear but not anger through encouraging self-talk), although some regulatory strategies are applied generally (e.g., withdrawal from situations that arouse negative affect).
- Emerging complexity in the social and personal goals underlying emotion regulation, based on growth in emotional and social understanding, as children learn to increasingly regulate their feelings to manage

social relations, improve cognitive efficiency, support self-esteem, and accomplish other psychologically sophisticated purposes.
- The emergence and growing stability of individual differences in emotion regulation goals, strategies, and general style, as individuals become emotion suppressers, avoiders, or expressors or adopt other emotional regulatory styles, as personality develops and consolidates.
- Enlistment into emotion regulation of other developing capabilities, such as attentional control, language, and strategic functioning.

Toddlerhood is at the beginning of most of these important developmental progressions.

The Significance of Early Emerging Emotion Regulatory Skills

The study of emotion regulation in toddlers is important, therefore, because this period is when many foundational developments in capacities for emotional self-management have their beginnings. Another reason is that individual differences in managing emotions in toddlers are associated with social competence, emotional well-being, and even risk for affectively related psychological disorders. With respect to social behavior with peers, for example, one research group reported that 2-year-olds who had difficulty managing their frustration in laboratory tasks were found to be less cooperative and more conflictual in interactions with other children (Calkins, Gill, Johnson, & Smith, 1999). Other researchers have reported that children who were more successful in managing emotions in stressful circumstances at age 3 also showed better preschool adjustment (Shields et al., 2001) and higher levels of cooperativeness and self-control in school at age 6 (Gilliom, Shaw, Beck, Schonberg, & Lukon, 2002).

Early emotion regulation is also predictive of cooperation with caregivers. Feldman and Klein (2003) reported that 2-year-olds who showed better emotion regulation during a standardized assessment were more cooperative during a clean-up task with their mothers (Calkins, Smith, Gill, & Johnson, 1998, did not find this association, however, using a somewhat different assessment of emotion regulation). In a longitudinal study, Stifter, Spinrad, and Braungart-Rieker (1999) reported that infants' emotion regulatory behaviors at 5 and 10 months predicted children's compliance at 30 months. Furthermore, emotion regulatory ability moderated the relations between temperamental negative reactivity and later compliant behavior: Infants with a highly reactive temperament were more defiant and noncompliant at 30 months only when they also had poor emotion regulation skills. By 18 months, however, differences in emotion regulation had a somewhat different association with subsequent compliance: Toddlers who were low in *both* temperamental reactivity and regulation exhibited the greatest subsequent noncompliance. Taken together, early-emerging differences in emotion regulation appear to be predictive of later capacities to cooperate with caregivers, with low emotion regulation foreshadowing noncompliance.

More broadly, early differences in emotion regulation may also predict young children's risk for psychological problems. The longitudinal research program of Shaw and his colleagues has shown that behaviors reflecting poor emotion regulation in infancy and toddlerhood (e.g., persistent fussiness, noncompliance, and aggression) predict later internalizing and externalizing problems in the preschool and childhood years (Shaw, Bell, & Gilliom, 2000; Shaw, Keenan, Vondra, Delliquadri, & Giovannelli, 1997; see also Keenan & Shaw, 2003). Based on these findings, his research team has concluded that the early origins of later psychopathology can be found in the combination of toddlers' affective vulnerability and aversive parenting, which has led them to the design of early screening and intervention approaches for families with very young children (Shaw, Dishion, Supplee, Gardner, & Arnds, 2006). In a similar vein, Calkins and Dedmon (2000) reported that 2-year-olds who had received high Child Behavior Checklist (CBCL) scores for externalizing behavior were found, in laboratory assessments, to exhibit significantly more frequent behaviors reflecting emotion dysregulation (such as venting distress, heightened negative affect, and distractability) compared to children with low externalizing scores.

Taken together, these studies suggest that individual differences in emotion regulation during the toddler years are important for later social competence and psychological functioning, and that attention to early-developing capacities for managing feelings is important. However, the literature on these topics remains underdeveloped. Beyond studies of predictive correlates, further research is needed to elucidate the developmental processes by which early emotion regulatory differences foreshadow later psychological functioning. As we shall see, for example, early differences in emotion regulation are also associated with temperamental individuality, parenting practices and the quality of parent–child relationships, each of which is also predictive of later social competence, cooperation, and psychological risk. It is possible, therefore, that differences in emotion regulation are part of the constellation of psychosocial outcomes that emerge from early parenting and temperament influences. The manner in which these antecedent influences interact in shaping later developmental outcomes, and the extent to which emotion regulation is a central mediator or moderator of their long-term effects, requires the design of future longitudinal research that can examine these developmental processes in concert. The value of clarifying these associations is reflected in the findings of a recent study from the NICHD Early Child Care Research Network (2004), which indicated that emotional dysregulation in mother–child interaction in 24- and 36-month-olds predicted children's later social and cognitive competencies, even after accounting for early maternal, relational, and family characteristics.

Studying Emotion Regulation in the Toddler Years

The importance of studying early emotion regulation, combined with the complexities of defining this phenomenon, makes research on the development of emotion regulation challenging (Cole, Martin, & Dennis, 2004; Thompson & Meyer, 2007). This is especially true for infants and toddlers, whose behavioral reactions to emotion elicitors are multidetermined and who cannot provide self-reports explaining their actions and their causes. Consequently, most studies of early emotion regulation rely on observations of behaviors presumed to reflect self-regulatory efforts, such as the child's gaze aversion, self-comforting, proximity seeking to mother, or other behaviors when negative emotion elicitors occur. In longitudinal research, these behavioral differences are then related to later social or emotional outcomes.

Besides the interpretive difficulties noted previously (i.e., that early differences in emotion regulation and later socioemotional outcomes may each be associated with common origins, such as temperament or parenting practices), there are other interpretive challenges to this research. First, researchers rarely independently validate that the behaviors they index as reflecting emotion self-regulation truly function in this manner. This is important because behaviors such as proximity seeking and gaze aversion are multidetermined. A child's orientation toward or away from the emotion elicitor can serve emotion regulatory purposes in some functional contexts but not others, for example, and these contexts are rarely distinguished and validated *a priori*. Second, differences in emotional arousal and emotion regulation are often confounded conceptually and behaviorally, with the result that their association may derive from their overlapping measurement rather than reflecting an empirical connection. Indeed, some researchers (such as Campos, Frankel, & Camras, 2004) argue that it is difficult if not impossible to conceptually distinguish emotional arousal from emotion regulation because of their common influences and assessment. The same problem with overlapping measurement is often also true of studies of the association between emotion regulation and its correlates (e.g., parenting practices), in which both emotion regulation and the correlate are studied in the same emotion-eliciting circumstances (such as mother–child interaction).

Third, developmental researchers are often interested in identifying stable individual differences in self-regulation that reflect emergent personality organization. But especially with young children, the influence of the situational context and functional goals related to emotion regulation make cross-contextual consistency the exception rather than the rule (Calkins et al., 1999; Grolnick, Bridges, & Connell, 1996). In studies with infants and toddlers, researchers are often studying situationally specific regulatory processes reflecting local rather than generalizable tendencies. The same is also likely to be true of efforts to distinguish children who are optimal or poor self-regulators across emotional, behavioral, attentional, cognitive, physiological, and other developmental domains (Calkins et al., 1998; but see Kochanska, Murray, &

Harlan, 2000). In short, because self-regulatory capabilities are only beginning to emerge in the early years, individual differences in emotion regulation are often situationally determined and are not necessarily stable over time or reflecting emergent personality qualities.

In response to these challenges, Cole and her colleagues (2004) have proposed a number of alternative research approaches to studying the development of emotion regulation These include assessing emotion independently of emotion regulatory processes (sometimes including microanalytic sequential analyses to examine their mutual influence), using multiple convergent measures of emotion regulation, and examining emotion self-regulation in contrasting situations with different expected emotional demands. These suggestions are valuable, and they underscore that considerable thoughtfulness, creativity, and hard work are required to study the complex unfolding of emotion self-management in the early years. Attention to issues of construct validation, the child's goals in the situation, and clarity of assessment are each also necessary. This requires studying emotion regulation in laboratory or naturalistic circumstances permitting clear inferences of the child's emotional goals for the situation, and a focus on behaviors that are directly associated with managing emotion in these particular situations.

THE DEVELOPMENT OF EMOTION REGULATION IN THE TODDLER YEARS

Consistent with its multifaceted quality, the development of emotion regulation between 1 and 3 years of age arises from physiological maturation, cognitive development, and relational influences. In particular, processes of brain maturation, conceptual growth in the child's understanding of emotion and self, temperamental individuality, and parenting practices each contribute to the growth of toddlers' capacities for emotion management.

Neurobiological Growth

Emotions are biologically basic but neurobiologically complex, entailing activation of multiple brain regions and neurohormonal processes (Fox & Calkins, 2003). Not surprisingly, the development of emotion regulation is also neurobiologically complex, involving the progressive maturation of excitatory systems and inhibitory processes in the brain and nervous system that have varying maturational timetables. The maturation of the hypothalamic–pituitary–adrenocortical (HPAC) axis, for example, is strongly associated with emotional behavior and extends through adolescence, but there are important declines in systemic lability during the first year that are influenced, in part, by caregiver responsiveness (Gunnar & Vasquez, 2006). At the same time, parasympathetic activity also matures during the early years to assume an increasingly important role in arousal regulation (Porges, Doussard-Roosevelt, &

Maiti, 1994). It is for these reasons that the reactive, all-or-none quality of the newborn's arousal becomes more graded, controllable, and environmentally sensitive before the end of the first year.

The neurobiological constituents of developing emotion regulation also involve regions of the prefrontal cortex, one of the most slowly maturing regions of the human brain governing a range of functions associated with working memory, planning, strategic functioning, and emotion regulation. Not surprisingly, multiple prefrontal regions are relevant to the strategic management of emotions, including the dorsolateral prefrontal cortex, orbitoprefrontal cortex, and the anterior cingulate cortex (Diamond, 2002; LeDoux, 1996; Posner & Rothbart, 2000). In various ways, the maturation of these regions enables developing capabilities for emotion regulation through maturing capacities for attentional control and redirection, the inhibition of impulsive responses and the substitution of reflective functioning, the enlistment of working memory into emotional processing, and other abilities. Although the prolonged neurobiological maturation of these areas helps to explain why emotion regulation has a very extended developmental timetable, the rudimentary early emergence of prefrontal capacities helps to explain developmental changes in emotionality in the first year (e.g., declines in unexplained fussiness and growing emotional responsiveness to external stimulation at 2–4 months and emotional response inhibition at 9–10 months) as well as providing a foundation for the achievements in emotion regulation in toddlerhood discussed in this chapter (see Thompson, 1994). Developing abilities to enlist attentional processes into emotional self-control, to inhibit immediate emotional reactions in favor of more constructive or socially appropriate responses, and to enlist prior knowledge networks into emotional responding each depend on the maturation of these regions of the prefrontal cortex.

Taken together, one of the reasons that the early years witness such remarkable advances in emotion self-management is because the neurobiological constituents of this capacity are maturing rapidly, although they still have a long way to go. These foundations make the toddler an emotive creature of considerably greater potential capacity for emotional self-control than the infant and also more capable of responding constructively to the incentives for emotion regulation from caregivers.

Conceptual Development in Understanding Emotion and the Self

Another reason that the toddler years are a period of such significant growth in emotion regulation is that young children are rapidly expanding their understanding of emotion. As noted earlier, developing capacities for emotion regulation are founded on a toddler's growing understanding of the causes and consequences of emotion and of strategies for emotion management (Thompson & Lagattuta, 2006). By age 2, for example, young children can be overheard making spontaneous references to emotions, the causes of emotion, and even emotion regulatory efforts (e.g., "I scared of the shark. Close my eyes" at 28 months—Bretherton, Fritz, Zahn-Waxler, & Ridgeway, 1986; see also Bartsch & Wellman, 1995; Wellman, Harris, Banerjee, & Sinclair, 1995). These early references to emotion reveal that even at this early age, toddlers appreciate the subjectivity of emotional experience, its referentiality (i.e., that people don't just feel, but they feel *about* something), the associations between particular emotions and specific situations that commonly elicit them, and the connections between emotions and other psychological states, such as perception and desires. By age 3, children have further associated emotions with beliefs and expectations about events (such as the surprise a visitor feels after seeing giraffes on a farm; Wellman & Banerjee, 1991). Although it will be quite some time before they acquire a psychologically sophisticated conception of emotion, toddlers are aware that emotion can be managed by fleeing, removing, restricting perception of, or ignoring emotionally arousing events based on their recognition of the connections between emotion and perception. They are also aware of the value of self-comforting and of seeking the assistance of caregivers for managing feelings (Thompson, 1990). Interestingly, toddlers' awareness of the association between emotions and (satisfied or unfulfilled) desires may actually *undermine* their emotional regulatory efforts when it causes them to become fixated on getting what they want as necessary to feeling better.

Emotion regulation is also affected by the growth of self-awareness. The period between ages 2 and 3 witnesses the emergence of representational self-awareness in toddlers' verbal self-referential behavior (e.g., "me big!"), verbal labeling of internal experiences such as emotions, assertions of competence and responsibility as autonomous agents, refusing assistance and insisting on "do it myself," growing sensitivity to evaluative standards and the emergence of conscience, assertions of ownership, and categorizing the self by gender and in other ways (see Thompson, 2006, for a review). Their more complex self-awareness is accompanied by the emergence of self-referential emotions during the second and third years as toddlers increasingly exhibit pride in their accomplishments (calling attention to their feats), guilt in their misbehavior (often accompanied by reparative behavior), shame when behavior reflects negatively on the self, and embarrassment when effusively praised (Lewis, 2000). Taken together, young children are beginning to regard themselves in more multidimensional and evaluative ways as they increasingly perceive themselves as objects of the attention and thought of others. Their emotional experiences increasingly incorporate their consciousness of how they are perceived and evaluated by others, which likely contributes to their motivation to learn how to manage their feelings, especially in the presence of others who matter to them. Emotion regulation in toddlers is thus motivated by their efforts to look good in the eyes of others, and by their need to manage feelings of embarrassment, guilt, and shame as well as other compelling feelings.

Finally, the most central conceptual advance of the toddler years is the growth of language, which permits young children access to others' thoughts and the capacity to share their thoughts with another. As we shall see later, the beginnings of parent–child conversation during the toddler years provides significant opportunities for young children to learn about emotions and the self and to acquire strategies of emotion management from their caregivers.

Temperament

Toddlers' temperamental individuality may be associated with the development of emotion regulation in at least three ways. First, certain temperamental qualities—particularly thresholds for the arousal of negative emotions—contribute to the intensity and persistence of emotionality that requires management. Some children simply face different challenges in regulating their emotions than do others because of their temperament. Second, other temperamental qualities, such as inhibition or effortful control, are directly associated with a young child's proneness to exert self-control in emotionally arousing situations. This is consistent with the view that a major feature of temperamental individuality is self-regulation (Rothbart & Bates, 1998). Finally, temperament may interact with caregiving influences to shape emotion regulation through the interaction of the child's needs for emotional support and the assistance provided by an adult. Because of their temperamental qualities, some children require greater assistance in emotion regulation than do other children, and they respond to the caregiver's initiatives in particular ways.

Studies have shown, in general, that toddlers who exhibit higher levels of negative arousal in situations designed to induce frustration or distress also enlist fewer effective strategies for managing their feelings and instead act in ways that tend to prolong or intensify their negative emotions (e.g., Buss & Goldsmith, 1998; Calkins & Johnson, 1998; Grolnick et al., 1996). As noted earlier, however, the concurrent assessment of emotion and emotion regulation presents interpretive difficulties: Is children's higher negative arousal a result of their use of less effective self-regulatory strategies, or are children's behavioral strategies and affective arousal coincident but functionally unrelated? More informative are studies showing that assessments of young children's temperamental reactivity are associated with independent observations of emotion regulation (Calkins & Dedmon, 2000; Calkins et al., 1999; NICHD Early Child Care Research Network, 2004). In one study, for example, maternal reports of the toddler's temperamental negative reactivity (high anger, low soothability) were associated with observations of ineffective emotion-related behaviors in frustration tasks, such as children's aggressive venting and focus on the distressing object, and less use of distraction and orienting toward mother (Calkins et al., 1999). Likewise, toddlers who are behaviorally inhibited, or who are high in temperamental fearfulness, tend to use different strategies for managing their arousal in stressful situations relative to toddlers who are low in fearful inhibition. In their encounters with a stranger, for example, infants and toddlers rated as temperamentally wary by their mothers averted gaze and avoided the stranger more than their temperamentally bolder counterparts (Mangelsdorf, Shapiro, & Marzolf, 1995), and Parritz (1996) found that wary temperament was associated with toddlers' greater self-comforting, proximity seeking, and whiny/demanding vocalizations to the mother.

Young children have other temperamental qualities that are more directly associated with emotion regulation. In light of the importance of distraction, gaze avoidance, and caregiver orientation to early emotion regulation, it is not surprising to find that individual differences in attentional self-control are associated with emotion regulation in young children (Belsky, Friedman, & Hsieh, 2001). Temperamental effortful control is also associated with individual differences in behavioral and emotional self-regulation in young children. *Effortful control* refers to one's capacity to inhibit a dominant response (such as an emotional reaction) and initiate a subdominant response according to situational demands (Rothbart & Bates, 1998). Toddlers who are high on effortful control exhibit greater capacities for emotional self-management and behavioral self-control in both contemporaneous and later assessments (Kochanska, Murray, & Coy, 1997; Kochanska et al., 2000). Such findings suggest that some children are temperamentally better equipped to exert self-control in emotion, attention, conduct, and other aspects of behavior.

Another way that temperament may be influential in the early development of emotion regulation is in how it interacts with caregiving influences. Consistent with the concept of "goodness of fit" between temperamental qualities and environmental supports or demands, researchers have found that certain parenting characteristics have different consequences for children who differ in temperament. In a study of the responses of 18-month-olds to moderate stressors, Nachmias and her colleagues reported that the interaction of toddlers' inhibited temperament with an insecure parent–child attachment relationship predicted elevations in postsession cortisol levels (Nachmias, Gunnar, Mangelsdorf, Parritz, & Buss, 1996). Only children who were both insecurely attached and highly inhibited experienced cortisol elevations; for inhibited toddlers in secure relationships, the mother's presence helped to buffer the physiological effects of challenging events, and uninhibited toddlers functioned well regardless of the security of attachment.

Temperament may be important as a moderator of the association between parenting and coping, and also as an influence on parents' perceptions of young children's emotional needs. Caregivers with temperamentally inhibited or difficult toddlers are likely to expend special effort to manage children's negative arousal, and as we shall see, their efforts may support or undermine children's developing self-regulatory capacities (Kennedy, Rubin, Hastings, & Maisel, 2004). Much more research is needed to explore how parental perceptions of children's temperamental qualities influence their emotional socialization efforts and, in this manner, developing emotion regulation.

Taken together, these studies indicate that temperamental qualities are an important influence on the development of emotion regulation capacities in toddlers, and that future studies must take into consideration the direct and indirect ways that temperament is relevant. Moreover, there are also suggestions that temperament may moderate the effects of parenting practices on toddler's emotion management, although more research on this topic is needed.

Parenting Influences and the Family Emotional Climate

In the study by Nachmias and colleagues (1996) described previously, toddlers' physiological regulation during stress was influenced by the broader security of the parent–child relationship and also by specific parenting practices. Postsession cortisol elevations were higher when mothers encouraged their offspring to approach the fear-provoking stimuli, and the mothers of inhibited toddlers were especially likely to do so (Nachmias et al., 1996). Consistent with these findings, research on the influence of parenting on the development of emotion regulation indicates that there are at least two ways that parents guide the growth of emotional self-control in young children (Thompson & Meyer, 2007). First, they do so through specific practices, such as how they respond supportively or critically to the emotions of offspring, directly intervene to manage toddlers' emotions, model emotion or emotion regulation at home, or socialize emotional development in other ways. Second, parents influence developing emotion regulation through the broader quality of the parent–child relationship that provides a resource of support, or insecurity, that influences toddlers' capacities to manage their feelings.

How parents respond in emotionally arousing situations significantly influences the emotion regulation of young children, as indicated by the Nachmias study. Other research shows that independent assessments of parenting practices are also associated with young children's emotion regulation. Feldman and Klein (2003) reported, for example, that parental warm control when eliciting the child's compliance and maternal sensitivity during free play were each associated with 24-month-olds' emotion regulation during a cognitive assessment (see also NICHD Early Child Care Research Network, 2004, for similar findings). Calkins and Johnson (1998) found that 18-month-olds who became more distressed during frustration tasks had mothers who were independently observed to be more interfering when interacting with their offspring, but the mother's positive guidance was associated with the child's constructive coping with frustration (see also Calkins et al., 1998). In a longitudinal study, Gilliom and colleagues found that maternal use of warm control in a teaching task with sons at age 1½ was associated with boys' constructive use of distraction in a frustration task at age 3½. Moreover, although maternal reports of difficult temperament at the earlier age did not predict later emotion regulatory strategies, there was an interaction of temperament and maternal control such that the children's temperamental difficulty did not predict later problems in emotion self-regulation when their mothers used warm control at the earlier age. In general, toddlers function better when their mothers are emotionally available to them during difficult challenges than when mothers are present but unengaged (Diener & Mangelsdorf, 1999). However, maternal strategies for directly managing children's emotions decline in frequency over the toddler period, suggesting a gradual transition to the child's more autonomous regulation of emotion (Grolnick, Kurowski, McMenamy, Rivkin, & Bridges, 1998; Spinrad, Stifter, Donelan-McCall, & Turner, 2004).

Taken together, these studies suggest that when caregivers provide sensitive support, especially during stressful challenges, their offspring develop more constructive approaches to managing emotions. This may occur as parents intervene to keep the toddler's distress manageable, which enables offspring to acquire and practice skills of emotional self-control. Supportive parental responding also contributes to the development of social expectations that adults will be emotionally helpful, and children's beliefs that their feelings are manageable. Moreover, when parents respond helpfully and supportively, it contributes to toddlers' beliefs that their feelings are valued and legitimate, by contrast with circumstances in which parents are denigrating, punitive, or dismissive, or when the child's negative emotions elicit the parent's personal distress (see Denham, 1998; Eisenberg, Cumberland, & Spinrad, 1998, for reviews). In the latter circumstances, young children may perceive their feelings as worthless, unimportant, or potentially dangerous. A toddler who is always told that "big boys (girls) don't cry" may struggle to manage feelings of sadness with this emotion judgment as a continuing influence.

There are many ways that parents sensitively help toddlers to regulate their feelings (Thompson, 1990, 1994). They distract the child from potentially frightening or distressing events, assist in solving problems that children find frustrating, and strive to alter the child's interpretation of negatively arousing circumstances (e.g., "It's just a game"). They also coach adaptive ways of reacting emotionally to difficult situations—sometimes as alternatives to the child's venting or another initially maladaptive response—that facilitate emotion regulation by enabling the child's feelings to be expressed with more constructive results. This can involve the common parental maxim to toddlers—"use words to say how you feel"—as well as enlisting an adult's assistance or problem solving rather than simply dissolving in loud wails. Sensitive parents also enlist social referencing to provide reassurance in challenging situations or caution in potentially dangerous circumstances (Klinnert, Campos, Sorce, Emde, & Svejda, 1983). Finally, parents also seek to manage the feelings of young offspring by proactively structuring children's experiences to make emotional demands predictable and manageable. They do this by creating daily routines (such as scheduling naps and meals) that accord with their knowledge of children's temperamental qualities and tolerance for stimulation, choosing child-care arrangements that are congenial to children's needs and capabilities and striving in other ways to create emotionally manageable daily routines. There has been little detailed study, however, of these parental practices by which a young child's emotional life is socialized and which create the context for the growth of emotion regulatory skills, and more research is needed.

Another way that sensitive parents contribute to the growth of constructive emotion regulation skills is through parent–child conversation (Thompson, 2006; Thompson, Laible, & Ontai, 2003). Although toddlers are not capable of being active conversationalists, their rapidly developing conceptual and linguistic skills and their interest in understanding their feelings (and those of others) combine, making them receptive partners in conversations concerning emotion and its management. In two studies, the frequency, complexity, and causal orientation of emotion-related conversations between mothers and their 3-year-olds predicted the child's emotion understanding at age 6 (Dunn, Brown, & Beardsall, 1991; Laible, 2004). These conversations are also likely to guide children's conceptions of emotion regulation. In a provocative ethnographic study, Miller and Sperry (1987) described the socialization of anger regulation and aggression by the mothers of three 2½-year-old girls growing up in a lower-income neighborhood in South Baltimore. Consistent with the need for assertiveness and self-defense in this environment, the mothers sought to "toughen" their young daughters by coaching, as well as modeling, reinforcing, and rehearsing specific strategies of anger expression and self-control that were adaptive to their community setting. As a consequence, their daughters developed a rich repertoire of expressive modes for conveying anger but were also capable of regulating its arousal and expression consistently with the rules of the subculture. Further research into how parents socialize emotion regulation in conversational contexts is warranted, especially because parents commonly coach offspring about the need to manage their feelings and often suggest specific strategies for doing so (Miller & Green, 1985).

These parental influences occur within the context of the broader emotional climate of the family (Dunsmore & Halberstadt, 1997). When toddlers must cope with frequent, intense negative emotion from other family members, particularly when it is directed to them, these experiences can overwhelm their capacities for emotion management. Moreover, in aversive family emotional climates young children are exposed to salient models of emotion dysregulation as well as experiences that are likely to shape children's normative expectations for how people typically behave emotionally and their affective schemas (e.g., emotions viewed as threatening, irrational, and/or uncontrollable). A large research literature indicates that an emotionally positive family climate is associated with children's adjustment and enhanced self-regulatory capacities, and an emotionally negative family climate is associated with more negative and mixed outcomes (Halberstadt, Crisp, & Eaton, 1999; Halberstadt & Eaton, 2002). These associations are stronger for infants and toddlers compared with older children, suggesting their particular sensitivity to the family emotional climate. This is consistent with longitudinal research indicating that as early as the child's second year, aversive family experiences are an important predictor of the development of clinically relevant conduct problems (Shaw et al., 2000). Differences in early family experiences are clearly relevant to the emergence of toddlers' capacities to manage their feelings constructively.

Security of Attachment

Parent–child relationships are the central feature of early family experiences because the impact of parental practices, parent–child conversation, and the family emotional climate is based on the relational context in which they occur. According to Cassidy (1994) and Thompson (1994; Thompson et al., 2003), differences in the security of parent–child attachment may be especially significant for the growth of emotion regulation. According to these theorists, the sensitivity of parental care and the trust inherent in parent–child conversation enable secure children to become more emotionally self-aware and to develop a more flexible capacity to manage their emotions appropriate to circumstances. By contrast, insecure children are more prone to emotional dysregulation, especially in stressful circumstances, that may be manifested in heightened, unmodulated levels of negative emotionality or, alternatively, in suppressing the expression of negative arousal and relying on nonsocial means to regulate emotion.

Even in early childhood, differences in the security of attachment appear to be associated with emergent emotion regulation capacities. In a longitudinal study over the first 3 years, Kochanska (2001) reported that over time, insecurely attached children exhibited progressively greater fear and/or anger, and diminished joy, in standardized assessments compared with secure children. Goldberg and her colleagues reported that even by age 1, the mothers of secure infants commented about both positive and negative emotions when interacting with them, while the mothers of insecurely attached infants either remarked rarely about the infant's feelings or commented primarily about negative emotions (Goldberg, MacKay-Soroka, & Rochester, 1994). By early childhood, securely attached preschoolers talk more about emotions in everyday conversations with their mothers, and their mothers are more richly elaborative in their discussions of emotion with them, which may help to explain why secure children are also more advanced in emotion understanding as early as age 3 (for reviews, see Thompson, 2006; Thompson et al., 2003; see also Laible & Thompson, 1998; Raikes & Thompson, 2006).

Although there has been relatively little research focused specifically on emotion regulation, there is evidence that children in secure relationships are better at managing negative emotions beginning early in life (see, e.g., Diener, Mangelsdorf, McHale, & Frosch, 2002; NICHD Early Child Care Research Network, 2004). In the Nachmias study, securely attached toddlers exhibited more competent coping with the stressful procedures than did insecurely attached children, although not higher cortisol elevations (Nachmias et al., 1996). Gilliom and his colleagues reported that boys who were securely attached at age 1½ were observed to use more constructive anger-management strategies at age 3½ (Gilliom et al., 2002). Secure toddlers were more likely to use distraction, ask questions about the frustration task, and wait quietly compared with insecurely attached boys.

These findings suggest that the relational context in which emotion regulation develops in the early years is important. Future research concerning parental influences on emotion regulation in toddlers should also explore whether toddlers' receptiveness to parental interventions and coaching is mediated by the broader security of the parent–child relationship (Laible & Thompson, 2007). Are children in secure relationships more responsive, for example, to parents' efforts to soothe their distress or to coach emotional regulatory strategies? Further exploration of this issue could help to elucidate how not only *what* happens but also *who* does it is important to toddlers' emotion regulation skills. Moreover, other early relationships may also be important influences on developing emotion regulation. Volling, McElwain, and Miller (2002) observed that toddler younger siblings were more likely to exhibit jealousy in triadic interactions with their mothers and older siblings when the sibling relationship was characterized by rivalry. The extent to which relational influences in the home have compounding influences on the growth of self-regulation in toddlerhood merits further attention.

SUMMARY AND CONCLUSION

There is a charming dissonance between public images of emotionally unregulated toddlers—the "terrible twos" subject to inexplicable temper tantrums—and the research account of this chapter. Although toddlers have far to go in their capacities to strategically regulate their emotions, research shows that many of the foundations of lifelong capacities for emotion management are established in the first 3 years of life. It is during this period, for example, that the neurobiological foundations of emotional reactivity become stable and cortical self-regulatory systems begin to mature. Toddlers are developing understandings of emotion, such as the associations between their feelings and psychological processes such as perception and desire, that equip them with the conceptual tools for rudimentary self-regulation of emotion. Temperament confers on the growth of emotion regulation unique individuality owing to the child's emotional reactivity and temperamental resources for self-control. The development of emotion regulation in toddlers is also profoundly influenced by caregivers. How parents respond to the emotional expressions of offspring, the emotional climate of the home, and the broader security and support of the parent–child relationship is among the important relational influences on the growth of emotional self-management in early childhood.

These multifaceted developmental influences are especially important because of emerging research evidence that toddlerhood is a period not only of emotional exuberance but also of emotional vulnerability. Research in developmental psychopathology reviewed earlier underscores that the origins of potentially significant forms of affective psychopathology can be found in early challenges to emotion regulation before the age of 3, especially in the interaction of the toddler's temperamental vulnerability and an emotionally aversive family environment. In short, toddlerhood witnesses the emergence of individual differences in capacities for emotion regulation that, for some, may foreshadow later difficulties with affective dysregulation.

Throughout this chapter, we have identified a number of important issues for future research that derive from the developmental processes we have profiled. These include more incisive inquiry into the origins of individual differences in toddlers' capacities for emotional self-control, the extent to which these differences are moderators of the influence of early temperament and/or family climate on later adjustment, how the security of attachment may influence young children's receptivity to the emotional socialization incentives of their caregivers, and the extent to which parents' perceptions of their child's temperamental individuality alter how they try to guide emotional growth and the development of emotional regulatory capacities in offspring. Further exploration of these questions is important not only for the insights it might yield into the early development of emotion regulation but for how it can advance basic understanding of emotional development in the early years. It is important to remember, however, the conceptual and methodological challenges of research in this area. Because our understanding of emotion regulation is based on the functions that self-regulatory strategies have for enabling individuals to achieve goal-corrected changes in their current emotional condition, developmental inquiry into the growth of emotion regulation must attend to the emotion goals underlying toddlers' self-management of emotion. For young children who cannot easily tell us why they are acting as they do, this is a methodological challenge.

Toddlers have many reasons for trying to regulate their feelings, of course. They do so in order to feel better when distressed, manage fear, enhance positive well-being, affirm relationships, engage in constructive coping, comply with social rules, and for many other reasons. As Bronson (2000) has noted, it is during toddlerhood that the developmental transition from primarily extrinsic regulation of emotions to the child's self-initiated self-regulated emotional experience ensues. The manner in which this occurs—colored by temperament, guided by close relationships, enlivened by an emerging sense of self, prepared by brain maturation, structured by emerging concepts of emotion—is a fascinating developmental story worthy of further study.

REFERENCES

Bartsch, K., & Wellman, H. (1995). *Children talk about the mind.* London: Oxford University Press.

Belsky, J., Friedman, S. L., & Hsieh, K. (2001). Testing a core emotion-regulation prediction: Does early attentional persistence moderate the effect of infant negative emotionality on later development? *Child Development, 72,* 123–133.

Bretherton, I., Fritz, J., Zahn-Waxler, C., & Ridgeway, D. (1986). Learning to talk about emotions: A functionalist perspective. *Child Development, 57*, 529–548.

Bronson, M. B. (2001). *Self-regulation in early childhood: Nature and Nurture.* New York: Guilford Press.

Buss, K. A., & Goldsmith, H. H. (1998). Fear and anger regulation in infancy: Effects on the temporal dynamics of affective expression. *Child Development, 69,* 359–374.

Calkins, S. D., & Dedmon, S. E. (2000). Physiological and behavioral regulation in two-year-old children with aggressive/destructive behavior problems. *Journal of Abnormal Child Psychology, 28,* 103–118.

Calkins, S. D., Gill, K. L., Johnson, M. C., & Smith, C. L. (1999). Emotional reactivity and emotional regulation strategies as predictors of social behavior with peers during toddlerhood. *Social Development, 8,* 310–334.

Calkins, S. D., & Johnson, M. C. (1998). Toddler regulation of distress to frustrating events: Temperamental and maternal correlates. *Infant Behavior and Development, 21,* 379–395.

Calkins, S. D., Smith, C. L., Gill, K. L., & Johnson, M. C. (1998). Maternal interactive style across contexts: Relations to emotional, behavioral, and physiological regulation during toddlerhood. *Social Development, 7,* 350–369.

Campos, J. J., Frankel, C. B., & Camras, L. (2004). On the nature of emotion regulation. *Child Development, 75,* 377–394.

Cassidy, J. (1994). Emotion regulation: Influences of attachment relationships. In N. A. Fox (Ed.), The development of emotion regulation and dysregulation: Biological and behavioral aspects. *Monographs of the Society for Research in Child Development, 59*(2–3, Serial No. 240), 228–249.

Cole, P. M., Martin, S. E., & Dennis, T. A. (2004). Emotion regulation as a scientific construct: Methodological challenges and directions for child development research. *Child Development, 75,* 317–333.

Denham, S. A. (1998). *Emotional development in young children.* New York: Guilford Press.

Diamond, A. (2002). Normal development of prefrontal cortex from birth to young adulthood: Cognitive functions, anatomy, and biochemistry. In D. T. Stuss & R. T. Knight (Eds.), *Principles of frontal lobe function* (pp. 466–503). New York: Oxford University Press.

Diener, M. L., & Mangelsdorf, S. C. (1999). Behavioral strategies for emotion regulation in toddlers: Associations with maternal involvement and emotional expressions. *Infant Behavior and Development, 22,* 569–583.

Diener, M. L., Mangelsdorf, S. C., McHale, J. L., & Frosch, C. A. (2002). Infants' behavioral strategies for emotion regulation with father and mothers: Associations with emotional expressions and attachment quality. *Infancy, 3,* 153–174.

Dunn, J., Brown, J., & Beardsall, L. (1991). Family talk about feeling states and children's later understanding of others' emotions. *Developmental Psychology, 27,* 448–455.

Dunsmore, J. C., & Halberstadt, A. G. (1997). How does family emotional expressiveness affect children's schemas? In K. C. Barrett (Ed.), *The communication of emotion: Current research from diverse perspectives* (pp. 45–68). San Francisco: Jossey-Bass.

Eisenberg, N., Cumberland, A., & Spinrad, T. L. (1998). Parental socialization of emotion. *Psychological Inquiry, 9,* 241–273.

Eisenberg, N., & Morris, A. S. (2002). Children's emotion-related regulation. In R. Kail (Ed.), *Advances in child development and behavior* (Vol. 30, pp. 190–229). San Diego, CA: Academic Press.

Feldman, R., & Klein, P. (2003). Toddlers' self-regulated compliance to mothers, caregivers, and fathers: Implications for theories of socialization. *Developmental Psychology, 39,* 680–692.

Fox, N., & Calkins, S. (2003). The development of self-control of emotion: Intrinsic and extrinsic influences. *Motivation and Emotion, 27,* 7–26.

Gilliom, M., Shaw, D. S., Beck, J. E., Schonberg, M. A., & Lukon, J. L. (2002). Anger regulation in disadvantaged preschool boys: Strategies, antecedents, and the development of self-control. *Developmental Psychology, 38,* 222–235.

Goldberg, S., MacKay-Soroka, S., & Rochester, M. (1994). Affect, attachment, and maternal responsiveness. *Infant Behavior and Development, 17,* 335–339.

Grolnick, W. S., Bridges, L. J., & Connell, J. P. (1996). Emotion regulation in two-year-olds: Strategies and emotional expression in four contexts. *Child Development, 67,* 928–941.

Grolnick, W. S., Kurowski, C. O., McManamy, J. M., Rivkin, I., & Bridges, L. J. (1998). Mothers' strategies for regulating their toddlers' distress. *Infant Behavior and Development, 21,* 437–450.

Gunnar, M., & Vazquez, D. (in press). Stress neurobiology and developmental psychopathology. In D. Cicchetti & D. Cohen (Eds.), *Developmental psychopathology: Risk, disorder, and adaptation* (2nd ed., Vol. 2, pp. 533–577). New York: Wiley.

Halberstadt, A. G., Crisp, V. W., & Eaton, K. L. (1999). Family expressiveness: A retrospective and new directions for research. In P. Philippot & R. S. Feldman (Eds.), *The social context of nonverbal behavior* (pp. 109–155). New York: Cambridge University Press.

Halberstadt, A. G., & Eaton, K. L. (2002). A meta-analysis of family expressiveness and children's emotion expressiveness and understanding. *Marriage and Family Review, 34,* 35–62.

Keenan, K., & Shaw, D. S. (2003). Starting at the beginning: Exploring the etiology of antisocial behavior in the first years of life. In B. B. Lahey, T. E. Moffitt, & A. Caspi (Eds.), *Causes of conduct disorder and juvenile delinquency* (pp. 153–181). New York: Guilford Press.

Kennedy, A. E., Rubin, K. H., Hastings, P. D., & Maisel, B. (2004). Longitudinal relations between child vagal tone and parenting behavior: 2 to 4 years. *Developmental Psychobiology, 45,* 10–21.

Klinnert, M., Campos, J., Sorce, J., Emde, R., & Svejda, M. (1983). Emotions as behavior regulators: Social referencing in infancy. In R. Plutchik & H. Kellerman (Eds.), *Emotion: Theory, research, and experience: Vol. 2. Emotions in early development* (pp. 57–86). New York: Academic Press.

Kochanska, G. (2001). Emotional development in children with different attachment histories: The first three years. *Child Development, 72,* 474–490.

Kochanska, G., Murray, K. T., & Coy, K. C. (1997). Inhibitory control as a contributor to conscience in childhood: From toddler to early school age. *Child Development, 68,* 263–277.

Kochanska, G., Murray, K. T., & Harlan, E. (2000). Effortful control in early childhood: Continuity and change, antecedents, and implications for social development. *Developmental Psychology, 26,* 220–232.

Kopp, C. B. (1989). Regulation of distress and negative emotions: A developmental review. *Developmental Psychology, 25,* 343–354.

Laible, D. (2004). Mother-child discourse surrounding a child's past behavior at 30 months: Links to emotional understanding and early conscience development at 36 months. *Merrill-Palmer Quarterly, 50,* 159–180.

Laible, D. J., & Thompson, R. A. (1998). Attachment and emotional understanding in preschool children. *Developmental Psychology, 34*(5), 1038–1045.

Laible, D. J., & Thompson, R. A. (2007). Early socialization: A relational perspective. In J. Grusec & P. Hastings (Eds.), *Handbook of socialization* (pp. 181–207). New York: Guilford Press.

LeDoux, J. (1996). *The emotional brain.* New York: Touchstone.

Lewis, M. (2000). Self-conscious emotions: Embarrassment, pride, shame, and guilt. In M. Lewis & J. Haviland-Jones (Eds.), *Handbook of emotions* (pp. 563–573). New York: Guilford Press.

Mangelsdorf, S. C., Shapiro, J. R., & Marzolf, D. (1995). Developmental and temperamental differences in emotion regulation in infancy. *Child Development, 66,* 1817–1828.

Miller, P. J., & Sperry, L. (1987). The socialization of anger and aggression. *Merrill–Palmer Quarterly, 33,* 1–31.

Miller, S. M., & Green, M. L. (1985). Coping with stress and frustration: Origins, nature, and development. In M. Lewis & C. Saarni (Eds.), *The socialization of emotions* (pp. 263–314). New York: Plenum Press.

Nachmias, M., Gunnar, M., Mangelsdorf, S., Parritz, R. H., & Buss, K. (1996). Behavioral inhibition and stress reactivity: The moderating role of attachment security. *Child Development, 67,* 508–522.

NICHD Early Child Care Research Network. (2004). Affect dysregulation in the mother-child relationship in the toddler years: Antecedents and consequences. *Development and Psychopathology, 16,* 43–68.

Parritz, R. H. (1996). A descriptive analysis of toddler coping in challenging circumstances. *Infant Behavior and Development, 19,* 171–180.

Porges, S. W., Doussard-Roosevelt, J. A., & Maiti, A. K. (1994). Vagal tone and the physiological regulation of emotion. In N. A. Fox (Ed.), Emotion regulation: Behavioral and biological considerations. *Monographs of the Society for Research in Child Development, 59*(Serial No. 240), 167–186.

Posner, M. I., & Rothbart, M. K. (2000). Developing mechanisms of self-regulation. *Development and Psychopathology, 12,* 427–441.

Raikes, H. A., & Thompson, R. A. (2006). Family emotional climate, attachment security, and young children's emotion understanding in a high-risk sample. *British Journal of Developmental Psychology, 24,* 89–104.

Rothbart, M. K., & Bates, J. E. (1998). Temperament. In W. Damon (Ed.) & N. Eisenberg (Vol. Ed.), *Handbook of child psychology: Vol. 3. Social, emotional, and personality development* (5th ed., pp. 105–176). New York: Wiley.

Saarni, C. (1999). *The development of emotional competence.* New York: Guilford Press.

Shaw, D. S., Bell, R. Q., & Gilliom, M. (2000). A truly early starter model of antisocial behavior revisited. *Clinical Child and Family Psychology Review, 3,* 155–172.

Shaw, D. S., Dishion, T. J., Supplee, L., Gardner, F., & Arnds, K. (2006). Randomized trial of a family-centered approach to the prevention of early conduct problems: 2–year effects of the family check-up in early childhood. *Journal of Consulting and Clinical Psychology, 74,* 1–9.

Shaw, D. S., Keenan, K., Vondra, J. I., Delliquadri, E., & Giovannelli, J. (1997). Antecedents of preschool children's internalizing problems: A longitudinal study of low-income families. *Journal of the American Academy of Child and Adolescent Psychiatry, 36,* 1760–1767.

Shields, A., Dickstein, S., Seifer, R., Giusti, L., Magee, K., & Spritz, B. (2001). Emotional competence and early school adjustment: A study of preschoolers at risk. *Early Education and Development, 12,* 73–96.

Spinrad, T. L., Stifter, C. A., Donelan-McCall, N., & Turner, L. (2004). Mothers' regulation strategies in response to toddlers' affect: Links to later emotion self-regulation. *Social Development, 13,* 40–55.

Stifter, C. A., Spinrad, T. L., & Braungart-Rieker, J. M. (1999). Toward a developmental model of child compliance: The role of emotion regulation in infancy. *Child Development, 70,* 21–32.

Thompson, R. A. (1990). Emotion and self-regulation. In R. A. Thompson (Ed.), *Socioemotional development. Nebraska Symposium on Motivation* (Vol. 36, pp. 383–483). Lincoln: University of Nebraska Press.

Thompson, R. A. (1994). Emotion regulation: A theme in search of definition. In N. A. Fox (Ed.), The development of emotion regulation and dysregulation: Biological and behavioral aspects. *Monographs of the Society for Research in Child Development, 59*(2–3, Serial No. 240), 25–52.

Thompson, R. A. (2006). The development of the person: Social understanding, relationships, self, conscience. In W. Damon & R. M. Lerner (Eds.), N. Eisenberg (Vol. Ed.), *Handbook of child psychology: Vol. 3. Social, emotional, and personality development* (6th ed., pp. 24–98). New York: Wiley.

Thompson, R. A., & Lagattuta, K. (2006). Feeling and understanding: Early emotional development. In K. McCartney & D. Phillips (Eds.), *The Blackwell handbook of early childhood development* (pp. 317–337). Oxford, UK: Blackwell.

Thompson, R. A., Laible, D., & Ontai, L. (2003). Early understanding of emotion, morality, and the self: Developing a working model. In R. Kail (Ed.), *Advances in child development and behavior* (Vol. 31, pp. 137–171). San Diego, CA: Academic Press.

Thompson, R. A., & Meyer, S. (2007). The socialization of emotion regulation in the family. In J. Gross (Ed.), *Handbook of emotion regulation* (pp. 249–268). New York: Guilford Press.

Volling, B. L., McElwain, N. L., & Miller, A. L. (2002). Emotion regulation in context: The jealousy complex between young siblings and its relations with child and family characteristics. *Child Development, 73,* 581–600.

Wellman, H., & Banerjee, M. (1991). Mind and emotion: Children's understanding of the emotional consequences of beliefs and desires. *British Journal of Developmental Psychology, 9,* 191–214.

Wellman, H., Harris, P., Banerjee, M., & Sinclair, A. (1995). Early understanding of emotion: Evidence from natural language. *Cognition and Emotion, 9,* 117–149.

Part IV

BIOLOGICAL AND CULTURAL PERSPECTIVES

14

The Cognitive Neuroscience of Early Socioemotional Development

MARTHA ANN BELL
CHRISTY D. WOLFE

Consideration of early socioemotional development is incomplete without concomitant examination of changes in cognition. In this chapter, we propose that developing relations between cognition and emotion must be considered in any conceptualization of socioemotional development (Bell & Wolfe, 2004; Gray, 2004; Rothbart, 2004). There has been much conceptual work proposing developing interrelations between cognition and emotion during very early childhood (e.g., Fox & Calkins, 2003; Fox, Henderson, Marshall, Nichols, & Ghera, 2005; Posner & Rothbart, 2000), as well as the suggestion that cognition and emotion are fully integrated by school age. Cognition–emotion integration in the school-age child may be demonstrated by the many self-regulatory activities that are essential for school readiness (Blair, 2002). There is, however, little empirical data on cognition–emotion, or self-regulatory, development and what research there is tends to focus on cross-sectional samples of infants (e.g., Keenan, 2002; Lewis, Koroshegyi, Douglas, & Kampe, 1997) and preschool children (e.g., Kerr & Zelazo, 2004; Rothbart, Ellis, Rueda, & Posner, 2003). There are no longitudinal studies on emerging cognition–emotion relations across very early development, despite speculations that this integration may have its foundation in infancy and may demonstrate major development shifts during the second and third years (Bell & Wolfe, 2004; Calkins & Fox, 2002).

In this chapter, we present a developmental framework for individual differences in the integration of cognition and emotion. Although this "integration" has been the focus of much recent speculation in the developmental literature, the manifestation of developing cognition–emotion relations can take many forms, each of which has very different implications for child outcome. For example, emotion and influences on emotion development may have an impact on cognition and, thus, cognitive outcome. Conversely, cognition and influences on cognitive development may affect the regulation of emotion and, thus, socioemotional outcome. Finally, cognition and emotion may become increasingly reciprocal over time, with interlocking developmental trajectories demonstrating the significance of both cognition and emotion as outcome measures. The focus of our research program is on individual differences in cognitive development; thus our most current work is designed to test the first and last of these models of cognition–emotion integration (see Figure 14.1).

We consider developing cognition–emotion relations within the larger context of "self-regulation," a construct with many definitions in the psychological literature (Baumeister & Vohs, 2004). We define self-regulation as conscious efforts to control one's inner states or responses with respect to thoughts, emotions, attention, and performance (Vohs & Baumeister, 2004). Thus, our conceptualizations of cognition and emotion might better be described as individual differences in "cognitive control" and "emotion con-

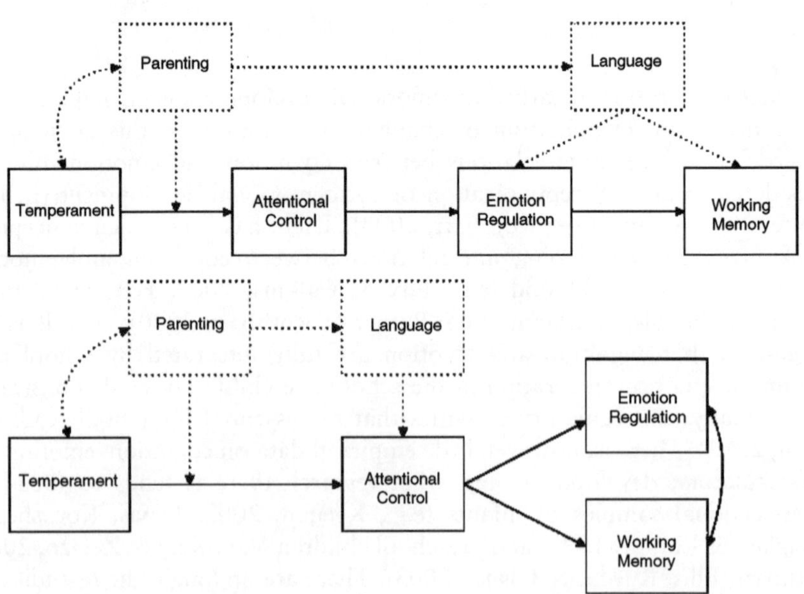

FIGURE 14.1. Two models of hypothesized cognition–emotion relations. In the top model, emotion mediates the relation between temperamentally based attentional control and cognition. In the bottom model, attentional control directly influences both emotion and cognition, with emotion and cognition being correlated. We hypothesize that cognition and emotion become increasing correlated across development.

trol." Within our self-regulation framework, we focus on "attentional control" as the mechanism for developing cognition–emotion relations and the two models we noted previously highlight how attentional control might promote developing cognition–emotion relations.

Our emphasis on attentional control comes from both the neuropsychology and temperament literatures because conceptual efforts to integration cognitive and emotional development may be most successful within a biologically based developmental framework. We consider the most compelling biological framework to be that of temperament-based attentional control, which is associated with the executive attention system (Rothbart, 2004). Rothbart and Bates (1998) have defined temperament as biologically based individual differences in emotional reactivity and the emergence of self-regulation of that reactivity beginning later in the first year of life, around 10 months of age (Rothbart, Derryberry, & Posner, 1994). The emergence of these early regulatory capacities is facilitated by the development of attentional control and thus may have implications for early and later cognitive development as well (Blair, 2002; Bush, Luu, & Posner, 2000; Fox, 1994; Ruff & Rothbart, 1996). Thus, we propose that attentional control is crucial to any investigation of the integration of cognition and emotion during infancy and early childhood.

In this chapter, we first examine the construct of attentional control, as we propose it is the mechanism for cognition–emotion integration. We next examine the cognitive construct of working memory and the socioemotional construct of emotion regulation because we propose that is specifically these two areas of development that are linked by the attentional control mechanism. In our examinations of attentional control, working memory, and emotion regulation, we focus on the neuropsychology of each construct. After examination of those three constructs, we illustrate our own attempts at integrating cognition and emotion by highlighting our current longitudinal work with children in their second year. Of course, development is a complex process. Thus, we end by briefly noting how caregiving behaviors and child language development may be linked to attentional control and, thus, are essential components in the study of cognition and emotion. Caregiving and language are included in our hypothesized models shown in Figure 14.1.

ATTENTIONAL CONTROL

Focus on attentional control as the catalyst for developing cognition–emotion relations results from current neuropsychological research. Posner recently proposed that the executive attention system, involving prefrontal cortex and components such as the anterior cingulate cortex, regulates both cognitive and emotion processing (Bush et al., 2000). In adults, this system is characterized by effortful, controlled attentional processing to either cognitive or emotion stimuli, and in particular the anterior cingulate cortex is activated during cognitive-attention and emotion-attention processing (Fichtenholtz et al., 2004; Yamasaki, LaBar, & McCarthy, 2002).

The functioning of the executive attention system begins to influence behavior during the later half of the first year of life (Ruff & Rothbart, 1996), a time when advances are beginning to be made in cognitive control (Diamond, Prevor, Callender, & Druin, 1997), attention control, (Rothbart et al., 1994; Ruff & Rothbart, 1996; Wilson & Gottman, 1996), and regulation of emotions (Calkins, Dedmon, Gill, Lomax, & Johnson, 2002; Ruff & Rothbart, 1996; van Bakel & Riksen-Walraven, 2004). Major advances in the development of the executive attention system continue throughout early childhood (Posner & Rothbart, 2000; Rothbart, Ellis, & Posner, 2004), a time when dramatic increases are seen in both cognitive and emotional control (Diamond et al., 1997; Kochanska, Murray, & Harlan, 2000). Because the executive attention system focuses on the emotion-attention and cognitive-attention functions of the frontal cortex, this may be the functional system that has the ability to connect cognitive and emotion development (Bell & Wolfe, 2004; Calkins & Fox, 2002; Fox et al., 2005).

As noted, the executive attention system has a long developmental period and begins to show some developmental changes in the last half of the first year of life (around 10 months of age), with major development occurring during toddlerhood (Derryberry & Rothbart, 1997; Rothbart et al., 1994; Rueda, Posner, & Rothbart, 2004). The executive attention system integrates thought and behavior and exerts control on emotional experience and expression. This has led to speculation that regulation is driven not only by positive/negative affect but also at the cognitive level. Rothbart has hypothesized that high attentional control is associated with low negative affect (Rothbart et al., 1994). Indeed, Rothbart's model of the development of temperament describes the process by which infants regulate distress using developing attentional abilities (Posner & Rothbart, 2000; Rothbart et al., 1994). Because of the beginnings of development of the executive attention system in the first year of life, infants who react strongly to events may initially be irritable but later develop the ability for sustained attention (Ruff & Rothbart, 1996). Thus, in Rothbart's model, the development of controlled attentional abilities precedes developing cognitive control, although to our knowledge this has not been empirically tested.

Attentional control associated with executive attention system develops rapidly during the toddler and preschool years and underlies what Rothbart calls "effortful control" (Rothbart & Bates, 1998; Rothbart et al., 2003). Effortful control focuses on the voluntary deployment of executive attention and involves the ability to withhold a dominant response in order to perform a nondominant response (inhibitory control), to detect errors, and to engage in planning. Longitudinal and cross-sectional studies demonstrate beginning advancements in voluntary deployment of executive attention around 30 months of age (Gerardi-Caulton, 2000; Kochanska et al., 2000; Rothbart et al., 2003), with stability across various episodes by 4 years of age (Kochanska

& Knaach, 2003). Our most current longitudinal work still in progress suggests that some children demonstrate executive attention by 24 months of age. Thus, controlled attentional abilities associated with the executive attention system demonstrate initial development at the end of the first postnatal year and progress on to rapid development during the second year.

Neuropsychology of Attentional Control

Although most of the work on the executive attention system and attentional control in infants and young children has focused on behavioral measures, heart rate (HR) has long been used to measure attention in infants and young children (e.g., Richards & Casey, 1992). During stimulus orienting, there is a large deceleration in HR associated with the orienting reflex. Following this is a period of sustained attention involving voluntary, subject-controlled information processing during which HR remains at a lower level and the variability in the HR is decreased (Richards, 2004; Richards & Casey, 1992). During sustained attention, infants and young children cannot be distracted from a central stimulus with a peripheral stimulus. Richards has speculated that the neural control of HR change associated with sustained attention originates from a cardioinhibitory center located in the frontal cortex (Richards & Hunter, 1998). Colombo suggests that processing during sustained attention might be similar to attentional processing associated with the executive attention system (Colombo, Richman, Shaddy, Greenhoot, & Maikranz, 2001). Thus, Colombo proposes that infants who exhibit longer periods of lowered HR (and concomitant longer periods of look duration) during visual attention tasks might do so because of better attentional control abilities. Richards has suggested that the same may be true in early childhood (Richards & Cronise, 2000).

Recent electrocortical work has indicated that the anterior cingulate cortex may indeed be associated with this HR-defined effortful, controlled attention during infancy. Using high-density electroencephalogram (EEG) recordings with infants, Richards (2004) has provided estimations of cortical sources of brain wave activity during HR-defined sustained attention. This source localization work implicates prefrontal cortex, including anterior cingulate. Recent functional magnetic resonance imaging (fMRI) work with adults also has highlighted anterior cingulate cortex in regulation of HR during effortful cognitive processing (Critchley et al., 2003; Luu & Posner, 2003). Thus, functioning of the anterior cingulate cortex may be manifested neuropsychologically in the HR response.

Recently, Posner and colleagues (Bush et al., 2000) have proposed that the attentional skills associated with the executive attention system and anterior cingulate serve to regulate both cognitive and emotional processing. Traditionally, the anterior cingulate has been viewed as having two major subdivisions to separately process cognitive and emotional information. The cognitive subdivision has interconnections with the prefrontal cortex, parietal cortex, and premotor and supplementary motor areas. This subdivision is activated by tasks that involve choice selection from conflicting information, which includes many working memory tasks (Bush et al., 2000). The emotion subdivision has interconnections with the orbitofrontal cortex, amygdala, and hippocampus, among other brain areas. This subdivision is activated by affect-related tasks, such as the emotional Stroop (Bush et al., 2000) and the classic odd-ball task using aversive photos that vary in emotional valence (Fichtenholtz et al., 2004). It appears that there is suppression of the affective subdivision during cognitive processing and likewise with the cognitive subdivision during affective processing; however, recent studies with adults point toward some interaction between cognition and emotion on Stroop-like or similar decision-making tasks (Bush et al., 2000). Thus, when considering the functionality and the neural connectivity of the anterior cingulate, the cognitive and emotion processes that were traditionally considered to be independent and separable can readily be understood as intricately bound and inseparable, especially on certain types of tasks. We propose that working memory and emotion regulation tasks can be used to investigate the development of these processes during infancy and early childhood.

WORKING MEMORY

The construct of working memory (Baddeley, 1986, 2000) has been the focus of a great deal of attention in the adult cognitive literature, and with good reason. Working memory is an essential component for everyday adult cognition because it underlies higher-order cognitive processes such as reasoning, planning, cognitive control, problem solving, and decision making (Logie, 1993). Working memory is needed when relating multiple pieces of information held in one's mind to each other or when inhibiting an interfering response while keeping information in one's mind (Diamond et al., 1997). Importantly, individual difference measures of working memory in adulthood are predictive of language comprehension, learning, and fluid intelligence (see Kane & Engle, 2002, for a review). Much less attention has been given to the *development* of working memory. Knowledge of the development of working memory is crucial, however. In a recent study of 7-year-old children, working memory was associated with English and mathematics achievement in school. Likewise, children with poor working memory performance at age 5 scored poorly on reading assessments at age 8 (Gathercole, Tiffany, Brisco, & Thorn, 2005). Clearly, there is a need to examine the development of this cognitive construct from its earliest origins and include in this examination possible contributors to individual differences in the development of working memory.

Our current research includes a longitudinal study that is unique in that it is the first to examine the development of working memory, and individual differences associated with that development, across the developmental time periods of infancy and early childhood. The only infancy-to-childhood study of the development of working memory of which we know is reported by Diamond and colleagues (1997). That project, however, had three groups of research participants—infants, toddlers, preschoolers—with short-term longitudinal methodology within each age grouping. Age-appropriate working memory tasks were used with each group. Thus, infants (6–12 months of age) performed the A-not-B task; toddlers (15–30 months of age) did A-not-B with invisible displacement; preschoolers (3½–7 years of age) did the day–night Stroop-like task. Within each age grouping, increases in performance were noted across age. That is, striking age-related performance with each developmental period was reported, but no across-development period assessments were made. We have argued that within-subjects studies are essential for the examination of individual differences in working memory performance because individual differences in the efficiency of brain functioning affect cognitive outcome (Bell & Adams, 1999). Our current longitudinal work provides that within-subjects data across infancy and early childhood. We highlight our protocol for the toddler assessment in a later section of this chapter.

Neuropsychology of Working Memory

Within the last decade there has been increasing focus on frontal lobe processing associated with working memory during infancy and childhood (e.g., Bell, 2001; Casey et al., 1995; Diamond et al., 1997; Roberts & Pennington, 1996). Developmental neuroscience research has demonstrated that individual differences in EEG activity recorded from frontal scalp locations are associated with performance on working memory tasks during both infancy and early childhood. We have reported that at 8 months of age, only infants with high performance on an infant working memory task (looking A-not-B) exhibit changes in frontal EEG power values from baseline to task; infants with low performance show no change in EEG from baseline to task (Bell, 2001, 2002, 2006). Changes in EEG activity from baseline to task are assumed to be indicative of changes in cortical functioning associated with task performance (Pivik et al., 1993). We have reported similar findings with 4½-year-old children; that is, children with high performance on a preschool working memory task (day–night Stroop) exhibit higher overall (baseline and task) EEG power values at the frontal regions than children with low performance on the same task (Wolfe & Bell, 2004). This focus on frontal activity is in agreement with Engle's model of working memory that has attentional control as the source of individual differences in working memory performance.

Working Memory and Attentional Control

In our research program, we focus on the construct of working memory as developed by Engle and colleagues (Engle, Kane, & Tuholski, 1999; Kane & Engle, 2002). Engle defines working memory as a system consisting of those highly activated long-term memory traces that are active above threshold as short-term memory representational components in the prefrontal cortex. Included in this characterization of working memory are the procedures and skills necessary to achieve and maintain that activation, as well as a limited-capacity, domain-free controlled attention component. This executive attention component is perhaps the most intriguing part of Engle's conceptualization of working memory because it is noted by Engle to be comparable to the construct of executive attention described by Posner's executive attention system (Engle et al., 1999).

The attentional capacity highlighted by Engle and colleagues is the capability of maintaining short-term memory representations in the presence of interference or response competition. Without this interference, information, goals, and response plans are easily retrieved from long-term memory. In the face of interference, however, it is likely that incorrect information and inaccurate responses are retrieved (Kane & Engle, 2002). Thus, this executive attention component is not needed for all cognitive processing but is called into action in circumstances that require inhibition of prepotent responses, error monitoring and correction, and decision making and planning (Engle et al., 1999). As would be expected, this domain-free executive attention ability can be used to predict performance on tasks requiring cognitive control, such as working memory and inhibitory control tasks (Kane & Engle, 2002).

It is precisely the predictive ability of attention that is the focus of Engle's research. Individual differences in executive attention, called "working memory capacity" by Engle and colleagues (Engle et al., 1999; Kane & Engle, 2002), are associated with a wide variety of cognitive abilities, including general fluid intelligence (Engle et al., 1999). We should emphasize that individual differences in executive attention are revealed only in situations that encourage or require controlled attention. Thus, the individual differences perspective in Engle's model reflects the ability of the individual to apply activation to short-term memory representations, to bring these representations into focus and to maintain them, and to do so in the face of interference or distraction (Engle et al., 1999; Kane & Engle, 2002). This suggests that individuals high in this controlled attention ability are more effective at blocking distracting, task-irrelevant information and maintaining a focus on pertinent information than individuals low in attention. Indeed, individuals ranked low on this attentional ability are more likely to break focus and orient to an irrelevant, attention-capturing external cue (Unsworth, Schrock, & Engle, 2004). Based on human and nonhuman primate literatures, Engle has hypothesized that individual differences in attentional control (i.e., working memory capacity) are associated with individual differences in the functioning of the prefrontal cortex (Engle et al., 1999; Kane & Engle, 2002). Engle asserts that his model is appropriate for research with children (Engle et al., 1999). Indeed, we use Engle's model of working memory because it includes the processes associated with controlled attention, such as inhibitory control of prepotent responses, specifies the role of the prefrontal cortex in the process of working memory, and allows for individual differences in working memory based on both the capacity for controlled attention and differences in prefrontal functioning. Researchers have begun to demonstrate some associations between attentional control characteristics and cognitive tasks involving working memory and inhibitory control in preschool children (Davis, Bruce, & Gunnar, 2002; Gerardi-Caulton, 2000; Wolfe & Bell, 2004). Researchers also have begun to demonstrate associations among these frontal lobe, executive function tasks and emotion-related aspects of self-regulation (Davis et al., 2002; Wolfe & Bell, 2004). It is the emotion-related aspects of self-regulation to which we now turn.

EMOTION REGULATION

Just as attentional control and working memory display dramatic developments during infancy and early childhood, so does emotion regulation (Calkins, 2004; Eisenberg, Smith, Sadovsky, & Spinrad, 2004; Kopp & Neufeld, 2003). Developmental changes in emotion regulation are demonstrated as the infant progresses from almost total dependence on caregivers for regulation of emotion state to independent self-regulation of emotions (Calkins, 2004). According to Kopp (1982, 1989; Kopp & Neufeld, 2003), early emotion regulation is influenced mainly by innate physiological mechanisms. Beginning around 3 months of age, some voluntary control of arousal is evident, with more purposeful control evident by 12 months, when developing motor skills and communication behaviors allow for interactions with caregivers. During the second year, infants begin to utilize language skills and increasing impulse control (Kopp, 1982, 1989), thus making the transition from passive to active methods of emotion regulation (Calkins, 2004). Kopp (1989) considers this emotion self-control to fully emerge between ages 3 and 4 years of age. Rothbart has suggested that the changes in self-control occurring between ages 3 and 4 years are related to the executive attention system (Rothbart et al., 2004).

Part of executive attention is the dimension of temperament known as effortful control, which Rothbart has defined as the ability to inhibit a dominant response in order to perform a subdominant response (Rothbart & Bates, 1998). Regulatory aspects of temperament typically are viewed as driven by individual differences in arousal and emotional reactivity (Rothbart et al., 2004). Effortful control, however, represents a behavioral system emerging in the second year that allows for voluntary control of arousal and emotion. Rothbart and colleagues (1994) have posited that the development of executive attention might underlie the effortful control of emotion. The developmental literature supports that association (Kochanska et al., 2000; Kochanska & Knaach, 2003).

Eisenberg's concept of emotion-related regulation (Eisenberg, Spinrad, & Smith, 2004) is similar to Rothbart's temperament construct of effortful control in its focus on voluntary control of emotion. Emotion-related regulation appears to also be strongly associated with attentional control and this type of regulation can occur prior, during, or after the elicitation of emotion.

Although there appears to be convergence among the emotion regulatory constructs highlighted by Rothbart, Eisenberg, Kopp, and Calkins in the preceding paragraphs, this appears not to be the case throughout the developmental literature. Recently, Cole, Martin, and Dennis (2004) discussed the lack of specificity in the developmental literature regarding the construct of emotion regulation. Such varied behaviors have been labeled as emotion regulation that many researchers have questioned the utility of the construct. In a paper that argued for the scientific utility of this developmental process, Cole and colleagues proposed a very specific definition of emotion regulation. To be specific, the term *emotion regulation* refers to two types of regulatory processes (Cole et al., 2004). Emotions can organize a child's thinking, learning, and action; in other words, outcomes related to activation of an emotion can be affected ("emotions as regulating"). Likewise, thinking, learning, and action can modify emotions; in other words, these factors can cause changes in an emotion ("emotions as regulated"). Thus, from Cole's point of view, emotion regulation can only be examined during an emotion experience, unlike Eisenberg's notion of emotion-related regulation, which also can be examined prior and after emotion elicitation. Although the Cole definition of emotion regulation incorporates cognition–emotion interactions, there is less emphasis on self-conscious, voluntary regulation of emotion.

Neuropsychology of Emotion Regulation

Similar to research on individual differences in working memory task performance, work focusing on emotions and emotional regulation has demonstrated individual differences in frontal EEG activity. Developmental evidence seems to suggest that electrophysiological differences in emotion regulation may be evident as early as the first year of life. Fox and colleagues have shown that infants who cry at maternal separation are more likely to exhibit right frontal EEG activation during rest (Bell & Fox, 1994; Davidson & Fox, 1989; Fox, Calkins, & Bell, 1994; Fox & Davidson, 1987). In addition, infants who display negative affect and high motor activity at 4 months of age are reported to exhibit right frontal activation at 9 months and inhibited behavior at 14 months (Calkins, Fox, & Marshall, 1996). For many infants, these individual differences in emotional regulation and EEG activation persist throughout the preschool years (Fox, Henderson, Rubin, Calkins, & Schmidt, 2001) and into middle childhood and beyond (Schmidt, Fox, Schulkin, & Gold, 1999). Fox (1994) has developed a model of differential activation of the left and right frontal cortices that relates differential asymmetry patterns to individual differences in emotion reactivity and emotion regulation. Fox (1994) proposes both cortical and subcortical influences on these brain electrical patterns. Thus, different levels of regulatory ability may be associated with frontal lobe activation asymmetries.

Measures of heart rate variability (HRV) and its variations of respiratory sinus arrhythmia and vagal tone have been linked to emotional reactivity and regulation. Infants with higher HRV are more emotionally expressive and reactive (Calkins et al., 2002; Porges, Doussard-Roosevelt, & Maiti, 1994; Stifter & Fox, 1990; Stifter, Spinrad, & Braungart-Ricker, 1999). This reactivity produces distress and irritability. As regulatory abilities develop, due to development of the executive attention system, the reactivity can lead to concentration when interest is paramount or to more expressive reactivity when other situations take precedent (Porges et al., 1994; Ruff & Rothbart, 1996). The suppression of HRV may be associated with coping behaviors involving attentional control during both infancy and early childhood (Bar-Haim, Fox, VanMeenen, & Marshall, 2004; Rothbart, Posner, & Boylan, 1990). Thus, individual differences in attention and the regulation of emotion may be mediated by autonomic activity (Ruff & Rothbart, 1996).

Emotion Regulation and Attentional Control

As previously noted, much of the neuropsychological work examining emotion regulation has conceptually linked developing regulatory abilities with development of the executive attention system. Ruff and Rothbart (1996) consider attention part of the larger construct of self-regulation, with individual differences in attention impacting the degree of success in the development of self-regulation. Developmentalists have followed suit by examining emotion regulation as a correlate of effortful control (e.g., Calkins & Fox, 2002), a special class of voluntary regulatory processes that develop with maturation of attentional mechanisms (Posner & Rothbart, 2000; Rothbart & Bates, 1998). Thus, in the developmental literature, regulation and attentional control are intricately linked.

RESEARCH ON CONNECTIONS BETWEEN COGNITION AND EMOTION

Our most current research is based on the general hypothesis that attentional control is critical in defining the developmental trajectories of both working memory and emotion regulation during infancy and early childhood. Specifically, we are testing the two models noted at the beginning of this chapter. Thus, one hypothesis is that emotion regulation mediates the relation between temperamentally-based attentional control and working memory (see Figure 14.1 top). The alternate hypothesis is that attentional control directly influences both emotion regulation and working memory and that emotion regulation and working memory become increasingly correlated with development (see Figure 14.1 bottom). We are testing these hypotheses with a longitudinal protocol that has assessments at 5 months, 10 months and 2, 3, and 4 years of age. Our previous longitudinal work incorporated assessments at 8 months and 4½ years (Wolfe & Bell, in press) and did not allow us to track the many changes that occur in working memory, emotion regulation, and attentional control with early development (e.g., Diamond et al., 1997). We are currently focusing on the 2-year data collection point for a cohort of 106 infants and parents who were recruited from nearby communities. All the children were healthy, full-term newborns. The average age of the parents at the child's birth was 30 for the mothers and 33 for the fathers, with no teenage parents in the sample. All parents have at least a high school diploma, and 78% of the mothers and 74% of the fathers have a college degree. Matching census data for the local geographic area, 89% of the children are Caucasian.

One of the greatest challenges in incorporating a 2-year assessment into our longitudinal protocol—aside from skillfully negotiating the application of the EEG and HR electrodes—involves administering tasks that are comparable to the infant tasks already experienced in the longitudinal investigation (i.e., tap the same cognitive, attention, and emotion skills of interest) and that the children understand and attempt. Because our longitudinal study will continue on to the preschool years, it also is crucial that these tasks likewise provide a smooth transition from our infant tasks to our preschool tasks. This section of the chapter highlights some of the ways in which we are measuring working memory, emotion regulation, and attentional control in our toddler sample at age 2 years. We are still in the midst of data collection, but we report some very preliminary behavioral findings on the 83 children we have seen thus far at the age two assessment. Although we do not report any EEG and HR data here, we do record EEG and HR during the working memory and attentional control tasks. We utilize emotion regulation tasks that allow the child the freedom to move about the room; thus, electrophysiological recordings are not available for emotion regulation.

Working Memory

As previously mentioned, our research focuses on the construct of working memory that includes controlled attention (Diamond, 2002; Engle et al., 1999; Kane & Engle, 2002). In all our infant work, we (Bell, 2001, 2002, 2005; Bell & Adams, 1999) have examined this working memory process with the A-not-B task (Diamond et al., 1997). Likewise, we have examined these cognitive skills in our previous preschool samples (ages 3½–4½ years) with age-appropriate working memory tasks (Wolfe & Bell, 2004), such as the Stroop-like day–night task (Diamond et al., 1997; Gerstadt, Hong, & Diamond, 1994), the tapping task (Diamond et al., 1997; Diamond & Taylor, 1996), the yes–no task (Wolfe & Bell, 2004), and the dimensional change card sort task (DCCS; Zelazo, Muller, Frye, & Marcovitch, 2003). All these tasks, however, are inappropriate for use with toddlers in their standard forms because they require language skills that are too advanced for most 2-year-old children. Thus, according to the developmental literature, the A-not-B task for infants is considered too easy for toddlers (although see Espy, Kaufmann,

McDiarmid, & Glisky, 1999), and the day–night types of tasks are too difficult for the 2- and 3-year-old age groups (see Diamond & Taylor, 1996; Gerstadt et al., 1994).

In our current research with 2-year-old children, we are utilizing a version of the A-not-B task that is appropriate for toddlers. As the child sits in a high chair and watches, we administer a version of this classic hiding task that incorporates elements of the invisible displacement strategy demonstrated by Diamond with toddlers (Diamond et al., 1997) and the A-not-B procedure used by Espy with preschoolers (Espy et al., 1999). First, we hide a ball under a colorful cup and move the cup to one side of the table. Next, we use a white screen to occlude the toddler's sight of the table while placing an empty cup of the same color as the hiding cup on the other side of the table. During the placement of the screen we count a 5-second delay period out loud. We do this to increase the working memory time load requirement (Pelphrey et al., 2004) and add an inference component. After the delay is counted, the screen is lifted, revealing the two cups, and the child is asked to look or point to the ball's location. Each child receives an initial trial with only the cup covering the ball in order to ensure that the gist of the task is understood and then the child receives a series of test trials with both cups where the ball is hidden twice on the same side before being hidden on the reverse side. As can be seen in Table 14.1, we are seeing a wide range of individual differences in performance on the A-not-B working memory task. This gives us confidence that this version of the task is age appropriate. For the preliminary analyses re-

TABLE 14.1. Descriptive Cognition and Emotion Data from 83 Children in the 2-Year Protocol

Task	Behavior ("best performance")	% of children
A-not-B working memory	1. No success on same-side trials with 4-second delay	7%
	2. Success on one same-side trial with 4-second delay	19%
	3. Success on two same-side trials with 4-second delay	46%
	4. Success on same-side and reversal trials with 4-second delay	28%
Mommy/me working memory	1. Refusal to participate	23%
	2. Success on naming control trials only	41%
	3. Success on teaching trials only	25%
	4. Success on test trials 1 and 2 (but not 3 and 4)	10%
	5. Success on test trials 1 through 4	1%
Crayon delay regulation	1. Colored on paper	42%
	2. Dumped out crayons	9%
	3. Picked up crayon box	5%
	4. Touched crayon box	17%
	5. Touched paper only	6%
	6. Did not touch crayons or paper	21%

ported below, performance on the A-not-B task is scored as percentage of correct responses.

We also utilize the Mommy/me task, a working memory task that is comparable to the preschool day–night task (Diamond et al., 1997; Gerstadt et al., 1994) and yes–no task (Wolfe & Bell, 2004). This is a task we created to use with 2-year-old children. Diamond and colleagues have stated that the day–night Stoop-like task is too difficult for 3-year-olds (Gerstadt et al., 1994). We reasoned that photos of mother and self might be more interesting for younger children than drawings of a sun and a moon, as used in the day–night task. This increased interest might allow us to assess working memory performance in the day–night Stroop-like manner. Specifically, in the Mommy/me task, a child is instructed to say "Mommy" to a Polaroid picture of herself and to say her own name to a Polaroid picture of her mother. Thus, like the day–night and yes–no tasks, the child is required to remember two rules and to inhibit a dominant response. As the child sits in a high chair, the experimenter first asks the child to name the individuals in the photos as a check to determine what name the child uses for her mother and for herself (naming control trials). Then the experimenter explains the rules of the "silly backwards game" and assesses the child's understanding by prompting her to say "Mommy" to her own photo and her name to the picture of her mother (teaching trials). Then the experimenter administers four trails without prompts (test trials). Again, as can be seen in Table 14.1, we are seeing a wide range of individual differences in performance on the Mommy/me working memory task, including of course many 2-year-old children who refuse to participate. This allows us to use the Mommy/me task as a "baseline" working memory assessment to examine trajectories of development in working memory performance at ages 3 and 4 years.

Emotion Regulation

During the infant portion of our longitudinal study, we employed the toy removal and arm restraint (Calkins et al., 2002) procedures to elicit distress/frustration and subsequent emotion regulation behaviors in the infants. To measure frustration and regulation in toddlers, we are using the difficult puzzle task (Smith, Calkins, Kean, Anastopoulos, & Shelton, 2004). Mothers are asked to work with their children on a set of three puzzles of increasing difficulty with respect to number of pieces (8 pieces, 12 pieces, 26 pieces). After mother and child work together on the first two easier puzzles, the experimenter requests that the child complete the final puzzle in her own while mother reads a magazine. Attached to the magazine is a note instructing mother to ignore her child's bids for help on the puzzle. Although we have not yet begun to code the behaviors on this task, anecdotally we have seen a wide range of frustration and regulation on this task. This has ranged from quiet determination to complete the puzzle by oneself to yelling and shoving the puzzle off the table.

We also are using the crayon delay task to measure regulation with our 2-year-old children. Typically used as an assessment of self-regulation or inhibitory control (e.g., the phone task in Vaughn, Kopp, & Krakow, 1984), rather than of emotion regulation, delay tasks offer an opportunity to capture regulatory abilities in a relatively low-stress situation. In this task, the experimenter places a newly opened box of crayons on the table along with a blank sheet of paper. As the experimenter places these items in front of the child, she tells the child that the child is going to draw a picture with the new crayons. However, before the child touches the crayons the experimenter tells the child that she has to leave the room to gather the things for the last game they will play together. The experimenter instructs the child to not touch the crayons until she returns to the room. The child's behavior is coded for level of regulation (i.e., no touch, touches paper, touches box, touches crayons, picks up crayon, and colors) during this taxing task, along with latency to touch the crayons. The experimenter returns after 60 seconds. As shown in Table 14.1, there is a wide range of behaviors on this delay task, as 21% of the children thus far have waited and not touched the crayons and 42% have colored on the paper. The remaining children touched only the paper, touched the crayons, picked up the crayon box, or dumped out the crayons. In the preliminary analyses reported below, the crayon delay latency is the time in seconds at which the child touched the crayons, with no touching scored as 60 seconds.

Perhaps our best measure of emotion regulation with this 2-year protocol is taken during the EEG and HR electrode application. Simply, we code whether or not the child accepts or rejects the electrodes. Other psychophysiological researchers who work with children have noted this procedure (Stifter et al., 1999). This measure of emotion regulation is particularly valuable in that it takes place in a stressful situation for the child—the EEG cap is a novel experience and arguably a stressful one for most 2-year-olds. Rodriguez and colleagues (2005) suggest that behaviors in a high-stress situation are more reflective of the child's regulatory abilities compared to a low stress situation. Very preliminary analyses of our current work, dividing the toddlers into two groups based on their willingness to wear the EEG and HR electrodes (approximately 73% of the children are accepting the EEG cap for the recording session), is indicating that accepting the electrodes is associated with inhibitory control abilities as measured by our warmup task pig–bull, modeled after the classic Simon-says task (Carlson, 2005). We will compare inhibitory or regulatory behaviors on the crayon delay and electrode acceptance tasks to behaviors on our third emotion regulation procedure, which involves the difficult puzzle. This puzzle procedure also allows for possible coding of maternal interactive style during a task that is frustrating for the child (Calkins et al., 2002).

As a final indicator of regulatory abilities, mothers are completing the Early Childhood Behavior Questionnaire (ECBQ; Putnam, Garstein, & Rothbart, 2006) at home prior to the lab visit. In the preliminary analyses we report next, we focus on the Inhibitory Control and Impulsivity scales of this temperament measure. Children who score high in Inhibitory Control are rated by their mothers as having the capacity to stop, moderate, or refrain from a behavior under instruction. Children who score high on Impulsivity are rated by their mothers as quickly initiating responses.

Attentional Control

Finally, we used a brief video to assess attentional control when the children in our sample were infants, but we quickly discovered that we need to employ a video to assist us during EEG and HR electrode application with the 2-year-old children. Thus, we are using a moving, novel toy for our attentional control assessment and we are coding for voluntary sustained attention to the toy. The experimenter hands the child the toy and instructs the child to hold and look at the toy without talking. The child has the toy for a maximum of 120 seconds and we code how long the child attends to the toy before discarding it or attending to other things in the room. We have just begun the coding of this task and are noting that all children will comply to the "sit and look without talking" instructions for a period of time, which appears to range from about 30 seconds to 120 seconds. After that, children typically will talk to mother about the toy, shove the toy off the table, or continue to physically orient to the toy but shift eye gaze to a nearby location. The children who shift eye gaze are especially intriguing, as it is our initial interpretation that they are attempting to comply with the experimenter's instructions but simply lose interest in the toy. Thus, we are coding not only the length attentional control but also behavior when attention to the novel toy ends. It may be that children who attempt to comply by shifting eye gaze may also be the children who exhibit more efficient strategies on our on our emotion regulation tasks.

We are utilizing two attentional scales from the ECBQ. Children who score high in attentional focus are rated by their mothers as being capable of sustained duration of orienting on an object of attention and as being capable of resisting distraction. Children who score high in attentional shifting are rated by their mothers as having the ability to transfer attentional focus from one activity or task to another.

Preliminary Findings

We are unable to test our hypotheses until all visits are complete and all coding is finalized, but we can examine relations among some of the variables of interest. Initial correlations among the A-not-B working memory task, the crayon delay regulatory task, and four ECBQ scales are shown in Table 14.2. We examined one-tailed correlations because we hypothesized the direction of the relations between the variables of interest. As expected, the crayon delay task is related to the ECBQ Inhibitory Control scale. Children with better compliance on the task (i.e., longer latency to touch) are rated by their mothers as higher on inhibitory control.

TABLE 14.2. Correlations between Cognitive and Emotion Regulatory-Type Measures

	A-not-B % correct	Crayon delay latency to touch	ECBQ attention focusing	ECBQ attention shifting	ECBQ impulsivity	ECBQ inhibitory control
A-not-B % correct	—	.16†			–26*	.24*
Crayon delay latency to touch		—				.27**
ECBQ attention focusing			—	.37***	–.18*	.29**
ECBQ attention shifting				—		.46***
ECBQ impulsivity					—	–.25*
ECBQ inhibitory control						—

Note. One-tailed tests.
†p <. 10; *p < .05; **p <. 01; ***p < .001.

Performance on the A-not-B working memory task is related to performance on crayon delay and to ECBQ scales. Higher performance on A-not-B is associated better compliance on crayon delay (i.e., longer latency to touch). The association between working memory and regulation is also seen with respect to the ECBQ scales. Higher performance on A-not-B is associated with lower impulsivity and high inhibitory control as rated by mother (see also Lee, Vaughn, & Kopp, 1983, for similar findings).

FUTURE DIRECTIONS

Many other factors in the developmental literature have been linked to individual differences in early outcome. Two factors in particular have major implications for the constructs of interest in our longitudinal research: maternal interactive style and child language. We briefly note how each factor may be associated with working memory, emotional regulation, and attentional control. Thus, the inclusion of maternal interactive style and child language would be of great benefit in the study of developing cognition–emotion relations in early development.

Maternal Interactive Style

Maternal interactive style has been shown to be related to emotion regulatory behaviors in infants and young children (Calkins, 2004; Calkins, Hungerford, & Dedmon, 2004; Calkins & Johnson, 1998; Diener, Mangelsdorf, McHale, & Frosch, 2002; Rodriguez et al., 2005), as well as to cognitive behaviors in early development (Landry, Smith, & Swank, 2003; Stams, Juffer, & van IJzendoorn, 2002). The view that nurturing and supportive maternal responses is vital for healthy psychosocial growth is incorporated into classic psychological theories. Although the environment, and specifically the caregiving environment, has been given such an essential role in early social development (Fox et al., 2005), not much attention has been given to the role of that same caregiving environment to the development of complex cognition. In the work that has been done, the focus has been on the effects of maternal behaviors on recognition memory (Miceli, Whiteman, Borkowski, Braungart-Rieker, & Mitchell, 1998). No work has examined the effect of caregiving on the development of attentional control or on working memory.

Colombo and Saxon (2002) have proposed, however, that infant cognitive status (e.g., length of attention or ability to remember over a length of time) interacts with some aspect of caregiver interaction across development. Over time, these interactive processes influence the child's cognitive outcome. Similarly, it may be that by supporting infants in the development of attentional skill, in part to relieve early infant distress (Ruff & Rothbart, 1996), caregivers are contributing to the attentional skills associated with later cognitive processing dependent on attentional control, such as working memory. This parent–child interaction may manifest itself differently in early childhood, when the relief of child frustration is paramount to a parent's interactions with young children (Calkins et al., 2002, 2004; Kopp, 1989, 1992). These parent–child interactions may likewise be associated with later cognitive processing in that they allow the child to develop self-regulatory skills essential before cognitions requiring cognitive control can occur. Thus, maternal behavior may also be essential for cognition, although how this is manifested across the infancy to early childhood time periods has not been investigated.

Child Language

It has been suggested that the development of language, along with the continued development of the frontal cortex, may underlie early childhood advances in voluntary control of behavior and action (Ruff & Rothbart, 1996). An association between language and self-regulatory aspects of development, especially those that involve attentional control, has been reported (Kaler & Kopp, 1990). It is this capacity of language to assist with regulatory aspects of development, especially those involving attentional control (Kopp, 1989), that make language a likely correlate of not only emotion development but cognitive development as well.

Developmental research indicates that there is an association between memory and language. Recognition memory scores during infancy are correlated with language comprehension and expression at ages 2½, 3, and 4 years (Rose, Feldman, Wallace, & Cohen, 1991). In children at 4 years of age, those with high working memory abilities produce more complex spoken language than children with low working memory abilities (Wolfe & Bell, 2004). Thus, language skills appear to contribute to the developmental trajectories of both cognition and emotion.

We did ask the mothers of our 2-year-olds to complete the MacAuthur–Bates Communicative Development Inventory. This checklist is used to document the child's production of spoken words and analyze early phases of grammar, specifically the complexity of the child's multiword utterances. We hypothesized that children with more total spoken words would be rated by their mothers as having less impulsivity and greater inhibitory control. We also hypothesized these children would have greater attentional focusing and attentional shifting. Thus far our hypotheses are supported, except those concerning impulsivity (see Table 14.3). We have similar hypotheses with respect to the complexity of utterances and the mean length of the utterances (MLU), with similar results (see Table 14.3).

FINAL REMARKS

We have proposed that the examination of early socioemotional development is incomplete without simultaneous consideration of changes in cognition. In this chapter, we have proposed that the investigation of associations between cognition and emotion is essential to any conceptualization of development and have illustrated our supposition with the examples of working memory and emotion regulation, with attentional control as the integrative mechanism

TABLE 14.3. Correlations between Language and ECBQ Temperament Measures

	ECBQ attention focusing	ECBQ attention shifting	ECBQ impulsivity	ECBQ inhibitory control
McArthur–Bates complex words	.40***	.41***	—	.41***
McArthur–Bates total words	.33**	.42***	—	.45***
McArthur–Bates mean length utterance	.30**	.39***	—	.32**

Note. One-tailed tests.

*p < .05; **p < .01; ***p < .001.

for these two constructs. We also summarized our current work with 2-year-old children and highlighted very preliminary data on cognition–emotion relations. These data represent the third wave of a five-wave longitudinal study examining the interrelations between cognition and emotion across infancy and early childhood.

The examination of working memory and emotion regulation in infants and toddlers is valuable in understanding the early developmental trajectories of these important psychological constructs. In school-age children, working memory performance is associated with school achievement, including reading and math. Emotion regulation is essential for appropriate and adaptive social behavior. Because of these critical outcomes, there is a need to track the development of these cognitive and emotion processes from their early origins and include in this examination their integration across development.

REFERENCES

Baddeley, A. D. (1986). *Working memory.* New York: Oxford University Press.

Baddeley, A. (2000). The episodic buffer: A new component of working memory? *Trends in Cognitive Sciences, 4,* 417–423.

Bar-Haim, Y., Fox, N. A., VanMeenen, K. M., & Marshall P. J. (2004). Children's narratives and patterns of cardiac reactivity. *Developmental Psychobiology, 44,* 238–249.

Baumeister, R. F., & Vohs, K. D. (2004). *Handbook of self-regulation: Research, theory, and applications.* New York: Guilford Press.

Bell, M. A. (2001). Brain electrical activity associated with cognitive processing during a looking version of the A-not-B object permanence task. *Infancy, 2,* 311–330.

Bell, M. A. (2002). Infant 6–9 Hz synchronization during a working memory task. *Psychophysiology, 39,* 450–458.

Bell, M. A. (2006). *The effects of temperament on cognitive processing at 8 months.* Manuscript under review.

Bell, M. A., & Adams, S. E. (1999). Equivalent performance on looking and reaching versions of the A-not-B task at 8 months of age. *Infant Behavior and Development, 22,* 221–235.

Bell, M. A., & Fox, N. A. (1994). Brain development over the first year of life: Relations between electroencephalographic frequency and coherence and cognitive and affective behaviors. In G. Dawson & K. W. Fischer (Eds.), *Human behavior and the developing brain* (pp. 314–345). New York: Guilford Press.

Bell, M. A., & Wolfe, C. D. (2004). Emotion and cognition: An intricately bound developmental process. *Child Development, 75,* 366–370.

Blair, C. (2002). School readiness: Integrating cognition and emotion in a neurobiological conceptualization of children's functioning at school entry. *American Psychologist, 57,* 111–127.

Bush, G., Luu, P., & Posner, M. I. (2000). Cognitive and emotional influences in anterior cingulated cortex. *Trends in Cognitive Sciences, 4,* 215–222.

Calkins, S. D. (2004). Early attachment processes and the development of emotional self-regulation. In R. F. Baumeister & K. D. Vohs (Eds.), *Handbook of self-regulation: Research, theory, and applications* (pp. 324–339). New York: Guilford Press.

Calkins, S. D., Dedmon, S. E., Gill, K. L., Lomax, L. E., & Johnson, L. M. (2002). Frustration In infancy: Implications for emotion regulation, physiological processes, and temperament. *Infancy, 3,* 175–197.

Calkins, S. D., & Fox, N. A. (2002). Self-regulatory processes in early personality development: A multilevel approach to the study of childhood social withdrawal and aggression. *Development and Psychopathololgy, 14,* 477–498.

Calkins, S. D., Fox, N. A., & Marshall, T. R. (1996). Behavioral and physiological antecedents of inhibited and uninhibited behavior. *Child Development, 67,* 523–540.

Calkins, S. D., Hungerford, A., & Dedmon, S. E. (2004). Mothers' interactions with temperamentally frustrated infants. *Infant Mental Health Journal, 25,* 219–239.

Calkins, S. D., & Johnson, M. C. (1998). Toddler regulation of distress to frustrating events: Temperamental and material correlates. *Infant Behavior and Development, 21,* 379–395.

Carlson, S. M. (2005). Developmentally sensitive measures of executive function in preschool children. *Developmental Neuropsychology, 28,* 595–616.

Casey, B. J., Cohen, J. K., Jezzard, P., Turner, R., Noll, D. C., Trainor, R. J., et al. (1995). Activation of prefrontal cortex in children during a nonspatial working memory tsk with functional MRI. *NeuroImage, 2,* 221–229.

Cole, P. M., Martin, S. E., & Dennis, T. A. (2004). Emotion regulation as a scientific construct: Methodological challenges and directions for child development research. *Child Development, 75,* 317–333.

Colombo, J., Richman, W. A., Shaddy, D. J., Greenhoot, A. F., & Maikranz, J. M. (2001). Heart rate-defined phases of attention, look duration, and infant performance in the paired-comparison paradigm. *Child Development, 72,* 1605–1616.

Colombo, J., & Saxon, T. F. (2002). Infant attention and the development of cognition: Does the environment moderate continuity? In H. E. Fitzgerald, K. H. Karraker, & T. Luster (Eds.), *Infant development: Ecological perspectives* (pp. 35–60). Washington, DC: Garland Press.

Critchley, H. D., Mathias, C. J., Josephs, O., O'Doherty, J., Zanini, S., Dewar, B. K., et al. (2003). Human cingulated cortex and autonomic control: Converging neuroimaging and clinical evidence. *Brain, 126,* 2139–2152.

Davidson, R. J., & Fox, N. A. (1989). The relation between tonic EEG asymmetry and ten-month-old infant emotional responses to separation. *Journal of Abnormal Psychology, 98,* 127–131.

Davis, E. P., Bruce, J., & Gunnar, M. R. (2002). The anterior attention network: Associations with temperament and neuroendocrine activity in 6–year-old children. *Developmental Psychobiology, 40,* 43–56.

Derryberry, D., & Rothbart, M. K. (1997). Reactive and effortful processes in the organization of temperament. *Development and Psychopathology, 9,* 633–652.

Diamond, A. (2002). Normal development of prefrontal cortex from birth to young adulthood: Cognitive functions, anatomy, and biochemistry. In D. T. Stuss, & R. T. Knight (Eds.), *Principles of frontal lobe function* (pp. 466–503). London: Oxford University Press.

Diamond, A., Prevor, M. B., Callender, G., & Druin, D. P. (1997). Prefrontal cortex cognitive deficits in children treated early and continuously for PKU. *Monographs of the Society for Research in Child Development, 62*(4, Serial No. 252).

Diamond, A., & Taylor, C. (1996). Development of an aspect of executive control: Development of the abilities to remember what I said and to "Do as I say, not as I do." *Developmental Psychobiology, 29,* 315–334.

Diener, M. L., Mangelsdorf, S. C., McHale, J. L., & Frosch, C. A. (2002). Infants' behavioral strategies for emotion regulation with fathers and mothers: Associations with emotional expressions and attachment quality. *Infancy, 3,* 153–174.

Eisenberg, N., Smith, C. L., Sadovsky, A., & Spinrad, T. L. (2004). Effortful control: Relations with emotion regulation, adjustment, and socialization in childhood. In R. F. Baumeister & K. D. Vohs (Eds.), *Handbook of self-regulation: Research, theory, and applications* (pp. 259–282). New York: Guilford Press.

Eisenberg, N., Spinrad, T. L., & Smith, C. L. (2004). Emotion-related regulation: Its conceptualization, relations to social functioning, and socialization. In P. Philippot & R. S. Feldman (Eds.), *The regulation of emotion* (pp. 277–306). Mahwah, NJ: Erlbaum.

Engle, R. W., Kane, M. J., & Tuholski, S. W. (1999). Individual differences in working memory capacity and what they tell us about controlled attention, general fluid intelligence, and functions of the prefrontal cortex. In A. Miyake & P. Shah (Eds.), *Models of working memory:*

Mechanisms of active maintenance and executive control (pp. 102–134). New York: Cambridge University Press.

Espy, K. A., Kaufmann, P. M., McDiarmid, M. D., & Glisky, M. L. (1999). Executive functioning in preschool children: Performance on A-not-B and other delayed response format tasks. *Brain and Cognition, 41,* 178–199.

Fichtenholtz, H. M., Dean, H. L., Dillon, D. G., Yamasaki, H., McCarthy, G., & LaBar, K. S. (2004). Emotion–attention network interactions during visual oddball task. *Cognitive Brain Research, 20,* 67–80.

Fox, N. A. (1994). Dynamic cerebral processes underlying emotion regulation. In N. A. Fox (Ed.), The development of emotion regulation: Biological and behavioral considerations. *Monographs of the Society for Research in Child Development, 59*(2–3, Serial No. 240), 152–166.

Fox, N. A., & Calkins, S. D. (2003). The development of self-control of emotion: Intrinsic and extrinsic influences. *Motivation and Emotion, 27,* 7–26.

Fox, N. A., Calkins, S. D., & Bell, M. A. (1994). Neural plasticity and development in the first two years of life: Evidence from cognitive and socio-emotional domains of research. *Development and Psychopathology, 6,* 677–698.

Fox, N. A., & Davidson, R. J. (1987). EEG asymmetry in ten-month-old infants in response to approach of a stranger and maternal separation. *Developmental Psychology, 23,* 233–240.

Fox, N. A., Henderson, H. A., Marshall, P. J., Nichols, K. E., & Ghera, M. M. (2005). Behavioral inhibition: Linking biology and behavior within a developmental framework. *Annual Review of Psychology, 56,* 235–262.

Fox, N. A., Henderson, H. A., Rubin, K. H., Calkins, S. D., & Schmidt, L. A. (2001). Continuity and discontinuity of behavioral inhibition and exuberance: psychophysiological and behavioral influences across the first four years of life. *Child Development, 72,* 1–21.

Gathercole, S. E., Tiffany, C., Briscoe, J., & Thorn, A. (2005). Developmental consequences of poor phonological short-term memory function in childhood: A longitudinal study. *Journal of Child Psychology and Psychiatry, 46,* 598–611.

Gerardi-Caulton, G. (2000). Sensitivity to spatial conflict and the development of self-regulation in children 24–26 months of age. *Developmental Science, 3,* 397–404.

Gerstadt, C. L., Hong, Y. J., & Diamond, A. (1994). The relationship between cognition and action: Performance of children 3½–7 years on a Stroop-like day–night test. *Cognition, 53,* 129–153.

Gray, J. R. (2004). Integration of emotion and cognitive control. *Current Directions in Psychological Science, 13,* 46–48.

Kaler, S. R., & Kopp, C. B. (1990). Compliance and comprehension in very young toddlers. *Child Development, 61,* 1997–2003.

Kane, M. J., & Engle, R. W. (2002). The role of prefrontal cortex in working-memory capacity, executive attention, and general fluid intelligence: An individual-differences perspective. *Psychonomic Bulletin and Review, 9,* 637–671.

Keenan, T. (2002). Negative affect predicts performance on object permanence task. *Developmental Science, 5,* 65–71.

Kerr, A., & Zelazo, P. D. (2004). Development of "hot" executive function: The children's gambling task. *Brain and Cognition, 55,* 148–157.

Kochanska, G., & Knaach, A. (2003). Effortful control as a personality characteristic or young children: Antecedents, correlates, and consequences. *Journal of Personality, 71,* 1087–1112.

Kochanska, G., Murray, K. T., & Harlan, E. (2000). Effortful control in early childhood: Continuity and change, antecedents, and implications for social development. *Developmental Psychology, 36,* 220–232.

Kopp, C. B. (1982). Antecedents of self-regulation: A developmental perspective. *Developmental Psychology, 18,* 199–214.

Kopp, C. B. (1989). Regulation of distress and negative emotions: A developmental view. *Developmental Psychology, 25,* 343–354.

Kopp, C. B. (1992). Emotional distress and control in young children. In N. Eisenberg & R. A. Fabes

(Eds.), *Emotion and its regulation in early development* (pp. 41–56). San Francisco: Jossey-Bass.

Kopp, C. B., & Neufeld, S. J. (2003). Emotional development in infancy. In R. J. Davidson, K. R. Scherer, & H. H. Goldsmith (Eds.), *Handbook of affective science* (pp. 347–374). New York: Oxford University Press.

Landry, S. H., Smith, K. E., & Swank, P. R. (2003). The importance of parenting during early childhood for school-age development. *Developmental Neuropsychology, 24,* 559–591.

Lee, M., Vaughn B. D., & Kopp, C. B. (1983). Role of self-control in the performance of very young children on delayed-response memory for location task. *Developmental Psychology, 19,* 40–44.

Lewis, M. D., Koroshegyi, C., Douglas, L., & Kampe, K. (1997). Age-specific associations between emotional responses to separation and cognitive performance in infancy. *Developmental Psychology, 33,* 32–42.

Logie, R. H. (1993). Working memory in everyday cognition. In G. M. Davies & R. H. Logie (Eds.), *Memory in everyday life* (pp. 173–218). Amsterdam: Elsevier.

Luu, P., & Posner, M. I. (2003). Anterior cingulate cortex regulation of sympathetic activity. *Brain, 126,* 2119–2120.

Miceli, P. J., Whiteman, T. L., Borkowski, J. G., Braungart-Rieker, J. M., & Mitchell, D. W. (1998). Individual differences in infant information processing: The role of temperamental and maternal factors. *Infant Behavior and Development, 21,* 119–136.

Pelphrey, K. A., Reznick, J. S., Davis Goldman, B., Sasson, N., Morrow, J., Donahoe, A., et al. (2004). Development of visuospatial short-term memory in the second half of the 1st year. *Developmental Psychology, 40,* 836–851.

Pivik, R. T., Broughton, R. J., Coppola, R., Davidson, R. J., Fox, N. A., & Nuwer, M. R. (1993). Guidelines for the recording and quantitative analysis of electroencephalographic activity in research contexts. *Psychophysiology, 30,* 547–558.

Porges, S. W., Doussard-Roosevelt, J. A., & Maiti, A. K. (1994). Vagal tone and the physiological regulation of emotion. In N. A. Fox (Ed.), The development of emotion regulation: Biological and behavioral considerations. *Monographs of the Society for Research in Child Development, 59,*(3, Serial No. 240), 167–186.

Posner, M. I., & Rothbart, M. K. (2000). Developing mechanisms of self-regulation. *Development and Psychopathology, 12,* 427–441.

Putnam, S. P., Gartstein, M. A., & Rothbart, M. K. (2006). Measurement of fine-grained aspects of toddler temperament: The Early Childhood Behavior Questionnaire. *Infant Behavior and Development, 29,* 386–401.

Richards, J. E. (2004). The development of sustained attention in infants. In M. I. Posner (Ed.), *Cognitive neuroscience of attention* (pp. 342–356). New York: Guilford Press.

Richards, J. E., & Casey, B. J. (1992). Development of sustained visual attention in the human infant. In B. A. Campbell, H. Hayne, & R. Richardson (Eds.), *Attention and information processing in infants and adults* (pp. 30–60). Hillsdale, NJ: Erlbaum.

Richards, J. E., & Cronise, K. (2000). Extended visual fixation in the early preschool years: Look duration, heart rate changes, and attentional inertia. *Child Development, 71,* 602–620.

Richards, J. E., & Hunter, S. K. (1998). Attention and eye movements in young infants: Neural control and development. In J. E. Richards (Ed.), *Cognitive neuroscience of attention: A developmental perspective* (pp. 131–162). Mahwah, NJ: Erlbaum.

Roberts, R. J., & Pennington, B. F. (1996). An interactive framework for examining prefrontal cognitive processes. *Developmental Neuropsychology, 12,* 105–126.

Rodriguez, M. L., Ayduk, O., Aber, J. L., Mischel, W., Sethi, A., & Shoda, Y. (2005). A contextual approach to the development of self-regulatory competencies: The role of maternal unresponsivity and toddlers' negative affect in stressful situations. *Social Development, 14,* 136–157.

Rose, S. A., Feldman, J. F., Wallace, I. F., & Cohen, P. (1991). Language: A partial link between infant attention and later intelligence. *Developmental Psychology, 27,* 798–805.

Rothbart, M. K. (2004). Temperament and the pursuit of an integrated developmental psychology. *Merrill-Palmer Quarterly, 50,* 492–505.

Rothbart, M. K., & Bates, J. E. (1998). Temperament. In N. Eisenberg (Ed.) & W. Damon (Series Ed.), *Handbook of child psychology: Vol. 3. Social, emotional, and personality development* (pp. 105–176). New York: Wiley.

Rothbart, M. K., Derryberry, D., & Posner, M. I. (1994). A psychobiological approach to the development of temperament. In J. E. Bates & T. D. Wachs (Eds.), *Temperament: individual differences at the interface of biology and behavior* (pp. 83–116). Washington, DC: American Psychological Association.

Rothbart, M. K., Ellis, L. K., & Posner, M. I. (2004). Temperament and self-regulation. In R. F. Baumeister & K. D. Vohs (Eds.), *Handbook of self-regulation: Research, theory, and applications* (pp. 357–370). New York: Guilford Press.

Rothbart, M. K., Ellis, L. K., Rueda, M. R., & Posner, M. I. (2003). Development mechanisms of temperamental effortful control. *Journal of Personality, 71,* 1113–1143.

Rothbart, M. K., Posner, M. I., & Boylan, A. (1990). Regulatory mechanisms in infant development. In J. T. Enns (Ed.), *The development of attention: Research and theory* (pp. 47–66). Dordrecht, The Netherlands: Elsevier Science.

Rueda, M. R., Posner, M. I., & Rothbart, M. K. (2004). Attentional control and self-regulation. In R. F. Baumeister & K. D. Vohs (Eds.), *Handbook of self-regulation: Research, theory and applications* (pp. 283–300). New York: Guilford Press.

Ruff, H. A., & Rothbart, M. K. (1996). *Attention in early development: Themes and variations.* New York: Oxford University Press.

Schmidt, L. A., Fox, N. A., Schulkin, J., & Gold, P. W., (1999). Behavioral and psychophysiological correlates of self-presentation in temperamentally shy children. *Developmental Psychobiology, 35,* 119–135.

Smith, C. L., Calkins, S. D., Kean, P., Anastopoulos, A. D., & Shelton, T. L. (2004). Predicting stability and change in toddler behavior problems: Contributions of maternal behavior and child gender. *Developmental Psychology, 40,* 29–42.

Stams, G.-J. J. M., Juffer, F., & van IJzendoorn, M. H. (2002). Maternal sensitivity, infant attention, and temperament in early childhood predict adjustment in middle childhood: The case of adopted children and their biologically unrelated parents. *Developmental Psychology, 38,* 806–821.

Stifter, C. A., & Fox, N. A. (1990). Infant reactivity: Physiological correlates of newborn and 5–month temperament. *Developmental Psychology, 26,* 582–588.

Stifter, C. A., Spinrad, T. L., & Braungart-Ricker, J. M. (1999). Toward a developmental model of child compliance: the role of emotion regulation in infancy. *Child Development, 70,* 21–32.

Unsworth, N., Schrock, J. C., & Engle, R. W. (2004). Working memory capacity and the antisaccade task: Individual differences in voluntary saccade control. *Journal of Experimental Psychology: Language, Memory, and Cognition, 30,* 1302–1321.

Van Bakel, H. J. A., & Riksen-Walraven, J. M. (2004). Stress reactivity in 15–month-old infants: Links with infant temperament, cognitive competence, and attachment security. *Developmental Psychobiology, 44,* 157–167.

Vaughn, B. E., Kopp, C. B., & Krakow, J. B. (1984). The emergence and consolidation of self-control from eighteen to thirty months of age: Normative trends and individual differences. *Child Development, 55,* 990–1004.

Vohs, K. D., & Baumeister, R. F. (2004). Understanding self-regulation: An introduction. In R. F. Baumeister & K. D. Vohs (Eds.), *Handbook of self-regulation: Research, theory, and applications* (pp. 1–9). New York: Guilford Press.

Wilson, B. J., & Gottman, J. M. (1996). Attention: The shuttle between emotion and cognition: Risk, resiliency, and physiological bases. In E. M. Hetherington, & E. A. Blechman (Eds.), *Stress, coping and resiliency in children and families* (pp. 189–228). Mahwah, NJ: Erlbaum.

Wolfe, C. D., & Bell, M. A. (2004). Working memory and inhibitory control in early childhood: Contributions from electrophysiology, temperament, and language. *Developmental Psychobiology, 44,* 68–83.

Wolfe, C. D., & Bell, M. A. (in press). The integration of cognition and emotion during infancy and early childhood: Regulatory processes associated with the development of working memory. *Brain and Cognition.*

Yamasaki, H., LaBar, K. S., & McCarthy, G. (2002). Dissociable prefrontal brain systems for attention and emotion. *Proceedings of the National Academy of Science, 99,* 11447–11451.

Zelazo, P. D., Muller, U., Frye, D., & Marcovitch, S. (2003). The development of executive function. *Monographs of the Society for Research in Child Development, 68*(3).

15

Biobehavioral Approaches to Early Socioemotional Development

KRISTIN A. BUSS
H. HILL GOLDSMITH

Several overarching ideas imply that developmentalists studying behavior during early childhood should incorporate biological factors into their theorizing and empiricism more fully. First is the observation that neuroscience and genetics are currently the major growth areas in the biobehavioral sciences. New concepts and methods that can enrich the study of young children's behavioral development have emerged from these burgeoning literatures. Within the field of developmental psychology, developmental cognitive neuroscience and developmental psychopathology are the major growth areas, partly because they solicit interdisciplinary input, much of which is biological. Also, biological investigations constrain our theories of behavioral development. Can we demonstrate biological substrates of children's behavioral phenotypes and show corresponding developmental changes in both the phenotypes and their substrates? Can variation in biological measures account for substantial individual differences in early childhood behavior? The answers to questions such as these should sharpen the delineation of behavioral phenotypes; better defined behavioral phenotypes will be useful for addressing questions having little to do with biology. Another current trend is detecting interactions of biological variables (e.g., specific genetic alleles) with experience or an environmental exposure to predict later developmental outcomes. These considerations imply that investigations at the behavioral level alone are insufficient to advance the field of early childhood development.

In this chapter, we apply some of the aforementioned considerations to early affective development, specifically focusing on negative emotions. The review of the literature focuses primarily on infants, toddlers, and preschool-age children to highlight the transitions across toddlerhood; however, we include studies of older children, adolescents, and young adults to address specific points and identify gaps in our knowledge of these processes in toddlerhood. We begin our review with behavior genetic evidence, primarily from twin studies, and include new data from two twin samples. We also review literature linking hypothalamic–pituitary–adrenocortical (HPA) axis activity with negative emotions and present new data from a sample of 24-month-olds. Finally we discuss research on autonomic and central nervous system influences on negative emotionality.

BEHAVIOR GENETIC APPROACHES TO EARLY EMOTIONAL DEVELOPMENT

Overview of Methodology and Concepts

The literature on the genetics of early emotional development is small when emotional development is defined narrowly as involving measurement of relatively "pure" emotion expression or reception. However, the literature on the genetics of emotion-relevant features of temperament and psychopathology in early development is more substantial. Prior to treating empirical data, we offer some general observations about genetic approaches.

The behavior genetic paradigm has many components, and research does not always proceed as logically as it might. Generally, the initial observation is that a phenotype "runs in families." Family studies do not distinguish genetic from environmental transmission but nevertheless establish vertical transmission of traits (from parent to offspring). Family studies are typically followed up by genetically informative designs demonstrating heritable influence on the phenotype, usually initially in twin studies and then in adoption studies or other family designs. This research sometimes suggests decomposition of the phenotype to highlight heritable or nonheritable features, sex-limited genetic effects, or age-related genetic effects. Longitudinal study with a genetically informative design allows for the examination of genetic influences on continuity and change of the phenotype. Within this type of empirical work, researchers typically examine environmental influences on the phenotype, possibly including study of gene–environment correlation and interaction. Controlling for genetic factors allows convincing demonstration of environmental effects. Particularly relevant to this chapter is the search for associated endophenotypes (e.g., neural substrates of the emotion phenotype that share the same genetic underpinnings).

Thus, the point of departure for genetic research is the demonstration of genetic variance associated with a phenotype. We can infer the relative strength of various classes of genetic and environmental factors from patterns of covariation among family members who have varying degrees of genetic overlap and who share environments or reside separately. The heritability statistic estimates the association between degree of genetic overlap and similarity on behavioral traits in relatives, and the environmental component can be divided into effects shared versus nonshared by relatives. Shared environmental effects explain similarity between twins and relatives in addition to that accounted for by common genes. Shared environmental variance also accounts for the similarity of genetically unrelated individuals who are reared together. The nonshared environmental variance is the remainder of the variance not explained by genes or by shared environment (see Turkheimer & Waldron, 2000, for a conceptual review). It includes the effects of experiences that are unique to each individual and independent of genetic factors. Nonshared environmental variance can be directly estimated from differences between monozygotic (MZ) cotwins. The estimate of nonshared environment is often confounded with measurement error. A common misunderstanding is that environmental effects are "what is left over" after genetic effects are estimated. Typical behavior-genetic methods treat genetic and shared environmental effects in an evenhanded manner, given the assumptions about how these effects can be partitioned. The more cogent criticism is that the genetic partitioning is based on sound theories of Mendelian inheritance whereas the environmental partitioning is based on familial units that might not be the most important markers of environmental influence. This basic biometric model can be expanded for longitudinal, multivariate analysis (Neale & Cardon, 1992). The method, its applicability to twin studies, and its limitations are explained in much more detail by Goldsmith (2003), Jang (2005), and Plomin, DeFries, McClearn, and Rutter (1997).

It is worth emphasizing that parents can exert strong experiential effects on their children's behavior in the absence of a shared environmental factor in biometric analyses. For example, hypothetically, aggressive fathers might induce inhibited behavior in children of a certain age. Such a hypothetical effect would not emerge in a univariate analysis of parent–offspring data of either aggressiveness or inhibition. Part of the solution to problems like this is use of multivariate analysis (McArdle & Goldsmith, 1990; Neale & Cardon, 1992). A more important part of the solution is integrating theories of how the environment works into these multivariate designs. Testing for environmental risk and protective factors in ways that are also sensitive to genetic factors requires programmatic application of several research strategies (Rutter, Pickles, Murray, & Eaves, 2001).

New Findings

As a simple illustration of the classic behavior-genetic approach to twin data on affective expression in toddlers, we present correlations indexing twin similarity for anger, sadness, and fear from an ongoing study (Van Hulle, Lemery, & Goldsmith, 2002). These parental report data (Table 15.1) derive from a

TABLE 15.1. Twin Similarity for Selected Scales from the Revised Toddler Behavior Assessment Questionnaire (Goldsmith, 1996)

	MZ R[a]	ssDZ R[b]	osDZ R[c]
Sadness	.69	.54	.58
Anger	.69	.34	.43
Object Fear	.78	.37	.26
Social Fear	.61	.06 (ns)	.13 (ns)

[a]MZ, monozygotic, or identical; n = 184 pairs.

[b]ssDZ, same-sex dizygotic, or fraternal; n = 170 pairs.

[c]osDZ, opposite-sex dizygotic; n = 164 pairs.

sample of 1,067 individuals with an average age of approximately 26 months. The families were recruited from statewide birth records and were unselected for characteristics other than volunteering for research.

Examining twin similarity in Table 15.1 leads to three main observations: (1) MZ twins are invariably rated more similar than dizygotic (DZ) twins; (2) same-sex and opposite-sex fraternal cotwins are equally similar at this young age; and (3) the pattern of MZ–DZ correlational differences varies such that DZ similarity approaches the MZ value for Sadness, DZ similarity is only about one-half the MZ value for Anger and Object Fear, and DZ twins do not show statistically significant similarity for Social Fear (shyness). The different patterns of MZ versus DZ similarity are consequential because they yield inferences about the degree of heritability (the ratio of variance associated with genetic differences to total variation). Falconer's (1989) simple formula for heritability is $h^2 = 2(R_{MZ} - R_{DZ})$, which follows from the biological fact that MZ twins share all of their segregating genes whereas DZ twins share only 50% on average and from the parsing of all environmental variance into between- and within-family components. Applying this formula to Sadness in Table 15.1 (and averaging the ss [same sex] DZ and os [opposite sex] DZ values), we would calculate $h^2 = 2(.69 - .56) = .26$. By an extension of the logic, the between-family, or shared, environmental variance for Sadness would be $2R_{DZ} - R_{MZ}$, or .43. Because these estimates of 26% heritability and 43% shared environmental variance are standardized, the remaining variance of 31% must reflect nonshared environmental variance and measurement error. These estimates are nonoptimal because they do not take into account sample sizes or any total variance differences for zygosity types, nor do they assess the fit of a model to the data so they should be interpreted with caution.

Univariate genetic and environmental variance estimates, such as those above, perhaps address issues of less contemporary interest than multivariate estimates. Using the same data that contributed to the Table 15.1 analyses, the phenotypic correlation between Sadness and Anger scales was .55, based on 1,067 individuals. Is that correlation of .55 due to shared genetic factors, shared environmental factors, or both? Again, using a simple illustration, we standardize scores and then correlate the Sadness score of one twin from each pair (Twin A) with the Anger of the other twin from the pair (Twin B), and vice versa. These correlations are done separately for zygosity groups. The resulting average correlations are .43 (MZ) and .36 (average of ssDZ and osDZ), which yields a bivariate heritability of only 14%, a shared environmental variance estimate of 29%, and nonshared environmental variance of 57%. Thus, we would conclude that about two-thirds of the association between anger and sadness is accounted for by shared environmental factors.

In cross-sectional data, these analyses can be extended to accommodate other variables, such as sex and age. The analyses can also accommodate the effects of measured genes (requiring molecular data) and measured environments (ranging from broad social class indicators to detailed observations of interpersonal interactions). In longitudinal data, any measure of individual differences in continuity or change that can be collected on a genetically informative sample can be analyzed for genetic and environmental associations. In an ongoing longitudinal twin study of emotional development from early infancy to age 3 years, mothers rated temperament on the Toddler Behavior Assessment Questionnaire (TBAQ; Goldsmith, 1996) at age 2 years and then on the Child Behavior Questionnaire (CBQ; Rothbart & Ahadi, 1994; Rothbart, Ahadi, & Hershey, 1994) at age 3 years. Complete longitudinal data are currently available for 142 pairs. After standardizing scores for each instrument, Table 15.2 presents results for two of the same TBAQ scales shown in Table 15.1, Anger and Social Fear, along with the parallel CBQ scales (Anger and Shyness). We averaged the z scores for the 2- and 3-year assessment for an estimate of toddler level, and we computed the signed difference from age 2 to 3 years as an estimate of change in relative rank order.

The results in Table 15.2 suggest that mean level measures are more heritable than change measures during the third year of life, perhaps partly due to

TABLE 15.2. Twin Similarity for Level and Change in Toddler Anger and Shyness

	MZ R[a]	DZ R[b]
Level (mean)		
Anger	.70	.43
Shyness	.79	–.18 (ns)
Change (signed difference)		
Anger	.40	.35
Shyness	.57	.27

[a]MZ, monozygotic, or identical; n = 51 pairs.

[b]DZ, dizygotic, or fraternal; n = 91 pairs (same-sex and opposite-sex pooled).

greater reliability. Genetic effects on change in Shyness, however, are apparent. As in the earlier examples, more complex model-fitting approaches such as McArdle and Goldsmith's (1990) would yield better estimates of the biometric effects on continuity and change. However, we bypass those here in favor of reviewing the broader literature.

Review of Genetic Studies of Negative Emotionality

We now turn to a selective review of genetic studies of early emotionality and temperament. A widely studied temperamental trait is behavioral inhibition (Kagan, Reznick, Clarke, Snidman, & Garcia-Coll, 1984; Kagan, Reznick, & Gibbons, 1989). In addition to ratings from parents and experiments, Matheny (1989) investigated the genetic basis of behavioral inhibition in toddlers using an observational rating of emotional tone. Twin data demonstrated substantial genetic variance in inhibition (MZ R = .79, DZ R = .26). In another study, Robinson, Kagan, Reznick, and Corley (1992) also found higher MZ than DZ similarity (average R = .55 vs. .23, respectively) for observational measures of behavioral inhibition. DiLalla, Kagan, and Reznick (1994) replicated this finding in 24-month-olds, and Manke, Saudino, and Grant (2001) examined genetic and environmental effects on membership in high-inhibition and low-inhibition groups at ages 14, 20, and 24 months. Generally, the degree of heritability was moderately high and consistent for high-inhibition group membership, for low inhibition, and for individual differences in the full range of inhibition. With up to 400 twin pairs, Emde and Hewitt (2001) summarized evidence that shyness, cheerfulness, and angry response to restraint were heritable and also influenced by shared environmental effects. In contrast, behavioral inhibition and empathy showed only additive genetic effects.

Genetic analyses also include consideration of gene–environment correlation and interaction, one example of which is Deater-Deckard and O'Conner's (2000) study of mutuality, the notion that healthy parent–child relationships exhibit emotional reciprocity and have a bidirectional, responsive quality. They used dyadic observational measures such as mutual eye gaze and shared positive emotion with mothers and a pair of their 3–4-year-old children, where the pairs were MZ or DZ twins, full siblings, or genetically unrelated adopted siblings. The similarity of siblings for the mutuality measures with their mothers suggested genetic influence based on child characteristics: MZ r = .61; DZ r = .26; full siblings, r = .25; and adopted siblings, r = –.04. Because the child-specific factors are heritable and the parent's contribution to mutuality constitutes an aspect of the child's environment, gene–environment correlation is induced in this situation. Further behavior-genetic studies of mutuality suggest that it is child specific and linked to child behavior problems (Deater-Deckard & Petrill, 2004).

Much of the behavior genetics literature on emotionality between infancy and kindergarten falls under the behavior problems rubric. Analysis of behavior problems in unselected community samples is hard to distinguish from analyses of individual differences in temperament/emotionality. A series of papers from The Netherlands examine multiple aspects of behavior problems. For instance, with nearly 10,000 3-year-old twins, Derks, Hudziak, van Beijsterveldt, Dolan, and Boomsma (2004) found moderate to strong genetic influences on all aspects of behavior problems rated by mothers and fathers. The large sample size provided power to detect modest shared environmental effects and sex differences in the degree of genetic effects as significant in some cases. In girls, aggressive behavior was more heritable and withdrawn behavior was less heritable than in boys (with reciprocal differences in the salience of shared environmental factors between girls and boys). A set of twin analyses from the U.K. samples also examines behavior problems in preschool children. Among the findings was that various anxiety problems (general distress, fears, and separation anxiety) share common genetic underpinnings and are individually moderately heritable (Eley et al., 2003); this study also demonstrated strong genetic effects on early obsessive–compulsive symptoms. Using only MZ twins from the same project, Asbury, Dunn, Pike, and Plomin (2003) showed that intrapair differences in symptoms—particularly externalizing symptoms—were associated with twin differences in parenting (both as reported by the parents). This putative effect of parenting on symptoms would be unconfounded by genetic differences due to the use of MZ twins.

Summary

The development of large panels of young twins and their families, the trend toward more differentiated measures of emotionality (including some observational measures), the inclusion of specific measures of both experience and candidate genes, and the better grounding behavior-genetic research in developmental theory are all positive signs that genetic research on early emotions is progressing. Another sign of progress is a focus on endophenotypes, to which we now turn.

PSYCHOPHYSIOLOGICAL APPROACHES TO EARLY EMOTIONAL DEVELOPMENT

Several key physiological systems influence negative affect (e.g., the amygdale, prefrontal cortex, autonomic nervous system, and neuroendocrine systems) (Davidson, Jackson, & Kalin, 2000). Interest in the role of physiological influence on emotions and emotional development stems, in part, from research in stress physiology. Neural substrates of the stress response include two integrated systems (Chrousos, 1998; McEwen, 1998; Meaney, 2001), both with connections to the limbic system, specifically the amygdala, anterior cingulate, and prefrontal cortex. The first of these is the limbic–hypothalamic–pituitary adrenocortical (L-HPA) axis and the second is the locus coeruleus–norepinephrine (LC-NE) system. At the outset we acknowledge these are overlapping and connected systems, but for purposes of this chapter, we address each individually. However, interconnections among these systems are crucial to understanding affective behavior, and we have conducted two studies in infants and toddlers to examine these links (e.g., Buss et al., 2003; Buss, Goldsmith, & Davidson, 2005).

Neuroendocrine Approach

Activity of the L-HPA system has been widely studied in animals and humans. The end product of this system, cortisol, can be measured in saliva samples, making it feasible to obtain from children in a variety of study designs (Kirschbaum & Hellhammer, 1989, 1994). Cortisol is the main glucocorticoid of the HPA system. The release of corticotropin releasing hormone (CRH) from the hypothalamus triggers a series of events culminating in the release of cortisol from the cortex of the adrenal glands. The production of cortisol is important to the body's response to stressful conditions (DeKloet, 1991; Gunnar, 1992).

Measurement of cortisol in saliva has made this a popular biological measure for research in infancy and childhood. Salivary cortisol represents the unbound level of hormone, which is the portion that elicits glucocorticoid effects. Basal cortisol is secreted in a circadian rhythm with the highest levels observed in the early morning (shortly after waking), followed by a steady decline throughout the day and evening, with the nadir occurring around midnight (Kirshbaum & Hellhammer, 1989, 1994). A few recent studies in toddlers and preschoolers have observed a flattening of the cortisol slope or a slight rise in the afternoon, possibly a result of napping (Buss, Davidson, Kabin, & Goldsmith, 2004; Dettling, Gunnar, & Donzella, 1999; Watmura, Sebanc, & Gunnar, 2002). Cortisol is also secreted under conditions of stress or threat. However, the magnitude of the stress response is affected by the time of sampling, such that cortisol reactivity will be greater during the lowest periods of the circadian cycle (Dallman et al., 1992). A variety of cortisol measures, both basal and reactive, have been reported. For instance, some studies report single measures of cortisol levels at different times across the day (e.g., morning peak and bedtime values), slope of decline across the day (calculated as difference score or regression line), area under the curve (a volumetric measure of cortisol level across at least three time points), reactivity measures (e.g., postlab visit minus prelab visit), and recovery from peak. Given the variability inherent in cortisol secretion and the reliability of assay procedures it is important to sample multiple days for reliable basal measures. Time of sampling, type of sampling procedure, drug use, sleep, and schedule changes are factors that introduce variation into studies on salivary cortisol and perhaps lead to inconsistencies in findings.

Under stressful conditions, basal regulation of the HPA system is overridden and elevations in cortisol are observed. Starting with the seminal work of Mason (1968), decades of research have shown that the psychological relevance of an event is a primary determinant of the HPA response to that event. Conditions of novelty and uncertainty can increase the magnitude of cortisol release. An individual's expression of negative affect in a situation is also associated with increased cortisol release. Although research has established the relation between negative affect and HPA activity, the differential impact of discrete emotions (e.g., fear, anger, and sadness) remains somewhat uncertain.

Cortisol and Fear/Sadness

Kagan, Snidman, and Arcus (1992) have suggested that extremely inhibited children are physiologically biased to become behaviorally inhibited in novel situations. One interpretation of "physiological bias" is that inhibited children show differences in basal physiological measures, such as increased cortisol levels, even when they are not overtly stressed. Greater physiological responses should also be apparent in the face of stress. In nonhuman primates, behavioral inhibition has been associated with basal HPA activity such that animals that spent more time freezing had higher cortisol levels (Kalin, Larson, Shelton, & Davidson, 1998). That is, basal HPA activity predicted which animals would behave in an inhibited way. In human toddlers, individual differences in basal cortisol were positively associated with observed inhibited behavior (Kagan, Reznik, & Snidman, 1987). In support of this finding, parent-reported shyness for their 14-month-olds was predictive of baseline cortisol several years later (Schmidt et al., 1997). Further support came from the finding that fear-related behaviors such as internalizing, self-isolation, and social withdrawal reported by parents and teachers were predicted by baseline cortisol levels measured 1½ years earlier (Smider et al., 2002). Despite the apparent replicability of these studies, the putative association between fear/withdrawal and cortisol reactivity is not always observed (e.g., Buss et al., 2003; Schmidt, Fox, Schulkin, & Gold, 1999).

Research on the HPA system has highlighted the complexity of the relation between physiology and emotional behavior. This is a field in which mediating and moderating variables play important roles. The work of Gunnar and colleagues demonstrates this complexity most clearly. For instance, elevations in cortisol correlated with distress in infants during maternal separations only when the caretaker was not interacting with the infant (Gunnar, Larson, Hertsgaard, Harris, & Brodersen, 1992). In another study, novelty elevated cortisol only in inhibited toddlers (Nachmias, Gunnar, Mangelsdorf, Parritz, & Buss, 1996). In summary, the availability of coping resources (e.g., attachment figure and responsive caregiver) or regulatory strategies can buffer the stress response (Gunnar, Brodersen, Nachmias, Buss, & Rigatuso, 1996). Gunnar (1994) concluded that the availability and appropriate use of coping resources, in combination with temperament, are the essential ingredients in reducing the likelihood of a cortisol stress response in the face of a challenge. Thus, a fearful temperament will be associated with a reactive cortisol profile only if the child has poor coping resources available or does not use those resources effectively. In other words, responses are mediated by an event's emotional impact, which, in turn, is determined by appraisal of the severity of demands in relation to the individual's coping resources (Frankenhaeuser, 1980; Stansbury & Gunnar, 1994; Gunnar, 1994).

Our work has produced similar findings. We found that the relation between cortisol levels and a specific withdrawal behavior, freezing, was only present in lower threat contexts—contexts in which most children were not distressed (Buss et al., 2004). Specifically, children who displayed more freezing in the context of readily available coping resources (e.g., toys and access to mother) showed the highest basal and reactive cortisol levels. In the same study, we also examined the associations between cortisol levels and two behavioral composites: a measure of inhibited behavior during a risk room task (similar to behavioral inhibition measures reported in the literature) and a composite of fear and withdrawal behaviors averaged across three stranger approaches. Both of these behavioral composites were uncorrelated with reactive cortisol, and behavioral inhibition was correlated with lower afternoon cortisol, an unexpected finding. These findings highlighted the importance of examining distinct affective behaviors, such as freezing, rather than assuming the equivalence of all fear behaviors. Moreover, the eliciting context was revealed as an important contributor to the association between cortisol and fear behavior. As mentioned earlier, in a study with 6-month-old infants, we failed to find the predicted association between withdrawal behaviors (both fear and sadness) and higher cortisol levels (Buss et al., 2003). However, we did find that greater relative right frontal electroencephalographic (EEG) asymmetry (putatively linked to withdrawal behaviors) was associated with both higher cortisol (at baseline and during a stranger approach) and also with more fear and sad behaviors.

Cortisol and Anger

Results for the relation between anger and cortisol are mixed. Three studies of anger reactivity and the HPA system in young children have revealed that aggressive or disruptive behaviors, combined with low frustration tolerance, are associated with higher cortisol levels (Dettling et al., 1999; Gunnar, Tout, deHaan, Pierce, & Stansbury, 1997; Tout, deHaan, Kipp, Campbell, & Gunnar, 1998). Once preschoolers have adjusted to the school environment, high levels of cortisol are associated with parent and teacher reports of aggression (Gunnar et al., 1997) and observations of aggression (Hart, Gunnar, & Cicchetti, 1995; Tout et al., 1998). Aggression in preschoolers has been associated with a greater rise in cortisol during the afternoon in day-care settings (Dettling et al., 1999). The model positing relations between fearful/anxious temperament and stress reactivity does not predict this finding. One explanation of the findings is that negative affect more generally—including both fear and anger—is associated with increases in cortisol. For example, in his work with temper tantrums, Potegal (2003) has found that only the frequency of tantruming (presumably largely an anger-related behavior) was associated with higher basal cortisol levels. However, another explanation is that the relation between anger/aggression and stress reactivity reflects anxiety expressed as aggression, which fits the adjustment to preschool findings but presumably does not fit the tantrum findings. There is support for this aggression-as-expression-of-anxiety hypothesis. Boys with conduct disorder comorbid with anxiety had elevated cortisol levels (McBurnett et al., 1991). In contrast, boys without comorbid anxiety had low cortisol levels.

Most of the work linking lower cortisol with anger has been examined in older children and adolescents and focuses on externalizing disorders and/or aggressive behavior. For example, aggression and hostility toward peers and teachers in second graders was associated with a reduced cortisol response to stress (Tennes & Kreye, 1985; Tennes, Kreye, Avitable, & Wells, 1986). Similar findings were reported by van Goozen and colleagues (1998; van Goozen, Matthys, Cohen-Kettenis, Buitelaar, & van Engeland, 2000) who demonstrated that children with disruptive behavior disorders had a weaker cortisol stress response compared with controls. The same pattern has been found for basal cortisol levels in relation to persistent aggressive behavior in a clinically referred sample of boys (McBurnett, Lahey, Rathouz, & Loeber, 2000).

Our own work suggests that anger and externalizing behaviors are associated with lower basal cortisol. In a sample of preschool children, we noted an association between low baseline levels of cortisol and externalizing behavior for father report of boys' behavior (Smider et al., 2002). In a sample of toddlers we found evidence differentiating anger from fear/sadness when examined in association with cortisol levels, as the next section reports.

New Findings of Anger and Basal Cortisol

We now turn to new findings differentiating approach-oriented (i.e., anger) and withdrawal-oriented (i.e., fear and sadness) negative affect with regard to cortisol levels. Eighty 24-month-olds and their mothers participated in two lab visits designed to address the associations among temperament dimensions of anger, fear, sadness, and physiological measures of basal and reactive cortisol and cardiac reactivity. Toddlers participated in several episodes designed to elicit different affective behaviors. These episodes were selected from the Locomotor and Preschool Laboratory Temperament Assessment Battery (Lab-TAB: Goldsmith & Rothbart, 1988; Goldsmith, Reilly, Lemery, Longley, & Prescott, 1994) and modified for use with toddlers (Buss & Goldsmith, 2000).

For the current set of analyses, we focused on basal cortisol in relation to anger, fear, and sadness temperament composites. Temperament composites were created by averaging facial, vocal, and bodily displays of each type of negative affect across multiple episodes. Both frequency and intensity of affective displays were included in the composites. The fear composite was created from behaviors indicative of fear and withdrawal during three fear-eliciting episodes: a risk room and two stranger approach interactions. The anger composite was created from behaviors indicative of anger and frustration during four frustration-eliciting episodes: toy removal, arm restraint, toy in locked box, and empty present episodes. The sadness composite was created from sadness behaviors across all seven of the episodes just mentioned. Saliva was collected on three consecutive days in the home (between the two lab visits). Parents were instructed to collect samples at each of four target times: in the morning (between 8:00 and 9:00 A.M.), at noon before lunch (between 11:00 A.M. and 12:00 P.M., in the afternoon (between 3:00 and 4:00 P.M.), and in the evening before bedtime (between 8:00 and 9:00 P.M.). Toddlers who provided at least two samples for each time period were included in the analyses (n = 54). Mean values for each of the four periods and for total cortisol volume were calculated (see Buss et al., 2004 for details). We conducted two sets of analyses. First we examined correlations between anger, fear, or sadness temperament composites and cortisol for each of the home sample measures. The fear temperament composite was not associated with any of the home cortisol measures and the sadness temperament composite was only marginally associated with home afternoon cortisol (r (54) = –.25, p < .10) and was in the opposite from expected direction. The anger composite was significantly associated with lower cortisol levels. Specifically, cortisol volume was associated with less anger across tasks (r(54) = –.31, p < .05). Anger was consistently associated with lower cortisol (r's = –.25, –.41, –.29, –.26 for morning, noon, afternoon, and evening cortisol respectively).

Because of the repeated measures nature of the home cortisol collection, multilevel modeling (MLM using SAS PROC MIXED) was used to estimate the effects of the slope of cortisol change on the relation between baseline cortisol and fear, sadness, or anger. This second set of analyses involved a series of two-level random coefficient models in which repeated observations (home cortisol samples) were nested within individuals (Raudenbush & Bryk, 2002; Snijders & Bosker, 1999). MLM uses all observations (sample size * repeated observations), which allows for a more powerful estimation of effects compared with averaging across cortisol samples (e.g., cortisol volume). Moreover, these models account for the nonindependence of observations in nested data. The intraclass correlation (calculated from a model with only random variation) for cortisol level across the sampling times was .41 indicating that 41% of the total variance in toddler cortisol levels was between toddlers. Thus, multiple observations within one toddler were more similar than observations among random toddlers.

We tested the following models. The unconditional model tests the effects of time on cortisol and thus represents a test of the average slope of cortisol across the day. Note that time was centered such that the zero point was the morning sample, which typically was the highest value. In the conditional model, the temperament measures were added to test the effects of each composite on cortisol levels. Each temperament composite was examined along with all possible interactions. In most cases, the full model as depicted below was not retained.

Unconditional model

Level 1: $\text{cortisol}_{ti} = \beta 0_i + \beta 1_{ati}$ (linear time) $+ \beta 2_{ati}^2$ (quadratic time) $+ e_{ti}$

Level 2: $\beta 0_j = \gamma 00 + \text{u}0_i$

$\beta 1_j = \gamma 10 + \text{u}1_i$

$\beta 2_j = \gamma 20 + \text{u}2_i$

Full conditional model (anger example)

Level 1: $\text{cortisol}_{ti} = \beta 0_i + \beta 1_{ati}$ (linear time) $+ \beta 2_{ati}^2$ (quadratic time) $+ e_{ti}$

Level 2: $\beta 0_j = \gamma 00 + \gamma 01$ (anger) $+ \text{u}0_i$

$\beta 1_j = \gamma 10 + \gamma 11$ (anger) $+ \text{u}1_i$

$\beta 2_j = \gamma 20 + \gamma 21$ (anger) $+ \text{u}2_i$

Turning first to the unconditional model, the fixed effects for time were not significant, suggesting that linear and quadratic slope were unrelated to cortisol level for the sample as a whole. However, the variance components for both linear and quadratic slope were significant, suggesting individual variability in cortisol slope. Although fixed effects were not significant, they were retained in the conditional models because the random effects were significant (Snijders & Bosker, 1999). Results for the series of conditional models were anticipated by the raw correlations reported above. Only the anger temperament measure was significantly associated with cortisol slope. The interactions between anger and time were not significant and the best fitting model was a main effects only model. The main effect of anger was significant suggesting that when anger was introduced into the model the level of cortisol was lower (t (59) = –2.19, $p < .05$). The unconditional and best fitting anger models are presented in Table 15.3. The fear and sadness models were not significant and will not be presented.

Summary

Both the extant literature and our new data imply that withdrawal-oriented behaviors such as fear and sadness are associated with higher basal levels and greater reactivity of cortisol levels although these associations do not invariably emerge. In contrast, approach-oriented behaviors such as anger and aggression tend to be associated with lower basal and reactive cortisol levels. Further support for this distinction between approach- and withdrawal-oriented affect in cortisol response was reported in a study of 4-month-olds' reactions to goal blockage (Lewis & Ramsey, 2005). Only infants who reacted with sadness to these situations evidenced higher reactive cortisol levels (Lewis & Ramsey, 2005). However, other studies in the cortisol literature do not report this pattern and/or fail to distinguish between fear/sadness and anger.

TABLE 15.3. Estimates for the Unconditional and Best Fitting Anger Model on Cortisol

Unconditional model		Anger model
Fixed effects	Coefficient (*SE*)	Coefficient (*SE*)
Intercept	.4904 (.09)	.4731 (.08)
Time	–.1693 (.11)	–.1649 (.11)
Time^2	.0405 (.04)	.0319 (.04)
Anger	—	–.1223 (.06)
Random effects	Parameter (*SE*)	Parameter (*SE*)
Level 2		
Intercept variance	.3062 (.08)	.2948 (.08)
Time variance	.3384 (.14)	.3343 (.14)
Time^2 variance	.0397 (.02)	.0393 (.02)
Residual variance	.1306 (.03)	.1316 (.03)

Autonomic Nervous System Approach

Research on the role of the autonomic nervous system (ANS) and negative affect is also closely linked with the stress physiology literature. Recall that the other neural substrate, the LC-NE system, is also a key system in the stress response (McEwen, 1998). Specifically, along with secretion of epinephrine and norepinephrine the LC elicits and regulates activity in the ANS through the hypothalamus in the service of the "fight or flight" response. The ANS plays a prominent role in cardiovascular (CV) activity and the developmental psychophysiology literature has focused on CV measures; thus we review this literature specifically. The heart is normally under tonic influence of both the sympathetic and parasympathetic branches of the ANS and circulating hormones. Efferent links in the autonomic control of the heart consist of sympathetic adrenergic and parasympathetic cholinergic fibers. Fibers from both branches terminate on cells in the sinoatrial (SA) node and can modify the intrinsic rate of the heart. Phasic heart rate acceleration (i.e., tachycardia) can result from an increase in sympathetic activity, a decrease in parasympathetic activity, or some combination of the two. Similarly, phasic heart rate deceleration (i.e., bradycardia) can result from a decrease in sympathetic activity, an increase in parasympathetic activity, or both.

Sympathetic influences on the heart can be neuronal via fibers originating from the spinal cord or hormonal via the adrenal medulla. The transmitter found in postganglionic fibers is NE. In addition, the adrenal medulla releases epinephrine (E) and to a lesser extent NE into the bloodstream. NE and E act on beta-1-adrenergic receptors to alter the spontaneous depolarization of SA nodal cells to produce an increase in heart rate and increase the strength of ventricular contraction. When activated, alpha 1-adrenergic receptors constrict blood vessels in the coronary and systemic circulation. Direct electrical stimulation of the sympathetic preganglionic fibers from the spinal cord elicits increased blood pressure, increased contractile force, and variable changes in heart rate. Sympathetic influences on cardiac dynamic events include alterations in ascending aortic flow (e.g., decreased ejection time and increased stroke volume), ventricular pressure (e.g., increased systolic pressure and decreased diastolic pressure), aortic pressure (e.g., increased pulse pressure), and ventricular volume (e.g., increased ejection rate and volume). The parasympathetic nervous system acts on the heart via the vagus (10th cranial) nerve. Cardiac vagal postganglionic fibers release acetylcholine (ACh) on the SA nodal cells. This neurotransmitter alters the course of the spontaneous depolarization of the cells to produce a decrease in firing and subsequent reduction in heart rate (i.e., negative chronotropic effect). In addition, at the atrioventricular node, ACh increases the refractory period of action potentials. Vagal activity can also slightly decrease the strength of ventricular contraction. Thus, increased activity of the parasympathetic branch and vagal innervation leads to a slowing of the heart. Furthermore, tonic levels of vagal input to the heart are mainly responsible for the normal resting heart rate.

CV Activity and Negative Emotions

The ANS literature has a long history of using physiological measures to differentiate emotions (see Cacioppo, Klein, Berntson, & Hatfield, 1993, for review). This research was sparked by the theories of James, Lange, and Cannon who stressed the importance of physiological systems for the experience of emotions. James' theory of emotions stated that emotions emerge from specific configurations of bodily responses (James, 1884, 1890). Lange was studying the bodily changes that accompanied sorrow, joy, and anger (Lange, 1922). At the same time, Cannon was studying changes in the sympathetic nervous system as reflected in the cardiovascular system during displays of intense fear and rage (Cannon, 1927). Ax (1953) was the first to empirically demonstrate that fear was associated with a decrease in heart rate relative to anger. Since that first study, findings have been inconsistent. Most studies are able to distinguish fear, anger, and sadness (i.e., basic negative emotions) from disgust and pleasure (e.g., Ekman, Levenson, & Friesen, 1983). However, cardiac differentiation between fear, anger, and sadness is less apparent. Cacioppo and colleagues (1993) suggest that potential patterns of differentiation are unlikely to be found using gross measures of response (e.g., heart rate). The sympathetic nervous system (SNS) and parasympathetic nervous system (PNS) dually innervate the heart and emotional stimuli are not likely to evoke reciprocal action of the SNS and PNS (Berntson & Quigley, 1991). Emotions may be better differentiated by focusing on measures of SNS and PNS activation (e.g., respiratory sinus arrythmia and preejection period). As a demonstration of this, Sinha, Lovallo, and Parsons (1992) showed that PEP differentiated anger from sadness such that larger decreases in PEP were found for anger.

In the developmental psychobiological literature, cardiac measures have also received a great deal of attention, especially within the fearful temperament and behavioral inhibition literatures. Most evidence for physiological differences between inhibited and uninhibited children comes from the investigation of heart rate reactivity, which indicates that inhibited children have higher and less variable heart rates (Kagan, Reznick, & Snidman, 1987, 1988; Kagan, Reznick, Snidman, Gibbons, & Johnson, 1988; Reznick et al., 1986). Measures of heart rate variability in these early studies were limited to heart period (HP) and HP variability (assessed by the standard deviation of a HP series). More recently, studies using respiratory sinus arrhythmia (RSA) or vagal tone (Porges, 1992), reflecting pure PNS cardiac activation, also find a relatively consistent pattern of findings with lower RSA being associated with greater fear. Newborn RSA predicted maternal ratings of fear (Stifter & Fox, 1990). High baseline RSA was associated with less fear and more approach to a stranger (Stifter, Fox, & Porges, 1989). However, the relation between HP or RSA and behavioral inhibition is not always present, especially when children are unselected (Asendorpf & Meier, 1993; Calkins & Fox, 1992; Marshall & Stevenson-Hinde, 1998). In addition to empirical support, psychobiological models of withdrawal behaviors consistently hypothesize a link between lower HR variability (as reflected in all the measures reported earlier) and withdrawal-related behaviors (e.g., Kagan, Reznick, & Snidman 1987, 1988; Porges, 1992). Thus, this hypothesized link is not unique to fear and should also include sadness. There is empirical support for this association in our own work in infants (Buss et al., 1998, 2003) and in toddlers (Buss, 2000; Buss et al., 2005). The association between sadness and RSA is also found in the extant literature demonstrating protection against risk for internalizing disorders (e.g., depression) when children are able to suppress RSA levels under challenge (e.g., El-Sheikh, 2001).

Fewer studies have investigated the relation between anger and cardiac reactivity in children. In contrast to fear and sadness, higher RSA has been associated with negative reactivity to a pacifier removal and mother report of frustration at 5 months (Stifter & Fox, 1990). Moreover, 18-month-olds who had higher scores on observed frustration and used more regulation strategies had higher RSA (Stifter & Jain, 1996). In contrast, baseline RSA and the ability to regulate RSA in infancy predicted preschool behavior problems (Porges, Doussard-Roosevelt, Portales, & Greenspan, 1996). Higher baseline RSA and greater changes in RSA were associated with less aggressive behaviors. Toddler boys at risk for developing aggression-related behavior problems had significantly lower RSA than boys not at risk (Calkins & Dedmon, 2000). In a recent longitudinal study of RSA suppression (i.e., ability to withdraw vagal influence under task demands), children with RSA suppression across tasks and from ages 2 to 4½ were rated as lower in negative emotionality (Calkins & Keane, 2004).

Kagan, Reznick, and Snidman (1997) have suggested that the relation between cardiac variability and behavioral inhibition represents SNS activity. However, HP and HP variability as measured in these studies is under tonic and phasic control of both branches of the ANS. Moreover, the RSA measure of variability is influenced by the PNS, and cardiac activity to new situations may be largely influenced by this system (Porges, 1992). To disentangle these influences, measures of SNS cardiac activity have recently emerged in the developmental literature. Specifically, preejection period (PEP) has been used because the SNS modulates PEP such that increases in sympathetic influence result in faster PEP (lower values) and are related to increased contractility of the heart. PEP reactivity is related to increases in task demands (Alkon et al., 2003) and to externalizing symptoms (Boyce et al., 2001). In our work with 24-month-olds, faster baseline PEP was associated with task-specific freezing behavior observed 1 week earlier (Buss, Davidson, Kalin, & Goldsmith, 2004). In another study, changes in HR and RSA were observed across an increasingly stressful lab visit, but PEP did not change in response to the tasks demands (Buss et al., 2005). This lack of association between task demands and PEP contrasts with other findings in children (Alkon et al., 2003). However, when we examined individual differences, we found that negative affect during a cognitive challenge was associated with slower PEP (i.e., less SNS reactivity) and that negative affect during a stranger approach was associated with faster PEP (i.e., greater SNS reactivity). Thus, there appears to be meaningful individual differences among interactions with negative affect, context (e.g., task demands), and SNS cardiac reactivity.

Summary

Although not all studies find expected associations between negative affect and HR, RSA, and PEP (e.g., Quas, Hong, Alkon, & Boyce, 2000), the preponderance of emerging results suggests that specific measures of cardiac reactivity and regulation (e.g., RSA suppression and PEP) help clarify negative affect-physiology associations. For instance, lower RSA and a failure to regulate RSA to task demands have consistently been associated with more fear and sadness behaviors and fewer anger and aggressive behaviors. Turning to the adjustment literature, we find that the ability to regulate PNS and SNS activity on the heart (i.e., RSA and PEP, respectively) is associated with fewer internalizing and externalizing symptoms.

Central Nervous System Approaches

In this section, we review the neural basis of negative emotion/temperament. In infants and young children, most of this work has utilized EEG whereas functional magnetic resonance imaging (fMRI) research is in its early stages. Building on the early theorizing and research of Cannon (1927) and Papez

(1937), researchers have investigated the neural circuitry of emotions both in animals (e.g., Davis, 1992, 1994; Kalin, 1993; LeDoux, 1992, 1996; Rolls, 1999) and in humans (e.g. Davidson, 1995; Davidson & Irwin, 1999). The neural structures that are recruited for emotion include, but are not limited to, the amygdala, bed nucleus of the stria terminalis, septum, hypothalamus, hippocampus, cingulate cortex, insular cortex, and the prefrontal cortex (including the dorsolateral, ventromedial, and orbitofrontal regions). The research agenda, pursued mostly in rats and monkeys, concerns the roles of these areas in reactions to emotion-eliciting stimuli, in pharmacological effects, and in the regulation of responses to stress. The investigation of fear and related states dominates the literature.

The amygdala has been implicated, most notably, in mediating the fear response. The amygdala appears to be crucial in extracting the emotional content of stimuli and, subsequently, in transducing the extracted affective value into autonomic, endocrine, and behavioral responses (Davis, 1992; LeDoux, 1992). Recent human neuroimaging studies have also highlighted the role of the amygdala in emotions, particularly negative emotions (Irwin et al., 1996; Morris et al., 1996; Whalen et al., 1998; see also Davidson & Irwin, 1999, for broader review). Much of this research has used recognition of fear versus happy faces under different conditions and tasks. These studies have identified greater signal increases in the amygdala for presentation of fear faces than happy faces, both during overt (Breiter et al., 1996; Morris et al., 1996) and masked presentation (Whalen et al., 1998). In a sample of children and adolescents, Baird and colleagues (1999) demonstrated amygdala activity to emotional faces compared with nonface images. Recently, Thomas and colleagues (2001b) showed increased amygdala activity for fear faces over neutral faces in adults, while in contrast, children showed more amygdala activity for the neutral faces. As suggested by Whalen (1998), the amygdala may be more sensitive to ambiguity than the actual emotional cues present in the stimuli.

In the developmental literature, Kagan and Snidman (1999) have speculated that behaviorally inhibited children differ in their threshold for amygdala activation. Recent neuroimaging evidence is converging to support this hypothesis. DeBellis and colleagues (2000) reported larger amygdala volumes in children with generalized anxiety disorder than in a group of controls. Using a masked-fear-faces presentation, Rauch and colleagues (2000) demonstrated exaggerated amygdala responses in patients with posttraumatic stress disorder (PTSD) in comparison to control subjects. Thomas, Drevets, and colleagues (2001a) demonstrated increased right amygdala activity to fear faces versus neutral faces for the anxious, but not depressed, children. In a follow-up study of inhibited children at 20 years of age, Schwartz, Wright, Shin, Kagan, and Rauch (2003) demonstrated that inhibited participants showed greater amygdale activity to novel versus neutral faces compared to uninhibited participants.

The prefrontal cortex (PFC) is also implicated in the neural circuitry of emotion. A large body of research with the PFC and emotion in humans has resulted in the idea of two main emotion or motivation systems: an approach system and a withdrawal system (Davidson & Irwin, 1999). The approach system is characterized by appetitive behavior and approach-related positive affect, whereas the withdrawal system is characterized by withdrawal behaviors. Anger, despite being a negatively valenced emotion, belongs to the approach system. These two systems are characterized by different patterns of anterior cerebral activity. Considerable evidence shows that approach-related behaviors, emotions, moods, and traits are characterized by greater relative left-prefrontal EEG activation. In contrast, withdrawal-related behaviors, emotions, moods, and traits are characterized by greater relative right-prefrontal EEG activation (see Davidson, 1992, 1995, for reviews).

According to Davidson's diathesis–stress model of anterior activation asymmetry, under conditions of stress or environmental challenge, individual differences in anterior asymmetry will increase the likelihood of specific emotional behaviors (Davidson, 1995). For instance, individuals with greater relative right frontal activation will be more likely to show withdrawal-related behaviors. In fact, behaviorally inhibited children show greater relative right frontal asymmetry at rest (Calkins, Fox, & Marshall, 1996; Davidson & Rickman, 1999; Fox et al., 1995) and during stressful tasks (Schmidt et al., 1999). Moreover, the children who had stable frontal EEG asymmetries from 4 years to 10 years of age also had more stable behavioral profiles (Davidson & Rickman, 1999). The association between fear behavior or distress and greater relative right frontal EEG activity has been consistently reported, even in temperamentally unselected samples of infants and children (e.g., Buss et al., 2003; Davidson & Fox, 1989; Fox & Davidson, 1988).

Anger has also recently been explored in the EEG asymmetry literature. In a series of studies, approach-motivated anger was associated with greater relatively left frontal activity (Harmon-Jones, 2003, for review). Although, to date, the bulk of this work has been conducted in adults, there are a few studies examining anger and EEG in children experiencing extreme temper tantrums. In a series of studies, Potegal and colleagues found converging evidence that tantrums in toddlers and preschoolers consist of two relatively independent sets of behaviors and emotional processes, anger and sadness/comfort seeking (which Potegal calls distress) (Carlson & Potegal, 2005; Potegal, 2005; Potegal & Davidson, 2003; Potegal, Kosorok, & Davidson, 2003). This anger/sadness distinction has also been found with EEG asymmetry in an examination of extreme groups—tantrum-prone versus non-tantrum-prone preschoolers (Potegal, Goldsmith, Chapman, Senulis, & Davidson, 1998). Children in the tantrum-prone group showed greater relative left baseline activation in the temporal leads compared to the non-tantrum-prone group. Moreover, across both groups, intensity of facial expressions of anger in the lab and parental report of anger (TBAQ Anger scale) was associated with greater relative left temporal baseline activation.

Summary

The EEG asymmetry work reviewed has solidified the role of motivation (approach vs. withdrawal) rather than affective valence (positive vs. negative) as the stronger influence on anterior cortical asymmetry, consistent with specific hypotheses differentiating anger from fear and sadness. However, the specific role of subcortical structures (e.g., amygdale) in withdrawal versus approach negative emotions remains unknown.

CONCLUDING THOUGHTS

In this chapter, we reviewed the biobehavioral literature in infancy and early childhood and provided new evidence for the role of biology in the development of discrete, negative affective behaviors. Behavior genetic evidence has shown that emotional behavior during the toddler period is as strongly influenced by genetic differences as during infancy or later childhood development. However, many lines of behavior-genetic evidence highlight environmental influence, such as our finding that variability in sadness is influenced by shared environmental variance. In the developmental psychobiology literature, converging evidence emphasizes the distinction between withdrawal-related negative emotions, such as fear and sadness, and approach-related negative emotions, such as anger. New findings suggest that individual differences in anger behaviors are more likely to be associated with lower cortisol levels whereas fear and sadness behaviors are more likely to be associated with higher cortisol levels.

However, our knowledge of these issues remains inchoate; expected findings sometimes are not obtained unless within-subject analyses are used and/or moderators, such as eliciting context, are taken into account. We are also just beginning to understand how biological variables interact with affective behavior to predict developmental pathways, such pathways toward later behavioral problems. Perhaps the overarching theme is that, like behavioral approaches, biological approaches to emotional development require careful measurement and close attention to issues of individual differences, context, and regulation.

ACKNOWLEDGMENTS

This research was supported in part by grants from the National Institutes of Health (Nos. R37-MH50560 and R01-MH59785; H. Hill Goldsmith, Principal Investigator), the Wisconsin Center for Affective Science (National Institutes of Mental Health Grant No. P50 MH52354; Richard J. Davidson, Center Director), and a National Institutes of Health, Predoctoral National Research Service Award (No. F31 MH11747) to Kristin A. Buss. We wish to express our appreciation to the families who participated in this project and to the dedicated staff of the UW Twin Center, the Wisconsin Twin Project, and the Laboratory for Affective Neuroscience.

REFERENCES

Alkon, A., Goldstein, L. H., Smider, N. A., Essex, M. J., Kupfer, D. J., & Boyce, T. W. (2003). Developmental and contextual influences on autonomic reactivity in young children. *Developmental Psychobiology, 42,* 64–78.

Asbury, K., Dunn, J. F., Pike, A., & Plomin, R. (2003). Nonshared environmental influences on individual differences in early behavioral development: A monozygotic twin differences study. *Child Development, 74,* 933–943.

Asendorpf, J. B., & Meier, G. H. (1993). Personality effects on children's speech in everyday life: Sociability-mediated exposure and shyness-mediated reactivity to social situations. *Journal of Personality and Social Psychology, 64,* 1072–1083.

Ax, A. F. (1953). The physiological differentiation between fear and anger in humans. *Psychosomatic Medicine, 15,* 433–442.

Baird, A. A., Gruber, S. A., Fein, D. A., Maas, L. C., Steingard, R. J., Renshaw, P. F., et al. (1999). Functional magnetic resonance imaging of facial affect recognition in children and adolescents. *Journal of the American Academy of Child and Adolescent Psychiatry, 38*(2), 195–199.

Berntson, G. G., Cacioppo, J. T., & Quigley, K. S. (1991). Autonomic determinism: The modes of autonomic control, the doctrine of autonomic space, and the laws of autonomic constraint. *Psychological Review, 98,* 459–487.

Boyce, T. W., Quas, J., Alkon, A., Smider, N. A., Essex, M. J., & Kupfer, D. J. (2001). Autonomic reactivity and psychopathology in middle childhood. *British Journal of Psychiatry, 179,* 144–150.

Breiter, H. C., Etcoff, N. L., Whalen, P. J., Kennedy, W. A., Rauch, S. L., Buckner, R. L., et al. (1996). Response and habituation of the human amygdala during visual processing of facial expression. *Neuron, 17,* 875–87.

Buss, K. A. (2000). *The physiology of emotional reactivity in toddlers: Endocrine and cardiac considerations.* Unpublished doctoral dissertation, University of Wisconsin–Madison.

Buss, K. A., Davidson, R. J., Kalin, N. H., & Goldsmith, H. H. (2004). Context specific freezing and associated physiological reactivity as a dysregulated fear response. *Developmental Psychology, 40,* 583–594.

Buss, K. A., & Goldsmith, H. H. (2000). *Manual and normative data for the Laboratory Temperament Assessment Battery—Toddler Version.* Psychology Department Technical Report, University of Wisconsin–Madison.

Buss, K. A., Goldsmith, H. H., & Davidson, R. J. (2005). Cardiac reactivity is associated with changes in negative emotion in 24-month-olds. *Developmental Psychobiology, 46,* 118–132.

Buss, K. A., Malmstadt, J., Dolski, I., Caranfa, D., Davidson, R. J., & Goldsmith, H. H. (1998). Vagal tone in infancy: Heritability, behavioral correlates and EEG. *Psychophysiology, 35*(Suppl. 1), S23.

Buss, K. A., Malmstadt Schumacher, J. R., Dolski, I., Kalin, N. H., Goldsmith, H. H., & Davidson, R. J. (2003). Right frontal brain activity, cortisol, and withdrawal behavior in 6-month-old infants. *Behavioral Neuroscience, 117,* 11–20.

Cacioppo, J. T., Klein, D. L., Berntson, G. G., & Hatfield, E. (1993). The psychophysiology of emotion. In M. Lewis & J. M. Haviland (Eds.), *Handbook of emotions* (pp. 119–142). New York: Guilford Press.

Calkins, S. D., & Dedmon, S. (2000). Physiological and behavioral regulation in 2-year-old children with aggressive/destructive behavior problems. *Journal of Abnormal Child Psychology, 28,* 103–118.

Calkins, S. D., & Fox, N. A. (1992). The relations among infant temperament, security of attachment, and behavioral inhibition at twenty-four months. *Child Development, 63,* 1456–1472.

Calkins, S. D., Fox, N. A., & Marshall, T. R. (1996). Behavioral and physiological antecedents of inhibited and uninhibited behavior. *Child Development, 67*(2), 523–540.

Calkins, S. D., & Keane, S. P. (2004). Cardiac vagal regulation across the preschool period: Stability, continuity, and implications for childhood adjustment. *Developmental Psychobiology, 45*(3), 101–112.

Cannon, W. B. (1927). The James–Lange theory of emotions: A critical examination and an alternative theory. *American Journal of Psychology, 39*, 106–124.

Carlson, G., & Potegal, M. (2005, October). *Are inpatient rages severe temper tantrums?* Paper presented at the 25th annual meeting of the American Academy of Child and Adolescent Psychiatry/Canadian Academy of Child and Adolescent Psychiatry, Toronto, Ontario, Canada.

Chrousos, G. P. (1998). Stressors, stress, and neuroendocrine integration of the adaptive response. The 1997 Hans Seyle Memorial Lecture. *Annals of the New York Academy of Sciences, 851*, 311–335.

Dallman, M., Akana, S., Schriber, K., Bradbury, M., Walker, C., Strack, A., et al. (1992). Stress, feedback and facilitation in the hypothalamo–pituitary–adrenal axis. *Journal of Neuroendocrinology, 4*, 517–526.

Davidson, R. J. (1992). Emotion and affective style: Hemispheric substrates. *Psychological Science, 3*, 39–43.

Davidson, R. J. (1995). Cerebral asymmetry, emotion and affective style. In R. J. Davidson & K. Hugdahl (Eds.), *Brain asymmetry* (pp. 361–387). Cambridge, MA: MIT Press.

Davidson, R. J., & Fox, N. A. (1989). Frontal brain asymmetry predicts infants' response to maternal separation. *Journal of Abnormal Psychology, 98*, 127–131.

Davidson, R. J., & Irwin, W. (1999). The functional neuroanatomy of emotion and affective style. *Trends in Cognitive Science, 3*, 11–21.

Davidson, R. J., Jackson, D. C., & Kalin, N. H. (2000). Emotion, plasticity, context and regulation: Perspectives from affective neuroscience. *Psychological Bulletin, 126*, 890–906.

Davidson, R. J., & Rickman, M. (1999). Behavioral inhibition and the emotional circuitry of the brain: Stability and plasticity during the early childhood years. In L. A. Schmidt & J. Schulkin (Eds.), *Extreme fear, shyness, and social phobia: Origins, biological mechanisms, and clinical outcomes* (pp. 67–87). New York: Oxford University Press.

Davis, M. (1992). The role of the amygdala in conditioned fear. In J. P. Aggleton (Ed.), *The amygdala* (pp. 255–306). New York: Wiley-Liss.

Davis, M. (1994). The role of the amygdala in emotional learning. *International Review of Neurobiology, 36*, 225–266.

Deater-Deckard, K., & O'Connor, T. G. (2000). Parent–child mutuality in early childhood: Two behavioral genetic studies. *Developmental Psychology, 36*(5), 561–570.

Deater-Deckard, K., & Petrill, S. A. (2004). Parent–child dyadic mutuality and child behavior problems: An investigation of gene–environment processes. *Journal of Child Psychology and Psychiatry, 45*, 1171–1179.

De Bellis, M. D., Casey, B. J., Dahl, R. E., Birmaher, B., Williamson, D. E., Thomas, K. M., et al. (2000). A pilot study of amygdala volumes in pediatric generalized anxiety disorder. *Biological Psychiatry, 48*(1), 51–57.

De Kloet, E. R. (1991). Brain corticosteroid receptor balance and homeostatic control. *Frontiers in Neuroendocrinology, 12*, 95–164.

Derks, E. M., Hudziak, J. J., van Beijsterveldt, C. E. M., Dolan, C. V., & Boomsma, D. I. (2004). A study of genetic and environmental influences on maternal and paternal CBCL syndrome scores in a large sample of 3-year-old Dutch twins. *Behavior Genetics, 34*, 571–583.

Dettling, A., Gunnar, M. R., & Donzella, B. (1999). Cortisol levels of young children in full-day childcare centers: Relations with age and temperament. *Psychoneuroendocrinology, 24*, 505–518.

DiLalla, L. F., Kagan, J., & Reznick, J. S. (1994). Genetic etiology of behavioral inhibition among 2-year-old children. *Infant Behavior and Development, 17*, 405–412.

Ekman, P., Levenson, R. W., & Friesen, W. V. (1983). Autonomic nervous system activity distinguishes among emotions. *Science, 221*, 1208–1210.

Eley, T. C., Bolton, D., O-Connor, T. G., Perrin, S., Smith, P., & Plomin, R. (2003). A twin study of anxiety-related behaviours in pre-school children. *Journal of Child Psychology and Psychiatry, 44*, 945–960.

El-Sheikh, M. (2001). Parental drinking problems and children's adjustment: Vagal regulation and emotional reactivity as pathways and moderators of risk. *Journal of Abnormal Psychology, 110*, 499–515.

Emde, R. N., & Hewitt, J. K. (2001). *Infancy to early childhood: Genetic and environmental influences on developmental change*. New York: Oxford University Press.

Falconer, D. S. (1989). *Introduction to quantitative genetics* (3rd ed.). New York: Longman.

Fox, N. A., & Davidson, R. J. (1988). Patterns of brain electrical activity during facial signs of emotion in 10-month-old infants. *Developmental Psychology, 24*(2), 230–236.

Fox, N. A., Rubin, K. H., Calkins, S. D., Marshall, T. R., Coplan, R. J., Porges, S. W., et al. (1995). Frontal activation asymmetry and social competence at four years of age. *Child Development, 66*(6), 1770–1784.

Frankenhaeuser, M. (1980). Psychobiological aspects of life stress. In S. Levin & H. Ursin (Eds.), *Coping and health* (pp. 203–223). New York: Plenum Press.

Goldsmith, H. H. (1996). Studying temperament via construction of the Toddler Behavior Assessment Questionnaire. *Child Development, 67*, 218–235.

Goldsmith, H. H. (2003). Genetics of emotional development. In R. J. Davidson, K. R. Scherer, & H. H. Goldsmith (Eds.), *Handbook of affective science* (pp. 300–319). Oxford, UK: Oxford University Press.

Goldsmith, H. H., Reilly, H. H., Lemery, K. S., Longley, S., & Prescott, A. (1994). *Manual for Preschool Lab-TAB*. Unpublished manuscript.

Goldsmith, H. H., & Rothbart, M. K. (1988). *Manual for the Laboratory Temperament Assessment Battery (v. 1)*. Unpublished manuscript.

Gunnar, M. R. (1992). Reactivity of the hypothalamic–pituitary–adrenocortical system to stressors in normal infants and children. *Pediatrics, 90*, 491–497.

Gunnar, M. R. (1994). Psychoendocrine studies of temperament and stress in early childhood: Expanding current models. In J. E. Bates & T. D. Wachs (Eds.), *Temperament: Individual differences at the interface of biology and behavior APA science volumes* (pp. 175–198). Washington, DC: American Psychological Association.

Gunnar, M. R., Brodersen, L., Nachmias, M., Buss, K. A., & Rigatuso, J. (1996). Stress reactivity and attachment security. *Developmental Psychobiology, 29*, 191–204.

Gunnar, M. R., Larson, M., Hertsgaard, L., Harris, M., & Brodersen, L. (1992). The stressfulness of separation among 9-month-old infants: Effects of social context variables and infant temperament. *Child Development, 63*, 290–303.

Gunnar, M. R., Tout, K., deHaan, M., Pierce, S., & Stansbury, K. (1997). Temperament, social competence, and adrenocortical activity in preschoolers. *Developmental Psychobiology, 31*, 65–85.

Harmon-Jones, E. (2003). Clarifying the emotive functions of asymmetrical frontal cortical activity. *Psychophysiology, 40*(6), 838–848.

Hart, J., Gunnar, M., & Cicchetti, D. (1995). Salivary cortisol in maltreated children: Evidence of relations between neuroendocrine activity and social competence. *Development and Psychopathology, 7*, 11–26.

Irwin, W., Davidson, R. J., Lowe, M. J., Mock, B. J., Sorenson, J. A., & Turski, P. A. (1996). Human amygdala activation detected with echo-planar functional magnetic resonance imaging. *Neuroreport: An International Journal for the Rapid Communication of Research in Neuroscience, 7*(11), 1765–1769.

James, W. (1884). What is an emotion? *Mind, 8*, 188–205.

James, W. (1890). *The principles of psychology* (Vol. I.). New York: Henry Holt.

Jang, K. L. (2005). *The behavioral genetics of psychopathology*. Mahwah, NJ: Erlbaum.

Kagan, J., Reznick, J. S., Clarke, C., Snidman, N., & Garcia Coll, C. (1984). Behavioral inhibition to the unfamiliar. *Child Development, 55*, 2212–2225.

Kagan, J., Reznick, J., & Gibbons, J. (1989). Inhibited and uninhibited types of children. *Child Development, 60*(4), 838–845.

Kagan, J., Reznick, J. S., & Snidman, N. (1987). The physiology and psychology of behavioral inhibition in children. *Child Development, 58,* 1459–1473.

Kagan, J., Reznick, J. S., & Snidman, N. (1988). Biological bases of childhood shyness. *Science, 240,* 167–171.

Kagan, J., Reznick, J. S., Snidman, N., Gibbons, J., & Johnson, M. O. (1988). Childhood derivatives of inhibition and lack of inhibition to the unfamiliar. *Child Development, 59,* 1580–1589.

Kagan, J., & Snidman, N. (1999). Early predictors of adult anxiety disorders. *Biological Psychiatry, 46,* 1536–1541.

Kagan, J., Snidman, N., & Arcus, D. M. (1992). Initial reaction to unfamiliarity. *Current Directions in Psychological Science, 1,* 171–174.

Kalin, N. H. (1993). The neurobiology of fear. *Scientific American, 268,* 94–101.

Kalin, N. H., Larson, C., Shelton, S. E., & Davidson, R. (1998). Asymmetric frontal brain activity, cortisol, and behavior associated with fearful temperament in Rhesus monkeys. *Behavioral Neuroscience, 112,* 286–292.

Kirschbaum, C., & Hellhammer, D. H. (1989). Salivary cortisol in psychobiological research: An overview. *Neuropsychobiology, 22,* 150–169.

Kirschbaum, C., & Hellhammer, D. H. (1994). Salivary cortisol in psychoneuoendocrine research: Recent developments and application. *Psychoneuroendocrinology, 19,* 313–333.

Lange, C. (1922). *The emotions.* Baltimore: Williams & Wilkins.

LeDoux, J. E. (1992). Emotion and the amygdala. In J. P. Aggleton (Ed.), *The amygdala: Neurobiological aspects of emotion, memory, and mental dysfunction* (pp. 339–351). New York: Wiley-Liss.

LeDoux, J. E. (1996). *The emotional brain.* New York: Simon & Schuster.

Lewis, M., & Ramsay, D. (2005). Infant emotional and cortisol responses to goal blockage. *Child Development, 76,* 518–530.

Manke, B., Saudino, K. J., & Grant, J. D. (2001). Extremes analysis of observed temperament dimensions. In R. N. Emde & J. K. Hewitt (Eds.), *Infancy to early childhood: Genetic and environmental influences on developmental change* (pp. 52–72). New York: Oxford University Press.

Marshall, P. J., & Stevenson-Hinde, J. (1998). Behavioral inhibition, heart period, and respiratory sinus arrhythmia in young children. *Developmental Psychobiology, 33,* 283–292.

Mason, J. W. (1968). A review of the psychoendocrine research on the pituitary–adrenal cortical system. *Psychosomatic Medicine, 30,* 576–608.

Matheny, A. P. (1989). Children's behavioral inhibition over age and across situations: Genetic similarity for a trait during change. *Journal of Personality and Social Psychology, 57,* 215–235.

McArdle, J. J., & Goldsmith, H. H. (1990). Alternative common-factor models for multivariate biometric analysis. *Behavior Genetics, 20,* 569–608.

McBurnett, K., Lahey, B. B., Frick, P. J., Risch, C., Loeber, R., Hart, E. L., et al. (1991). Anxiety, inhibition, and conduct disorder in children: II. Relations to salivary cortisol. *Journal of the American Academy of Child and Adolescent Psychiatry, 30,* 192–196.

McBurnett, K., Lahey, B. B., Rathouz, P. J., & Loeber, R. (2000). Low salivary cortisol and persistent aggression in boys referred for disruptive behavior. *Archives of General Psychiatry, 57,* 38–43.

McEwen, B. S. (1998). Protective and damaging effects of stress mediators. *New England Journal of Medicine, 338,* 171–179.

Meaney, M. J. (2001). Maternal care, gene expression, and the transmission of individual differences in stress reactivity across generations. *Annual Review of Neuroscience, 24,* 1161–1192.

Morris, J. S., Frith, C. D., Perrett, D. I., Rowland, D., Young, A. W., Calder, A. J., et al. (1996, October 31). A differential neural response in the human amygdala to fearful and happy facial expressions. *Nature, 383,* 812–815.

Nachmias, M., Gunnar, M., Mangelsdorf, S., Parritz, R., & Buss, K. A. (1996). Behavioral inhibition and stress reactivity: The moderating role of attachment security. *Child Development, 67,* 508–522.

Neale, M. C., & Cardon, L. R. (1992). *Methodology for genetic studies of twins and families.* Dordrecht, The Netherlands: Kluwer Academic.

Papez, J. W. (1937). A proposed mechanism for emotion. *Archives of Neurology and Psychiatry, 38*, 725–743.

Plomin, R., DeFries, J. C., McClearn, G. E., & Rutter, M. (1997). *Behavioral genetics* (3rd ed.). New York: Freeman.

Porges, S. W. (1992). Vagal tone: A physiological marker of stress vulnerability. *Pediatrics, 90*, 498–504.

Porges, S. W., Doussard-Roosevelt, J. A., Portales, A. L., & Greenspan, S. I. (1996). Infant regulation of the vagal "brake" predicts child behavior problems: A psychobiological model of social behavior. *Developmental Psychobiology, 29*, 697–712.

Potegal, M. (2003, April). *Preliminary observations on salivary cortisol baseline and transients associated with tantrums in 3 year olds.* Paper presented at the 2003 biennial meeting of the Society for Research in Child Development, Tampa, FL.

Potegal, M. (2005, April). *Tantrums in externalizing, internalizing and typically developing 4 year olds.* Paper presented at the 2005 biennial meeting of the Society for Research in Child Development, Atlanta, GA.

Potegal, M., & Davidson, R. (2003). Temper tantrums in young children: I. Behavioral composition. *Journal of Developmental and Behavioral Pediatrics, 24*, 140–147.

Potegal, M., Goldsmith, H. H., Chapman, R., Senulis, J., & Davidson, R. (1998, July). *Tantrums, temperament, and temporal lobes.* Paper presented at the meeting of the International Society for Research on Aggression, Ramapo, NJ.

Potegal, M., Kosorok, M. R., & Davidson, R. (2003). Temper tantrums in young children: II. Tantrum duration and temporal organization. *Journal of Developmental and Behavioral Pediatrics, 24*, 148–154.

Quas, J., Hong, M., Alkon, A., & Boyce, T. W. (2000). Dissociations between psychobiologic reactivity and emotional expression in children. *Developmental Psychobiology, 37*, 153–175.

Rauch, S. L., Whalen, P. J., Shin, L. M., McInerney, S. C., Macklin, M. L., Lasko, N. B., et al. (2000). Exaggerated amygdala response to masked facial stimuli in posttraumatic stress disorder: A functional MRI study. *Biological Psychiatry, 47*(9), 769–776.

Raudenbush, S. W., & Bryk, A. S. (2002). *Hierarchical linear models: Applications and data analysis methods.* Thousand Oaks, CA: Sage.

Reznick, J. S., Kagan, J., Snidman, N., Gersten, M., Baak, K., & Rosenberg, A. (1986). Inhibited and uninhibited children: A follow-up study. *Child Development, 57*, 660–680.

Robinson, J. L., Kagan, J., Reznick, J. S., & Corley, R. (1992). The heritability of inhibited and uninhibited behavior: A twin study. *Developmental Psychology, 28*, 1030–1037.

Rolls, E. T. (1999). *The brain and emotion.* Oxford, UK: University Press.

Rothbart, M. K., & Ahadi, S. A. (1994). Temperament and the development of personality. *Journal of Abnormal Psychology, 103*, 55–66.

Rothbart, M. K., Ahadi, S. A., & Hershey, K. L. (1994). Temperament and social behavior in childhood. *Merrill-Palmer Quarterly, 40*, 21–39.

Rutter, M., Pickles, A., Murray, R., & Eaves, L. (2001). Testing hypotheses on specific environmental causal effects on behavior. *Psychological Bulletin, 127*(3), 291–324.

Schmidt, L. A., Fox, N. A., Rubin, K. H., Sternberg, E. M., Gold, P. W., Smith, C. C., et al. (1997). Behavioral and neuroendocrine responses in shy children. *Developmental Psychobiology, 30*, 127–140.

Schmidt, L. A., Fox, N. A., Schulkin, J., & Gold, P. W. (1999). Behavioral and psychophysiological correlates of self-presentation in temperamentally shy children. *Developmental Psychobiology, 35*, 119–135.

Schwartz, C. E., Wright, C. I., Shin, L. M., Kagan, J., & Rauch, S. L. (2003). Inhibited and uninhibited infants "grown up": Adult amygdalar response to novelty. *Science, 300*, 1952–1953.

Sinha, R., Lovallo, W. R., & Parsons, O. A. (1992). Cardiovascular differentiation of emotions. *Psychosomatic Medicine, 54*, 422–435.

Smider, N. A., Essex, M. J., Kalin, N. H., Buss, K .A., Klein, M. H., Davidson, R. J., et al. (2002). Salivary cortisol as a predictor of socio-emotional adjustment during kindergarten: A prospective study. *Child Development, 73,* 75–92.

Snijders, T. A. B., & Bosker, R. J. (1999). *Multivariate analysis: An introduction to basic and advanced multilevel modeling.* Thousand Oaks, CA: Sage.

Stansbury, K., & Gunnar, M. R. (1994). Adrenocortical activity and emotion regulation. In N. A. Fox (Ed.), The development of emotion regulation: Biological and behavioral considerations. *Monographs of the Society for Research in Child Development, 59*(Serial No. 240), 108–134.

Stifter, C. A., & Fox, N. A. (1990). Infant reactivity: Physiological correlates of newborn and five-month temperament. *Developmental Psychology, 26,* 582–588.

Stifter, C. A., Fox, N. A., & Porges, S. W. (1989). Facial expressivity and vagal tone in five- and ten-month-old infants. *Infant Behavior and Development, 12,* 127–137.

Stifter, C. A., & Jain, A. (1996). Psychological correlates of infant temperament: Stability of behavior and autonomic patterning from 5 to 18 months. *Developmental Psychobiology, 29,* 379–391.

Tennes, K., & Kreye, M. (1985). Children's adrenocortical responses to classroom activities and tests in elementary school. *Psychosomatic Medicine, 47,* 451–460.

Tennes, K., Kreye, M., Avitable, N., & Wells, R. (1986). Behavioral correlates of excreted catecholamines and cortisol in second-grade children. *Journal of the American Academy of Child Psychiatry, 25,* 764–770.

Thomas, K. M., Drevets, W. C., Dahl, R. E., Ryan, N. D., Birmaher, B., Eccard, C. H., et al. (2001). Amygdala response to fearful faces in anxious and depressed children. *Archives of General Psychiatry, 58*(11), 1057–1063.

Thomas, K. M., Drevets, W. C., Whalen, P. J., Eccard, C. H., Dahl, R. E., Ryan, N. D., et al. (2001). Amygdala response to facial expressions in children and adults. *Biological Psychiatry, 49*(4), 309–316.

Tout, K., deHaan, M., Kipp Campbell, E., & Gunnar, M. R. (1998). Social behavior correlates of cortisol activity in child care: Gender differences and time-of-day effects. *Child Development, 69,* 1247–1262.

Turkheimer, E., & Waldron, M. (2000). Nonshared environment: A theoretical, methodological, and quantitative review. *Psychological Bulletin, 126*(1), 78–108.

van Goozen, S. H., Matthys, W., Cohen-Kettenis, P. T., Buitelaar, J. K., & van Engeland, H. (2000). Hypothalamic–pituitary–adrenal axis and autonomic nervous system activity in disruptive children and matched controls. *Journal of the American Academy of Child and Adolescent Psychiatry, 39,* 1438–1445.

van Goozen, S. H., Matthys, W., Cohen-Kettenis, P. T., Gispen-deWied, C., Wiegant, V. M., & van Engeland, H. (1998). Salivary cortisol and cardiovascular activity during stress in oppositional defiant disorder boys and normal controls. *Biological Psychiatry, 43,* 531–539.

Van Hulle, C. A., Lemery, K. S., & Goldsmith, H. H. (2002). Wisconsin Twin Panel. *Twin Research, 5,* 1–4.

Watamura, S. E., Sebanc, A. M., & Gunnar, M. K. (2002). Rising cortisol at childcare: Relations with nap, rest, and temperament. *Developmental Psychobiology, 40,* 33–42.

Whalen, P. J. (1998). Fear, vigilance, and ambiguity: Initial neuroimaging studies of the human amygdala. *Current Directions in Psychological Science, 7*(6), 177–188.

Whalen, P. J., Rauch, S. L., Etcoff, N. L., McInerney, S. C., Lee, M. B., & Jenike, M. A. (1998). Masked presentations of emotional facial expressions modulate amygdala activity without explicit knowledge. *Journal of Neuroscience, 18*(1), 411–418.

16

The Sociocultural Context of Transitions in Early Socioemotional Development

SUSAN M. PEREZ
MARY GAUVAIN

> By the age of 2, children have become creatures of their cultures: they can make meaningful utterances, initiate interaction, and display complicated likes and dislikes.
>
> —MUNROE AND MUNROE (1994, p. 72)

Many changes in the second and third years of life serve as critical transitions of social, emotional, and cognitive development and, thereby, pave the way for further psychological growth. As in other periods of development, these changes are a product of the child's emerging capabilities and the social and cultural context in which the child develops. In this chapter we discuss the sociocultural context of early socioemotional development. We suggest that it is essential to take the social and cultural context into account both in describing the normative developmental changes that take place during this period and in explaining how this development occurs and variation in this process. Moreover, it is important to consider the maturational changes and needs of the child and the contributions of the sociocultural context as interactive and dynamic. Both the nature and mechanisms of sociocultural influence change as children's capabilities develop and their social world expands.

What makes toddlerhood a unique and transitional period of development and how is this period of growth situated in the social and cultural context? In her age-related classifications of children, Margaret Mead (1949) distinguished children in the following way: She called children from birth to 1 year of age "lap children," children in the second and third years were "knee children," 4- and 5-year-olds were "yard children," and 6- to 10-year-olds were "community children." These age groupings simultaneously describe children in terms of their physical and cognitive capabilities and their relation to the world, including the extent to which their abilities require supervision and protection by elders (Whiting & Edwards, 1988). Lap and knee children require almost constant supervision. A primary distinction, however, is that lap children have limited independent mobility. Therefore, they are almost always in physical or visual contact with a caregiver on whom they rely for much of their movement and for the provision of resources, support, and protection. In contrast, knee children are ambulatory and they can obtain resources, explore the world, regulate social distance, and seek protection on their own. Both lap and knee children are inexperienced and their knowledge of the world and its hazards are limited, but the independent mobility of knee children makes them more susceptible to injury as well as invites unique opportunities for learning (National Center for Health Statistics, 2000). As a result, when children move from being lap to knee children, sociocultural contributions to development change. In all cultural communities, knee children exact substantial attention and receive less nurturance and more control from caregivers than lap children do (Edwards, 1989). However, cultures differ in the identity of the caregivers and in the extent of supervision and control directed toward children at this age (Weisner & Gallimore, 1977). Reasons for these cultural differences include subsistence level, maternal workload, family size, and contributions from social supports (Whiting & Edwards, 1988).

What this description suggests is that in the second and third years of life children are almost always in the company of others. Their developing capabilities, including new physical, cognitive, and communicative skills, make way for new types of social experiences and transactions, which reflect broader cultural values and practices. Although several theoretical perspectives contend that social and cultural experiences play a formative role in early development (Bronfenbrenner & Morris, 1998; Super & Harkness, 1986; Rogoff, 2003), carving out the details of this complex process and understanding the common developmental themes and their variations across social and cultural conditions are difficult. Efforts to trace this process have taken several tacks. Some researchers concentrate on ways in which the broader cultural context, instantiated in practices, values, and beliefs regulate opportunities for psychological development (Goodnow, Miller, & Kessel, 1995; Sigel, McGillicuddy-DeLisi, & Goodnow, 1992). Other researchers examine how social interactions between children and their caregivers, as well as other regular social partners, affect how development occurs (Gauvain, 2001). An underlying assumption in both approaches is that children are born into and participate in a culture *and* in a social system within that culture. The proximal social system represents the broader cultural context largely via the types of activities and social roles in which participants engage. In addition, it represents its own particular qualities through the unique history of its members and how individuals interpret and act on the shared practices and values of the culture. In specific situations, these cultural and social forces are molded to fit with the capabilities and needs of the child, defined by developmentally related capabilities and expectations as well as the child's own individual characteristics, including temperament, cognitive skills, and interests.

There are a number of critical changes in children's capabilities in the second and third years that set the stage for, and constrain, children's social and cultural participation. Children in all cultures experience substantial alteration in their daily lives and in how they are treated by others. In many cultures, this is the time when children are weaned from the breast, sleeping and social arrangements change, maternal care is shared with or transferred to other people, oftentimes siblings, and children begin to move out into the world and assert their own will (Edwards, 1989; Martini & Kirkpatrick, 1992). How much stress ensues from these changes, for both children and parents, varies widely across cultures and family situations. There are also important changes in children's cognitive capabilities, most significantly the ability to represent and operate on symbols, including the understanding and use of language, which has enormous impact on children's social life. In addition, children's social competence increases, their sense of self develops, and they have better understanding and control of emotions. Together, these changes affect how children experience and interact with the world and learn to function independently or interdependently to become contributing members of society (Edwards, 1989).

A sociocultural approach to the study of early socioemotional development provides a useful framework for investigating the role of interpersonal processes that serve to inculcate children into the beliefs, values, and practices of the community in which they will become competent and mature members and meet parental expectations and socialization goals (Miller & Goodnow, 1995). This perspective offers insight into development that is not available in other approaches. Unlike traditional approaches that separate social, emotional, cognitive, and language development, a sociocultural approach strives to integrate these aspects of psychological growth because, together, they constitute competent cultural participation—the goal of human development. A sociocultural perspective also attempts to delineate the underlying, organized forces in the social and cultural context of psychological growth, what Super and Harkness (1986) refer to as the *developmental niche*. In so doing, this approach has the potential to provide a more detailed description of the psychological context of development than is presently available. Finally, a sociocultural approach emphasizes learning as a primary mechanism of development. Historically, many socialization models included learning, but it was conceptualized as a relatively passive process. Contemporary sociocultural approaches view learning as a dynamic process in which cultural members, even very young members, function as active mental agents who, within the realm of their abilities, make sense of and adapt the information provided by the social and cultural context to meet their own needs and circumstances (Shweder et al., 1998). This process is inherently sociocognitive, including contributions from the individual and the social group. It is an individual process in that psychological change occurs in the person's own mind. It is social in two ways. Knowledge gets into the mind largely through social experiences of one sort or another (Vygotsky, 1978), and much of the knowledge that is in the mind is social in origin and, therefore, shared with others. Further specification as to how this process operates and affects particular points of development is needed, however. Recently, several studies have addressed this topic in relation to the periods of infancy, middle childhood, and adolescence (see Cole, Cole, & Lightfoot, 2005).

In this chapter we take the view that a sociocultural approach has much to offer to an understanding of development during the period of toddlerhood. We begin with a brief overview of the sociocultural perspective and the ways in which social processes that contribute to socioemotional development in the second and third years of life are integrated with cultural experience. We discuss research that examines three areas of development that are widely studied in this age group because of their importance to development at this time, specifically play, attention, and the regulation of emotion. We aim to demonstrate some of the unique contributions offered by a sociocultural approach to an understanding of socioemotional development and apply this understanding, by way of illustration, to these specific areas of development during toddlerhood.

A SOCIOCULTURAL APPROACH TO PSYCHOLOGICAL DEVELOPMENT

A sociocultural approach to psychological development emphasizes the roles of social, symbolic, and material resources in organizing and supporting human development (Rogoff, 2003; Tomasello, 1999; Vygotsky, 1978). Culture, a system of shared meaning and activity, provides the context for child development (Cole, 1996). Culture is instantiated in values and practices as well as conceptions or beliefs about childhood and development, which shape the ways in which communities approach child socialization (Shweder et al., 1998). Cultural practices, in conjunction with cultural beliefs about development and the capabilities of the child at the time, determine the types of activities available to children, the nature of children's participation in these activities, and children's opportunities to develop skills through social processes as they engage in activities (Miller & Goodnow, 1995). For instance, cultures differ as to whether adults or children are primarily responsible for children's learning and development, whether children are mostly segregated from or integrated into adult activity, and whether direct instruction, observation, or joint activity is the primary means of advancing children's skills (Gauvain, 2005). Cultures also differ in the skills that are considered important and emphasized in activities (e.g., individualistic goals such as academic success vs. collectivistic goals such as social responsibility toward the group) (Greenfield, Keller, Fuligni, & Maynard, 2003).

Although research based on a sociocultural approach has focused extensively on cognitive development, the role of social and cultural processes as a means of advancing capabilities can be applied readily to social and emotional development. Because social, emotional, and cognitive development are coordinated and integrated across development, many of the same underlying processes that have been identified in research on cognitive development may be at play in the social transmission of skills in the areas of social and emotional development. These processes include opportunities for children to acquire skills through social interaction, ongoing participation in activity with the guidance of more experienced partners, and the support and direction provided by tools of thinking and routine behavioral practices available in the culture (Rogoff, 2003). Such experiences allow children to participate in their culture, whether this participation involves solving a cognitive problem, managing a social conflict, or regulating an emotion, at a level at which they would not be capable on their own. These interactions and experiences serve as mechanisms for development; are directed toward the achievement of particular sets of skills, values, and beliefs; and will eventually lead to children becoming competent members of their community (Gauvain, 2001; Rogoff, 2003).

Social interaction, especially between children and more experienced partners and targeted toward the child's *zone of proximal development* (Vygotsky, 1978), provides an immediate context for facilitating more mature functioning. Research on processes like scaffolding (Wood, Wood, & Middleton, 1978) and guided participation (Rogoff, 2003) has shown that children are active participants in these processes and that different patterns of interaction between children and more skilled individuals have different consequences for development. To contribute optimally to children's growth, these processes need to be responsive to the child's needs, with responsibility transferred from the more experienced partner to the child as the child gains competence.

While considering social interaction between caregivers and children a mechanism for development, it is important to remember that these interactions are embedded within the context of a relationship that includes the partners' knowledge of each other, their emotional bond, and their prior experiences with each other. Socialization goals and practices are influenced by characteristics of parents and children that are relatively stable over time and affect social interaction, such as parenting style and child temperament, and by the socioemotional experiences the interactive partners have with each other, or their *shared social history* (Gauvain & DeMent, 1991). Adult guidance is influenced by such factors as parental expectations, task goals, and the child's need for assistance (Garner, 1995; Wood et al., 1978). These factors are also related to caregiver perceptions of a child's ability to participate in particular activities and the amount of responsibility the child can assume.

Research has identified several social and cultural processes that provide opportunities for children as young as 1 and 2 years of age to learn cognitive skills that, in turn, contribute to socioemotional development. These processes include attention regulation (Chavajay & Rogoff, 1999), collaborative activity (DeLoache, 1984); conversation (Mullen & Yi, 1995), cultural practices specific to age-related expectations (Gaskins, 1999), instruction (LeVine et al., 1994), guided participation (Rogoff, Mistry, Göncü, & Mosier, 1993), joint attention (Morales et al., 2000), modeling and observational learning (Bauer & Dow, 1994), negotiation (Litowitz, 1993), parental beliefs or ethnotheories (Harkness & Super, 1996), scaffolding (Valsiner, 1984), shared intentions (Tomasello, 1999), shared narratives and storytelling (Mistry, 1993), and social referencing (Repacholi, 1998). In addition, many important cognitive changes that occur in the second and third years of life have been studied in ways that are based on or consistent with a sociocultural perspective, including concept formation (Gelman, Coley, Rosengren, Hartman, & Pappas, 1998), event memory (Ratner, 1980), planning (Benson, 1994), problem solving (Gauvain & Fagot, 1995), understanding of mind (Carpendale & Lewis, 2004), symbolic representation in language (Hollich, Hirsch-Pasek, & Golinkoff, 2000), numerical understanding (Saxe, Guberman, & Gearhart, 1987), and pretense (Farver & Wimbarti, 1995).

Although research is limited, efforts to examine social and cultural processes in relation to socioemotional development in the second and third years have been fruitful. In the next section we use a sociocultural perspective to discuss three specific areas of early socioemotional development: play, attention, and emotion regulation. We focus on these areas of development because, during the transition to toddlerhood, they reflect inherently social processes, largely take place in the social context, and rely on support and guidance from caregivers. These processes illustrate the importance of social interaction in early socioemotional development. As such, these areas of socioemotional development are likely to be influenced by the larger sociocultural context in which development occurs. As the ecological systems approach suggests, broad or more distal cultural beliefs and practices can organize proximal parenting practices and parent–child social interactions (Bronfenbrenner & Morris, 1998). Thus, we might expect to see differences across cultural communities in the goals and socialization practices pertaining to these areas of socioemotional development.

It is important to point out that many of our examples are drawn from research in Western communities and primarily include European American samples. Although we find this research useful for illustrating some of the social and cultural contributions to development in toddlerhood, it paints a narrow portrait of the cultural experiences children have at this time. For instance, this research tends to concentrate on the interactions of toddlers and single caregivers, usually mothers. However, cross-cultural research indicates that multiple caregivers are more common around the world for children of this age than are single caregivers (Seymour, 2004), which challenges assumptions about the importance of exclusive early relationships with a primary caregiver (Tronick, Morelli, & Ivey, 1992). Although our illustrations were constrained by the available psychological literature, we hope that research on toddlerhood expands to include samples that are more representative of the range of young children's experience both within and across cultural communities. Broadening research in this way will likely lead to fundamental changes in theories of psychological development (Seymour, 2004), changes that are likely to recognize the inextricable connection between psychological development and the sociocultural context in which development occurs.

THE SOCIOCULTURAL CONTEXT OF SOCIOEMOTIONAL DEVELOPMENT IN TODDLERHOOD

During toddlerhood, children acquire skills in many areas relevant to overall socioemotional functioning, including increased mobility, language development, and advances in cognition, self-development, and emotion regulation. These advancements reflect a time of transition because they result in changes in how the child interacts with the world and, in turn, the ways in which parents and others perceive the child and approach socialization and interaction with the child. An important feature of a sociocultural approach to early socioemotional development is its attention to how social, cognitive, and emotional aspects of psychological growth inform and influence each other. For instance, the development of emotional competence depends, in part, on cognitive skills that develop in social context such as language, attention regulation, and problem-solving ability (Saarni, 1999). Language development occurs in social context through processes such as child-directed speech and joint attention (Hoff, 2001); attentional processes are subject to socialization goals consistent with cultural values, beliefs, and practices (Chavajay & Rogoff, 1999; Zukow-Goldring, 1997); and more skilled partners scaffold the development of problem-solving skills (Gauvain, 2001).

Thus, from a sociocultural perspective this age period is transitional not only because children are in the midst of developing many important and powerful skills but also because the ways in which these skills form and develop occur under the tutelage of more skilled partners in the cultural context of development. Thus, children's emerging abilities and the sociocultural context in which these abilities are nurtured organize children's daily experiences and have long-term developmental consequences for children's overall socioemotional functioning. For instance, research with Western samples has demonstrated that the quality of parent–child interaction in the form of cognitive stimulation versus restrictiveness in toddlerhood predicts self-regulatory competence in middle childhood (Olson, Bates, Sandy, & Schilling, 2002); parent–child relationships with high levels of negative affect in the first 36 months of life predict children's difficulty in cognitive and social development through preschool and first grade (NICHD Early Child Care Research Network, 2004); mother–child conflict at 30 months predicts children's emotional understanding at age 3 (Laible & Thompson, 2002); parent–child relationships characterized by shared positive affect, cooperation, and responsiveness in the second year predict displays of moral emotions, such as guilt and empathy, in preschool and early school-age children (Kochanska, 2002); and, maternal strategies for regulating children's emotional reactions at 30 months predict children's regulation of emotion at age 5 (Spinrad, Stifter, Donelan-McCall, & Turner, 2004). The nature and quality of caregiver–child interactions in toddlerhood have important implications for children's socioemotional development and functioning. However, cross-cultural research with non-Western samples suggests that during this time, other relationships may also begin to play significant roles in child development. Observations by Tronick and colleagues (1992) of Efe infants and toddlers (the Efe are a foraging community in Africa) indicate that from 1 to 3 years of age children spend less time with their mothers and more time with peers. By age 2, about half of the time children had peers as their social companions; by age 3, 70% of the children's social contact time was with peers.

The following sections elaborate on the theme of adult guidance and socialization practices in the second and third years. First, we discuss the developmental progression of children's play in the toddler years. Play simultaneously incorporates and contributes to children's development of language, cognition, emotion, and social skills at this time and patterns of children's play vary with the cultural context in which the child is socialized. Second, we discuss the development of attention in the toddler period. Attentional skills contribute greatly to a toddler's ability to regulate emotion, are important for social competence and learning, especially in social context, and are subject to socialization that varies with cultural context. Finally, we discuss the early development of emotion regulation. Emotion regulation has immediate and long-term implications for children's socioemotional functioning, relies on emerging cognitive skills as well as support from more experienced social partners, and is subject to socialization practices that vary with the larger cultural context. Figure 16.1 provides a summary of the developmental milestones and similarities and differences across social and cultural contexts in these areas of socioemotional development in toddlerhood.

The Sociocultural Context of Play in Toddlerhood

The Importance of Play and Key Developments in the Toddler Period

Play is an important activity of early childhood that both reflects and contributes to children's cognitive and social skills (Göncü, Tuermer, Jain, & Johnson, 1999). Play exists in a variety of forms, including physical, object,

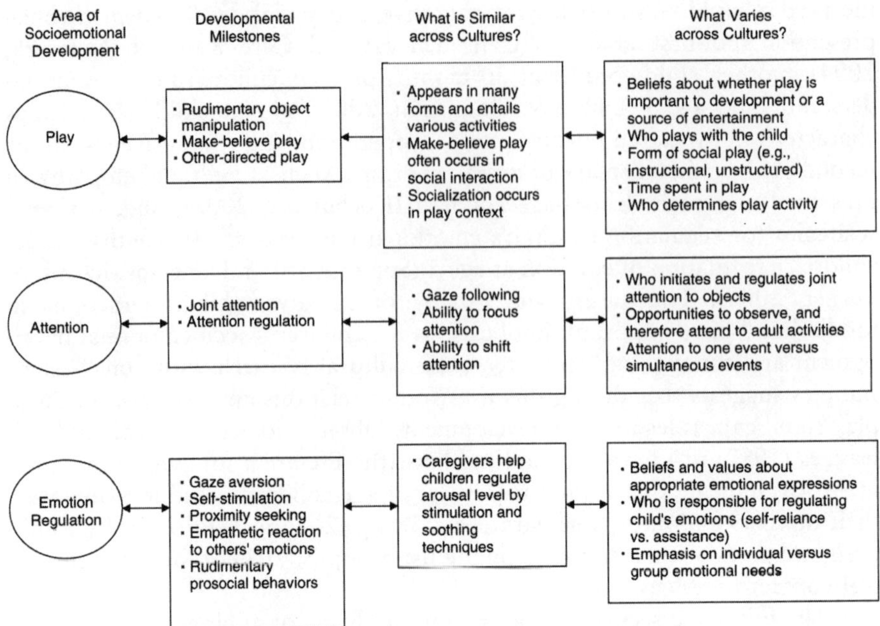

FIGURE 16.1. Developmental milestones and cultural similarities and variations in play, attention, and emotion regulation in toddlerhood.

and pretend play, all of which have been described in a wide range of cultures (Smith, 2004). Play has both immediate and delayed benefits for young children. Immediate benefits of play include the establishment and maintenance of social relationships, especially with peers, and practice with communication skills, social roles, and reciprocal turn taking (Bjorklund & Pelligrini, 2002). Delayed benefits include the accumulation of cognitive and language skills (Zukow, 1986), opportunities to practice or prepare for adult roles and behaviors (Göncü et al., 1999), and decreased likelihood of developmental delays later in childhood (Tamis-LaMonda, Shannon, Cabrera, & Lamb, 2004). Užgiris and Raeff (1995) describe play as involving a variety of activities, such as talking, touching, interacting, and sharing attention, that give children experience with skills they will need to participate in future cultural interactions.

Play in toddlerhood advances from rudimentary object manipulation to pretend play, which emerges at about 15 months of age and reflects changes in symbolic thinking (Farver, 1999). Prior to age 2, make-believe or pretend play involves the use of realistic toys, such as pretending to drink from a cup but not pretending to drink from a hat (Tomasello, Striano, & Rochat, 1999), which illustrates limitations in symbolic thinking. Pretending with less realistic toys begins to emerge after age 2 and in the third year toddlers are able to imagine events and objects without the support of concrete objects. At this time, play also advances from being self- to other-focused.

Social and Cultural Processes in the Development of Play

Although children sometimes play alone, play is often a social activity. Certain forms of play, such as pretend or symbolic play, are more likely to emerge when children, especially toddlers, play with someone else rather than alone. Haight and Miller (1992) found that among middle-class American toddlers, roughly 80% of pretend play took place in the context of mother–child interaction. The nature of these interactions also changed with development. When their children were 12 months of age, mothers initiated most play episodes, but by the time children were 24 months old both mothers and toddlers initiated play.

From a sociocultural perspective, social pretend play is particularly significant to development. It relies on the abilities, which emerge in the second and third years of life, to think about that which is not immediately present and be able to communicate these ideas to a partner (Howes, 1985). This type of transaction is the first instance in which children engage in social interactions based on commonly understood symbols rather than the literal meaning of an object. Such transactions are foundational to the ability to understand and participate in culture (Nelson, 1996). For instance, in a Mayan community in the Zinacantán region of Mexico in which siblings are the primary companions of toddlers, Maynard (2002) found that much of the cultural instruction that older siblings offer to younger siblings took place in the context of play. The play of 3- to 11-year-old children with their younger, toddler-age siblings was frequently based on everyday tasks such as washing, cooking, and taking care of dolls, and it involved both makeshift items, like leaves and dirt, and household items, like tortilla presses and bathing tubs. These play episodes provided many opportunities for young children to learn about and practice these types of cultural tasks as well as gain experience with language.

The role of adults in children's play differs according to whether parents view play as important to children's development, whether they consider themselves appropriate play partners for children, and the extent to which they enjoy or engage in pretend play with children (Haight, Parke, & Black, 1997). With a sample from the United States, Haight and colleagues (1997) found that both mothers and fathers regard pretend play as important to children's cognitive development. However, mothers' beliefs about the importance of pretend play to development and their own role as a play partner were associated with the time spent in pretend play with children. In contrast, fathers' own preference for pretend play was positively associated with the time spent in pretend play. These findings suggest that even within an American sample, beliefs about pretend play and the ways in which adults support children in this activity reflect parent's individual views, such as those related to gender roles.

Research has examined whether there are differences across cultures in parents' beliefs about play and the practices associated with these cultural beliefs. Martini and Kirkpatrick (1992) found that Marquesan mothers, who work most of the day, believe that toddlers are more interested in playing with older children, especially siblings and cousins, rather than with adults. For these mothers, such play is beneficial because toddlers, who mothers believe strive to be like older children, have the opportunity to observe older children and learn important skills from them. Consistent with Haight and colleagues (1997), Farver (1999) found that European American mothers viewed play with young children as important to their social and cognitive development whereas Mexican mothers viewed play as a form of entertainment. Consistent with these beliefs, European American mothers engaged in a great deal of face-to-face and didactic play while Mexican mothers generally did not play with their children and expected them to play with peers or older siblings. Thus, cross-cultural research indicates that cultural beliefs regarding the purpose of play and how best to meet developmental goals are related to parent–child play patterns when children are toddlers.

In contrast to observations in the United States that suggest that toddlers are greatly interested and involved in symbolic play, Gaskins (1999) found that Mayan toddlers played less overall and spent little of their playtime in symbolic play. To understand this difference, it is critical to examine the cultural context. In this Mayan community, adult work takes precedence over child activity and, consequently children, even very young children, get little direction from adults as to what to do with their time. Children determine their activities on their own or with the help of older children, primarily siblings. The play activities of Mayan toddlers are rarely acknowledged or supported by adults, except when they interfere with an adult's activities or use household objects in inappropriate ways. When symbolic play occurs, it is often in the context of mixed-age peer groups and older children have responsibility for structuring the play, such as deciding on themes and assigning roles. Because young children in this community spend much of their time in culturally valued activities other than play, such as observing other people's daily activities, Gaskins challenges the idea that play is central to early development and suggests that play is but one of many culturally supported activities that may contribute to development in early childhood.

Conclusions and Future Directions

Cross-cultural research has demonstrated that patterns of adult–child interaction during play are related to socialization goals that reflect parental expectations for toddler's socioemotional development and functioning. Mosier and Rogoff (2003) examined differences across cultures in children's opportunities to develop prosocial skills, such as cooperation with others, during play episodes. In the United States toddlers are often required to adhere to the same rules of play as older children as a means of training children to cooperate with others. However, in Mayan communities socialization emphasizes both freedom of choice and responsibility to the group. Toddlers are not expected to understand the rules, nor is their misbehavior construed as intentional. With time and experience, it is expected that toddlers will come to cooperate voluntarily with others, reflecting cultural values of collectivism and group harmony. Consistent with this interpretation, Mosier and Rogoff found that during play episodes Mayan toddlers were allowed more free will than children in the United States and that Mayan toddlers often cooperated in these play episodes without prompting from others.

The types of skills toddlers can acquire through play reflect the goals and values of the larger culture as expressed in the ways that social partners organize and are involved in children's play. Experiences during play provide toddlers with practice in all types of skills valued in the culture, including culturally appropriate ways of interacting with others and displaying and satisfying one's own needs in social context. The next section expands our discussion by examining the development of attention in relation to the experiences toddlers have in social and cultural context.

The Sociocultural Context and the Development of Attention

The Importance of Attention and Key Developments in Toddlerhood

Attention includes the ability to select and orient to sensory stimuli and is important for maintaining focus on and achieving short- and long-term goals (Ruff & Rothbart, 1996). Processes involved in the development of attention in toddlerhood include attention regulation skills, such as joint attention, and the role of attention regulation skills, including the abilities to focus and shift attention, in early socioemotional development. Joint attention involves the ability to look reliably and flexibly toward the place or object where another person, usually a social partner, is looking (Carpenter, Nagell, & Tomasello, 1998). Joint attention is central to many processes that are critical to socioemotional development in toddlerhood. It directs children's attention toward certain information in the environment and communicates to young children that other people can play instrumental roles in identifying objects worthy of attention. Joint attention is associated with the development of language (Morales et al., 2000) and social cognition, including perspective taking and understanding the mental states of others (Carpendale & Lewis, 2004). Finally, it aids in the understanding of others as intentional agents, a chief component of social cognition and cultural participation (Tomasello, 1999). Thus, this socially based attentional process plays a fundamental role in the use and regulation of attention in early childhood.

The ability to regulate attention, both in the form of attention focusing and attention shifting, is considered a basic cognitive process as well as a dimension of temperament (Rothbart & Posner, 2001). This ability is important to early learning in that it allows the individual to select and attend to important aspects of the environment while filtering out or ignoring aspects that are not relevant to the activity at hand. Consequently, it is influential to cognitive, social, and emotional functioning. For example, in the regulation of emotion, the ability to focus on alternative stimuli, as in distraction strategies, assists in modulating emotional reactivity (Kopp, 1989). In turn, the ability to regulate emotionality and focus on relevant stimuli in the environment aids in sustaining successful social interactions. Thus, attention regulation, sometimes referred to as an executive control process (Rothbart & Bates, 1998), has long-term consequences for cognitive and emotional development as well as socioemotional functioning (Ruff & Rothbart, 1996).

The development of attention relies, in part, on the development of neural connections and brain structures, such as the frontal cortex, associated with higher-order thinking (Johnson, 2005). Attention develops early and rapidly and changes from a reactive or involuntary process at birth to a self-regulative process that begins to emerge at around 12 months of age (Ruff & Rothbart, 1996). Individual differences in this ability, as in the amount of time it takes to orient to novel stimuli and how long attention to a particular stimulus is sustained, can be identified as early as the first year (Rothbart & Bates, 1998). By 18 months children are quite competent at directing their gaze, they can discriminate visual targets that are relatively close in space, and they can search outside their immediate visual range for a target object (Butterworth, 1995).

The development of attention is informed by children's experience in social context as evidenced by advances in children's ability to engage in joint attention. At 12 months, infants can locate the visual target that is the object of another person's gaze correctly. By 18 months of age, the process of joint attention is increasingly integrated with language—for example, a child will change gaze direction to look where the mother is looking when she uses an object label (Baldwin, 1991). Advances in the ability to participate in joint attention late in the first year are associated with advancements in other areas of development, such as emotion. For example, the emotional valence of the communication influences what children learn about the object of shared reference, which is refined in the second and third years in the process of *social referencing* (Feinman, 1982). The coordination of social, emotional, and cognitive development, evident in changes in the process of joint attention over the first few years, illustrates the integration of these skills, particularly during developmental transitions.

Social and Cultural Processes in the Development of Attention

Even the earliest forms of attention that appear involuntary are subject to social experience (see Gauvain, 2001). For instance, efforts by caregivers to regulate infant distress change as the child develops. There is a shift from using direct physical soothing techniques, such as holding and rocking, to indirect techniques that involve distracting infants by orienting their attention to other stimuli, which can help reduce distress (Rothbart & Posner, 2001).

Both adults and children are active participants in joint attention. Adults direct the child's attention to external entities as well as monitor the child's focus of attention and adjust their gaze to correspond to this focus. Children contribute by using the attentional, emotional, and social skills they have available. These processes, in turn, have implications for early socioemotional development. For instance, children's play at 12 months of age is more advanced (i.e., it is more functional and relational) during joint attention episodes than when children this age are not engaged in joint attention (Bigelow, MacLean, & Proctor, 2004). Also, when adults alternate their gaze between the infant and an event and also emote in response to the event, infants point at the event more (Liszkowski, Carpenter, Henning, Striano, & Tomasello, 2004). In contrast, when adults react emotionally to the infant without alternating their gaze to the event or only look to the event, infants decrease the amount of pointing across trials. Thus, what toddlers can learn from joint attention episodes depends, in part, on the emotional quality of the interaction.

The development of attention, including processes of joint attention and abilities at focusing and shifting attention, varies across cultures. Although cross-cultural research indicates some similarities across very different communities in the development of joint attention (Adamson & Bakeman, 1991), cultural variation in the communicative styles and cultural practices that caregivers use to establish joint attention are also evident. For example, among the !Kung San, a hunting-gathering society in Africa, adults neither encourage nor prohibit the young child's exploration of objects (Bakeman, Adamson, Konner, & Barr, 1990). However, if the child initiates interactions by offering objects to caregivers, joint attention and object exploration follow the same course observed in other communities. Thus, research suggests that culture provides a framework that organizes the initiation of joint attention episodes and the communicative exchanges that occur in these situations.

Other research has indicated that differences across cultures in the structure of daily activities and the ways in which children are involved in these activities have consequences for the development of attention and attention regulation. Opportunities for young children to observe adult activities in their community, whether adults or children are in charge of regulating children's attention during joint activities, and whether children are socialized to focus on one event at a time or engage in simultaneous attention to several ongoing events differ substantially across cultural communities (Rogoff et al., 1993; Zukow-Goldring, 1997). Such differences reflect values in the community about the course and goals of development.

In a comparison of European American and Mayan families, Rogoff and colleagues (Chavajay & Rogoff, 1999; Rogoff et al., 1993) found group differences in beliefs about children's development, which were reflected in the socialization of attention and attention regulation. European American families tended to value accelerating the pace of development and parents viewed themselves as instrumental in this process. To this end, European American toddlers were frequently observed to be engaged in dyadic interactions with a parent in which the adult was responsible for structuring and directing the course of the interaction, which was largely focused on instruction. Concentrated attention by the child on one event at a time was encouraged. In contrast, Mayan parents did not emphasize accelerating development and they viewed children as responsible for expressing their own interests and maintaining their own motivation and learning. Mayan toddlers had more opportunity to observe adult activity, were typically involved in group versus dyadic interactions, were expected to learn by watching others rather than through verbal instruction, and often attended to multiple simultaneous events.

Conclusions and Future Directions

Attention development in the toddler period not only reflects maturational changes but is also an interactional skill that emerges from joint participation in social context. These interactions are situated in cultural context and thus attention, a seemingly basic cognitive or temperamentally rooted skill, reflects developmental goals, beliefs, and practices defined by culture. The cognitive, social, and emotional skills that young children develop through the socialization of attention rely on the types of interaction that take place between adults and children, which in turn influence children's opportunities to learn in social context. Future research on the development of attention in the toddler years from a sociocultural perspective could provide more comprehensive understanding of this foundational ability. Attentional processes have enormous consequence for development, especially when children enter school and the ability to regulate attention is critical to success. Variation across cultural contexts in the development of this ability and the intricate and essential role of social experience in the way this process develops in early childhood suggest many fruitful avenues of study. Such research could have wide-ranging impact on both developmental theory and the application of these ideas.

The Sociocultural Context of the Development of Emotion Regulation

The Importance of Emotion Regulation Skills and Key Developments in Toddlerhood

This section reviews the early development of emotion regulation skills. The development of emotional competence, partly evidenced by awareness of one's emotional states and knowledge and strategy use regarding emotion regulation and emotional self-presentation, plays a central role in children's development and socioemotional functioning (Saarni, Mumme, & Campos, 1998). Emotional competence, and specifically emotion regulation, is considered to be particularly important in social contexts in that it helps determine how an individual interprets and navigates transactions with others (Saarni, 1999). Consistent with the functionalist perspective, emotions are viewed as intra- and interpersonally regulating, that is, emotions regulate the behavior of the self and the behavior of others (Saarni et al., 1998).

The development of emotion in social context and the reciprocal relation among emotional, social, and cognitive development are evident early in development. Baron-Cohen (2005) emphasizes both this contextual nature and reciprocal relation in his model of empathizing. This model attempts to capture the apparently unique human capacity to identify the thoughts and emotions of others and to respond with appropriate emotion. By the beginning of the second year, children are able to engage in joint attention as well as have empathic reactions to another's emotional state. Together, these capabilities contribute to social and emotional competence in the form of prosocial behaviors such as helping because they function to identify another's intentional state and accompany that knowledge with a motivation to assist.

The contribution of the social and cultural context to emotional development is particularly clear in the development of emotional regulatory skills. Emotion regulation refers to the processes involved in coping with positive and negative emotions as they become overarousing, persist for long periods of time, or interfere with goals (Kopp, 1989). The ability to regulate emotional arousal contributes to children's social competence. Because emotion has the potential to disrupt ongoing cognitive activity due to the activation of action tendencies associated with that emotion, emotion regulation is important for facilitating performance on tasks requiring inhibition, sustained attention, or replacement of current for long-term goals (Frijda & Mesquita, 1998).

There are several changes in emotion regulation during the transition from infancy to toddlerhood. Although during the first few months infants are capable of some emotion regulation strategies such as gaze aversion, self-stimulation, and proximity seeking to caregivers (Cole, Martin, & Dennis, 2004), they are largely reliant on external regulators, usually caregivers, to assist in emotion regulation, particularly when arousal levels are high. Caregivers are responsible for detecting children's emotional signals and helping the child regulate his or her level of arousal by providing appropriate stimulation or soothing behaviors. Research has demonstrated that the quality of these early exchanges (Garner, 1995), through the establishment of interactional synchrony between caregivers and children (Harrist & Waugh, 2001), predicts independent regulatory ability and socioemotional functioning in early childhood. In toddlerhood, as cognitive and social skills develop and there is increased ability to regulate emotion independently, emotional development reflects mutually influential interactions between caregivers and children. Thus, children are active participants or cocreators of their emotional experience. They integrate what they have learned in the context of social interaction into their own emotional experience and in their emotional transactions with others (Saarni, 1999).

Social and Cultural Processes in the Development of Emotion Regulation

Research has suggested that during interactions with toddlers in emotionally arousing or frustrating situations, the extent of maternal support, emotional availability, and interaction styles effects immediate and long-term functioning. In the short term, maternal interactions that involve guidance and sensitivity, versus directive or controlling behavior, are associated with the degree to which toddlers display distress in frustrating situations, whether toddlers attempt to use adaptive emotion regulation strategies on their own, and how effective toddlers are at modulating their own emotional arousal. In the long term, interactions with mothers in toddlerhood are related to children's overall socioemotional functioning in early and middle childhood (Calkins & Johnson, 1998; Diener & Mangelsdorf, 1999; NICHD Early Child Care Research Network, 2004; Spinrad et al., 2004). Thus, the quality of such interactions has implications for children's experience of emotional arousal and independent attempts at emotional self-regulation. The emotional interactions of caregivers and young children are, in turn, situated within a particular cultural ecology. Research suggests that the development of emotion regulation is a cultural process as caregivers socialize children's emotion regulation skills according to the values, norms, beliefs, and expectations of the culture (Friedlmeier & Trommsdorff, 1999). Cultural value systems with regard to emotion regulation include ideas about the extent and type of emotional expressions that are appropriate, even by very young children (Mead, 1963; Whiting & Edwards, 1988). For instance, industrialized Western nations are characterized by an orientation toward individuality (Keller et al., 2004) and socialization goals focus on the development of autonomy and independence (Kagitibaasi, 1996). In contrast, Eastern nations are often characterized by an orientation to interdependence and socialization goals focus on children's connections with others and social expectations. As a result, children reared within an independent sociocultural orientation, in comparison to those reared within an interdependent orientation, tend to be encouraged to regulate their emotions independently from an earlier age and to regulate emotions verbally or seek support through eye contact rather than through physical contact (Friedlmeier & Trommsdorf, 1999; Keller et al., 2004).

The view that Western cultures exclusively emphasize independence and non-Western cultures exclusively emphasize interdependence may be overstated, however. This view tends to position cultural descriptions of the development of competence in a relativistic form: how the values and practices of a community compare with Western values and practices rather than in terms of a primary long-term goal of all cultures, which is to foster the development of competent human beings *and* community members (Martini & Kirkpatrick, 1992). To accomplish these goals, children need to have an emotional sense of self as well as an emotional connection to the community at large. For instance, in Marquesa, a traditional Polynesian community, children are raised to be sensitive and responsive to the needs of others and to be self-reliant (Martini & Kirkpatrick, 1992). In toddlerhood, this means that children are encouraged to join the sibling group and be cooperative and nondemanding. Mothers report that toddlers are most interested in being with their siblings and cousins and that they cry when these partners leave them. Concern about toddlers being cooperative and undemanding of caregivers is important because by the time children are 18 to 24 months of age, mothers are often pregnant with another child and toddlers must learn that they cannot be as reliant on mother as they had been previously. Self-reliance at this time is encouraged in a number of ways. Toddlers learn that expressions of anger, frustration, and sadness are not tolerated and that they are expected to comfort themselves. They are also encouraged to imitate their older siblings by entertaining themselves and doing household chores. Martini and Kirkpatrick (1992) observed that toddlers learn to read contextual cues to determine when they need to be obedient and when they can express their own will, such as standing up to adult authority. In such instances, if the child reads a situation correctly, a parent may be proud of the child who is expressing personal autonomy and coming to understand that "willfulness has its place" (p. 211). In short, Marquesan toddlers are learning to be emotionally competent individuals as well emotionally connected members of the group.

Conclusions and Future Directions

Although there are few studies that explicitly examine the role of the social and cultural context on the development of emotion regulation in toddlerhood, the research findings discussed here highlight the importance of establishing whether current models of emotion regulation development apply across different sociocultural contexts. The development of emotion regulation skills is critical for children's overall socioemotional competence as well as for cultural maintenance. Emotional arousal can interfere with social and cognitive activities and with performance on tasks involving delay or inhibition. Better understanding of the contribution of social and cultural experience to the development of emotional self-regulation, which has its roots in toddlerhood, will increase knowledge of early development and has implications for long-term socioemotional functioning.

CONCLUSIONS

In this chapter we used a sociocultural framework to examine socioemotional development in toddlerhood. Because of the immaturity of the human organism at birth, children are reliant on caregivers to guide and shape growth in the first years of life. Thus, advancements in social, emotional, and cognitive skills arise from maturational processes in conjunction with the guidance provided by more experienced partners and the broader cultural context, contributions explicitly recognized by a sociocultural approach. Attention to the social and cultural processes that contribute to early socioemotional development is necessary for understanding not only *what develops* but also the mechanisms or underlying processes involved in *how* this development occurs.

Research indicates that there is both commonality and variation in the ways in which the social and cultural context contributes to early socioemotional development. What is common across contexts is that early development largely takes place in the family and kin context and through social interaction and activity participation. Some of this commonality is rooted in the maturationally based capabilities and constraints of the child at this point in development and some stems from the inherently social nature of the species. What varies across contexts is the ways in which caregivers view and approach socialization and how these are reflected in the opportunities children have to participate in activities that shape their development. Socialization goals and the social interactions that reflect these goals vary in relation to the beliefs, values, and practices of the cultural context of development. Differences across cultural contexts stem from traditions and preferences of the community and do not represent deficits in childrearing practices.

In this chapter we reviewed research in three areas—play, attention, and emotion regulation—which are central to socioemotional development in toddlerhood. These three areas are subject to socialization, largely situated in the family or kin context, and influenced by the larger cultural context via the beliefs, values, and practices of caregivers and through the routine activities in which young children are engaged. In addition, play, attention, and emotion regulation illustrate the integrative nature of social, emotional, and cognitive areas of development during this time of transition. Changes observed in play patterns over the course of toddlerhood reflect underlying changes in cognitive ability, attentional control, self-regulation, and social skills. Similarly, attention relies on temperament and cognitive ability, and it contributes to and benefits from learning in social context, which relies on the utilization of emotion regulation strategies. Finally, emotion regulation contributes to socioemotional functioning but also relies on and enhances the development of cognitive skills and social competence. Thus, although these three processes are discussed separately, they are closely related and reciprocal influences on development.

While recognizing the importance of maturational influences on the development of these processes, the research we reviewed stresses the importance of examining the role of the social and cultural context. This type of examination is especially critical during the toddler period when children spend most of their time with family and kin yet are able to move about on their own and use their experiences to carve out their own skills and sense of self. Through social interaction, defined in large part by cultural values, beliefs, and practices, the foundations for many skills that will contribute to later socioemotional competence are established. Variations in play patterns are associated with cultural beliefs with regard to children's primary play partners and the importance of play for development. These, in turn, affect how play is situated in early development and what children learn from play. Socialization of attention is associated with variation in children's involvement in interactions with adults and adult activities and with values regarding the ability to focus attention on one event at a time versus being able to attend to several simultaneous events. Children's development and utilization of emotion regulation strategies are associated with cultural beliefs about appropriate displays of emotion and the view of children in relation to the larger group.

Attention to cultural sources of variation aids in our understanding of similarities and differences across groups in the underlying processes involved in socioemotional development in very early childhood. In addition, when differences do exist across groups, the sociocultural perspective calls for an interpretation that recognizes that children are developing skills necessary to become competent members of their community. This view differs from one that assumes a homogenous pattern of maturation and the achievement of normative developmental milestones. Although Margaret Mead distinguished "knee children" from younger and older children over 50 years ago, her view of this period of childhood as unique on both maturational and cultural grounds remains descriptive of how children develop in the second and third years of life. However, it is important to remember that Mead's description is developmental; it not only characterizes what development is like for children at a particular point in time but also describes where children are headed next. The experiences of "knee children" help ready them to become "yard children," for whom experiences stretch beyond the immediate homestead and into more contact with nonfamily adults. The social, emotional, cognitive, and language skills honed in toddlerhood and coordinated with the social and cultural context of development facilitate this shift by enabling yard children to fit in with, and benefit from, the social and cultural experiences awaiting them.

REFERENCES

Adamson, L. B., & Bakeman, R. (1991). The development of shared attention during infancy. In R. Vasta (Ed.), *Annals of child development* (Vol. 8, pp. 1–41). London: Kingsley.

Bakeman, R., Adamson, L. B., Konner, M., & Barr, R. G. (1990). !Kung infancy: The social context of object exploration. *Child Development, 61*, 794–809.

Baldwin, D. A. (1991). Infants' contribution to the achievement of joint reference. *Child Development, 62*, 875–890.

Baron-Cohen, S. (2005). The empathizing system: A revision of the 1994 model of the mindreading system. In B. J. Ellis & D. F. Bjorklund (Eds.), *Origins of the social mind: Evolutionary psychology and child develop* (pp. 468–492). New York: Guilford Press.

Bauer, P. J., & Dow, G. A. A. (1994). Episodic memory in 16– and 20–month-old children: Specifics are generalized, but not forgotten. *Developmental Psychology, 30*, 403–417.

Benson, J. B. (1994). The origins of future orientation in the everyday lives of 9- to 36-month-old infants. In M. M. Haith, J. B. Benson, R. J. Roberts, & B. F. Pennington (Eds.), *The development of future-oriented processes* (pp. 375–407). Chicago: University of Chicago Press.

Bigelow, A. E., MacLean, K., & Proctor, J. (2004). The role of joint attention in the development of infants' play with objects. *Developmental Science, 7,* 518–526.

Bjorklund, D. F., & Pellegrini, A. D. (2002). *The origins of human nature: Evolutionary developmental psychology.* Washington, DC: American Psychological Association.

Bronfenbrenner, U., & Morris, P. A. (1998). The ecology of developmental processes. In W. Damon & R. M. Lerner (Eds.), *Handbook of child psychology* (5th ed., Vol. 1, pp. 993–1028). New York: Wiley.

Butterworth, G. (1995). Origins of mind in perception and action. In C. Moore & P. J. Dunham (Eds.), *Joint attention: Its origins and role in development* (pp. 29–40). Hillsdale, NJ: Erlbaum.

Calkins, S. D., & Johnson, M. C. (1998). Toddler regulation of distress to frustrating events: Temperamental and maternal correlates. *Infant Behavior and Development, 21,* 379–395.

Carpendale, J. I. M., & Lewis, C. (2004). Constructing an understanding of mind: The development of children's social understanding within social interaction. *Brain and Behavioral Sciences, 27,* 79–151.

Carpenter, M., Nagell, K., & Tomasello, M. (1998). Social cognition, joint attention, and communicative competence from 9 to 15 months of age. *Monographs of the Society for Research in Child Development, 63*(Serial No. 255), 1–174.

Chavajay, P., & Rogoff, B. (1999). Cultural variation in management of attention by children and their caregivers. *Developmental Psychology, 35,* 1079–1090.

Cole, M. (1996). *Cultural psychology: A once and future discipline.* Cambridge, MA: Harvard University Press.

Cole, M., Cole, S. R., & Lightfoot, C. (2005). *The development of children* (5th ed.). New York: Worth.

Cole, P. M., Martin, S. E., & Dennis, T. A. (2004). Emotion regulation as a scientific construct: Methodological challenges and directions for child development research. *Child Development, 75,* 317–333.

DeLoache, J. S. (1984). What's this? Maternal questions in joint picture book reading with toddlers. *Quarterly Newsletter of the Laboratory of Comparative Human Cognition, 6,* 87–95.

Diener, M. L., & Mangelsdorf, S. C. (1999). Behavioral strategies for emotion regulation in toddlers: Associations with maternal involvement and emotional expressions. *Infant Behavior and Development, 22,* 569–583.

Edwards, C. P. (1989). The transition from infancy to early childhood: A difficult transition, and a difficult theory. In V. R. Bricker & G. H. Gossen (Eds.), *Ethnographic encounters in Southern Mesoamerica: Essays in honor of Evon Z. Vogt, Jr.* (pp. 167–175). Austin: University of Texas.

Farver, J. M. (1999). Activity setting analysis: A model for examining the role of culture in development. In A. Göncü (Ed.), *Children's engagement in the world: Sociocultural perspectives* (pp. 99–127). New York: Cambridge University Press.

Farver, J. M., & Wimbarti, S. (1995). Indonesian toddlers' social play with their mothers and older siblings. *Child Development, 66,* 1443–513.

Feinman, S. (1982). *Social referencing and the social construction of reality in infancy.* New York: Plenum Press.

Friedlmeier, W., & Trommsdorff, G. (1999). Emotion regulation in early childhood. *Journal of Cross-Cultural Psychology, 30,* 684–711.

Frijda, N. H., & Mesquita B. (1998). The analysis of emotions: Dimensions of variation. In M. F. Mascolo & S. Griffin (Eds.), *What develops in emotional development?* (pp. 273–295) New York: Plenum Press.

Garner, P. W. (1995). Toddlers' emotion regulation behaviors: The roles of social context and family expressiveness. *Journal of Genetic Psychology, 156,* 417–430.

Gaskins, S. (1999). Children's daily lives in a Mayan village: A case study of culturally constructed roles and activities. In A. Göncü (Ed.), *Children's engagement in the world: Sociocultural perspectives* (pp. 25–61). New York: Cambridge University Press.

Gauvain, M. (2005). Sociocultural contexts of learning. In A. E. Maynard & M. I Martini (Eds.),

Learning in cultural context: Family, peers, and school (pp. 11–40). New York: Kluwer Academic.

Gauvain, M. (2001). *The social context of cognitive development*. New York: Guilford Press.

Gauvain, M., & DeMent, T. (1991). The role of shared social history in parent–child cognitive activity. *Quarterly Newsletter of the Laboratory of Comparative Human Cognition, 13,* 58–66.

Gauvain, M., & Fagot, B. (1995). Child temperament as a mediator of mother–toddler problem solving. *Social Development, 4,* 257–276.

Gelman, S., Coley, J. D., Rosengren, K. S., Hartman, E., & Pappas, A. (1998). Beyond labeling; The role of maternal input in the acquisition of richly structured categories. *Monographs for the Society for Research in Child Development, 63*(1, Serial No. 253).

Göncü, A., Tuermer, U., Jain, J., & Johnson, D. (1999). Children's play as cultural activity. In A. Göncü (Ed.), *Children's engagement in the world: Sociocultural perspectives* (pp. 148–170). New York: Cambridge University Press.

Goodnow, J. J., Miller, P. J., & Kessel, F. (1995). *Cultural practices as contexts for development*. San Francisco: Jossey-Bass.

Greenfield, P. M., Keller, H., Fuligni, A., & Maynard, A. (2003). Cultural pathways through universal development. *Annual Review of Psychology, 54,* 461–490.

Haight, W., & Miller, P. (1992). The development of everyday pretend play: A longitudinal study of mothers' participation. *Merrill-Palmer Quarterly, 38,* 331–349.

Haight, W. L., Parke, R. D., & Black, J. E. (1997). Mothers' and fathers' beliefs about and spontaneous participation in their toddlers' pretend play. *Merrill-Palmer Quarterly, 43,* 271–290.

Harkness, S., & Super, C. M. (1996). *Parents' cultural belief systems: Their origins, expressions, and consequences*. New York: Guilford Press.

Harrist, A. W., & Waugh, R. M. (2001). Dyadic synchrony: Its structure and function in children's development. *Developmental Review, 22,* 555–592.

Hoff, E. (2001). *Language development* (2nd ed.). Belmont, CA: Wadsworth/Thomson.

Hollich, G. J., Hirsch-Pasek, K., & Golinkoff, R. M. (2000). Breaking the language barrier: An emergentist coalition model for the origins of word learning. *Monographs of the Society for Research in Child Development, 65*(3, Serial No. 262).

Howes, C. (1985). Sharing fantasy: Social pretend play in toddlers. *Child Development, 56,* 1253–1258.

Johnson, M. H. (2005). *Developmental cognitive neuroscience* (2nd ed.). Oxford, UK: Blackwell.

Kagitcibaasi, C. (1996). *Family and human development across cultures: A view from the other side*. Mahwah, NJ: Erlbaum.

Keller, H., Yovsi, R., Borke, J., Kartner, J., Jensen, H., & Papaligoura, Z. (2004). Developmental consequences of early parenting experiences: Self-recognition and self-regulation in three cultural communities. *Child Development, 75,* 1745–1760.

Kochanska, G. (2002). Mutually responsive orientation between mothers and their young children: A context for the early development of conscience. *Current Directions in Psychological Science, 11,* 191–195.

Kopp, C. B. (1989). Regulation of distress and negative emotions: A developmental view. *Developmental Psychology, 25,* 343–354.

Laible, D. J., & Thompson, R. A. (2002). Mother–child conflict in the toddler years: Lessons in emotion, morality, and relationships. *Child Development, 73,* 1187–1203.

LeVine, R., Dixon, S., LeVine, S., Richman, A., Leiderman, P. H., Keefer, C. H., et al. (1994). *Child care and culture: Lessons from Africa*. Cambridge, UK: Cambridge University Press.

Liszkowski, U., Carpenter, M., Henning, A., Striano, T., & Tomasello, M. (2004). Twelve-month-olds point to share attention and interest. *Developmental Science, 7,* 297–307.

Litowitz, B. E. (1993). Deconstruction in the zone of proximal development. In E. A. Forman, N. Minick, & C. A. Stone (Eds.), *Contexts for learning* (pp. 184–196). New York: Oxford University Press.

Martini, M., & Kirkpatrick, J. (1992). Parenting in Polynesia: A view from the Marquesas. In J. L.

Roopnarine & D. B. Carter (Eds.), *Parent–child socialization in diverse cultures: Vol. 5. Annual advances in applied developmental psychology* (pp. 199–222). Norwood, NJ: Ablex.

Maynard, A. E. (2002). Cultural teaching: The development of teaching skills in Maya sibling interactions. *Child Development, 73*, 969–982.

Mead, M. (1949). *Male and female*. New York: William Morrow.

Mead, M. (1963). Socialization and acculturation. *Current Anthropology, 4*, 184–188.

Miller, P. J., & Goodnow, J. J. (1995). Cultural practices: Toward an integration of culture and development. In J. J. Goodnow, P. J. Miller, & F. Kessel (Eds.), *Cultural practices as contexts for development* (pp. 5–16). San Francisco: Jossey-Bass.

Mistry, J. (1993). Cultural context in the development of children's narratives. In J. Altarriba (Ed.), *Cognition and culture: A cross-cultural approach to cognitive psychology* (pp. 207–228). Amsterdam: Elsevier.

Morales, M., Mundy, P., Delgado, C. E. F., Yale, M., Messinger, D. Neal, R., et al. (2000). Responding to joint attention across the 6– through 24–month age period and early language acquisition. *Journal of Applied Developmental Psychology, 21*, 283–298.

Mosier, C. E., & Rogoff, B. (2003). Privileged treatment of toddlers: Cultural aspects of individual choice and responsibility. *Developmental Psychology, 39*, 1047–1060.

Mullen M. K., & Yi, S. (1995). The cultural context of talk about the past: Implications for the development of autobiographical memory. *Cognitive Development, 10*, 407–419.

Munroe, R. L., & Munroe, R. H. (1994). *Cross-cultural human development*. Prospect Heights, IL: Waveland Press.

National Center for Health Statistics. (2000). *Health, United States, 2000*. Hyattsville, MD: Centers for Disease Control and Prevention.

Nelson, K. (1996). *Language in cognitive development: The emergence of the mediated mind*. Cambridge, UK: Cambridge University Press.

NICHD Early Child Care Research Network. (2004). Affect dysregulation in the mother–child relationship in the toddler years: Antecedents and consequences. *Development and Psychopathology, 16*, 43–68.

Olson, S. L., Bates, J. E., Sandy, J. M., & Schilling, E. M. (2002). Early developmental precursors of impulsive and inattentive behavior: From infancy to middle childhood. *Journal of Child Psychology and Psychiatry, 43*, 435–447.

Ratner, H. H. (1980). The role of social context in memory development. In M. Perlmutter (Ed.), *Children's memory* (pp. 49–67). San Francisco: Jossey-Bass.

Repacholi, B. M. (1998). Infants' use of attentional cues to identify the referent of another person's emotional expression. *Developmental Psychology, 34*, 1017–1025.

Rogoff, B. (2003). *The cultural nature of human development*. New York: Oxford University Press.

Rogoff, B., Mistry, J., Göncü, A., & Mosier, C. (1993). Guided participation in cultural activity by toddlers and caregivers. *Monographs of the Society for Research in Child Development, 58*,(7, Serial No. 236).

Rothbart, M. K., & Bates, J. E. (1998). Temperament. In N. Eisenberg (Ed.), *Handbook of child psychology: Vol. 3. Social, emotional and personality development* (5th ed., pp. 105–176). New York: Wiley.

Rothbart, M. K., & Posner, M. I. (2001). Mechanism and variation in the development of attentional networks. In C. A. Nelson & M. Luciana (Eds.), *Handbook of developmental cognitive neuroscience* (pp. 353–363). Cambridge, MA: MIT Press.

Ruff, H. A., & Rothbart, M. K. (1996). Attention in early development: Themes and variations. New York: Oxford University Press.

Saarni, C. (1999). *The development of emotional competence*. New York: Guilford Press.

Saarni, C., Mumme, D. L., & Campos, J. (1998). Emotional development: Action, communication, and understanding. In N. Eisenberg (Ed.), *Handbook of child psychology: Vol. 3. Social, emotional and personality development* (5th ed., pp. 237–309). New York: Wiley.

Saxe, G. B., Guberman, S. R., & Gearhart, M. (1987). Social processes in early number development. *Monographs of the Society for Research in Child Development, 52*(2, Serial No. 216), 3–162.

Seymour, S. (2004). Multiple caretaking of infants and young children: An area in critical need of a feminist psychological anthropology. *Ethos, 32,* 538–556.

Shweder, R. A., Goodnow, J. J., Hatano, G., LeVine, R. A., Markus, H., & Miller, P. (1998). The cultural psychology of development: One mind, many mentalities. In R. M. Lerner (Ed.) & W. Damon (Series Ed.), *Handbook of child psychology: Vol. 1. Theoretical models of human development* (pp. 865–937). New York: Wiley.

Sigel, I. E., McGillicuddy-DeLisi, A. V., & Goodnow, J. J. (1992). *Parental belief systems: The psychological consequences for children* (2nd ed.). Hillsdale, NJ: Erlbaum.

Smith, P. K. (2004). Play: Types and functions in human development. In B. J. Ellis & D. F. Bjorklund (Eds.), *Origins of the social mind: Evolutionary psychology and child development* (pp. 271–291). New York: Guilford Press.

Spinrad, T. L., Stifter, C. A., Donelan-McCall, N., & Turner, L. (2004). Mothers' regulation strategies in response to toddlers' affect: Links to later emotion self-regulation. *Social Development, 13,* 40–55.

Super, C. M., & Harkness, S. (1986). The development niche: A conceptualization of the interface of child and culture. *International Journal of Behavioral Development, 2,* 545–569.

Tamis-LaMonda, C. S., Shannon, J. D., Cabrera, N. J., & Lamb, M. E. (2004). Fathers and mothers play with their 2– and 3–year-olds: Contributions to language and cognitive development. *Child Development, 75,* 1806–1820.

Tomasello, M. (1999). *The cultural origins of human cognition.* Cambridge, MA: Harvard University Press.

Tomasello, M., Striano, T., & Rochat, P. (1999). Do young children use objects as symbols? *British Journal of Developmental Psychology, 17,* 563–584.

Tronick, E. Z., Morelli, G. A., & Ivey, P. K. (1992). The Efe forager infant and toddler's pattern of social relationships: Multiple and simultaneous. *Developmental Psychology, 28,* 568–577.

Uzgiris, I. C., & Raeff, C. (1995). Play in parent–child interactions. In M. H. Bornstein (Ed.), *Handbook of parenting* (Vol. 4, pp. 353–376). Mahwah, NJ: Erlbaum.

Valsiner, J. (1984). Construction of the zone of proximal development in adult–child joint action: The socialization of meals. In B. Rogoff & J. V. Wertsch (Eds.), *Children's learning in the "zone of proximal development"* (pp. 65–76). San Francisco: Jossey-Bass.

Vygotsky, L. S. (1978). *Mind in society: The development of higher psychological processes.* Cambridge, MA: Harvard University Press.

Weisner, T. S., & Gallimore, R. (1977). My brother's keeper: Child and sibling caretaking. *Current Anthropology, 18,* 169–190.

Whiting, B. B., & Edwards, C. P. (1988). *Children of different worlds: The formation of social behavior.* Cambridge, MA: Harvard University Press.

Wood, D., Wood. H., & Middleton, D. (1978). An experimental evaluation of four face-to-face teaching strategies. *International Journal of Behavioral Development, 1,* 131–147.

Zukow, P. G. (1986). The relationship between interaction with the caregiver and the emergence of play activities during the one-word periods. *British Journal of Developmental Psychology, 4,* 223–234.

Zukow-Goldring, P. (1997). A social ecological realist approach to the emergence of the lexicon: Educating attention to amodal invariants in gesture and speech. In C. Dent-Read & P. Zukow-Goldring (Eds.), *Evolving explanations of development: Ecological approaches to organism–environment systems (pp. 199–250).* Washington, DC: American Psychological Association.

Part V

INDIVIDUAL DIFFERENCES AND APPLICATIONS

17

Social Relations, Self-Awareness, and Symbolizing

A Perspective from Autism

R. PETER HOBSON

If the title of this chapter carries an echo of G. H. Mead's (1934) classic work *Mind, Self and Society*, then all to the good. Mead traced the origins of symbolic thinking, and with this a special form of mentality that is distinctive to humans, to fundamental features of role taking in communication. He proposed that foundational for symbolizing is a set of goings-on where one person anticipates that the response called out *in* the other by the self corresponds with the response called out in the self *by* the other. Symbolizing entails that one is separate from other people yet connected with others through aspects of experience that are coordinated and (knowingly) communicated.

This chapter represents an ambitious reworking of Mead's thesis: ambitious, for three reasons: (1) because I try to specify some of the processes that make genuinely mutual and reciprocal communicative exchange possible; (2) because I attempt to trace how, beyond the first year of life, toddlers acquire the kind of understanding of self and other that gives rise to the ability to symbolize and thereby restructure conceptual growth; and (3) for the reason that I argue the case for the interpersonal and emotional bases of self-awareness and symbolizing predominantly through citing research with individuals who are, by and large, lacking insight into self, other, and symbol—those with early childhood autism.

Such an approach entails much that is controversial. Perhaps most obviously, it is far from straightforward to draw conclusions about early toddlerhood from research with children who are often beyond toddler age, and especially so if the children have developmental disorders. Suppose we discover something new and unusual about the interpersonal relations of, say, 6-year-old children with autism. How are we to decide whether we have identified an impairment that is "basic" to autism and that might have been present from early in life and disrupted the children's cognitive development, or whether we have unearthed socioemotional sequelae to primary cognitive disability? How could one justify the claim that here we gain a purchase on toddler-level psychological processes in children who have had so much happening in the years beyond toddlerhood to obscure, modify, and transform what might or might not have been awry in those early years?

I have two responses to this challenge. First, if we are willing to suspend disbelief and pay close attention to the *qualities* of psychological functioning in relatively older children with autism, then examine the evidence for continuities in such functioning from the earliest years, what had seemed farfetched claims for developmental linkage may come to assume plausibility. When the atypical developmental pathway followed by young children with autism is brought in relation to what can be observed in typically developing toddlers, this yields a new vision of *both* typical *and* atypical development. It remains to apply further tests of the authenticity of this vision, of course, but that is the way of science. Second, there is now a substantial body of research concerning children with autism who are at or not far beyond the stage of toddlerhood, and I cite many such studies in this contribution. Often, the children have been matched with typically developing toddlers, usually according to mental rather than chronological age, so one can make direct comparisons between the behavior of children with autism and that of younger but developmentally typical peers.

Having pleaded my case, it may be helpful to offer a map of what is to come. I begin with a brief synopsis of those aspects of toddlerhood on which I am concentrating. This amounts to a thumbnail sketch of developments that receive more adequate and detailed treatment in other chapters of this volume. With theoretical intent, I foreground certain features of what is described and offer suggestions concerning the nature of the developmental processes at work. Subsequently, I turn to the case of autism and summarize a set of studies that, in my view, help us to clarify not only what is atypical about these children's interpersonal relations, self-awareness, play, language, and thought but also something of the essence of interpersonal relations, self-awareness, play, language, and thought in typically developing toddlers. To conclude, I step back and with more than a nod of acknowledgment to G. H. Mead, Vygotsky, and Freud, consider how we might reframe our account of the early development of mind.

ON TODDLERHOOD

It is impossible to isolate toddlerhood from what goes on before and after the second and third years of life. Nature has little respect for our chronological categories, any more than it has for our wish to classify the components of mental life into what is cognitive, what is conative, and what is affective. Of course, it makes sense to consider the cognitive, conative, and affective dimensions of the relations between young children and the world, especially because we need to understand how older children and then adults come to acquire new ways of thinking, of being motivated, and of feeling toward people and things, that are partly separable from each other. Yet especially when we consider the earliest years of life, we need to remember that what we conceive of as cognitive or affective aspects of psychological functioning may grow out of a very young child's relations with the world and with other people that are inseparably cognitive *and* affective in nature. It is arguable—and indeed, I argue—that the emergence of distinctively human forms of self-awareness and cognition depend on this being so.

The end of the first year sets the stage for the dazzling psychological developments that will ensue over children's subsequent 2 years of life. In the realm of social relations, the typically developing 12-month-old is relating to other people with newfound capacities for imitation and communicative exchange in one-to-one encounters, and more than this, is relating to another person's relatedness to him- or herself and a shared environment. A number of researchers have documented the catalogue of accomplishments that characterize what Trevarthen (Trevarthen & Hubley, 1978) called the period of secondary intersubjectivity. For example, children are following the eye gaze and pointing of others, they request help and respond to requests of help from others, they indicate and show things to other people, often with gaze checking, they initiate as well as accept invitations to play, and they imitate conventional gestures and actions with objects. They are also beginning to utter greetings ("Hi!") and name-like words and pretending to carry out adult activities such as using the telephone (e.g., Bretherton, McNew, & Beeghly-Smith, 1981; Carpenter, Nagell, & Tomasello, 1998). This potential for the child to become engaged with other individuals in such a way as to adjust his or her orientation to the world *through* the other draws on a child's constitutional propensities, of course, but is also realized in the context of past as well as present experiences with caregivers. For example, Hobson, Patrick, Crandell, Garcia-Perez, and Lee (2004) reported how infant 12-month-olds whose mothers showed high sensitivity and low intrusiveness toward them in a teaching task (and presumably, many other settings) were more likely than infants of insensitive mothers to orientate to an unfamiliar adult in such a way as to share engagement with objects and events in the world.

A critical thing to appreciate about these features of a 1-year-old's social relations is how they constitute stepping-stones from the period of infancy when a baby is relating *either* to other people *or* to the things and events in his or her surroundings to a time in the middle of the second year of life when the toddler will acquire *concepts* of self and other as individuated centers of consciousness who have their own, person-anchored subjective experiences of the world (Hobson, 1993). A challenge we face is to account for the developmental transitions that occur during this short time and to identify the interpersonal as well as intraindividual processes through which such changes are effected—and, of course, to trace the repercussions that ensue for cognitive as well as emotional growth.

To address these issues, I begin by noting just some of the advances in social relations and thinking that are observed in typical development over the second and into the third years of life. Only in relation to such a sketch can one appraise those unusual features of development that characterize children with autism and related disorders. For the present purposes, my intention in reviewing such contrasts is not only to highlight how the study of typically developing toddlers is vital for deepening our understanding of autism, but also to recruit a perspective on autism in order to achieve fresh insight into the processes and mechanisms of typical development.

SELF- AND OTHER-AWARENESS

The grounding for human beings' understanding of self and other is their experiences of relating to others. For example, one could not know what a person (with a mind) *is* unless one were able to relate to persons as persons, which means relating to others with feelings (Hamlyn, 1974). Or, to put this differently, a child's growing awareness of the difference between persons and things is founded on the child's propensity to *experience* people differently from things. From early in the first year of life, when an infant perceives another person's body and bodily expressive actions, this entails that the infant him- or herself experiences socially coordinated feelings and tendencies to action.

With subsequent development, of course, as a great deal in this volume illustrates, young children's increasingly sophisticated *understandings* of self and other also affect how they relate to others. For our purposes, consider just two simple examples. The first comes from Hoffman (1984) and concerns Marcy, a girl of 20 months. Marcy wanted a toy that her sister was playing with. When she asked for it, her sister refused to give it to her. Marcy paused, apparently reflecting what to do, and then went straight to her sister's rocking horse. This was her sister's favorite toy, and she never allowed others to touch it. Marcy climbed up on the horse, and keeping her eye on her sister, cried "Nice horsey! Nice horsey!" Her sister put down the toy Marcy wanted and came running angrily, whereupon Marcy climbed down from the horse, ran directly to the toy, and grabbed it.

For my second example, I quote from Charlotte Buhler (1937):

> The following experiment is very illustrative. The adult forbids the child to touch a toy that is within the child's reach. He then turns away or leaves the room for a moment. All the 1–2-year-olds understand the prohibition as cancelled at the moment that contact with the adult is broken, and play with the

> toy. If the adult returns suddenly, 60 per cent of the children of 1;4 and 100 per cent of those of 1;6 show the greatest embarrassment, blush, and turn to the adult with a frightened expression. From 1;9 on they attempt to make good what has happened by returning the toy quickly to its place. From two years on they attempt to motivate the disobedience, for example, by claiming the toy as their own. After the age of two the child expresses will, insistence on its own rights, and possessive impulses in its relation with adults. (pp. 66–67)

In the first example, we can observe how before her second birthday, Marcy relates to her sister not only as someone who might be induced to feel things and act accordingly, but also as an individual with her own preferences and vulnerabilities. Moreover, at least on the face of it, we witness Marcy reflecting on a problem, and on her own course of action to deal with it. Of the second example, Buhler noted that a certain degree of self-evaluation is inherent in the independent planning of the young child who holds fast to his or her goals. Indeed in this phase of life, improvements in executive function may have much to do with a child's growing ability not only to reflect on but also to relate with feelings toward him- or herself in relation to the world.

Buhler's passage brings out further important features of young toddlers' social relations. In particular, the return of a prohibiting adult is enough to trigger a new embarrassed state that appears to express not only the toddler's experience of the returning adult as external figure, but also his or her experience of him- or herself-in-relation-to-the-other. It is not merely that the toddler remembers the other, in the way a cat might register its owner's arrival by leaping from a forbidden perch; the toddler also seems to have a picture of him- or herself as having acted disobediently in relation to the other as prohibiting, or perhaps a sensitivity toward the other's potential attitude toward him- or herself as naughty. All this has intense emotional and relational coloring.

Such important descriptive studies have now been complemented by an impressive range of systematic investigations into the 1 year-olds' growing propensity to comply and cooperate with others and to engage in coordinated role-responsive interactions (e.g., Brownell & Carriger, 1990; Hay, 1979; Kaler & Kopp, 1990), studies of 2-year-olds' reactions to mishaps (Cole, Barrett, & Zahn-Waxler, 1992), and research on the processes whereby young children internalize aspects of parental relatedness toward themselves as they develop self-evaluative emotions (e.g., Forman, Aksan, & Kochanska, 2004; Kelley, Brownell, & Campbell, 2000; Kochanska, Coy, & Murray, 2001). Alongside this, there is complementary evidence concerning the qualities and implications of self–other differentiation. From around the age of 18 months, for example, toddlers not only make self-descriptive utterances such as "my book" or "Mary eat" (Kagan, 1982) but also show silly or coy behavior in front of a mirror (Lewis & Brooks-Gunn, 1979)—and there is evidence that personal pronoun usage and self-recognition may reflect common development in self-concepts that are also relevant for advanced pretend play (Lewis & Ramsay, 2004). Home recordings of conversations between mothers and their young children recorded by Dunn, Bretherton, and Munn (1987) reveal how by 24 months of age, children may take an active part in talking about people's feeling states such as those of sadness, distress, happiness, affection, and tiredness. Emotional role taking and self-regulation, and emotional understanding and self-reflective awareness, appear to be developing hand-in-hand. Also bound up with these developments is a growing capacity to symbolize.

SYMBOLIC PLAY AND LANGUAGE

There are inexhaustible subtleties in the development of symbolic play and language during the second and into the third years of life, but I shall select just two features for discussion. The first is that in order to play symbolically, a child must be aware that she is *choosing* to make one thing stand for another, or inventing imaginary objects, or whatever. Note that this entails a degree of self-consciousness. If she were not aware of introducing new meanings for the purposes of play, she would be making a mistake or even hallucinating, but not playing (Leslie, 1987). Much of the fun of playing appears to arise from the child exercising her potential to adopt this and then that perspective in re-presenting to herself, and often to others, imaginary happenings. Moreover, she is emotionally invested in the meanings with which she imbues the materials of play, perhaps especially when these involve human characteristics. Such features of play may hold the key to how play develops. Critically, play entails awareness of self-as-bringing-meanings, and the child needs to recognize the critical distinction between objects with given meanings and what might be called human takes (or perhaps gives) on reality.

When we turn from the emergence of symbolic play to the emergence of (symbolic) language, one of the added complexities is that language functions in different ways. It is expressive as well as referential, for example, and as speech act theorists such as Grice (1957) and Searle (1969) insisted, it serves the purposes of social action as well as information exchange. Having said this, there is an important commonality with symbolic play: Language takes off when a toddler grasps something about the way in which arbitrary signifiers can carry human meanings. Moreover, what an individual uses a word to mean when addressing me is a meaning I can anchor in that word when addressing someone else. Beyond this, meanings are sensitive to contexts of use, and more specifically, they relate to the situation-as-construed by the person or persons expressing themselves through words. All this is woven into the ways language is acquired. For example, Tomasello and colleagues (e.g., Tomasello, 1999; Tomasello & Barton, 1994) have provided elegant illustration of how toddlers between the ages of 18 and 24 months learn the meanings of words by interpreting what speakers mean, and intend to mean, at the time they utter those words. When an adult said he was going to find the "toma" and searched among a number of buckets containing strange objects, it was only when the adult smiled with satisfaction at finding an object and stopped his searching that the child attributed the word to the object then in focus. Language learning is bound up with appreciating what an adult is doing and intending and feeling when speaking, not just with witnessing object labeling.

From a developmental perspective, there appear to be two contrasting ways to conceptualize the emergence of symbolic play and context-sensitive, flexible language—and the new level of self-awareness that these entail. The one way is to suppose that play and/or language emerge according to their own timetables for reasons that are largely independent of the patterning of social relations, and then they are woven into the fabric of interpersonal transactions. The other way (which I have considered at greater length in Hobson, 1993) is to posit that it is largely through developments in social relations, and the understandings to which they give rise, that symbolic play and language (or at least, critical aspects of language) emerge. Specifically, there may be something basic about a toddler's propensity to assume the psychological orientation of other people and at the same time to register others' subjective perspectives as having otherness. Note that *basic* here means that such processes occur *prior to understanding* what it is to take a perspective. Although, arguably, such a propensity underlies the typically human forms of sharing emotional states during early infancy, the clearest manifestations are those of joint attention, social referencing, and the like, observable at the end of the first year of life. Then, about 6 months later, as I have already noted, toddlers achieve *insight* into what it means to be a self, namely, someone with a person-specific psychological orientation to the world. Around the same time, moreover, the child assumes his or her own capacity *as* a self to introduce new perspectives on objects and events in symbolic play. Language takes off as the child grasps how people express and communicate their person-anchored meanings through uttered sounds (now words). According to this account, such forms of social experience provide the structure for a more explicit conceptual grasp of what it means to have, to change, and to introduce new perspectives on objects and events, and to anchor these perspectives in symbols.

There are many possible sources of evidence that bear on our choice between these alternatives, or more subtle mixes of the two. One source is what we observe in atypical development. It is time to turn to the case of autism.

THE CASE OF AUTISM

The Social Relations of Children with Autism

If one dwells on the abilities and disabilities of children with autism, it is difficult to avoid concluding that human development is not "of a piece." In some domains, these children can seem able and adroit, while in others—especially in the sphere of relating to other people, but also in the flexibility and generativity of their thinking and play—they are seriously, sometimes tragically, limited. It was in 1943 that the American psychiatrist Leo Kanner first described autism, and I cite one of his clinical case descriptions to present the syndrome. Here he describes 6-year-old Frederick attending his clinic for the first time:

> He was led into the psychiatrist's office by a nurse, who left the room immediately afterward. His facial expression was tense, somewhat apprehensive, and gave the impression of intelligence. He wandered aimlessly about for a few moments, showing no sign of awareness of the three adults present. He then sat down on the couch, ejaculating unintelligible sounds, and then abruptly lay down, wearing throughout a dreamy-like smile. . . . Objects absorbed him easily and he showed good attention and perseverance in playing with them. He seemed to regard people as unwelcome intruders to whom he paid as little attention as they would permit. When forced to respond, he did so briefly and returned to his absorption in things. When a hand was held out before him so that he could not possibly ignore it, he played with it briefly as if it were a detached object. He blew out a match with an expression of satisfaction with the achievement, but did not look up to the person who had lit the match. (p. 224)

Here we have a vivid picture of a child who was unconnected, on an emotional level, with the people around him. More than this, he related to people in a way that seemed uncomprehending of their very status as people—and here one may note a stark contrast with typically developing infants, never mind toddlers—in that he played with the hand and not the person whose hand it was, or was satisfied with blowing out the match but did not share that pleasure with the person who held it. Thus it was that Kanner commented on the children's "profound aloneness" in relation to others, such that "people, so long as they left the child alone, figured in about the same manner as did the desk, the bookshelf, or the filing cabinet" (p. 246). He concluded by suggesting that the children "have come into the world with innate inability to form the usual, biologically provided affective contact with people" (p. 250).

Already we are confronted with a problem I alluded to earlier, namely, the question that might be raised in relation to Kanner's claim about what is innate and present from the beginning of life, when the children he is studying are long past infancy. In the last decade, evidence has emerged not to prove, but to render more probable, that (with certain caveats about the universality of the claim for all children who manifest the syndrome) children with autism do have profound social impairment of very early onset. Their limitations extend beyond a lack of responsiveness to other people's relations toward themselves to a (relative) failure to attune to others' attitudes toward a shared world.

Beyond clinical descriptions of individual cases, three sources of evidence pertain to the manifestations of autism in infancy and toddlerhood. The first and most equivocal of these are videotapes or home movies of the early lives of children subsequently diagnosed to have autism (e.g., Baranek, 1999; Osterling & Dawson, 1994). These suggest that aspects of social engagement such as looking at others and orienting to the child's own name may be relatively absent during the first year.

The second source of evidence is parental report (e.g., Dahlgren & Gillberg, 1989; Lord, Storoschuk, Rutter, & Pickles, 1993; Stone & Lemanek, 1990). For example, Wimpory, Hobson, Williams, and Nash (2000) interviewed parents of very young children who were referred with difficulties in relating to and communicating with others. At the time of interview, the undiagnosed children were between 32 and 48 months old, and it was only subsequently that 10 children diagnosed with autism were compared with 10 children, matched for age and developmental level, who did not have autism. This meant that when parents were asked about the children's behavior in the first 2 years of life, they were recalling events from only 6 to 24 months previously, and their memories were not distorted by knowledge of autism. The parents' reports indicated that not one of the infants with autism had shown frequent and intense eye contact, engaged in turn taking with adults, or used noises communicatively, whereas half of the control children were reported to show each of these kinds of behavior. There were also fewer infants with autism who greeted or waved to their parents, who raised their arms to be picked up, who directed feelings of anger and distress toward people, who were sociable in play, or who enjoyed and participated in lap games. Then in addition, there were group differences in the infants' ways of relating to other people with reference to objects and events in the environment. For example, not one of the infants with autism but at least half the infants in the control group were reported to offer or give objects to others in the first 2 years of life. The same was true of pointing at objects or following others' points. Few children with autism were said to show objects to others, and not one was said to have looked between an object of interest and an adult, for example, when the infant wanted something out of reach. They appeared to be not only less connected with other people for their own sake but also less connected with or less able to share others' affective attitudes to a shared world (Kasari, Sigman, Mundy, & Yirmiya, 1990).

The third body of evidence comes from direct observation of toddlers with autism. Sigman, Kasari, Kwon, and Yirmiya (1992) videotaped 30 young autistic children with a mean age of under 4 years and closely matched nonautistic retarded and typically developing children in the presence of an adult who appeared to hurt herself by hitting her finger with a hammer, simulated fear toward a remote-controlled robot, and pretended to be ill by lying down on a couch for a minute, feigning discomfort. In each of these situations, children with autism were unusual in rarely looking at or relating to the adult. When the adult pretended to be hurt, for example, children with autism often appeared unconcerned and continued to play with toys. When a small remote-controlled robot moved toward the child and stopped about 4 feet away, the parent and the experimenter, who were both seated nearby, made fearful facial expressions, gestures, and vocalizations for 30 seconds. Almost all the nonautistic children looked at an adult at some point during this procedure, but fewer than half the children with autism did so, and then only briefly. The children with autism were not only less hesitant than the mentally retarded children in playing with the robot but also played with it for substantially longer periods of time. It seemed that they were less influenced by the fearful attitudes of those around them. Similar studies have now been conducted with 20-month-olds (Charman et al., 1997), where for example, only 4 of 10 children with autism but every one of the nonautistic children looked to the face of an investigator who expressed pain, and the children with autism very rarely switched their gaze between an activated toy and adult to check out the toy. Here again we find evidence that children with autism are relatively "unengaged" not only in one-to-one interpersonal–affective transactions but also with another person's emotional attitudes toward objects and events in the world.

Perhaps I should try to distill what these observations may tell us about typical early development. It is part of knowing what a person is, that one finds oneself relating to persons in a personal way. Such relations involve, among other things, being sensitive and responsive to expressions of feeling in the other, and engaging in emotionally coordinated interactions. One striking illustration is when infants of 2 months are confronted with their mother assuming a "still-face" posture and show a typical pattern of discomfort and dysregulation (originally, Tronick, Als, Adamson, Wise, & Brazelton, 1978). Although there is development in the specificity with which particular bodily expressions of emotion are perceived and reacted to, and with this, development in the range of mutually patterned states involving an infant and others, this represents the elaboration of the category of the person in the infant's experience, not its emergence. Primary intersubjectivity is a dyadic phenomenon. It entails psychological connection *with* another person, in the sense that each participant is engaged with what is expressed *through* the other's body. And such a connection provides the grounding not only for our experience (and ultimately, understanding) of other people *as* people but also for our engagement with others' attitudes to a shared world. In each of these respects, individuals with autism are partly deprived of what it takes to apprehend other people as centers of subjectivity and consciousness.

Here it needs to be acknowledged that despite the evidence I have cited, it has yet to be established whether as infants, children with autism are indeed limited in achieving intersubjective engagement with other people. This is a matter that may be difficult to resolve, insofar as the criteria for such engagement are in dispute, and infants at risk are difficult to recruit and study. Some workers have taken the view that it is only with the onset of triadic person–person–world relations that the developmental trajectory of children with autism deviates from that of other children. Others would continue to stress that there may be domain-general cognitive, rather than emotional/intersubjective, sources to the children's developmental psychopathology, for instance, in their inability to achieve "central coherence" in thinking such that they cannot integrate diverse information and achieve social sensitivity (e.g., Happé, 2000). I would simply highlight the importance of the motivational-cum-emotional process of being affected by and drawn toward the attitudes of other people in joint attention and social referencing, because this is conspicuous for its absence among children with autism—and because this is *also* conspicuous for its limited quality in one-to-one interpersonal transactions, as Kanner observed.

Whatever the case in this regard, we might also note one further, especially interesting, aspect of the social relations of children with autism. This is the way in which they are able to copy the goal-directed actions of someone else, and are even prone to echo the behavior of others. By contrast, they find it hard and/or are rarely moved to imitate a range of emotional expressions, bodily movements, and pantomimed actions (e.g., Curcio, 1978; Dawson & Adams, 1984; DeMyer et al., 1972; Hammes & Langdell, 1981; Rogers, Hepburn, Stackhouse, & Wehner, 2003; Sigman & Ungerer, 1984). Why should this be? Might this profile of imitative abilities and disabilities be connected with unusual qualities of self- and other-awareness in the children?

Self- and Other-Awareness

Clinical descriptions convey how in many circumstances, children with autism appear to lack the kinds of self-consciousness and self-awareness that render typically developing toddlers so charming and delightful, and at times so challenging. The account provided by Gerhard Bosch is especially illuminating. In attempting to delineate "the particular mode of existence of an autistic child" (Bosch, 1970, p. 3), Bosch illustrated how the child often seems to lack a sense of possessiveness as well as self-consciousness and shame, to be delayed in "acting" on others by demanding or ordering, and to be missing something of the " 'self-involvement,' the acting with, and the identification with the acting person" (p. 81). He also suggested that "counter-attack or defense is impossible because the child has no experience of attacking or defensive relationship with others" (p. 99). Perhaps most prescient of all, Bosch emphasized that "delay occurs in the constituting of the other person in whose place I can put myself . . . [and] . . . in the constituting of a common sphere of existence, in which things do not simply refer to me but also to others" (p. 89).

It is important that Bosch framed his account of self- and other-awareness not merely in the currently fashionable terms of "mental representation" but instead with reference to interpersonal involvement, social agency, attacking and defensive stances, and possession. These aspects of social life are striking by their relative absence in individuals with autism, precisely because they are so striking for their presence in typically developing toddlers. It is not that young children with autism are completely without certain forms of self-awareness. For example, they often remove surreptitiously placed rouge from their faces when they perceive themselves in a mirror (Dawson & McKissick, 1984; Neuman & Hill, 1978; Spiker & Ricks, 1984). What most children with autism do not show is the coyness so typical of young normal or learning disabled children without autism. Thus, for example, the child with autism can make use of his own reflection to register what it means to have his own body marked, and he is likely to act accordingly in trying to remove the mark from his face. What is far less certain is whether such behavior is motivated by a concern with the way he looks to other people, and with the evaluative attitudes that others may entertain in seeing him marked in an unusual manner. He perceives a body in a mirror, and he recognizes that this is the body toward which he can act in a body-self-directed way; but he may not conceive of himself as self in the minds of others (Hobson, 1990b).

Consider the study conducted by Kasari, Sigman, Baumgartner, and Stipek (1993) with mentally retarded young children with and without autism (mean age 42 months), and mental age–matched normal toddlers (mean age 23 months). Each subject completed a puzzle, and the experimenter and parent reacted neutrally; then the child completed a second puzzle, and after 3 seconds, both adults gave praise. Although the children with autism were like mentally retarded and typically developing children in being inclined to smile when they succeeded with the puzzles, those with autism were less likely to draw attention to what they had done or to look up to an adult, and less likely to show pleasure in being praised. There seemed to be something missing or abnormal in the children's feelings toward the approval and attention they might gain from (and the experiences they might share with) the adults present. Their pride assumed a strangely asocial form. In further assessments of pride in high-functioning children and young adolescents with autism, with mean age approximately 12 years and around average IQ (Capps, Yirmiya, & Sigman, 1992: see also Kasari, Chamberlain, & Bauminger, 2001), the children could cite situations eliciting pride but provided instances that were less personal and in some ways more stereotyped (e.g., finishing one's homework or winning games) than was the case with control children.

So, too, with regard to guilt. Kasari and colleagues (2001) describe how high-IQ children with autism can report feeling guilt, but compared with control children they provide fewer self-evaluative statements and are more likely to describe situations in terms of rule breaking, disruptiveness, and damage to property rather than those of causing physical or emotional harm to others. For children with autism, guilt appears to be defined in terms of memorizable rules and actions such as taking toys from school, stealing cookies, running away, and so on, rather than in interpersonal, empathic terms.

Similar results emerge when the focus turns to embarrassment. According to Capps and colleagues (1992) and Kasari and colleagues (2001), children with autism are liable to give examples of embarrassing situations that are external and uncontrollable, whereas matched typically developing children often give more specific and personal examples that relate to controllable events. Especially frequent are reports of feeling embarrassment because of teasing by others, a relatively rare response from children without autism; but references to the presence of an audience are relatively infrequent. Complementary findings have emerged from a recent program of research into social emotions among children and adolescents with autism (Chidambi, 2003; Hobson, Chidambi, Lee, & Meyer, 2006). For example, interviews with parents of children with autism indicated how these children show almost no clear signs of embarrassment, whereas such feelings were striking among the matched comparison group. Although the children with autism were said to be affected by the moods of others, there were few who showed clear expressions of pity and guilt. We interpreted these findings in terms of the children's limited propensity and/or ability to experience "person-centered" feelings that are configured by the ability to identify with other people's attitudes.

Yet it is not the case that all supposedly complex emotions are equally atypical in expression among children with autism. Jealousy, an emotion that might well be related to the attachment system and that may not entail identifying with others' feelings, is a case in point. In the interview study already mentioned, the two groups were almost identical insofar as equal numbers with and without autism were said to manifest clear jealousy, and very few in either group showed none at all. Bauminger (2004) reported that in two jealousy-eliciting conditions—one in which the child's parent praised another child's picture while ignoring his or her own child's and another in which the parent engaged in affectionate play exclusively with the other child—the majority of high-functioning children with autism (mean age 11 years) displayed clear indications of jealousy, and there was not a group difference from control participants in this respect. On the other hand, the children with autism tended to express themselves by acting toward the parent rather than looking at him or her. In separate tests, the children with autism were less proficient in recognizing jealousy in a picture, and only half could produce personal and affective (as opposed to social-cognitive) examples of jealousy, whereas all the control children could do so.

These latter findings, of a difficulty encountered by children with autism in describing their own jealousy and (apparently) understanding the nature of jealousy, are reminiscent of three other reports. Lee and Hobson (1998) conducted "self-understanding interviews" with participants with autism between 9 and 19 years of age (and verbal mental ages from 4 to 10 years) and reported that they contrasted with children who did not have autism in being restricted in the feelings they expressed about themselves, and in failing to mention friends or being members of a social group. Bauminger and Kasari (2000) described how children with autism between the ages of 8 and 14 years spoke of loneliness but failed to refer to the more affective dimension of being left out of close intimate relationships. As Bauminger (2004) suggests, children with autism appear to find difficulty in considering interpersonal relationships when reflecting on their emotional experiences.

What insights might we gain from such observations? It is not merely that our attention is drawn to contrasts between typically developing toddlers and children with autism. We also discover something about the developmental fabric of self-consciousness, and the ways in which specifically social experiences—indeed, specific *kinds* of social experience—are woven into diverse qualities of self-awareness. This is intriguing for our understanding of self-consciousness in typical development, of course. Evidence from autism suggests that there are dissociable aspects of self-consciousness in front of a mirror, of pride, even of guilt and embarrassment. The aspects that are relatively missing among children with autism are those for which interpersonal engagement with and sensitivity to the attitudes of others appear to be critical. It is likely that in typically developing toddlers, such engagement and such sensitivity is constitutive of, and perhaps developmentally foundational for, the qualities and intensity of self-consciousness they display.

Symbolic Play

By and large, children with autism are severely restricted in their capacity for flexible, creative symbolic play (e.g., Riguet, Taylor, Benaroya, & Klein, 1981; Wing, Gould, Yeats, & Brierly, 1977). For example, Ungerer and Sigman (1981) and Sigman and Ungerer (1984) presented children with autism between 2½ and 6½ years who were cognitively matched not only with mentally retarded children but also typically developing toddlers between 16 months and 3 years, with a set of toys that included dolls, toy furniture, a brush, and so on. They initially modeled four symbolic acts and then observed the children's play. One of the categories of play recorded was that of symbolic play, which involved using one object as if it were another object, or according agency to a doll, or creating absent objects or people. The children with autism were observed to show a degree of symbolic play, but this was less frequent, was less varied, and involved fewer integrated acts than in the case of the participants without autism. On the other hand, as several investigators have noted (e.g., Jarrold, Boucher, & Smith, 1993; Lewis & Boucher, 1988), it may be possible to prompt elements of symbolic play even when a child's spontaneous play appears to be sparse. This raises the question: Why does play matter so much to children without autism but so much less so to those with autism? Or, to express this differently, "Why do toys and other symbolic artifacts *engage* us so?" (Hobson, 1993, p. 164).

I restrict myself to one theoretical and one empirical set of observations. From a theoretical perspective, we need to explain how a child recognizes that the symbols of play are different from what they symbolize, or to express this differently, that the meaning I ascribe is dissociable both from the object or event that originally carried that meaning, and from the object to which I now attribute the meaning symbolically. If I make this box a pretend-bed, I knowingly apply bed-meanings to something that yields up its identity for the purposes of play. My proposal is that it is by relating to *other people's* attitudes to the world that a toddler is lifted out of his or her own one-track way of apprehending objects and events and is moved to adopt different perspectives (Hobson, 1990a). In a critical development over the course of the first half of the second year, the toddler comes to understand these *as* different person-anchored perspectives. Having identified with the ways that other people relate to the world and to him- or herself, the toddler becomes able to relate to *his or her own* relations with the world. This is tantamount to achieving self-awareness of one's potential to apply alternative perspectives. It is here that we see the dawn of self-reflection. Now the child can realize his or her potential, knowingly to transpose attitudes from his or her original targets to new, symbolic media. No wonder the materials of play come to matter, in that what is most important to a child is often that which is re-created and modified through self-initiated, relatively controllable and distanced symbolic means. At the same time, the interpersonal playfulness of play, the joy of sharing and coordinating attitudes with others, is carried into the theater of the individual's own mind. The creativity and fun of playful imagination bears the hallmark of its interpersonal origins.

The empirical observations come from a recently completed study of symbolic play among children with autism (Hobson, Meyer, & Lee, 2006). In a nutshell, the results were that two matched groups of able children with and without autism, between 7 and 14 years and with verbal mental ages between 2 and 10 years, were similar in their flexible use of play materials, and even their ability to make one thing stand for another—yet there was indication that the *process* through which this was achieved was different among participants with autism, in that they were rated as showing less fun and being less invested in the materials of play and less creative. It was even possible to achieve interrater reliabilities in judgments of the children's awareness of themselves as creating new meanings, and here, too, the children with autism scored less highly. The upshot is that if one evaluates play from a social–developmental rather than an individualistic cognitive–computational perspective, then one finds a relation between the quality of children's engagement with others' attitudes toward the world (including toward the world of play) and the quality of the children's attitudes to their own alternative takes on the world and their engagement in playful symbolizing.

Language

Here I could not hope to survey the domain of early language development in children with autism, never mind appraise this in relation to the emergence and early differentiation of language in typically developing toddlers. Instead, I highlight some features of the children's language that appear to be especially telling for their underlying social–relational abnormalities.

The first thing to note is how a substantial proportion of children with autism never learn how to speak. They appear unable to grasp what speech is for, or how it operates. This seems to be more than a linguistic problem, because often their communicative gestures are also limited. In these cases it seems that very basic kinds of engagement with others needed to underpin mutual communicative exchange, and to give motivation and sense to intending to communicate, is missing. Children who cannot share or otherwise coordinate their experiences, and intend to do so, cannot communicate except insofar as they can make sounds or movements to get things done.

To provide an overview of the kinds of linguistic abnormality in the language of individuals with autism, one can return to Kanner's (1943) original account. Kanner observed how the children he studied often echoed the words or phrases of other people, often retaining the intonation; how they were liable to confuse the personal pronouns "I" and "you"; how they would make idiosyncratic utterances that could only be understood with reference to the contexts in which the child acquired the words; and how they showed literal speech that appeared to reveal a failure to grasp connotative meanings. Other features one might add to this list are abnormalities in the tone and rhythm of speech (which may be flat and monotonous, or sing-song), difficulties in initiating or sustaining a conversation with someone else, and what has been called pedantic literalness, not least in failing to differentiate between what is old and what is new to a listener. And to take up the matter of "getting things done," Wetherby and Prutting (1984) recorded how a small group of young children with autism who were in the prelinguistic and early stages of language development would regulate an adult's behavior to achieve an environmental end such as getting food, but none attracted and directed the adult's attention to him- or herself or to an object as an end in and of itself. They requested objects and showed protest, but unlike language-matched typically developing children, none showed off, commented on or labeled things, or acknowledged the adult who was interacting with them.

The upshot of all this is that one needs to question how far children with autism listen to someone speaking, as well as speak themselves, with the same kinds of understanding of communicative intention, and the same kinds of expressive and communicative intent, as do people without autism. Or, to put this in developmental context, if a great deal of language learning depends on a toddler apprehending and drawing inferences from what an adult is intending to communicate in using speech—and in particular, the aspects or elements of situations the adult has in mind, or the nuances of relatedness to the listener the adult is highlighting or adjusting (as in being polite)—and if, more than this, the child then needs not only to identify such things but also *identify with* the adult's speech acts in expressing those things—then perhaps the speech of children with autism reveals in which respects such factors shape early language development.

There is one respect in which the language of children with autism appears to provide especially clear instances of limitation in the kinds of reciprocal role-taking adjustment to speaker–listener meanings that Mead highlighted for typical communication. This is where words, phrases, or sentences appear to be adopted wholesale and without adjustment to the stance of a speaker in a given context. Echollia is a striking example, but so, too, it is likely that the children's erratic use of personal pronouns (e.g., Bosch, 1970; Fay, 1979; Lee,

Hobson, & Chiat, 1994) reflects their relative incomprehension that such terms refer to people with reference to whoever is talking. *I* for me when I speak becomes *I* for you when you speak. The point here is that language is rooted in *a person's* psychological orientation, in what a speaker intends and means from a particular vantage point that (once again) needs to be identified with if the varieties of language use are to be appreciated.

Fresh Insights from Imitation in Autism

Thus far, the phenomena of autism (at least as I have framed them) appear to point to something abnormal in affected children's ability to move to the perspective of someone else, to adopt that perspective for themselves, and to come to understand what a human perspective *is*. It is important that in this context, "perspective" means more than visual perspective or even point of view, in that it encompasses the manifold ways in which an individual can hold a stance or mode of relating to the world. Although in recent years, much attention has been given to the limitations in "theory of mind" apparent in children with autism (see, e.g., chapters in Baron-Cohen, Tager-Flusberg, & Cohen, 2000), the starting point for theory of mind theorizing was not so much a concern with interpersonal relatedness but a concern with children's *concepts* of mind such as those of belief, desire, and intention. In many cases, the theoretical perspective adopted was computational in style, and the developmental account was framed in terms of representations and metaprepresentations and the computations (such as decoupling representations) that could be performed on these (e.g., Leslie, 1987). Here it might be noted that computers do not have concepts, nor is it obvious that they could derive concepts of belief in the absence of the ability to hold beliefs. True, the theory of mind approach has now stretched back in developmental time to encompass what are considered to be precursor abilities in infancy, especially those entailed in joint attention, but the danger remains that such a drift may bring with it a continuing preoccupation with what is cognitive in early development, and a less than thorough reappraisal of how there might be emotionally configured social–relational foundations for cognitive representations, concepts, and the like.

We have already considered a domain, that of symbolizing, in which social–developmental factors might *explain* how a child's cognitive system acquires enhanced computational resources. Yet there remains the challenge to analyze how specific components or properties of social relations achieve the developmental results that (arguably) they do. Recent studies in imitation serve to illustrate how the structure of self–other relations, and in particular the movements in psychological stance effected by the process of identification, may be critical in providing the basis for children's *understanding* of persons with their own subjective takes on the world.

In a methodologically novel study, Hobson and Lee (1999) tested matched groups of children with and without autism between 9 and 19 years (and verbal mental ages between 4 and 13 years) for their ability to imitate a person demonstrating four novel goal-directed actions on objects in two contrasting styles. It is difficult to define what style means, but two actions may be distinguished according to the style with which they are executed, even when they have in common both a goal and a means to that goal. In one condition, the demonstrator made a toy policeman on wheels move along by pressing down on its head *either* with his wrist cocked *or* with extended index and middle fingers. In other conditions, he showed either gentle or harsh styles of action. The results were as follows. The children with autism were perfectly able to copy the demonstrator's actions, for example, in pressing down the policeman's head to make him move. On the other hand, they contrasted with control participants insofar as very few adopted the demonstrator's style of acting on the objects. Instead of adopting the wrist or two-finger approach to activating the toy, for example, most of them pressed down on the policeman's head with the palm of a hand. Here we stressed a contrast between children's ability to observe and copy intended actions per se, relatively intact in autism, and the propensity to identify with and thereby imitate a *person's* expressive mode of relating to objects and events in the world.

Our hypothesis is that (most) children with autism are limited in a particular form of imitation through which an individual assumes the *stance* of the other. When a typically developing toddler *identifies with* someone else, he or she perceives actions and attitudes anchored in the other person's bodily located orientation toward the world in such a way that these are assimilated to the individual's own bodily located orientation. One expression of this is when an individual imitates someone else's self-oriented action, so that the action becomes oriented to the individual's (rather than the copied person's) self, and this proved to be another feature that distinguished children with autism in the Hobson and Lee (1999) study. For example, one condition involved the demonstrator holding a piperack against his own shoulder in order to strum it with a stick, either harshly or gently. Here a substantial majority of the control participants identified with the demonstrator and positioned the piperack against their own shoulder before strumming it. By contrast, most of the children with autism positioned the piperack at a distance in front of them, on the table. Therefore not only with respect to style but also with respect to self-orientation, the children with autism did not assume the manner with which the other person executed actions, even though they copied the actions per se.

In subsequent studies, we have introduced systematic variation between the style and strategy/goal of an action (Hobson, Lee, & Meyer, 2003; Meyer & Hobson, 2003). For example, we demonstrated that in comparison with matched participants without autism, children with autism aged between 6 and 15 years (mean verbal mental age 6 years) were especially unlikely to imitate style when this is incidental to the goal of actions, whereas when a particular style of action was necessary to achieve a result (e.g., pulling bluetack slowly to stretch it, rather than abruptly to pull it apart), there was little group difference.

We have also devised a fresh approach to investigating self–other orientation (Meyer & Hobson, 2004). In one study, we tested 32 children between the ages of 6 and 14 years, half with autism and half without autism but instead with learning difficulties or developmental delays. The children with and without autism were group-matched for chronological age, language ability, and visual–motor integration skills. Their verbal mental ages ranged from 2 to 13 years. Sitting on the floor opposite a participant, the investigator demonstrated four actions, each of which was presented in two different ways. For example, she picked up a small wheel with a metal handle (a castor from furniture) and rolled it from left to right either directly in front of herself *or*, leaning forward, across the front of the participant; another example was where she *either* lifted a blue box from its position in front of herself, placed it on top of a box positioned in front of the participant, and then returned it to the starting point *or* lifted the box closest to the participant, placed that on top of the box nearest herself, then returned it to its original position. After returning the object(s) to their original positions, the investigator instructed the child: "Now you."

The children's subsequent actions were scored as reflecting *identification* if the child copied the investigator's stance (i.e., the action in relation to self or other). For example, identification occurred when the children imitated the tester's close-to-self orientation by rolling the wheel close to him- or herself or copied close-to-other orientation by rolling the wheel close to the tester. As we predicted, the children with autism were significantly less likely to imitate the self–other orientation of the actions. While half the children in the comparison group copied the self–other orientation of the actions on at least half of the eight trials, for example, only 3 of the 16 children with autism did so; and from a complementary perspective, six of the participants with autism imitated self–other orientation on fewer than two occasions, while only one participant in the comparison group did so as infrequently as this.

Yet these results do not necessarily reflect the kinds of interpersonal engagement implicated in our hypothesis about identification, which pertains to interpersonal linkage, interpersonal differentiation, and intersubjective coordination and movement. To address this issue, we drew on the program of research inspired by the work of Mundy and Sigman and their colleagues (Mundy & Sigman, 1989; Sigman, Mundy, Sherman, & Ungerer, 1986), as well as by others such as Loveland and Landry (1986), indicating that joint attention, and especially the initiation of joint attention, reflects something very basic about the impairments in intersubjective engagement that characterize autism. We focused on what it means to share experiences (Hobson, 1989). Joint attention *of a certain kind* occurs when one person shares experiences of the world with another. True sharing involves movement toward and adoption of aspects of the other person's psychological stance vis-à-vis objects or events and coordination with one's own now-expanded subjective state. The important thing here is that one participates in the other person's state and maintains awareness of otherness in the person with whom one is sharing, while also being affectively involved from one's own standpoint.

Therefore, we extended the self–other imitation study just described (Hobson & Hobson, 2007). Our new hypothesis was that specifically sharing looks (reflecting identification) would have a positive relation to the propensity to imitate self–other orientation. Unlike other kinds of looks, those we called sharing looks involved a deeper gaze, which conveyed personal involvement (what Kanner, 1943, probably meant by the phrase *affective contact*). With a single prediction in mind, we took a closer look at the videotapes of self–other imitation in the aforementioned study. The demonstration and imitation sequences of the self–other-orientation study were coded by an independent naive judge (reliable with a second rater) for (1) direction of gaze—to the tester, object, or away and (2) quality of joint attention looks—sharing, checking (i.e., glancing "at" the tester to see what she might do), or orientating to the speech or movement of the tester. Given the skepticism we have encountered about rating such looks, I should note that interrater reliabilities in judgment have been high (in this study, two independent judges agreed in classifying 24 of 27 looks). Results were that children with autism spent less than half as much time looking at the tester and significantly more time looking at the objects, relative to children in the comparison group. This difference was not specific to a particular quality of joint attention look, as the pattern was similar for sharing, checking, and orienting looks. The percentage of time spent looking at the tester overall, as well as frequency of checking and orienting joint attention looks, were *not* related to imitation of self–other orientation in either group. By contrast, as predicted, *sharing looks* were specifically and significantly associated with the children's propensity to imitate self–other orientation, both within and across the two groups.

These results complement the findings of Carpenter, Pennington, and Rogers (2002), who administered a battery of social-cognitive measures, including facial and manual imitation tasks, to children with autism between 3 and 5 years (and with a mean verbal mental age of approximately 2 years) and a matched comparison group of children with developmental delays. These researchers also tracked whether or not, at any point, the children showed evidence of joint engagement, defined as a spontaneous look to the tester and back to the object. Whether or not the children with autism showed evidence of joint engagement (75% of the children with autism did so) was significantly associated with their performance on the imitation tasks, as well as many of the other social-cognitive measures. Results from the present study extend such findings to reveal that a specific type of joint attention—namely, "sharing"—is directly related to the children's imitation of self–other orientation. If sharing looks are another manifestation of the propensity to be moved by (and often, to) others' subjective orientation, then this should come as no surprise.

TODDLERHOOD REVISITED

How might we now reappraise the psychological development of the typically developing 1- and 2-year-old? How do the phenomena of autism reshape or even transform our view of how development proceeds over these critical early years of life and inform our notions of what it is that has developed? For example, how are we to understand the nature of interpersonal relations, or self-consciousness or self-regulation, or creative flexible symbolic play and language? The study of autism promises to help us find a framework for addressing these questions. I am going to propose that the human infant's and toddler's capacity to *identify with* other people is critical for cognitive as well as social development. Here, in brief, is why I think this is so.

First, we have to consider the background of the first year of life. Human infants are not like chimpanzee infants. True, each kind of infant (and young children with autism, come to that) enjoy rough-and-tumble play with grown-ups. But there is a quality of interpersonal engagement, what phenomenologists have called dwelling in the experiences of the other person, that is distinctive to humankind. It is present from around 2 months of age, and it is a source of joy for a caregiver and any other adult fortunate enough to receive the young infant's favors. I believe that already, as the teasing of infants around the middle of their first year testifies (Reddy, 1991), we see the first signs of a linkage-cum-differentiation between babies and other people that will soon become more sophisticated modes of sharing experiences. This is an emotional business, with dimensions that are cognitive (e.g., people are distinguished from things, unless the things are disguised as people) and conative (e.g., infants are motivated to orient to, and engage with, people, especially friendly and responsive ones).

In passing, I should note there are complementary theoretical perspectives on the matters with which I have been concerned. For example, Barresi and Moore (1996) have offered a somewhat (but not radically) different account of how young children coordinate first-person and third-person perspectives. In my view, these authors' explanation in terms of an intentional schema and the role of imitating goal-directed actions underestimates the developmental significance of infants being moved to the orientation of others through engagement with bodily expressed attitudes. Or again, both Meltzoff (e.g., 2002) and Tomasello (e.g., 1999) have stressed how infants experience others as "like me," but each appears to think that *understanding* of self and other as having minds arises through the application of analogy *from* one's own case *to* that of other people. According to my scheme, understandings of self and other are two sides of the same coin: A child comes to grasp that each is a person with his or her own mental orientation, on the basis of increasing differentiation among interchangeable person-anchored stances that implicate coordinated interpersonal experience. Indeed, it may well be the case that, as Bråten (1998) has suggested, human infants are born with the propensity to experience the bodily expressed subjective states of other people *both* in their own feelings *and* as in some sense "other."

Whatever the case in these respects, all this is water under the bridge for the toddler. Except that the 1-year-old tottering around the room, like the adult watching her, is still in the thrall of both primary and secondary intersubjectivity, where she is prone to monitor her caregiver's attitudes to the world, drawn to show or point or otherwise share experiences with the other, and inclined to imitate another person's actions. Moreover, these actions are not just copied. Take the videotape I have been reviewing just now, of a child very early in her second year who watched, wide-eyed, as an adult put a glittering ring of tinsel on her head, and who then gleefully put the ring on her own head. What could be more unremarkable? And yet, what a remarkable thing to happen. Or again, consider the 1-year-old who waves good-bye. A commonplace occurrence, except that it is not so commonplace for children with autism. In one study (Hobson & Lee, 1998), we made videotapes of the greetings and farewells of *teenagers* with and without autism, and in all cases of the individuals with autism who waved, the waves were strange and unconvincing, often ill-directed or limp or somehow not really waves. These individuals had not adopted other people's waves, with the communicative and outward-facing expressiveness that waves entail, and made this gesture their own.

What all this seems to suggest is that in the earliest phases of toddlerhood, children are engaged with others in a special way. Take the specialness of showing objects to someone else, something that children with autism (or chimpanzees, come to that) rarely do. This seems to express the young child's engagement with the other person's bodily expressed attitude to the object, or perhaps more accurately, to the object-as-shown-by-the-child. It is not just that the child uses other people to find out about the world, but also that she uses the world to explore relations with other people.

Take the specialness of imitation. It is not just that the child copies someone else's actions—where putting a ring on the person's head might be copied by the action of trying to put the ring on that same person's head—but rather, the child assimilates the other's action with regard to the other's self as a potential action she (the child) can make toward her own self.

Take the specialness of personal pronoun learning. The child naturally associates an utterance (e.g., "Mine!") as expressing the other person's attitude with which the child can identify, so that she can give linguistic expression to the same attitude *when it is hers,* by the very same expression "Mine!"

Take the specialness of linguistic communication. When the adult uses a word to designate something—and the something may be actions in the future, not merely things or events that are present—the child interprets these in terms of what makes sense, and what the adult may be trying to communicate, from the adult's point of view.

Take the specialness of the almost 2-year-old's newfound capacities for empathy with others, where the other's preferences or feelings are (at least in part) understood from the other's stance; or signs of so-called self-conscious emotions in which toddlers appear to take attitudes toward themselves as if from an outside perspective of someone else.

Or, finally, take the specialness of symbolic play, in which the toddler must (logically must, if this is really to count as choosing to make this stand for that) be aware of applying new, self-selected meanings to the vehicles of symbolic play when he or she engages in make-believe pretend. How are we to interpret how all these things have entered the repertoire of children so young?

Observations of children with autism who are so limited in each and every one of these respects may help us to understand all this. For we have seen how children with autism are not *engaged with* other people, and the attitudes and subjective states other people express through their bodies, in the way that is so special to typically developing toddlers. No wonder they are (mostly) stuck in their own one-track, matter-of-fact world, relatively uninclined (rather than disinclined) to share experiences with others. Often they are unmoved by the attitudes of others toward a shared world. They tend to acquire a language that is often fixed in meaning and unresponsive to the person- and perspective-dependent nuances (pragmatics) that give language such richness. They are un-self-conscious in *some* but not all respects, and they relatively lack the refinement of feeling that comes with coyness, guilt, and shame embedded in self–other relatedness. Last but not least, they are mostly uncreative and lacking in investment and fun when it comes to symbolic play. All this is manifest well before the developmental stage in which the children might be expected to have acquired a so-called theory of mind manifest in concepts of belief, intention, and so on.

I do not want to belabor the point, but there is so much in a toddler's world that depends on, because it arises out of, a child's identification with the attitudes of others (Hobson, 2002/2004). To identify with someone else is to feel something of the other's psychological stance, and potentially to make that one's own, but at the same time (at least initially) to feel the stance as the other's. That is what sharing means—not just catching a feeling-state from someone else but having feelings for the other person and with the other person who is recognized to be other. So, too, it is a developmental achievement when the child *conceptualizes* him- or herself as one person in a community of separate yet connected individuals, each a center of consciousness who can construe the world in this way or that. In symbolic play, it is not just that the child knows him- or herself to be deploying person-dependent (i.e., self-created) meanings, important though this is, but also that the symbolic vehicle is known to be symbolic and not the thing itself, available to carry meanings that a child ascribes to and embodies in objects with otherness. More than this, if this account is correct, the very creativity and generativity of symbolic play and much of the wealth of the imagination are the products of two closely related qualities of mind: (1) the provisionality and flexibility of symbols that can fix and carry meanings and be combined and recombined in infinite variety, and (2), the fluidity that comes with role taking through perspectives that originate in identifiable-with person-anchored attitudes and actions toward the world. Movements in attitude that are interpersonal in source become movements in attitude and thought within the toddler's own mind. And, of course, the speed and flexibility of such movement should come as no surprise, when we reflect on the lightning-fast movements in mind induced by the spoken or written word (if I say "child," see how swiftly this has moved you in thought).

In remains for me to be true to my promise, and to return to G. H. Mead, Vygotsky, and Freud. Mead (1934) envisaged how symbols are embedded in reciprocal communication, and how they give rise to what one might call the mental space needed for reflective thought and imagination. Vygotsky (1962) recognized that the higher functions of the human mind arise through the interiorization of interpersonal processes. Freud (1917/1957) traced how the process of identifying with others is critical for establishing an inner world in which one relates to oneself as well as to others—and elsewhere, incidentally, suggested that identification is the basis for empathy. Each had insight into a feature of human psychology that is in danger of being lost to our academic (but not quite to our clinical) discipline—that goings-on between people become goings-on within the individual mind.

I have been making the case (elaborated in Hobson, 2002/2004) that by virtue of their limited capacity for identifying with others in feeling, children with autism are largely deprived of those characteristics of mind that depend on intersubjective experience. What we discover is that the list of such propensities and abilities is startlingly long and extends to vital aspects of cognitive as well as social development. The central theme of this chapter has been how from early on in life, our engagement with other people is not only constitutive of human forms of sharing, including those expressed through joint attention with others, but also the source of vital components of reflective self-awareness. One such component is the ability to know what it means to adopt multiple perspectives, and it is this that underpins flexible, creative symbolic thinking. Another is the propensity to define one's individuality in relation to others; another is to regulate one's own feelings and actions as if from a semiexternal perspective. For the human styles of mind, self, and society to develop, we need specifically human forms of personal relatedness with others. Both children with autism, who face serious obstacles to becoming fully engaged in our cultural as well as social community, and typically developing toddlers, for whom developments in social relations and changes in self-awareness and thinking are often closely intertwined, have a great deal to teach us about all this.

ACKNOWLEDGMENTS

This chapter was completed while I was a Fellow at the Center for Advanced Study in the Behavioral Sciences, Stanford, California. I am very grateful to have had the chance to spend thinking time with colleagues in the United States.

REFERENCES

Baranek, G. T. (1999). Autism during infancy: A retrospective video analysis of sensory-motor and social behaviors at 9–12 months of age. *Journal of Autism and Developmental Disorders, 29*, 213–224.

Baron-Cohen, S., Tager-Flusberg, H., & Cohen, D. J. (2000). *Understanding other minds: Perspectives from developmental cognitive neuroscience* (2nd ed.). Oxford, UK: Oxford University Press.

Barresi, J., & Moore, C. (1996). Intentional relations and social understanding. *Behavioral and Brain Sciences, 19*, 107–154.

Bauminger, N. (2004). The expression and understanding of jealousy in children with autism. *Development and Psychopathology, 16*, 157–177.

Bauminger, N., & Kasari, C. (2000). Loneliness and friendship in high-functioning children with autism. *Child Development, 71*, 447–456.

Bosch, G. (1970). *Infantile autism* (D. Jordan & I. Jordan, Trans.). New York: Springer-Verlag.

Bråten, S. (1998). Infant learning by altercentric participation: the reverse of egocentric observation in autism. In S. Bråten (Ed.), *Intersubjective communication and emotion in ontogeny: A sourcebook* (pp. 105–126). Cambridge, UK: Cambridge University Press.

Bretherton, I., McNew, S., & Beeghly-Smith, M. (1981). Early person knowledge as expressed in gestural and verbal communication: When do infants acquire a "theory of mind"? In M. E. Lamb & L.R. Sherrod (Eds.), *Infant social cognition: Empirical and theoretical considerations* (pp. 333–373). Hillsdale, NJ: Erlbaum.

Brownell, C. A., & Carriger, M. S. (1990). Changes in cooperation and self–other differentiation during the second year. *Child Development, 61*, 1164–1174.

Buhler, C. (1937). *From birth to maturity.* London: Kegan Paul.

Capps, L., Yirmiya, N., & Sigman, M. (1992). Understanding of simple and complex emotions in non-retarded children with autism. *Journal of Child Psychology and Psychiatry, 33*, 1169–1182.

Carpenter, M., Nagell, K., & Tomasello, M. (1998). Social cognition, joint attention, and communicative competence from 9 to 15 months of age. *Monographs of the Society for Research in Child Development, 63*(4, Serial No. 255).

Carpenter, M., Pennington, B. F., & Rogers, S. J. (2002). Interrelations among social-cognitive skills in young children with autism. *Journal of Autism and Developmental Disorders, 32*, 91–106.

Charman, T., Swettenham, J., Baron-Cohen, S., Cox, A., Baird, G., & Drew, A. (1997). Infants with autism: An investigation of empathy, pretend play, joint attention, and imitation. *Developmental Psychology, 33*, 781–789.

Chidambi, G. (2003). *Autism and self-conscious emotions.* Unpublished doctoral thesis, University College, London.

Cole, P. M., Barrett, K. C., & Zahn-Waxler, C. (1992). Emotion displays in two-year-olds during mishaps. *Child Development, 63*, 314–324.

Curcio, F. (1978.) Sensorimotor functioning and communication in mute autistic children. *Journal of Autism and Childhood Schizophrenia, 8*, 281–292.

Dahlgren, S. O., & Gillberg, C. (1989). Symptoms in the first two years of life: A preliminary population study of infantile autism. *European Archives of Psychiatry and Neurological Sciences, 238*, 169–174.

Dawson, G., & Adams, A. (1984). Imitation and social responsiveness in autistic children. *Journal of Abnormal Child Psychology, 12*, 209–226.

Dawson, G., & McKissick, F. C. (1984). Self-recognition in autistic children. *Journal of Autism and Developmental Disorders, 14*, 383–394.

DeMyer, M. K., Alpern, G. D., Barton, S., DeMyer, W. E., Churchill, D. W., Hingtgen, J. N., et al. (1972.) Imitation in autistic, early schizophrenic, and nonpsychotic subnormal children. *Journal of Autism and Childhood Schizophrenia, 2*, 264–287.

Dunn, J., Bretherton, I., & Munn, P. (1987). Conversations about feeling states between mothers and their young children. *Developmental Psychology, 23*, 132–139.

Fay, W. H. (1979). Personal pronouns and the autistic child. *Journal of Autism and Developmental Disorders, 9*, 247–260.

Forman, D. R., Aksan, N., & Kochanska, G. (2004). Toddlers' responsive imitation predicts preschool-age conscience. *Psychological Science, 15*, 699–704.

Freud, S. (1957). Mourning and melancholia. In J. Strachey (Ed. & Trans.), *Standard edition of the complete psychological works of Sigmund Freud* (Vol. 14, pp. 243–258). London: Hogarth Press. (Original work published 1917)

Grice, H. P. (1957). Meaning. *Philosophical Review, 66*, 377–388.

Hamlyn, D. W. (1974). Person-perception and our understanding of others. In T. Mischel (Ed.), *Understanding other persons* (pp. 1–36). Oxford, UK: Blackwell.

Hammes J. G. W., & Langdell, T. (1981). Precursors of symbol formation and childhood autism. *Journal of Autism and Developmental Disorders, 11*, 331–346.

Happé, F. (2000). Parts and wholes, meaning and minds: Central coherence and its relation to theory of mind. In S. Baron-Cohen, H. Tager-Flusberg, & D. J. Cohen (Eds.), *Understanding other minds: Perspectives from developmental cognitive neuroscience* (pp. 203–221). Oxford, UK: Oxford University Press.

Hay, D. F. (1979). Cooperative interactions and sharing between very young children and their parents. *Developmental Psychology, 15*, 647–653.

Hobson, J. A., & Hobson, R. P. (2007). Identification: The missing link between joint attention and imitation? *Development and Psychopathology, 19*, 411–431.

Hobson, R. P. (1989). On sharing experiences. *Development and Psychopathology, 1*, 197–203.

Hobson, R. P. (1990a). On acquiring knowledge about people and the capacity to pretend: Response to Leslie. *Psychological Review, 97*, 114–121.

Hobson, R. P. (1990b). On the origins of self and the case of autism. *Development and Psychopathology, 2*, 163–181.

Hobson, R. P. (1993). *Autism and the development of mind.* Hove, Sussex, UK: Erlbaum.

Hobson, R. P. (2002/2004). *The cradle of thought.* New York: Oxford University Press.

Hobson, R. P., Chidambi, G., Lee, A., & Meyer, J. (2006). Foundations for self-awareness: An exploration through autism. *Monographs of the Society for Research in Child Development, 71* (Serial No. 284), 1–165.

Hobson, R. P., & Lee, A. (1998). Hello and goodbye: A study of social engagement in autism. *Journal of Autism and Developmental Disorders, 28*, 117–126.

Hobson, R. P., & Lee, A. (1999). Imitation and identification in autism. *Journal of Child Psychology and Psychiatry, 40*, 649–659.

Hobson, R. P., Lee, A., & Meyer, J. (2003, April). *Identification in autism.* Paper presented at the biennial meeting of the Society for Research in Child Development, Tampa, FL.

Hobson, R. P., Meyer, J., & Lee, A. (2006, June). *Interpersonal dimensions of pretending and playing: A fresh perspective from autism.* Paper presented at the International Conference for Infant Studies, Kyoto, Japan.

Hobson, R. P., Patrick, M. P. H., Crandell, L. E., Garcia-Perez, R. M., & Lee, A. (2004). Maternal sensitivity and infant triadic communication. *Journal of Child Psychology and Psychiatry, 45*, 470–480.

Hoffman, M. L. (1984). Interaction of affect and cognition in empathy. In C. E. Izard, J. Kagan, & R. B. Zajonc (Eds.), *Emotions, cognition and behaviour* (pp. 103–131). Cambridge, UK: Cambridge University Press.

Jarrold, C., Boucher, J., & Smith, P. (1993). Symbolic play in autism: A review. *Journal of Autism and Developmental Disorders, 23*, 281–307.

Kagan, J. (1982). The emergence of self. *Journal of Child Psychology and Psychiatry, 23*, 363–381.

Kaler, S. R., & Kopp, C. B. (1990). Compliance and comprehension in very young toddlers. *Child Development, 61*, 1997–2003.

Kanner, L. (1943). Autistic disturbances of affective contact. *Nervous Child, 2*, 217–250.

Kasari, C., Chamberlain, B., & Bauminger, N. (2001). Social emotions and social relationships: Can children with autism compensate? In J. A. Burack, T. Charman, N. Yirmiya, & P. R. Zelazo (Eds.), *The development of autism* (pp. 309–323). Mahwah, NJ: Erlbaum.

Kasari, C., Sigman, M., Bauminger, P., & Stipek, D. J. (1993). Pride and mastery in children with autism. *Journal of Child Psychology and Psychiatry, 34*, 352–362.

Kasari, C., Sigman, M., Mundy, P., & Yirmiya, N. (1990). Affective sharing in the context of joint attention interactions of normal, autistic and mentally retarded children. *Journal of Autism and Developmental Disorders, 20*, 87–100.

Kelley, S. A., Brownell, C. A., & Campbell, S. B. (2000). Mastery motivation and self-evaluative affect in toddlers: Longitudinal relations with maternal behavior. *Child Development, 71,* 1061–1071.

Kochanska, G., Coy, K. C., & Murray, K. T. (2001). The development of self-regulation in the first four years of life. *Child Development, 72,* 1091–1111.

Lee, A., & Hobson, R. P. (1998). On developing self-concepts: A controlled study of children and adolescents with autism. *Journal of Child Psychology and Psychiatry, 39*, 1131–1141.

Lee, A., Hobson, R. P., & Chiat, S. (1994). I, you, me and autism: An experimental study. *Journal of Autism and Developmental Disorders, 24*, 155–176.

Leslie, A. M. (1987). Pretense and representation: The origins of "theory of mind." *Psychological Review, 94*, 412–426.

Lewis, M., & Brooks-Gunn, J. (1979). *Social cognition and the acquisition of self*. New York: Plenum Press.

Lewis, M., & Ramsay, D. (2004). Development of self-recognition, personal pronoun use, and pretend play during the 2nd year. *Child Development, 75,* 1821–1831.

Lewis, V., & Boucher, J. (1988). Spontaneous, instructed and elicited play in relatively able autistic children. *British Journal of Developmental Psychology, 6*, 325–339.

Lord, C., Storoschuk, S., Rutter, M., & Pickles, A. (1993). Using the ADI-R to diagnose autism in preschool children. *Infant Mental Health Journal, 14*, 234–252.

Loveland, K. A., & Landry, S. H. (1986). Joint attention and language in autism and developmental language delay. *Journal of Autism and Developmental Disorders, 16*, 335–349.

Mead, G. H. (1934). *Mind, self and society.* Chicago: University of Chicago Press.

Meltzoff, A. N. (2002). Elements of a developmental theory of imitation. In A. N. Meltzoff & W. Prinz (Eds.), *The imitative mind: Development, evolution, and brain bases* (pp. 19–41). Cambridge, UK: Cambridge University Press.

Meyer, J. A., & Hobson, R. P. (2003, April). *"The way you do the things you do" (when copying) may tell of autism.* Paper presented at the second International Symposium on Imitation in Animals and Artifacts, University of Wales, Aberystwyth.

Meyer, J. A., & Hobson, R. P. (2004). Orientation in relation to self and other: The case of autism. *Interaction Studies, 5*, 221–244.

Mundy, P., & Sigman, M. (1989). The theoretical implications of joint-attention deficits in autism. *Development and Psychopathology, 1*, 173–183

Neuman, C. J., & Hill, S. D. (1978). Self-recognition and stimulus preference in autistic children. *Developmental Psychobiology, 11*, 571–578.

Osterling, J., & Dawson, G. (1994). Early recognition of children with autism: A study of first birthday home videotapes. *Journal of Autism and Developmental Disorders, 24*, 247–257.

Reddy, V. (1991). Playing with others' expectations: Teasing and mucking about in the first year. In A. Whiten (Ed.), *Natural theories of mind* (pp. 143–158). Oxford, UK: Blackwell.

Riguet, C. B., Taylor, N. D., Benaroya, S., & Klein, L. S. (1981). Symbolic play in autistic, Down's, and normal children of equivalent mental age. *Journal of Autism and Developmental Disorders, 11*, 439–448.

Rogers, S. J., Hepburn, S. L., Stackhouse, T., & Wehner, E. (2003). Imitation performance in toddlers with autism and those with other developmental disorders. *Journal of Child Psychology and Psychiatry, 44,* 763–781.

Searle, J. R. (1969). *Speech acts*. Cambridge, UK: Cambridge University Press.

Sigman, M. D., Kasari, C., Kwon, J.-H., & Yirmiya, N. (1992). Responses to the negative emotions of others by autistic, mentally retarded, and normal children. *Child Development, 63*, 796–807.

Sigman, M., Mundy, P., Sherman, T., & Ungerer, J. A. (1986). Social interactions of autistic, mentally retarded and normal children and their caregivers. *Journal of Child Psychology and Psychiatry, 27*, 647–656.

Sigman, M., & Ungerer, J. A. (1984). Cognitive and language skills in autistic, mentally retarded, and normal children. *Developmental Psychology, 20*, 293–302.

Spiker, D., & Ricks, M. (1984). Visual self-recognition in autistic children: Developmental relationships. *Child Development, 55*, 214–225.

Stone, W. L., & Lemanek, K. L. (1990). Parental report of social behaviors in autistic preschoolers. *Journal of Autism and Developmental Disorders, 20*, 513–522.

Tomasello, M. (1999). *The cultural origins of human cognition*. Cambridge, MA: Harvard University Press.

Tomasello, M., & Barton, M. (1994). Learning words in nonostensive contexts. *Developmental Psychology, 30*, 639–650.

Trevarthen, C., & Hubley, P. (1978). Secondary intersubjectivity: Confidence, confiding and acts of meaning in the first year. In A. Lock (Ed.), *Action, gesture and symbol: The emergence of language* (pp. 183–229). London: Academic Press.

Tronick, E., Als, H., Adamson, L., Wise, S., & Brazelton, T. B. (1978). The infant's response to entrapment between contradictory messages in face-to-face interaction. *Journal of the American Academy of Child and Adolescent Psychiatry, 17*, 1–13.

Ungerer, J. A., & Sigman, M. (1981). Symbolic play and language comprehension in autistic children. *Journal of the American Academy of Child Psychiatry, 20*, 318–337.

Vygotsky, L. S. (1962). *Thought and language* (E. Hanfmann & G. Vakar, Trans.). Cambridge, MA: MIT Press.

Wetherby, A. M., & Prutting, C. A. (1984). Profiles of communicative and cognitive-social abilities in autistic children. *Journal of Speech and Hearing Research, 27*, 364–377.

Williams, J. H. G., Whiten, A., & Singh, T. (2004). A systematic review of action imitation in autistic spectrum disorder. *Journal of Autism and Developmental Disorders, 34*, 285–299.

Wimpory, D. C., Hobson, R. P., Williams, J. M., & Nash, S. (2000). Are infants with autism socially engaged?: A study of recent retrospective parental reports. *Journal of Autism and Developmental Disorders, 30*, 525–536.

Wing, L., Gould, J., Yeates, S. R., & Brierly, L. M. (1977). Symbolic play in severely mentally retarded and in autistic children. *Journal of Child Psychology and Psychiatry, 18*, 167–178.

18

A Systemic Approach to Assessment of Normative and Atypical Socioemotional Function in Toddlers

Hiram E. Fitzgerald
Jessica Barnes
Jason Almerigi

Scientific study of toddler development and the toddler in context must be driven by theoretical models that embrace life-course continuities and discontinuities, guided by measurement strategies sensitive to development in context and grounded in systems theory. Systemic approaches to assessment provide an avenue for understanding continuities and discontinuities in the development of emotions and emotional behavior, and for addressing significant deviations from normative developmental pathways. For example, significant progress has been made toward understanding the organization and development of emotion-related regulation during infancy and toddlerhood. Emotion-related regulation has been defined "as the process of initiating, avoiding, inhibiting, maintaining, or modulating the occurrence, form, intensity, or duration of internal feeling states, emotion-related physiological, attentional processes, motivational states, and/or the behavioral concomitants of emotion in the service of accomplishing affect-related biological or social adaptation or achieving individual goals" (Eisenberg, 2006, p. 134; see also Eisenberg & Spinrad, 2004). Self-regulation refers to the deliberate and effortful control of impulse, attention, behavior, and affect, and to the emergent ability to regulate one's behavior, to suppress behaviors associated with negative emotions, to delay gratification, and to work toward future goals.

According to Eisenberg and colleagues (2000), behavioral regulation involves the voluntary activation or inhibition of behavior associated with internal states (throwing or not throwing a block when frustrated), whereas emotional regulation consists of the modulation of internal processes through the monitoring and regulation of internal feeling states and physiological reactions to those feeling states (an implicit component of the attachment relationship). Of these two components of self-regulation, behavior regulation is easier to assess because it can be directly observed or reported. Assessing the physiological components of emotion regulation typically requires specialized techniques that are best used in basic research laboratories or medical settings (Fox & Fitzgerald, 1990; Karmel & Gardner, 2006).

Developmental scientists have also achieved a deeper understanding of the complex interplay among individual, family, and contextual factors that shape life-course outcomes, including those influencing emotion-related regulation. To fully understand the development of emotion-related regulation requires study of both direct and indirect influences on the individual, particularly within the context of interpersonal relationships. During the toddler years there is substantial within- and between-individual variation in the differentiation of emotion-related regulation. Some presenting state characteristics of the toddler may endure; others will change. Similarly, some qualities of self–other relationships will endure and others will change. Determining which factors affect toddler development immediately and over the life course requires continued analysis of the transactions between children and their multiple environments. Such analyses are driven by assessment. In this chapter we focus on assessment of socioemotional development during the toddler years, the transitional years from infancy to preschool that capture moving from crawling to walking, babbling to talking, motor exuberance to behavioral control, impulse gratification to the ability to delay.

A SYSTEMS APPROACH TO ASSESSMENT

This chapter approaches early assessment from a systemic framework (Figure 18.1; Fitzgerald, Zucker, & Yang, 1995). We stress four levels of analysis relevant to study of the structure and function of any system, including the biopsychosocial matrix that influences the organization of self-regulation. The first level in this analysis is to identify and describe the individual components of the system, from both distal and proximal perspectives. Presenting state characteristics include the child's characteristics (temperament, soothability, normative functioning), sibling characteristics, parental perceptions of the child, and parental characteristics. Second, the structural and functional connections of subunits must be identified and described (e.g., assessing sibling relationships, parent–child interactions, marital conflict, and family resources).

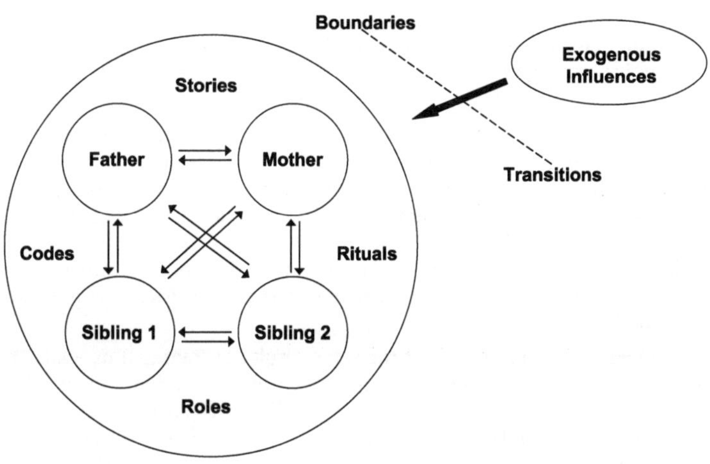

FIGURE 18.1. Systems approach to assessment of individual and family functioning. Adapted from Fitzgerald, Zucker, and Yang (1995) and Loukas, Twitchell, Piejak, Fitzgerald, and Zucker (1998).

Third, one must identify and describe the systemic properties of the system that emerge from the dynamic interactions among members of the family system (e.g., assessing the impact of family traditions, values, beliefs, resources, and cohesiveness on individual behavior). Finally, one must identify adjunctive systems that may have direct or indirect effects on family functioning (e.g., assessing the impact of supplemental child care on individual behavior and interpersonal relationships, neighborhood quality, and parental work environment). Such systemic analysis requires use of a variety of measurement tools, sensitivity to their psychometric properties, including factor structures and instrument validity and reliability (Table 18.1), and the impact of the measurement context on child functioning.

THE IMPORTANCE OF ASSESSMENT EARLY IN DEVELOPMENT

The prevalence of children with learning disabilities, speech and language handicaps, mental retardation, emotional disturbances, poor self-regulatory skills, aggressive behavior, substance abuse disorders, and poor school achievement is unacceptably high worldwide. For example, approximately 17% of all children in the United States have one or more developmental disability and 20% of all school-age children have attention problems. There is increasing evidence that problem behaviors emerging early in development structure setting events that affect the quality of interactions young children have with their caregivers and their experienced environments and guide children onto

TABLE 18.1. Psychometric Issues to Be Considered When Selecting Measurement Tools for Cross-Sectional and Longitudinal Research Methodologies

Reliability

- *Internal consistency.* Do the items in an instrument measure the same construct (aggression, temperament, activity level, persistence, impulsivity, etc). It is often reported as Cronbach's alpha statistic. Acceptable reliability coefficients for screening tools are. 80 or greater, that for diagnosis and intervention are .90 or greater (Wasserman & Bracken, 2003). Using shortened forms of measurement tools requires recalibration to determine whether the short form still reliably measures the construct. For instruments with multiple subscales, strong internal consistency is most important at the subscale level.
- *Test–retest.* Does the instrument yield the same results on repeated assessment occasions? Test–retest assesses stability of results over time. It is critical for longitudinal research designs in order to assess change or stability in a particular construct over time. Many assessment tools are age-period-specific, such that items assessing a construct at one age period may not be appropriate for another age period. For example, items appropriate for assessing antisocial behavior in a toddler may be completely different from items assessing antisocial behavior in a school-age child. Choosing an instrument developed to assess a particular construct over a long time span is the preferred solution.
- *Interrater.* Do different individuals rating the same behavior agree in the ratings they assign to that behavior? High interrater reliability is essential for observational data (direct observation, videotaped interactions). Cohen's kappa is a frequently used statistic for interrater reliability. Training procedures used to secure high interrater reliability must be described in detail to assure replication of results. In large-scale multisite national studies, centralized training ensures high interrater reliability across sites. Fidelity checks are used to ensure that high interrater reliability is maintained in longitudinal studies.

Validity

- *Content.* Do the items in an instrument adequately assess all aspects of the construct? Good content validity begins with having a solid understanding of published literature in the specific content domain (e.g., social competence, emotion regulation, and behavioral undercontrol). The issue is somewhat complicated in that some items may reflect aspects of different constructs) leading to high correlations among different assessment tools.
- *Criterion.* Do results of one instrument correlate with results of another instrument presumed to measure the same construct? Concurrent and predictive validity are types of criterion validity.
- *Concurrent.* Does one measure of a behavior correlate highly with another measure of the same behavior when both are assessed at the same time? For example, does one measure of child aggression correlate highly with another measure of child aggression?
- *Predictive.* Does the measure administered at one time period predict a measure of child performance at another time period? For example, does a measure of temperament at age 2 predict the child's temperament at age 10? Do indicators of dysregulation (sleep disturbance) at age 3 predict early-onset psychopathology at age 10?

developmental pathways that can lead to undesirable consequences (Gottman, Katz, & Hooven, 1996).

Longitudinal studies provide convincing evidence that emotional difficulties and behavior problems originating during the first 3 years of life are highly likely to be sustained and expressed later in development. Data from the Dunedin Multidisciplinary Health and Development Study indicate that children with difficult temperamental characteristics at age 3 were more likely to have externalizing behavior problems between ages 9 and 15 and to be convicted for violent offenses at age 18 (Moffitt, Caspi, Rutter, & Silva, 2001). Eisenberg and Spinrad (2004) report that children with poor regulation, high impulsivity, or negative emotions are more likely to express externalizing behaviors and poor social skills during childhood. Children experiencing problems with attention and impulse control, in particular the clinical syndrome of attention-deficit/hyperactivity disorder, are at elevated risk of academic and achievement difficulties, a range of health problems (including accidental injury and death), antisocial behavior, substance use and abuse, and interpersonal problems (Nigg, 2006). Much the same can be said about etiological studies of aggression (Shaw, 2006) (toddlers have the highest rates of aggressive behavior of any developmental period), or risk for alcoholism (Fitzgerald & Zucker, 2006). Because such problems are heterogeneous, assessing and identifying sources of variation that influence emergent characteristics is essential if one is to design effective interventions or to develop prevention programs that can alter life-course pathways.

Evidence suggests that persistent exposure to risky rearing environments increases the probability that children will be guided onto developmental pathways that promote and sustain problem behaviors over the life course (Table 18.2—Fitzgerald, & Zucker, 2006; Zucker et al., 2000). The challenge is to discover which factors regulate the organization of developmental pathways. Evidence clearly supports the critical influence of individual, parent–child relationship, family, and contextual characteristics for shaping life-course change or promoting stability. The systemic approach is essential to understand normative aspects of emergent systems that guide attempts to discern the meaning of variations from normative life-course pathways.

When studying the etiology of disorganized behavior, it is important to determine the extent to which behaviors under investigation are context specific or can be generalized across settings. For example, if behavior problems are only evident in the home, it suggests that family dynamics should be the focus of prevention or intervention efforts. However, if the problems generalize across contexts, then intervention efforts must be more complex and far-reaching. For very young children, supplemental child-care settings are the contexts that provide opportunities to address issues of context specificity. So, assessment must provide for observation of children in multiple settings, the most common of which involves center-based care, family day care, or preschool (Fitzgerald, Mann, Cabrera, & Wong, 2003).

TABLE 18.2. Developmental Psychopathology: Continuity and Discontinuity Pathways

The continuity pathway with origins in infancy and early childhood

Preschool
Externalizing behavior problems, social withdrawal, poor school readiness

Childhood
Behavior problems, oppositional behavior, impulsivity, social withdrawal, poor school performance

Late middle childhood
Family disorganization (divorce/separation, loss of job, health or social problems of other family member); poorer parent monitoring

Adolescence
Earlier onset of alcohol and other drug involvement, heavier alcohol and other drug problems, delinquency, depression

Adulthood
Antisocial personality disorder, mood disorder, substance abuse disorder

Two discontinuity pathways suggesting differentiation occurring during the transition from elementary to middle school

Discontinuity pathway I	Discontinuity pathway II
Preschool	
School readiness, behavior within normal limits, adaptive temperament	School readiness, behavior within normal limits, adaptive temperament
Childhood	
Good school adaptation and performance; good friendship network	Good school adaptation and performance; good friendship network
Late middle childhood	
Family disorganization (divorce/separation, loss of job, health or social problems of other family member); poorer parent monitoring; shift in more deviant peer network; increasing emergence of externalizing behavior, developing pattern of internalizing problems	Family disorganization (divorce/separation, loss of job, health or social problems of other family member); shift in peer network; increasing emergence of externalizing behavior
Adolescence	
Alcohol and other drug involvement, minor delinquency; poor or adverse outsider response or parent response; undependability of both parents, less available prosocial network	Alcohol and other drug involvement; poor or adverse parent or outsider response and/or clinical course

Note. Adapted from Fitzgerald and Zucker (2006); Fitzgerald, Zucker, Puttler, Caplan, and Mun (2000); and Zucker, Chermack, and Curran (2000).

Another aspect of assessment concerns the theoretical models, psychometric properties, and standardization samples used to develop measurement tools. Roggman, Fitzgerald, Bradley, and Raikes (2002) address this issue within the context of assessing paternal behavior. They note that measurement tools used to assess paternal behavior are often the same as or adapted versions of tools developed to study maternal behavior. Whereas there are advantages to adapting established instruments for use with fathers, the potential disadvantages relate to whether the meaning of items is the same for fathers and mothers, or whether observational rating scale behavioral definitions are ecologically the same for fathers and mothers. For example, in observational studies of the impact of intrusiveness, observers code behaviors according to a common definition of intrusiveness based on maternal behavior. But, from the toddler's perspective paternal intrusiveness may be more likely to be perceived as an invitation to play than as an act of intrusion in ongoing behavior (Roggman et al., 2002). Many of these same concerns apply to use of instruments in different cultural contexts (Tomlinson, Swartz, & Landman, 2006).

THE CONTEXT OF ASSESSMENT DURING THE TODDLER YEARS

The systemic approach to assessing emotional development during the toddler years that we present in this chapter is built around a set of broadly confirmed findings about the course of human development. First, individual differences are an integral aspect of early development. Although there are many well-documented stages, levels, and transition points during the early postnatal years, there is rich diversity in how individual children negotiate their distinct pathways. Second, every individual develops within a context, and context matters. It makes a difference whether one is born into a family with extensive economic and human resources, versus one that is isolated and lacking necessities. For example, early development focuses on relationships. Attachment relationships structure early social–emotional development through positive parent–infant interactions. Healthy attachments synergistically enhance protective factors while simultaneously dampening the impact of risk factors that might otherwise push the child onto nonoptimal developmental pathways. The focus of most of this work has been on the mother–infant relationship and on the impact of out-of-home childcare settings on child development (Fitzgerald et al., 2003). As noted previously, innovations in family interaction research offer new methodologies to examine how fathers fit into the evolution and quality of the family alliance, particularly as it is relates to development of self-regulation (Fitzgerald, McKelvey, Schiffman, & Montanez, 2006).

GENERAL GUIDELINES FOR ASSESSING VERY YOUNG CHILDREN

There are several reasons why assessment of very young children requires special consideration and care. Some of the issues requiring attention include reactions to strangers and strange places (for laboratory settings), language barriers, rapid transitions from one developmental stage to the next, and contextual factors (including who is the informant for nonobserved behavior). To address these issues, researchers must develop instruments and methodologies that are sensitive to the young child's developmental stage and context. A work group assembled by Zero to Three: National Center for Infants, Toddler, and Families developed a set of guidelines to address the methodological issues facing researchers conducting infant and toddler assessment (Zero to Three, 2005). These principles include:

1. Using an integrated developmental model to determine the child's level of functioning within various contexts.
2. Using multiple sources of information and varied methods of assessment.
3. Using a determined sequence for assessment that integrates information from multiple sources and varied methods.
4. Placing primary importance on the relationship between the child and the primary caregiver.
5. Having a thorough understanding of developmental sequences and timetables.
6. Attending to the child's functional capacities and patterns of organizing experiences.
7. Focusing on the child's competencies and strengths.

The intent of the guidelines is to help ensure that the importance of context and developmental stages receive proper attention (Advisory Committee on Services for Families with Infants and Toddlers, 1996) in any assessment of young children's adaptive behavior and functioning.

REASONS FOR ASSESSMENT

Assessment refers to the processes used to make evaluative decisions relative to interventions or prevention programs targeting individuals, families, or programs (Meisels & Fenichel, 1996). There are at least four key reasons for assessing young children: (1) to establish normative parameters of development, including expected variation within (longitudinal) and between (cross-sectional) individuals; (2) to screen children to determine whether they are at risk for significant deviations from normative pathways of development; (3) to diagnosis children in order to identify the specific parameters of a problem, to link it with "causal" context events, and a set of possible interventions; (4) to determine whether a particular intervention or prevention program is effective; and (5) to determine whether children have the necessary skills to successfully negotiate life-course challenges.

CLINICAL ASSESSMENT: SCREENING AND DIAGNOSIS

Screening is used to identify children who may be at risk for developmental delay whether due to established risks (acquired through genetic, congenital, or perinatal influences), biological risks (acquired congenitally or during the perinatal period), or environmental risks (acquired due to postnatal exposure to adverse environmental factors). Screening involves a brief evaluation of the child in order to identify the presence of indicators of functional delay. Often, it is only those children with existing developmental delays or who are at high risk for such delays who are screened to determine the extent of deviation from normative development. However, it is important to screen for auditory and visual problems on a wider scale, given the primacy of sensory functioning in the perception of emotional and relational cues.

Increasing concerns that fewer children are entering kindergarten with requisite skills for school success have led to increased screening and diagnostic assessment for their readiness to learn. Foundational skills are often assessed during the toddler years to determine if special attention is required to assist children in acquiring these skills. The most common foundational skills assessed in early childhood are literacy, numeracy, and socioemotional skill. Literacy and numeracy skills provide an important foundation for later learning. Those children who have not yet learned the basic literacy and numeracy skills at kindergarten entry will have difficulty learning with the rest of the class, straining peer and adult relationships in the classroom. Socioemotional skills are also a key aspect of school readiness. In particular, self-control is a foundational skill that allows young children to regulate behavior with peers and adults to increase positive interactions and allows children to focus in the classroom (Leppanen & Hietanen, 2001). Currently, researchers have noted increases in behavioral undercontrol that are alarming.

Because screening provides a brief glimpse of child functioning, it probably overlooks some children who require more intense testing and, conversely, identifies some children as at risk when they actually are not. These are known as false-negative and false-positive screening results. To help reduce such errors, screening tests should meet criteria for sensitivity and specificity. Sensitivity indicates that the test is able to successfully identify at-risk infants, with a minimum of 80% of the children with problems receiving failing scores. Specificity indicates that the test accurately identifies children who are not at risk, with a minimum of 90% of the children without problems passing the test. Considering these issues, it is important to view screening as a first step in a multistep process that includes further procedures at diagnosis for those individuals identified at risk through the screening and an understanding that the screening process may have missed a portion of the sampled population who are at risk.

If screening suggests or if the presenting state characteristics are sufficiently suggestive of problem areas, a formal diagnostic assessment may be undertaken. The purpose of diagnosis is to confirm the presence and extent of a problem and then to classify the toddler into a category that enables targeted intervention. The French psychiatrist Rene Spitz (1965) was the first individual to formally propose a diagnostic classification scheme for infants. Today, the prevailing diagnostic classification system for infant mental health is that developed by Zero to Three (2005). This system posits five axes (Clinical Disorders, Relationship Classification, Medical and Developmental Disorders and Conditions, Psychosocial Stressors, and Emotional and Social Functioning). Diagnostic classifications provide mental health specialists with common definitions of disorders, even when classifications may be too broad. For example, classifying a toddler as autistic fails to account for the wide variation among autistic children. Specialists now refer to autistic spectrum disorders so that interventionists are alerted to a set of characteristics while simultaneously being notified that each child will require individualized assessment to determine the full extent of autistic behaviors (Akshoomoff & Stahmer, 2006).

ASSESSMENT IN THE CONTEXT OF PREVENTIVE-INTERVENTION PROGRAMS

From one perspective, all reasons for assessing behavior during the early years of life is to determine which children are at risk for poor developmental outcomes, and which interventions successfully alter risk status over time. Nearly all developmentalists adhere to the principle that risk cumulates over time and that the greater number of risk factors one is exposed to, the greater the likelihood of poor developmental outcomes. This sometimes is referred to as an additive or strong continuity model of development (Fitzgerald, Davies, & Zucker, 2002). From another perspective, risk is viewed from a more probabilistic or discontinuity model of development (Zucker, Fitzgerald, & Moses, 1995). This framework places greater significance on the interplay between the individual's genetic history, level of environmental risk, and length of exposure to familial and other structures that serve to maintain poor developmental pathways or that alter such pathways. Regardless of whether one operates from an additive or a probabilistic model of cumulative risk, the key to resolving negative outcomes lies in the strategies employed to prevent the formation of negative pathways or to intervene with sufficient power that the toddler will be guided onto more positive and affirming pathways. For example, from a probabilistic risk perspective, families experiencing heightened risk factors are prime candidates for prevention programs (see Figure 18.2). The level of intervention or prevention will be guided by the severity of risk. Vulnerable children/families require the most intense intervention/prevention

		Environment	
		High risk	Low risk
Genotype	High risk	Vulnerable	Resilient
	Low risk	Troubled	Nonchallenged

FIGURE 18.2. Probabilistic model of risk for poor developmental outcomes. Adapted from Fitzgerald and McKelvey (in press) and Zucker, Wong, Puttler, and Fitzgerald (2003).

efforts, and troubled children/families require moderate intervention/prevention efforts. Nonchallenged children/families most likely benefit from natural support networks and interactions with significant others over the life course (Fitzgerald & McKelvey, in press; Zucker, Wong, Puttler, & Fitzgerald, 2003). Regardless of the approach used to intervene with development or to prevent negative pathways, the goal is to shift toddlers and their families toward resilient and nonchallenged life-course pathways.

Planning an intervention program for an individual child requires a careful assessment of that child's strengths and weaknesses as well as those of the child's caregivers and the caregiving environment. For clinical interventions, this is best done by a multidisciplinary team, each assessing specialized domains of child functioning and then coordinating their assessments into an individualized family intervention plan. For research studies, the goal is to collect sufficient information to determine which factors contribute to program success and which do not. Data sampling must include information from the child, the child's caregivers, and the ecological context within which caregiving takes place. Sometimes preventive-intervention studies involve locally specific samples, but such studies now more frequently involve thousands of families participating in rigorous randomized evaluation designs (Raikes & Emde, 2006).

The implementation of a number of large-scale national studies during the past decade has focused attention on a particular issue concerning child assessment. Such studies include the national evaluation of Early Head Start (Raikes & Emde, 2006). In each of these, investigators must make decisions about the breath and depth of assessment and the time demands on participants for data collection. These decisions often lead to use of abbreviated forms or subscales of assessment instruments, practices that challenge the original normatively established reliability and validity of the instruments (Fitzgerald, in press).

SOURCES OF INFORMATION ABOUT CHILD FUNCTIONING

From a systemic perspective, it is essential to observe the child's behavior in a rich variety of contexts, including those that involve parent–child interactions.

Such observations and analyses can be performed in the present by a trained clinician or researcher, or they can be performed later through the use of videotape. It is also important to gain information from as many other sources as possible, including reports from others who interact with the child. Study of the emergence of behavior regulation generally relies on data gathering from three sources: the child (directly assessing child behavior), parents (parent and other caregiver reports of child competencies), and observers (others rating the behavior of children alone or in the context of social interactions). In the section that follows, we address some issues about source of information and present selected examples of assessment tools that are widely used in research with toddlers.

Child as Primary Informant

Gaining information directly from the child is essential for determining the child's developmental status, reaction to structured and unstructured situations, and behavior in varying contexts. One can select from a variety of standardized tests to determine current level of functioning (Table 18.3). Usually, the examiner includes the child in a relatively formal assessment setting, but in community-based scale studies data often are collected in a home setting, a child-care facility, or some other "natural" setting. Regardless of the situation, establishing a positive relationship with the child prior to assessment will likely result in more optimal performance for both children and their caregivers. This is especially the case when assessing parent–child interactions. When assessment occurs in natural settings, it is important to try to isolate the child (and parent) from the influence of other siblings or adults. Distractions most often negatively impact performance, reducing both the reliability and validity of the assessment. Ideally, assessments in the home involve two assessors who can work separately with the child and parent, or one can monitor the other children in the home while the parent–child dyad are involved in the assessment process. The basic premise for including assessment tools in this category is that the infant or toddler's actual behavior is the information evaluated by the assessor. For example, the toddler resists opening a gift or does not resist; inhibits behavior in a stop–go task or does not, and so on. Little is dependent on an observer interpreting a behavior or scoring some ongoing structured task on qualities such as persistence, attention getting, and the like.

Caregiver as Primary Informant

Gaining information from caregivers is a critical aspect of early assessment. One not only gains information about the child but also gains important information about the parents' perceptions of child behavior, childrearing practices, and knowledge of children's developmental and psychological status. There are three general approaches to gaining assessment information from parents: questionnaires, interviews, and direct observation.

TABLE 18.3. Assessment of Emotion-Related Regulation: Child as Primary Informant

Construct	Tool	Description
Behavioral control	Gift delay	The Gift (Present) delay evaluates the child's ability to delay gratification (Funder, Block, & Block, 1983). Subsequent to the child's intellectual assessment session, the child is thanked for his or her participation and told he or she can have a present. As the present is being shown, the examiner apologizes to the child and says there is one more task he or she must first complete. The child is shown a complex block design task and is told he or she must first complete this task before getting his or her present. Reliability (interrater) and validity (concurrent and predictive) are acceptable.
Behavioral inhibition	Delay tasks	These observational tasks (delay of gratification [M & M], speed of motor activity [rolling car], stop motor activity [stop–go], ability to lower voice during excitement [whisper]) assess behavioral regulation of 3- to 5-year-old children (Eisenberg, 2006; Kochanska, Murray, & Harlan, 2000). In the delay of gratification task the inability to wait is reflective of impulsivity. Snack delays usually involve waiting to eat crackers or "cold" cereal with the administrator controlling the delay interval. When gift delay is used with older toddlers, a gift is placed on a table close to the child who then is asked to wait and not touch the gift bag until the examiner returns to the room. The examiner leaves the room for a period of time. An observer then views the child through a viewing window and measures the time that transpires before the child touches the bag. After a fixed time, the examiner returns to the room. These tasks are best suited for use in structured laboratory situations. Reliability (interrater) and validity (concurrent) are acceptable (Kochanska & Knaack, 2003).
Observed persistence	Puzzle box task	Children are presented with a box that contains a puzzle with geometrically shaped pieces. The box is created in a way that allows the child's hand movements to be observed by the experimenter but not by the child. However, the box design permits children to look at their hand movements by lifting the cover on the front of the box. When given the box, children are told by the experimenter to complete the puzzle without looking and that if the task is completed in a certain length of time (4–5 minutes), they will receive a prize. An observed persistence proportion score is then created from the time the child persisted on the task rather than being off task or cheating (Eisenberg et al., 1996).
Emotional expressions	Puppet tasks	Children's ability to identify emotion in facial expressions, emotion expression identification, and emotion situation has been assessed via cloth puppets with prototypical facial expressions of happy, sad, angry, and afraid drawn (Denham, McKinley, Couchoud, & Holt, 1990). In this series of tasks, children are first asked to identify the emotions displayed on the puppet faces. Second, the children are asked to identify the emotion that another would feel using a vignette told by the puppeteer. The third task assesses the children's ability to identify another's feelings in a situation where the other person feels differently from the child.

(*continued on next page*)

TABLE 18.3. *(continued)*

Construct	Tool	Description
Emotion naming and recognition	Adapted Kusche Affective Interview (KAI-R)	Miller et al. (2005) adapted two measures from the KAI-R (Kusche, Greenberg, & Beilke, 1988) to assess spontaneous emotion naming skills and emotion recognition in preschool- and school-age children. In the first measure, children are asked to name all the different feelings they can think of and are prompted with "any more" until they said no. Children receive one point for each emotion named on a list of common target emotions (e.g., happy, sad, angry, and scared; 10 possible emotions total). For the measure that assesses emotion recognition, children are shown 10 pages that display four drawings of children depicting different emotions on each page. The children are asked to identify which person on the displayed page shows a specific emotion. The 10 target emotions include love, sad, scared/afraid, excited, mad/angry, surprised, frustrated, proud, worried, and happy. Children receive 0 points on this measure for an incorrect answer (e.g., "sad" for "happy"), 1 point for an answer that is the correct valence but wrong emotion (e.g., "mad" for "scared"), and 2 points for a correct answer. Scores on this measure are calculated to reflect the mean number of points a child receives for each item (ranging from 0 to 2).
Emotion recognition	Diagnostic Analysis of Nonverbal Accuracy (DANVA2)	The DANVA2 (Nowicki & Duke, 1994) is often used to determine a child's ability to identify emotions in others. The test consists of 24 photographs of Caucasian children making facial expressions of fear, sadness, anger, and happiness. Support for the overall construct validity of the DANVA2 was obtained in a study of children between the ages 3 and 10 (Nowicki, Glanville, & Demertzis, 1998). Findings consistently demonstrated with the DANVA2 include: (1) mean accuracy increases with age from age 3 to age 33; (2) DANVA2 scores are related to indices of social competence for all age groups (from age 3 to college age); (3) DANVA2 scores are not related to IQ as assessed by standardized IQ measures but are related to academic achievement.
School readiness	Lollipop Test	The Lollipop Test is an individually administered, criterion-referenced screening test of school readiness used with children 3 years of age or older. The Lollipop Test consists of four subscales: identification of colors and shapes, and copying shapes; picture description, position, and spatial recognition; identification of numbers and counting; and identification of letters and writing. Reliability (internal consistency) and validity (concurrent and predictive) are acceptable (Chew & Morris, 1989; Eno & Woehlke, 1995).
Receptive vocabulary	Peabody Picture Vocabulary Test—Revised (PPVT-R)	The PPVT-R (Dunn & Dunn, 1981) is an individually administered, norm-referenced measure of hearing vocabulary. Each form of the PPVT-R contains five training items, followed by 175 test items arranged in order of increasing difficulty. Each item has four black-and-white illustrations arranged in a multiple-choice format. The participant must choose the illustration that best depicts the meaning of the word that has been orally presented by the examiner. Reliability (internal consistency) and validity are acceptable.

(continued on next page

TABLE 18.3. *(continued)*

Construct	Tool	Description
Language	Preschool Language Scale—Fourth Edition (PLS-4)	The PLS-4 (Zimmerman, Steiner, & Pond, 2002) is an individually administered test used to identify language disorders or delays in children from birth through 6 years of age. The PLS-4 is composed of two subscales: auditory comprehension and expressive communication. The auditory comprehension scale assesses the child's ability to understand language. The expressive communication scale assesses the child's vocal development and ability to communicate with others. Different aspects of the child auditory comprehension and expressive communication are assessed at different ages.
General development	Brigance Inventory of Early Development II—social–emotional subscale	This criterion-based measure of development encompasses 200 skills across 11 domains: preambulatory motor, gross motor, fine motor, self-help, speech and language, general knowledge and comprehension, readiness, basic reading skills, manuscript writing, basic math, and social and emotional development, for children from birth to 7 years. Direct child and parent assessment and parent observations administered by an examiner trained in child development and familiar with the measure. Reliability (test–retest, internal consistency) is acceptable (Glascoe, 2000).
Cognitive development (see BBRS, Table 18.5)	Bayley Scales of Infant Development—Second Edition (BSID-II)	The BSID-II is a standardized assessment of cognitive development for children ages 1 to 42 months of age. The Mental Scale provides a normalized standard score, the Mental Development Index (MDI) evaluating perception, memory, habituation, learning, vocalizations, higher level problem solving and cognitive skills thought to underlie cognitive structures. The test administrator has specific instructions for the preparation and administration of each item. The BSID-II is reported to take about 30 minutes to administer for children under 15 months and about 60 minutes for older children. Reliability (internal consistency) and validity (concurrent) are acceptable. (Bayley, 1993).
Social problem solving	Wally Social Skills and Problem Solving Game (Wally)	The Wally assesses both the qualitative and quantitative dimensions of a child's social problem solving. It uses a game-fantasy approach and 13 brightly colored pictures of hypothetical problem situations related to object acquisition and friendship skills. The themes presented in the situations are as follows: Rejection (#1), Making a mistake (#2, 6), Unjust treatment (#3), Victimization (#4, 7), Prohibition (#5), Loneliness (#8), Being cheated (#9), Disappointment (#10), Dilemma (#11), Adult disapproval (#12), Attack (#13). Reliability (internal consistency) is acceptable (Webster-Stratton, Reid, & Hammond, 2001).

Questionnaires are a cost-effective way to gather information because they can be self-administered. Questionnaires that have strong metrics for reliability and validity allow one to contrast results against normative standards. The researcher can select a variety of questionnaires to assess parent perceptions of their children across a wide domain of behaviors including those comprising self-regulation (impulsivity, frustration, aggression, delay of gratification, depressive mood). The advantages of questionnaires are that they can be self-administered, have normative standards, and have extensive, behavior specific questions, allowing a researcher to assess a wide range of functional domains. However, these advantages are also their disadvantage because outcomes are restricted to the questions asked as well as individual differences in the interpretation of the questions. Therefore, questionnaires are often supplemented with interviews (see Table 18.4).

Interviews enable the investigator to probe more deeply in the dynamics of parenting, child behavior, and family life. Unstructured interviews use open-ended questions that are tailor-made to particular families. The situation is similar to a conversation, guided by the skills of the interviewer and by the overall goal of the interview (e.g., to gain deeper understanding of the contexts of child aggressive behavior). Because of the conversational aspect of the unstructured interview, it can facilitate development of a trusting relationship between examiner and parent and set the stage for continued involvement in, for example, longitudinal studies. Interviews also can be structured. For example, in the national evaluation of Early Head Start, a structured interview was used to ensure that every parent was asked the same set of questions, emulating the normative aspect of questionnaires (Administration on Children, Youth, & Families, 1999; Paulsell, Kisker, Love, & Raikes, 2002; Raikes & Emde, 2006). Even the probes associated with questions were predetermined. Because structured interviews also reflect conversation, they too can help to relax parents and allow them an opportunity to reflect on their child's behavior or their own views about parenting in an informal context.

Observer as Primary Informant

There also are a variety of assessment settings in which individuals are trained to observe targeted behaviors. Naturalistic observation can take place in laboratory settings, with relatively rigorous control, or in homes, playgrounds, child-care centers, and other settings where less control of ecological context is possible (McCabe, Robello-Britto, Hernandez, & Brooks-Gunn, 2004). What one trades off for enhancing ecological validity one loses in rigor with respect to control of the factors that may be influencing the toddler's behavior. Observational assessment approaches generally require formal procedures to train observers to criteria, usually attempting to establish interrater reliabilities of about .90. While ensuring reliable assessments, the danger is that most observational tools are guided by underlying theoretical concepts and highly defined observational criteria. Whether such concepts and criteria apply beyond the sample used to develop the tool remains an open question. For example, one may develop a scoring procedure for rating eye-to-eye contact during parent–child interactions and then use the observational technique with individuals from cultures where eye-to-eye contact has a different meaning than in the culture where the tool was developed. Failing to see such contact may lead the observer's highly reliable rating to have little validity because of cultural influences on the intersubjective self or shared meaning of the act (Fitzgerald, 2006). Nevertheless, there is general consensus that efforts

TABLE 18.4. Assessment of Socioemotional Development: Parent/Caregiver as Primary Informant

Tool	Construct	Description
Behavior problems	Infant Toddler Social–Emotional Assessment—Revised (ITSEA)	The ITSEA, appropriate for children ages 12–36 months, consists of four global domains (Internalizing, Externalizing, Regulatory, and Competence Domains), as well as 17 individual scales across these domains, which are supported by confirmatory factor analyses (Carter, Briggs-Gowan, Jones, & Little, 2003). The Internalizing domain includes the following subscales: Activity/impulsivity, Aggression/Defiance, Peer Aggression. The Internalizing domain includes Depression/Withdrawal, General Anxiety, Separation Distress, Inhibition to Novelty. The Regulatory dimension includes Sleep, Negative Emotionality, Eating, Sensory Sensitivity. Scales within the Competency domain include: Compliance, Attention, Imitation/Play, Mastery Motivation, Empathy, and Prosocial Peer Relations. The items are scored on a 3-point scale ranging from "not true/rarely," "somewhat true/sometimes," to "very true/often." The ITSEA may be given in an interview format as well. Reliability (internal consistency, test–retest) and validity (concurrent) are acceptable (Briggs-Gowan & Carter, in press).
Behavior problems	Brief ITSEA (BITSEA)	The BITSEA consists of 60 items, drawn from the ITSEA, and is scored on the same 3-point scale. The BITSEA, intended for use with 1- and 2-year-old children, is composed of two scales: Problem (49 items) and Competence (11 items). Reliability (internal consistency) is acceptable.
Behavior problems	Child Behavior Checklist (CBCL)	The CBCL can be completed by each parent independently (Achenbach & Edelbrock, 1983). The CBCL has been normed on children 2 to 16 years of age. It yields standardized scores on eight narrow-band subscales, two broad-band subscales concerning externalizing and internalizing behavior, and a total behavior problems score. Scales are based on ratings of 1,728 children and are normed on a new national sample of 700 children. In all its forms and revisions, the CBCL is the most widely used measure of children's behavior problems and is available in many languages. Reliability and validity are acceptable.
Behavior problems	Child Behavior Rating Scale—Revised (CBRS)	The CBRS is an 84-item questionnaire concerning child behavior (Noll & Zucker, 1985). The items are divided into 49 desirable child behavior items (e.g., minds, shows affection, plays preference [e.g., realistic role playing, fantasy roles, quiet games, active games] and appropriately expresses anger), and 35 undesirable child behavior items (e.g., pushes or hits, wets, interrupts, and inappropriately expresses anger). The questionnaire asks parents for two types of information: frequency and importance of increasing the performance rate for desirable behavior or decreasing the performance rate for undesirable behaviors. Frequency of occurrence is assessed first by asking respondents to rate each item on a 7-point scale (anchor points: 1 = Never, 7 = Always). After assessing frequency, respondents are asked to use two different methods to indicate the importance of changing the performance rate for various of their child's behaviors. In the first method, respondents are asked to select and list in descending order of importance up to six items (behaviors) from the desirable behavior list that they would most like their child to do more often. Respondents repeat this procedure for the undesirable behavior list by selecting and listing up to six items that they would most like their child to do less often. Reliability (internal consistency) and validity (concurrent, predictive) are acceptable.

(*continued*)

TABLE 18.4. (*continued*)

Tool	Construct	Description
Emotion regulation, temperament	Infant Behavior Questionnaire—Revised (IBQ-R)	Rothbart's IBQ-R (see Rothbart, 1981; Rothbart, Ahadi, Hershey, & Fisher, 2001) is appropriate for infants through 12 months. The IBQ-R assesses dimensions of Activity Level, Distress to Limitations, Approach, Fear, Duration of Orienting, Smiling and Laughter, Vocal Reactivity, Sadness, Perceptual Sensitivity, High Intensity Pleasure, Low Intensity Pleasure, Cuddliness, Soothability, and Falling Reactivity/Rate of Recovery. One can use a set of subscales when assessing emotion regulation: Duration of Orienting, Low Intensity Pleasure, Soothability, and Cuddliness. Reliability and validity are acceptable.
Emotion regulation, temperament	Early Childhood Behavior Questionnaire (ECBQ)	The ECBQ, used with toddlers from 13 to 36 months of age, assesses the following dimensions: Activity Level, Attentional Focusing, Attentional Shifting, Cuddliness, Intensity Pleasure, Impulsivity, Inhibitory control, Low-Intensity Pleasure, Motor Activation, Perceptual Sensitivity, Positive Anticipation, Sadness, Shyness, Sociability and Soothability (see Rothbart, 1981; Rothbart et al., 2001).
Temperament	Carey Temperament Scales	This assesses child temperament from 1 month to 12 years of age. The parent (caregiver) questionnaire is divided into five age groupings, with 75–100 descriptions of behavior, each rated on a 6-point scale based on frequency of occurrence. It requires about 20 minutes to administer and an early high school reading level. It is scored and interpreted by a licensed professional. Norms are based on white samples from Eastern United States. Reliability (test–retest, internal consistency) is acceptable (Carey & McDevitt, 1978).
Temperament	Dimensions of Temperament Scale—Revised (DOTS-R)	The DOTS-R is a 54-item questionnaire that assesses 11 aspects of temperament: Activity Level-general, Activity Level-sleep, Approach–Withdrawal, Flexibility–Rigidity, Mood, Rhythmicity—Sleep, Rhythmicity—Eating, Rhythmicity—Daily Habits, Task Orientation (and Distractibility, Persistence for young adults). There is a parent report for preschool-age to elementary-age children, self-report and other-report at older ages. It requires about 30–45 minutes depending on reading level. Reliability (internal consistency) and validity (concurrent) are acceptable (Windle & Lerner, 1986).
Social, emotional, and behavioral regulation	Achenbach System of Empirically Based Assessment	This self-administered 99-item checklist assesses behavior and language. The behavioral measures divide into two syndromes, externalizing and internalizing behavior problems, and a variety of subscales in each syndrome. Items are relevant for children between the ages of 1½ and 5 years. There are two versions, one for parents and one for caregivers/teachers. The language survey is used to identify the child's best multiword phrases from a list of 310 words. Two broad syndromes are identified: externalizing and internalizing. A nationally representative sample was used for developing norms. Reliability (test–retest, interrater, internal consistency) and validity (concurrent, predictive) are acceptable (Achenbach & Rescorla, 2000).

(*continued*)

TABLE 18.4. (*continued*)

Tool	Construct	Description
Self-regulation	Infant–Toddler Symptom Checklist (ITSC)	The ITSC is a screening tool for rating the child's self-regulation and temperament. It focuses on assessing potential problems related to child behaviors such as fussiness, sleep difficulties, eating problems, and rapid transitions in negative moods. The normative information involved a small sample so should be viewed cautiously. It was used in the ECLS-B national study and results from that study provide useful information relevant to low-income samples. Validity (concurrent, predictive) is acceptable (DeGangi, Poisson, Sickel, & Wiener, 1995).
Behavior problems and stress	Parenting Stress Inventory	This is a screening measure of child behavior problems and stress as perceived by the parent. One hundred twenty items (long form) or 36 items (short form) are factored into 13 subscales across four domains—total stress, child domain, parent domain, life stress—rated on a 5-point scale. It requires 30 minutes to complete and a fifth-grade reading level. Interpretation requires a trained specialist. It is available in several languages. Reliability (test–retest, internal consistency) and validity (concurrent, predictive) are acceptable (Abiden, 1990).
Developmental delay	Parents' Evaluation of Developmental Status—Social–Emotional Scale	This is a general measure used to screen for developmental delay or childhood disorders (birth to age 8). It assesses nine domains—global/cognitive, expressive language and articulation, receptive language, fine motor, gross motor, behavior, social-emotional, self-help, and school—and is completed by parent or by caregiver. It comprises 10 questions, rated as yes, no, or a little, and requires 10 minutes to administer and a fifth-grade reading level (English, Spanish, and Vietnamese). Reliability (test–retest, interrater, and internal consistency) and validity (concurrent, predictive) are acceptable (Glascoe, 2006).
Social–emotional functioning	Vineland Social–Emotional Early Childhood Scales	This tool measures social–emotional functioning—interpersonal relationships, play and leisure time, coping skills—for children birth to 72 months of age. It is designed to identify the need for further assessment and to assist in planning interventions. It is a semistructured interview consisting of 122 items that are rated across five options from usually performs to don't know. It is nationally representative and used to develop norms. The interviewer–assistant parent report requires about 25 minutes. The administration, scoring, and interpretation require a trained examiner. Reliability (test–retest, interrater, internal consistency) and validity (concurrent) are acceptable (Raggio & Massingle, 1993).
Developmental delay	Ages and Stages Questionnaire—Personal–Social Functioning Scale	This is a general screening instrument used to detect developmental delay. It includes subscales for communication, gross motor, fine motor, problem solving, and personal–social functioning. It assesses children ages 4 months to 60 months. Parent-completed questionnaires are organized into age intervals. Each age interval has 30 items. Parents rate frequency of occurrence. It requires about 15 minutes to complete and a sixth-grade reading level (English, Spanish, French, and Korean). Reliability (test–retest, interrater, internal consistency) and validity (concurrent, predictive) are acceptable (Bricker & Squires, 1999).

(*continued*)

TABLE 18.4. *(continued)*

Tool	Construct	Description
Temperament and self-regulation	Temperament and Atypical Behavior Scales	This scale measures temperament and self-regulatory behavior in children from 11 to 71 months. It consists of a 15-item screener and a 55-item assessment. It is designed to identify the need for additional assessment and for interventions. It is completed by parent or an individual familiar with the child's behavior and has no nationally established normative standards. It takes 10–30 minutes to complete, depending on which form used. Reliability (test–retest, internal consistency) and validity (predictive) are acceptable (Neisworth, Bagnato, Salvia, & Hunt, 1999).
Depression	Preschool Feelings Checklist	This checklist is used to screen for depression in children (36–66 months of age). Parents or caregivers rate items as "yes–no." It requires about 10 minutes to complete. Reliability (internal consistency) and validity (predictive) are acceptable (Luby, Heffelfinger, Koenig-McNaught, Brown, & Spitznagel, 2004).
Opposition defiant behavior or conduct disorders	Eyberg Child Behavior Inventory—Parent (ECBI); Sutter–Eyberg Student Behavior Inventory—Revised—Teacher (SESBI-R)	These are measures of behavior problems in the home or school settings from the parent's or teacher's perspective, for children ages 2–16 years. The ECBI consists of 36 items and the SESBI-R consists of 38 items. Each child behavior is rated twice: once for intensity (a 7-point scale rating for frequency), and one for problem (yes–no decision as to whether the behavior is perceived to be a problem. They have no nationally representative normative sample. They take 15 minutes to complete and require a sixth-grade reading level. Graduate-level clinical skills are required for interpretation. Reliability (test–retest, interrater, internal consistency) and validity (concurrent, predictive) are acceptable (Eyberg & Pincus, 1999).
Regulatory disorders	Infant–Toddler Symptom Checklist	This is a measure to screen for sensory and regulatory disorders for children 7 to 30 months of age. The checklist focuses on nine domains: self-regulation, attention, sleep, eating or feeding, dressing, bathing, and touch, movement, listening and language, looking and sight, and attachment/emotional functioning. It is a series of five age-specific questionnaires to be completed by parent report or through an interview. Most items list a behavior that is rated as "never or sometimes," "most times," or "past." It has moderate predictive validity. It has a nonnational sample, predominately white. The parent/caregiver report of interview requires about 10 to 20 minutes to complete. It may be scored and interpreted by highly training program staff (DeGangi et al., 1995).
Behavior problems	Devereux Early Childhood Assessment (DECA)	The DECA comprises parent, teacher, or caregiver ratings of 2- to 5-year-old children's protective factors (27 items including initiative, self-control, attachment) and 10 behavior problems. It is rated on a 5-point scale from never to very frequently during past 4 months. It has nationally representative normative standards. It is scored and interpreted by a trained individual. Reliability (test–retest, interrater, internal consistency) and validity (predictive) are acceptable (LeBuffe & Naglieri, 1999).

(continued)

TABLE 18.4. (*continued*)

Tool	Construct	Description
Developmental screening	Denver Developmental Screening Test—Personal–Social Scale (DDST)	The DDST is a screening tool for four areas: personal–social, fine-motor adaptive, language, and gross motor (birth to age 6). It has 125 items. The child's performance is rated on a pass–fail basis. It includes a Prescreening Developmental Questionnaire consisting of 91 parent-completed items from the total set. The normative sample is drawn from Colorado. It takes 10–20 minutes for direct child assessment and parent report obtained by a trained examiner. Reliability (test–retest, interrater) is acceptable (Frankenburg, Fandal, & Thornton, 1987).
Vocabulary development	MacArther Communicative Development Inventory (CDI)	There are three versions of the CDI: Level I (infants, 8–16 months), Level II (toddlers, 16–30 months), and Level III (toddlers 30–36 months). The CDI may be used with developmentally delayed children as long as chronological age does not exceed the upper age limit of the measures. The CDI II contains a vocabulary checklist of 75 words. The parent is asked to identify which words the toddler says, as well as comment on whether or not the toddler has begun to combine words (not yet, sometimes, often). The CDI III includes a 75-word vocabulary list as well as questions concerning production of multiword sentence. If multiword sentence use is reported, additional questions assess word combinations, use of language, and length of sentences. Reliability (internal consistency) is acceptable (Fenson et al., 1993).
Developmental assessment	Infant Development Assessment—Emotion and Feeling State Scale (IDA)	The IDA is a comprehensive, multidisciplinary, family-centered process designed to improve early identification of children birth to 3 years of age who are developmentally at risk. The IDA is an integrated process that includes the Provence Birth-to-Three Developmental Profile. It is used to assess a child's developmental level and status in eight domains: gross motor, fine motor, relationship to inanimate objects, self-help, language, relationship to persons, emotions and feeling states, and coping. Reliability and validity are acceptable (Provence, Erikson, Vater, & Palmeri, 1995).
Antisocial behavior	Antisocial Behavior Checklist	Parental antisocial behavior is defined by parents' responses to the following four questions: *Have you ever been expelled from school? Have you ever been fired or laid off from a job because of behavior, attitude, or work performance? Have you ever been put in jail, arrested or convicted of a crime, other than drunk driving? Have you ever had a drinking or drug problem or have other people thought you had one?* Affirmative responses of 0 or 1 are indicative of low antisocial behavior while an affirmative response to two or more questions is characterized as high antisocial behavior. The four-item questionnaire is an adaptation of the Antisocial Behavioral Checklist developed by Zucker, Noll, Ham, Fitzgerald, and Sullivan (1994) and has been useful in studies conducted as part of the national evaluation of children in Early Head Start.
Depression	Center for Epidemiologic Studies—Depression Scale (CES-D)	The CES-D is a 12-item self-report measure of depressive symptoms in community populations (Radloff, 1977; Ross, Mirowsky, & Huber, 1983). Parents report the number of days in the past week they experienced a particular symptom. Symptoms include poor appetite, restless sleep, loneliness, sadness, and lack of energy. Items are coded on a 4-point scale from rarely (0) to most days (3). Scores on the scale range from 0 to 36. Items are scored on a 4-point Likert scale indicating the frequency and intensity of the symptom during the previous week.

(*continued*)

TABLE 18.4. (*continued*)

Tool	Construct	Description
Emotional expressiveness	Self Expressiveness in the Family Questionnaire (SEFQ)	The 40-item SEFQ examines the frequency of emotional expressiveness of an individual within the family context. Respondents are asked to consider each hypothetical, affective scenario and rate how frequently the individual expresses him- or herself in each situation. A 9-point likert scale is used ranging from "not at all frequently" (1) to "very frequently" (9). The measure consists of two main scales: one positive and one negative, and a total score may be calculated as well. Reliability (internal consistency) is acceptable (Halberstadt, Parke, Cassidy, Stifter, & Fox, 1995).
Neighborhood violence	Neighborhood risk	Neighborhood risk is defined by parents' yes–no responses to five questions concerning neighborhood violence (e.g., "Have you heard or seen a violent crime take place in your neighborhood," "Have you known someone who was a victim of a violent crime in your neighborhood?"). An affirmative response on two or more questions signifies high neighborhood risk. The neighborhood risk short questionnaire was developed from items used to assess antisocial behavior in the Michigan Longitudinal Study (Zucker et al., 1995) and has been successfully used in studies of children and families participating in the national evaluation of Early Head Start (Fitzgerald et al., 2006).
Family environment	Family Environment Scale (FES)	The FES is a 90-item scale created to measure relationship dimensions, personal growth dimensions, and system maintenance dimensions within the family environment. For this study we use the FES Conflict subscale of five items that measure the expression of aggression and anger as well as conflicted interactions of the family. Items are rated on a 4-point scale, with 4 indicating high agreement with statements such as "We fight a lot," "We hardly ever lose our temper." Reliability (internal consistency) is acceptable (Moos & Moos, 1976).
Family support	Family Support Scale	Parent satisfaction with available social support services for families with young children. It is an 18-item questionnaire with each item rated on a 5-point scale. It takes approximately 10 minutes to complete. It is administered, scored, and interpreted by trained staff. Reliability (test–retest, internal consistency) and validity (concurrent) are acceptable (Dunst, Jenkins, & Trivette, 1984).
Family support	Family Support Scale	Parent satisfaction with available social support services for families with young children. It is an 18-item questionnaire with each item rated on a 5-point scale. It takes approximately 10 minutes to complete. It is administered, scored, and interpreted by trained staff. Reliability (test–retest, internal consistency) and validity (concurrent) are acceptable (Dunst, Jenkins, & Trivette, 1984).
Child-rearing attitudes	Adolescent–Adult Parenting Inventory (AAPI-2)	The AAPI-2 is designed to assess the parenting and childrearing attitudes of adult and adolescent parent and preparent populations. There are five constructs in this inventory: inappropriate expectations of children, parental lack of empathy toward children's needs, strong belief in the use of corporal punishment as means of discipline, reversing parent–child role responsibilities, and oppressing children's power and independence (Bavolek & Keene, 1999).

(*continued*)

TABLE 18.4. *(continued)*

Tool	Construct	Description
Behavior, social, and emotional functioning	Parent–Child Rating Scale (P-CRS)	The P-CRS is a 39-item measure that assesses children's behavioral, social, and emotional functioning from a parent's perspective. It measures a child's problem behaviors and competencies along three problem dimensions (Acting Out, Shy–Anxious, Learning Problems) and four competence dimensions (Frustration Tolerance, Assertive Social Skills, Task-Orientation, and Peer Social Skills) (Hightower, 1994).
Disorder in home environment	Confusion, Hubbub, and Order Scale (CHAOS)	The CHAOS is a measure of disorder and confusion in the home environment. There are 15 statements completed by parent or caregiver, each rated on a 4-point scale reflecting degree to which statement matches the home environment. It requires 10 minutes to complete and is scored and interpreted by trained staff. Reliability (test–retest, internal consistency) and validity (concurrent) are acceptable (Matheny, Wachs, Ludswig, & Phillips, 1995).
Coping strategies	F-COPES	The F-COPES is used to assess the pattern of coping strategies used by families facing everyday problems or difficulties. It has 30 items and five subscales: three assess external family coping (acquiring social support from relatives, friends, neighbors, and extended family; seeking spiritual support; and mobilizing the family to acquire and accept help from community resources and services). Two subscales assess how families handle problems internally: reframing, which assesses the family's capacity to redefine stressful situations in order to make them more manageable, and passive appraisal, which measures the inactive or passive behaviors a family might employ. Reliability (internal consistency) is acceptable (McCubbin, Olson, & Larsen, 1991).

should always be made to obtain assessment information from observers other than the toddler's parent or relative (see Table 18.5).

Because human development is always an interplay between normative species-driven processes and individual transactions with the environment, assessment during the early years should always be anchored in systemic models of development. Child behavior, therefore, must be viewed in multiple contexts and must involve input from multiple data sources, including those external to the family, such as the quality of family support systems, neighborhood climate and other factors that may affect the quality of the child's social relationships and ability to exercise self-control. Ideally, information from each informant represented in Tables 18.3 through 18.5 will be taken into account when assessing the developmental status of the target child.

CONCLUSION

Modern approaches to assessment during the early years of development are steeped in systemic models of early organizational processes. Such approaches require data collection from the individual child, the child in relational interactions with his or her caregiver(s), and includes gathering of data about the

TABLE 18.5. Observer as Primary Informant

Tool	Construct	Description
Depression, relationship disorders	Alarm Distress Baby Scale (ADBS)	The ADBS (Guedeney & Fermanian, 2001) is used in clinical settings with infants from 2 to 24 months of age to identify sustained withdrawal behavior. The scale consists of eight items (facial expression, eye contact, general level of activity, self-stimulating gestures, vocalizations, briskness of response to stimulation, relationship and attraction) rated by a home visitor or clinician from 0 (*No unusual behavior*) to 4 (*Severe unusual behavior*). A cutoff score of 5 was reported to have a sensitivity of .82 and a specificity of .78 for detecting developmental risk in the infant in the year after the administration. Reliability (internal consistency) and validity (concurrent) are acceptable.
Emotion regulation	Bayley Behavior Rating Scale (BBRS)	The BBRS measures the child's behavior during the Bayley Scales of Infant and Toddler Development assessment (Bayley, 1993). The Emotion Regulation component of the BBRS measures the child's ability to change tasks and test materials and handle frustration. The interview assesses the child's behavior by scoring 7 items on a 5-point scale, with 5 indicating more positive behavior, such as low levels of frustration and high levels of cooperation. Items include positive affect, negative affect, motor control, attention to task, social engagement, and ability to adapt to transitions during the testing situation. In the ECLS-B national study, items were included to assess caregiver's perceptions of child performance in the testing situation to performance in general. A third edition of the BSID was published in 2005 and includes a new test of social-emotional functioning, including self-regulation (Psychological Corporation).
Attachment	Attachment Q-set (AQS)	The AQS assesses infant attachment behavior in the home (Waters & Deane, 1985). It consists of 90 items designed to describe children's behaviors during periods of interactions with their parents. The items are sorted into nine piles according to a predefined, rectangular distribution as outlined by AQS procedures. The AQS method has several advantages over other types of measures. The Q-set methodology requires that more attention be given to each item as compared to rating scale procedures, and it is expected to limit social desirability because only a specified number of items can be identified as "most characteristic" of subject. Waters's statistical protocol for computer analysis can be used to compare coder pile assignments to a distribution representing a prototypically secure child. Using this method, security scores range from +1.00 (perfectly secure child) to –1.00 (prototypically insecure). The score is the correlation between the subject's Q-set and that of a prototypically secure child. Some investigators consider the AQS to represent a "gold standard" for measuring attachment (see van IJzendoorn, 1995).
Attachment	Toddler Attachment Sort–45 (TAS45)	The TAS45 is a version of the AQS developed for the ECLS-B national study for administration by laptop. The TAS45 yields measures of secure, avoidant, resistant, and disorganized attachment. Training procedures ensure high interrater reliability. Full details about the TAS45 and other measures used in the ECLS-B are available at *nces.ed.gov/ecls/Birth.asp* (Andreassen & West, in press).

(*continued*)

TABLE 18.5. (*continued*)

Tool	Construct	Description
Emotional responsiveness	Preschool classroom observations	Fabes and Eisenberg (1992) have outlined a method of completing observations of children's emotional and regulation responsiveness in natural settings. When cues of anger or sadness are identified during 10-minute observations of children in play areas, the experimenter records the cause of the emotion and the regulation response to the emotion. This type of observational method requires extensive training of the experimenters who conduct the observations.
Parent–child interaction	Three-Bag Assessment	Mothers and toddlers participate in a semistructured interaction called the Three-Bag Assessment. During the task, mother and child are asked to play with three different sets of toys, each placed within separate bags, labeled "1," "2," or "3." Each dyad is given 10 minutes to play with the toys, with the only restriction being that they must play with the toys in the bags in numerical order, beginning with bag "1." Six parental behavioral scales and three child behavior scales were developed by Brady-Smith, O'Brien, Berlin, Ware, and Fauth (2000), based on existing scales used in the NICHD Study of Early Child Care (Owen et al., 1993). Child subscales used in the national evaluation of Early Head Start included Sustained Attention and Child Engagement of the Parent. Parental subscales included Parent Supportiveness and Negative Regard of the Child. All parent and child subscales are scored on a 1–7 scale from low expression of the behavior to high expression of the behavior
Mother–child interaction	Nursing Child Assessment Satellite Training—Teaching Scale (NCATS)	The NCATS was used at some sites involved in the national evaluation of Early Head Start. Designed as a direct observation measure, it has been used during video sessions with later scoring by trained coders. The NCATS is a standardized assessment tool that measures caregiver sensitivity to the child's behaviors, responsiveness to distress, socioemotional growth fostering, cognitive growth fostering, and child's clarity of cues and responsiveness to caregiver. There is a standardized training procedure for coders and standardized norms for evaluating outcomes. Reliability (interrater, internal consistency) and validity (concurrent, predictive) are acceptable (Summer & Spietz, 1995).
Family environment	Home Observation for Measurement of the Environment (HOME)	The HOME is a widely used instrument designed to provide systematic measurement of the family environment. The Infant/Toddler: 0–3 looks at parent responsivity, parent acceptance, organization, learning materials, involvement, and other adult involvement in the child's life. The Early Childhood: 3–6 looks at child's access to learning materials, parents' ability to provide language stimulation, parent responsivity, parental ability to provide academic stimulation, parent modeling, parental acceptance, and other adult involvement in the child's life (Caldwell & Bradley, 1984). Reliability (internal consistency, interrater) and validity (concurrent, predictive) are acceptable.

(*continued*)

TABLE 18.5. (*continued*)

Tool	Construct	Description
Emotional–social functioning	Functional Emotional Assessment Scale	This is a measure of emotional and social functioning and caregivers' support of their child's emotional development. It assesses children 7–48 months and measures regulation and interest in the world; forming relationships; intentional two-way communication; development of a complex sense of self; representational capacity and elaboration of symbolic thinking and thematic play. Trained observers rate the child's developmental status based on observations of caregiver–child play interactions. Ratings are based on live or videotaped observations. Observational ratings require about 20 minutes. It is a nonrepresentative normative sample. Reliability (test–retest) and validity (predictive) are acceptable (Greenspan, DeGangi, & Wieder, 2001).

context within which the child and his or her caregivers live. Any strategy that fails to approach assessment from a systemic framework fails to provide insights into child functioning that allow translation into programs that may facilitate changes in child behavior. This is as true for assessments performed in small- or large-scale research projects as it is for assessments performed in the service of determining effective clinical interventions. As evidenced in this chapter, the armamentarium of measures for assessing social–emotional development during the early years of human development is full. The key to successful measurement, therefore, is understanding the child's performance within a broader context of developmental processes and ensuring that all contexts inform the assessment protocol so that research results and clinical insights are guided by a deep understanding of the assessment process.

REFERENCES

Abiden, R. R. (1990). *Parenting Stress Index*. Charlottesville, VA: Pediatric Psychology Press.

Achenbach, T., & Edelbrock, C. (1983). *Manual for the child behavior checklist and revised child behavior profile.* Burlington, VT: University Associates in Psychiatry

Achenbach, T. M., & Rescorla, L. A. (2000). *Manual for the ASEBA preschool forms and profiles.* Burlington: University of Vermont Department of Psychiatry.

Administration on Children, Youth, and Families. (1999). *Leading the way: Characteristics and early experiences of selected first-wave Early Head Start programs: Vol. I. Cross-site perspectives*. Washington, DC: U.S. Department of Health and Human Services.

Advisory Committee on Services for Families with Infants and Toddlers. (1996). *The statement of the advisory committee on services for families with infants and toddlers*. Washington, DC: U.S. Department of Health and Human Services.

Akshoomoff, N. A., & Stahmer, A. (2006). Early intervention programs and policies for children with autistic spectrum disorders. In H. E. Fitzgerald, B. M. Lester, & B. Zuckerman (Eds.), *Crisis in youth mental health: Vol. 1. Childhood disorders* (pp. 109–132). Westport, CT: Praeger.

Andreassen, C., & West, J. (in press). Measuring socioemotional functioning in a National Birth Cohort Study. *Infant Mental Health Journal.*

Bavolek, S. J., & Keene, R. G. (1999). *Adult–Adolescent Parenting Inventory 2: Administration and development handbook*. Park City, UT: Family Development Resources.

Bayley, N. (1993). *Bayley Scales of Infant Development* (2nd ed.). San Antonio, TX: Psychological Corporation.

Brady-Smith, C., O'Brien, C., Berlin, L., Ware, A., & Fauth, R. C. (2000). *Child–Parent Interaction Rating Scales for the Three-Bag Assessment (36 months)*. Unpublished scales, National Center for Children and Families, Teachers College, Columbia University.

Bricker, D., & Squires, J. (1999). *Ages and Stages Questionnaires: A parent completed child monitoring system* (2nd ed.). Baltimore: Brookes.

Briggs-Gowan, M. J., & Carter, A. S. (in press). Applying the Infant–Toddler Social & Emotional Assessment (ITSEA) and Brief-ITSEA in early interventions. *Infant Mental Health Journal.*

Caldwell, B., & Bradley, R. (1984). *Home Observation for Measurement of the Environment.* Little Rock: University of Arkansas.

Carey, W. B., & McDevitt, S. C. (1978). Revision of the Infant Temperament Questionnaire. *Pediatrics, 61*, 735–739.

Carter, A. S., Briggs-Gowan, M. J., Jones, S. M., & Little, T. D. (2003). The Infant–Toddler Social and Emotional Assessment (ITSEA): Factor Structure, Reliability, and Validity. *Journal of Abnormal Child Psychology, 31*(5), 495–514.

Chew, A. L., & Morris, J. D. (1989). Predicting later academic achievement from kindergarten scores on the Metropolitan Readiness Tests and the Lollipop Test. *Educational and Psychological Measurement, 49*(2), 461–465.

DeGangi, G. A., Poisson, S., Sickel, R. Z., & Wiener, A. S. (1995). *Infant/Toddler Symptom Checklist: A screen tool for parents.* Tuscon, AZ: Psychological Corporation.

Denham, S. A., McKinley, M., Couchoud, E. A., & Holt, R. (1990). Emotional and behavioral predictors of preschool peer ratings. *Child Development, 61*(4), 1145–1152.

Dunn, L. M., & Dunn, L. M. (1981). *Peabody Picture Vocabulary Test—Revised manual for Forms L and M.* Circle Pines, MN: American Guidance Service.

Dunst, C. J., Jenkins, V., & Trivette, C. M. (1984). The Family Support Scale: Reliability and validity. *Journal of Individual, Family, and Community Wellness, 1*, 45–52.

Eisenberg, N. (2006). Emotion-related regulation. In H. E. Fitzgerald, B. M. Lester, & B. Zuckerman (Eds.), *Crisis in youth mental health: Vol. 1. Childhood disorders* (pp. 133–155). Westport, CT: Praeger.

Eisenberg, N., Fabes, R. A., Guthrie, I. K., Murphy, B. C., Maszk, P., Holmgren, R., et al. (1996). The relations of regulation and emotionality to problem behavior in elementary school children. *Development and Psychopathology, 8*(1), 141–162.

Eisenberg, N., Guthrie, I. K., Fabes, R. A., Shepard, S., Losoya, S., Murphy, B. C., et al. (2000). Prediction of elementary school children's externalizing problem behaviors from attention and behavioral regulation and negative emotionality. *Child Development, 71*(5), 1367–1382.

Eisenberg, N., & Spinrad, T. L. (2004). Emotion related regulation: Sharpening the definition. *Child Development, 75*, 334–339.

Eno, L., & Woehlke, P. (1995). Use of the Lollipop Test as a predictor of California Achievement Test scores in kindergarten and transitional first-grade status. *Psychological Reports, 76*(1), 145–146.

Eyberg, S., & Pincus, D. (1999). *Eyberg Child Behavior Inventory and Sutter–Eyberg Student Behavior Inventory—Revised. Psychological Assessment Resources.* Odessa, FL: Psychological Assessment Resources.

Fabes, R. A., & Eisenberg, N. (1992). Young children's coping with interpersonal anger. *Child Development, 63*, 116–128.

Fenson, L., Dale, P. S., Reznick, J. S., Thal, D., Bates, E., Hartung, J. P., et al. (1993). *The MacArthur Communicative Development Inventory.* San Diego, CA: Singular.

Fitzgerald, H. E. (2006). Cross cultural research during infancy: Methodological considerations. *Infant Mental Health Journal, 27*, 612–617.

Fitzgerald, H. E., Davies, W. H., & Zucker, R. A. (2002). Growing up in an alcoholic family: Structuring pathways for risk aggregation. In R. MacMahon & R. DeV Peters (Eds.), *The effects of parental dysfunction on children* (pp. 127–146). New York: Kluuwer Publications.

Fitzgerald, H. E., Mann, T., Cabrera, N., & Wong, M. M. (2003). Diversity in caregiving contexts.

In R. M. Lerner, M. A. Easterbrooks, & J. Mistry (Eds,), *Handbook of psychology Vol 6: Developmental psychology* (pps. 135–167). New York: Wiley.

Fitzgerald, H. E., & McKelvey, L. M. (in press). Mental health: Prevention and intervention. In M. M. Haith & J. B. Benson (Eds). *Encyclopedia of early childhood.* Oxford, UK: Elsevier.

Fitzgerald, H. E., McKelvey, L. M., Schiffman, R. F., & Montanez, M. (2006). Exposure to neighborhood violence and paternal antisocial behavior on low-income families and their children. *Parenting: Research and Practice, 6*, 243–258.

Fitzgerald, H. E., & Zucker, R. A. (2006). Pathways of risk aggregation for alcohol use disorders. In K. Freeark & W. S. Davidson III (Eds.), *Crisis in youth mental health: Vol. 3. Issues for families, schools, and communities* (pp. 249–271). Westport, CT: Praeger.

Fitzgerald, H. E., Zucker, R. A., & Yang, H.-Y. (1995). Developmental systems theory and alcoholism: Analyzing patterns of variation in high risk families. *Psychology of Addictive Behaviors, 9*, 8–22.

Fox, N., & Fitzgerald, H. E. (1990). Autonomic function in infancy. *Merrill–Palmer Quarterly, 36*, 27–51.

Frankenburg, W. R., Fandal, A. W., & Thornton, S. M. (1987). Revision of Denver Prescreening Development Questionnaire. *Journal of Pediatrics, 110*, 653–657.

Funder, D., Block, J., & Block, J. (1983). Delay of gratification: Some longitudinal personality correlates. *Journal of Personality and Social Psychology, 44*(6), 1198–1213.

Glascoe, F. P. (2000). *IED-II Standardization and validation manual.* North Billerica, MA: Curriculum Association.

Glascoe, F. P. (2006). *Parents' evaluation of developmental status.* Nashville, TN: Ellsworth & Vandermeer Press.

Gottman, J. M., Katz, L. F., & Hooven, C. (1996). Parental meta-emotion philosophy and the emotional life of families: Theoretical models and preliminary data. *Journal of Family Psychology, 10*, 243–268.

Greenspan, S. I., DeGangi, G., & Wieder, S. (2001). *The Functional Emotional Assessment Scale (FEAS) for Infancy and Early Childhood: Clinical and research applications* (pp. 73–217). Bethesda, MD: Interdisciplinary Council on Developmental and Learning Disorder.

Guedeney, A., & Fermanian, J. (2001). A validity and reliability study of assessment and screening for sustained withdrawal reaction in infancy: The alarm distress baby scale. *Infant Mental Health Journal, 22(5), 559–575.*

Halberstadt, A. G., Parke, R. D., Cassidy, J., Stifter, C. A., & Fox, N. (1995). Self-expressiveness within the family context: Psychometric support for a new measure. *Psychological Assessment*, 7, 93–103.

Halpern, R., Gingliani, E. R., Victoria, C. G., Barros, F. C., & Horta, B. L. (2000). Risk factors for suspicion of developmental delays at 12 months of age. *Journal of Pediatrics (Rio Journal)*, 76, 421–428.

Hightower, A. D. (1994). *Parent Child Rating Scale.* Rochester, NY: Primary Mental Health Project.

Karmel, B. Z., & Gardner, J. M. (2006). Learning disabilities and mental health issues: Predictions from neonatal regulation, attention, and neurobehavioral assessments. In H. E. Fitzgerald, B. M. Lester, & B. Zuckerman (Eds.), *Crisis in youth mental health: Vol. 1. Childhood disorders* (pp. 83–108). Westport, CT: Praeger.

Kochanska, G., & Knaack, A. (2003). Effortful control as a personality characteristic of young children: Antecedents, correlates, and consequences. *Journal of Personality, 71*, 1087–1112.

Kochanska, G., Murray, K. T., & Harlan, E. T. (2000). Effortful control in early childhood: Continuity and change, antecedents, and implications for social development. *Developmental Psychology, 36*(2), 220–232.

Kusche, C. A., Greenberg, M. T., & Beilke, B. (1988). *The Kusche affective interview.* Unpublished manuscript, University of Washington, Seattle.

LeBuffe, P. A., & Naglieri, J. A. (1999). The Devereux Early Childhood Assessment (DECA): A measure of within-child protective factors in preschool children. *NHSA Dialog: A Research-to-Practice Journal for the Early Intervention Field, 3*(1), 75–80.

Leppanen, J. M., & Hietanen, J. K. (2001). Emotion recognition and social adjustment in school-aged girls and boys. *Scandinavian Journal of Psychology, 42*(5), 429–435.

Loukas, A., Twitchell, G. R., Piejack, L. A., Fitzgerald, H. E., & Zucker, R. A. (1998). The family as a unity of interactive personalities. In L. L'Abate (Ed.), *Handbook of family psychopathology* (pp. 35–59). New York: Guilford Press.

Luby, J. L., Heffelfinger, A., Koenig-McNaught, A., Brown, K., & Spitznagel, E. (2004). The preschool feelings checklist: A brief and sensitive screening measure for depression in young children. *Journal of the American Academy of Child and Adolescent Psychiatry, 43*, 708–717.

Matheny, A. P., Wachs, T. D., Ludwig, J. L., & Phillips, K. (1995). Bringing order out of chaos: Psychometric characteristics of the Confusion, Hubbub, and Order Scale. *Journal of Applied Developmental Psychology, 16*, 429–444.

McCabe, L. A., Robello-Britto, P., Hernandez, M., & Brooks-Gunn, J. (2004). Games children play: Observing young children's self-regulation across laboratory, home and school settings. In R. DelCarmen-Wiggins & A. Carter (Eds.), *Handbook of infant, toddler, and preschool mental health assessment* (pp. 491–521). New York: Oxford University Press.

McCubbin, H. I., Olson, D. H., & Larsen, A. S. (1991). F-COPES (Family Crisis Oriented Personal Evaluation Scales). In H. I. McCubbin & A. I. Thompson (Eds.), *Family assessment inventories for research and practice* (pp. 193–207). Madison: University of Wisconsin Press.

Meisels, S. J., & Fenichel, E. (Eds). (1996). *New visions for the developmental assessment of infants and young children.* Washington, DC: Zero to Three: National Center for Infants, Toddlers, and Families.

Miller, A. L., Gouley, K. K., Seifer, R., Zakriski, A., Eguia, M., & Vergnani, M. (2005). Emotion knowledge skills in low-income elementary school children: Associations with social status and peer experiences. *Social Development, 14*(4), 637–651.

Moffitt, T. E., Caspi, A., Rutter, M., & Silva, P. A. (2001). *Sex differences in antisocial behavior.* Cambridge, UK: Cambridge University Press.

Moos, R. H., & Moos, B. S. (1976). A typology of family social environments. *Family Process, 15*(4), 357–372.

Neisworth, J., Bagnato, S., Salvia, J., & Hunt, F. (1999). *TABS Manual for the Temperament and Atypical Behavior Scale: Early Child Indicators of Developmental Dysfunction.* Baltimore: Brookes.

Nigg, J. T. (2006). Attention deficits and hyperactivity-impulsivity in children: A multilevel overview of causes and mechanisms. In H. E. Fitzgerald, B. M. Lester, & B. Zuckerman (Eds.) *Crisis in youth mental health Vol 1: Childhood disorders* (pp. 157–182). Westport, CT: Praeger.

Noll, R. B., & Zucker, R. A. (1985). *Child Behavior Rating Scale: School-age revision.* Unpublished document, Michigan Longitudinal Study, University of Michigan Addiction Research Center, Ann Arbor, MI

Nowicki, S., & Duke, M. P. (1994). Individual differences in the nonverbal communication of affect: The Diagnostic Analysis of Nonverbal Accuracy Scale. *Journal of Nonverbal Behavior, 18*(1), 9–35.

Nowicki, S., Glanville, G., & Demetrzis, A. (1998). A test of the ability to recognize emotion in the facial expressions of African American adults. *Journal of Black Psychology, 24*(3), 335–350.

Owen, M. T., Norris, C., Houssan, M., Wetzel, S., Mason, J., & Ohba, C. (1993, September). *24-Month Mother–Child Interaction Rating Scales for the Three Boxes Procedure.* Paper presented at the NICHD Study of Early Child Care Research Consortium, Washington, DC.

Paulsell, D., Kisker, E. E., Love, J. M., & Raikes, H. H. (2002). Understanding implementation in early head start programs: Implications for policy and practice. *Infant Mental Health Journal, 23*, 14–35.

Provence, S., Erikson, J., Vater, S., & Palmeri, S. (1995). *Infant and Toddler Developmental Assessment: The IDA Procedures Manual and Provence Birth to Three Developmental Profile.* Chicago: Riverside Press.

Radloff, L. S. (1977). The CES-D Scale: A Self-Report Depression Scale for Research in the General Population. *Applied Psychological Measurement, 1*, 385–401

Raggio, D. J., & Massingale, T. W. (1993). Comparison of the Vineland Social Maturity Scale, the

Vineland Adaptive Behavioral Scales—survey form, and the Bayley Scales of Individual Development, with infants evaluated for developmental delays. *Perceptual and Motor Skills, 77*, 931–937.

Raikes, H., & Emde, R. N. (2006). Early Head Start: A bold new program for low-income infants and toddlers. In N. F. Watt, C. Ayoub, R. H. Bradley, J. E. Puma, & W. A. LeBoeuf (Eds.), *The crisis in youth mental health: Vol. 4. Early intervention programs and policies* (pp. 181–206). Westport, CT: Praeger.

Robinson, J. L., & Fitzgerald, H. E. (2002). Early Head Start: Investigations, insights and promise. *Infant Mental Health Journal, 23*, 250–257.

Roggman, L. A., Fitzgerald, H. E., Bradley, R. H., & Raikes, H. (2002). Methodological, measurement, and design issues in studying fathers: An interdisciplinary perspective. In C. S. Tamis-LeMonda & N. Cabrera (Eds.), *Handbook of father involvement: Multidisciplinary perspectives* (pp. 1–30). Mahwah, NJ: Erlbaum.

Ross, C. E., Mirowsky, J., & Huber, J. (1983). Dividing work, sharing work, and in-between: Marriage patterns and depression. *American Sociological Review, 48*, 809-823.

Rothbart, M. (1981). Measurement of temperament in infancy. *Child Development, 52*, 569–578.

Rothbart, M. K., Ahadi, S. A., Hershey, K., & Fisher, P. (2001). Investigations of temperament at three to seven years: The Children's Behavioral Questionnaire. *Child Development, 72*, 1287–1604.

Shaw, D. S. (2006). The development of aggression in early childhood. In H. E. Fitzgerald, B. M. Lester, & B. Zuckerman (Eds.), *Crisis in youth mental health: Vol. 1. Childhood disorders* (pp. 183–204). Westport, CT: Praeger.

Spitz, R. A. (1965). *The first year of life*. New York: International Universities Press.

Summer, G., & Spietz, A. L. (1995). *NCAST caregiver/parent–child interaction teaching manual* (2nd ed.). Seattle: NCAST Publications, University of Washington.

Thomas, A., & Chess, S. (1977). *Temperament and development*. New York: Brunner/Mazel.

Tomlinson, M., Swartz L., & Landman, M. (2006). Insiders and outsiders: Levels of collaborative research partnerships across resource divides. *Infant Mental Health Journal, 27*, 532–543.

van IJzendoorn, M. H. (1995). Adult attachment representations, parental responsiveness and infant attachment: A meta analysis and the predictive validity of the adult attachment interview. *Psychological Bulletin, 117*, 387–403.

Wasserman, J. D., & Bracken, B. A. (2003). Psychometric considerations of assessment procedures. In J. Graham & J. Naglieri (Eds.), *Handbook of assessment psychology* (pp. 43–66). New York: Wiley.

Waters, E., & Deane, K. E. (1985). Defining and assessing individual differences in attachment relationships: Q methodology and the organization of behavior in infancy and early childhood. In I. Bretherton & E. Waters (Eds.), Growing points of attachment theory and research. *Monographs of the Society for Research in Child Development, 50*(1–2, Serial No. 209).

Webster-Stratton, C., Reid, J., & Hammond, M. (2001). Social skills and problem solving for children with early-onset conduct problems: Who benefits? *Journal of Child Psychology and Psychiatry, 42*, 943–952.

Windle, M., & Lerner, R. M. (1986). Reassessing the dimensions of temperament individuality across the life span: The revised Dimensions of Temperament Survey (DOTS-R). *Journal of Adolescent Research, 1*, 213–230.

Zero to Three. (2005). *Diagnostic classification of mental health and developmental disorders of infancy and early childhood: Revised edition (DC:0-3R)*. Washington, DC: Author.

Zimmerman, I. L., Steiner, V. G., & Pond, R. E. (2002). *Preschool Language Scale* (4th ed.). San Antonio, TX: Psychological Corporation.

Zucker, R. A., Chermack, S. T., & Curran, G. R. (2000). Alcoholism: A life span perspective on etiology and course. In A. J. Sameroff, M. Lewis, & S. M. Miller (Eds.), *Handbook of developmental psychopathology* (pp. 569–587). New York: Kluwer Academic/Plenum Press.

Zucker, R. A., Fitzgerald, H. E., & Moses, H. (1995). Emergence of alcohol problems and the several alcoholisms: A developmental perspective on etiologic theory and life course trajectory. In D.

Cicchetti & D. Cohen (Eds.), *Manual of developmental psychopathology: Vol. 2. Risk, disorder and adaptation* (pp. 677–711). New York: Wiley.

Zucker, R. A., Fitzgerald, H. E., Refior, S. K., Puttler, L. I., Pallas, D. M., & Ellis, D. A. (2000). The clinical and social ecology of childhood for children of alcoholics: Description of a study and implications for a differentiated social policy. In H. E. Fitzgerald, B. M. Lester, & B. Zuckerman (Eds.), *Children of alcoholics: Selected readings* (pp. 109–142). New York: Garland Press.

Zucker, R. A., Noll, R. B., Ham, H. P., Fitzgerald, H. E., & Sullivan, L. S. (1994). *Assessing antisociality with the Antisocial Behavior Checklist: Reliability and validity studies.* East Lansing: Michigan Longitudinal Study, Michigan State University.

Zucker, R. A., Wong, M. M., Puttler, L. I., & Fitzgerald, H. E. (2003). Resilience and vulnerability among sons of alcoholics. In S. S. Luthar (Ed.), *Resilience and vulnerability: Adaptation in the context of childhood adversities* (pp. 76–103). Cambridge, UK: Cambridge University Press.

Index

Page numbers followed by *f* indicate figure, *t* indicate table

B

D

T

U

V

W

Z